Sport, Mediation and Arbitration

Asser International Sports Law Series

Editors
Robert C.R. Siekmann and Janwillem Soek

ISSN 1874–6926

Partners of the ASSER International Sports Law Centre

C/M/S/ Derks Star Busmann
ATTORNEYS AT LAW CIVIL LAW NOTARIES TAX ADVISERS

WILKENS C.S.
TRANSLATORS & INTERPRETERS

Legal League
Football lawyers association

BIRD & BIRD

Field R

LCA
avvocati e commercialisti d'impresa studio associato

WISTRAND
LAW FIRM

KLEVEN & KRISTENSEN

TOLUN Consulting Sport Law Center
With Us, The Solution is Well Within Reach...

DF Advocates
Deguara Farrugia Advocates

LAWIN
LIDEIKA, PETRAUSKAS, VALIŪNAS ir PARTNERIAI

KĻAVIŅŠ & SLAIDIŅŠ
Attorneys at Law
LAWIN

FRORIEP RENGGLI
ATTORNEYS AT LAW | GENEVA | ZURICH | ZUG | LAUSANNE | LONDON | MADRID

T.M.C. ASSER INSTITUUT
ASSER INTERNATIONAL SPORTS LAW CENTRE

SPORT, MEDIATION AND ARBITRATION

by

Ian S. BLACKSHAW

T•M•C•ASSER PRESS

Published by T·M·C·Asser press
P.O. Box 16163, 2500 BD The Hague, The Netherlands
<www.asserpress.nl>

T·M·C·Asser press' English language books are distributed exclusively by:

Cambridge University Press, The Edinburgh Building, Shaftesbury Road,
Cambridge CB2 2RU, UK,
or
for customers in the USA, Canada and Mexico:
Cambridge University Press, 100 Brook Hill Drive, West Nyack, NY 10994-2133, USA
<www.cambridge.org>

ISBN 978-90-6704-307-6
ISSN 1874-6926

Cover photograph: 'Painterly Realism of a Football Player' by Kazimir Malevich, 1915.
Courtesy of the Heirs of Kazimir Malevich.

**T.M.C. Asser Instituut – Institute for Private and Public International Law,
International Commercial Arbitration and European Law**

Institute Address: R.J. Schimmelpennincklaan 20-22, The Hague, The Netherlands; Mailing Address: P.O. Box 30461, 2500 GL The Hague, The Netherlands; Tel.: +3170 342 0300; Fax: +3170 3420 359; Internet: www.asser.nl.
Over forty years, the T.M.C. Asser Institute has developed into a leading scientific research institute in the field of international law. It covers private international law, public international law, including international humanitarian law, the law of the European Union, the law of international commercial arbitration and increasingly, also, international economic law, the law of international commerce and international sports law.
Conducting scientific research, either fundamental or applied, in the aforementioned domains, is the main activity of the Institute. In addition, the Institute organizes congresses and postgraduate courses, undertakes contract-research and operates its own publishing house.
Because of its inter-university background, the Institute often cooperates with Dutch law faculties as well as with various national and foreign institutions.

FOREWORD

It is a pleasure to write this Foreword to the second, expanded edition of Ian Blackshaw's well-respected book on the extra-judicial settlement of sports disputes through mediation and arbitration.

Prof Blackshaw is a master of his subject who explains in clear and straightforward terms the various forms of alternative dispute resolution (ADR) methods available for dealing with a wide range of different kinds of sports disputes, which are on the increase, not least because of the huge sums of money that are nowadays at stake in sport at the elite level. As I have written elsewhere, "[t]*he unique investment of competitive egos, emotions, expectations, and money in international sports almost guarantees a dividend of highly charged disputes*.....[and] [t]*he structure for resolving them is complex*."

Dispute resolution, is one of the most critical issues which overshadow the sports arena. As Prof Blackshaw rightly points out however, ADR is "*not a panacea*" for settling all kinds of sports disputes, and so the role of the courts must not be underestimated. This is true in both Europe and the United States of America, where I practice and teach international sports law.

The expanded version of this book includes a more in-depth study of the functions and role of the Court of Arbitration for Sport (CAS), based in Lausanne, Switzerland, and also a review of the contribution of CAS to an emerging so-called '*Lex Sportiva*'. Subjects that fascinate and intrigue me, I might add. Also, an account of the services offered by the Arbitration and Mediation Center of the World Intellectual Property Organization, based in Geneva, Switzerland, for settling sports-related disputes – not necessarily IP related ones – is a very useful and important addition to the book, especially the settlement by WIPO of sports-related domain name disputes. Whether one regards the Internet as a blessing or a curse, it is definitely here to stay and impact more and more on sports bodies, sports persons and sports marketers, as indeed Prof Blackshaw points out.

The book also covers the use of 'advisory opinions' by CAS and the value of settling sports disputes by 'expert determination' through WIPO. Both of these forms of ADR have an important place in the hierarchy of sports disputes resolution and accordingly are worthy of consideration by parties wishing to settle disputes quickly, inexpensively, and – above all – fairly and effectively.

Let me congratulate Prof Blackshaw in producing an altogether well-rounded, well-researched and well-written book – in the much-acclaimed Asser International Sports Law series (Editors: Dr Robert Siekmann and Dr Janwillem Soek) – on a subject of critical importance to the sporting world – and beyond. It is a book that I heartily recommend to all those involved in sports disputes around the world; and, I would add, one that will most certainly be on my bookshelf for constant referral and consultation.

June 2009

James A.R. NAFZIGER
President of the International Association of Sports Law (I.A.S.L.)
Thomas B. Stoel Professor of Law
Willamette University College of Law
Salem, Oregon
United States of America

SUMMARY OF CONTENTS

TABLE OF CONTENTS

LIST OF ACRONYMS

AAA	American Arbitration Association
AARRO	Afro-Asian Rural Reconstruction Organisation
ABA	American Bar Association
ACAS	Arbitration and Conciliation Advisory Service
ADR	alternative dispute resolution
AFL	Australian Football League
AHD	Ad Hoc Division
AIBA	Association Internationale de Boxe Amateur
AIWF	Association of Winter Olympics International Sports Federations
ANOC	Association of National Olympic Committees
ANZSLA	Australian and New Zealand Sports Law Association
AOC	Australian Olympic Committee
ASA	Amateur Swimming Association
ASC	Australian Sports Commission
ASF	Swiss Football Association
ASOIF	Association of Summer Olympics International Sports Federations
ATF	Supreme Court Decisions
ATHOC	Athens Olympic Organizing Committee
BALM	British Association of Lawyer Mediators
BAS	Belgian Arbitration Commission for Sport
BASL	British Association for Sport and the Law
BIRPI	Bureaux for the Protection of Intellectual Property
BOA	British Olympic Association
BOIC	Belgian Olympic and Interfederal Committee
BWLA	British Weightlifters Association
CAS	Court of Arbitration for Sport
CEDR	Centre for Effective Dispute Resolution
CFAs	Conditional Fee Agreements
CIA	Concordat sur l'arbitrage
CJI	International Judicial Panel
CNOSF	Comité National Olympique et Sportif Français
COC	Canadian Olympic Committee
CONI	Italian Olympic Committee
CPD	Continuing Professional Development
CPR	Center for Public Resources
DG SANCO	Directorate-General for Health and Consumer Protection
DRC	FIFA Dispute Resolution Chamber
EC	European Community
ECC- Net	European extra-judicial network
ECHR	European Court of Human Rights
ECJ	European Court of Justice
ECODIR	Electronic Consumer Dispute Resolution Platform
EEA	European Economic Area
EU	European Union
FA	Football Association of England and Wales
FAI	Irish Football Association
FAT	FIBA Arbitral Tribunal
FEI	International Equestrian Federation
FFSA	Fédération française des sociétés d'aviron
FFV	French Sailing Federation

FIBA	Fédération Internationale de Basketball
FIFA	Federation Internationale de Football Association
FIFPro	Fédération Internationale des Associations de Footballeurs Professionnels
FILA	International Federation of Associated Wrestling Styles
FIM	International Motorcycling Federation
FIN-NET	network for financial services
FINA	international swimming federation
FIS	International Ski Federation
FISA	International Rowing Federation
FJO	Federal Act on Judicial Organization
FPJ	Portuguese Judo Federation
GR	General Regulations
HFF	Hellenic Football Federation
HTTA	Hellenic Table Tennis Federation
IAAF	International Association of Amateur Athletic Federations
IBF	International Badminton Federation
ICAAN	Internet Corporation for Assigned Names and Numbers
ICADR	International Centre for Alternative Dispute Resolution
ICAS	International Council of Arbitration for Sport
ICC	International Chamber of Commerce
ICSID	International Centre for the Settlement of Investment Disputes
IFCAI	International Federation of Commercial Arbitration Institutions
IFs	international sports federations
IIHF	International Ice Hockey Federation
IOC	International Olympic Committee
IP	Industrial Property
IPC	International Paralympic Committee
ITC	International Transfer Certificate
JSAA	Japan Sports Arbitration Agency
KBRSF – FRBSE	Royal Belgian Federation for Equestrian Sports
LCIA	London Court of International Arbitration
LDIP	Swiss Federal Law on Private International Law
LEN	European Swimming League
NAA	National Athletics Association
NADP	National Anti-Doping Panel
NAF	National Arbitration Forum
NBA	National Basketball Association
NCAA	The National Collegiate Athletic Association
NGBs	National Governing Bodies
NOCs	National Olympic Committees
NRL	Australian National Rugby League
NSDC	Australian National Sports Dispute Centre
ODR	online dispute resolution
OG	Olympic Games
PCT	International Applications for Patents
PIL Act	Swiss Act on Private International Law
PSC	Players' Status Committee
RFU	Rugby Football Union
RSTP	Regulations on the Status and Transfer of Players
SAEC	Sports Assembly Executive Committee
SDRCC	Sport Dispute Resolution Centre of Canada
SDRP	Sport Dispute Resolution Panel
SOCOG	Sydney Organising Committee for the Olympic Games
SPFA	Scottish Professional Footballer's Association
TCC	Technology and Construction Court
TFS	Swiss Federal Tribunal
UCI	International Cycling Union
UDRP	Uniform Domain Name Dispute Resolution Policy
UEFA	Union of European Football Associations

UIAA	International Mountaineering and Climbing Federation
UMA	Uniform Mediation Act
USAW	United States of America Wrestling Association
USOC	United States Olympic Committee
WADA	World Anti-Doping Agency
WBC	World Boxing Council
WHA	Welsh Hockey Union
WHU	Welsh Hockey Union
WIPO	World Intellectual Property Organisation
WIPO ECAF	WIPO Electronic Case Facility
WSA	Welsh Sports Association
WTO	World Trade Organization
WWF	World Wrestling Federation

Part I
Alternative Dispute Resolution in General and Mediation in Particular

CHAPTER 1
GENERAL INTRODUCTION

1.1 The Business of Sport

Sport is now big business accounting for more than 3 percent of world trade. In the European Union, sport has developed into a discrete business representing more than 2 percent of the combined GNP of the 27 Member States.

This phenomenal growth in the value of the Sports Industry is largely due to the increase in the broadcast coverage of sports events and the exponential rise in the fees paid by broadcasters for the corresponding rights. For example, an estimated three billion people watched the spectacular opening ceremony of the 2008 Beijing Olympic Summer Games; and the TV rights to English FA Premier League for the three seasons, 2007-2010, have been sold by auction for a staggering GBP 1.7 billion.

Increased television coverage has also led to a spectacular rise in the value of sports sponsorship, by national and multinational companies wishing to associate themselves and their products and services with major national and international sports events, such as the Olympic Games. It is not surprising, therefore, that the world-wide market for sports sponsorship has steadily grown into a multi-billion dollar industry

The increase in leisure time in the developed world has also played a significant part in the meteoric rise of the Sports Industry with more people participating in and watching sport than ever before. This, in turn, has seen the rise of sports men and women as sports personalities with salaries, especially footballers, many of whom are now earning GBP 150,000 per week and also benefiting from lucrative sponsorship and endorsement deals. Their incomes are now akin to the fabulous incomes of Hollywood 'stars'. In fact, sport is now firmly a part of the world-wide entertainment industry and an important one at that!

Likewise, the increasing importance of intellectual property (IP) and the commercialisation of the corresponding IP rights (IPRs) in the sporting arena is another phenomenon that should not be overlooked. Indeed, without the legal recognition and protection afforded to sports IPRs, many major and other sports events, including the Olympic Games and the FIFA World Cup, would never be viable financially, to the detriment of the athletes themselves and also to the great disappointment of sports fans and followers throughout the world. Equally, leading sports persons would not be able to commercially exploit their corresponding personality and image rights.[1]

All of this, combined with the development and inexorable rise in the use and application of the Internet and other new forms of media, including mobile phones, to deliver

[1] See further on this important and developing subject: Ian S. Blackshaw and Robert C.R. Siekmann, eds., *Sports Image Rights in Europe* (The Hague, T.M.C. Asser Press 2005).

sports programming, content and information (e.g., the latest cricket score), the value of the Sports Industry is set to continue growing even further in the future.

Indeed, according to Sepp Blatter, the President of FIFA, the World Governing Body of Football, and I would agree with him, sport is now a product in its own right, and there is much to play for not only on but also off the field of play. As such, the number of sports-related disputes is on the increase.

So, the question, quite naturally, arises: how best to resolve these disputes? The traditional – that is, through the Courts – or the modern way – that is extra-judicially? In other words, by some form of alternative dispute resolution (ADR) method.

1.2 The Need for Alternative Dispute Resolution Mechanisms in Sport

With all this money and wealth circulating in sport, winning is now everything – the privilege and satisfaction alone of taking part is passé. In other words, the Olympic motto has nowadays lost its currency. And, with the increasing use of performance enhancing drugs by sports persons, it seems to be a case of winning at all costs! For top sports persons, winning means money and riches. So, in line with the old adage, where there is money to be fought over there are likely to be disputes, it is not surprising that sports litigation is also on the increase.

This raises the question, given the special characteristics and structures of sport, well recognised around the world and not least by the EU Commission in Brussels in its evolving Policy on Sport and not least in its 2007 'White Paper on Sport', how best to resolve sports disputes. By traditional or modern means? In other words, through ADR methods.

ADR may be defined as any process that leads to the resolution of a dispute through the agreement of the parties without the use of a judge or arbitrator; and has become very popular over the years amongst companies, business people and organisations around the world, including sports bodies, such as the International Olympic Committee, which established the Court of Arbitration for Sport (CAS) in 1983 to settle sports disputes 'within the family of sport'.[2]

Extra-judicial settlement of various kinds of disputes through ADR methods has developed because the Courts – and, indeed, traditional forms of arbitration like those conducted through the International Chamber of Commerce in Paris, France – are often slow; procedurally complex, technical and inflexible; and quite expensive. Apart from all that, the outcomes of judicial proceedings are generally unpredictable. Litigation is, therefore, something of a lottery! Added to which, Judges are not always *au fait* with the background to certain kinds of business disputes, especially those involving technical matters.

This is particularly true when it comes to sports disputes, in view of the special characteristics and dynamics of sport – not least, the need for swift results where sporting deadlines are often in play – particularly recognised by the European Union and referred to as the 'specificity of sport'.[3]

---

[2] See further on the organisation and activities of the CAS: Ian S. Blackshaw, Robert C.R. Siekmann and Janwillem Soek, eds., *The Court of Arbitration for Sport 1984-2004* (The Hague, T.M.C. Asser Press 2006).

[3] See further generally on the value of resolving sports disputes by ADR the chapter by Ian Blackshaw on 'Alternative Dispute Mechanisms in Sport', in Ian Blackshaw Mark James, John O'Leary, Roger Welch, Ian Blackshaw, Simon Boyes and Andrew Caiger, *Sports Law*, 3rd edn. (London, Cavendish Publishing 2006).

Furthermore, the Courts themselves are actively encouraging and promoting the use of various forms of ADR in suitable cases. For example, the Lord Chief Justice of England and Wales, Lord Phillips of Worth Maltravers, has recently extolled the merits and virtues of ADR as an alternative to litigation in a speech given on 29 March, 2008 at the new International Centre for Alternative Dispute Resolution in New Delhi, India. In view of the importance of his remarks, the full text of this speech is reproduced in Appendix I to this book.

In this work, we will examine the possibilities of using, instead of the traditional forms of litigation and heavy duty arbitration, such as that offered by the International Chamber of Commerce in Paris, which also, I should add, has its place in the scheme of things in particular cases and circumstances, alternative forms of dispute resolution, including mediation, med-arb, expert determination and arbitration by such bodies as the Court of Arbitration for Sport, based in Lausanne, Switzerland, and the Arbitration and Mediation Center of the World Intellectual Property Organization, based in Geneva, Switzerland, as a means of settling sports disputes.

To put the subject into context and by way of background, we will first take a look at the attitude of the Courts generally to their being involved in sports disputes.

CHAPTER 2
THE COURTS AND SPORTS DISPUTES

2.1 Generally

Generally speaking, the use of alternative methods of resolving disputes, including arbitration, conciliation and mediation, is not opposed by the Courts.

Indeed, in many jurisdictions around the world, the Courts are very sympathetic and often actively encourage the amicable extra-judicial settlement of disputes of various kinds, not least in the sporting field.

2.2 The Position in England

In England, there is a long established legal tradition that the Courts do not generally intervene in sports disputes. They prefer to leave matters to be settled by the sports bodies themselves, considering them to be in the words of Vice Chancellor Megarry in the case of *McInnes* v. *Onslow-Fane*[4] ' ... far better fitted to judge than courts'.

And, Lord Denning, a former Master of the Rolls, went further and expressed the point in the following succinct and characteristic way in *Enderby Town Football Club Ltd* v. *Football Association Ltd*[5]: '... justice can often be done in domestic tribunals better by a good layman than a bad lawyer'.

However, the English Courts will intervene when there has been a breach of the rules of natural justice[6] and also in cases of 'restraint of trade', where livelihoods are at stake.[7] Although it may be added that the British sprinter, Dwain Chambers, failed in the English High Court on 18 July, 2008 to get the lifetime ban imposed on him by the British Olympic Association (BOA) for a doping offence committed in 2003, for which he was banned for two years, on the grounds that the Court did not consider that the BOA ban constituted an unreasonable restraint of trade! Some commentators have remarked that the outcome of this case was another example of the reluctance of the English Courts to intervene in sports disputes, leaving them to be dealt with by the sports governing bodies themselves.[8]

2.3 The Position in the United States of America

Incidentally, a similar legal situation exists in the United States.[9] In *Harding*, the Federal District Court made the following observations:

---

[4] [1978] 1 *WLR* 1520, at p. 1535.
[5] [1971] 1 Ch. 591, at p. 605.
[6] *Revie* v. *Football Association*, *The Times*, 19 December 1979.
[7] *Greig* v. *Insole* [1978] 3 *All ER* 449.
[8] See the author's critique of this decision in 3/4 *The International Sports Law Journal* (ISLJ) (2008).
[9] See *Harding* v. *United States Figure Skating Association* [1994] 851 F Supp 1476.

> 'The courts should rightly hesitate before intervening in disciplinary hearings held by private associations.... Intervention is appropriate only in the most extraordinary circumstances, where the association has clearly breached its own rules, that breach will imminently result in serious and irreparable harm to the plaintiff, and the plaintiff has exhausted all internal remedies. Even then, injunctive relief is limited to correcting the breach of the rules. The court should not intervene in the merits of the underlying dispute.'

2.4 The Position in Canada

In Canada, the situation is similar to that in the United States of America.[10] In *McCaig*, the Judge made the following pertinent remarks about the role of the Courts in the resolution of sports disputes:

> '... The bodies which heard the appeals were experienced and knowledgeable in the sport of sailing, and fully aware of the selection process. The appeal bodies determined that the selection criteria had been met ... [and] as persons knowledgeable in the sport ... I would be reluctant to substitute my opinion for those who know the sport and knew the nature of the problem.'

2.5 The Position in the European Civil Law Countries

2.5.1 Generally

In the European civil law countries too, the Courts are generally amenable to the parties trying to settle their disputes by arbitration and other extra-judicial methods, and will adjourn proceedings in cases where there is an express contractual requirement to refer disputes to, say, arbitration, to allow this process to be pursued. Only in the event of failure to reach an extra-judicial solution, and in some other very limited cases, will the Courts be prepared to entertain a suit and adjudicate on the dispute.

Also, generally speaking, the Courts will not intervene in sporting disputes, which concern the 'rules of the game' of the sport concerned.

The position in Switzerland provides a good example of these general principles.

2.5.2 Switzerland

Under Article 190(2) of the Swiss Federal Code on Private International Law of 18 December, 1987 a decision of the CAS, which is treated as an arbitral award under Swiss Law, can only be challenged in the following circumstances:

> 'a) if a sole arbitrator was designated irregularly or the arbitral tribunal was constituted irregularly;
> b) if the arbitral tribunal erroneously held that it had or did not have jurisdiction;
> c) if the arbitral tribunal ruled on matters beyond the claims submitted to it or if it failed to rule on one of the claims;
> d) if the equality of the parties or their right to be heard in an adversarial proceeding was not respected;
> e) if the award is incompatible with Swiss public policy'.

---

[10] See *McCaig* v. *Canadian Yachting Association & Canadian Olympic Association* [1996] Case 90-01-96624.

Also, the Swiss Federal Tribunal (the highest Court) has held, as part of a seminal ruling of 15 March, 1993 on the juridical nature of awards made by the CAS, that any judgement, that has as its sole object the application of games rules, is '... in principle, outside a juridical control'. We will return to this important case later in the section on the CAS.

2.5.3 Spain

In some jurisdictions, for example, Spain, there is a legal requirement for the parties in dispute to attempt a resolution through conciliation proceedings conducted before a Judge ('acto de conciliacion') before being permitted to proceed with an ordinary legal action before the Courts. In such proceedings, the Judge explores with the parties in dispute the possibilities of their settling their dispute amicably.

2.5.4 Italy

There is a similar situation in Italy in relation to the settlement of sports disputes, where parties to such disputes are obliged first to refer their disputes to a special Chamber of Conciliation and Arbitration for Sport (*Camera di Conciliazione e Arbitrato per lo Sport*) – a kind of Italian CAS.

2.6 The Position in the Rest of the World

A similar situation is developing in other parts of the world too, as sport is a global phenomenon and sports disputes are an increasingly common occurrence throughout the world. So, solutions need to be found quickly, informally, effectively and inexpensively to resolve sports disputes of various kinds, including commercial ones, which, with so much money at stake, are continually on the rise.

It should be added, however, that ADR is not a panacea for all ills and is not appropriate in cases, where, for example, injunctive relief or a legal precedent is required to resolve the dispute. In such cases, the Courts are the most appropriate forum for settling disputes.

CHAPTER 3
ALTERNATIVE DISPUTE RESOLUTION (ADR)

Before looking at the pros and cons of using Mediation to settle sports disputes, it would be useful to put the subject of ADR into context and look at what it is and the reasons for its growth and popularity in general.

3.1 WHAT IS ADR?

3.1.1 **Generally**

Like many other innovative business practices, ADR originated in the United States and has quickly spread around the world. For example, a number of US organisations, including one appropriately called 'JAMS/ENDISPUTE' has been providing an ADR service to individuals and companies for more than twenty years, claiming a settlement rate of 90 percent.

ADR has been defined by the ADR Group, which is based in Bristol in the UK and claims to be the UK's first and largest private commercial dispute resolution service, as follows: 'Any process that leads to the resolution of a dispute through the agreement of the parties without the use of a judge or arbitrator.'

The ADR Group was established in 1989 by a group of lawyers, businessmen and professional mediators to provide a 'quick and inexpensive means of resolving disputes without the need to resort to the courts'.

The ADR Group has affiliated offices in the USA, Canada and throughout the EU, and mediates in more than 12,000 cases annually, claiming a 94 percent settlement rate. The Group offers services in dispute prevention and management and training courses in negotiation and mediation.

The other body providing ADR services in the UK is the Centre for Effective Dispute Resolution (CEDR), which is based in the City of London. CEDR was established one year after the ADR Group in 1990. CEDR also offers training programmes and its members include leading lawyers and law firms and many 'blue chip' companies. CEDR claims an 85 percent settlement rate.

ADR has grown out of the need to provide parties to a dispute with an alternative to litigation as a means of settling their disputes. Over the years, litigation has come to be regarded, especially by businessmen, as an expensive, inflexible and dilatory method of dispute resolution. Arbitration, originally seen and embraced by the commercial community, as a quicker and less expensive way of settling disputes, is also now regarded as suffering from similar defects.

3.1.2 The 'Woolf reforms' in England

The English Courts have responded to these complaints by promoting attempts to settle cases in the early stages of the litigation process as part of new reforms of the Rules of Civil Procedure introduced on 26 April, 1999 by Lord Woolf. Writing in *The Times* on 4 April, 2000, Frances Gibb, the newspaper's legal editor, noted:

> 'Gladiatorial-style litigation is losing its appeal. In its place, mediation – a conciliatory way to tackle disputes outside the courtroom – is finally taking off. These are the findings of a survey [by "MORI"] into Lord Woolf's shake-up of civil justice. The message one year on is that the reforms have promoted a 'cultural shift' towards mediation.'

In fact, to encourage attempts at mediation, the Courts may impose an adverse order for costs on a party refusing to mediate who is considered to have acted unreasonably.

As the former Lord Chancellor, Lord Irvine of Lairg, told the CEDR Civil Justice Audit Conference, held in London on 7 April, 2000: 'There is no doubt that ADR can provide quicker, cheaper and more satisfactory outcomes than traditional litigation. I want to see ADR achieve its full potential.'

It is interesting to note, *en passant*, that, in the 1995 unreported case of *Lennox Lewis* v. *The World Boxing Council and Frank Bruno*, the High Court ordered Lewis to try to settle the dispute with Bruno and the WBC over a fight with Mike Tyson, as required by the WBC Rules, by compulsory mediation, which the Judge considered would be 'a perfectly proper independent process of mediation'.

3.2 Advantages of ADR

As CEDR, the Centre for Effective Dispute Resolution, another UK provider of ADR services, puts it:

> 'All disputes, whether in difficult business negotiations or full-scale litigation, can become a drain on resources, sapping money, time and management focus, and destroying important commercial relationships.'

ADR addresses these particular issues and, again, according to CEDR, offers the following advantages:

- speed – ADR processes can be set up quickly and usually last only one or two days;
- cost savings – ADR costs a fraction of litigation;
- confidentiality – ADR is confidential, thus avoiding any unwanted publicity;
- control and flexibility – unlike a court hearing, the parties themselves remain in full control of the ADR process and any settlement agreed. If no settlement is reached, the parties retain their rights to sue. In other words, the ADR process is conducted on a 'without prejudice' basis;
- commercial focus – the parties' commercial and/or personal interests influence the outcome, thereby making more creative settlements possible;
- business relations – ADR processes, being closer to business negotiations than adversarial courtroom procedures, can be better preserved or restored;

- independence – parties can benefit from rigorous and confidential analysis of their position by a genuinely independent mediator.

ADR can be used in conjunction with litigation and arbitration and in national and international disputes. It can also be used in almost any area of law or business (see later).

But, as the former Lord Chancellor, Lord Irvine of Lairg, has also pointed out in the Inaugural Lecture to the Faculty of Mediation and ADR in London on 27 January, 1999: 'ADR is not a panacea, nor is it cost-free.'

Indeed, it is worth setting out the text of the complete Lecture, which the reader will, I think, find interesting and informative:

Lord Irvine of Lairg
The UK Lord Chancellor

Inaugural Lecture to the Faculty of Mediation and ADR
Wednesday, 27 January 1999 London

Let me begin with a quotation for everyone who still thinks that the concept of alternatives to combative, court-based, Olympian dispute resolution is today's modishness. It is from *The Charitable Arbitrator*, written in 1688, by the so-called 'Prior of St Pierre', who was evidently no fan of litigation. If you are minded to satirise lawyers in print, a pseudonym may have been then, as now, a shrewd move! He wrote:

> '... to be a good mediator you need more than anything patience, common sense, an appropriate manner, and goodwill. You must make yourself liked by both parties, and gain credibility in their minds. To do that, begin by explaining that you are unhappy about the bother, the trouble and the expense that their litigation is causing them. After that, listen patiently to all their complaints. They will not be short, *particularly the first time around.*'

The Academy of Experts has worked hard in recent years to improve the standards of dispute resolution in this country. I am delighted to be here today, to deliver the inaugural lecture of this Faculty of Mediation and ADR. I hope that this lecture – like the Faculty itself – will continue to take forward the essential public debate about ADR.

The modern development of ADR has its origins in the United States of America in the 1970s as a reaction against the high cost and long delays of litigating business disputes. ADR has now come to be recognised internationally as an effective alternative to highly expensive and rigid adversarial systems.

ADR has spread primarily through the influence of the institutions. These include the international arbitration organisations, national and regional arbitration and conciliation centres, national arbitration institutions, professional institutions and national courts. Whilst not dependent on government endorsement, this can provide additional impetus. The International Chamber of Commerce, recognising that the conduct of formal arbitration or litigation may be costly, time consuming, and entail considerable disruption for the parties involved, has always had a procedure for conciliation and two thirds of all ICC arbitration cases are resolved through negotiation before the imposition of an award. Other major international arbitration organisations to offer conciliation services include the American Arbitration Association, the London Court of International Arbitration, the World Intellectual Property Organisation and the International Centre for the Settlement of Investment Disputes. Building on this international framework, most national arbitration centres and organisations now actively promote the use of ADR.

In the UK the Centre for Dispute Resolution (CEDR) was launched with the support of the Confederation of British Industry in 1990 to promote ADR in dispute handling. CEDR promotes ADR, trains and accredits mediators and arranges mediations and they claim a 95 per cent success rate in resolving disputes. The Academy of Experts, although its main purpose is to promote the better use of experts, is also at the forefront in the development of ADR processes and was the first UK body to establish a register of qualified mediators. The British Association of Lawyer Mediators was set up in 1995 with the aim of promoting mediation in the UK and of the role of lawyers in mediation and the maintenance of high professional standards. The City Disputes Panel, was founded in 1994 to settle financial disputes in the financial services industry. Its panellists are dedicated to the resolution of financial disputes through mediation, evaluation, determination and arbitration. Also the use of ADR has been established in the UK in resolving family and divorce disputes, employment disputes, environmental disputes, and community or neighbourhood disputes.

The Government freely recognises that ADR has a significant part to play in the delivery of civil justice. In Opposition, we advocated the development of alternatives to litigation, including the use of legal aid to fund access to mediation, arbitration and tribunals. Almost four years ago, at the Labour Party Annual Conference of 1995, we drew attention in our Policy Statement to what we considered to be: 'An imbalance between public provision for traditional litigation on the one hand and mediation services on the other.'

We also made it plain that we proposed to use the existing legal aid budget 'to expand access to alternative forms of dispute resolution such as mediation, arbitration and tribunals'. Last year, I approved the LAB's decision to make legal aid available for mediation.

And in Government we have continued to encourage the use of mediation, most notably in the area of family law, where it is a central tenet of divorce law reform. The importance of mediation and ADR in family law cases can scarcely be understated, given the high incidence of family breakdown and the appalling social consequences which result.

Those of you here who heard me deliver the CEDR conference Keynote Address last November will know that I have no doubt whatsoever of the considerable potential benefits which ADR can deliver, for the system of civil justice, and for the individuals and parties who seek redress through that system. I spoke then of cost-effectiveness; of high approval ratings from those who have used mediation or other alternatives; of the wide endorsement and support that so many experienced judges and senior lawyers have for ADR processes. I wholeheartedly share their enthusiasm, and their desire to develop this potential to its fullest extent.

Equally, I recognise that ADR is not dependent on Government endorsement. It is a thriving, autonomous, profitable industry. In his address to the CEDR Conference, Professor Karl Mackie referred to 'a recognition that ADR is a serious market opportunity for professional firms, a significant management tool for companies'.

Private sector companies and individuals are increasingly choosing to investigate alternatives to the courts and arbitration. Institutions such as CEDR itself, and the City Disputes Panel, are reporting rapidly increasing caseloads. It is also significant that much of this new work is international – an affirmation of London's position as the leading centre for international commercial dispute resolution.

The courts have taken their own steps to ensure that the potential benefits of ADR are, at the very least, given ready consideration by the parties before them. A pilot mediation scheme at the Central London County Courts was set up in 1996. Mediations continue to take place regularly. Those who have participated in them generally express a high degree of satisfaction with the process. I wish to pay tribute tonight to the mediators themselves – some of whom have been provided by the Academy of Experts – for their enthusiasm and support for this pioneering scheme.

I am also pleased to commend the introduction of a mediation initiative in the Technology and Construction Court – a new court which I opened last October. It is well recognised that heavy construction cases in particular are suitable for mediation, and we know from experience both in this country – but particularly in other jurisdictions such as Hong Kong, the United States and Australia – that mediation can be a, if not the, most effective way of resolving such disputes, often within the life time of the contract, and at very considerable cost savings to the parties.

The Court of Appeal continues to support ADR actively. Specialist panels of senior, widely experienced lawyers have been set up, to assist in mediating pending appeals. At the setting down stage, the Master of the Rolls now writes to both parties, urging them to consider ADR. Should they decide not to, they are invited to indicate why. This protocol helps, not only to impress upon appellant and respondent that the Court sees ADR as a serious option, but to gather direct empirical information why it is not entertained by some.

The Commercial Court issued a Practice Direction in 1993, stating that judges of the court wished to encourage parties to consider ADR. This was strengthened in a further direction, in 1996, allowing judges to consider whether a case is suitable for ADR at the interlocutory stage, to invite the parties to try it if appropriate, and to arrange early neutral evaluation.

The active support and participation of the judiciary sends a clear message to litigants and their legal representatives. ADR is not some fashionable quirk – it is a valid avenue of settlement, recognised and even promoted by the courts.

Further a discretionary power for judges will come from the new Rule 26.4, which I have approved, part of that tranche of the civil justice reforms which are due to come into effect this April. The new Rule will enable judges, at their own volition, or if requested by both parties, to stay cases they consider may be amenable to some other, more satisfactory form of resolution, such as mediation. Now, within a process driven by the imperative to keep adjournments and delays to a minimum, this Rule is remarkable in recognising that there may actually be a time benefit in delaying full proceedings, to see if quicker, more satisfactory resolution can be brought about by mediation.

This Government's increased focus on the potential benefit of ADR is, to some extent, a recognition of what the market-place is demonstrating. ADR clearly can succeed – it can deliver great benefits to parties in dispute. Individuals and companies are increasingly willing to pay for the services of mediators and arbitrators because they believe that they can achieve a more satisfactory resolution to their dispute than they are likely to secure through the full process of the court. And for parties who have, or want to leave, 'ongoing' commercial relationships, mediation is of particular value.

Let me make this point clearly. I have no doubt whatsoever that ADR has a role – an expanding role – within the civil justice system. But my Government and my Department's support is neither unconditional, nor is it absolute. There are serious and searching questions to be answered about the use of ADR. I believe that anybody who is genuinely committed to the better development of ADR is not only aware of these concerns, but shares my determination to see them addressed fully. It is in the interests of those who provide ADR to try to ensure that their services are professional, governed by universally-recognised competencies; and, above all, to ensure that they provide a service that people do need.

Professor Mackie referred in his speech to a 'gravy boat' trailing in the wake of current ADR opportunities. It is perhaps an expression that lawyers should avoid. Nobody wants to be accused of lapping at that trough. There may indeed be profits to be made from the provision of alternatives to court-based dispute resolution. But I can assure you that this Government will not be suborned into swelling them.

I want to set out my key concerns to you this evening – because I want you – the practitioners, the interested academics and experts, the experienced lawyers – to help us to find the answers. It is particularly appropriate to use the forum of this inaugural address to put these questions unequivocally on record. And I would ask anyone with views on these questions – based on comparative studies, or with the unique insights borne of experience – to pass your thoughts on to me. Your help in this will be of the greatest value.

The central objective of ADR is to encourage and promote the settlement of disputes without the need to start litigation. If that cannot be achieved, ADR still aims to assist in achieving a negotiated settlement before the trial itself starts. To succeed, ADR settlements must be fair and just, to the satisfaction of both parties in dispute. A settlement achieved without trial must be a sound and valid outcome in itself, not a compromised measure deemed by one or the other party to have short-changed them of something a trial would have achieved.

Some unstinting admirers of ADR assert that all disputes are suitable for ADR, and can benefit from it. I doubt that such unlimited enthusiasm does much to help promote wider use of ADR in the long run. Courts have a vital – indispensable – part to play in the resolution of many categories of dispute. It is, at best, naïve to claim that mediation and its alternatives can adequately equate to this role. An obvious example is the establishment of significant judicial precedent – this can arise in any category of case in dispute. Or consider the issues of cases which set the rights of the individual against those of the State. The experience of the United States suggests this is an extremely sensitive area, which must be approached with extreme care.

I think the use of ADR in administrative cases is of necessity limited. There may be more to be gained from the development of the ombudsman system, though I appreciate that ombudsmen are more concerned with the resolution of grievances, than with the resolution of disputes over conflicting rights.

But this is our current position: we do not have sufficient analytical information about ADR to claim, with certainty, that it can be useful in every category of case. We must undertake a comprehensive process of research and consideration, to answer with certainty the question: what kinds of case are suitable for ADR.

Another key area to be addressed in the development of ADR is, who are the beneficiaries? And how do they benefit? In the broadest sense, our civil and criminal reforms are driven by the need to improve access to justice. Widening the means by which everyone can gain a degree of redress for wrongs done, which lives up to expectations. Providing alternatives to the court-based resolution process must clearly be a step in the right direction.

But each step must be taken with an eye to its effect on all players in the system. Improved access to the courts will inevitably increase the burden of the workload in the courts. The introduction of the small claims arbitration scheme in 1985 was hugely popular and successful. Yet the very success of this measure imposed an unexpectedly significant burden on the county courts and the District Judges charged with administering it.

Consider, for example, the impact on the courts of ADR becoming a significantly more active part of proceedings. We would have to be sure that the Court Service actually had the capacity to deliver this substantive new function. And not at the expense of existing procedures, or other reforms – either in funding or time. Advocates of tangible Government support for ADR have argued that the Court Service will eventually benefit, through a reduction in procedural delays, or a saving of judicial time in court. This may prove to be true. But they, and we, must be able to demonstrate that the wider use of ADR in the courts is economically viable. We will need to measure and evaluate these schemes through widespread monitoring, and through pilots. And those who are active in campaigning for an expansion of ADR will need to co-operate fully in this process of assessment.

The principal argument commonly advanced in support of ADR is the potential for cost savings to the parties themselves. But again, this assumption is not straightforward. When cases do settle through ADR – particularly if this is at an early stage of litigation – very substantial cost savings can be realised. But every case which takes the option of attempting some alternative form of dispute resolution incurs an additional element of cost which does not arise if the conventional route is followed. In doing so, both parties are, in essence, taking a speculative gamble – that the investment of additional money in ADR will be rewarded by a successful pre-trial resolution, or at least a shorter case.

And the simple fact is, that some parties will lose the gamble. And ex port facto, they will have wasted time and money on testing the possibility of an alternate resolution – waste which would have been avoided had they chosen to stick to the conventional process of settling their dispute through the courts. The cost of gambling on successful ADR is not borne by the mediators and arbitrators, but by the parties themselves, and by civil justice itself.

Now this is not a matter of trifling costs, or a few days' delay. Those of you with professional or personal experience of ADR will acknowledge that it is often a demanding, skilled and sophisticated process. Proponents of mediation will readily cite statistics relating to saved court time and costs in some of the most complex business disputes. They are perhaps less ready to collate information on the costs arising from failed arbitrations. To ignore these elements – to make no determined attempt to weigh them up against the well-promoted benefits of ADR – is, at best, not balanced.

I don't wish to minimise the less measurable benefits which ADR can bring to parties in dispute. Those who have used it successfully report notably high levels of satisfaction with the actual outcomes achieved, and with the route taken to achieve settlement. ADR can reduce acrimony and aggression which is, regrettably, a common factor in court-based disputes. The benefit of this in mediated family disputes is, I think, very generally accepted.

Last October, speaking at the closing session of the fourth European conference on family law, in Strasbourg, I was pleased to acknowledge the wide international appreciation of the potential of mediation in family cases. I drew attention to the many positive benefits of the family mediation process. In reducing conflict; in encouraging a constructive and forward- looking perspective to the plans and aims of both parties. In securing agreements with a better chance of being adhered to, because they are based on step-by-step decisions reached and accepted by the individuals themselves. In the basic potential for financial savings.

So, we should not ignore the benefit of empowering the parties in less personal, emotional contexts. They too can appreciate a process of settlement which actually leaves them with the conviction that they have received a more truly satisfactory outcome, than that which follows months of stressful, fraught litigation. There is a convincing argument that parties feel more genuine satisfaction from an outcome achieved through a mediated solution.

By definition, practitioners of ADR have the most opportunity to benefit. Those who are able to offer competent and successful ADR and mediation services will find they are part of a burgeoning – and a profitable – new profession.

Lawyers in particular have a great opportunity to increase the range of services they can offer to their clients. That announcement last year from the Legal Aid Board that I referred to – that franchise legal aid will be available for mediation – should also cultivate the interest of many in the legal profession – including perhaps some who have remained sceptical to date.

It is clear that there is much greater awareness and interest in ADR amongst professionals from various disciplines and within the business community than was the case only five years ago or so. One good measure of ADR's growing importance is the number of mediators undergoing institutional training courses, and the fact that the Law Society and other professional bodies are devoting considerable attention to drafting appropriate ethical standards and guidelines for mediators.

New business opportunities will present the legal profession – indeed, all professions whose members are working to develop these alternatives – with considerable challenges. Certainly, compared to the majority of relevant professional organisations, ADR is not governed by any commonly agreed codes of practice, guidelines for training or professional conduct. The degree to which the public – and this Government – will put its faith in ADR, will depend greatly on the level of responsibility which those who wish to practise it can demonstrate.

So I hope that my comments, this evening and elsewhere, have demonstrated my unequivocal support for the better development of ADR. It has already begun to have a significant effect on the overall approach to civil justice. This will continue, and it will expand. My Department has taken active steps in the last year to forge links with leading providers of ADR and mediation services. Their willingness to co-operate with my officials, to offer advice, and to participate in pilot studies in the courts, is greatly appreciated, and augurs well for the future.

It is in our common interest to go forward – but festina lente – we must proceed slowly, on the basis of sound analysis and evaluation. This is a lesson which other jurisdictions have learned at a price. America, which often takes the lead in innovative legal practices, is raising serious questions over the claims made for the efficacy of ADR in the courts there. Professor Hazel Genn's thorough scrutiny of the pilot mediation work carried out in the Central London County Court, suggests that much the same challenges may be levelled at ADR in this country.

Perhaps one of the most alarming findings from Professor Genn's Report was that, throughout the time of the pilot exercise, only five per cent of the parties who might have elected to try mediation, actually did so. Only 5%. This was in spite of concerted efforts to encourage take-up.

In part, of course, this can be attributed to a lack of understanding – both of what mediation is, and of how successful and satisfying it can be for those in dispute. In part, it stemmed from concerns over cost. But we must be careful, and certain, that we are promoting and developing a service which meets a genuine – if undiscovered – need. Providers must take particular care that it is not the other way round.

So I want to emphasise this. We need more, detailed, analytical information, answering the specific concerns which I have touched upon tonight, and others. Do people know and understand enough about ADR? Can it really be of benefit to a majority of cases? Under what circumstances is it not the right avenue? Can its benefit be had at a reasonable cost to the system as a whole, and the individual parties? What consideration should we give to an element of compulsion?

This last question is particularly difficult. Many supporters of ADR argue strongly that the current low take-up of pilot schemes comes from lack of knowledge of its potential, and a general resistance to change and the unknown. Only with an element of compulsion, they claim, will those whose reluctance is through ignorance be able to make an informed choice. But to some extent, evidence from America suggests that compulsion does not improve settlement rates. Moreover, there are fundamental constitutional issues about the right of the individual to access of justice in the courts. I have no ready answer for you this evening – the only rational answer at this time is that we must scrutinise, consider and take great care before we act.

Very difficult too is the question of costs sanctions if mediation fails. I suggested earlier that ADR adds an extra layer of costs to the litigation process. How should these costs be dealt with by the trial Judge where mediating has failed? Is it right for the Judge simply to award costs, without making an investigation of what actually happened in the mediation? That would involve the breach of a cardinal principle of ADR, its confidentiality. Is it sufficient – as some have suggested – simply to invite the Judge to exercise his own judgement as to whether this is a case in which ADR ought to have been tried? And if he thinks it should have been but it was not, should he express that opinion in his costs award? Should we ask the mediators, when mediation has failed, to indicate how they think the Judge should exercise his discretion with respect to costs? These questions are increasingly being asked – and they need answers.

I also referred earlier to the responsibility of the professional organisations who want to see greater use of ADR in this country. It is not the habit of the Government to constrain the activities of professional bodies. But if we are to support the expenditure of the justice budget on ADR, we will need to be sure that this industry does not become monopolistic or covert. Practitioners must demonstrate a united approach to developing standards of competence and effective training. A regime of self-regulation measurable by the Government, and by the people whom you will be looking to as clients.

ADR is, I believe, entirely consistent with the principle of the better delivery of justice.

I am optimistic about ADR's future place in the system – but I am required to be a sceptic. As Lord Chancellor, I am charged with the responsibility to ensure that what I endorse can deliver – can make a positive contribution to the justice system in total. It is therefore my duty to ask the difficult questions, and to test the answers to the limit.

ADR has many supporters. But they too have a responsibility to proceed with care. ADR is not a panacea, nor is it cost-free. But I do believe that it can play a vital part in the opening of access to justice. But to do so, it must be properly implemented, properly developed and properly regulated. So let us proceed together, with caution, and in the clear light of experience and consideration. For, if ADR can live up to the hopes of its most passionate advocates, we may together bring about one of the most far-reaching, significant – and universally appreciated – reforms to civil justice.

Now let me end on a more lyric note. It is from *The Lover Arbitrator*, written in 1799. Volnay, a lawyer, is asked to arbitrate a separation between husband and wife. He agrees, with this morally uplifting sentiment:

> 'Neither accused nor arbitrator, I'll always be a conciliator, Although a lawyer by profession To reconcile is my obsession. And so my business always ends With no more clients, just more friends. '

What forms of ADR are available?

3.3 Forms of ADR

ADR takes various forms and these have been defined, again by the ADR Group, as follows:

Conciliation – The intervention of an independent third party in order to bring the disputing parties together to talk.

Mediation – A voluntary private dispute resolution process in which a neutral person helps the parties to reach a negotiated settlement. The neutral third party would ordinarily play a more pro-active role than in conciliation. The mediator has no power to make any decision or award.

The *Mini-Trial* – A voluntary non-binding procedure allowing both parties to present their case before senior executives from each party. They would normally do so in the presence of a neutral 'expert' who would assist the parties to settle and who may if necessary give a legal or technical view of the merits of the case or likely litigation outcome. This procedure has been described as being 'structured to reconvert a legal dispute back into a business dispute'. The neutral 'expert' could also be a mediator.

Neutral Evaluation – The use of a neutral to evaluate the facts and offer an opinion designed to help the parties reach a settlement.

The last two forms of ADR are, in essence, species of Expert Determination. This is particularly valuable and useful dispute mechanism in cases involving technical issues that need to be resolved. For example, in the sports field, an overrun on the quoted costs in the building or refurbishing of a sports stadium or arena could be quickly settled with the intervention of an independent and suitably qualified expert, whose decision the parties agree to accept as binding on them.

Med-Arb – A blend of mediation and arbitration in which the issues in dispute are identified –but not settled – by the mediator and subsequently determined by an arbitrator in an arbitration proceeding.

Although a popular form of ADR, Michael F. Hoellering, in an interesting overview of Med-Arb, entitled 'Mediation & Arbitration – A Growing Interaction',[11] came to the general conclusion that, although there is an expanding culture that favours combining arbitration with conciliation, each operates best when functioning separately. He also pointed out that:

> '... throughout the general business community, appreciation of mediation has now reached the point that it is standard [American Arbitration Association] policy to inform disputants of its availability at the beginning of every arbitration, and to provide a mediation "window" which the parties can take advantage of at any stage of the arbitration process'.

And added by way of example:

> 'in ...[an] ... arbitrated case, in which liability was determined in a series of interim awards, the chairman of the arbitral tribunal was asked to mediate the damage issue. He did so, successfully, after resigning as chairman of the tribunal.'

[11] *Dispute Resolution Journal* (Spring 1997) at pp. 23-25.

CHAPTER 4
MEDIATION IN GENERAL

4.1 INTRODUCTORY

According to the ADR Group, CEDR, JAMS and other ADR service providers, the most popular form of ADR is Mediation with high success rates.

Mediation is also taking off in the rest of Europe, which, according to Jane Player, head of litigation at the London law firm of DLA, 'is more receptive to mediation because on the whole the continent is less adversarial [with] fewer large law firms with strictly litigation departments [and] lawyers [who] do both corporate and litigation'.

Why is Mediation so popular and successful? The ADR Group claims a settlement rate of 80 percent of the mediation cases it handles; whilst CEDR and JAMS/ENDISPUTE claim success rates of 85 percent and 90 percent respectively.

4.2 ADVANTAGES OF MEDIATION

Mediation enjoys the following main advantages:

Mediation is quick – it can be arranged within days or weeks rather than months or years as in the case of litigation and can also be conducted in a very short time.

It is less expensive – quick settlements save management time and legal costs.

It is confidential – adverse publicity is avoided and unwanted parties, such as competitors or journalists, are not present.

It covers wider issues, interests and needs – underlying issues and hidden agendas are exposed making creative solutions possible to satisfy the needs of all the parties.

It is informal – a common sense and straightforward negotiation results.

It allows the parties to retain control – the parties make the decisions rather than control being handed over to a judge or an arbitrator.

It is entirely 'without prejudice' – the parties have nothing to lose, their rights are not affected by the mediation, thus litigation can be commenced or continued if the mediation fails to produce an agreed settlement.

As Sam Passow, head of research at CEDR, has put it in a report, entitled, 'Hands across the Table', by Kelly Parsons in *The European Lawyer* in July 2000:

> 'Mediation differs from other alternative dispute resolution methods, such as arbitration, because the outcome or solution is not imposed. It has to be concluded voluntarily by the parties on either side. The mediator facilitates by evaluating the dispute and proposing solutions, but does not make a judgment as happens in an arbitration or independent expert determination. This means the parties own the outcome, it is their problem but also their solution. Therefore they are more likely to get an outcome that they can live with.'

So, what is mediation?

4.3 The Concept of Mediation

Mediation is not a new thing. People have been mediating – that is, trying to reconcile differences between individuals and groups – for thousands of years. The Bible and other ancient texts are full of examples. Indeed, the Roman Catholic Church emerged during the Middle Ages as an effective arbitrator (for which read 'mediator') between Christian sovereigns. As Henry T. King Jr. and Marc A. Le Forestier point out in a fascinating article, entitled 'Papal Arbitration – How the Early Roman Catholic Church Influenced Modern Dispute Resolution':[12]

> 'To avoid war between Christian sovereigns, an arbitrator with inherent authority and a divine commission to do justice was made available.... Papal sovereignty permitted secular kings to submit to papal arbitration ... Within the framework of the divine right of kings, the pope was a proper arbitrator because he too derived his position from divine right.'

However, in the last twenty years or so, mediation, as a method of settling commercial disputes, has grown in popularity in the business community and has taken on certain features and characteristics.

Many learned books have been written and seminars given on the theory of mediation and the underlying principles of negotiation, as well as manuals published on its practical application to a range of disputes and issues.

It is beyond the scope of this work to go into the theory of mediation and the part played by psychology and its practical application in a dispute situation and context. Suffice to say, that mediation, if not a science, is certainly an art, and there is need for mediators to be properly trained in it. Many professional training and accreditation courses are available, and many litigators have taken or are taking advantage of them. Mediation is growing as a new legal practice area to satisfy a developing need amongst a wide range of clients.

4.4 What is Mediation?

Mediation is a voluntary, non-binding, 'without prejudice' process that uses a neutral third party (mediator) to assist the parties in dispute to reach a mutually agreed settlement without having to resort to a court. It differs from litigation and arbitration in that a binding decision is not imposed on the parties by a judge or an arbitrator. The main advantage of the mediation process is to permit the parties to work out their own solution to their dispute with the assistance of the mediator.

Mediation is a natural extension of the most common method of resolving disputes, namely, negotiation. However, negotiations either break down or cannot be commenced for a variety of reasons. Mediation gives the parties in dispute the option to start or continue negotiations in a controlled setting. If the mediation is not successful, the parties are still free to go to court or arbitration, so nothing has been lost.

---

[12] *Dispute Resolution Journal* (Summer 1997) at pp. 74-80.

4.5 Common Concerns about Mediation Answered

Many people regard agreeing to mediation as an admission of failure. This is not the case. As previously mentioned, negotiations break down for various reasons, and so mediation gives the parties the chance of keeping the negotiations going. The negotiations have not failed until mediation has been attempted.

Putting the dispute in the hands of a mediator does not involve any loss of control by the parties. On the contrary, the control remains with the parties, as the mediator has no authority to render any decision or force any settlement. A settlement is only reached if and when the parties consider that the settlement proposed is fair and reasonable.

Mediation does not create extra work for the parties in dispute. In fact, in the long run, mediation saves time. The parties do have to invest some time and effort in the mediation, but most cases submitted to mediation settle, saving further time. Even in the minority of cases in which mediation does not lead to a settlement, the time spent on the mediation reduces the time needed for preparing for a trial.

Neither does mediation create extra costs. Mediation reduces costs related to litigation through the early settlement of the dispute. It also, as already mentioned, reduces the trial preparation time required in those cases, which do not settle.

Many people shy away from mediation because they think that an opponent will use the mediation to gain more information about their case. In the mediation process, each party is completely in control of the information disclosed. If a party does not wish the other side to know something, they can keep it to themselves or disclose it to the mediator in confidence. However, if the information is something that might persuade the other party to accept a settlement, or is something they will find out about later on through the civil procedural legal process of '*discovery*', there is little, in those particular circumstances, to be lost by freely disclosing that information.

The parties are entirely free to choose the mediator. In fact, they must agree on his or her appointment. Organisations, such as CEDR, that offer mediation services, have a list of trained mediators with details of their qualifications and experience.

Most mediations are quick, lasting a few hours or a few days, but the mediator will continue to work with the parties as long as they wish to continue with the mediation.

It is often said that arbitration rather than replacing litigation tends to lead to litigation. On the other hand, mediation is not just an extra step in the dispute resolution process; it is usually the final step as most cases settle.

As already mentioned, nothing is lost if the mediation is not successful. Because the mediation process is conducted on a 'without prejudice' basis, the parties are free to go to court or arbitration. It is as if the mediation did not take place. Nothing revealed in the mediation can be used by either party and neither can the mediator be required to give evidence on behalf of either party in any subsequent court or arbitration proceedings.

However, it is possible for both parties to waive their right to confidentiality and 'without prejudice' privilege, but what happens if one party refuses to do so? Can a judge in subsequent legal proceedings, look behind the curtain of confidentiality and 'without prejudice' privilege? See the following interesting article on this fundamental point, which was first published in *the New Law Journal*, on 15 May 2008:

Tony Allen[13]

Mediation: protection by privilege and confidentiality? A review of *Cumbria Waste Management and another v Baines Wilson*

Following closely on the saga of the Bournemouth Airport car park in *Earl of Malmesbury v Strutt & Parker* [2008] EWHC (TCC) comes another case dealing with the confidentiality of the mediation process, namely *Cumbria Waste Management Ltd and Lakeland Waste Management Ltd v Baines Wilson* [2008] EWHC 786 (QB), heard in the Birmingham Mercantile Court by HHJ Frances Kirkham. In *Malmesbury,* the Earl strangely conceded (along with his opponents) that the judge should hear the offers that each had made to the other at the mediation. As a direct result of that, Jack J found that the Earl's position at the mediation had been wholly unreasonable, and based part of his adverse costs sanction package on that. It is fundamental to that decision that it was not the judge who peered uninvited behind the veil normally drawn over without prejudice offers exchanged at mediations, but both parties who invited him there by specifically waiving any privilege. However, *Cumbria and Lakeland v Baines Wilson* deals with a case where one party at a mediation would not waive privilege.

There had been two mediations, in fact, with different mediators, both cases being defended by DEFRA and arising out of the 2001 foot and mouth outbreak (presumably the waste requiring management included diseased cattle carcasses). Cumbria sued DEFRA for £4.5 million but settled at mediation for £3.9 million. Lakeland sued DEFRA for £1.72 million but settled through mediation for £1.4 million. Both were based on standard CEDR Model Agreements.

Both Cumbria and Lakeland had instructed solicitors Baines Wilson (BW) to advise and negotiate on the service agreements between DEFRA and themselves, and they now brought proceedings against BW alleging professional negligence which had caused them to lose the difference between their invoiced claims (plus presumably interest) and the settlements which emerged from the mediation, asserting that they had been reasonable to settle, but that the discounts they had been forced to concede were as a result of BW's negligent advice.

BW sought disclosure of a wide range of documentation relating to the mediation, and it is this that is the subject of the judgment of HHJ Kirkham. The essential issues were:

(1) whether disclosure could be ordered contrary to one party's wishes by virtue of an exception to 'without prejudice' privilege; and
(2) whether the confidentiality provisions of the mediation agreement also (and separately) preclude disclosure at the behest of one of the mediation parties.

Cumbria and Lakeland took a neutral stance over disclosure (perhaps wisely thinking that to protest too much might be misinterpreted as a sign of weakness over what might be disclosed), but DEFRA opposed it, arguing that it might reveal generally their attitude to claims of this kind when there are a number similar such cases confronting DEFRA. In appearing in these proceedings DEFRA expressly declined to waive its asserted privilege and its right to confidentiality. The judge was shown the mediation agreements but no documentation claimed to be privileged.

Both mediators reportedly took the view that the privilege belonged to the parties and not to them, though the second mediator said that she would normally counsel against the parties agreeing to share such matters with the court (advice clearly not tendered in the Bournemouth airport case). She also drew attention to the fact that the disclosure sought was so broad as to encompass any notes made by the mediator or by parties in private mediation sessions.

BW argued that it was unfair on them to have no access to documents relating to the terms on which the claims by Cumbria and Lakeland were compromised with DEFRA if the former were seeking to claim that BW were liable for the shortfall through negligence. In terms of the confidentiality clause in the CEDR form of agreement, BW argued that it was both novel and wrong to assert that A and B can validly contract for confidentiality so as to exclude C from seeing documents, when C has a proper interest in seeing them. As to without prejudice privilege, BW argued that this had

[13] Solicitor and Director of CEDR.

been waived when it was asserted by Cumbria and Lakeland that it had been reasonable for them to settle on discounted terms.

Judge Kirkham reviewed the main authorities on these points, looking particularly at *Muller v Linsley & Mortimer* [1996] 1 PNLR 74, which on the face of it was decided on very similar facts. She held however that in *Cumbria* it was the defendant (DEFRA) which was seeking protection from disclosure and not the claimants, a situation not discussed in *Muller.* She therefore refused to find that DEFRA had lost without prejudice privilege about what happened at the mediation.

Interestingly, she went on to consider the extent and force of the confidentiality provision in the mediation agreement, not a topic covered by direct authority in relation to mediation confidentiality. The main source material for the debate on this was Toulson & Phipps' textbook on confidentiality (with some passing references to *Rush & Tomkins v Granada Television* [[1989] AC 1280). She relied on a passage which stated:

> '*Mediation and other forms of dispute resolution have assumed unprecedented importance within the court system since the Woolf reforms of civil procedure. Formal mediations are generally preceded by written mediation agreements between the parties that set out expressly the confidential and "without prejudice" nature of the process. However, even in the absence of such an express agreement, the process will be protected by the "without prejudice" rule set out above.*'

HHJ Kirkham found that on both grounds of 'without prejudice' privilege and based on contracted confidentiality as between the parties, it would be wrong to order disclosure of the mediation documents. In particular, she wanted mediators to be free to conduct mediations without fear that their notes might be disclosed to others. She saw this as an exception to the general rule that confidentiality is not a bar to disclosure of material to a court.

This is a bold decision and reinforces the security of what goes on at mediations which has apparently been under investigation in several recent decisions such as *Brown and Rice v Patel* [[2007] EWHC 625 (Ch), *Chantry Vellacott v Convergence Group* [[2007] EWHC 1774 and the *Malmesbury* case. So far as I am aware, all previous cases where mediation content has been reported to a judge have involved specific waiver of privilege by the parties, for better or worse. What *Cumbria* suggests is that courts might indeed be prepared to find that there is a special mediation privilege worthy of judicial protection because the parties (and the mediator) formally contract in writing to keep the mediation process confidential. The judge in *Brown v Rice and Patel* doubted whether such a privilege yet exists, but *Cumbria* suggests that it might. *Muller* may still act as something of a brake on that, though this concerned informal 'without prejudice' correspondence rather than a formal mediation.

One related but unresolved point relates to the fact that 'without prejudice' protection almost certainly belongs only to the parties and not to the mediator. But the mediator also signs up to the confidentiality clause in the mediation agreement. Might therefore a mediator have to be consulted before any disclosure is made of what transpired at a mediation? In *SITA v Watson Wyatt* [[2002] EWHC 2025 and 2401 (Ch), the parties purportedly waived privilege to report to the judge (for different manifestations of self- interest) what a mediator was alleged to have said at a mediation, a decision that I criticised at the time. Does *Cumbria* suggest that this should never happen in future? I am sure that confidentiality will and should never be used to conceal wrongdoing by a mediator, but short of this it is hard to see why a mediator should not receive the benefit of acting confidentially in that sensitive role as much as the parties, remembering that there are two levels of confidentiality operating at a mediation offered for the benefit of the parties – overall confidentiality of the process, and confidentiality of private meetings with each party during the process.

This is going to be a continuing debate before judges at first instance, with doubtless a future opportunity for the Court of Appeal to give further guidance. Judicial instincts on the whole rightly seem to be that the mediation process is deserving of protection from undue scrutiny.

4.6 When is Mediation Appropriate?

Mediation is not suitable for all kinds of disputes and in all circumstances.

Mediation will never work unless the parties are genuinely willing to reach an amicable settlement of their dispute and ready to make compromises in the process.

Equally, not all types of dispute are suitable for mediation (more on this later when we look at the use of mediation for settling sports disputes).

Mediation should be seriously considered by parties in a dispute in the following circumstances:

- when they wish to control the outcome of the dispute rather than leave the decision to a judge or arbitrator;
- when they wish to preserve or restore a business relationship;
- when they wish to settle if they can get acceptable terms from the other side;
- when they wish to save the costs of preparing for a trial which may never take place;
- when they wish to avoid or limit the risks of going to trial;
- when they wish to have a quick settlement, including preferring to settle for less now than perhaps more later;
- when they consider that the legal and/or technical complexities of the case are in danger of eclipsing the economic and commercial realities;
- when they prefer to settle a dispute in private;
- when they feel that an injection of common sense or communication is needed to reach a settlement;
- when they believe that a few hours of concentrated effort is likely to produce an acceptable settlement.

4.7 When Should a Dispute Be Referred to Mediation?

A dispute can be referred to mediation at any time, but certain times have been identified by experience as being opportune.

According to the ADR Group, there are four 'windows of opportunity' for referring a dispute to mediation. They may be summarised as follows:

- when each party to a dispute has taken legal advice and before the dispute escalates. A process called a mediated Pre-Litigation Review can be helpful at this stage. The parties meet to decide whether they really wish to litigate and what information they need in order to make an informed decision;
- when a writ has been served. Until then the defendant may not recognise the seriousness of the dispute to warrant mediation;
- when discovery has taken place and the parties have a clear idea of the situation;
- when the case is ready for trial and before the parties have incurred the heavy costs of a trial.

However, it is possible to mediate at any stage of a dispute and, if the mediation proposal is refused, there is no reason why it cannot be proposed again at a later stage.

4.8 Dispute Management

In deciding whether mediation is suitable in any given dispute, the ADR Group, based on their experience of successful mediation, have developed for the use of lawyers, accountants, claims personnel and business people alike the following helpful 'flow diagram' of file review procedures.

CHAPTER 5
MEDIATION IN PRACTICE

Having decided to try to settle a dispute by mediation, how does one go about doing it? Obviously, the first thing is to begin the process.

5.1 How to Start a Mediation

In practice, the party interested in mediation contacts one of the mediation service providers, such as the ADR Group or CEDR, and discusses, in complete confidence the nature of the dispute and its suitability for mediation. If the case is considered to be suitable, the next step is to discuss the possibility of mediation with the other side. This is often done through solicitors or the mediation service provider. According to the ADR Group, an indirect suggestion to mediate is often more effective than a direct approach by one of the parties.

If the other side agrees to mediate, the parties need to choose a mediator who is acceptable to them. The mediation service providers maintain lists of qualified mediators with details of their qualifications and experience to help the parties to decide on the most suitable mediator for their particular dispute.

The next stage is to set a date, time and place for the mediation to commence, which is mutually convenient to the parties. This date should be as far ahead as necessary to give the parties the time they need to prepare fully for the mediation.

The parties are asked to sign an Agreement to Mediate (the terms of this Agreement are discussed later) and also provided with notes on how to prepare for the mediation. They are also required to confirm that they have authority to settle the case at the mediation if agreement is reached.

About a week before the date on which the mediation is scheduled to commence, the mediator will call the parties to introduce him/herself and to answer any preliminary questions the parties may have on the mediation.

The next step is to actually mediate.

Before describing how mediation works in practice, it would be useful to identify the sort of qualities that a mediator should possess, also describe the Agreement to Mediate the parties will have to sign before the mediation begins and how to prepare for the mediation.

5.2 Qualities Required by a Mediator

5.2.1 **Generally**

Much has been discussed and written on what makes a good and effective mediator. For example, writing as long ago as 1688 – mediation is not, in fact, that new! – the Prior of St. Pierre had this say:

I.S. Blackshaw, Sport, Mediation and Arbitration

> '... to be a good mediator you need more than anything patience, common sense, an appropriate manner, and goodwill. You must make yourself liked by both parties, and gain credibility in their minds. To do that, begin by explaining that you are unhappy about the bother, the trouble and the expense that their litigation is causing them. After that, listen patiently to all their complaints.'

Although, as in the above quotation, a number of general qualities and attributes have been identified, much depends on the nature of the dispute and the context in which it has arisen. In the final analysis, to use a sporting metaphor: it is a question of 'horses for courses'!

5.2.2 **Particular qualities**

However, in an insightful article, entitled 'Strategic Considerations in Choosing a Mediator', published by JAMS/ENDISPUTE, an appropriately named Washington DC based provider of mediation and arbitration services, who describe themselves as 'the resolution experts', Dr David S. Ross, an attorney and mediator with ten years experience, sets out some of the main considerations in selecting a mediator.

In this article, he points out upfront that 'Because the mediation process is only as effective as the mediator who manages it, choosing the right mediator is critical'.

According to Ross, the most important qualities needed in a mediator are the following:

- mediation experience;
- mediation process skills;
- substantive expertise;
- reputation for neutrality;
- creativity;
- strong interpersonal skills; and
- the ability to help parties reach agreements.

He strongly advocates obtaining references on any mediator proposed, pointing out that most mediators provide references on request. He goes further than this, however, and advises that parties should take the time to speak directly to individuals who have used the mediator proposed and obtain their feedback on the mediator's abilities and competence, especially strengths and weaknesses and mediation style.

He also underscores the need for the mediator to have 'substantive expertise' that is, specialist knowledge in the particular field in which the dispute arises. He notes that, as more mediators are specialising in specific substantive areas, parties are able to choose a mediator with both 'substantive expertise' and 'mediation process skills', regarding both as essential qualities.

He also stresses the importance of mediator 'empathy' and defines the ability to 'empathize' as the capacity to 'demonstrate an understanding of the feelings and needs of another person'. And he adds:

> 'Empathic mediators can build strong, trusting relationships with parties, leading to more open and effective communication ... [which] drives the mediation process, creating opportunities for joint problem solving ... .'

Finally, he addresses the tantalising gender issue: do female mediators have particular advantages over male mediators. Although he ducks the issue, he does seem to imply that, again, it depends on the nature of the dispute and the gender of the parties themselves. But what he does say with more certainty is that if a party is 'highly emotional, then a mediator with strong interpersonal skills should be a priority'. He also adds for good measure that the parties have a common interest in choosing a mediator who makes them 'feel comfortable and confident'. We will return to this and other qualitative issues when we take a look at mediating sports disputes later.

In a fascinating book, entitled *Mediating Dangerously: The Frontiers of Conflict Resolution*,[14] Ken Cloke, Director of the Dispute Resolution Center in Santa Monica, California, USA, looks at what it takes to be what he calls a 'dangerously good mediator'. Amongst many pertinent issues, he raises the question: 'do you want to be professional or effective?' And suggest that, on occasions, mediators must let their hair down to gain attention, trust and honest involvement of the disputants. 'The goal here' he says 'is to be authentic, which can only happen if you are seen as truly mediating from the heart.' And poses the question: 'When appropriate, will/can you wear your heart on your sleeve?'

Professor Karl Mackie, the Chief Executive of CEDR, a leading authority on ADR in the UK (he is Professor of ADR at Birmingham University), has also opined on the essential qualities of a good mediator. In an article in the *Maritime Review* of 1997, he wrote:

> 'Mediation is the ADR technique which enables the parties to resume, or sometimes to begin, negotiations. The very presence of a mediator changes the underlying dynamic of the negotiating process. The mediator brings negotiating, problem-solving and communication skills to the process, deployed from a position of independence and neutrality, making real progress possible where direct negotiations have stalled.'

So, a good mediator needs to be a skilled negotiator, trouble-shooter and communicator as well.

5.2.3 Professionality of the mediator

On the subject generally of the qualities required of a mediator, one further important matter needs to be addressed. That is, the professionality of the mediator. Mediation is still a relatively new method of dispute resolution and many parties may be reluctant to try it because they are not sure of the professional status of the mediator.

To what extent, for example, can the parties rely on the mediator acting impartially and avoiding any conflicts of interest? If the mediator is a lawyer, he will presumably be bound by the rules of the Law Society or The Bar Council in discharging his duties as a mediator. In such a case, if the mediator contravenes those rules, he or she can be disciplined. But mediators are drawn from a variety of professions and none. So, to protect the public from an unscrupulous mediator and ensure high standards amongst mediators, many of the organisations providing mediation services have anticipated this and issued their own Codes of Conduct.

---

[14] Jossey-Bass 2001.

5.2.4 Codes of Conduct

As a sample, the text of the 'Professional Code of Practice for Solicitors' of the ADR Group, drawn from the Society of Professionals in Dispute Resolution, is set out in Appendix II to this book.

As you will see, the ADR Group Professional Code of Practice for Solicitors is designed to operate in conjunction with any other Professional Code of Conduct that may be applicable in the circumstances. As all the mediators appointed by the ADR Group are English solicitors, they are also subject to The Law Society of England and Wales' Code of Practice for Civil/Commercial Mediation. In particular, it may be noted that, under Article 8 of the ADR Group Code of Practice for Solicitors, solicitor mediators are required to have Professional Indemnity Cover in respect of their acting as mediators.

The ADR Group Code of Practice for Solicitors covers such matters as impartiality, confidentiality, conflicts of interest, disclosure of fees and advertising and promotion. In practice, the rules dealing with potential and actual conflicts of interest (Art. 3) are of particular importance.

It is not clear what is the legal status of this Code. It seems to fall into the category of other self-regulating Codes of Practice. However, if the mediator contravenes any part of the Code, this will provide support in any claims for 'wilful misconduct' or 'gross negligence' brought by a party against the mediator under the terms of the 'Mediation Agreement' (see next section). For comparative purposes and also because they are not limited to professional lawyer-mediators, the terms of the new CEDR Code of Conduct, which are EU compliant (see following paragraph), are set out in Appendix III to this book.

Standards in mediation have also caught the attention of the European Commission, which is very interested in promoting Alternative Dispute Resolution generally and establishing minimum standards throughout the European Union (EU). In April 2002, the Commission published a discussion paper (Green Paper) on ADR. In July 2004, the Commission organised the launch of a Code of Conduct for Mediators, which was approved and adopted by a large number of Mediation experts; and in October 2004 the Commission adopted and submitted to the European Parliament and the Council a proposal for a Directive on certain aspects of mediation in civil and commercial matters. The Directive was adopted on 21 May 2008. The Green Paper, the Code of Conduct and the Directive on Mediation all form part of the current work on establishing an area of freedom, security and justice, and particularly on improving access to justice in the EU. It is the European Commission's view that encouraging the use of Mediation and other forms of ADR assists in the resolution of disputes and helps to avoid the worry, time and cost associated with court-based litigation and so assists EU citizens in a real way to secure their legal rights. The background to these initiatives and the latest situation on the EU Code of Conduct of Mediators and the EU Directive on Mediation are set out in Appendix IV to this book.

5.3 The Agreement to Mediate

Once the parties have agreed to mediate, they need to start the process by signing a Mediation Agreement.

Before, however, looking at how to prepare for a mediation and how a typical mediation is conducted and proceeds in practice, we will look at the terms and conditions to be found in the normal standard Agreement to Mediate, often referred to as a 'Model Mediation Agreement', that the parties to a mediation are required to sign before commencing the mediation.

5.3.1 CPR European Model Mediation Agreement

For the purposes of our review, we will use the Model Mediation Agreement ('Agreement') used in Europe by the CPR Institute for Dispute Resolution (CPR), based in New York. The full text of this document is set out in Appendix V to this book.

As will be seen, in the clause defining the parties to the Agreement, the mediator is joined by a trainee. This is normal practice, so that future mediators can obtain 'on the job' training, which is now becoming more commonplace in most professions. However, according to the 'Procedure', as mentioned and defined in the following paragraph, the trainee does not take any active part in the mediation process, neither does he charge any fee and may only observe the process if the parties agree.

After defining the nature of the 'Dispute' that has arisen between the parties, the Agreement confirms that the parties have agreed to mediate following the CPR Model Procedure for Mediation of Business Disputes in Europe ('Procedure'), the text of which is set out in Appendix V to this book, and appoint the mediator. The Procedure is, therefore, incorporated in the Agreement by reference and is fully binding on all the parties to the Agreement.

The Agreement then goes on to define the duties and obligations of the parties and the mediator, including the trainee. In particular, all the parties to the Agreement expressly agree to be bound by the Procedure, including the 'without prejudice' and confidentiality provisions set out in Paragraph 9. In these days of litigation management, there is a specific relaxation of the obligation of secrecy to allow the parties to inform the court of 'the schedule and overall status of the mediation for purposes of litigation management'.

As with all confidentiality obligations, the parties are free to disclose things if they all agree to do so, and also are not bound by the confidentiality provisions if required by law or the court to make any disclosures.

To reinforce the 'without prejudice' status of the mediation process, there is a specific obligation on the parties to the dispute not 'to require the mediator to give evidence in any subsequent litigation about the dispute except in the case of an allegation of misconduct during the mediation proceedings'.

The Agreement expressly provides that the mediator, which also includes the trainee, shall not be liable for any act or omission in the mediation, except where such is the result of the mediator's 'own wilful misconduct or gross negligence'.

As time is of the essence in a mediation, there is a declaration by the mediator and the trainee that they do not have any previous commitments which would 'significantly' delay the 'expeditious' conduct of the mediation process and neither will they make any such commitments.

Again, consonant with the crucial need for the mediator and the trainee to be entirely neutral (actually referred to as 'neutrals' by JAMS/ENDISPUTE), there are express obligations on the part of the mediator and the trainee to disclose, inter alia, any prior business or professional relationships or 'any other circumstances' which may affect their impartiality.

These obligations are supplemented by other ones regarding future relationships, requiring the mediator and the trainee, as well as any other person assisting them in the mediation, not to 'personally' work on any matter for or against any party, regardless of specific subject matter, for six months after the cessation of their services in the mediation. The mediator and the trainee and anyone else affected by this restriction can be released from it with the consent of all the parties. It may be noted, *en passant*, that this restriction amounts to a 'restraint of trade' clause and, as such, must be reasonable in all respects if it is to be legally enforceable.

The Agreement is completed by remuneration and governing law and jurisdiction clauses. The fees and expenses of the mediator are to be shared equally by the parties and no part of them shall accrue to CPR – this provision is designed to protect the independence and integrity of CPR. Again, *en passant*, I would note that the governing law and jurisdiction clause is vague and needs more precision and substance to avoid it being legally unenforceable for uncertainty.

5.3.2 **'Ground Rules of Proceeding'**

For the sake of completeness, as the Procedure is also made part of the Model Mediation Agreement, as explained above, one or two comments on its provisions should be made. Perhaps the most important of these provisions are those contained in Paragraph 3, which lay down the so-called 'Ground Rules of Proceeding'.

In particular, the mediation is a voluntary process, depending on the co-operation of the parties, and the mediator does not issue a binding decision.

The Procedure also deals with other practical matters, including what happens in the event that the parties to the dispute fail to agree. In such a case, the mediator is required to discuss with the parties the possibility of their agreeing on another form of ADR to settle their dispute.

In any case, each of the parties is free to withdraw from the mediation at any time on giving written notice to the mediator and the other party or parties.

If the dispute goes to arbitration, the mediator may not be an arbitrator.

5.4 How to Prepare for Mediation

The key to success in mediation or, indeed, in any other form of negotiation is to follow the boy scouts' motto and 'be prepared!'

In a helpful practical booklet, entitled, *Making the Most of Mediation*, the ADR Group devote a section on how to prepare for mediation. They point out that a common reason for mediation not producing a settlement agreement is that one side or the other has failed to prepare sufficiently for the mediation.

Although preparing for a mediation is less time consuming and expensive than for a court trial or arbitration, mainly because there is no formal presentation of evidence or cross-examination of witnesses, the parties need to be clear about what they wish to achieve and be ready to evaluate settlement offers from the other side.

The ADR Group offers a preparation strategy, which, they claim, will enable parties to go into a mediation with 'confidence'.

This strategy may be summarised as follows:

- Check that you have all the information needed to value your case (e.g., expert reports, counsel's opinion, and medical evidence).
- Make sure that you have authority to settle the case.
- Make sure you know all the facts and what witnesses you can call on if the case goes to trial.
- Determine the particular questions you wish the mediator to ask the other side (mediators only have the power the parties give them)
- Identify and analyse the legal issues.
- Consider what you wish the mediator to have in advance – ideally a two-page summary of the facts and the arguments.
- Decide on your tactics – what you wish to disclose to the other side. If you are not sure of its relevance or value, discuss in confidence with the mediator.
- Consider how best you can use the mediator – not only is the mediator a channel of communication, but also can play devil's advocate, be a problem solver and source of new ideas and approaches.
- Work out a mediation plan and how best you can persuade the other side to your point of view and position.
- Be realistic about what you want and how best to persuade the other side that you are being realistic.

With this in mind, prepare your opening statement, which should be designed to impress the other side with your grasp of the facts and the strength of your arguments.

Decide who is to do what, especially if you are represented by a solicitor, but be ready to participate actively in the private meetings.

In other words, as in any kind of negotiation – and mediation essentially is an assisted negotiation – careful preparation, planning and structuring of the process pays dividends.

5.5 How Mediation Works in Practice

5.5.1 Getting started

Most mediations start rather formally.

In the early stages, the parties, who may act alone or with their legal representatives (if one party is legally represented and the other not, the mediator normally encourages the unrepresented party to obtain independent legal advice), tend to argue about the facts of the dispute and state their respective legal positions.

Later on, in the private sessions with the mediator, the mediation usually becomes more informal with the parties discussing settlement options and trading settlement positions back and forth.

5.5.2 The role of the mediator

The mediator acts as a facilitator to get the parties to open up and discuss matters and try to reach a settlement of their dispute. As one satisfied client of a CEDR organised mediation put it: 'The mediator did a first class job – facilitating the discussion rather than trying to take charge'.

And added for good measure: 'I think we would have regarded the mediation process as productive even if it had not culminated in a settlement.'

The mediator controls the procedural aspects of the mediation, but there are no formal rules of procedure or evidence. In international mediations, the mediator decides on the language in which the mediation is conducted and whether and what documents should be translated.

The mediator holds individual meetings (known in mediation-speak as 'caucuses') and joint meetings with the parties and, in consultation with them, fixes the time and place of each session and the agenda. The mediation is to be conducted expeditiously. Only if authorised by the party concerned to do so, does the mediator disclose to the other side anything that is discussed or revealed to the mediator by that party.

Like any kind of negotiation, the mediation is a developing and evolving process and its success depends on the skills of the mediator to bring the parties closer together to try to reach a settlement. As a satisfied client of the ADR Group put it:

> 'The mediation was principally to discuss quantum and try and resolve the enormous gap between the two sides ... We must say, before it took place we were a little sceptical but we were impressed by the way the negotiations were handled by the mediator ... We feel that we secured a very reasonable settlement when balancing the risks for costs and damages ... We therefore feel that in the sort of case where the parties have reached an impasse and their valuations are poles apart, mediation is worth trying before the last resort of trial.'

However, the mediator does not impose any solution on the parties. But, if they are unable to reach a settlement and, if all the parties and the mediator agree, the mediator will produce for the parties a non-binding written recommendation on settlement terms. The mediator will not attempt to anticipate what a court might decide, but, based on all the circumstances of the particular case, will set out what the mediator would suggest could be appropriate terms on which to settle the dispute.

No formal record or transcript of the mediation proceedings is made – the mediation is conducted on an entirely confidential basis. Only the parties can agree to disclose or publish anything.

Any settlement reached, as a result of the mediation, will not be legally binding on the parties until it has been incorporated in a Settlement Agreement signed by or on behalf of the parties.

5.5.3 General steps in the mediation process

Although each mediation is unique and follows its own particular course, most mediations tend to follow a certain broad general framework, which Professor Karl Mackie of CEDR has usefully identified as follows:

> '1. Preliminary contact between the parties and the mediation organisation (or mediator) to:
>   - agree to mediation;
>   - agree terms of mediation including dates, duration, location, representation, legal framework, costs documentation;
>   - agree on a named mediator.
>
> 2. Limited, brief written summaries of the case submitted by the parties in advance to:
>   - inform the mediator;
>   - focus the parties on the real issues.

3. Initial joint meeting at which:
   - the mediator clarifies the process and establishes the ground rules;
   - the parties present a summary of their case to each other;
   - the issues are clarified.
4. Private, confidential meetings between the mediator and each party separately to:
   - examine important issues and needs of each party;
   - encourage openness about weaknesses as well as strengths;
   - discuss options for settlement.'

5.5.4 The role of the parties in the mediation

Although the success or failure of the mediation process largely depends upon the skills of the mediator, the attitude, co-operation and preparedness of the parties also play an important part. With this in mind, the ADR Group has issued some guidelines to help parties get the most out of a mediation. They throw further light on the nature of the mediation process and are worth summarising as follows:

- Ensure that whoever attends the mediation is totally prepared, has authority to make decisions, and all who need to attend are present.
- Allocate sufficient time for the mediation: start early and stay as long as it takes.
- Be punctual at sessions: being late may give a wrong impression.
- Your opening statement should deal with the facts of the case and, if the other side has gone first, indicate where you agree or disagree with them.
- Stay calm and be realistic.
- Only use emotive language, if you feel genuinely aggrieved about something and wish the other side to know it.
- Avoid making your opening demands too specific. For example, if you say 'I will only settle for x amount', the other side will stop listening and start thinking why you should not get it.
- Keep an open mind throughout. Mediation is a creative process and often reveals possibilities for agreement of which the parties may not be aware.
- Be persistent. Every mediation has a 'low point' when agreement seems unlikely. This is normal and most cases go on to settle. A break for reflection by the parties often helps in such cases.

As previously mentioned, mediation is essentially a negotiation and its success will often depend upon following the so-called 'golden rule of negotiation', namely: 'Do not go for the last penny – in a good negotiation everybody wins something!'

5.6 The Costs of Mediation

One of the attractions of mediation as a dispute resolution method is that, compared with litigation and arbitration, it is cheaper.

In general, the parties to the mediation pay their own mediation costs and expenses (including the costs of any legal representative) and share equally the fees and expenses of the mediator and those of the mediation service provider. The mediation fees are usually in accordance with an 'ad valorem' scale of fees. This is the case of mediations conducted under the auspices of CEDR and UK Sport Resolutions.

However, in some cases the costs may be paid by one party as part of the settlement and, on certain occasions, the party proposing mediation may offer to fund the entire cost of the mediation.

The ADR Group operates a different – more flexible – system of charging for its mediation services as follows. But in all cases, charges by the ADR Group for mediations are always agreed in advance.

For the 'average' case, which takes between 5 and 7 hours, the mediation costs are based on a per party per hour basis. For cases, which may take less time, the ADR Group offers a half-day (three-hour) mediation for a fixed fee.

For relatively low value cases (under GBP 25,000), the ADR Group recommends a ninety-minute mediation on what they call a 'Mediated Settlement Day' for a fixed fee.

The ADR Group also – quite enterprisingly – offers telephone mediations for smaller or less complex cases at a lower rate.

The ADR Group also offers a mediated Pre-Litigation Review (PLR) process, which is designed to help the parties to a dispute to decide whether or not to proceed with litigation. The cost of a PLR is negotiated on a case by case basis.

Finally, the ADR Group can also provide mediations on a daily consultancy basis to resolve disputes within organisations or advise on dispute prevention.

Irrespective of who pays for the mediation, the mediator is always paid by the ADR Group to avoid any suggestion of bias that might arise if the parties or party (as the case may be) pays the mediator direct.

ADR Group mediations are conducted in accordance with a prescribed 'Mediation Procedure' which parties pursuing Mediations under the auspices of the ADR Group are taken to have accepted. The ADR Group Mediation Procedure Rules are reproduced in Appendix VII to this book.

CHAPTER 6
MEDIATION 'ONLINE'

6.1 THE RISE OF THE INTERNET

With the rise and increasing use of the Internet, it is not surprising that mediation 'on line', using video conferencing, is now being offered to parties in dispute. Where? In the States, of course! It will be interesting to see how this method of mediating develops. It would certainly seem to be attractive in international commercial disputes and, with access to the 'world wide web' becoming more widespread and the cost of going 'on line' becoming cheaper and quicker, it must save time and money, both of which are precious commodities as far as business people are concerned.

For further information on the potential of online dispute resolution (ODR) for settling a wide range of commercial and other disputes, includes sports-related ones, please refer to a book with the intriguing title *Online Dispute Resolution: Resolving Conflicts in Cyberspace* by E. Katsh and J. Rifkin, published in 2001 by Jossey-Bass London.

In his address to the 2001 Annual Conference of the International Federation of Commercial Arbitration Institutions (IFCAI), William K. Slate II, President and Chief Executive Officer of the American Arbitration Association, focused on the role of 'on line' dispute resolution in the burgeoning field of 'e-commerce'. In his view, 'on line' dispute resolution is to the arbitration field what the ATM card was to the banking and financial industry, and over time more conflicts will migrate to 'on line' methodologies. The following article, entitled 'Online Dispute Resolution: Click Here to Settle Your Dispute'[15] is based on Slate's remarks to the IFCAI Conference, which was held in Prague in the Czech Republic:

William K. Slate II
Online Dispute Resolution: Click Here to Settle Your Dispute

The focus of this article is online dispute prevention and resolution in e-commerce. But before looking discretely at arbitration and the world of technology, I think it important to first step back and see 'technology' as a great deal more than just a tool or modern gadget, but as the larger force that is driving the new globalization system where the world has become increasingly an interwoven place.

This globalization system is characterized by a single word: the Web! In the words of Thomas Friedman, the author of a compelling book on this subject entitled *The Lexus and the Olive Tree,* '... in the globalization system we reach for the Internet, which is a symbol that we are all increasingly connected and nobody is quite in charge'.

So what then is the essence of globalization driven by technology? James Surowicki, a business columnist, has said: 'It is the notion that innovation replaces tradition. The present-or perhaps the future-replaces the past. Nothing matters so much as what will come *next,* and what will come *next* can only arrive if what is here .now gets overturned!'

While this makes the globalization system a terrific place for innovation, it clearly makes it a difficult place to live, since most people prefer some measure of security about the future, as compared to a life lived in almost constant uncertainty.

[15] *Dispute Resolution Journal*, November. 2001/January 2002, at pp. 10-14.

So, you may well ask, does this globalized economy driven by ever newer and newer technologies have implications, indeed impacts on arbitral institutions and dispute resolution processes? And, the answer is of course – yes – and very much so!

E-Commerce Market

The e-commerce market, in terms of two generic groups, consists of sales between businesses, or B2B, and also sales between businesses and consumers, known as B2C. While the expected growth for both areas is astronomical, I do have some figures on the expected growth in the business-to-business area.

B2B e-commerce transactions worldwide will grow from $145 billion in 1999 to $7.9 trillion in 2004. Over $1.2 trillion of B2B e-commerce sales were made in the year 2000. Over $6.3 trillion of B2B e-commerce sales will occur by 2005. Thus, analysts are predicting that 2B2 e-commerce sales will grow six fold over the next five years. At the same time it is expected that access to. the Internet will grow by over 100 million users in the next four years, bringing the total to over 3 50 million users by 2005.

Online Dispute Resolution

In the short span of a couple of years the proliferation and varied uses for online dispute resolution services has exploded. The World Intellectual Property Organization and. a handful of other institutional providers are daily resolving Internet domain name disputes through an online arbitration process.

At last count, over 3,000 such cases have been filed. When a party registers a domain name they agree to submit any disputes to the online arbitration process. The fees are kept low for consumers and the process is simple and quick.

In the United States we see parties also using online dispute resolution services, and in the past year no fewer than 12 new entities have emerged providing online dispute resolution options.

And so, for example, there are online business services available today with names such as Cyber-Settle, and Click 'N Settle, where if you have a simple dispute about a number, as in dollars and cents numbers, you can submit it to one of these services which operates on an algorithm based computer program. The parties get up to three opportunities for a 'match' (a meeting of the minds) with the party on the other side. In this exercise each party is offering a figure to the computer. The entire process is technology driven with no human-being involved in the decisional process.

You may ask, who would do that? Well, one of the providers boasts 5,000 cases handled last year and the prediction of at least 10,000 cases in the current year. It is true that the referenced cases are primarily automobile insurance matters where fault or liability is clear and the parties needed simply to agree on a dollar figure. Nonetheless, parties' willingness to use these processes opens the door, and warms up the business community for more possibilities.

On a larger volume scale, SquareTrade, a San Francisco-based online dispute resolution provider (largely for B2C transactions for eBay, an online auction site), reports handling over 40,000 cases involving buyers and sellers worldwide since their launching in February 2000.

The underlying point here is that online dispute resolution is already very much with us. This holds out the specter of 24/7 (24 hours a day, 7 days a week) of online dispute resolution possibilities. I have come to believe that online dispute resolution is to the arbitration field what the ATM card was to the banking and financial industry; a breakthrough in technology that led to around-the-clock. service, accessible from anywhere in the world.

On the arbitration side, the traditional paradigm of a neutral replicating a courtroom has already given way to the resolution of disputes where only a dollar figure is involved and no neutral and no hearing room exist. Interestingly, the providers of algorithmic services have turned anonymity in the decisional process into an advantage-just a computer program that matches numbers.

The business-to-consumer sector of e-commerce is an area in which policymakers in Europe, the U.S., and the rest of the world will look very closely out of an interest in protecting the consumer from the strength and the will of big business.

Commissions in Europe, the U.S., and Japan, including the European Commission, are actively studying the business-to-consumer online area and attempting to establish cross-border standards. The European Commission estimates that annually some 15% of thousands of business-to-consumer online transactions will require some form of alternative dispute resolution methods and the Commission, of course, wants to insure that it is a fair process.

E-Commerce in the B2B Environment

On a much larger business scale, and more consistent with the traditional work of arbitral institutions, is the need to provide services for e-commerce business-to-business transactions. In, this context one should consider a variety of business transactions where the Internet is utilized as the medium for exchange.

At a very simplistic level this involves a corporation that offers its goods and services for sale over the Internet and a buyer enters into a contract for the sale and delivery of goods or services on the Web.

Another model involves the growth of so called B2B vertical, digital marketplaces, where companies move all of their supply chain operations onto the Internet. In so doing, they join competitors to create an exchange where they buy all of their supplies together online.

One of the first of these so-called vertical exchanges is composed of General Motors, Daimler-Chrysler, and Ford, and is known as Covisint. This joining with other competitors and suppliers uses computers and Web sites to buy and sell goods, trade market information, and run back-office operations, such as inventory control. In the end they predict they will save billions of dollars by moving all these shared purchases onto the Internet.

At last count there were over 300 vertical business-to-business marketplaces buying everything from energy to paper goods to airline parts. The number of business transactions for just one of these B2B marketplace exchanges is in the hundreds of thousands of individual transactions annually. And of course, these online transactions will incur traditional problems, such as late delivery, the condition of goods, and standard breach of contract.

The pertinent question is this: will parties to e-commerce transactions, particularly those involving B2B online markets, want to resolve their problems in court or even by traditional alternative dispute resolution methods such as offline arbitration? The answer is probably no to both questions.

They will want to resolve matters online, have their complaint filed online, their documents *considered* online, their hearing *held* online, their decision *rendered* online, and be serviced by institutional providers.

The speed and volume of transactions of business-to-business online vertical markets will not tolerate inordinate time bumps in the process. It is simply economically too inefficient. Hence, online dispute resolution will be deemed not only highly desirable, but by many, required.

Of course, in the near term complex matters will continue to go offline to the traditional route, but over time more conflicts will migrate to online methodologies.

B2B E-Commerce Survey

We, at the American Arbitration Association, knew from the information just provided that B2B e-commerce is growing rapidly, and that as business relationships change, the nature of disputes might change as well. As a consequence, we determined to ascertain whether or not this shift to e-commerce and the use of e-commerce exchanges is as prevalent as forecasted and, if so, what the impact might be on disputes and how organizations might move to address them. Thus, the AAA conducted a survey by contracting with an independent research firm.

The study was based on 100 interviews with senior executives and corporate counsel of Fortune 1,000 or similar large firms. In total, interviews were conducted with 40 general counsel, 45 CEOs, CFOs and COOS; and 15 CIOs and CTOs. In response to questions regarding the impact of a dispute on their business; two out of three (68%) said that they would be concerned about a B2B dispute with a major supplier. Forty-six percent of the respondents said an e-commerce dispute with a major trading partner would have an impact on their business. While 57% say that managing supply chains online will create new and different types of disputes.

In response to questions concerning their involvement in business-to-business e-commerce most of the respondents or 91% said that they are already involved in B2B e-commerce. Ninety-five percent said that they expect their involvement with B2B e-commerce to grow in the next year and 35 % of those responding said they expected that involvement to grow significantly.

When asked what they saw as major challenges in the B2B e-commerce environment, 91% said they had concerns about issues of integrity and security. Eighty-six percent said they had concerns about the effectiveness of technology and 9% were concerned about cost issues.

In regard to B2B e-commerce dispute management, 51% of those responding say their company incorporates dispute clauses into all contracts. Frankly, I would have thought the number would have been higher. Forty percent say they assigned staff other than the general counsel to manage disputes. Forty-one percent have set guidelines for conducting B2B e-commerce relationships. And finally, 27% assign general counsel to manage these disputes.

When asked what additional business-to-business guidelines were needed, the respondents coalesced around four answers. The one receiving the most answers was 'how to resolve disputes quickly.' This harkens back to my earlier observation that once companies have committed to e-commerce relationships they do not want to have to resort, except where necessary, to traditional conflict management modalities.

Other areas in which survey respondents said additional guidelines are needed were in the area of pricing/billing, confidentiality, and delivery and shipments. The latter item has to do with keeping delivery and shipments going while disputes are promptly resolved.

Is it expected that new types of disputes will emerge' as a result of increased e-commerce? The majority of executives and general counsel say that moving their supply chain online will create new or different types of disputes. They believe that those 'new classes of disputes' would include information-related issues, security/privacy issues, and ordering.

So, in summary with regard to the E-Commerce Readiness Survey, three major points emerged: 1) 95% of those responding expect their company's involvement in B2B e-commerce to increase; 2) however, 64% of those responding said their company does not yet have a plan in place to deal with B2B e-commerce disputes; and 3) almost 70% expressed a felt need for additional guidelines, for e-commerce rules to assist in managing disputes.

E-Commerce Protocol

Related to the felt need for guidelines, the American Arbitration Association with the involvement of a number of major global corporations earlier this year developed an E-Commerce Protocol for the management of online disputes. Ultimately 20 global corporations signed the Protocol as charter signatories.

It is in large measure an e-commerce dispute management 'wake-up call.' The basic idea was to have a vehicle for encouraging businesses to think about the management of disputes in the e-commerce context. The principal components of the Protocol are fairness, continuity of business, clear dispute management policies, a range of options for the parties to avail, and a commitment to the use of technology.

The E-Commerce Protocol was the first step to address fairness and confidence in the integrity of transacting business in the electronic environment. Trust for all parties in this new business medium is critical to its use and success. The Protocol has now been joined by new online rules, which support the Protocol and are specific processes to be followed in conducting dispute resolution online.

And, as every institutional provider would appreciate, it is important to have a specifically trained e-commerce panel of neutrals available, competent in the use of technology to receive, send, and consider legal and business issues online. The AAA has developed a training curriculum and identified a cadre of individuals from our global panel to be a part of a discrete roster of e-commerce arbitrators and mediators.

New Services for e-commerce

Along with rules and processes for handling disputes in B2B e-commerce, new technologies have evolved to help improve the efficiency of dispute resolution and provide information that all participants in the conflict management process can use to help prevent disputes. Some of the most notable new approaches are:

Online Claims Submission This terminology refers to the capability to permit a claimant to submit claims directly through the Internet for one type or multiple types of claims, including claims that may still be processed largely offline.

Online Algorithmic ADR This dispute resolution method utilizes the Internet and an automated set of rules to assist parties in simple disputes to be able to reach agreement without the involvement of mediators or arbitrators.

Online Assisted ADR This process contemplates combining Internet access and online applications to dispute resolution services such as document sharing, postings, case status, and mediator or arbitrator selection, and instructional exchanges instantly, anytime, anywhere and *in support* of offline, traditional meetings or hearings.

Online ADR Today this means dispute resolution services that are accomplished completely online, including documents only arbitrations, algorithmic methods, and limited subject matter mediations. All interactions are accomplished through the Internet, through chat rooms, posting boards, and, if necessary, conference calls, and Web-based meetings. This is not an effective method today to do complex cases or full arbitration solutions.

Online DRM (Dispute Risk Management) This process extends the continuum of dispute resolution (negotiation to litigation) to that of dispute risk management, focusing on: risk assessment, prevention, and containment in addition to dispute resolution. These online services allow all participants in the B2B e-commerce process to actively find and share ways to prevent missed expectations entirely or contain disagreements before they expand into a dispute.

As we continue to build dispute information into conflict management databases, it is inevitable that information will accumulate to assist like parties in avoiding disputes when certain conditions or actions emerge. This knowledge will lead to increased opportunities to engage in dispute avoidance mechanisms, and provide new opportunities to assist organizations in reducing disputes; as well as improve the fairness and integrity in B2B e-commerce.

The Future

As I summarize a few points and look over the horizon to the days ahead, I will attempt to avoid the result that a well-known U.S. law professor noted when he said that 'people who live by crystal balls are destined to eat glass.'

First, for those of us who would like things to remain just the way they are right now-which is all of us-the question must be asked-will there still be traditional arbitrations-only modestly affected by technology? The answer is yes, of course, but I strongly believe there will be a fewer number of those cases with each passing year. Therefore, if one aspires to a long life, you will have to get online.

As business-to-business e-commerce grows there is a significant opportunity for institutions (particularly as contrasted to ad hoc neutrals) to engage B 2B online markets and provide a range of services from the low-tech online claims submission to online assisted methodologies all the way to dispute risk management.

A challenge here for traditional thinkers is to begin to ponder a new paradigm where arbitration and related services are not offline with parties coming to institutions in the traditional way, but where institutions are an integral part of the very technology systems which are enabling the operation of B2B e-commerce to flourish. Here institutions must move quickly in. order to remain relevant!

I also believe the growth of arbitration and resolution of international commercial transactions will produce straight-line upward growth in the use of online modalities as the world business communities become more homogeneous in their practices, and interdependent in their dealings across national borders.

The e-commerce world has clearly signaled that national borders, with each ensuing year, will mean less and less in the global marketplace. Indeed, it is my belief that the use of online technology to resolve disputes will grow very quickly to the extent that one year from now we will all be amazed at the exponential use of online options.

Finally, we expect to see in the coming days greater movement in the direction of 'dispute avoidance' before parties ever reach the stage of requiring mediation and arbitration. This is already taking place in the construction field, both domestically and internationally, through the use of 'partnering facilitation' dispute review boards and other holistic approaches to anticipating disputes.

Once again, I think that this will be further facilitated by the use of online competencies where the collection of data about disputes, including the frequency and the nature and circumstances in which they arise, will enable parties to *anticipate* with a greater degree of accuracy pressure points where disputes might arise.

Think about it, with all of the pertinent information online and readily available, parties will be able to resolve more disputes or address potential disputes among themselves. To the extent a third party is needed, this will require a new kind of dispute resolution facilitator who will work with parties in an anticipatory way to avoid disputes and hence utilize well-developed negotiation skills.

6.2 Telephone Mediation

Mediation by telephone has also now become popular and more use of this medium is being made, where practical, time, financial, and other considerations may dictate and apply. As mentioned above, the ADR Group offers a telephone mediation service.

However, 'face-to-face' discussions are, in my view, more preferable as personal interaction and 'body language' are fundamental elements in the success of any mediation, which is essentially a negotiation conducted in the physical presence of the parties and the mediator.

Incidentally, it is not unknown – and is becoming more popular and frequent – for 'hearings' before the CAS to be held and evidence of witnesses to be taken by telephone – using conference calls and other 'hook-ups' – where the parties and their representatives (especially their lawyers) are spread across more than one continent or in different hemispheres.

6.3 Online Dispute Resolution

6.3.1 **Introductory remarks**

With the inexorable rise in so-called 'e-commerce' (on-lone purchases and sales of goods and services) resulting from the increasing and widespread use of the Internet, there has been a corresponding increase in the number of Internet-related disputes. This has lead to the creation of a dispute resolution process known as online dispute resolution (ODR).

Typically, this method of settling disputes can be applied to resolve conflicts relating to Internet commerce or any other dispute where the parties appreciate the efficiency and cost savings associated with an innovative dispute resolution facility.

The UK-based ADR Group has been pioneering the use of ODR in conjunction with <themediationroom.com> which is a specialist technology provider. The software driving the technology is designed to the highest specification and can be applied to simple disputes or to more complex ones involving, for example, multi-party cross border disputes.

6.3.2 **Internet disputes**

As internet usage continues to expand, it becomes increasingly necessary to design efficient mechanisms for resolving Internet disputes, because traditional mechanisms, such as litigation, are often time-consuming, expensive and disproportionate to the value of the initial transaction.

The ADR Group has been at the forefront of this development process in the UK and has pioneered an effective and user friendly ODR system for the resolution of Internet disputes. Parties to an Internet dispute are able to communicate with a trained mediator through a confidential 'web-file' over a secure Internet site. The mediator works with both parties to help them resolve their differences online.

Consumer rights are protected throughout the process as the consumer is free to walk away at any stage.

To assist the settlement processes, the ADR Group has worked with key clients in the retail trade and insurance sectors to offer a non-binding recommendation if mediation is not successful within a predetermined time frame. This system provides certainty to the dispute resolution process by facilitating effective dispute management and managing litigation risk.

ODR has a multitude of applications and the ADR Group is already working with a number of organizations, who use ODR services to support a high volume of dispute resolution, as well as provide an alternative process for their own internal disputes.

6.3.3 How the ODR process works

When an online case begins, a dispute 'web-file' is opened and the parties in dispute and their representatives are invited to interact online. The parties must then follow a three-stage strict security process in order to participate in the online mediation.

Each dispute file contains a set of message areas. The message areas displayed will vary for each participant. The reason for this is because each participant is strictly controlled as to access to and, use of, the message areas. If they have access to an area, then the system will control whether such access allows the participant to post messages or only to read them. For example, one area will be accessible only to the mediator and one party and his or her lawyer, if any, and another by the mediator and the other party and his or her lawyer. In this way the mediator can have private and confidential sessions with each side as in physical mediation. There will be another area in which the mediator can post messages to both sides, who can read them but not respond to them, and also, at his/her option (some mediators prefer not to), he/she can access an area where he/she can keep private notes to which no-one else has access.

Every time a message is posted to one of the message areas, everybody with power to read such messages receives a system generated e-mail alerting him or her to the fact that a new message has been posted with a link to the site.

Multiple party disputes are also catered for and in all versions full confidentiality can be maintained within the various groupings of participant.

6.3.4 How to refer an online case

The following online referral form is used:

Claimant:

First Name:

Company Address:

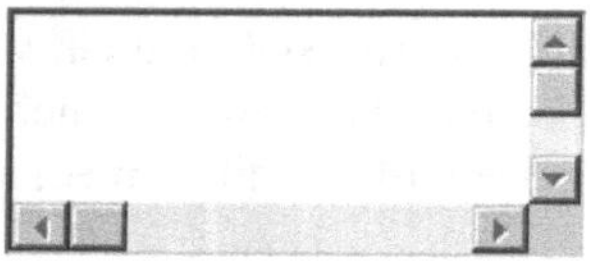

Defendant:

First Name:

Company Address:

Phone Number: Phone Number:

Nature of claim and brief description:

Approximate amount of dispute: Complexity (low / medium / high):

Claimant's Solicitor / Advisor: Defendant's Solicitor / Advisor:

First Name: First Name:

Firm: Firm:

Address: Address:

DX: DX:

Phone Number: Phone Number:

Fax Number: Fax Number:

Email: Email:

Ref: Ref:

Is this a court referred mediation?	Yes: ☐ No: ☐
Have all party(ies) agreed to mediation	Yes: ☐ No: ☐
If the mediation has not been proposed with the other party(ies), is ADR Group to approach them?	Yes: ☐ No: ☐
Is it usual for the mediation fee to be split equally between the parties.	Yes: ☐ No: ☐
Is there an alternative arrangement in this case?	Yes: ☐ No: ☐

Are there any other issues you or your client consider important and which may be relevant to in the choice of mediator? Yes: ☐ No: ☐

How did you hear about ADR Group?

6.3.5 Online dispute resolution training programme

This programme has been designed for the ADR professional who wishes to offer an additional mediation capability. Successful completion of the course will enable such persons to conduct mediation sessions online or as tool to support preparation of traditional 'face-to-face' mediations.

The programme is web-based and guides participants through ODR by covering the process and core competencies. Communication techniques and strategies for the online environment will be developed. Practical mediation simulations are supported by assessment and feedback.

The programme has been jointly developed by <themediationroom.com> and the ADR Group.

The programme comprises three sections:

Section 1: Preparation for the on-line mediation environment;
Section 2: Core competencies and communication techniques with practical guides for all mediation phases;
Section 3: Mediation management and final assessment (simulated mediation).

The programme is delivered through the platform of <themediationroom.com> which is the underlying software used by the ADR Group for conducting 'live' online mediations. In this way, delegates will not only build knowledge and skills required to conduct online mediation, but also develop practical experience in using the software.

The programme does not provide accreditation as a mediator and is ideally suited as follow-up training to the ADR Group's Civil and Commercial Foundation Mediation training (or another recognised mediation accreditation course).

The programme provides the following learning outcomes:

- how to develop trust in the unseen mediator;
- to understand the range of appropriate procedures and techniques for communication and time management;
- how to adapt discourse for the online environment;
- how to use ODR as a mediation preparation tool in 'face-to-face' mediation;
- details of available ODR systems, current trends, benefits and limitations;
- how to market your ODR skills in all areas.

6.3.6 Who should undertake the programme?

ADR professionals who are about to complete their training or are already practicing as a mediator.

6.3.7 Coaching and assessment

Each delegate is assigned an online coach from the ADR Group Training Faculty. Feedback and mentoring will be provided online within each trainee's own private and secure 'web-file'. Final course assessment will be conducted by an independent assessor. Delegates who successfully complete the programme will be awarded the ADR Group's 'Certificate of Accreditation in Online Mediation'.

6.3.8 Continuing Professional Development (CPD)

The CPD allocation for the course is 16 CPD hours as recognised by the Law Society of England and Wales, the Bar Council and the ADR Group's panel membership requirement.

6.3.9 Membership

On completion of the ODR training programme, delegates will be offered the opportunity to join the international ODR panel.

6.3.10 Programme fee

The cost of the ODR training programme amounts to GBP 375 (excluding VAT) per delegate, with ADR Net members receiving a 10 percent discount on this charge.

6.3.11 ODR panel membership

On completion of the ADR Group Online Distance Learning Training Programme, delegates will receive automatic ODR panel membership status for the duration of one year. This will enable panel members to receive and refer online cases through the ADR Group.

6.3.12 Annual fee

ODR Panel members will be entitled to renew their membership on a yearly basis at a fee of GBP 100 (excluding VAT) per annum. ADR Net members will receive automatic renewal inclusive of their membership package.

6.4 Settling Sports Domain Name Disputes

The phenomenal rise in the popularity and use of the internet – not least in relation to sports content – has spawned its own peculiar kinds of disputes and produced a particular kind of 'mediation' or alternative dispute resolution process for settling them. For example, 'cybersquatting', which is abusive registration of 'domain names', is subject to a particular form of adjudication process under the auspices of the World Intellectual Property Organisation (WIPO), a specialised agency of the UN, with its headquarters in Geneva, Switzerland.

Abusive registration of a domain name occurs where:

- a domain name complained of is identical or confusingly similar to a trade mark of another;
- is registered by a party who has no rights or legitimate interest in that domain name; and
- the domain name in question is registered and used in bad faith.

All three conditions must be satisfied for the complainant to succeed.

As to the bad faith requirement, the ICAAN (Internet Corporation for Assigned Names and Numbers) Uniform Domain Name Dispute Resolution Policy provides examples of acts, which prima facie constitute evidence of bad faith. The list is not exhaustive but illustrative.

The examples are as follows:

- offering to sell the domain name to the trade mark owner or its competitor;
- an attempt to attract for financial gain internet users by creating confusion with the trade mark of another;
- registration of a domain name in order to prevent the trade mark owner from reflecting his trade mark in a corresponding domain name; and
- registration of the domain name in order to disrupt the business of the competitor.

All claims of 'cybersquatting' on the Net are decided on their own particular facts and merits, in line with the above bad faith criteria and other circumstances which are indicative of bad faith.

Using the WIPO adjudication procedure, a number of sports disputes have been quickly and effectively settled – not surprisingly over the internet itself!

For a more detailed look at the settlement of sports-related disputes, including sports domain name disputes, through the WIPO Arbitration and Mediation Center adjudication process, see Part Three of this book at page 191 et seq.

CHAPTER 7
MEDIATION BY SPORTS BODIES

7.1 INTRODUCTORY

A number of Sports Bodies offer mediation as a means of settling sports disputes – or more correctly 'sports-related' disputes.

We will take a look at the Court of Arbitration for Sport (CAS); the UK Sports Resolutions body; the former Australian National Sports Dispute Centre (NSDC); the relatively new Sport Dispute Resolution Centre of Canada (SDRCC) and the Japan Sports Arbitration Agency (JSAA).

Although not *in stricto sensu* a mediation body, but in a number of respects close to being one, we will also examine the important FIFA Dispute Resolution Chamber (DRC), particularly with reference to the settling of compensation disputes under the revised International Football Transfer Rules.

Again, *en passant*, although not strictly a form of mediation, it is worth mentioning that the International Association of Amateur Athletic Federations (IAAF) offers parties in dispute so-called 'Paper Only' Arbitrations, which are more flexible and designed to speed up the dispute settlement process. They are also cheaper avoiding the costs associated with a hearing. Paragraphs 9 and 10 of Rule 23 of the IAAF Handbook (Division II Constitution) provide as follows:

> '9. Where a matter has been referred to the Arbitrators under Rule 21.3 then, in place of an oral hearing, an athlete may request that the Arbitrators reach their decision solely on the basis of written submissions. Details of the applicable procedures are to be found in the "IAAF Arbitration Guidelines".
> 10. The Arbitrators shall have the power to decide all matters of fact and law, as well as the powers specified in the IAAF Arbitration Guidelines'.

The IAAF Arbitration Guidelines contain the following provisions on 'Paper Only' Arbitrations:

> '1. Where a 'paper only' arbitration has been requested, the following additional procedures will apply:
> a) Within 28 days of the reference, the athlete shall prepare a full statement of his case, attaching any necessary documentation in support.
> b) Within 21 days of the receipt by the IAAF of the athlete's statement, the IAAF shall prepare a statement in response, a copy of which shall be delivered to the athlete's Member federation.
> c) The athlete shall have the opportunity to submit a reply to the IAAF's statement of response. Such reply shall be delivered to the IAAF within 10 days of the delivery of the statement in response. If it so chooses, the IAAF may submit a reply.
> d) The IAAF may request that any member federation or Area Group Association submits a statement for consideration by the arbitrators. This statement shall be submitted within 21 days of the request of the General Secretary. A copy of the statement shall be

I.S. Blackshaw, Sport, Mediation and Arbitration

given to the athlete by his member federation. The athlete shall be given the opportunity to reply. The reply shall be submitted within 10 days of the receipt of the statement by the athlete.

e) The general secretary may, in his absolute discretion, lengthen or shorten the time available for the service of any of these documents.

f) Once all statements and replies have been received by the IAAF, they shall be dispatched to the arbitrators forthwith. The arbitrators shall consider the evidence and may request any further information necessary from the athlete, the IAAF, the Area Group Association or member federation involved.

g) The arbitrators shall reach their decision within 28 days. On any given issue, the decision of a majority of the arbitrators shall be regarded as the decision of the Arbitration Panel. No minority opinion shall be delivered. The decision shall be communicated to the General Secretary who shall inform all relevant parties forthwith.

h) The decision shall be final and binding on all parties and upon all IAAF Members. The arbitrators shall not be obliged to give any reason for their decision.

i) The decision shall have immediate effect. The fact of referral and the arbitrators shall be reported in the next notice being sent by the General Secretary to all members of the IAAF.'

7.2 The Court of Arbitration for Sport (CAS)

7.2.1 **General introduction**

The CAS is an arbitration body created by the International Olympic Committee (IOC) in 1983. Also known by its French acronym 'TAS' (Tribunal Arbitral du Sport), it is based in Lausanne, Switzerland, and has two permanent outposts in Sydney, Australia, and New York, USA. During the Olympic Games, it operates an Ad Hoc Division, which was set up on 28 September, 1995 for the Centennial Olympic Games held in Atlanta in 1996.[16]

The CAS has a minimum of 150 arbitrators from 37 countries, who are specialists in arbitration and sports law.[17] They are appointed for four-year renewable terms and must sign a 'letter of independence'. The CAS also has a permanent President.

CAS arbitrators are not generally obliged to follow earlier decisions or obey the sacred Common Law principle of *stare decisis* (binding precedent).[18] However, in the interests of comity and legal certainty they are usually prepared to do so.

The CAS is dedicated to hearing and settling any disputes directly or indirectly relating to sport, including commercial issues, for example, a dispute over a sponsorship contract. Any natural person, for example, an athlete, or legal person, for example, a sports association or a company, may bring a case before the CAS. The parties must agree to do so in writing.

It should also be mentioned that the working languages of the CAS are French and English and, in the absence of agreement between the parties, the CAS shall select one of the two languages as the language of the proceedings. The parties can choose another language provided the Court agrees, in which case the CAS may order the parties to pay all or part of the translation costs (Rule 29 of the CAS Procedural Rules).

---

16 See Heiko T. van Staveren, 'Why Does Sport Need Its Own Jurisdiction?', in W.P. Heere, ed., *International Law and The Hague's 750th Anniversary* (The Hague, T.M.C. Asser Instituut 1999) pp. 229-232; Matthieu Reeb, 'The Role of the Court of Arbitration for Sport', ibid., pp. 233-238; and James A.R. Nafziger, 'The Court of Arbitration for Sport and the General Process of International Sports Law', ibid., pp. 239-250. See also M. Reeb, 'The Court of Arbitration for Sport', 3(4) *Sports Law Bulletin* (2000) p. 10.

17 At the time of writing, there are around threehundred.

18 See case of *UCI* v. *J.*, 7 NCB, CAS 97/176 Award of 28 August, 1998, p. 14.

The CAS also offers non-binding Advisory Opinions on potential disputes similar to the concept of 'expert determination' in the commercial world. The CAS Code of Sports-related Arbitration including the Rules governing these Advisory Opinions, the latter which, in a number of respects, are akin to Mediation, are dealt with later in detail and are set out in Appendix XIX. A more detailed look at CAS Arbitrations, Advisory Opinions and other matters are covered in Part Two of this book at page 149 et seq.

7.3 CAS Mediation

The CAS also offers a mediation service,[19] which was introduced on 18 May, 1999.[20] And, as Ousmane Kane, the former Senior Counsel to the CAS and, during his tenure as such, responsible for mediation, has remarked:

> 'The International Council of Arbitration for Sport took the initiative to introduce mediation alongside arbitration. As the mediation rules encourage and protect fair play and the spirit of understanding, they are made to measure for sport.'[21]

Article 1, Paragraph 1 of the CAS Mediation Rules (Rules), which are set out in Appendix VIII, defines mediation in the following terms:

> 'CAS Mediation is a non-binding and informal procedure, based on a mediation agreement in which each party undertakes to attempt in good faith to negotiate with the other party, and with the assistance of a CAS mediator, with a view to settling a sports-related dispute.'

Article 2 of the Rules defines a 'mediation agreement' as follows:

> 'A mediation agreement is one whereby the parties agree to submit to mediation a sports-related dispute which has arisen or which may arise between them.
> A mediation agreement may take the form of a mediation clause inserted in a contract or that of a separate agreement.'

In other words, an express or an *ad hoc* mediation reference clause.

Although mediation is expressly excluded (in Para. 2 of Art. 1 of the Rules) for disciplinary and doping cases, for obvious reasons, mediation is very appropriate for settling the commercial/financial issues and consequences (for example, loss of lucrative sponsorship and endorsement contracts), which often follow from a doping case, particularly where the sports person concerned was wrongly accused of being a drugs cheat. For example, Dianne Modahl would probably have been better advised to try to settle her claims for compensation against the British Athletic Federation through mediation rather than through the courts.[22]

---

19 See booklet *Mediation Guide*, published by and available from CAS.

20 There are currently some 65 CAS mediators.

21 On the value of mediation generally for settling sports disputes, see Ian S. Blackshaw, '*Mediating Sports Disputes – National and International Perspectives*'(The Hague, T.M.C. Asser Press 2002) and on CAS mediation, see Ian S. Blackshaw, 'Settling Sports Disputes by CAS Mediation', 3 *CAS Newsletter* (November 2005) at pp. 4-7.

22 *Modahl* v. *British Athletic Federation* [2001] *All ER* (D) 181 (October). See also Ian S. Blackshaw, 'Modahl Loses Appeal For Compensation', 4(6) *Sports Law Bulletin* (November/December 2001) pp. 1, 3-4.

If the parties in dispute prefer to settle their differences by mediation – and many do because of the special characteristics and dynamics of sport[23] – the CAS model mediation clause is as follows:

> 'Any dispute, any controversy or claim arising under, out of or relating to this contract and any subsequent of or in relation to this contract, including, but not limited to, its formation, validity, binding effect, interpretation, breach or termination, as well as non-contractual claims shall be submitted to mediation in accordance with the CAS Mediation Rules.'

If mediation proves to be unsuccessful, although mediation providers usually claim a success rate of around 85 percent, the CAS recommends the following additional clause to be inserted in a contract to cover the above contingency:

> 'If, and to the extent that, any such dispute has not been settled within 90 days of the commencement of the mediation, or if, before the expiration of the said period, either party fails to participate or continue to participate in the mediation, the dispute shall, upon the filing of a Request for Arbitration by either party, be referred to and finally settled by CAS arbitration pursuant to the Code of Sports-related Arbitration. When the circumstances so require, the mediator may, at his own discretion or at the request of a party, seek an extension of the time limit from the CAS President.'

Thus, the CAS offers disputing parties the possibility of a 'Med-Arb' dispute resolution process: mediation to identify the issues; and arbitration to settle them.

Whilst on the subject of mediation, it may be noted, *en passant*, that in a landmark ruling in the English Courts in the case of *Cable & Wireless PLC* v. *IBM United Kingdom* [2002] 2 *All ER* (Comm) 1041, Mr Justice Colman held that an agreement to refer disputes to mediation is contractually binding. In this case, IBM called on Cable and Wireless to mediate a dispute that had arisen under a contract in which the parties had agreed to mediate future disputes. Cable and Wireless refused to do so, claiming that the reference to mediation in the contract was legally unenforceable because it lacked certainty and was like an unenforceable agreement to negotiate. The judge rejected this argument, holding that the agreement to try to resolve a dispute, with identification of the procedure to be used, was sufficient to give certainty and, therefore, legal effect to the clause. It may be added that, in England too, parties, who, under Court rules, refuse to try – or even *consider* the possibility of mediating – to settle their disputes by mediation at an early stage in the litigation process, may run the risk of being denied their legal costs if ultimately successful, contrary to the normal rule that 'costs follow the event'.[24]

Because of its popularity in the sporting world, many International and National Sports Federations now include specific provisions for mediation of appropriate sports disputes in their Statutes and Constitutions. As to the legal validity of a so-called CAS arbitration or mediation 'clause by reference' in such Statutes and Constitutions, see the decision of

---

[23] See the case of Richie Woodhall and Frank Warren involving a time-critical dispute under certain management and promotion agreements entered into between them, which was settled within 72 hours by mediation, discussed at p. 182 in Ian S. Blackshaw, *Mediating Sports Disputes – National and International Perspectives* (The Hague, T.M.C. Asser Press 2002).

[24] See *Susan Dunnett* v. *Railtrack PLC* [2002] EWCA Civ 302; and *Leicester Circuits Limited* v. *Coats* [2003] EWCA Civ 333. But see also *Halsey* v. *Milton Keynes General NHS Trust* and *Steel* v. *Joy and Halliday* [2004] EWCA Civ 576; [2004] 4 *All ER* 920, collectively known as the *Halsey* case and described by Lord Phillips of Worth Maltravers as 'the most important English judgement about ADR' (see Appendix I to this book).

the Swiss Federal Tribunal of 31 October 1996 in the case of *N.* v. *Federation Equestre Internationale*.[25] In that case, the Court held that by agreeing to abide by the rules of the Federation, which included a provision to refer all disputes exclusively to the CAS, the sports person concerned was bound to submit the dispute to the CAS, even though he had not expressly agreed to CAS arbitration or mediation. So-called 'sports association law' applied in such a case.

7.4 Procedural Aspects of CAS Mediations

Under Article 3 of the Rules, except where the parties agree otherwise, the version of the Rules in force at the time the written request for mediation (required under Art. 4 of the Rules) is filed at the CAS Court Office shall apply.

Article 4 provides that the written request shall contain: 'the identity of the parties and their representatives (name, address, telephone and fax numbers), a copy of the mediation agreement and a brief description of the dispute'.

Upon filing the mediation request, the administrative fee stipulated in Article 14 of the Rules must be paid; and the day on which this request is received by the CAS Court Office shall be considered as the date on which the mediation proceedings commenced.

Pursuant to Article 6 of the Rules, the CAS President chooses the mediator from the list of CAS mediators drawn up in accordance with the provisions of Article 5. The mediator appointed must be and remain independent of the parties (ibid.). The parties may be represented or assisted at their meetings with the mediator (Art. 7). The representative must have full authority to settle the dispute alone, without consulting the party whom he is representing (ibid.).

Under Article 8 of the Rules, the procedure to be followed in the mediation shall either be agreed by the parties themselves or determined by the mediator. This is a slight deviation from the general principle that the mediator is the one who controls the procedural aspects of the mediation. But the parties are required to 'cooperate in good faith with the mediator and … guarantee him the freedom to perform his mandate to advance the mediation as expeditiously as possible'.

The role of the mediator is laid down in Article 9 of the Rules, which recognises the basic concept of mediation, namely, that the mediator acts as a facilitator and may act in any manner '… he believes to be appropriate' but may not impose any solution of the dispute on either of the parties.

Article 10 of the Rules provides for the confidentiality of the mediation process subject to the normal exception of making any disclosure as required by the law. And further provides that:

> 'No record of any kind shall be made of the meetings… [and] [a]ll the written documents shall be returned to the party providing these upon termination of the mediation, and no copy therefore shall be retained.'

Article 10 also makes provision for the mediation to be conducted on a 'without prejudice' basis, expressed in the following terms:

---

[25] *Nagel/FEI*, CAS-Digest I, p. 585.

> 'The parties shall not rely on, or introduce as evidence in any arbitral or judicial proceedings:
> views expressed or suggestions made by a party with respect to a possible settlement of the dispute;
> admissions made by a party in the course of the mediation proceedings;
> documents, notes or other information obtained during the mediation proceedings;
> proposals made or views expressed by the mediator;
> the fact that a party had or had not indicated willingness to accept a proposal.'

Article 11 of the Rules deals with the questions of when and how the mediation may be terminated and provides as follows:

> 'Either party or the mediator may terminate the mediation at any time.
> The mediation shall be terminated:
> by the signing of a settlement by the parties;
> by a written declaration of the mediator to the effect that further efforts at mediation are no longer worthwhile; or
> by a written declaration of a party or the parties to the effect that the mediation proceedings are terminated.'

Article 12 of the Rules requires that any settlement of the mediation must be in writing and signed by the mediator and the parties. And further provides that:

> 'Each party shall receive a copy thereof. In the event of any breach, a party may rely on such copy before an arbitral or judicial authority.
> A copy of the settlement is submitted for inclusion in the records of the CAS Court Office.'

Article 13 of the Rules deals with the question of failure to settle and includes the following important provision – absolutely fundamental to the process of mediation:

> 'In the event of failure to resolve a dispute by mediation, the mediator shall not accept an appointment as an arbitrator in any arbitral proceedings concerning the parties involved in the same dispute.'

7.4.1 CAS mediation costs

Article 14 of the Rules deals with the equally important subject of the costs of CAS mediations. Until the CAS administrative fee is paid by each party, the mediation proceedings cannot be started; and the CAS Court Office may require the parties to deposit an equal amount as an advance towards the CAS mediation costs. The parties are required to pay their own mediation costs and, unless otherwise agreed, share equally the other final costs, which include the CAS fee, the mediator's fees, calculated on the basis of the CAS fees scale, a contribution towards the costs of the CAS, and the costs of witnesses, experts and interpreters.

7.4.2 CAS mediation symposium

Following the introduction of the CAS Mediation Service in 1999, the CAS held a symposium in Lausanne on 4 November, 2000 to promote this aspect of its work. Three Papers were presented by Bernard Foucher, President of the French Institute of Mediators; Christopher Newmark, a Partner in the London Office of the Baker & Mckenzie Law Firm and a CEDR Registered Mediator; and William K. Slate II, President and CEO of the American Arbitration Association. For ease of reference, we set out below the texts of these Papers. The one by Bernard Foucher on 'Mediation as a Method of Settling Sports Disputes under French Law' was given in French.

Bernard Foucher[26]
Conciliation as a way of resolving sports related disputes in France

LA CONCILIATION COMME MODE DE RÈGLEMENT DES CONFLITS SPORTIFS EN DROIT FRANÇAIS

Le système de la conciliation a été introduit par la loi no 92-652 du 13 juillet 1992 relative à l'organisation et à la promotion des activités physiques et sportives (article 19), à partir d'un amendement parlementaire.

Il aménage dans le domaine du sport, un mode de règlement des conflits tout à fait original, qui emprunte à la fois à l'arbitrage et à la médiation, sans être juridiquement ni l'un, ni l'autre, et qui a pour objectif de limiter l'intervention du juge étatique dans les contentieux sportifs.

Depuis maintenant sept ans, le système de 'la conciliation à la française' a fait ses preuves. La loi du 6 juillet vient de le confirmer et de le renforcer.

Quel est ce mécanisme original? (I); Comment a-t-il fonctionné? (II).

I– LE MÉCANISME DE LA CONCILIATION
A– L'organisation de la conciliation.

Qui est chargé d'assurer la conciliation?

Dans sa dernière version, c'est-à-dire celle du 6 juillet 2000, la loi attribue au CNOSF '*une mission de conciliation dans les conflits opposant les licenciés, les groupements sportifs et les fédérations agréées, à l'exception des conflits mettant en cause des faits de dopage*'.

□ Ce n'est pas une nouveauté. Déjá la loi du 25 octobre 1975, dite loi 'Mazeaud' avait prévu à l'article 14 que: '*Le CNOSF arbitre à leur demande, les litiges opposant les licenciés, groupements et fédérations. Un décret en Conseil d'Etat détermine les conditions d'application du présent décret*'. Mais faute de décret d'application à l'époque, cette mission n'avait jamais été exercée.

La loi de 1984 avait elle aussi confiée une mission de conciliation au CNOSF, mais cette mission restait facultative.

□ La loi de 1992 lui confiera une mission de conciliation obligatoire dans certains cas, mais sans autre précision quant à l'organisation de cette mission.

Le CNOSF s'est donc dans un premier temps organisé lui-même en établissant une liste de conciliateurs et en regroupant ces conciliateurs en une 'conférence des conciliateurs' ayant, à sa tête un président.

La liste des conciliateurs a été arretée par le Conseil d'administration du CNOSF, sur proposition du bureau et après agrément des candidatures par la commission juridique.

L'idée a été de retenir des candidatures qui présentaient un double profil: des compétences juridiques et une connaissance approfondie des institutions sportives.

Actuellement cette liste comporte 14 noms et comprend:

- des professeurs de droit (4)
- des magistrats de l'ordre administratifs (2)
- des magistrats de l'ordre judiciaire (3)
- des avocats (4)
- une expert comptable (1)

---

[26] Président de la Conférence des Conciliateurs, Secrétaire général des tribunaux administratifs et des cours administratives d'appel.

Quant au président de la conférence des conciliateurs, un certain nombre de pouvoirs d'organisation des audiences de conciliation et d'instruction des dossiers lui avaient été reconnus par un 'règlement de concillation' adopté là encore, par le Conseil d'administration du CNOSF.

Enfin, pour gérer les demandes de conciliation, le CNOSF a mis en place un service de la conciliation comprenant notamment 3 assistants de conciliation qui assurent la gestion des dossiers, et a mis à disposition des locaux pour permettre la tenue des audiences de conciliation.

□ Pour donner plus de rigueur juridique à toute cette organisation, la loi du 6 juillet 2000 est venue officialiser l'existence de la 'Conférence des conciliateurs', ainsi que celle du président de la conférence des conciliateurs qui se trouve investi, de par la loi cette fois-ci, d'un certain nombre de prérogatives.

De même, la loi vient renforcer sérieusement l'obligation de confidentialité des conciliateurs qui en cas de violation de cette obligation s'exposent à des sanctions pénales.

B– Le champ d'application de la conciliation.
Sur quels litiges porte la conciliation?
A l'exception de ceux mettant en cause des faits de dopage, tous les litiges opposant les licenciés, les groupements sportifs et les fédérations peuvent être soumis à la conciliation. Mais il convient de faire une distinction entre les conflits qui relèvent d'une procédure de conciliation facultative et ceux qui relèvent d'une procédure de conciliation obligatoire.

□ Les conflits qui relèvent d'une procédure obligatoire demeurent les plus nombreux.

Selon la définition retenue sur le nouvel article 19 issu de la loi du 6 juillet 2000, il s'agit des conflits qui résultent '*d'une décision susceptible ou non de recours interne, prise par une fédération dans l'exercice de prérogatives de puissance publique ou en application de ses statuts*'.

La condition posée par la loi de 1992 qui exigeait que le conflit concerne une fédération titulaire de la délégation du ministre chargé des sports, n'est donc pas reprise et il suffit que le conflit concerne une fédération seulement agréée.

La plupart des décisions réglementaires ou individuelles concernant l'organisation et le fonctionnement de la discipline sportive, dont la fédération a la gestion, relèvent donc de la conciliation obligatoire. Il en est de même des décisions de la fédération qui concernent le fonctionnement interne de l'association et mettent en cause l'application des statuts.

Le conflit relevant d'une procédure de conciliation obligatoire ne pourra alors être directement soumis au juge. La saisine du juge sera en effet sanctionnée par une irrecevabilité.

□ Un certain nombre de conflits sont exclus de la procédure de conciliation obligatoire mais ils pourront toujours faire l'objet d'une procédure de conciliation facultative, si les parties l'acceptent.

Il en est ainsi des litiges concernant des contrats de travail ou des contrats commerciaux (sponsoring – droits de télévision ....).

C– La procédure de la conciliation.
Comment fonctionne la conciliation?
La procédure de conciliation comporte un certain nombre de mesures contraignantes destinées à assurer l'efficacité du système.

Toutefois, ces règles de procédures, insuffisamment détaillées dans la loi de 1992 ont dû être complétées en pratique, et sont améliorées et définies par la loi du 6 juillet 2000.

1– La saisine du conciliateur.
□ Elle est faite par toute partie au litige au moyen d'une demande adressée au président de la conférence des conciliateurs. C'est celui-ci:

→ qui est chargé de désigner un ou plusieurs concillateurs en fonction de la difficulté de l'affaire;
→ qui est chargé de procéder à une instruction sommaire de la recevabilité de chaque affaire et de rejeter directement les demandes qui ne concernent pas des litiges relevant de la procédure de conciliation obligatere ou des demandes qui lui paraissent manifestement infondées ou irrecevables.

La loi du 6 juillet 2000 confirme l'attribution de ces pouvoirs du président de la conférence des conciliateurs, pouvoirs qu'il détenait au préalable de manière un peu sommaire du 'règlement de la conciliation'.

□ Elle peut intervenir avant l'épuisement des voies de recours internes devant les instances fédérales.

Cette disposition, qui n'est pas remise en cause par la loi du 6 juillet 2000, est motivée par le souci de ne pas bloquer le litige dans des délais d'examen trop longs par les organes de recours de la fédération.

□ Elle entraîne l'interruption des délais de recours juridictionnels éventuels.

□ Elle entraîne la suspension de la décision contestée.

On perçoit l'intérêt de cette mesure. Si la décision est déjà exécutée, quel est en effet l'intérêt de rechercher une conciliation? Cette mesure constitue donc un moyen incitatif pour engager le plus rapidement la discussion et parvenir à un compromis.

Mais on s'est interrogé sur son application. D'une part le texte n'était pas très clair sur la durée précise de la suspention. D'autre part, les fédérations manifestaient à son égard quelques critiques lorsque la saisine du conciliateur avait essentiellement pour but de pouvoir bénéficier de l'effet suspensif et revêtait alors un caractère dilatoire.

Ex: Alors qu'un joueur de football a commis sur le terrain une faute grave et indiscutable entraînant une sanction de suspension de plusieurs matches, la simple saisine du conciliateur entraîne la susponsion de la sunction et 'l'autoriserait' à participer au match suivant.

C'est pourquoi un aménagement avait été apporté par 'le règlement de conciliation'. Il consistait à considérer que ce n'était pas la saisine du conciliateur qui entraînait la suspension de la décision contestée, mais la décision du président de la conférence des conciliateurs se prononçant sur la recevabilité de la demande. Une marge de manoeuvre était ainsi laissée au président de la conférence des conciliateurs qui en différant sa décision sur la recevabilité de la demande et sur la désignation d'un conciliateur différait aussi 'l'effet suspensif'.

La loi du 6 juillet 2000 vient donner une base légale et compléter cet aménagement: '*lorsque le conflit résulte de l'intervention d'une decision individuelle, l'exécution de cette décision est suspendue à compter de la notification à l'auteur de la décision de l'acte désignant un conciliateur*'. L'effet suspensif ne trouvera donc plus à s'appliquer que pour les actes individuels. La loi accorde même un pouvoir supplémentaire au président de la conférence des conciliateurs: celui-ci '*peut lever ladite suspension dans le cas où la décision contestée est motivée par des actes de violence caractérisée*'.

2– L'intervention du conciliateur.

□ Le conciliateur doit se prononcer dans le délai d'un mois à compter de sa saisine.

□ À l'issue d'une 'audience de conciliation' le conciliateur doit formuler des propositions de conciliation aux parties.

□ Les propositions doivent être acceptées par les parties, mais il existe, un système d'approbation tacite.

En effet, la proposition est présumée acceptée, sauf opposition notifiée au conciliateur et aux parties dans le délai d'un mois à compter de la notification de la proposition du conciliateur.

II– LA PRATIQUE DE LA CONCILIATION

A– Le nombre d'affaires traitées.

La conciliation a fait ses premiers pas en 1993. Sept ans plus tard, elle a examiné son millième dossier.

Le tableau suivant permet de retracer son activité au 1er septembre 2000.

<table>
<tr><td colspan="4">1141
dossiers enregistrés</td></tr>
<tr><td colspan="3">913
dossiers soumis à une procédure de concillation</td><td>228
dossiers directment rejetés pour irrecevabilité</td></tr>
<tr><td rowspan="2">239
dossiers ont fat l'objet d'un accord entre les parties lors de l'audience de conciliation</td><td colspan="2">674
dossiers ont donné lieu à des propositions de conciliation</td><td></td></tr>
<tr><td>421
dossiers où les propositions de coniciliation ont été acceptées</td><td>253
dossiers où les propositions de coniciliation ont été refusées</td><td></td></tr>
<tr><td colspan="2">660
dossiers où le litige a été résolu (soit un taux de 73%)</td><td>70
dossiers où le litige a été porté devant les tribunaux</td><td></td></tr>
</table>

Ce tableau appelle les brefs commentaires suivants:

– Le mécanisme de la conciliation a démarré lentement les deux ou trois premières années. Il est aujourd'hui bien connu des acteurs du monde sportif, et le nombre de dossiers enregistrés se situe aux alentours de 160 par an.
– Un nombre significatif de ces dossiers (1/5 environ) a été rejeté pour irrecevabilité, soit parce que la demande était manifestement infondée ou tardive, soit parce que le litige ne relevait pas du champ d'application de la procédure de conciliation obligatoire. Mais dans ce dernier cas, une procédure de conciliation facultative, où le conciliateur intervient alors à titre de 'bons offices' peut-être engagée si les parties l'acceptent explicitement.
– Une situation n'a pas d'explication précise. C'est celle qui résulte de l'écart entre, le nombre de litiges non résolus (253) et le nombre de litiges portés devant les tribunaux (70). Il s'agit de cas où très généralement, la proposition faite par le conciliateur a été refusée par la fédération, et où l'autre partie ne 'poursuit' pas. Il est probable que celle-ci ne souhaite pas faire de procédure juridictionnelle ... à moins que la proposition du conciliateur, même non suivie d'effet, ait permis de lui donner une satisfaction 'suffisante'.

B– Le type d'affaires traités.

Il n'est pas possible de donner une liste exhaustive des litiges soumis à la conciliation, ni de les identifier, au risque d'ailleurs d'enfreindre le principe de la confidentialité. Les questions soumises au conciliateur sont très variées et concernent toutes les disciplines sportives, ou presque.

Le nombre d'affaires traitées permet surtout de repérer les litiges qui reviennent le plus souvent devant le conciliateur, et de dresser ainsi une typologie du contentieux sportif en portant un diagnostic sur ce contentieux. Ce diagnostic n'est pas inutile car il permet de renseigner les fédérations notamment, sur les points faibles de leurs réglementations ou de leurs décisions.

Cinq types de litiges peuvent cependant être plus clairement distingués.

1 – Les litiges relatifs à l'application des réglementations fédérales.

Ce sont les plus nombreux. Ils concernent essentiellement:

a) les licenciés.

– *Litiges concernant la délivrance les licences mais aussi la régularité des licences.*
Beaucoup de litiges ont, un temps concerné, par exemple, les manquements aux mentions obligatoires que doit comporter une licence (attestation de certificat médical, mentions incomplètes ou erronées ...).
Ces problèmes entraînent des réactions en chaîne, puisque la participation d'un joueur 'non' licencié ou 'non régulièrement' licencié à une compétition peut remettre en cause les résultats de la compétition.

- *Litiges concernant les mutations de licenciés.*
  Certaines fédérations encadrent ces mutations par des règles tellement contraignantes que le conciliateur en arrive à se demander si ces règles ne constituent pas une entrave illicite à la liberté d'association et au respect du droit à la pratique sportive affirmé par l'article 1er de la loi sur le sport.

b) Les groupements sportifs.
- *Litiges concernant des refus d'affiliation souvent fondés sur de circonstances de fait étrangers à la réglementation sportive.*
- *Litiges liés d'une manière générale à l'application de la réglementation sportive.*
  Ce domaine est très vaste et très varié. Pour cibler quelques litiges importants, nous pouvons relenir:
  - D'une part, les problèmes résultant de l'organisation et du fonctionnement des compétitions.
    À titre d'exemples: le droit de participer à une compétition sous réserve d'inscrire plusieurs équipes, ou un nombre de joueurs minimum
    le problème de la participation aux compétitions, de sportifs étrangers.
    (NB: s'agissant du sport professionnel l'application de l'arrêt BOSMAN ne pose plus, aujourd'hui de difficultés, mais s'agissant du sport non professionnel, la participation de sportifs étrangers pose toujours des difficultés).
    le problème de report de matches pour terrains impraticables.
    le problème des décisions d'arbitrage.
    (NB: il existe sur ce point une irrecevabilité de principe, sauf s'il est constaté une erreur dans l'application du règlement: l'arbitre prend une décision que le règlement sportif ne lui permettrait pas de prendre (pas faute technique d'arbitrage mais faute 'juridique' d'arbitrage)).
  - D'autre part, les problèmes résultant de décisions d'accession au professionnalisme.
- *Litiges liés à des modifications de règlements sportifs (modification en cours de saison ou de compétition par exemple).*

À partir de ce premier type de litiges, plusieurs constatations s'imposent:

- Celle tout d'abord d'une inflation de réglementation de la part des fédérations qui en arrivent à mettre en place des 'usines à gaz'. Plus la réglementation est dense, détaillée, pointilliste, plus elle risque d'être confuse et donc source d'interprétation et de litiges.
- Celle ensuite d'une confusion entre les décisions de nature 'administrative' et de nature 'disciplinaire'(les procédures applicables seront pourtant différentes).
  Par exemple: le refus de mutation d'un joueur, qui ne remplit pas les conditions réglementaires n'est pas une sanction. Il ne résulte pas d'une faute, mais du non respect des conditions posées.
- Celle enfin de dispositions réglementaires souvent imprécises voire lacunaires:
  Exemple:
  - *la suspension de terrain, s'applique t-elle à toutes les compétitions ou à certaines d'entre elles?*
  - *la suspension de joueurs est-elle prononciée pour une durée ou pour un nombre de matches défini?*

2 – Les litiges relatifs aux sanctions disciplinaires.

Ces litiges représentent environ 30% des demandes de conciliation.

C'est un domaine très sensible, d'autant que l'effet suspensif de la saisine du conciliateur revêt ici toute son importance et son particularisme, ainsi qu'il a déjà été indiqué.

Dans ces litiges, le conciliateur suit la même démarche que le juge, et en particulier le juge administratif.

Il examine la régularité de la décision (c'est-à-dire la légalité externe) en s'appuyant notamment sur le décret de 1993. Celui-ci prévoit en effet un certain nombre de règles de procédure que certaines fédérations ignorent encore, ou n'appliquent pas (double degré de 'juridiction'; composition des instances disciplinaires de 5 membres au moins, et majorité d'entre eux n'appartenant pas au comité directeur; respect du droit de la défense; motivation de la décision, qui ne doit pas être stéréotypée).

Il examine le contenu de la décision (c'est-à-dire la légalité interne) en s'appuyant notamment sur deux principes: la sanction doit être prévue par un texte (principe de la légalité des peines); la sanction doit être proportionnée à la faute.

À partir de ce type de litiges, plusieurs remarques doivent être faites:

- Souvent la décision disciplinaire est entachée d'une procédure irrigulière qui l'exposerait à une annulation irrémédiable par le juge.
- L'appréciation du principe de proportionnalité est généralement mal comprise. Certaines fédérations se dotent d'un barème de sanctions extrêmement détaillé, au point de ne plus laisser aux organes disciplinaires une marge d'appréciation, et donc une possibilité de respecter le principe de proportionnalité.
- Ce type de litiges peut exposer le système de la conciliation à une difficulté d'application résultant de la nécessité de faire 'valider' en principe, la proposition de conciliation par l'organe disciplinaire (à priori indépendant de l'autorité fédérale présente à la conciliation).

3 – Les litiges relatifs aux sélections et notamment aux sélections nationales.

Ce sont des litiges résultant généralement du refus de sélectionner un athlète, Ils sont difficiles à gérer par le conciliateur. En effet, ces litiges portent en réalité sur des appréciations subjectives des qualités des athlètes, et procèdent souvent d'un climat de défiance entre l'athlète et la fédération.

Dans ces litiges, l'athlète n'attend ni plus ni moins du conciliateur, qu'il lui donne son 'billet' de sélection à la sortie de l'audience.

De plus, ces litiges doivent souvent être réglés 'en urgence'.

Dans ces litiges, le conciliateur ne peut certainement pas se substituer à l'appréciation qui a pu être faite par les spécialites (sélectionneur – directeur technique national) sur les capacités d'ensemble de l'athlète à participer à une compétition, et imposer la sélection de l'athlète. Il s'agit en effet d'une appréciation paticulièrement discrétionnaire.

Cependant, le concillateur peut d'une part, vérifier s'il existe des règles pré-établies de sélection et dans ce cas exiger leur respect. Certaines fédérations encadrent en effet la procédure de sélection en retenant des critères objectifs, tels que la réalisation de résultats sportifs ou de minima exigibles (seront sélectionnés les 2 premiers, par exemple ...). D'autres, au contraire, laissent une totale liberté au selectionneur pour faire ses choix. Dans le premier cas, si la fédération a entendu se lier par des critères précis, le conciliateur veillera au respect de l'application de ces critères. Dans le second cas, le conciliateur ne discutera même pas du choix du sélectionneur, sauf à considerer que celui-ci s'est fondé sur des considérations totalement étrangères à la valeur sportive de l'athlète (il s'agirait presque d'une selection déguisée ou d'un détournement de pouvoir).

Le conciliateur peut d'autre part, obtenir la meilleure transparence possible des motifs de refus de sélection. Il est vrai que le droit, la jurisprudence n'obligent pas les fédérations de motiver un refus de sélection. Mais de nombreux litiges révèlent que les athlètes ont saisi le conciliateur parce qu'ils s'estimaient écartés de la sélection sans en connaître les raisons. Une simple explication réduira les tensions et mettra un terme au litige.

4 – Les litiges concernant le contrôle de la gestion des clubs professionnels.

Ce n'est pas un domaine quantitativement important. Mais c'est un domaine délicat.

Il touche en effet à la situation financière des clubs et à leur devenir.

Certaines disciplines sportives ont mis en place une branche 'professionnelle' avec des organismes spécifiques (les ligues nationales). La nécessité d'avoir un secteur professionnel viable a conduit à assurer un contrôle de la gestion des clubs professionnels, et à confier à des organes de contrôle de gestion le soin d'apprécier la situation financière de ces clubs. Des décisions peuvent alors être prises pour refuser une accession ou un maintien en professionnalisme en raison d'une situation financière insuffisante ou dégradée.

Or ce domaine touche à une conception un peu nouvelle du sport. En effet il ne suffit pas d'être le meilleur sportivement, et de se prévaloir de résultats sportifs pour accéder à un championnat professionnel, il faut aussi se prévaloir de critères extra-sportifs (bonne situation financière, et même, autres critères matériels). Le conciliateur se trouve donc saisi de décisions de refus d'accession ou de maintien en professionnalisme pour des raisons tenant à la gestion et la situation financière d'un club examinées par des organes de contrôle de gestion.

Le conciliateur ne peut certainement pas refaire l'expertise financière. Il n'en a ni les moyens metériels, ni les compétences techniques. Mais il peut vérifier si la procédure prévue à bien été respectée (délais pour présenter les documents comptables – nature des pièces produites – double examen parfois prévu, par un organisme d'appel), et si la décision repose sur des faits exacts, n'est pas entachée d'un détournement de pouvoir ou ne comporte pas une erreur manifeste d'appréciation.

Quel constat faire de ce type de litiges?

Il est double. D'une part, la réglementation est souvent imprécise en la matière (que veut dire 'une situation financière saine'? à quel moment précis apprécier la situation financière du club?). D'autre part, ce type de litiges aboutit à une véritable dérive contentieuse, où l'éthique sportive est balayée.

Que penser du contentieux généré par le club classé dernier de sa division et relégué sportivement, qui va mettre en cause la montée du club arrivé en tête de la division inférieure et acquise sportivement, en se bornant à contester l'examen qui a été fait de la situation financière de ce dernier?

5 – Les litiges relatifs à l'application des statuts fédéraux.

Ces litiges sont distincts de ceux précédemment évoqués dans la mesure où ils ne résultent pas de la mise en oeuvre de prérogatives de puissance publique, mais de l'application des statuts fédéraux réglementant la vie associative de la fédération, et dans la mesure aussi, où ils relèvent ensuite généralement à la competence du juge judiciaire.

Les litiges concernent surtout:

= *Le contentieux résultant de l'application des statuts de la fédération.*
  Le conciliateur va s'attacher à ce que ces statuts soient respectés et que les décisions internes à la vie de l'association soient conformes à ces statuts.
  Le problème intéressant s'est posé de savoir s'il fallait avant de veiller à l'application des statuts, vérifier si ces statuts étaient conformes aux statut types annexés au décret n° 85-236 du 13 février 1985 modifié, conformité permettant et validant en principe, l'agrément ministériel.
  L'option a plutôt été de s'en tenir à la stricte application des statuts qui tiennent lieu de loi à l'association (la non conformité aux statuts-types pose alors le problème de la légalité de l'agrément accordé par le ministre, mais reste étrangère au seul litige concernant l'application des statuts).
= *Le contentieux électif qui couvre à la fois la régularité des candidatures et la régularité des votes.*
= *Le contentieux résultant de la tenue des assemblées générales (convocations irrégulières – débats irriguliers – tenues d'assemblées ordinaires ou extraordinaires).*
= *Le contentieux résultant des relations entre fédération et organes déconcentrés.*

Trois remarques s'imposent à partir de ce type de litiges:

- Ils se doublent la plupart du temps de considérations personnelles.
- Ils résultent souvent d'un manque de rigueur, notamment dans la tenue des assemblées générales. Ce manque de rigueur est 'acceptable' lorsque la vie de l'association est 'paisible'. Il devient source de litiges lorsque la vie de l'association est conflictuelle.
- Ces litiges n'offrent que peu de solutions au conciliateur qui ne peut se limiter qu'à proposer par exemple, de refaire l'assemblée générale ou les élections.

C – Le mode de traitement des affaires.

1 – La tenue d'une audience de conciliation.

Chaque affaire qui a été déclarée recevable est examinée 'lors d'une audience de conciliation' qui réunit le conciliateur désigné et les parties concernées par le litige. Ces parties sont généralement le demandeur et le défendeur qui est le plus souvent une fédération sportive. Mais dans certains cas, une partie tierce, intéressée par la résolution du litige peut être invitée à participer à l'audience.

L'audience ne saurait être empreinte de formalisme, mais elle doit se dérouler dans le respect du principe du contradictoire et du débat équitable,

Il importe surtout que les parties présentes à l'audience, qui par ailleurs doivent veiller à garder une confidentialité des débats, soient suffisamment représentatives, et capables de s'engager efficacement pour accepter les solutions éventuellment proposées. Cette remarque concerne essentiellement les représentants des fédérations qui ne sauraient venir 'assister' à une audience de conciliation sans avoir la capacité de décider au nom de la fédération et de s'engager dans la conciliation. Il y va bien sûr de l'intérêt de l'audience de conciliation et de ses chances de succès.

2 – L'acquisition d'une 'culture de la conciliation'.

L'expérience acquise au fil des dossiers et des audiences de conciliation permet de considérer qu'il existe bien une 'culture de la conciliation' qui doit être bien comprise de l'ensemble des participants.

Le conciliateur tout d'abord, doit faire preuve d'une capacité d'écoute (il doit permettre aux parties de s'exprimer et de 'se parler'), de patience (il faut désamorcer des situations conflictuelles générant parfois une certaine agressivité entre les parties) de conviction et de persuasion (il faut essayer de convaincre et non d'imposer).

Les parties ensuite, doivent être capables d'admettre l'idée du compromis. À la différence d'un procès devant le juge qui se termine par un 'vainqueur' et un 'vaincu', la conciliation doit permettre de dégager une solution consensuelle où il n'y a ni vainqueur, ni vaincu. Mais pour y parvenir, chaque partie doit souvent admettre d'abandonner une partie des ses prétentions et accepter le compromis.

Il n'est pas rare enfin que les parties soient représentées par un avocat. Là aussi, l'attitude de l'avocat en conciliation ne doit pas être tout à fait la même que celle de l'avocat en procès. Devant le juge il doit défendre son client avec pour but essentiel d'imposer sa solution. Devant le conciliateur il doit développer une capacité de facilitation du litige et non de blocage du litige, même parfois au prix d'un recul dans la ligne de défense de son client.

3 – La recherche d'une solution équilibrée.

L'intérêt essentiel du mécanisme de la conciliation est de faciliter l'adoption d'une solution équilibrée à la résolution d'un litige sportif.

L'intrusion du droit dans le domaine du sport ne s'est pas faite sans heurts et la résolution de litiges sportifs par le juge étatique n'est pas toujours adaptée (délais de réponse trop longs, inefficacité de solutions juridiques à des situations spécifiques de l'activité sportive).

La conciliation permet précisément de régler différemment les conflits en tenant compte de la spécificité sportive et en recherchant des solutions qui essaient de préserver un équilibre entre les intérêts des parties et un équilibre entre l'ordre sportif et l'ordre juridique.

Le mode de traitement des affaires pourra alors, en conciliation, être à géométrie variable. Soit une conciliation entre les parties est envisageable et la solution proposée sera plus pragmatique que juridique, soit une conciliation n'est pas envisageable et la solution proposée restera essentiellement juridique.

En conclusion, le bilan de la 'conciliation à la française' mérite d'être défendu.

Certes le mécanisme de la conciliation n'est pas exempt de toute critique. Le juriste pourra y trouver matière à interrogations. Les dispositions de l'article 19 sont-elles suffisamment précises? Quelle est la valeur juridique de la proposition de conciliation? Comment assurer juridiquement son exécution?

La fédération, placée le plus souvent en position de défendeur, pourra y trouver matière à critiques. L'effet suspensif est-il opportun? La saisine du conciliateur avant l'épuisement des voies de recours internes est-elle souhaitable? Comment mettre en application certaines propositions du conciliateur? *(par exemple pour les propositions concernant les mesures disciplinaires, faut-il revenir à l'organe disciplinaire?).* La conciliation obligatoire n'est-elle pas tout simplement une atteinte intolérable à l'autorité fédérale?

Le requérant pourra y trouver matière à insuffisance. L'encadrement procédural n'est-il pas trop contraignant? Pourquoi le mécanisme de la conciliation obligatoire est-il limité à certains litiges? Pourquoi le conciliateur n'a-t-il pas le pouvoir de faire ou de décider?

Mais au delà de toutes ces questions, le mécanisme de la conciliation apparaît pour les litiges sportifs comme un système original, efficace et adapté.

- □ Il est original dans la mesure où il se distingue:
  - → du recours au juge, où le rnode de règlement du conflit est imposé et où la solution retenue a force exécutoire;

→ du recours à l'arbitrage, où le mode de règlement du conflit est librement accepté et où la solution retenue a force exécutoire;
→ du recours à la médiation où le mode de règlement du conflit est librement accepté et où la solution retenue n'a pas force exécutoire.

Dans la conciliation à la française, le mode de règlement du conflit est en effet imposé, mais la solution retenue n'a pas force exécutoire.

□ Il est efficace et adapté dans la mesure où:
→ Il évite le recours au juge qui n'est pas le censeur naturel de l'activité sportive;
→ Il permet de résoudre les litiges dans 'la famille du sport';
→ Il permet de disposer d'une expertise juridique à partir de l'analyse faite par le conciliateur et de ses propositions;
→ Il permet de disposer d'une solution rapide, gratuite, pragmatique qui peut concilier sport et droit.

C'est en ce sens que la conciliation est bien une procédure au service du sport.

Christopher Newmark[27]
Is Mediation Effective for Resolving Sports Disputes?

A. Introduction
This paper gives an overview of the use of mediation for resolving sports disputes. As a preliminary matter it is perhaps helpful to make it clear where we are in the evolution of mediation in sports disputes, at least in Europe. To use an American sporting metaphor, we have barely got off first base. The Court of Arbitration for Sport ('CAS'), which introduced its mediation rules in May 1999, has not carried out any sports mediations yet. Nor has the LCIA, the other lead organiser of this conference. This does not mean that these institutions do not have sensible mediation rules. They do. It is just that mediation in this specialist area is in its infancy, especially in the international arena.

In the UK, where the use of mediation for general commercial disputes has grown exponentially over the last 18 months, the Centre for Dispute Resolution ('CEDR'), which is the leading commercial mediation provider, has assisted in about 10 sports mediations in total. I will be referring to one of these which hit the sporting headlines later. A new body, the Sport Dispute Resolution Panel ('SDRP'), is about to undertake its first sports mediation.

These statistics suggest that, as in all areas of ADR, the US is still well ahead of the game in the use of mediation for resolving sports disputes. We will hear from William Slate from the AAA about the use of mediation in the US for sports related disputes, and we can probably learn most by examining the US experience. But we can also learn by going back to basics, by looking at what the process of mediation actually is and what it offers, and by then looking at some of the types of dispute that arise in the sporting world. This process, which is the focus of the next two sections of this paper (Sections B and C below), should show us where there are matches and where mediation is likely to have a role. In Section D, the paper then examines some of the practical issues that users and providers of mediation should give careful consideration to as they develop mediation services and insert mediation clauses in their contracts.

B. What does mediation offer?
This is not the place to embark on a complete A-Z of the mediation process. I will however remind us all of some of the key features of mediation which always need to be borne in mind when considering its application for a dispute:

- **Mediation is nothing more than 'supercharged' settlement negotiation.** The process can be misunderstood to be more complex than it is. It is certainly powerful, it certainly has many

---

[27] Christopher Newmark is a partner in the London office of Baker & McKenzie and a CEDR registered mediator. Andrea Dahlberg and David Green of Baker & McKenzie assisted with the research for this paper.

subtleties and dynamics which give it advantages over direct negotiation, but, fundamentally, it is a process which involves negotiation with a view to arriving at a compromise agreement. As a basic rule, where a dispute is capable of resolution by means of a negotiated settlement agreement, mediation is viable.

- **Mediation is *usually* consensual – i.e. the parties attend the mediation by agreement.** The word usually is italicised because we will need to come back to this in the context of 'mandatory' mediation imposed by the rules of governing bodies.
- **The mediator does not give a decision, but acts as a facilitator to assist the parties in achieving a settlement.** Styles of mediation differ. Some mediators are more evaluative than others. Parties sometimes request mediators to propose solutions. But the key distinction between mediation and adjudicative dispute resolution processes remains.
- **Mediation can be (and usually is) very fast.**
- **Mediation is always private and confidential (provided that confidentiality is upheld by the courts).**
  In the common law countries, the confidentiality of the mediation process is a given. In civil law countries, the attitude of the courts is less clear.
- **A successful mediation invariably requires some compromise on the part of all parties.** Mediated agreements where one party effectively capitulates are not unknown, but they are rare. Compromise of some sort is invariably involved, but this does not mean that the result always 'splits the baby'.
- **The outcome of a mediation cannot bind third parties who did not participate in the mediated settlement.** This is fundamental and of particular relevance in the sporting context. Where the interests of third parties need to be taken into account, then those parties need to buy into the mediation process so they can be bound by its outcome.
- **A settlement achieved in a mediation is only enforceable as a contract (unless it is subsequently embodied in an arbitration award or court order).** This is sometimes raised as a weakness of the process. However, this feature of mediation goes back to the underlying nature of the process – it is just a negotiation hopefully leading to a contractual agreement.
- The terms of the settlement agreement are in the hands of the parties and are not limited to the normal remedies associated with courts or tribunals. This is of course a feature of direct negotiations as well. But the intervention of the mediator creates an environment in which creative solutions are more likely to be explored.

C. Sports disputes in all their different shapes and sizes

This diagram does not purport to depict all relationships in the sporting world – but it does pick out some of the key relationships. And wherever there is a relationship there is potential for a dispute. The disputes differ in nature. In the introduction to this paper, reference is made to 'sports disputes' as if that is a term of art or describes a clearly defined set of disputes. In fact the term is imprecise and is used to refer to the miscellany of disputes arising out of the world of sport. Some such disputes are purely commercial contractual disputes (e.g. those between a competitor and a sponsor). Others are regulatory (e.g. 4 dispute between a competitor and a governing body over eligibility) or quasi criminal (e.g. disciplinary or doping disputes). A selection of characteristic disputes (which can be illustrated with real examples) and their suitability for mediation are described below. As will be seen, whilst mediation clearly has something to offer for some, it is inappropriate for others.

Disputes arising when a national sporting body bans an athlete for a doping offence and the athlete appeals the decision.

The case of the German long distance runner, Dieter Baumann, illustrates this type of dispute. Baumann was found to have an excessive amount of the steroid nandrolone in his blood and was therefore automatically suspended from participating in any sport by the National Athletics Association ('NAA') in Germany. Baumann then claimed that his toothpaste was contaminated by the drug and that he was the victim of a conspiracy. The NAA refused to lift the suspension as, according to its rules, if an athlete tests positive, the burden is on the athlete to prove his innocence. Baumann filed for injunctive relief in two German courts but both courts upheld the NAA's ruling. Baumann then appealed to the NAA's own tribunal which, perhaps surprisingly, stated that a conspiracy was a viable possibility and lifted the ban. This allowed Baumann to become a member of the German Olympic team and he flew to Sydney this summer to compete. Unfortunately for Baumann, the International Athletics Association then barred him from participating.

Instinctively it is easy to conclude that this type of dispute is not suitable for mediation. The reason is that a doping offence is a quasi-criminal matter. It is not a matter capable of being settled by negotiation. A ruling of innocence or guilt is required. The rights of other competitors are also affected. Those that do not take drugs need to see that sanctions which are known and understood are imposed against drug takers. The sporting bodies need to send a clear deterrent message to other drug users. A private dispute resolution process aimed at compromise is therefore wholly inappropriate.

The CAS mediation rules recognise this and so expressly exclude such disputes from mediation with these words:

> '*CAS mediation is provided solely for the resolution of disputes related to the CAS ordinary procedure. A decision passed by the organ of a sports organization cannot be the subject of mediation proceedings before the CAS. All disputes related to disciplinary matters, as well as doping issues, are expressly excluded from CAS mediation.*' (CAS Mediation Rules, Art 1)

What about the disputes which may result from the imposition of a ban?

The US runner Harry 'Butch' Reynolds tested positive for the steroid nandrolone and was banned by the IAAF. He was banned for two years and, having failed to have the ruling set aside, brought a battery of legal proceedings against the IAAF and the Athletics Congress seeking monetary compensation. His claims included breach of contract, defamation, denial of due process and tortious interference with business relations. This resulted in the IAAF banning Reynolds from the 1992 Olympics. Subsequently Reynolds succeeded in obtaining a default judgment for more than $27 million including treble punitive damages and attempted to enforce the judgment against four of the IAAF's creditors. A further four years of appeals followed and resulted in Reynolds' case finally being dismissed for lack of jurisdiction – a matter that the IAAF had always contested.

Claims for compensation like this one are capable of compromise – especially where complex legal and jurisdictional issues arise. They raise questions such as: Where can the governing body which imposed the ban be sued (if anywhere)? Which law applies to the suit against actions of the governing body? These complexities and uncertainties make litigation even more hazardous and costly and, in such circumstances, mediation may become significantly more attractive. In England, part of the reason for the growth in the use of mediation a couple of years ago was not because lawyers and their clients thought it was a fantastic process. It was because they felt that they had to find an alternative to the cost, delays and uncertainties of the litigation process.

Disputes arising after disciplinary proceedings (other than those relating to doping).

The Football Association of England and Wales ('FA') banned the Arsenal manager, Arsene Wenger, from the touchline for twelve matches and fined him four weeks wages on 10 October this year for an alleged confrontation with an official. Wenger was found guilty by the FA of 'threatening behaviour and physical intimidation'. He pleaded not guilty at a disciplinary commission hearing and has said he will appeal the FA's decision. He was the first person to be charged under the FA's new hard-hitting disciplinary code of conduct. The fine alone amounts to about €100,000 and the ban, set to begin on 30 October this year, will affect his ability to work effectively for a considerable period.

Is this dispute concerning the severity of a punishment a matter capable of settlement? It is certainly a closer call dm the Baumann case. One can perhaps envisage a negotiation where the competitor pledges better behaviour in return for a lighter sentence. But ultimately it remains a disciplinary matter where a point of principle is concerned and the governing body cannot be seen to compromise its own rules. Mediation is also typically considered inappropriate where one party needs to make a public example of a case in order to deter others. This would appear to be such a situation.

Disputes between a competitor and a governing body arising from the selection process for a representative event.

An interesting example of this type of dispute is the litigation and arbitration which arose in the last few weeks from a dispute as to which of two wrestlers should represent the US on the Greco-Roman US Wrestling Team at the Olympic Games in Sydney. Our Chicago office acted for the United States of America Wrestling Association ('USAW'), which is the national governing body for amateur wrestling, runs the Olympic trials and nominates wrestlers to the US Olympic Committee which rules on which athletes are on the team.

What happened was this: Keith Sieracki defeated Matt Lindland 2-1 in the deciding bout of the Olympic trials. USAW accordingly nominated Sieracki for the Olympic team. Lindland protested but two levels of protest committees agreed with the referee's decision on the mat. Lindland then took his case to arbitration under the rules of the USAW arguing not that the referee's judgment had been wrong, but that the referee had misapplied the rules. This, argued Lindland, made the decision one which was capable of appeal. Surprisingly, the arbitrator ordered a re-match. Sieracki protested and referred the matter to a second arbitration which was to operate effectively as an appeal of the first decision. In the meantime, Lindland won the re-match, but the USAW declined to change its nomination.

The day before the final hearing in Sieracki's arbitration, Lindland filed an action to enforce the first arbitration award (which had resulted in the re-match that Lindland had won). The Federal Court denied enforcement and Lindland appealed to the 7th Circuit Court of Appeals. Within 24 hours, after no oral argument, the 7th Circuit reversed the District Court and enforced the arbitration award and required USAW to nominate Lindland.

At about the same time that day, the second arbitration (filed by Sieracki) was concluded and the arbitrator ordered USAW to nominate Sieracki. In compliance with both the court order and the second arbitration award, USAW nominated both -wrestlers. The US Olympic Committee ('USOC') delayed its selection beyond the stated deadline and Lindland brought a contempt motion against USAW (at midnight on a Friday) to compel it to name only Lindland. On Saturday, the USAW was compelled to nominate Lindland.

The USOC ignored this nomination and selected Sieracki. Lindland then sought to compel the USOC, who was not a party to the first arbitration, to accept the USAW nomination and name Lindland to the US Olympic Team. USOC appealed to the 7th Circuit.

Meanwhile Sieracki filed his own motion to enforce the second arbitration award in the Colorado Federal Court and the application was transferred to the Chicago Federal Court. The Chicago Federal Court denied enforcement of the second award simply because Lindland had enforced his award first. Sieracki then appealed this decision to the 7th Circuit. Again after no oral argument, the same appellate panel of the 7th Circuit upheld both decisions, compelling USOC to name Lindland and denying Sieracki's motion to enforce the second arbitration award. USOC sought a stay of enforcement from the United States Supreme Court and this was denied.

Lindland then went to the Olympic Games in Sydney and won a silver medal.

This case was unprecedented in the 7th Circuit. There were three separate appeals, plus additional motions in a period of 2 weeks. The 7th Circuit had not had this level of activity on such an urgent basis, even in death penalty cases.

With this level of procedural complexity and uncertainty, and with the need for a speedy solution, one might think that the ingredients were ideal for mediation. However, although this was not a disciplinary dispute, a final, non-negotiated decision was required all the same. The mediator could hardly have proposed a compromise – 'Lindland, you can go to Sydney, but Sieracki, don't worry, you can go to Athens in 2004'.

Even though mediation may not seem appropriate in such cases, the English court has, on, at least one occasion, been prepared to send parties off to mediation where the rules of the governing body require this. In *Lennox Lewis -v- The World Boxing Council and Frank Bruno* (unreported transcript, 3 November 1995), Lewis brought an action against the World Boxing Council ('WBC') based in Mexico and against Bruno who lived in England. Lewis wanted to stop both these parties from acting so as to allow Bruno to fight Mike Tyson for the WBC title instead of Lewis. Lewis, having served the proceedings on Bruno in England, obtained leave ex parte to serve the WBC in both Mexico and Puerto Rico. The English court subsequently ruled that the action against Bruno was just a ploy so as to enable Lewis to found jurisdiction in England against the WBC, the real defendant in the case. The court refused the relief sought and sent Lewis off to the US to conduct compulsory mediation under the WBC rules. This is interesting for a number of reasons:

- The WBC's rules provide for compulsory mediation for all claims against the WBC without distinguishing between disputes which may be suitable for mediation and those which may not.
- It is an indication of the English court's willingness to support the dispute resolution procedures of a sports governing body where those procedures provide for mediation.
- The Judge even rejected Lewis' claim that because any mediation would be under the auspices of the WBC itself, it would not be impartial. In this regard the Judge appeared to be influenced by the fact that the WBC rules did not deny Lewis access to a court if the mediation did not resolve the matter. The Judge stated:

'I see no reason to assume that such compulsory mediation process which will be carried out in Dallas pursuant to the clause will not be a perfectly proper independent process of mediation. But in any event, I see no reason to take the view that whatever the defects of the mediation process the plaintiff will be bound to accent its consequences, because in my judgment the effect, so far as I can understand it, of the exclusive jurisdiction clause, bearing in mind as I do that it is not a provision governed by English law, is that there is a backstop of litigation in the courts of Dallas as the final means of resolving any dispute between (in this case) the plaintiff and the WBC.'

Transfer disputes involving players, their clubs and, on occasions, their governing bodies.

In 1999, in a case in which our Zurich office was involved, a Canadian ice hockey player was in dispute with his former Swiss club and the International Ice Hockey Federation (IIHF) in connection with the player's intended transfer to a team in Canada. Because the player had an ongoing contract with the Swiss team, the IIHF objected to the transfer and refused to give the player the necessary release. A settlement with the club was reached so that the player could join the Canadian club. Prior to that, the Swiss team managed to have all other Swiss teams (which were members of Switzerland's premier league) sign a 'gentlemen's agreement' according to which they would not contact the player for at least two years. Two months later the player wanted to come back to Switzerland and was offered a job by one of the Swiss teams (despite the agreement). His former club intervened and requested that the Swiss National Hockey League not allow the player to play for this new club. The case was then referred to the Hockey League's (internal) judicial body (a single judge) who after a short procedure decided in favour of the hockey player.

In retrospect, mediation might have been a very useful tool to settle the dispute. These kinds of disputes are basically commercial disputes involving contractual relations between players and teams. Where, as in this case, the governing body (the IIHF) was involved, there may be issues of principle which need to be adhered to in order to protect the interests of other players and teams and the integrity of the governing bodies' rules. It would by dangerous to mandate mediation in every such case, but it may certainly have a role when used appropriately on a case by case basis.

Contractual disputes between competitors and managers, promoters etc.

In 1999 the boxer, Richie Woodhall, a WBC super middle weight champion and Frank Warren, Woodhall's boxing promoter, were engaged in an entrenched contractual disput. Woodhall was angry about a contract he had signed with Warren, claiming that it meant that a third party received money every time he fought (and that he had not previously been made aware of that fact). Woodhall was also unhappy about delays in payment for his fights. In the press, Warren vigorously defended his position and denied the claims. Litigation commenced before the English courts and both parties stated publicly that they were heading for court.

As a last ditch attempt to achieve a settlement, the parties agreed to mediate and they approached CEDR. CEDR appointed a mediator, found a venue and, working with the parties, had all the documentation ready within two days. After a further two days the mediation was concluded and accorded in a binding contract. The press and sports commentators were amazed at the speed of the process and its successful outcome. Before the parties entered mediation they were engaged in a war of words on television and in the press. Their relationship appeared to be very acrimonious. The mediation resulted in new contracts being drawn up which were acceptable to both parties. Both parties' lawyers and the parties themselves were full of praise for the mediation process. Frank Warren said '*It was important to all to bring this matter to a speedy conclusion. We have shaken hands and look forward to resuming our successful partnership.*' ('How to settle disputes – without a legal punch up', by Francis Gibb, The Times, 3 August 1999).

The benefits to the parties were speed, confidentiality and the ability to get on quickly with their business. Relationships can of course be very important in sport, and mediation, because of its non-adversarial nature, can assist in preserving these relationships. In this case speed was essential to the resolution of this dispute. Both parties also stood to gain by continuing their successful relationship after the resolution of the problem.

The rugby league coach, Ellery Hanley, found himself subject to an indefinite suspension after he made some unflattering comments about his club's directors. Both sides called in legal advisers (Hanley using the same firm that had represented Woodhall). Hanley received the backing of over 1,000 supporters who staged a sit-in protest. The support Hanley received showed that sacking him would be an unwise option for the club. However, his comments had been made publicly and the directors wanted an apology. The situation seemed to be deadlocked. However, after a full day of discussions a compromise was reached which was acceptable to both parties. Ellery Hanley publicly apologised and returned to his position after just 10 days suspension. Like the Woodhall and Warren case, the dispute was one which was capable of settlement through negotiation, and in both cases, mediation was the most effective way of structuring the negotiations.

Disputes between teams as to the organisation of their sport.

As this paper is being written the Rugby Football Union ('RFU') is attempting to resolve a major dispute over automatic promotion and relegation between the top two divisions in English rugby union involving 26 professional football clubs. The RFU has failed to resolve the dispute and is now proposing to the clubs that they mediate the dispute, although the clubs themselves appear less than enthusiastic with the idea. While the Chairman of the RFU has been reported as saying that he hopes the clubs will recognise that appointing an independent third party with specialist skills in resolving major and difficult issues is the right way forward, the Head of English First Division Rugby has been quoted to say: '*It wouldn't make any difference if they brought the Queen in to arbitrate*' (The Guardian, 20 Oct 2000).

This example illustrates the importance of the consensual nature of mediation. It is very difficult to force it on people. The RFU may think mediation is a good idea, but if the teams who are in dispute don't, it is unlikely to work. Watch this space.

D. Some important practical issues concerning the use of mediation

In England, reluctance to embrace mediation for general commercial disputes has given way to unbridled enthusiasm. Mediation clauses are being inserted into contracts and institutions are building mediation into their dispute resolution procedures. All the signs are that this heady enthusiasm for mediation may soon break out in continental Europe. Whilst those who have experienced the benefits that mediation can offer will approve of these developments, some care needs to be taken. There are few horror stories to tell (it is early days), but it is already clear that there are some trip wires ready to catch the unwary. This section addresses a few of these.

Getting to mediation

How parties arrive at mediation has a significant bearing on the mediation itself. The usual routes to me on are:

- By an agreement between the parties reached before any dispute has arisen and typically recorded in the dispute resolution provisions of a contract. As in the *Lewis v Bruno and WBC* case described above, that contract might take the form of the rules of a governing body to which the individual or team is said to be bound.
- By an agreement between the parties reached after **a** dispute arises but before litigation or arbitration have been commenced.
- By an agreement between the parties reached in the course of either litigation or arbitration.
- By reason of a court order which either compels or 'recommends' that the parties should use mediation before proceeding with litigation.

Before drafting a mediation clause, either in a contract or in the rules of a governing body, consider the following issues:

Clauses compelling the use of mediation
A clause which simply provides that the parties to a dispute will consider the use of mediation, but which does not compel its use, is straightforward and harmless. It overcomes the hesitancy to recommend mediation that parties often feel, but it does not require the use of mediation in cases where it is not appropriate for any reason. The perceived problem with such clauses is that they are likely to be ignored because they have no teeth. As a result, there is an increasing tendency for lawyers to draft 'binding' mediation clauses, often as part of a tiered dispute resolution procedure starting with negotiation, moving on to mediation and ending in either arbitration or litigation. These binding clauses may seem attractive, but they are, in the author's experience, fraught with danger for the following reasons:

- The jury is still out in the court rooms of most jurisdictions as to whether such clauses are actually enforceable. Where one party refuses to mediate even where there is a clause requiring him to do so, should courts or arbitrators decline to entertain proceedings until the mediation phase has been completed? This is not a straightforward question, particularly where, in the context of the rules of sporting bodies which are based in another jurisdiction, there may also be uncertainty as to which law governs the issue.
- One party may successfully argue that its conduct prior to mediation is covered by the same confidentiality as would have been applicable in the mediation itself If such confidentiality is upheld, it may make it difficult, if not impossible, for a court or tribunal to attribute fault where a mediation has failed to happen.
- The development of a fundamental right of access to a court has been marked in recent years. In Europe this development has come under Article 6 of the European Court of Human Rights (ECHR). Whilst the ECHR has been around since 1950, the powerful right of access to justice has been developed substantially in recent cases, most notably in *Osman v UK*. Any attempt to restrict the ability of a party to 'have their day in court' is now potentially under attack. However, at least under the ECHR, rights under Article 6 are not absolute. They can be waived. Also the rights protect parties in regard to the 'determination' of the dispute as a whole, not merely one, informal stage. Provided that parties have recourse to courts or arbitrators if the mediation fails, it is unlikely that Article 6 will be successfully invoked.
- Although good drafting can probably get around the difficulty in most countries, the need for one party to commence litigation urgently either to get injunctive relief or to prevent a limitation period from expiring, can run counter to the requirement to spend time mediating before litigating.
- In order to succeed in mediation, the parties need enough information about the strengths and weaknesses of their position in order to take an informed view on settlement. In some cases, parties do not have that information until after a formal dispute resolution process has been commenced and they have had the opportunity to set out claims clearly and exchange information.
- Once the dispute arises, it may be patently unsuitable for mediation.
- Where the mediation clause is contained in the rules of a governing body, there may be a dispute as to whether such rules actually bind the other party. Lennox Lewis argued that he was not bound by the dispute resolution rules of the WBC because he was not a member of the WBC. The English court rejected this argument at the hearing on jurisdiction, but it remained a live issue. Such debates can complicate, not simplify the dispute resolution process.

Who is to act as mediator?
It is imperative that all parties in the mediation have confidence in the skills of the mediator and, even more importantly, the mediator's independence and impartiality. Where disputes arise in specialist areas, the protagonists usually want a mediator who is steeped in that specialist area. For example, in the sporting context, rugby teams arguing about the system of relegation and promotion between the divisions of their league, instinctively want a mediator who knows rugby inside out. The problem is that such individuals, by virtue of being steeped in the sport, are often not perceived as being wholly independent or impartial. Somewhere in their history, they are likely to have expressed views that could make them seem biased.

The problem is likely to be exacerbated if a sports governing body uses a fixed panel of mediators. Those mediators may, over time, become tainted with association with the governing body, and become distrusted by parties who are in dispute with the governing body. This will be all the more so if the mediations are administered by the governing body itself.

Both these factors suggest that the mediation services offered by bodies such as the CAS and SDRP, which have access to a large number of mediators who have experience in sports disputes generally, but do not have direct affiliations with any of the parties, will prove to be the most successful.

Mediation used in combination with arbitration
Parties may start an arbitration, trust their arbitrator, and decide to ask him or her to mediate. Should he accept the invitation? In the course of a mediation, the parties may realise that they are not going to be able to reach agreement, but that they would like to take advantage of the knowledge gained by the mediator and ask him or her to switch roles and become an arbitrator. Can he accept that invitation?

On the face of it these are simple requests and the neutral arbitrator or mediator should be able to do what the parties want, provided he or she feels suitably qualified to do so. However, the combination of mediation and arbitration where the same neutral is involved can give rise to real difficulties, which one needs to be wary of.

- If the parties know before the mediation phase that the mediator may become arbitrator if no settlement is reached, they may be disinclined to be frank with the mediator during the mediation phase. This may prevent the mediation from being effective.
- If a mediator has become an arbitrator, what information gleaned during the mediation phase of the case can the arbitrator use in arriving at an award? Will the use of information obtained in confidence from one party render the award vulnerable to attack or render it unenforceable?

These are not insurmountable problems. An increasing number of institutions which have traditionally offered arbitration services are now offering mediation services. CAS, the LCIA, the AAA, and, shortly the ICC are notable examples. These institutions have an important role to play in developing systems and safeguards that enable users of their services get the best out both mediation and arbitration.

Conclusion
Mediation has an important role to play in settling certain types of sports disputes. We are bound to see its use grow. The mere fact that more sports dispute resolution bodies establishing their own mediation rules and promoting its benefits will ensure this. But for mediation to succeed it should not be made mandatory. It will be most successful when used because it is suitable in the particular circumstances of each case. When it retains this flexibility – particularly in relation to use and timing – it will greatly assist the sporting world in the effective management and resolution of disputes.

William K. Slate II
The Growth of Mediation and Mediation in Sports Disputes in the US

Good morning. As the program suggests my remarks to you are bifurcated somewhat to the extent that I first address the growth of mediation and thereafter discuss mediation in sports disputes in the

U.S. Suffice it to say there is a great deal more to say about the former (i.e. growth generally) than can be said at the present time regarding mediation in sports disputes in the U.S. or to my knowledge any place else for that matter.

As to the growth of mediation in the U.S. and the world, it is certainly enjoying a heyday. At the American Arbitration Association, we see mediation, as a percentage of cases growing at a faster rate than arbitration. To be clear here, however, we are doing considerably more arbitrations day-to-day than mediations, but the growth factor of mediations is still quite evident. And, while mediation has reached a state of maturity in the states such as California, where private mediation and court-referenced mediation involve thousands of cases a year, we also see significant growth in other parts of the world. In Latin America, both Columbia and Argentina have statutes which contribute in significant ways to the utilization of mediation in a broad range of cases from civil cases to small claims to family matters. At a conference just held in Washington, DC last week, co-sponsored by the Inter-American Development Bank and the American Arbitration Association, a representative from the Columbian government stated that mediation has potentiated the availability of quasi-judicial processes to women in a way that the traditional court system has failed to deliver.

In the UK, CEDR (Centre for Dispute Resolution) advises that mediators are successful in about 85% of the cases involving business problems. Apparently one of the reasons for the tremendous increase in mediation in the UK is the new Civil Procedure Rules devised by Lord Harry Woolf, which replaced the old High Court and County Court rules on April 26, 1999. The growth of mediation is reported in other parts of Europe including Germany and France, where in Paris this past summer a program devoted to mediation was held at the House of the Paris Bar and co-sponsored by the Paris Bar and the Dispute Resolution Section of the American Bar Association. Reports were given in that meeting to suggest that mediation is taking a strong foothold now in Paris.

In returning to the U.S., a recent survey of 530 of the largest corporations in the U.S. reveal that 88% say they use mediation to resolve disputes while 79% use arbitration. Also in the U.S., a number of entities have emerged on the Internet, which provide online mediation services. The process of course necessitates high levels of security and a protected 'chat room' where a technology proficient mediator and the parties come together for a discussion and a mediated result. I have not seen any case numbers to date, but that is a capacity which all institutions will have very shortly if they do not already offer such a service. And, in speaking of online capabilities as related to mediation, it is very clear to us that the online disposition of business-to-business (B2B) conflicts which will arise out of vertical integrated marketplaces will further encourage the use of online mediation disposition when one realizes that the tens of thousands of online transactions, which will take place in vertical marketplaces cannot tolerate the inefficiency of going off-line to resolve traditional business disputes. Thus, a range of technology methodologies which incorporate mediation will clearly insight the growth of mediation as an alternative.

At the American Arbitration Association, we see contractual clauses increasingly employing mediation backed up by final and binding arbitration. As an institutional practice, we offer mediation to all parties who file arbitrations as an alternative. Thus, throughout the course of a given calendar year we have a significant number of cases which come to us with arbitration clauses which are 'converted' to mediations. Indeed this is occurring to a modest degree in our International Center where parties coming to the Center from different countries, different cultures, and different languages are willing to attempt mediation in somewhere between 7-10% of our international cases. However, in the international context the question does arise as to the effectiveness of the enforcement of foreign awards outside of the context of the United Nations Convention on the recognition and enforcement of foreign arbitral awards. There are 111 countries who are parties to the New York Convention, and of course parties may also seek enforcement, if appropriate, under the Inter-American Convention, popularly known as the Panama Convention. While an agreement signed after a mediation would have the same effect as a binding commercial contract, at least one writer, James D. Wangelin, who both writes and practices actively in international commercial arbitration, has observed that some parties have avoided the court system or mediation for reasons that include concern that a judgment or mediation award will not be recognized or enforced in a foreign jurisdiction, while arbitration awards, on the other hand, are widely recognized and enforced. So, will mediation be used increasingly in the resolution of complex, multinational commercial disputes – undoubtedly. However, I do not believe, for the reasons just articulated, that it will be an overnight success story internationally.

Arbitration, after all, has taken about 75 years to reach this point of international maturity and global acceptance.

Well, how does all of this growth of mediation across every conceivable field, from employment to environmental to international relate to the use of mediation to resolve sports disputes? Apparently, precious little, if at all, if one confines sports disputes to the area of 'individual athlete participation issues.' Our research to date suggests that as to disputes involving athletes (drug use, eligibility, identity, selection to participate by an NGB), no cases have been found as ICAS (which has a new set of mediation rules, of course), at the USOC or at the American Arbitration Association where we are by federal statute the place where NGB or USOC disputes end up – no cases received.

As to athletes, the reasons for reliance on arbitration are fairly obvious. A decision on drugs/no drugs – participate or non-participation in an event, are the kinds of issues about which there is (a) very little if any middle ground; and (b) acceptance of a non-participation result is totally unacceptable to the athlete. Does this mean that mediation has no place in disputes involving athletes? I think the answer is no, but it would appear to me that its applications are limited. Might an athlete for a minor infraction agree to limited non-participation in lieu of a more extended ban? Perhaps, but then the question might arise as to whether such a result (if it involved drugs for example) is in the best interest of the governing body or the sport. And, while it needn't be the 'tail wagging the dog' the time required to reach a mediated result – even one backed up by final and binding arbitration – would very likely take too long in the midst of a major sporting event such as the Olympic Games. In such a setting, a focused, time-limited arbitration can and does produce the required timely result. So, at the end of the day, in what I am labeling as 'individual athlete participation issues' I find little incentive on the part of either side to pursue mediation.

That having been said, a host of other sports related disputes do lend themselves quite suitably to mediations. Here I have in mind a range of controversies surrounding licensing, trademark, and logo usage. I also believe that greater use of mediation might be employed as to relationships among sports entities including vying federations. Likewise there are a number of typical business issues surrounding organized sports for which mediation is appropriate including contractual disputes, sponsorship disputes, and commercial/advertisement disputes. Indeed, a number of disputes in the categories just referenced have resulted in negotiated settlements which if not mediations were clearly the first cousin to mediations.

There is one interesting development in the United States which perhaps holds out the specter of some application to athletes and sports. I have in mind here the development of a Uniform Mediation Act (UMA) which is in draft form and is the product of the National Conference of Commissioners on Uniform State Laws. Before 1980, not a single state in the U.S. had legislation requiring ADR. Today each state has multiple statutes, and in 1998 the United States Congress reinforced the use of ADR by adopting the Alternative Dispute Resolution Act of 1998. While leaving broad discretion to the courts to select the particular forms of ADR to be included in their own local programs, the Act requires all federal district courts to adopt some form of ADR and this generally means some form of mediation. Well, the Uniform Mediation Act, which would have implications principally for the states in its draft form is being discussed as a vehicle, not only for the range of civil disputes, but also to be utilized as an alternative in addressing criminal misdemeanor matters. I mention this only as a parenthetical reference since the draft is still in circulation and the debate about it continues as we speak. Nonetheless, since arguably some of the issues surrounding individual athletes, such as drugs and identity cases, have quasi-misdemeanor elements associated with them, then I ponder whether a Uniform Mediation Act that encourages experiences in the misdemeanor realm might in due course offer examples and experience that would be applicable to individual athlete disputes.

In closing I would note the disaffection which the speaker has with his own remarks since it is infinitely more interesting to offer positive ideas and suggestions in a form such as this as contrasted with concluding that the principal subject seems to have limited application to the issue at hand. Having said that I do believe mediation will continue to flourish and a host of issues, particularly the business related ones, which are so much a part of amateur and professional sports today. I do, however, conclude for the present that mediation's role will be a quite limited one, at least for the near term in the resolution of disputes involving individual athletes and their understandable desire to be allowed to participate in the events to which they have devoted themselves. Thank you very much for your kind attention.

7.4.3 CAS mediations to date

To date, there have been a number of mediations conducted by CAS in relation to administrative sporting disputes involving Sports Federations and the exercise of their regulatory functions. Details are sketchy because of the confidentiality requirements.

There have also been a number of commercial disputes settled by CAS Mediation. These cases have included disputes with a sports management agency over the commercialisation of a cyclist's image rights and some financial disputes between athletes and their advertising agencies in relation to substantial commission payments.

As the CAS mediation service becomes more widely known, it is expected that more sports disputes, including commercial and financial ones, will be referred to CAS for settlement under the Mediation Rules, thus proving the suitability of mediation for resolving sports disputes quickly, confidentially and relatively inexpensively.

7.5 Sport Resolutions (UK)

The UK has its own dedicated sports disputes resolution body offering a variety of ADR solutions to a wide range of sports disputes.

7.5.1 Background

Sport Resolutions (UK) (Sport Resolutions) is the new name of the UK Sports Dispute Resolution Panel (SDRP).[28] Its Dispute Resolution Manager/Solicitor is Susan Humble, whose legal background is in litigation.

The original SDRP was largely the 'brain child' of an English Lawyer, Charles Woodhouse, CVO, a former Legal Adviser to the Commonwealth Games Foundation. It was established on 1 January, 2000 and is headquartered in London. It was set up to provide sports governing bodies, commercial organisations and individuals throughout the UK with 'a simple, independent and effective mechanism ... to resolve their differences fairly, speedily and cost effectively'. It is modelled on the Court of Arbitration for Sport.

Sport Resolutions is now the independent alternative dispute resolution service for sport in the United Kingdom, offering arbitration, mediation and tribunal appointment and administration services. Sport Resolutions (UK) is also the independent provider of the National Anti-Doping Panel (NADP)[29] and Tribunal Service for sport in the United Kingdom. Sport Resolutions plays a major role in developing and planning dispute resolution services which help to maintain high standards of conduct and fair play both on and off the field of play.

Sport Resolutions has experience of appointing to and administering over 250 disputes, across 50 sports, with three-quarters of enquiries and referrals coming from Olympic, Paralympic and English high performance sports. The remaining quarter of enquiries and referrals come from community sport – the so-called 'grass roots'.

---

[28] The author acknowledges, with thanks, the material supplied by Sport Resolutions (UK) (the trading name of The Sports Dispute Resolution Panel Ltd.), who are at the forefront of providing sport and all its stakeholders in the UK with an effective mechanism for resolving their differences.

[29] The National Anti-Doping Panel, an independent body established to determine sports anti-doping cases in the United Kingdom.

Sport Resolutions delivers its services through its expert panels of mediators and arbitrators, all leaders in the field and recruited for their unique understanding of the UK sporting system.

Sport Resolutions has recently reviewed its structure to put in place a new management team. In April 2007, SDRP appointed Gerard Elias QC as its new Chairman, along with four independent non-executive directors, with legal, commercial, accounting and administrative experience. A small Management Board now meets every four to six weeks to take the business forward.

In July 2007, the Sport Resolutions Board agreed a new vision to be the dispute resolution service of choice for all sports in the United Kingdom and has recently established a new business plan to deliver an exciting new range of services.

In March 2008, the Sports Dispute Resolution Panel Limited moved to new offices in Fleet Street, London and adopted Sport Resolutions (UK) as its new trading name.

A number of sports bodies in the UK have now incorporated into their Rules and also their Contracts referral of disputes to sports resolutions (UK). For example, the British Olympic Association now includes in its Commercial Contracts a standard dispute resolution clause, which provides firstly for mediation and, if that fails, then arbitration. This clause is in the following terms:

> 'In the event of a dispute arising out of or in relation to this Agreement including any question regarding its existence, validity or termination, the parties shall first seek amicable settlement of the dispute by mediation in accordance with the Mediation Procedure of Sports Resolutions (UK) in London in force at the date the dispute is referred to mediation.'
>
> If the dispute is not settled by mediation within sixty days of the appointment of the mediator, or such further period as the parties agree in writing, the dispute shall be referred to and finally resolved by arbitration under the Sports Resolutions (UK) Rules for Arbitration, which Rules are deemed incorporated by reference in this Clause.
>
> The number of arbitrators shall be one.
>
> The seat of the arbitration shall be London.
>
> The Agreement is governed and shall be construed in accordance with English Law.'

Likewise, several commercial companies and firms engaged in sports marketing and promotion in the UK are also now using a similar dispute resolution clause in their Agreements.

The standard Sports Resolutions' Mediation and Med-Arb Clauses are respectively as follows:

7.5.2 Mediation standard clause

> 'The parties hereby agree that if they are in dispute they will refer the matter to Sport Resolutions (UK) (a trading name of The Sports Dispute Resolution Panel Ltd. – Company No. 3351039) for resolution by mediation in accordance with Sport Resolutions' Mediation Procedure (as amended from time to time).'

7.5.3 Combined mediation/arbitration clause

> 'In the event of a dispute arising out of or relating to this Agreement, the parties shall first seek settlement of the dispute by mediation in accordance with the Mediation Procedure of Sport Resolutions (UK) (a trading name of The Sports Dispute Resolution Panel Ltd. – Company No. 3351039) in force at the date the dispute is referred to mediation.

If the dispute is not settled within [...] days of the mediation being instituted, or such other period as the parties shall agree in writing, the dispute shall be referred to and finally resolved by arbitration under the Sport Resolutions' Arbitration Rules (in force from time to time) which Rules are deemed to be incorporated by reference to this Clause.'

7.5.4 Sports Resolutions (UK) Mediation Rules

Sports Resolutions' mediation service was originally set up with advice and assistance from CEDR and exhibits many of the features characteristic of the mediation process offered by CEDR, but adapted to a sporting context.

The Rules of its Mediation Procedure ('the Mediation Rules') are set out in Appendix IX to this book. A few comments on these Rules now follow.

The parties to the mediation must enter into a Mediation Agreement based on the Sports Resolutions Model Mediation Agreement (Rule 2.1), the text of which is set out in Appendix IX to this book.

The mediator is chosen by the parties from a list maintained by the SDRP and, in case they are not able to agree on the mediator, Sport Resolutions Executive Director will appoint the mediator (Rule 3.1). The former SDRP published its first list of approved mediators in September 2000.

Rule 3.5 lays down the legal status of the mediator as an 'independent contractor'. In other words, the mediator is not acting as an agent or employee of the Sport Resolutions and so no legal liability attaches to the Sport Resolutions for any wrongful or unlawful act or omission of the mediator.

The Mediation Rules also provide for the mediation to be on a 'without prejudice' basis. These principles are reinforced by the detailed provisions of Rules 3.6, 11.2 and 9.2 respectively. Rule 3.6 provides as follows:

> 'None of the Parties to the Mediation Agreement will call the Mediator or Sport Resolutions (or any employee, consultant, officer or representative of Sport Resolutions) as a witness, consultant, arbitrator or expert in any litigation or arbitration in relation to the dispute and the Mediator and Sport Resolutions will not voluntarily act in any such capacity without the written agreement of all the parties.'

Rule 11.2 provides as follows:

> 'All documents (which include anything upon which evidence is recorded including tapes and computer discs) or other information produced for, or arising in relation to, the mediation will be privileged and not admissible as evidence or discoverable in any litigation or arbitration connected with the dispute except any documents or other information which would in any event have been admissible or discoverable in any such litigation or arbitration.'

Rule 9.2 provides as follows:

> 'The referral of the dispute to mediation does not affect any rights that may exist under Article 6 of the European Convention on Human Rights. If the dispute is not settled by mediation, the Parties rights to a fair trial are unaffected.'

As with all mediations, the Mediation Rules also state that the mediation shall be confidential (Rule 11.1), except, of course, to the extent it may be necessary to implement or enforce any Settlement Agreement (see later). It may be noted, *en passant*, that the latest version of the Mediation Rules does not contain the provision in the previous version requiring the parties to also keep confidential the fact that the mediation is to take place or has in fact taken place. This, in the opinion of the author, is an unfortunate omission and in any subsequent revision of the Mediation Rules should be rectified. The whole purpose and interest of mediation to the sporting world is that the process should be entirely confidential.

The confidentiality of the mediation process is reinforced by Rule 7.1, which provides as follows: 'No formal record or transcript of the mediation will be made.'

Rule 10 provides for a stay of any court or arbitration proceedings pending the mediation, if the parties so agree.

Any settlement reached in the mediation will only be legally effective if incorporated into a Settlement Agreement, signed by or on behalf of the parties (Rule 8).

Under the previous SDRP Mediation Rules, Rule 13 excluded liability of the SDRP and the mediator for acts or omissions in the mediation except in cases of fraudulent or wilful misconduct. This exclusion has been dropped from the revised Sports Resolutions' Mediation Rules. Notwithstanding, liability of the Mediator or Sports Resolutions for any wrongdoing will be determined in accordance with general legal principles. Under well established general principles of tort (*Donoghue* v. *Stevenson* [1932] AC 562 and the subsequent line of cases), I would consider that the Mediator and Sport Resolutions owe the parties to the mediation a legal duty of care and, in the event of its breach and resulting damage, a legal action would lie against the Mediator and Sport Resolutions for Common Law negligence.

The usual rules apply in relation to the payment by the parties of fees, expenses and costs of the mediation under the provisions of Rule 12.

7.5.5 Sports Resolutions Mediation Agreement

As mentioned above, the parties to a Sports Resolutions Mediation are required to enter into their standard Mediation Agreement, a draft of which is set out in Appendix X to this book.

7.5.6 Sports Resolutions Advisory Opinions

Like the CAS, Sports Resolutions issues non-binding Advisory Opinions, which, as previously mentioned, are of practical importance in assisting the parties to identify the legal issues arising in connection with their dispute.

The corresponding Advisory Opinion Rules, which are self-explanatory, are set out in Appendix XI to this book.

7.5.7 Sports Resolutions Code of Conduct

Sports Resolutions' Panel Members are subject to a Code of Conduct, the text of which is set out in Appendix XII to this book.

The provisions of this Code of Conduct apply to 'all Members of the Panel of Arbitrators, the Panel of Mediators, and any other Panel(s) operated from time to time by Sport Resolutions' (Clause 1.2).

The Code requires Members to carry out their duties 'expeditiously and professionally' (Clause 2.6) and also to 'disclose at the earliest possible time anything which might be perceived as a conflict of interest' (Clause 2.3).

Furthermore, the Code requires from Members 'a relationship of trust and confidence' which it describes as 'paramount' (Clause 3.2).

Under the provisions of Clause 3.3 of the Code '[a]ny breach of this Code may result in action being taken against the Member concerned including but not limited to Sport Resolutions absolute discretion to withdraw membership of the Panel'.

7.6 The Former Australian National Sports Dispute Centre (NSDC)

Let us now take a brief look at how they handle sports disputes extra-judicially 'down under'. Until recently, sports disputes were settled by mediation, arbitration and 'expert determination' under the auspices of the NSDC, the background to the setting up of which was as follows.

7.6.1 **Background**

According to the NSDC:

> 'Sporting disputes have become an epidemic in Australia in the last five years. No longer are sports disputes settled by a friendly argument between mates over a beer. Sport is big business. Even amateur sports cannot escape the potential for a dispute. Faced with potential high costs, time delay and pressure associated with Court proceedings, sports organisations have been crying out for an alternative.'

So, the NSDC, based in Sydney, Australia, was established in January, 1996, to provide 'an inexpensive, fast and effective means of resolving sports disputes'.

The background to the setting up of the NSDC is described in the following extract from an article by Brian Doyle, a leading Australian Sports Lawyer and former President of the Australian and New Zealand Sports Law Association, who was involved in the setting up of the NSDC:[30]

> 'In 1992 the Australian and New Zealand Sports Law Association (ANZSLA) at its annual conference held a session specifically directed towards dispute resolution. At that time there were no facilities available in Australia that could effectively avoid the civil court system with all its disadvantages of expense, delay and the fracturing of sporting relationships.'

The meeting urged the establishment of a registry of the Court of Arbitration for Sport to cover the Oceania region, and the Executor Director of the Confederation of Australian Sport (the umbrella organisation that lobbies on behalf of most Australian sports) called

30 'Sports Dispute Resolution in Australia', 3/4 *Sports Law Bulletin* (2000) at p. 13.

for the establishment of an independent disputes resolution to be established for all sports when he said:

> 'The reality is that there are going to be severe disputes in sport which inevitably end up in the courts. Sports is emotional, it involves complicated commercial arrangements, it is often about personal and organisational power. It is multi-faceted and involves a veritable kaleidoscope of opinions – nearly all of them 'expert'. Ask an athlete, a coach, an administrator and a neutral observer about a sporting issue and receive four different perspectives.'

Shortly after that Conference ANZSLA prepared an issues paper on the role of alternative dispute resolution in sport, and that eventually led to the establishment of the ANZSLA Dispute Resolution Scheme which was launched at the Auckland annual conference in 1995.

The service had a number of arms:

- mediation;
- arbitration;
- providing assistance to sporting judiciaries/tribunals; and
- providing suitable people to carry out expert investigations.

The proposal for a separate mediation service was to overcome what we saw as a problem within the Court of Arbitration for Sport where the arbitrators were firstly to try to settle the dispute. Most people involved in mediation or arbitration accept that to try to settle a dispute, and in doing so hear the issues and the arguments, can cause a difficulty in then sitting as an arbitrator.

Perhaps the CAS arbitrators got over this by paying lip service to the requirement to mediate. There was an overwhelming response from qualified arbitrators and mediators with that special interest in sport that we required, and panels were formed throughout the States of Australia and in New Zealand. The value of having qualified people available to conduct independent inquiries was seen in the appointment of the then President of ANZSLA Hayden Opie to investigate problems within the gymnastics section of the Australian Institute of Sport. Allegations had been raised by (mostly) parents of some of the younger girls attending the Institute as to the conduct of some of the staff. Mr. Opie conducted a long and very searching inquiry that required him to travel throughout Australia before presenting a very thorough report to the Australian Sports Commission.

The service suffered from lack of resources and funds but was nevertheless able to provide assistance to a number of sports in dispute.

In 1996 the establishment of an Oceania Registry of the Court of Arbitration for Sport in Sydney was announced. With the Olympic Games of 2000 being conducted in that city it was considered a priority to have a court up and running in the lead in to the Games.

At the same time the Australian Olympic Committee, the Confederation of Australian Sport, the Australian Sports Commission (ASC – the arm of the Federal Government that administers sport in Australia) and ANZSLA reached agreement on the establishment of a National Sports Dispute Centre Pty Limited (NSDC). Each of these organisations jointly owns an equal share in and operates the Centre, with a Director from each organisation and an appointed Registrar who is assisted in carrying out his duties by funding from the ASC.

The NSDC essentially took over the ANZSLA Dispute Resolution Service ... To some degree there may be competition between the NSDC and CAS ... The value of the NSDC has been proved. It future success will depend upon financing from the Australian Sports Commission, its ability to continue to publicise itself and the enthusiasm of the lawyers who sit as mediators, arbitrators or investigators.

7.6.2 The present day

Sadly, through lack of interest and funding, the NSDC is 'dead'. According, again, to Brian Doyle, the NSDC was originally owned by four parties: the Australian Olympic Committee (AOC); the Australia New Zealand Sports Law Association (ANZSLA); the Confederation of Australian Sport (Confederation); and the Australian Sports Commission (Commission). During Brian Doyle's time as President of the ANZSLA, the AOC pulled out, referring all the sports disputes of its members to the CAS. The Confederation at that time was undergoing difficulties, changing its name and not showing great interest in dispute resolution. The following Brian Doyle's resignation as President of the ANZSLA, letters were written to all of the sports federations and major and minor sports leagues asking for their views on the NSDC. Only ten of these sports organisations confirmed their support. The silence from the rest of them was 'deafening'! The Commission then withdrew its financial support, and, without that support, the ANZSLA under its new President, Simon Rofe, could no longer continue and, likewise, the NSDC was wound up in 2006.

The result of all this is that now all major sports disputes are referred to the CAS. During its existence, the NSDC dealt effectively with a wide range of sports disputes and its demise, therefore, is to be regretted.

7.6.3 Mediation in 'racial vilification' cases

A word or two now follows on dealing with racial vilification in sport, which has – for some time – been a problem in Australian Football and Rugby. This has led to the introduction of so-called 'Vilification Codes' in an effort to combat this form of discrimination in sport. And mediation and conciliation processes have been used successfully in Australia to deal with this problem.

In an interesting article, entitled, 'Combating vilification: The AFL and NRL Anti-vilification Rules'[31] Ian Warren discusses the role of ADR in general and mediation in particular in relation to dealing with breaches of the so-called 'Vilification Codes', introduced by the Australian Football League (AFL) and Australian National Rugby League (NRL), to combat racial vilification.

This is defined in Rule 30 of the AFL Code as: 'conduct which threatens, disparages, vilifies or insults another ... on the basis of that person's race, religion, colour, descent or national or ethnic origin'.

And in similar, but more extensive terms, racial vilification is defined in Rule 2 of the NRL Code as:

> 'conduct which offends, insults, humiliates, intimidates, threatens, disparages or vilifies another person on the basis of that person's race, religion, colour, descent, nationality, ethnic origin, gender, sexuality, marital status, status as a parent, disability or HIV/AIDS status'.

---

[31] 9/4 *The Australia New Zealand Sports Law Association Commentator* (March 2000).

As regards Rule 30, Warren notes in his article that it has become part of the AFL culture and, accordingly, racial vilification is no longer tolerated by the AFL He goes on to point out that, according to reports in *The Australian* newspaper in April 1999, from the passage of this Rule in 1996 to the end of the 1997 season a total of seventeen cases had been heard, all of which were successfully resolved by mediation.

He suggests that mediation has been successful because:

> 'Concepts of offence and harm often have subjective connotations, particularly within the context of sporting activity ... [and] ... [t]here is a vast range of behaviours, actions and words which might be deemed racially harmful in any given context. Conciliation [for which read "mediation"] processes are specifically aimed to consider these issues in an informal environment sensitive to the requirements of the parties.'

He also cites the case of the AFL player Sam Newman, who appeared on the nationally televised 'Footy Show' with his face painted black, after AFL star Nicky Winmar, who is black, failed to appear on the programme as scheduled. Newman and Winmar settled this racial slur by entering into a 'voluntary conciliation agreement' – again for 'conciliation' read 'mediation' – independently of Rule 30 after complaints about the parody were made to both the network and the AFL.

On the other hand, Warren points out that all cases falling under Rule 2 of the NRL Code are subject to 'preliminary conciliation conducted by an authorised Complaints Officer' – again for 'conciliation', read 'mediation' and for 'Complaints Officer', read 'Mediator'.

Warren then goes on to make some interesting comments – worthy of consideration in a wider context – about the usefulness or otherwise of requiring confidentiality in dealing with complaints under both the AFL and NRL Codes as follows:

> 'It is difficult to compare the effectiveness of the AFL's and NRL's racial vilification codes. The critical issue lies in the frequency of complaints and the efficacy with which they are resolved. In this respect confidentiality requirements have a dual and often contradictory purpose. On the one hand they preserve the confidentiality of the victim's harm and the offender's shame at confronting that harm. This is common justification for the requirement of confidentiality and informality under many models of alternative dispute resolution. On the other hand confidentiality is often compromised by extensive media and public scrutiny of suspected breaches of the Rules both before and after any mediation ... As sports organisations become more accepting of legal representation in disciplinary proceedings, it is to be expected that greater synthesis of available information on the conduct and outcomes of these proceedings will be required to contest disputes in the future. This may erode the confidentiality rule with both positive and negative consequences.'

It is certainly true that, without sufficient information on mediations of sports disputes that have actually taken place and, in certain cases, without knowing either whether the mediation was successful or not, due to confidentiality constraints, it is very difficult, if not impossible, to make an evaluation of the efficacy of past mediations generally and whether to advise invoking the process in particular future cases. Precedent does have its uses. What works in one case may well work in another similar case (the Common Law *in consimili casu* principle).

Finally, he cites the interesting case of Peter Everitt and the novel and creative way in which he himself dealt with his admitted breach of Rule 30 for the second time. Again for 'conciliation' read 'mediation' and for 'deed of agreement' read 'settlement agreement'. He describes and explains the unusual resolution of this case as follows:

> 'After considerable debate over the availability of the conciliation process and the role of the Tribunal, Everitt offered his own punishment at a private meeting which was later ratified by the victim, the clubs concerned and the AFL in a formal "deed of agreement". Everitt agreed to step down from football for four matches and paid $20,000 of his football earnings to an indigenous development program in which he voluntarily participated. While this might be viewed as an unusual way to side-step the league's formal conciliation and tribunal procedures, it also suggests that clubs and individuals are willing and able to devise and implement their own forms of mediation and punishment alongside the League's formal rules.'

The case underscores the point that justice and honour can be done and seen to be done just as effectively through a mediation process as through a judicial process in a tribunal – in the right circumstances.

7.7 The Sport Dispute Resolution Centre of Canada (SDRCC)

A brief mention should also be made of the Sport Dispute Resolution Centre of Canada (SDRCC).

In April, 2004, this sports disputes resolution body, modelled on the lines of the CAS but taking into account the Canadian dispute resolution tradition, officially commenced its operations. The setting up and the activities of the SDRCC – the so-called 'Canadian CAS' – are well described and analysed juridically by Dr Hilary Findlay in her contribution, entitled 'Form Follows Function: Crafting Rules for a Sport-Specific Arbitration Process – "The Canadian CAS"' in the Asser Sports Law Series book on *The Court of Arbitration for Sport 1984-2004*.[32]

She makes some pertinent observations in her conclusions as to what is necessary for setting up an effective sport-specific arbitration mechanism and identifies the following three important criteria as follows:

> ' ... what is the appropriate scope of review afforded to the adjudicator in an arbitration, what is the appropriate standard of review to determine an "error" in the original decision, and, lastly, what is the appropriate scope of authority of the adjudicator in crafting a remedy'.[33]

Let us hope that the Canadian experiment with extrajudicial settlement of sports disputes within the Canadian sport system will achieve a greater and more long-standing success than its Australian NSDC equivalent!

7.8 The Japan Sports Arbitration Agency (JSAA)

For the sake of completeness, a brief remark or two should also be made about the Japan Sports Arbitration Agency (JSAA), which was established on 7 April, 2003 and has been operational since 1 June, 2003, since when at least five arbitral awards have been rendered.

---

32 Edited by Ian S. Blackshaw, Robert C.R. Siekmann and Janwillem Soek (The Hague, T.M.C. Asser Press 2006) at pp. 280-293.

33 Ibid., at p. 291.

Its objectives are stated in Article 3 of the Statutes of the Agency, namely: '… to support the development of sports by administering services to efficiently settle disputes between, among others, athletes and sports associations through arbitration'.

The JSAA is modelled on the Court of Arbitration for Sport.

For further information on the background, the structure, the applicable rules and the cases handled to date by the JSAA, see the chapter, entitled 'The Activities of the Japan Sports Arbitration Agency' by Masato Dogauchi in the Asser Sports Law Series book on *The Court of Arbitration for Sport 1984-2004*.[34]

7.9 The FIFA Dispute Resolution Chamber

The FIFA Dispute Resolution Chamber (DRC) is an important sports disputes resolution body handling an estimated several hundred football-related cases each year. Not all of these cases are published on the FIFA official website; but only those of 'general interest'. For example, on 15 August, 2008, FIFA published the decision of the DRC in the Adrian Mutu case, who was sacked by Chelsea Football Club in October 2004, and fined GBP 20,000 and banned by the English FA from football for seven months, after failing a drugs test for cocaine. Chelsea brought a claim against the player in the DRC for damages for breach of contract. A FIFA statement read:

> 'We can confirm that a decision has been taken by the Dispute Resolution Chamber (DRC) regarding the case of the player Adrian Mutu and Chelsea Football Club (England), and that the decision has been notified to the parties concerned.
>
> The claim for compensation of Chelsea Football Club, regarding the breach of a contract which was signed between the two parties on 12 August 2003, has been partially accepted. The player Adrian Mutu will have to pay the amount of EUR 17,173,990 to Chelsea Football Club.'

Generally speaking, the decisions of the DRC are based on general principles of labour law, but on some points/issues the DRC makes its own kind of law, which may be described as a *lex sportiva*, as the so-called 'specificity of international professional football' is one of the considerations to be taken into account by the DRC in reaching their decisions in appropriate cases.

7.9.1 **Background**

The world governing body of association football, FIFA, was established in 1904 for the purpose of achieving, on a global basis, uniformity, equality and certainty in football, and improving the game, both on and off the field of play. To realise these goals, FIFA first set up the Players' Status Committee (PSC), one of its Standing Committees,[35] with the aim of deciding all international football disputes.

In 2001, FIFA set up the DRC to take over certain disputes from the PSC relating to the international status and transfer of players. Its competence extends to cases concerning labour disputes, with an international dimension, and also to disputes regarding training compensation and the so-called solidarity contribution.

---

[34] Ibid., at pp. 300-312.

[35] FIFA Statutes 2008, effective as of 1 August, 2008, Art. 34.1(o).

The PSC is required to set up and monitor compliance with the Regulations on the Status and Transfer of Players (RSTP), the latest version of whose provisions namely December 2004/October 2007, are set out in Appendix XIII to this book, and also to determine the status of players for various FIFA competitions.[36] Its competence is governed by the provisions of the RSTP. The PSC is also be responsible for the work of the Dispute Resolution Chamber in accordance with the RSTP and the Rules Governing the Procedures of the Players' Status Committee and the Dispute Resolution Chamber.[37]

For further information regarding the background and history of the DRC and, in particular, the influence and effect of the European Court of Justice Decision in *Bosman*[38] on the corresponding rules and operating arrangements, see the recent book entitled, *The Jurisprudence of the FIFA Dispute Resolution Chamber* by Frans de Weger.[39]

7.9.2 **The nature composition and operation of the DRC**

The DRC is not an arbitral court, such as the CAS. The decisions of the DRC are not, therefore, international arbitral awards, and can only be enforced through the statutes and regulations of FIFA. In other words, within the so-called 'football family'. As such, the decisions of the DRC are of great importance and have a huge impact on the international football world. The members of FIFA, the national associations, must fully comply with all decisions of FIFA, such as decisions of the DRC.[40] In turn, the national associations must take measures to ensure that their own members, the national players and clubs, also fully comply with these decisions.[41]

The DRC meets in the form of a panel composed generally of at least three members, including the chairman or the deputy chairman.[42] According to the FIFA Commentary, the composition of the DRC must be based on the fundamental principle of equal representation of players and clubs. Ten members represent the players and are proposed by FIFPro, the international union for professional football players; and ten club members are proposed by the national associations and leagues from around the world from amongst their clubs.

The FIFA Executive Committee then formally appoints the proposed members, together with the chairman and the deputy chairman.[43] In this respect, it is very important that the members of the DRC do not perform different functions in the same matter. They will explicitly refrain from attempting to influence other bodies and committees and they must maintain strict confidentiality concerning any and all information that may come to their attention in the exercise of their duties and not mentioned in the decision. In particular, they are strictly obliged to respect the secrecy of deliberations.[44] The decisions of the DRC are made by a simple majority vote of the members; each of the members, includ-

---

36 Ibid., Art. 49.1.

37 Ibid., Art. 49.2.

38 Case C-415/93 *Union Royale Belge de Societes de Football v. Bosman* [1995] *ECR* I-4921.

39 Published by the T.M.C. Asser Press, The Hague, 2008, at pp. 2-8.

40 Ibid., Art. 13.1(d).

41 Ibid., Art. 65.2.

42 According to the FIFA Statutes, the composition, specific duties and powers of the individual committees, such as the DRC, will be stipulated in special organisation regulations. The composition of the DRC is therefore laid down in the before-mentioned Procedural Rules as well as the RSTP, edition 2005.

43 FIFA Commentary, explanation Art. 24, p. 72. Procedural Rules, Art. 4.

44 Procedural Rules, Art. 5 Para. 7.

ing the chairman, has one vote each. In the event of a tie, the chairman has a casting vote. Abstentions are not permitted! The decisions will be communicated to the parties in writing, although in urgent cases, the decision may be given orally immediately, with written confirmation following within the next twenty days.[45]

However, if the case is of a comparatively simple nature, then it may be handled and decided by a single judge: the so-called DRC Judge. In that event, the members of the DRC will appoint a DRC Judge for the clubs and one for the players from amongst their members.[46] Members of the DRC may not adjudicate in cases in which they have a personal or direct interest. In other words, a potential conflict of interests' situation. In such cases, the member concerned is required to withdraw from the proceedings in good time and give reasons for being unable to act.[47]

When deciding cases, the DRC applies the RSTP, whilst taking into account all relevant arrangements, laws and/or collective bargaining agreements that exist at national level, as well as the specificity of sport.[48] In practice, the RSTP rules are the main source of law for the DRC when deciding a dispute relating to the international transfers of players, their status and their eligibility to participate in organised football.[49] These fundamental rules are compulsorily and uniformly applied throughout the world.[50] They aim to regulate international transfer law when deciding a dispute between member associations and they also establish basic principles that guarantee uniform and equal treatment of all participants in the international football world.[51]

The RSTP rules are complemented by the Rules Governing the Procedures of the PSC and the DRC (the Procedural Rules). The Procedural Rules deal with such matters as the composition of the DRC, its jurisdiction and the applicable law.

The DRC is required to render a decision within sixty days of filing the case and the DRC Judge is required to render his or her decision within thirty days.[52] Reasons must be given for the decision.[53] There is time limit of two years for bringing proceedings before the DRC.[54]

In general, proceedings before the DRC or the DRC Judge are free of charge.[55] However, if one of the parties generates unnecessary costs as a result of its conduct, the DRC may impose the costs on the party concerned, irrespective of the outcome of the case.[56]

7.9.3 **Appeals from the DRC**

In its Circular 827, FIFA outlined that after 'intense and very constructive discussions with the International Council of Arbitration for Sport', FIFA finally agreed to recognise the

---

[45] Ibid., Art. 13 Para 2.
[46] RSTP, edition 2005, Art. 24 Para. 2.
[47] Procedural Rules, Art. 7 Para. 1.
[48] RSTP, edition 2005, Art. 25 Para. 6.
[49] The RSTP also set up rules regarding the release of players for association teams and the player's eligibility to play for such teams.
[50] FIFA Commentary, explanation Art. 1 Para. 1, p. 8.
[51] FIFA Commentary, explanation Art. 1 Para. 2, p. 8.
[52] RSTP, edition 2005, Art. 25.1.
[53] Procedural Rules, Art. 13 Para. 4.
[54] RSTP, edition 2005, Art. 25.5.
[55] Ibid.; and Procedural Rules, Art. 15 Para. 2.
[56] RSTP, edition 2005, Art. 15 Para. 1.

jurisdiction of the CAS to act as a final appeal body for decisions taken by the DRC with effect from 11 November 2001.[57]

Article 62.1 of the FIFA Statutes provides that the decisions of the DRC may be appealed before the CAS.[58] This possibility is also mentioned in the decisions of the DRC itself. The provisions of the CAS Code of Sports-Related Arbitration will govern these appeals and the CAS will primarily apply the various regulations of FIFA and, additionally, Swiss Law to them.[59]

Appeals against final decisions rendered by FIFA legal bodies and against decisions passed by confederations, members or leagues must be lodged with the CAS within 21 days of notification of the decision in question.[60] Each decision of the DRC expressly stipulates that the 'statement of appeal' must be sent to the CAS directly within 21 days of receipt of notification of the decision concerned and that it will furthermore contain all the elements as required by the directives of the CAS, a copy of which is enclosed with the decision. Within a further ten days following the expiry of the time limit for filing the 'statement of appeal', the appellant must file a brief stating the facts and legal arguments on which the appeal to the CAS is based.[61] Within the following twenty days from the receipt of the grounds for the appeal, the respondent must then submit his 'statement of defence' to the CAS.[62]

Finally, it should be noted that cases may only be referred to the CAS after all other internal FIFA channels have been exhausted.[63] The CAS, however, is expressly excluded from handling appeals arising from: (a) violation of the Laws of the Game; (b) suspensions of up to four matches or up to three months; and (c) decisions against which an appeal to an independent and duly constituted arbitration tribunal recognised under the rules of the association or confederation may be made.[64] Appeals to the CAS will not generally have a suspensive effect. However, the appropriate FIFA body or, alternatively, the CAS itself, may order an appeal to have such an effect.[65]

By way of example, the recent Decision of the DRC in the important *Andrew Webster* Case, which was subsequently appealed to the CAS, is set out in Appendix XIV to this book.[66]

7.9.4 **Final remarks**

It should be noted that recourse to the ordinary courts of law for settling disputes is, as a general principle, expressly prohibited by FIFA, unless expressly provided for in the FIFA regulations.[67]

---

57 Circular 827 dated 10 December 2002.

58 See Ian S. Blackshaw, Robert C.R. Siekmann, Janwillem Soek, eds., *The Court of Arbitration for Sport 1984-2004* (The Hague, T.M.C. Asser Institute 2006) generally and, in particular, the chapter in this book by Christian Krähe, entitled, 'The Appeals Procedure before the CAS', at pp. 99-104.

59 FIFA Statutes, Art. 62.2.

60 Ibid., Art. 63.1; CAS Procedural Rules, Art. R49.

61 In conformity with Point 4 of the Directives.

62 CAS Procedural Rules, Art. R55.

63 FIFA Statutes, Art. 63.2.

64 Ibid., Art. 63.3.

65 Ibid., Art. 63.4.

66 DRC Case 47936, 4 April 2007.

67 FIFA Statutes, Art. 64.2.

Furthermore, the Member Associations of FIFA are required to insert a clause in their statutes or regulations, stipulating that it is prohibited to take disputes in their Associations or disputes affecting Leagues, members of Leagues, clubs, members of clubs, players, officials and other Association officials to ordinary courts of law, unless the FIFA regulations or binding legal provisions specifically provide for or stipulate recourse to the ordinary courts of law. Instead of recourse to the ordinary courts of law, provision shall be made for arbitration. Such disputes shall be taken to an independent and duly constituted arbitration tribunal recognised under the rules of the Association or Confederation or to the CAS. Furthermore, the FIFA Member Associations shall also ensure that this stipulation is implemented in their Association, if necessary by imposing a binding obligation on its members. The Associations shall also impose sanctions on any party that fails to respect this obligation and ensure that any appeal against such sanctions shall likewise be strictly submitted to arbitration, and not to the ordinary courts of law.[68]

FIFA and, it may be said, so many other international sports governing bodies and organisations have a general policy of excluding the ordinary courts from being involved in disputes. But such attempts, if not qualified, to oust the jurisdiction of the courts, are void under English Law and also under many other legal systems around the world, as being contrary to 'public policy' (*ordre public*). This is particularly so in several jurisdictions in relation to the settlement of labour disputes by legal proceedings.

However, such provisions if reworded to the effect that recourse to the ordinary courts of law is only permitted after all internal procedures for dispute resolution within the sports body or organisation concerned have been exhausted this is generally valid. See, for example, the decision in the leading English case of *Scott* v. *Avery*.[69]

Finally, the decisions of the DRC are relatively speedy; rendered by football specialists; and enforceable through the FIFA disciplinary channels and procedures. Hence, as mentioned at the beginning of this section, the DRC is not short of cases!

7.10 The FIBA Arbitral Tribunal (FAT)

7.10.1 **Introductory remarks**

Established two years ago in May 2007 – with very little fanfare outside the world of basketball – FIBA – the International Basketball Federation – set up its own dispute resolution body, know by the acronym 'FAT' – the FIBA Arbitral Tribunal – with the laudable objectives of settling disputes speedily, informally, inexpensively and effectively. So far, the FAT has dealt with 37 cases, with 20 more pending at the time of writing.

The FAT, which is the brainchild of Dr Dirk Reiner-Martens, a former Secretary-General of FIBA and well-known sports arbitrator, has its seat in Geneva, Switzerland, where FIBA itself is based; and offers arbitration under Swiss Law. It is independent of FIBA, and the language of its arbitrations is English. Hearings are by application only and appeals from FAT awards lie to the CAS, which is based in Lausanne, Switzerland. All its arbitrators have CAS experience and its President is Professor Gabrielle Kaufmann-Kohler of Geneva University, who is well-known in CAS circles.

---

68 Ibid. Art. 64.3.

69 [1865] 5 HL Cas.811.

However, exceptionally, no appeals lie from awards of the FAT or appeals to the CAS to the Swiss Federal Tribunal. These are expressly renounced by the parties to the FAT (see below). In fact, to date, at least, there have been no appeals to the CAS or legal challenges to FAT awards.

The FAT is proving to be an effective body within the European world of basketball. In fact, the FAT standard form arbitration clause is now commonplace in European basketball contracts. However, the FAT is also growing in popularity outside Europe in other countries such as China, the Lebanon and Saudi Arabia.

7.10.2 The FAT standard-form arbitration clause

The standard express contractual reference to FAT arbitration takes the following form:

> 'Any dispute arising from or related to the present contract shall be submitted to the FIBA Arbitral Tribunal (FAT) in Geneva, Switzerland and shall be resolved in accordance with the FAT Arbitration Rules by a single arbitrator appointed by the FAT President.
>
> The seat of the arbitration shall be Geneva, Switzerland.
>
> The arbitration shall be governed by Chapter 12 of the Swiss Act on Private International Law (PIL), irrespective of the parties' domicile. The language of the arbitration shall be English.
>
> Awards of the FAT can be appealed to the Court of Arbitration for Sport (CAS), Lausanne, Switzerland. The parties expressly waive recourse to the Swiss Federal Tribunal against awards of the FAT and against decisions of the Court of Arbitration for Sport (CAS) upon appeal, as provided in Article 192 of the Swiss Act on Private International Law.
>
> The arbitrator and CAS upon appeal shall decide the dispute *ex aequo et bono*.'

As will be seen, FAT arbitration is handled by a single arbitrator – rather than a panel of three which is more common in CAS cases – and this helps to speed up the process of getting a FAT award. Also, short deadlines are set for the parties to reply; and submissions are made on line.

Likewise, time is saved by the fact that the dispute is decided on an *ex aequo et bono* basis – in other words, by applying general rules of justice and fairness, including, of course, the rule of *due process* – obviating the need to refer to any particular national or international law. This basis also applies to the determination of any appeals from the FAT to the CAS. This possibility is foreseen in Article R45 of the CAS Code of Sports-related Arbitration (2004 edition).

In general, a decision of the FAT is made within six weeks of the end of the proceedings; and, this, in turn, is usually within three to four months of the date of the filing by the claimant of the request for arbitration.

7.10.3 The FAT request for arbitration

Arbitration by FAT is commenced by filing a written request for arbitration, a template of which is as follows:

Request for Arbitration

To the
FIBA Arbitral Tribunal

Fédération Internationale de Basketball
51-53, Avenue Louis Casaï
1217 Meyrin/Geneva
Switzerland
By facsimile to: +41-22-5450099
By E-mail: FAT Secretariat *[ctrl + click]*

Date:

The Claimant(s)

Name of the Claimant		[Second Claimant, if applicable]
Full Address:		
Telephone:		
Facsimile:		
E-Mail:		

Counsel (if applicable):

Name:	
Company:	
Full Address:	
Telephone:	
Facsimile:	
E-Mail:	

hereby request(s) that an arbitration be commenced against

the Respondent

Name of the Respondent:	
Full Address:	
Telephone:	
Facsimile:	
E-Mail:	
Contact person of the Respondent	

according to the Arbitration Rules of the FIBA Arbitral Tribunal ("FAT Rules") in force at the time of the filing of this Request for Arbitration.

The Claimant and the Respondent are parties to an arbitration agreement dated
according to which this dispute shall be submitted to the FAT.

Copy of the Arbitration Agreement

[must be] attached ☐.

The Claimant requests that any communication to him/her/it concerning this arbitration be made as per the FAT Rules

☐ to the Counsel specified above.
☐ to the Claimant specified above, as no Counsel is appointed.

1. Facts and Legal Arguments

2. Request for Relief
[*e.g. salaries, agent fees, compensation, late payment fee, interests, costs of the arbitration, legal fees and expenses, other requests*]
Claimant(s) request(s):

3. Evidence
All written evidence on which the Claimant intends to rely is attached hereto.

4. Request for Hearing and for Examination of (a) witness(es) [not mandatory]
The Claimant requests that a hearing be held
and that Mr/Mrs is/are to be examined as witness(es) .

Witness(es):

Name:		[Second Witness, if applicable]
Full Address:		
Telephone:		
Facsimile:		
E-Mail:		

5. Costs
The Claimant(s) recognise(s) that the arbitration will not proceed until a non-reimbursable handling fee of EUR 3,000 is received in the FIBA bank account as follows:

Beneficiary: FIBA (Arbitral Tribunal)
Bank: UBS Lausanne, Switzerland
Account No.: 0243-509384.60F
IBAN: CH48002432435093846OF
Swift: UBSWCHZH80A

A copy of the bank transfer voucher is attached to the Request of Arbitration.
The costs of the arbitration will be fixed by the Arbitrator at a later point in time.

Signature ________________________________
Name and Title in print:

POWER OF ATTORNEY

The undersigned hereby appoints

Mr. / Ms ....
[name(s) of representative(s)]

each individually to fully and generally represent the undersigned, including the right to grant sub-power of attorney, vis-à-vis third parties and courts / courts of arbitration in the matter of

[Claimant(s) vs. Respondent]
before the FIBA Arbitral Tribunal (FAT)

This power of attorney can be transferred and continues to be valid in case of death or legal incapacity of the undersigned. It shall include, but not be limited to, the authority to

- make and receive statements and declarations of any nature, in particular, to receive service of process;
- represent the undersigned in any litigation / arbitration as well as enforcement and ancillary proceedings,
- enter into settlement agreements, and
- accept on behalf of the undersigned money and other valuables.

....
Place, Date

....
Signature

....
Name of the Undersigned in Print

As will be seen, the request for arbitration, which is similar to the one filed with the CAS, is accompanied by a Power of Attorney in favour of the claimant's (legal) representative.

The claimant is also required to pay an administration fee of EUR 3,000; and, in addition, the claimant and the respondent share an advance payment of the arbitrator's fees. These fees are determined according to the value and complexity of the dispute. If the respondent fails to pay its share of these fees, the claimant can pay that share; and all these factors are taken into account in any final award that is made on costs by the FAT.

7.10.4 The FAT procedural rules

Arbitrations before the FAT are conducted in accordance with the FIBA Arbitral Tribunal Arbitration Rules of December 2007. These can be downloaded from the FIBA official website to be found at <www.fiba.com>.

These Rules are subject to the FIBA Arbitral Tribunal Regulations, which form part of section L.2 of the FIBA Internal Regulations, which provide as follows:

> '**L2 FIBA Arbitral Tribunal (FAT)**
> **L2.1 General Principles**
> L2.1.1 FIBA establishes an independent FIBA Arbitral Tribunal (FAT) for the simple, quick and inexpensive resolution of disputes arising within the world of basketball in which FIBA, its Zones, or their respective divisions are not directly involved and with respect to which the parties to the dispute have agreed in writing to submit the same to the FAT.
> L2.1.2 FAT awards can be appealed to the Court of Arbitration for Sport (CAS), Lausanne, Switzerland.
> L2.1.3 The FAT is primarily designed to resolve disputes between clubs, players and agents.
> L2.1.4 It is recommended that parties wishing to refer their possible disputes to the FAT use the following arbitration clause in their contracts:
>
> *'Any dispute arising from or related to the present contract shall be submitted to the FIBA Arbitral Tribunal (FAT) in Geneva, Switzerland and shall be resolved in accordance with the FAT Arbitration Rules by a single arbitrator appointed by the FAT President.*
> *The seat of the arbitration shall be Geneva, Switzerland.*
> *The arbitration shall be governed by Chapter 12 of the Swiss Act on Private International Law (PIL), irrespective of the parties' domicile.*
> *The language of the arbitration shall be English.*
> *Awards of the FAT can be appealed to the Court of Arbitration for Sport (CAS), Lausanne, Switzerland. The parties expressly waive recourse to the Swiss Federal Tribunal against awards of the FAT and against deci-*

sions of the Court of Arbitration for Sport (CAS) upon appeal, as provided in Article 192 of the Swiss Act on Private International Law.
The arbitrator and CAS upon appeal shall decide the dispute ex aequo et bono.'

L2.2 The FAT Arbitration Rules
Arbitration proceedings before FAT will be conducted in accordance with the FAT Arbitration Rules which are available from the FIBA Secretariat on request and which are available also on the FIBA website.

Any proposed changes to the FAT Arbitration Rules shall be prepared by the FIBA Legal Commission and shall be submitted to the FIBA Central Board for approval.

The proceedings are governed by the version of the FAT Arbitration Rules in force at the time of the filing of a request for arbitration.

L2.3 Seat of the FAT
The FAT has its seat in Geneva, Switzerland.

L2.4 Financing
The financing of the FAT is guaranteed by FIBA, it being understood that the FAT is designed to be self-financing.

L2.5 The FAT President / the FAT Vice President
The FAT President and the FAT Vice President shall be appointed by the FIBA Central Board for a renewable term of 4 years between the ordinary sessions of the FIBA Congress. They shall have legal training.

The FAT Vice President shall substitute for the FAT President in case of the latter's inability to exercise the functions assigned to him under the FAT Arbitration Rules, including instances where the FAT President is prevented from exercising his functions due to a conflict of interest.

L2.6 The Duties of the FAT President
The FAT President shall have the following duties:

a) To ensure the proper functioning of the FAT, inter alia, by establishing administrative guidelines for the tribunal.
b) To establish a list of at least three (3) FAT arbitrators for a renewable term of four (4) years between the ordinary FIBA Arbitral Tribunal page 3 of 3 sessions of the FIBA Congress. The FAT arbitrators shall have legal training and shall have experience with regard to sport.
c) To appoint, on a rotational basis, a FAT arbitrator to the individual arbitration proceedings before the FAT.
d) To establish a system of remuneration for the FAT arbitrators.
e) To exercise those functions assigned to him under the FAT Arbitration Rules.

L2.7 Honouring of FAT Awards
L2.7.1 In the event that a party to a FAT Arbitration fails to honour a final award or any provisional or conservatory measures (the 'first party') of FAT or of the Court of Arbitration for Sport upon appeal against a FAT award, the party seeking enforcement of such award (the 'second party') shall have the right to request that FIBA sanction the first party. The following sanctions can be imposed by FIBA:

a) a monetary fine of up to EUR 100,000; this fine can be applied more than once; and/or
b) withdrawal of FIBA-license if the first party is a player's agent; and/or
c) a ban on international transfers if the first party is a player; and/or
d) a ban on registration of new players and/or a ban on participation in international club competition if the second party is a club.

The above sanctions can be applied more than once.

L2.7.2 The second party shall send to FIBA with his request a complete file of the FAT/CAS proceedings. The decision on the sanction is taken by the Secretary General or his delegate. Before taking his decision he shall give the first party an opportunity to state his position.

L2.7.3 The decision to sanction the first party shall be subject to appeal to the FIBA Appeals Tribunal according to the Internal Regulations governing Appeals.'

7.10.5 **Enforcing FAT awards**

As will be seen from the above provisions in L2.7.1, failure to honour a FAT award may give rise to a number of sanctions being imposed by FIBA on the party concerned. These sanctions include: a monetary fine; the withdrawal of a FIBA Agent's Licence; a ban on the international transfer of players; and a ban on the registration of new players.

To date, apparently there is only one case in which the party concerned has failed to comply with a FAT award.

As will also be seen from the above provisions in L2.7.3, FIBA sanctions are appealable to the FIBA Appeals Tribunal in accordance with the corresponding Regulations.

7.10.6 **Concluding remarks**

The FAT is proving to be an effective and, therefore, popular body for resolving disputes in the sport of basketball and, perhaps, this wining formula/model may be adopted by other sports bodies for the settlement of their disputes. That remains to be seen, of course.

However, not all sports may wish to adopt the *ex aequo et bono* basis of decision making and/or exclude further appeals to external courts or tribunals – in other words, the ordinary courts of the land which may otherwise have jurisdiction in dealing with disputes. In this connection, there is always the legal problem of ousting the jurisdiction of the courts, which in many jurisdictions is not legally possible – at least, until all internal remedies of the sports body concerned have been exhausted. See, for example, the English House of Lords decision in the case of *Scott* v. *Avery* [1856] 5 HL Cas 811.

But what may be said with more certainty is that the FAT can expect to have a heavier caseload in the foreseeable future, as the dispute resolution procedures of the FAT are invoked by more countries outside Europe. This, of course, will necessitate the appointment of more FAT arbitrators, who currently comprise a rather select and limited band of pioneers!

CHAPTER 8
AMERICAN ARBITRATION ASSOCIATION (AAA)

8.1 Background

In the United States, under the Ted Stevens Olympic and Amateur Sports Act of 1978 – usually referred to as the 'Amateur Sports Act' – National Governing Bodies (NGBs) of each sport are required to submit all disputes within the scope of this Act to binding arbitration by the American Arbitration Association (AAA).

The Act also entitles Olympic, Pan American and Paralympic athletes and other parties dissatisfied with rulings of the United States Olympic Committee (USOC) to be reviewed by the AAA.

The decisions of NGBs, under the provisions of the USOC Constitution, are subject to arbitration by the AAA.

The AAA has an extensive experience of conducting Mediations and Arbitrations and the corresponding Rules are set out in full in Appendix XV to this book.

8.2 Should CAS Replace AAA?

Although the AAA has much experience of conducting Arbitrations of many kinds, in view of the developing role of the CAS in settling international sports disputes, there is a growing feeling, in some quarters, that the Amateur Sports Act should be amended to substitute the CAS for the AAA as the designated arbitral body to determine disputes between athletes and USOC and/or its NGBs.

For a view on this and the pros and cons of introducing such a requirement, the following contribution to this ongoing debate by American Lawyer, Paul H. Haagen, entitled, 'Have the Wheels Already Been Invented? The Court of Arbitration for Sport as a Model of Dispute Resolution' is both interesting and instructive:

'The sports community faces the same problems that any other community faces when dealing with a dispute: how to resolve the matter in a way that is efficient and cost effective, and seen by interested parties to be fair. It faces those problems, however, in a context in which both the parties to the dispute and interested third parties are likely to view any resolution through the jaundiced eye of partisanship. The cries of anguish that issue from the crowds at every sporting event, convinced that an injustice is perpetrated by each referee's call (and many non-calls), are only the most audible indication of the difficulty of adjudication in the context of intense competition.

In addition, there is often a need for a very rapid response. If the eligibility of an athlete is challenged on the eve of a competition, the question must either be decided very quickly or the competition will be seriously disrupted and distorted. Even when the context does not require an immediate decision, athlete careers are frequently so short that justice delayed is justice denied. In addition, the disputes are often about arcane matters, only poorly understood by persons outside the sports com-

I.S. Blackshaw, Sport, Mediation and Arbitration

munity, and take place against the background of legal norms that are relatively undeveloped. When we add to this that they can also involve very substantial amounts of money, and access to competitions that may define an athlete's sense of self, the potential intensity of the conflict becomes clearer.

The nature of many disputes in sports, moreover, precludes the easiest and happiest forms of dispute resolution. In general, they must be decided. They cannot merely be settled. There are few win/win situations, and a not inconsiderable number of lose/lose ones.

When these disputes take place not against the background of local or national competition, but international competition, each of the difficulties noted above is made more intense by the overlay of differing cultural and legal expectations, and increased levels of suspicion of the motives and good faith of others. Few competitors, and few of their supporters, are prepared to believe that anyone else's domestic adjudicatory process, whether in the courts or in some non-judicial forum, will produce fair or consistent results. They are certainly right to be skeptical. The handling of athletic disputes in domestic courts has not been among the greatest of judicial success stories. The individuals who run international sport have been vocal and open in their contempt for the interference of domestic tribunals, especially those of the United States, in the running of what they regard as their internal affairs.

Sixteen years ago, the IOC attempted to address these problems by creating the Court of Arbitration for Sport, or CAS. CAS was designed to be an international arbitral body capable of resolving disputes in the field of sports. It consists of two 'divisions': the Ordinary Arbitration Division, which handles matters of first instance, and the Appeals Arbitration Division, which deals with appeals from the decisions of federations, associations and other sports bodies. Sixty 'well-known jurists who also have a good knowledge of sports related issues' were appointed to serve as potential arbitrators. Both CAS and the arbitrators were, according to the pronouncements of the IOC, 'completely independent from the IOC, in the exercise of their duties'. If the IOC was impressed with the independence of CAS, others were not. Despite the pronouncement of independence, there were powerful indicia of dependence. The IOC had created CAS, it selected half of CAS's members, it administered and supervised CAS, it provided all of CAS's 'running costs', and CAS was physically located on the grounds of the IOC in Lausanne, Switzerland.

In 1993, the question of CAS's complete independence was challenged in court.

The Swiss Federal Tribunal in the *Gundel* decision held that CAS did, in spite of the entanglements, offer 'the guarantees of independence upon which Swiss law makes onditional the valid exclusion of ordinary judicial recourse,' but noted that the close ties between the IOC and CAS left open the question of whether it was sufficiently independent to serve as a valid arbitral body in a case involving the IOC. This opinion spurred a restructuring designed to make CAS more independent of the IOC. The critical reforms were the creation of ICAS, the International Council of Arbitration for Sport, to supervise and regulate CAS, the insulation of CAS from direct IOC supervision, and the change in the method of selection and an increase in the number of potential arbitrators. Under the reformed system, there are 150, 30 chosen from among those proposed by the IOC, 30 from among those proposed by the IFs, 30 from among those proposed by the NOCs, 30 chosen after 'appropriate consultations with a view to safeguarding the interests of athletes, and 30 chosen from among persons independent of the bodies responsible for proposing arbitrators.

In 1996, CAS added two additional courts, one at the National Dispute Resolution Center in Sydney, Australia and the other in Denver, Colorado, substantially increasing its potential attractiveness to non-European athletes.

The reformed CAS appears to address many of the most pressing problems surrounding the resolution of athletic disputes, and it has aroused considerable interest that it may provide a workable forum for adjudicating these disputes. It was recently proposed, for example, that the USOC externalize the adjudications process relating to doping by turning it over entirely to CAS.

In the remaining time, I want to raise the question of whether it will be possible to use CAS in this way and whether, given its current structure and modes of operation, such use would be desirable. As with most discussions of alternatives to current methods of dispute resolution, the answer depends in large measure on what one takes to be the baseline. It is easy to fall into the trap of comparing ideal litigation with actual arbitration, or the theoretical benefits of arbitration with the evident short comings of litigation. Here the analysis is complicated by the fact that to date there have been relatively few reported decisions from CAS, and even fewer involving difficult, contentious issues. That said, for those of you who like to look at the end of books first, my answer to the first question will be a qualified yes, and the answer to the second is that there will be some significant benefits and some significant problems.

1. The first issue to be faced is whether it is possible consistent with US law to require resort to CAS. At present, the answer is likely to be both no, but there is reason to believe that Congress may be willing to change the law. Although the language of the Amateur Sports Act is not entirely clear, the Act it is likely to be interpreted to require that arbitration of sports related disputes be AAA arbitration. If there is Sufficient support for CAS in the American sporting community, it seems likely that the Act would be amended to permit the parties to agree to CAS arbitration.
2. The second issue is assuming that the Amateur Sports Act permits the use of CAS arbitration will CAS arbitration be available to deal with such disputes? Within the field of sport, CAS has very broad jurisdiction to hear cases in which the parties have agreed to submit their disputes to CAS. Until relatively recently, there was a substantial likelihood that the US courts would refuse to enforce pre-dispute arbitration agreements by denying a recalcitrant party access to the courts. The dramatic shift in attitude in the US courts toward arbitration and toward the enforceability of contracts to arbitrate makes it almost certain that they would be enforced today. Even adhesive contracts imposed on persons with no realistic alternatives but to sign them will be treated a enforceable agreements to arbitrate, at least in any situation in which the arbitration process meets at least minimal standards of due process.
   As a practical matter, getting the signed agreements from participating may be an administrative headache for the various federations. Attempting to solve the administrative problems may in turn raise legal issues. Will, for example, an agreement entered into on-line, but that is not followed up with a hard copy signature page, constitute a valid agreement enforceable agreement to arbitrate. There will also be serious questions about the enforceability of agreements entered into by or on-behalf of minors in those jurisdictions that do no by statute specifically provide that they are enforceable. Assuming that there are no problems relating to minors and the administrative problems associated with actually getting valid signatures on the agreement to arbitrate, these agreements should be legally enforceable.
3. Assuming that CAS accepts the case will the Swiss courts treat CAS as a valid arbitral body? In light of the reforms, the answer is almost certainly yes. The *Gundel* case went a long way toward recognizing CAS as a valid arbitral body even under the old structure. It is difficult to believe that the reforms will not have removed their remaining doubts.
4. Assuming that the Swiss courts treat CAS as a valid arbitral body, will the US courts enforce the arbitral decisions without subjecting them to judicial review? Under the New York Convention, and the developing interpretation of arbitration law in the US, the answer is again almost certainly yes.

Thus we have in CAS a body able to render enforceable arbitral decisions.

Will this body deliver on the promise of speedy, cost effective justice, that is both fair to the parties and seen by the parties to be fair? No one knows. The record to date is too incomplete.

Is the structure of the organization such that it seems likely that it will? Here the answer seems to be mixed. There are some hopeful signs, and some reasons for concern.

The usual claims for arbitration are that it will be quick and relatively inexpensive. The CAS rules do, in fact, encourage quick resolution. They provide for relatively short time periods for the formation of the panels and for the rendering of opinions. There are a number of procedural devices that make it possible to deal with matters expeditiously. CAS has created special ad hoc bodies, such as the one at the Atlanta Olympics, where the need to timely adjudication was particularly acute.

Nothing guarantees that there will not be delays, but the structure favors quick resolution.

Similarly, the costs of proceeding through CAS seem reasonable for most situations. There will, however, be ones that raise serious concerns. CAS does not provide counsel for those unable to provide counsel for themselves, although at Atlanta it did encourage volunteers to provide free services. It also permits on a discretionary basis the apportioning of costs among the parties in accordance with their ability to pay. Whether this is enough to insure fairness is open to question, but then it should be borne in mind that many of these same criticisms could be leveled at the courts as well. What may be of more moment than the equitable concerns is the legal validity of any agreement to arbitrate that does not address them. Where employees are forced as a condition of employment to submit disputes with their employer to mandatory arbitration, the United States Court of Appeals has held that the employer must pay the costs of the arbitration in certain circumstances. It seems likely that the courts might hold federations that impose a requirement that competitors agree as a condition of participation to mandatory arbitration would be subject to a similar due process requirement, at least in any situation in which an athlete would be denied access to CAS because that athlete did not have the resources to bring the case.

Much of the attractiveness of CAS turns on the fact that the arbitrators are all persons ostensibly with expertise in sport. The value of expertise is immediately and intuitively obvious. Anyone who has ever litigated or arbitrated a case can tell horror stories of attempting to convey complex information to judges or arbitrators who are incompetent and uninformed. Expert panels can much more quickly focus on the issues genuinely in dispute, thus reducing costs and delay. They do not need to be brought up to speed. Many matters that would need to be explained to non-experts either will not need to be explained at all, or will be able to be explained much more efficiently.

Expertise is, however, a problematic concept. What constitutes expertise is left to the nominating bodies and ICAS. Nowhere is it defined. Nor is expertise, however defined, in one aspect of sport necessarily easily transferrable to another. A person expert in the organization of the International Olympic Committee may have no greater ability to deal with the science underlying a claimed challenge to a doping violation than any random member of the judiciary. Some may have less.

Experts are easily confused with persons who merely have a vested interest, and the unhappy history of expert courts in this country ought to serve as a caution.

President Taft created the Commerce Court for reasons that closely track those being given in favor of CAS – that it would permit the rapid and uniform resolution of often arcane regulatory disputes involving the Interstate Commerce Commission, a rapid and uniform resolution not available through the regular courts. Two and a half years later, the experiment was abandoned. The concentration of one type of dispute in a single body, it turned out, favored capture and corruption more than efficiency. One of the expert judges was discovered to have been accepting bribes from the railroads, and Congress or the Supreme Court ended up reversing virtually all of its decisions. The point here is not that CAS will so quickly fall prey to the same problems. The point is rather: 1) that expertise is not so easily established when we are dealing with an organization with as broad a mandate as CAS, that is for any relevant decisional group it may not be all that expert and 2) that expertise does not necessarily promote fairness.

These complaints notwithstanding, it seems likely that CAS arbitrators will have sufficient familiarity with sport related issues that they will be especially adept in dealing with cases that do not raise fundamental, structural questions. Was the handling of a particular urine sample compromised? – where the only question is one about establishing whether the taking of the sample conformed to standard procedures. Was the taking of a substance not specifically banned and about which there was lack of data about the performance enhancing effect grounds for stripping an athlete of an Olympic medal? Here the importance of familiarity with the usual ways of doing things, of the conventional understandings of athletes is enormously important.

Where the dispute does raise fundamental, structural questions, familiarity with and allegiance to the usual way of doing things is likely to be a hindrance. For example, if the question is whether existing tests for endogenous substances are adequate to constitute adequate proof of doping, then the question of meaning of expertise – and of genuine independence from the bodies with a vested interest in the regulation of sport becomes more pressing. To date, the reported decisions from CAS are reasonably comforting in their balance.

On the other hand, to date CAS has not ruled on hard questions that might affect the interests of federations, NGBs, NOCs or the IOC. One example of the experience to date may be illustrative of the current state of our information. In 1997, CAS reversed the decision of FINA to suspend for two years a water polo athlete who took a prescription drug to control asthma. Under FINA's rules, the athlete was entitled to take the drug, but was required to declare that he had done so. Operating under a misapprehension, caused in part by the failure of the IF to keep its various NGBs informed of changes in the rules, the athlete failed to report that he had used an inhaler to control asthma and was suspended from competition for two years from July 26, 1995 to July 26, 1997. The IF represented to CAS that it did not regard the athlete as a cheat. Rather, it believed that he had made a good faith mistake, but that it had no flexibility under its regulations to impose a lighter sanction or no sanction at all. CAS upheld the finding of a doping violation, but noted that it had greater authority with regard to the imposition of penalties and 'cancelled' the sanctions – or presumably only the three and a half months that were remaining of them. It is comforting that an athlete who took a substance that he was entitled to take, and whose only violation was the good faith failure to report the taking of it, and whose position was supported by both his national federation and the IF, could have the equity of his position vindicated. It was not a hard case. Whether the only partial independence of CAS will permit it the independence to take on the hard case and to protect athletes in accordance with the 'fundamental principles of law' that govern CAS proceedings remains an open question. Given the continuing control, albeit indirect, that the IOC exercises over CAS, there is strong reason to believe that such cases are not likely to get the serious review that they would get from a court or from a more independent, general body like AAA.

Searching review is, of course, only one value. Especially when we are talking about matters in international sports, the need for confidence in the consistency and uniformity of decisions may be equally pressing. What does CAS promise here? By centralizing decisions in a single body, and removing those decisions from both domestic and sport based tribunals, it may be possible to achieve greater uniformity. It should be noted, however, that not all federations are currently prepared to accept the jurisdiction of CAS either on matters of first instance or on appeal. Thus, even if CAS were to achieve consistency among those matters submitted to it, it could not deal with matters excluded by federations from its purview. What about consistency among those matters submitted to it.

There are a large number of potential arbitrators, drawn from around the world, and coming out of distinctly different legal traditions, who could be called on to decide any given case. It strains credulity to believe that they are likely to decide cases similarly. Moreover, like most arbitral bodies, CAS is not bound by precedent. Even if it were, it would be difficult for subsequent panels follow the lead of earlier panels, because of the incompleteness of the reported cases. This is admittedly a more pressing concern for persons trained in the Common Law, and especially those trained in the United States. Civil Lawyers have learned to live with sparse case reports. But if it is a more obvious concern for those of us trained in the Common Law, it is a more general problem as well. As Craig Masback has noted, there is a pressing need in international sports for what he has called a *lex sportiva*, a stable body of law that is transparent and consistent. Both the transparency and the consistency will certainly lead to greater confidence in and acceptance of decisions – especially those rendered by a body that is foreign to the participants, applying principles of law unfamiliar to them, and imposed on them by the very bodies that they are now in conflict with.

Has the wheel already been invented? Yes and no. The reformed CAS constitutes an important innovation in the search for a reliable, efficient forum for the resolution of sports related disputes. It has many of the positive features of sport specific arbitral bodies and has gone further than previous organizations to create the kind of externalization and independence that will be necessary to achieve credible results. It remains, however, closely tied to the IOC, the NOCs and the federations.

These ties will inevitably raise questions about the independence of CAS, particularly among those forced to resort to it.

The procedures established by CAS, like those of most arbitral bodies, have all of the advantages that come with greater informality and all of the disadvantages of them as well. There are questions about whether CAS has the authority to reach the full range of remedies available through the courts.

There is a wheel out there. How good it is remains to be seen.'

8.3 Article 59 of the Olympic Charter

In any case, pursuant to Article 59 of the Olympic Charter,[70] 'any dispute arising on the occasion of, or in connection with, the Olympic Games shall be submitted exclusively to the Court of Arbitration for Sport, in accordance with the Code of Sports-Related Arbitration'.

In practice, as a condition of entry to the Games, athletes and all other participants in the Olympic Games in whatever capacity, which includes coaches, trainers and officials, are required to sign a waiver agreeing to the exclusive jurisdiction of the CAS for the settlement of such disputes pursuant to Paragraph 6 of the bye-law to Article 45 of the Olympic Charter in the following terms:

[70] 7 July 2007.

'Understanding that, as a participant in the Olympic Games, I am participating in an exceptional event which has ongoing international and historical significance, and in consideration of the acceptance of my participation therein, I agree to be filmed, televised, photographed, identified and otherwise recorded during the Olympic Games under the conditions and for the purposes now or hereafter authorized by the International Olympic Committee ("IOC") in relation to the promotion of the Olympic Games and Olympic Movement.

I also agree to comply with the Olympic Charter currently in force, in particular, with the provisions of the Olympic Charter regarding the eligibility for the Olympic Games (including Rule 41 and its Bye-law), the mass media (Rule 49) and the allowable trademark identification on clothing and equipment worn or used at the Olympic Games (bye-law to Rule 51).

I also agree that any dispute arising on the occasion of or in connection with my participation in the Olympic Games shall be submitted exclusively to the Court of Arbitration for Sport, in accordance with the Code of Sports-related Arbitration (Rule 59).

I also agree to comply with the World Anti-Doping Code and with the IOC Code of Ethics. All relevant and applicable provisions and rules have been brought to my attention by my National Olympic Committee and/or my National Sports Federation or International Sports Federation.'

8.4 International Sports Arbitration Generally

On the subject of using Arbitration for settling sports disputes generally, a leading US Sports Lawyer and Academic, Professor James A.R. Nafziger of Willamete University College of Law, USA, and President of the International Association of Sports Law, who has contributed the Foreword to this book, has written a most interesting article, entitled 'Arbitration of Rights and Obligations in the International Sports Arena'.[71]

It is reproduced in full as follows:

James A.R. Nafziger[72]
Arbitration of Rights and Obligations in the International Sports Arena

Arbitration of disputes related to international sports competition is a growth industry. Certainly one of the most important developments in sports law during the past few years has been the expanded role of the Court of Arbitration for Sport ('CAS').[73] Business is also brisk for the American Arbitration Association and other national arbitral bodies around the world.[74] Many of the disputes have involved the eligibility of athletes on the eve of sanctioned international competition.[75]

---

71 35/2 *Valparaiso University Law Review* (Spring 2001), pp. 357-377.

72 Thomas B. Stoel, Professor of Law, Willamette University College of Law; Vice President, International Association of Sports Law. This article is based on the author's remarks at a conference in Chicago on November 2 and 3, 2000, entitled, 'Arbitrating Sports Disputes: A World View'. This conference was organized by the Valparaiso University School of Law. The author thanks Christopher Cipoletti and Steven J. Thompson for their assistance in the preparation of this article.

73 See Matthieu Reeb, 'The Role of the Court of Arbitration for Sport', in Wybo P. Heere, ed., *International Law and The Hague's 750th Anniversary* (1999), p. 233; James A.R Nafziger, 'The Court of Arbitration for Sport and the General Process of International Sports Law', in Wybo P. Heere ed., *International Law and The Hague's 750th Anniversary* (1999), p. 239.

74 Newspaper headlines tell the story. See, e.g., Jess Bravin, 'Ready, Set, Arbitrate!: Here is This Year's New Hot Olympic Event. Arbitration', *Wall Street Journal*, August 18, 2000, at A1, A6; Vicki Michaelis, 'Roster Disputes Go Down to the Wire', *USA Today*, August 24, 2000, at 1C.

75 See, e.g., Lauri Tarasti, *Legal Solutions in International Doping Cases: Awards by the IAAF Arbitration Panel 1985-1999* (2000); Matthieu Reeb ed., *Recueil des Sentences du TAS/Digest of CAS Awards 1986-1998* (1998).

I. GROWTH OF INTERNATIONAL SPORTS ARBITRATION

In 1988, not a single demand for arbitration was filed during the run-up to the Olympic Games in Seoul.[76] By contrast, in 2000, the docket prior to the Sydney Games numbered some eight cases in the United States alone[77] and six times that number in Australia.[78] Arbitration of international sports disputes in Europe is also common.[79] The growth industry of international sports arbitration is clearly multinational. Hailing, as I do, from the state that brought you Tonya Harding in 1994,[80] Mary Decker Slaney in 1996, 1997, 1998 and 1999,[81] and Matt Lindland in 2000[82] – three very different individuals, but all seasoned veterans of arbitration – I hope you appreciate that we Oregonians are doing our part to fuel this industry. And, as Matt Lindland's silver medal in Sydney attests, we are getting better at quality control within the industry.

What accounts for this 'Atrendy Olympic event,'[83] this 'burgeoning Olympic sport of arbitration,'[84] as it has been called? Several explanations are immediately apparent. Video taping and electronic records of trials and final events provide better evidence to resolve disputes and thereby encourage more challenges to decisions. More obviously, perhaps, issues involving doping and the use of other performance-enhancing agents have sparked a substantial amount of arbitration. Even though the identification, testing, and sanctioning of prohibited substances and techniques are more effective today than even five years ago, the circumstances of their procurement, distribution and use are subtle and often ambiguous, giving rise to more disputes. And speaking of agents, the growing role of professional agents and sports lawyers has given athletes a keener eye for infractions of their rights, procedures for implementing those rights, and alternative remedies for redressing their grievances. Today's athletes have a better idea of their rights and are prepared to act on them regardless of the traditional etiquette against doing so on the eve of competition. They also know that the stakes of eligibility are much higher than they used to be.

In responding to these developments, arbitration has become a preferred means for resolving sports-related disputes. In the United States, this trend is in part the result of the Ted Stevens Olympic and Amateur Sports Act[85] – otherwise known as the Amateur Sports Act which endorses arbitration to resolve disputes in the sports arena. The law requires National Governing Bodies ('NGBs') for each sport to agree to submit all disputes within the scope of the Act to binding arbitration by the American Arbitration Association ('AAA'). The law also entitles Olympic, Pan American and Paralympic athletes, or other parties aggrieved by decisions of the United States Olympic Committee ('USOC'), to a review of their grievances by the AAA.[86] Under the USOC Constitution, NGB decisions are subject to arbitration by the AAA.

Beyond the United States, at the global level, many international sports federations ('Ifs') have entered into agreements with the CAS for binding arbitration of disputes between them and their constituents. In turn, IFs normally require their member organizations to provide for arbitration of their disputes with athletes. Athletes selected for the Olympics and other international competition must now sign a waiver form by which they agree to exclusive CAS jurisdiction over au disputes involving doping and other issues of eligibility.[87] In *Ragheeb v. IOC*,[88] the CAS confirmed that it

---

76 Bravin, *supra* note 74.

77 Michaelis, *supra* note 74 at 1C.

78 Id..

79 See, e.g., Luc Silance, Les Sports et le Droit 406-08, 417-18 (1998) (referring particularly to Belgian and French practice).

80 See James A.R. Nafziger, 'International Sports Law as a Process for Resolving Disputes', 45 *INT'L & Comp. L.Q.* (1996) pp. 130, 140-142.

81 See Tarasti, *supra* note 75.

82 See *infra* Parts II-III.

83 Michaelis, *supra* note 74.

84 Jere Longman, 'On the Olympics: Athletes Are Taking the Trials from the Arenas to the Courts, New York Times, August 23, 2000, at C23.

85 36 U.S.C.A. §§ 220501-220509 (West Supp. 2000) ('Ted Stevens Olympic and Amateur Sports Act').

86 36 U.S.C.A § 220529 (West Supp. 2000).

87 Olympic Charter 74 (2000).

88 The decision of *Ragheeb* v. *IOC* is a decision of the Court of Arbitration for Sport. This decision is unpublished and on file with CAS in Lausanne, Switzerland. *Ragheeb* v. *IOC*, CAS (August 30, 2000) (on file with CAS).

could review an issue of eligibility only on the basis of such an arbitration agreement or a specific accreditation of an athlete for competition by the IOC. Because of the emerging role of the CAS in resolving these kinds of disputes at the international level, one commentator has suggested that the Amateur Sports Act should be amended to substitute the International Council of Arbitration for Sport, which is the parent organization of CAS, in place of the AAA as the designated arbitral body to hear all disputes between athletes and the USOC or its designated NGBs.[89]

For all these reasons, international sports arbitration is a growth industry. Litigation, on the other hand, is number two and, therefore, has to try harder. But courts have found it hard to try harder. Courts of law are, first of all, very reluctant to review eligibility and other decisions by sports bodies involving access to competition. When they do undertake such review, the process is often time-consuming and risky.[90] Although that may also be true for arbitration, on balance, arbitration is less costly, more expeditious, and more flexible in responding to new circumstances. The 1998 Amendments to the Amateur Sports Act that bar athletes from litigating eligibility decisions within twenty-one days before major competition also encourage arbitration unless the newly created USOC ombudsman is successful in facilitating a resolution of the dispute.[91]

II. RECENT DEVELOPMENT: *LINDLAND V. U.S.A. WRESTLING*

Arbitration is not, however, without its problems. For one thing, any third-party settlement of grievances by athletes is apt to be controversial. After all, good sportsmanship is supposed to avoid squabbling. Disputes are supposed to be resolved on the playing field. But legal disputes are inevitable. When they do arise, any review process on the eve of major competition may affect team morale, compete for the attention of sports organizations at the expense of athletes, consume valuable training time for the competitors, and sap their energy.[92] Even so, the enthusiasm of Tammy Thomas, Lisa Raymond, Matt Lindland, Julie Smith and other claimants to pursue their rights to participate in international competition appeals to us more than the apathy of certain men's tennis and basketball players whom we might like to have seen in Sydney.

What, then, are the hurdles in the path of arbitration and how can they be cleared? In addressing this question, the dispute between Matt Lindland and the United States of America Wrestling Association ('U.S.A. Wrestling') is a good place to begin.

In one sense, the *Lindland* case is unusual because it does not involve the dominant theme in international sports arbitration of doping. The case does, however, raise a number of significant issues about the structure for resolving eligibility disputes and the role of arbitration in this structure. Lindland demonstrates what happens when function follows form in dispute resolution.

On June 24, 2000, in Bout #244 of the Greco-Roman Wrestling trials to determine the United States Olympic team, Keith Sieracki beat Matt Lindland 2-1 in a best-of-three series to gain a berth

---

[89] Edward E. Hollis III, Note, 'The U.S.A. Olympic Committee and the Suspension of Athletes: Reforming Grievance Procedures Under the Amateur Sports Act of 1978', 71 *Ind. L.J.* (1995) pp. 183, 200.

[90] See generally, James A.R. Nafziger, 'International Sports Law: A Replay of Characteristics and Trends', 86 *Am. J. Intl.* (1992) pp. 489, 508-510.

[91] The amended law provides as follows: (a) General. [...] In any lawsuit relating to the resolution of a dispute involving the opportunity of an amateur athlete to participate in the Olympic Games, the Paralympic Games, or the Pan-American Games, a court shall not grant injunctive relief against the corporation within 21 days before the beginning of such games if the corporation, after consultation with the chair of the Athletes' Advisory Council, has provided a sworn statement in writing executed by an officer of the corporation to such court that its constitution and bylaws cannot provide for the resolution of such dispute prior to the beginning of such games. (b) Ombudsman. (1)The ... ombudsman for athletes... shall – (A) provide independent advice to athletes at no cost about the applicable provisions of this chapter (citation omitted) and the constitution and bylaws of the corporation, national governing bodies, a paralympic sports organizations [Sic], international sports federations, the International Olympic Committee, the International Paralympic Committee, and the Pan-American Sports Organization, and with respect to the resolution of any dispute involving the opportunity of an amateur athlete to participate in the Olympic Games, the Paralympic Games, the Pan-American Games, world championship competition or other protected competition as defined in the constitution and bylaws of the corporation; (B) assist in mediating any such disputes. 36 U.S.C.A. §220509 (1994 & West Supp. 2000).

[92] See Michaelis, *supra* note 74.

on the team in the seventy-six kilogram (167.5-pound) class.[93] In accordance with U.S.A. Wrestling rules, the three mat officials included a referee, a judge, and a mat chairman. Lindland immediately protested the officiating of his loss, claiming that Sieracki had applied an illegal hold by using his legs and had also attempted to flee a hold in violation of the rules of both the international wrestling federation ('FILA') and U.S.A. Wrestling.[94] Lindland's protest complied with the Protest Procedures of U.S.A. Wrestling and special procedures for the 2000 Olympic trials. The Protest Committee, however, refused to overturn the decision against Lindland on the basis that it involved judgment calls by mat officials that were beyond the Committee's competence to review. For good reason, mat decisions are simply not subject to change on review. Lindland appealed the denial of his protest to U.S.A. Wrestling's Standing Greco-Roman Sport Committee. He argued before this body, in a telephonic bearing on July 13, 2000, that the mat officials had not simply misinterpreted U.S.A. Wrestling rules, but had misapplied them. For proof of his claim, he demanded that the Committee view a videotape of the match despite an organizational rule against the use of videotaped evidence.

Six days later, on July 19, 2000, the Standing Committee denied Lindland's appeal, four to one, largely on the basis of the discretion vested in mat officials to make or not make penalty calls. As a result, U.S.A. Wrestling added Sieracki's name to the roster of nominations to be submitted to the USOC for the 2000 Olympic team. Lindland then brought a demand for arbitration in Chicago of his grievance against U.S.A. Wrestling,[95] as he was entitled to do under the Amateur Sports Act.[96] Such proceedings are usually referred to as Article IX arbitrations, after Article IX of the USOC Constitution.[97] In accordance with the Amateur Sports Act, the winner of the disputed event, Keith Sieracki, was not a party to the arbitration between Lindland and U.S.A. Wrestling.

In the Chicago arbitration, Lindland argued that U.S.A. Wrestling had not provided procedures for the prompt and equitable resolution of his grievance, as the Amateur Sports Act requires.[98] This requirement formed the legal framework of the proceedings that followed. The gist of Lindland's arguments was that the Greco-Roman review committee had failed to follow U.S.A. Wrestling's own rules and had fashioned new ones to suit its interests, for example, by recusing four committee members who might have supported Lindland's claim. The arbitrator, Daniel Bums, agreed with Lindland and ordered a rematch between the two competitors. Sieracki participated in the rematch under protest. This time Lindland won 8-0. U.S.A. Wrestling, however, simply added Lindland to its Olympic eligibility list as an alternate, leaving Sieracki as its nominee to the USOC for the Olympic team. Lindland responded by seeking enforcement of the arbitral award in the federal District Court for the Northern District of Illinois. The court dismissed his action, without a written opinion, apparently for lack of federal jurisdiction.[99] Now, let us return to the arbitral award.

---

93 For a summary and chronology see Gary Mihoces, 'Grappling with a Decision Lindland Goes to Sydney, While Sieracki Stays Home', *USA Today*, September 14, 2000, at 1C.

94 The Official Rules of FILA (the Fédération Internationale des Luttes Associées) (1999) are the international rules of wrestling. These rules have largely been adopted by USA Wrestling with some modifications. Article 61 of the FILA Rules provides as follows: A. In Greco-Roman Wrestling it is forbidden to grasp the opponent below the hips or to squeeze him with the legs. All pushing pressing or 'lifting' by means of contact with the legs on any part of the body of the opponent is also strictly forbidden. In Greco-Roman wrestling unlike Free Style wrestling it is necessary to accompany the opponent to the ground. B. In Free Style wrestling, a scissor lock with the feet crossed is forbidden on the head, the neck or the body. Art. 57 of the FILA Rules provides as follows: 'Fleeing a hold occurs when the defending wrestler openly refuses contact in order to prevent his opponent from executing or initiating a hold.' Id. Art. 59 of the FILA Rules ('Illegal Holds') establishes several duties of the referee in the event of a prohibited act by a competitor. Id. Lindland claimed the referee failed to fulfill these duties.

95 *Lindland* v. *United States Wrestling Ass'n, Inc.*, Am. Arb. Ass'n No. 30-190-00443-00 (August 9, 2000) (Burns, Arb.).

96 U.S.C.A. § 220529 (West Supp. 2000).

97 This provision implements the provision in the Amateur Sports Act for arbitration of grievances against the USOC. U.S. Olympic Committee Const., Art. IX.

98 36 U.S.C.A. § 220522(a)(13) (West Supp. 2000) ('An amateur sports organization is eligible ... to continue to to be recognized, as a national governing body only if it ... provides procedures for the prompt and equitable resolution or grievances of its members.'). 36 U.S.C. § 220503(8) assigns the following purpose to the USOC and therefore, by delegation, to the NGBS: 'to provide swift resolution of conflicts and disputes involving amateur athletes, national governing bodies, and amateur sports organizations, and protect the opportunity of any amateur athlete, coach, trainer, manager, administrator, or official to participate in amateur athletic competition.'

99 See *Lindland* v. *United States Wrestling Ass'n, Inc.*, 230 F.3d 1036, 1038 (7th Cir. 2000).

After the Chicago award but prior to the rematch, Sieracki filed his own arbitration demand in Denver before A. Bruce Campbell, seeking confirmation of his status as the sole nominee in his weight class for the Greco-Roman wrestling team.[100] Lindland counterclaimed to the opposite effect. So, we have the prospect of a rematch of dispute resolution as well as wrestling. As we shall see, however, the prospect of repetitive dispute resolution by virtue of a second round of arbitration in Denver was fuzzy because some of the issues in Denver were materially different from those in the Chicago arbitration. The Denver arbitrator first determined the arbitration was proper and. allowed all evidence offered by the parties except the videotape of Bout #244. Sieracki won this second round of arbitration. After four conferences in which all parties in the overall dispute participated, Arbitrator Campbell determined that Sieracki was not bound by the Chicago Award because he had not been a party to it. He found no evidence that the mat officials in Bout #244 had misapplied the rules or otherwise abused their authority. He also found that U.S.A. Wrestling's procedural arrangements, including the review committee's refusal to hear the team coach's testimony or to view video tape of the match, had not prejudiced either wrestler, did not constitute an irregularity or impropriety, and did not justify setting aside the grievance process. The Denver Award concluded by ordering U.S.A. Wrestling to withdraw Lindland's name from the eligibility list for the team and to confirm Keith Sieracki as the sole nominee on the team roster to be submitted to the USOC.

Just a few hours after the Denver Award, however, the Seventh Circuit Court of Appeals reversed the lower court in its refusal to enforce the Chicago Award in Lindland's favor and issued a mandate to U.S.A. Wrestling to enforce the award by nominating Lindland to the USOC.[101] When Lindland sought to enforce this decision, however, the district court refused again on the basis that it lacked jurisdiction.[102] Lindland then obtained a writ of mandamus from the Circuit Court that ordered the lower court to enforce the Chicago Award.[103] At this point U.S.A. Wrestling and the USOC were faced with what appeared to be contradictory orders.

Since arbitration is not normally subject to issue and claim preclusion,[104] each of the wrestlers therefore was free to seek judicial confirmation of the arbitral award in his favor under § 9 of the Federal Arbitration Act.[105] Lindland, who was back in the federal courts for the second time, specifically requested a court order to compel the USOC to send his name to the IOC despite the USOC's argument that it could not do so because it had already sent Sieracki's name to the IOC. The Denver court, on the other hand, transferred the Sieracki action to the Chicago federal court, where the opposing federal actions were consolidated. (One might well ask what would have happened if the federal district court in Denver had not transferred the Sieracki action to the federal court in Chicago for consolidation of the two actions.)

After consolidation of the two actions, the Northern District of Illinois court, in the face of the mandamus order issued by the Seventh Circuit, directed the USOC to substitute Lindland for Sieracki as U.S.A. Wrestling's sole nominee to the USOC and denied Sieracki's petition to confirm the Denver Award in his favor. In compliance with the district court order, the USOC requested the IOC to replace Sieracki with Lindland as a member of the Olympic team. It also appealed the court ruling that required it to take this action. U.S.A. Wrestling appealed each of the mandated district court decisions to the Seventh Circuit, which upheld both orders.[106] In the end, less than two weeks before the beginning of the Olympic Games, United States Supreme Court justice Stevens (also from Chicago, incidentally) denied a request by the USOC for a stay of the Seventh Circuit's mandamus order.[107]

---

[100] *Sieracki* v. *United States Wrestling Ass'n, Inc*., Am. Arb. Assn No. 30-190B00483-00 (August 24, 2000) (Campbell, Arb.). Since this second arbitration did not fall within the prescribed process for reviewing a grievance under the Amateur Sports Act, it had the rather odd posture of a friendly action between the like-minded Sieracki and USA Wrestling as a means to confirm the latter's decision in Sieracki's favor, to challenge the fairness of the Chicago arbitration, and to question whether the notice and circumstances of the rematch were fair. See id.

[101] Lindland, 230 F.3d at 1040.

[102] *Lindland* v. United *States Wrestling Ass'n., Inc.,* 227 F.3d 1000 (7th Cir. 2000).

[103] Id.

[104] *Brotherhood of Maint. Of Way Employees* v. *Burlington N R.R*., 24 F.3d 937, 939-41 (7th Cir. 1994).

[105] 9 U.S.C. § 9 (1994).

[106] *Lindland* v. *United States Wrestling Ass'n, Inc*., 227 F.3d 1000 (7th Cir. 2000).

[107] See Jess Bravin, 'High Court Ensures Wrestler's Trip to Olympics', *Wall Street J*., September 7, 2000, at B19 (noting that justice Stevens denied the request for review without comment).

From the record, it appears that the case was very ably, indeed admirably argued by counsel for the parties. In view of the time constraints, the advocacy was exemplary. And reasonable minds can certainly differ on the outcome of the case. I personally have no quarrel with it. But I do want to question several of its legal premises. Fundamentally, the Chicago Award was based on a determination that U.S.A. Wrestling's review of Lindland's protest was procedurally defective. The arbitrator found that the organization's rules were inadequate to deal with the issues that arose in the case concerning possible conflict of interest, recomposition of the review committee, and restrictions on testimony.[108] The materiality of these defects is questionable,[109] as was the advisability of ordering a rematch rather than a recomposition and reconvention of the Protest Committee.[110] Simple mathematics reveals that if Lindland's corner coach in Bout #244 had recused himself, as would surely be appropriate, and if all of the remaining three committee members who recused themselves had instead voted in Lindland's favor, the result at most would have been a tie, which would have been insufficient to reverse the original decision in favor of Sieracki.[111]

Even so, the bases for review within U.S.A. Wrestling, as the process developed, are murky. What is clear is that the by-laws and rules of U.S.A. Wrestling did not provide any real guidance on appropriate procedures for reviewing a protest of this sort.[112] As a result, simply reconvening the Protest Committee might not have overcome apprehensions about the fairness of the administrative process.

U.S.A. Wrestling's refusal to entertain videotaped evidence except for during-match viewing by mat officials and for viewing flagrant misconduct and allegations of brutality is also questionable. The rule against videotaped evidence is designed to shield judgment calls from endless challenge and dispute. The rule thus protects the integrity of officiating and avoids substituting arbitrators for referees. Nevertheless, excluding videotaped evidence clearly conflicts with the rules of FILA, the international wrestling federation.[113] Moreover, the governing law of the Amateur Sports Act seems to contemplate a freer evidentiary environment by stating that '[t]he parties may offer any evidence

---

108 See *Lindland* v. *United States Wrestling Ass'n, Inc.*, Am. Arb. Ass'n No. 30-190-00443-00 (August 9, 2000) (Burns, Arb.).

109 See *Sieracki* v. *United States Wrestling Ass'n, Inc.*, Am Arb. Ass'n No. 30-190-00483-00 (August 24, 2000) (Campbell, Arb.).

110 In the Chicago arbitration, the justification in the " Conclusion and Award" follows: Changed situations of Committee participants, the question of the President of USA will attend and vote [sic], the exigencies of the present circumstances of final team selection, the fact that a crucial witness's testimony was chilled at the first hearing, the potential atmosphere of a reconvened full Committee, and the very lack of guidance in USA Wrestling by-laws and rules, when grouped together, are convincing that Lindland cannot be put back to the same position he was on July 12, and cannot receive the prompt and equitable resolution of his grievance that he has been promised. For example, one excluded member of the Committee was a fellow wrestler with a grievance *pending* at that time. That grievance has now been finally resolved. Another mistake made in fashioning the July 13 Committee, [sic] was the erroneous belief that some members of the Greco-Roman Sports Committee had also *voted* on that Protest Committee, and they were excluded for that reason. In fact, only one member had actually *voted* at the Protest Committee and that was the president of the USA Wrestling, who testified he was an *ad hoc* member of the Committee and may have attended one Committee meeting over the past several years. As significant is the lack of guidance and advance notice on these issues to Lindland, and Committee members, as he attempted to process his protest.

111 See *Sieracki,* Am. Arb, Ass'n No. 30-190-00483-00, at. 1 (f).

112 The Chicago award found: 'USA Wrestling has not provided any written rules, regulations, bylaws, or precedential authority justifying its actions and decisions regarding: 1) the determination of the number and identities of the Greco-Roman Sports Committee when hearing appeals such as Lindland's, 2) grounds for excluding sitting Committee members from participating and deliberating in appeals such as Lindland's; 3) limitations on the nature and extent of the testimony of witnesses; 4) who is permitted to appear and participate in the hearing.' *Lindland,* Am Arb. Ass'n No. 30-190-00483-00, at Findings of Fact 9.

113 In the event of a protest, Art. 63 of the Official Rules of FILA clearly encourages the use of videotape. See *supra* note 94. To the contrary, one of the few modifications of the FILA rules by USA Wrestling provides as follows: "Under no circumstances shall the use of video tapes or films of a bout be considered or shown in the evaluation of any protest. Elements of the FILA Protest procedures may be applied as determined by the protest committee. U.S.A. Modifications, Article 63, U.S.A. Wrestling Protest Procedures (1999). The Denver Award wisely sidestepped the issue of whether USA Wrestling's rules are Aless or more wise than those of FILA. *Sieracki,* Am. Arb. Ass'n No. 30-190-00483-00, at II-6.

they desire and shall produce any additional evidence the arbitrators believe is necessary to an understanding and determination of the dispute. The arbitrators shall be the sole judges of the relevance and materiality of the evidence offered.'[114]

Reasonable minds may, of course, differ on the advisability of allowing videotaped evidence. What is hard to dispute, however, is the complexity of the legal process which extended over a period of two and-one-half months and involved thirteen stages of dispute resolution.[115] Surely that was an unlucky thirteen, not just for Sieracki, but for the reputation of dispute resolution related to international sports competition. In the cogent words of Matt Lindland's wife, '[t]hey're probably going to have to change the rules after this one.'[116]

III. THE SEVENTH CIRCUIT OPINIONS

The formal process for resolving the *Lindland* dispute merits consideration. I would argue that, although the selection of Lindland to the Olympic team was a reasonable outcome of the dispute, the premises of the Seventh Circuit's orders to that effect are shaky. Indeed, *Lindland* is a good example of the difficulty that federal courts have had in defining their role in disputes involving the eligibility of athletes for international competition.[117]

At the heart of the Seventh Circuit's opinions, written by Judge Frank Easterbrook, is a conclusion that the Chicago Award was valid while the Denver Award was invalid.[118] The rationale was that because the Chicago Award had been upheld by a court of law, any later award, namely the one in Denver, could not purport to countermand it. Once the court had ordered U.S.A. Wrestling and the USOC to substitute Lindland for Sieracki on the Olympic team, that was it. Although the Seventh Circuit's confirmation of the Chicago Award is certainly reasonable, its negative conclusion about the Denver Award is much less compelling. While acknowledging the lack of issue and claim preclusion in arbitration, the court's opinion enlists two principal arguments against the Denver Award, concluding therefore that it was 'doubly flawed.'[119] First, Judge Easterbrook concluded that the Denver Award was, in his words, *ultra vires* because, unlike the Chicago Award, it was not conceived as an appeal of a USOC or NGB decision under the Amateur Sports Act. But he failed to appreciate that, unlike the Chicago arbitration, which was premised in the Amateur Sports Act, the Denver arbitration was brought under the USOC's Grievance Procedures for Code of Conduct and Team Selection 2000 Olympic Games.

Second, Judge Easterbrook construed Rule 48 of the Commercial Arbitration Rules of the American Arbitration Association to bar the Denver Award as a redetermination of the merits of a claim already decided.[120] But Rule 48 merely bars a redetermination of the merits in a *modification of a single award.* What makes the double arbitration in *Lindland* so interesting is that the two awards involved different parties and, to an extent, different issues. Not only did the Circuit Court minimize these differences, but it took Denver Arbitrator Campbell to task for deciding, in the courts words, to 'ignore' Rule 48 'utterly'[121] and thereby to flout the judicial confirmation of the Chicago Award. But Campbell had reason to ignore Rule 48 because it simply did not apply.

Judge Easterbrook's opinion emphasized that the winner of a contested event is normally not a party to an Article IX proceeding. That is certainly true and appropriate under the law. But there were four material differences between the Chicago and Denver arbitrations. First, the Denver claimant, Sieracki had been unable to appear formally in the Chicago arbitration. Although that did not in any way call into question the Chicago Award, by the same token it enabled him to demand relief in Denver from the mandatory rematch ordered by the Chicago Award. Judge Easterbrook seems to have been bothered by Sieracki's timing of this demand prior to the event itself. But what was Sieracki supposed to do to vindicate his position after the award in the Chicago arbitration to which he was

---

114 36 U.S.C.A. § 220529(5) (West Supp. 2000).

115 See *Lindland* v. *United States Wresthng Ass'n.*, 230 F.3d 1036, 1037-38 (7th Cir. 2000) (noting the several stages of litigation); Michaelis, *supra* note 74, at 1 C.

116 Michaelis, *supra* note 74, at 1 C.

117 *See* Nafziger, *supra* note 80, at 134-142 (discussing the *Reynolds and Harding* cases).

118 *Lindland* v. *United States Wrestling Ass'n*, Inc., 227 F-3d 1000, 1005 (7th Cir. 2000).

119 Id. at 1003.

120 Id. at 1004.

121 Id.

not a party? Perhaps he should have waited a few days until he had lost the rematch before pursuing a judicial remedy. But, under the time constraints imposed by the Amateur Sports Act, it was probably wise for him to get off the mat and get moving again. In any event, he had standing under the 2000 Protest Rules to demand arbitration. Surely, the Denver arbitrator was acting properly in hearing the demand of an athlete whose original selection to the team was in jeopardy.

Although many Article IX disputes involving allegations against an athlete impact only indirectly on other identifiable competitors, an either-or eligibility issue of the sort at issue in *Lindland* is materially different. Article IX's exclusion of the disputed winner of an event in an arbitration of that dispute presents a serious issue. It is simply unfair to ignore the winner's interests on the basis that arbitration of a grievance under the Amateur Sports Act excludes the winner as a party. In the Denver arbitration, on the other hand, both of the contesting wrestlers, as well as U.S.A. Wrestling, made appearances.

Second, the Denver arbitration, although it considered Lindland's protest *de novo,* also heard new issues related to the rematch that occurred while the Denver arbitration was pending. It simply is not correct to conclude, as the Seventh Circuit opinion does, that '[t]he whole point of the Campbell proceeding [Denver arbitration] was to redecide issues.'[122] That may have been part of the point but by no means the whole point. Judge Easterbrook's opinion itself acknowledges that Sieracki initiated his arbitration, 'protesting the result of the rematch.'[123] Moreover, unlike the issues raised by Lindland in the Chicago arbitration, Sieracki's demand in Denver sought a determination that he should be the sole nominee to the Greco-Roman Olympic team, to the exclusion of Lindland.

Third, it is reasonable to view the Denver arbitration as a fresh proceeding, unaffected in part by the Seventh Circuit order that confirmed the Chicago Award. After all, the rematch had converted Sieracki, the original winner, into a loser. Surely, Sieracki, the 'new' loser, so to speak, should have been entitled to the same right to demand the same kind of arbitration as Lindland, the 'old' loser, so to speak, had enjoyed. Thus, Sieracki could claim the arbitrability of his grievance under either the Code of Conduct and Team Selection or, arguably, under a theory that the results of the rematch could be contested as a fresh action and hence that the second arbitration in Denver was proper under the same provision of the Amateur Sports Act which Lindland had legitimately invoked.

Even if one does not accept the recharacterization of the Denver arbitration as a fresh action, perhaps because Sieracki had not exhausted the internal protest and grievance procedures required by law,[124] it nevertheless seems clear that the complex of dispute resolution was more of a muddle than the Seventh Circuit seems to have appreciated. For instance, the opinions failed to appreciate the very real dilemma faced by U.S.A. Wrestling and the USOC in the face of two inconsistent awards. Instead, one of judge Easterbrook's opinions intimates that NGB's like U.S.A. Wrestling are 'scofflaws,'[125] chastises the USOC for insisting that 'it is entitled to do as it pleases – defying injunctions to its heart's content,'[126] and surmises a conspiracy between U.S.A. Wrestling and the USOC in contempt of court.[127] These observations may or may not be correct, but that kind of fighting language by an appeals court, without adequate proof, is disconcerting.

That said, one of the Circuit Court opinions does hint at some productive new directions for resolving these kinds of disputes. In Judge Easterbrook's words, conflicting instructions may not be an 'irremediable evil. Injunctions create property rights, which may be altered by private agreements. Bargaining among Sieracki, Lindland and U.S.A. Wrestling could lead to a settlement that would relieve U.S.A Wrestling of any incompatible obligations.'[128] Judge Easterbrook caps this observation with a challenge: 'Definitive resolution of the right way to handle conflicting awards, after one has been confirmed, may await another day.'[129]

---

122 Id.

123 Id. at 1003.

124 See 36 U.S.C.A. § 220529 (West Supp. 2000); *Dolan* v. *U.S. Equestrian Team. Inc.*, 608 A.2d (N.J. Super. Ct. App. Div. 1992). Sieracki, on the other hand, was seeking to vindicate his initial victory under severe time constraints.

125 *Lindland* v. *United States Wrestling Ass'n, Inc.*, 227 F.3d 1000, 1008 (7th Cir. 2000).

126 Id. at 1007.

127 Id. at 1006.

128 Id. at 1003.

129 Id.

I am quite sure that that day has not yet arrived. I do want to ask, however, what can be done, specifically, to improve the process. Let me say again that I think both the Chicago and Denver arbitral awards in *Lindland* were creditable. Neither was spoiled by any of the defects of corruption, fraud or evident partiality for which the Arbitration Act allows an award to be set aside.[130] Even if one were to agree that a first award ordinarily should bar a second award, the two awards in this case differed substantially from each other.[131] Consequently, judge Easterbrook's misunderstanding of the express reach of the first award,[132] his caustic appraisal of the second award, and his injudicious name-calling were simply off the mat. The problem lay not in the arbitration itself but in the structure of dispute resolution that encourages proliferation and, worse yet, redundancy of proceedings.

IV. IMPROVING THE STRUCTURE OF DISPUTE RESOLUTION

Let me offer several suggestions to improve the structure. First, in reviewing arbitrations under federal law, the courts should proceed cautiously. Judicial relief from the decisions of sports bodies should be reserved for cases where due process violations are patent, and the violations dispositive, as they were not in *Lindland.* The financial stakes for athletes, absent issues of labor law,[133] do not alone provide a compelling basis for judicial intervention. To quote another Seventh Circuit judge, Richard Posner: '[T]here can be few less suitable bodies than the federal courts for determining the eligibility, or the procedure for determining the eligibility, of athletes ...'[134] The *Harding* court in Oregon also had it right, I think, in cautioning that:

> Intervention [by the courts] is appropriate only in the most extraordinary circumstances, where [a national governing body] has clearly breached its own rules, that breach will imminently result in *serious* and irreparable harm to the plaintiff, and the plaintiff bas exhausted all internal remedies. Even then, injunctive relief is limited to correcting the breach of the rules. The court should not intervene in the merits of the underlying dispute.[135]

Second, repetitious proceedings and the complexity they entail, particularly in eligibility cases, could be avoided by amending the Amateur Sports Act and the USOC Constitution to enable an individual winner of a disputed competition to participate in a single arbitration alongside the individual claimant, NGB and, as appropriate, the USOC. It is simply unfair to presume that a contested winner's interests are fully represented by an NGB.[136] A unified arbitration would then bar subsequent arbitration. In team sports, the problem of standing to appear is considerably more complicated. Even so, as a starter, team members of a class potentially affected by an eligibility decision might simply elect one of their number to represent their common interests.

Third, the Amateur Sports Act should be interpreted or, if necessary, amended to avoid arbitration of a referee's decision so long as a claimant has had the benefit of a full and fair review by the

---

130 See 9 U.S.C.A. § 10(a) (supp. V 1999).

131 See *supra* notes 122-123 and accompanying text.

132 Despite Judge Easterbook's argument that the Denver Award purported to rescind the Chicago Awards order to place Lindland on the Olympic team not only does the Denver Award contain no such attempted rescission, but the Chicago Award, in the first instance, did not actually order Lindland's selection to the USA Olympic team. See *Lindland* v. *United States Wrestling Ass'n, Inc.*, Ani. Arb. Ass'n No. 30-190-00443-00 (August 9, 2000) (Burns, Arb.)

133 Compare the following timely observation: 'U.S. courts and international federations must begin viewing amateur athletics in a more employment-related light, as substantial sums of money are at stake when suspensions of Olympic athletes occur. In the U.S.A., amateur athletes have traditionally not been viewed as employees due to the strict NCAA regulations prohibiting college athletes from receiving financial rewards for their talents.' Mary K. Fitzgerald, 'The Court of Arbitration for Sport; Dealing with Doping and Due Process during the Olympics', 7 *Sports Law. J.* (2000) pp. 213, 236.

134 *Michels* v. *United States Olympic Comm.*, 741 F.2d 155,159 (7th Cir. 1984).

135 *Harding* v. *United States Figure Skating Ass'n*, 851 F. Supp. 1476,1479 (D. Or. 1994)

136 U.S. Olympic Comm. Const., Art. IX, § 2 (providing that a demand or arbitration must designate Asuch USOC member, normally an NGB, as an adverse party). See *also Lindland* v. *United States Wrestling Ass'n, Inc.*, 230 F.3d 1036, 1039 (7th Cir. 2000). As Judge Easterbrook's opinion points out, this is in keeping with the arrangement in labor arbitration that an employee who is discharged from employment may arbitrate a grievance with his employer but need not designate as an additional party a replacement who may be dischargeable by an award in favor of the grievant.

appropriate NCB, unless that body would itself permit such a review.[137] In *Lindland,* the Chicago Award steered clear of scrutinizing judgment calls. The Denver Award, on the other hand, seemed to comment fairly directly on the judgment of the mat officials. A procedural rule barring review of such judgment calls in all but the most egregious cases would help avoid understandable suspicions by the media and the public that arbitrators can make second caus. In the Lindland-Sieracki match, there were three mat officials, all of whom appear to have satisfied U.S.A. Wrestling's requirement that they understood the rules and avoided wrongful, dishonest, intentionally improper, or bad faith conduct.[138] Even if they failed to take account of illegal wrestling maneuvers in violation of the rules of the game, such bad judgment calls or inaction should not be subject to arbitration or litigation in the absence of evidence that they had simply failed to understand the rules or that they abused their authority.

Fourth, we should make it clear that the merits not only of judgment calls but of the rules of the game themselves are generally beyond the competence of arbitration or litigation. After all, technical rules are constantly under review and reform by the IOC, IFs and NGBs themselves. One commentator has therefore proposed that the Amateur Sports Act be amended to provide that the jurisdiction of courts under the Act should be limited to determinations of whether responsible sports organizations have complied with their own rules of eligibility, presumably within an acceptable margin of discretion. This proposal would bar courts from evaluating the merits of a dispute, confining their review to an evaluation of procedural due process.[139]

In drawing a line between nonreviewable game rules and reviewable rules, procedures and practices, two cases of the CAS are instructive. The first arose out of an incident during the 1996 Atlanta Games.[140] In reviewing a referee's disqualification of an athlete, known as 'Boxer M, ' for landing a below-the-belt punch on his opponent, the CAS applied international custom, particularly from the United States, France, and Switzerland. The CAS concluded from this general practice that a technical decision, standard or rule – in other words, a nonreviewable game rule – is shielded from arbitral or judicial scrutiny unless the rule or its application by sports officials is arbitrary, illegal, or the product of a wrong or malicious intent against an athlete.[141] In such cases, the rule or its application is reviewable. Sanctions appearing to be excessive or unfair on their face are also reviewable. The rationale for the *Boxer M* decision was two-fold: that IFs have the responsibility to enforce rules, and referees or ring judges are in a better position than arbitrators to decide technical matters.[142]

In the second CAS case, the AOC Advisory Opinion, the CAS considered the reviewability of a decision by the international swimming federation ('FINA'), less than a year before the 2000 Olympic Games, to approve the use of full-body ('long john') swimsuits.[143] These highly elastic suits, which were first marketed by Speedo, attempted to stimulate natural sharkskin. The suits were designed to increase a swimmer's speed and endurance, to reduce drag, and possibly to enhance the buoyancy of the swimmer. The FINA Bureau, after lengthy discussion, ruled that 'the use of these swimsuits does not constitute a violation of the FINA Rules.'[144] In response to this ruling, the Australian Olympic Committee ('AOC'), nervous about possible claims of unfairness at the Sydney Games, asked the CAS for an advisory opinion under its Rule 60. The AOC inquired whether the FINA ruling had complied with FINA's own rules and whether, m any event, use of the suits would raise contestable issues of fairness. In a thorough and thoughtful opinion, the CAS properly advised that FINA had reached its decision in compliance with its own rules and that its ruling which was

---

137 Longman, *supra* note 84, at D8 ('There is no quicker way to kill spectator interest than to have a game played and the outcome decided a month later by lawyers').

138 *Sieracki* v. *United States Wresting Ass'n, Inc.*, Am. Arb. Ass'n No. 30-190-0m83-00, II-1, 2, (August 24, 2000) (Campbell Arb.).

139 Hollis, *supra* note 89.

140 Reeb, *supra* note 75, at 413 (*M.* v. *Ass'n Internationale de Boxe Amateur*) (CAS Ad Hoc Division, Atlanta 1996).

141 Id.

142 Id.

143 Advisory Opinion Delivered by the Ct. of Arbitration for Sport at the request of the Australian Olympic Committee, TAS 2000/C/267 ACO (Richard M. McLaren, Sole Arbitrator) (on file with author).

144 Id. at 12.

tantamount to approval of bodysuits, did not raise any reviewable issues of unfair procedure, bad faith, conflict with general principles of law, or unreasonableness.[145]

Fifth, NGBs and other sports associations, under the supervision of IFs, should draft more explicit and uniform rules of eligibility and remedies for relief of legitimate grievances by athletes. Sheer chaos reigns today, and that is grossly unfair to athletes. For example, NGBs should clarify the precise weight that they will give to career records and recent international performance in determining eligibility when team tryouts alone are not determinative. Such clarification would have avoided the arbitration to determine the composition of the U.S. Women's softball team in Sydney and another arbitration involving the U.S. women's cycling team.[146] The demand by Tammy Thomas, winner of the 500-meter women's trial for the 2000 Olympics, against Christine Witty, whom the United States cycling federation selected on the basis of her superior two-year performance profile, was a variation on the *Lindland* case. Although an arbitrator ordered a ride-off to settle the controversy, much like the *Lindland* wrestling rematch, Witty, unlike Sieracki, simply refused to show up and promptly filed her own arbitration action.

Let me underscore the need, for reasons of fairness, to harmonize rules and remedies to make them as uniform and predictable as possible, across the range of sports. For example, serious questions of equity and due process arise whenever a track-and-field athlete is barred for life for ingesting a substance that is permitted (or was permitted) in baseball. Similarly, the Amateur Sports Act should make it clear that ad hoc measures, such as rematches, should be only a last resort when reconstitution of a defective eligibility review process would be grossly unfair or impossible.

V. OBLIGATIONS OF ATHLETES

Finally, my most far-reaching suggestion for reform is that arbitral awards should take account of obligations or duties as well as rights of athletes. We often forget that the framework for protection of human rights includes obligations or duties as well. It is a trade-off. Rights arise out of reciprocal relations within a community. They are confirmed by social contract. Article 29 of the Universal Declaration of Human Rights establishes that '[e]veryone has duties to the community in which alone the free and full development of his personality is possible.'[147] Similarly, the African Charter on Human and Peoples' Rights acknowledges obligations and duties of individuals toward society,[148] and the American Declaration of the Rights and Duties of Man establishes ten specific duties.[149]

To be sure, this authority only confirms the reciprocal nature, in very general terms, of the social contract putting human rights into play. None of the human rights instruments comes close to identifying specific duties of athletes or to providing any specific legal basis for imposing duties on them. Still, the general authority provides a normative foundation for more specific requirements. The Olympic Charter, for example, establishes that '[t]he practice of sport is a human right.'[150] Several decisions of the CAS have elaborated on the obligation of athletes to serve the community interest in ensuring fairness and a level playing field for all. For example, in several doping cases, the CAS established a duty of athletes to disclose information coming to their attention about doping to the detriment of competition.[151]

Although the ideal of athletes as role models is often romanticized and exaggerated, athletes unquestionably influence young people.[152] Therefore, in reviewing claims, arbitrators should con-

---

[145] Id. at 19-21. But see Janwillem Soek, 'You Don't Win Silver – You Miss the Gold', *Int'l Sports L.J.* (September 2000) at p. 15 (criticizing the advisory opinion for assuming the existence of a dispute between the ACC and FINA and thereby failing to resolve the issue of fairness of the controversial bodysuits).

[146] Bravin, *supra* note 74, at A 1.

[147] Art. 29, Universal Declaration of Human Rights, G.A. Res. 217A, U.N. GAOR, 3rd Sess. Pt. 1, Resolutions, at 71, U.N. Doc. A/810 (1948); see Keba Mbaye, 'Sport and Human Rights', *Olympic Rev.*, December 1998-January 1999, at 8-12.

[148] African Charter on Human and People's Rights, O.A.U. Doc. CAB/LEG/67/3 Rev. 5, Arts. 27-29 (1981).

[149] American Declaration of the Rights and Duties of Man, O.A.S. Res. XXX, O.A.S. Off. Rec. OEA/Ser. L/V/1.4, Arts. 29-38 (1965).

[150] Olympic Charter, Fundamental Principle 8 (2000).

[151] Reeb, *supra* note 75, at 142, 143, 158.

[152] See, e.g., René Lefort and Jean Harvey, 'What's in a Garne?', *The Unesco Courier*, April 1999, at 18.

sider the special obligations or duties that athletes owe to society as well as their rights. In reviewing disputes involving the status of athletes, the issue ought to be what is in the best public interest, not just what is in the best interest of particular sports.[153] In that light, it is difficult to justify the outcome of the *Sprewell* arbitration. Latrell Sprewell's physical, indeed nearly homicidal, assault on Head Coach Peter Carlesimo and the Golden State Warriors' team trainer, followed by his angry return from the locker room to reiterate his threats and repeat his assaults, surely warranted the most severe penalty. Accordingly, the National Basketball Association ('NBA'), in consultation with the Warriors, imposed a one-year, 82-game suspension from NBA play without pay – the most severe sanction that the NBA had ever imposed on a player. The Warriors also terminated the remaining years in Sprewell's Uniform Player Contract with the Golden State Warriors.[154]

However, the arbitrator hearing Sprewell's demand for relief mitigated the suspension to the remaining 68 games of the season and reinstated Sprewell's contract with the Warriors.[155] The Grievance Arbitrator's generous treatment of Latrell Sprewell unfortunately minimized the social consequences of his decision. In all fairness, the Grievance Arbitrator was fundamentally concerned about the issue of due process insofar as there had been no precedent for the severe penalty of a one-year suspension and termination of Sprewell's guaranteed contract. Perhaps, though, precedent, like consistency, can be a hobgoblin. Perhaps serious physical assault should be treated the same in the sports arena and sports arbitration as on the streets.

By the same token, sports organizations have ethical obligations to society, too. This expectation underlies an arbitral decision that upheld the most severe penalty ever imposed by the NBA.[156] The Minnesota Timberwolves had received this sanction for secretly conspiring with an athlete to avoid the NBA's salary cap, a requirement that is further elaborated in the league's collective bargaining agreement with the players' association. Ethical issues of this sort are particularly serious when, as in this case, an athlete and a sports association conspire to violate fundamental organizational rules.

Although sports and athletes are special, their special status means a higher standard of conduct. In the words of one observer, 'players are highly visible in the community, and that carries a public obligation.'[157] Sport is also highly visible in the community. As we arbitrate rights and perhaps take account of obligations within the international sports arena, the public interest should be paramount. Surely that is an appropriate world view for arbitrating sports disputes in the early twenty-first century.

---

153 See Paul C. Weiler and Gary R. Roberts, *Sports and the Law: Text, Cases, Problems* 86 (#3) (2nd edn. 1998).

154 See 'Latrell Sprewell Reinstatement Ruling', in Walter T. Champion, jr., *Fundamentals of Sports Law* 442 (Cum. Supp. 1999).

155 Sprewell later brought action in the federal district court against the NBA and the Golden State Warriors claiming thirty million dollars in damages on the basis that the arbitral award against him was racially discriminatory. See *Sprewell* v. *Golden State Warriors*, C98-2053-VRW, 1999 WL 179682 (N.D. Ca. March 26, 1999). Sprewell's action and a revised version of it were both dismissed as meritless suits in 1998 and 1999, respectively. On review, the Ninth Circuit Court of Appeals upheld the lower court. *Sprewell* v. *Golden St. Warriors*, 231 F.3d 520 (9th Cir. 2000).

156 See David DuPree and Vicki Michaelis, 'Smith Cap Ruling Upheld', *USA Today*, November 10, 2000, at 1C (summarizing the arbitrator's approval of a penalty that denied the Timberwolves first-round draft picks during the next five NBA drafts and fined them USD 3.5 million).

157 John Gibeaut, 'When Pros Turn Cons', *ABA J.*, July 2000, at 108.

CHAPTER 9
THE INTERNATIONAL CHAMBER OF COMMERCE (ICC)

9.1 INTRODUCTORY

As previously mentioned, sport is now a global business and, as such, many sports-related disputes are international in nature and scope. For almost eighty years, international business disputes of various kinds have been successfully referred to arbitration by the International Chamber of Commerce (ICC), based in Paris. The ICC International Court of Arbitration has gained a good reputation amongst business people. But, as disputes over the years have become more complex and, in turn, arbitration has become more technical, time-consuming and costly, other forms of dispute resolution have grown up and been developed by other organisations and also by the ICC.

In fact, since 1976, the ICC has operated an International Centre for Expertise, which appoints experts to issue non-binding reports on issues of a primarily technical nature, in order to help parties resolve related disputes amicably. Another form of 'expert determination'.

9.2 ICC MEDIATION SERVICE

9.2.1 **Background**

As part of this drive to offer new forms of dispute resolution, the ICC introduced on 1 January, 1988, new rules on conciliation – the so-called ICC Rules of Optional Conciliation. These Rules were replaced with new so-called ICC ADR Rules on 1 July 2001. In effect, they are Mediation Rules and they are reproduced in Appendix XVI.

Before commenting on them, it is interesting to note, *en passant*, that, so far as the ICC is concerned, the idea of conciliation to settle commercial disputes is not that new. In fact, the very first dispute successfully resolved by the ICC, following the establishment of its Arbitration service in 1923, was settled by conciliation. The dispute, between French and Belgian parties concerning the quality of a consignment of walnut wood, was settled after an hour's discussion!

9.2.2 **ICC Mediation Rules**

The purpose of the ICC ADR Rules (ICC Mediation Rules) is set forth in the Preamble to them as follows:

> 'Amicable settlement is a desirable solution for business disputes and differences. It can occur before or during the litigation or arbitration of a dispute and can often be facilitated through the aid of a third party (the "Neutral") acting in accordance with simple rules. The parties can agree to submit to such rules in their underlying contract or at any other time.

The ICC sets out these amicable dispute resolution rules, entitled the ICC ADR Rules (the "Rules"), which permit the parties to agree upon whatever settlement technique they believe to be appropriate to help them settle their dispute. In the absence of an agreement of the parties on a settlement technique, mediation shall be the settlement technique used under the Rules.'

The ICC Mediation Rules are the product of extensive discussions between the ICC and dispute resolution experts and representatives of the business community from 75 countries around the world. Their aim is to offer an alternative method of resolving disputes amicably in the best way to suit the particular needs of the parties in dispute.

A distinctive feature of these Rules is the freedom offered to the parties to follow the dispute resolution mechanism most conducive to reaching a settlement in a given case. As will be seen, in the absence of a specific agreement to the contrary, the parties are taken to have opted for Mediation (Art. 5.2).

Under Article 5.3 of the Rules, the Mediator (the 'Neutral') is free to conduct the dispute settlement process 'as the Neutral sees fit', but must be 'guided by the principles of fairness and impartiality and by the wishes of the parties'. And each party is required to 'co-operate in good faith with the Neutral' (Art. 5.5).

Article 3 of the Rules deals with the selection of the Mediator, who is required to provide the ICC with a CV and a 'statement of independence' (Art. 3.2).

Likewise, the Mediation, including its outcome, is 'private and confidential' (Art. 7.1) and conducted on a 'without prejudice' basis (Art. 7.2). This latter article provides as follows:

'Unless required to do so by applicable law and in the absence of any agreement of the parties to the contrary, a party shall not in any manner produce as evidence in any judicial, arbitration or similar proceedings:

a) any documents, statements or communications which are submitted by another party or by the Neutral in the ADR proceedings, unless they can be obtained independently by the party seeking to produce them in the judicial, arbitration or similar proceedings;
b) any views expressed or suggestions made by any party within the ADR proceedings with regard to the possible settlement of the dispute;
c) any admissions made by another party within the ADR proceedings;
d) any views or proposals put forward by the Neutral; or
e) the fact that any party had indicated within the ADR proceedings that it was ready to accept a proposal for a settlement.'

Furthermore, the Mediator must act impartially and, generally speaking, may not testify in '... any judicial, arbitration or similar proceedings concerning any aspect of the ADR proceedings' (Art. 7.4).The Mediation is started by a written Request under Article 2.A.1, together with the payment of a 'non-refundable registration fee' pursuant to Article 4.1 of USD 1,500; and the parties are free to terminate the Mediation at any time after it has commenced, without being required to give any reason, and in the other circumstances specified in Article 6.1.

Any settlement reached as a result of the Mediation is not binding on the parties unless and until it is incorporated into a 'settlement agreement' and signed by them (Art. 6.1.a).

As is usual nowadays, the Rules contain a 'Disclaimer' in Article 7.5 in the following terms: 'Neither the Neutral, nor the ICC and its employees, nor the ICC National Committees shall be liable to any person for any act or omission in connection with the ... proceedings.'

Of course, the extent to which, legally speaking, such a denial of liability will be valid and enforceable will depend upon the circumstances of each particular case and the applicable law.

As is also usual, the costs of the Mediation are shared equally by the parties, except as may be provided otherwise in any settlement agreement, and the parties are responsible for their own expenses (Arts. 4.5 and 4.6). A Schedule of the Costs is contained in the Appendix to the Rules.

9.2.3 Advantages of ICC Mediation Rules

In summary, as will be seen, the ICC Mediation Rules are:

- simple and concise (there are only seven articles);
- flexible and user friendly (no procedural restraints are placed on either the Mediator or the parties);
- require full confidentiality from every person involved in the Mediation in whatever capacity;
- time effective (the Mediator can set time limits for the parties to present their arguments); and
- cost effective (the costs are substantially lower than an ICC Arbitration and shall not, in any event, exceed USD 10,000 (Appendix B)).

As is normal, Mediation under the ICC ADR Rules should only be attempted and is only likely to be successful in appropriate cases where the parties in dispute are prepared to compromise, that is, are ready, able and willing to reach an amicable settlement of their dispute.

Anyone wishing to mediate under the ICC ADR Rules can include a corresponding clause in their contracts. The ICC offers a range of reference clauses to suit the parties' needs and the particular circumstances. These optional clauses are set out in Appendix XVI, including a very flexible and practical 'Optional ADR Clause' in the following terms:

> 'The parties may at any time, without prejudice to any other proceedings, seek to settle any dispute arising out of or in connection with the present contract in accordance with the ICC – ADR Rules.'

9.3 Why Use ICC Mediation?

Mediation under such a prestigious, experienced, professional and independent body as the ICC – considered to be the world's leading business organisation – offers another reliable dispute resolution tool that is available to parties involved in all kinds of international commercial disputes, including sports-related ones, which, in relation to the latter, it is suggested, may be overlooked by them at their peril.

Furthermore, as doubts have been and continue to a certain extent, in some quarters, to be expressed about the independence of the CAS, despite the creation and interposition of the International Council for the Arbitration of Sport, pursuant to the 'Paris Agreement' of 22 June, 1994, parties to international sports disputes may also wish to consider using the services of a completely independent, long established and respected body such as the ICC.

See the decisions of the Swiss Federal Tribunal in the cases of *Elmar Gundel* v. *FEI/CAS*[158] and *Raducan* v. *International Olympic Committee*.[159] Also, see later on the settlement of sports-related disputes by arbitration through the Court of Arbitration for Sport in Part Two of this book.

In view of their importance, English versions of these judgements are now reproduced for ease of reference:

Extract of the judgement of March 15, 1993, delivered by the 1st Civil Division of the Swiss Federal Tribunal in the case G. versus Fédération Equestre Internationale and Court of Arbitration for Sport (CAS) (public law appeal) (translation)

A. G. is a professional rider who is part of the German jumping team. He is a member of the Buchloe riding club and the holder of a licence for national and international competitions. On the occasion of the annual renewal of his licence, G. has each time undertaken to comply with the rules of the German Equestrian Federation, which refers to the rules enacted by the International Equestrian Federation for international competitions.

The International Equestrian Federation (FEI), which has its seat in Lausanne, is an association composed solely of National Federations (NF). It deals, in particular, with international competitions and establishes the rules governing the organization of international meetings. In the interest of the present case, it is appropriate to quote the following provisions from its statutes (18th edition, effective 21st March 1991):

'Article 051 – PREAMBLE

1. The FEI is located in Switzerland, as an incorporated body under the Swiss Civil Code, Book 1, Title 11, Chapter III. In all matters of civil litigation, the FEI is subject to Swiss Law. All civil actions (litigations) shall be brought before the Swiss Courts of the city in which the FEI is located.

...

4. All Individuals and Bodies, National Federations and Organizing Committees, Officials, Horse Owners, Persons Responsible and Competitors involved in any activities within the jurisdiction of the Statutes, Regulations and Rules, undertake to recognize the authority and responsibilities of Officials, Ground Juries, Appeal Committees, the Judicial Committee and the CAS in the performance of the duties required of them under the Statues, Regulations and Rules, and undertake not to resort to any other legal procedures in matters coming within the responsibilities of these bodies.

...

6. In order to ensure that the execution of these responsibilities is carried out according to the highest standards of justice and equity, the following bodies and procedures are established:
   6.1 A Judicial Committee to decide on all cases which are outside the competence of any other body established under the Statutes, Regulations and Rules.
   6.2 The Court of Arbitration for Sport (CAS) – created by the IOC – to hear all appeals against the decisions of any competent body established under the Statutes, Regulations and Rules.
   6.3 An Arbitration Procedure (Art. 057).

Article 052 – JUDICIAL COMMITTEE

...

4. The Judicial Committee shall decide all cases not in the competence of the Ground Jury and Appeal Committee of an International Equestrian Event submitted to it through the Secretary General. These cases may be:
   4.1 Cases of infringement of the Statutes, Regulations and Rules.

---

158 15 March 1993 [1993] I Civil Court (Swiss Fed Trib).

159 4 December 2000 [2000] II Civil Court (Swiss Fed Trib).

4.2 Cases of violation of the common principles of behaviour, fairness and accepted standards of sportsmanship.
4.3 Cases of disagreement on the interpretation of the Statutes, Regulations and Rules.

Article 053 – COURT OF ARBITRATION FOR SPORT (CAS)
1. The CAS shall hear all the admissible appeals reported by the Secretary General against decisions taken by Appeal Committees in the first instance and by the Judicial Committee (052.4). The parties concerned shall undertake to comply with the Statutes and Regulations of the CAS and to accent and enforce in good faith its decision.

...

6. There is no appeal against the decision of the Appeals Tribunal, except in the case of the expulsion of a National Federation which must be confirmed by the General Assembly.

Article 057 – ARBITRATION
1. Any dispute between National Federations or between National Federations and the Bureau or other body of the FEI which the Judicial Committee considers to be outside the scope of the Statutes, Regulations or Rules shall be settled definitively by a Court set up in accordance with the Statutes and Regulations of the "COURT OF ARBITRATION FOR SPORT".
2. The parties shall undertake to conform to the aforesaid Statutes and Regulations and to execute in good faith the award made.
3. The Court of Arbitration shall make a definitive award and the parties shall waive the right to any appeal, in accordance with Article 192 of the Swiss Federal Law on Private International Law (LDIP). The parties shall agree to have the seat of the Court of Arbitration at Lausanne (Switzerland) and to apply Swiss Law.'

In its General Regulations (GR) of 23rd July 1990, the FEI established the procedure to be followed in order to settle disputes, and fixed, in particular, the competence of its Judicial Committee (art. 168) and that of the CAS (art. 169), together with the conditions and terms and modalities of the appeal (art. 173). Annex F to the said GR contains the Statute and Regulations of the CAS, in which no distinction is made between the original and appellate jurisdiction.

B. G. took part with the horse 'Life is Life' in the international jumping event (CSIO) in Aachen between 16th and 19th June 1991. He won prize money representing a total of 40,000 marks. On the occasion of this event, the horse in question was designated for a medications control, which entailed the taking of a double sample of urine and blood. Analysis of the first sample of urine, performed by the Horseracing Forensic Laboratory Ltd in Newmarket (GB), revealed the presence of a prohibited substance, isoxsuprine. At the request of the German Equestrian Federation, an analysis of the second urine sample was performed in the presence of Professor Donike of Cologne; this gave the same result as the first.

In its decision of 5th December 1991, the FEI Judicial Committee, considering that isoxsuprine came under the category of substances prohibited by the FEI Veterinary Regulations, pronounced the disqualification of the rider G. and his horse 'Life is Life' from all the competitions of the Aachen CSIO and the withdrawal of the prize money won on this occasion. It further suspended the rider from international equestrian competitions for three months, imposed a fine of 1,500 francs on him and taxed the costs of the procedure to him.

Ruling on the appeal by G. on 10th September 1992, the CAS partially allowed this appeal in that it confirmed the disqualification of the rider and his horse, hut reduced the period of suspension to one month and the fine to 1,000 francs. As for the costs of the procedure, it taxed these 2/3 to the appellant and 1/3 to the FEI.

C. G. lodged a public law appeal in the meaning of arts. 191 para. 1 LDIP and 85 let. c OJ. He concluded in favour of the judgements pronounced on 5th December 1991 by the FEI and 10th September 1992 by the CAS being annulled. Accessorily, he requested the annulment only of the latter judgement and the fixing of a 30-day time limit to institute an ordinary action before the competent state court.

By presidential decision of 23rd September 1992, a request by the appellant for the granting of suspensive effect was rejected.

The exchange of documents was limited to the question of the admissibility of the appeal. In their respective answers, the FEI and the CAS both supported the argument of the admissibility of the appeal such as it relates to the judgement of the CAS of 10th September, excluding the FEI decision of 5th December 1991.

In Law

1. The public law appeal is inadmissible insofar as it relates to the decision taken on 5th December 1991 by the FEI Judicial Committee. Indeed, not only was it lodged late (art. 89 para. 1 OJ), but it also relates to a decision which is not contestable by such means, given that the Committee, as a body of the FEI, merely expressed the will of this association, a party to the dispute, and therefore did not pronounce, an international arbitral award which alone would have been subject to a public law appeal in the meaning of arts. 85 let. c OJ and 190 et seq. LDIP.
2. The appellant received, first of all, the operative provisions of the CAS award, dated 10th September 1992, the grounds of the award being sent to him later, viz. 15th October 1992. Written notification of the grounds of the award is provided under art. 61 of the CAS Statute. For this reason, both the first notice of appeal of 17th September 1992 and the two supplementary statements of case of 13th October and 6th November 1992 were lodged before expiry of the time for appeal (art. 89 para. 2 OJ; ATF 106 la 239). Thus, the request made by the appellant in his document of 13th October 1992 for a second exchange of documents to be ordered becomes purposeless upon examination of the grounds cited in support of it.
3. The public law appeal is opened against the CAS award only on the double condition that such judgement actually be an international arbitral award in the meaning of arts. 176 et seq. LDIP, and that it concern points of law, and therefore that it does not have as its sole object games rules whose application is, in principle, outside all juridical control (ATF 118 11 15 et seq. preamble 2,108 11 15,103 la 410 et seq.).
   a) The seat of the CAS is in Lausanne and the appellant is domiciled in Germany. The condition of an international connection, laid down in art. 176 para. 1 LDIP, is thus fulfilled in this particular case.
   b) The arbitral award, in the meaning of art. 189 LDIP, is a judgement pronounced, on the basis of an arbitration agreement, by a non-state court to which the parties entrust the task of settling a case of a patrimonial nature (art. 177 para. 1 LDIP) of an international nature (art. 176 para. 1 LDIP). According to the judicial practice of the Federal Tribunal, a true award, ranking with the judgement of a state court, presupposes that the arbitral tribunal pronouncing it offers sufficient guarantees of impartiality and independence as follow from art. 58 Cst. (ATF 117 la 168 preamble 5a, 107 la 158 preamble 2b). Failing this, the award would constitute merely a civil judgement enforceable in the whole of Switzerland (art. 61 Cst.; ATF 97 1 489 preamble l). In this latter judgement, the Federal Tribunal, applying these principles, considered that an arbitral tribunal, which was the body of an association having the quality of party to the action did not offer sufficient guarantees of independence. The decisions taken by such bodies indeed constitute only a simple expression of will by the association concerned; such decisions are acts falling within the scope of administration and not judicial acts. Therefore it is not possible to consider them as arbitral awards, from the point of view of both the Concordat sur l'arbitrage (CIA) and chapter 12 of the LDIR For this reason, such decisions cannot be contested either by means of a composition appeal (art. 36 CIA) or by the means of appeal provided under art. 190 LDIP (HEINI, Die gerichtliche Überprufung von Vereinsstrafen, in: Freiheit und Verantworturig im Recht, FS Arthur Meier-Hayoz, p. 223 et seq.; JOLIDON, Commentaire du Concordat suisse sur l'arbitrage, Introduction no. 68, and no. 235 ad art. l; LALIVE/POUDRET/REYMOND, Le droit de l'arbitrage interne et international en Suisse, no. 1.2 ad art. 1 CIA and no. 2 ad art. 176 LDIP; CORBAT, Les peines statutaires, thesis Fribourg 1974, p. 130 et seq.). In fact, to pronounce an award in one's own case is quite simply not compatible with the guarantee of independence (ATF 52 1 75; HEINI, Op. cit., p. 228; GULDENER, Schweizerisches Zivilprozessrecht, 3rd edition, p. 604), so that it matters little, in this respect, to know whether the personal independence of the members of the arbitral tribunal called upon to settle the dispute could be safeguarded

by means of the rules on the challenge (of another opinion: JOLIDON, Arbitrage et sport, in: Recht und Wirtschaft heute, FS MAX KUMMER, p. 633 et seq., 643/644).
The above-mentioned principles apply also in the hypothesis where the person affected by the award of the body of the association is only indirectly a part of it, in other words when only associations or other artificial persons may become members, as sections, of the umbrella association. The indirect member may also contest the decisions of the association, pursuant to art. 75 CC, or have examined by the judge the punishments (penalties provided for by the regulations) which have been imposed upon him (RIEMER, Commentaire bernois ad art. 60 et seq. CC, Systematischer Teil no. 511,515 and 529, and no. 18 ad art. 75 CC). In the case of punishments, this juridical protection must be accorded even to the person who is not a member of the association, if such person is subject to the rules established by the association, for example when such a measure is a condition to be fulfilled in order to be able to take part in an event organized by the association. Here again, the contested decision must be open to free and independent juridical control, control which may be entrusted to an arbitral tribunal on condition that such tribunal constitutes a true judicial authority and not the simple body of the association interested in the outcome of the. dispute (RIEMER, no. 18 and 85 ad art. 75 CC; HEINI, op. cit., p. 229; *passim,* Das Schweizerische Vereinsrecht, p. 55/56 and 60 et seq.; KUMMER, Spielregel und Rechtsregel, p. 48 et seq.; SCHERRER, Rechtsfragen des organisierten Sportlebens in der Schweiz, thesis Zurich 1982, p. 150 et seq.; BODMER, Vereinsstrafe und Verbandsgerichtsbarkeit, thesis St Gallen 1988, p. 204 et seq.; SCHWAB/WALTER, Schiedsgerichtsbarkeit, 4th edition, p. 274 et seq.). As indicated above, on the occasion of the annual renewal of his licence, the appellant undertook to respect the rules established by the German Equestrian Federation; in doing so, he indirectly submitted to the rules of conduct enacted by the International Equestrian Federation, in particular to the juridical procedure developed by such association to contest the penalties imposed by it. In conformity with these rules of procedure, after having brought an appeal against the decision of the Judicial Committee, he concluded a complementary arbitration agreement with the FEI in which he admitted the jurisdiction of the CAS to rule on his appeal. Consequently, in view of the above, the point of knowing whether the decision at present being contested is an arbitral award which can be brought before the Federal Tribunal depends on the juridical situation of the CAS with regard to the FEI.
The idea of creating an arbitral tribunal which would be seized of litigation directly or indirectly linked with sport was put forward in 1983 by Juan Antonio Samaranch, President of the International Olympic Committee (IOC). The CAS is an autonomous arbitral institution on an organizational level, but without artificial personality, whose seat is in Lausanne. Having a Statute, which entered into force on 30th June 1984, given to it by the IOC and completed by a set of Regulations adopted on the same date, it rules, by an arbitral award, on cases submitted to it by parties and bearing on rights which they freely dispose of (art. 3). *Ratione materiae,* it is competent to hear disputes of a private nature arising out of the practice or development of sport (art. 4). The CAS is composed of a maximum of 60 members, chosen, for a renewable period of four years, from among persons having had legal training and being recognized as competent in the field of sport (art. 6). The IOC, the International Federations (IFs) and the National Olympic Committees (NOCS) each appoint fifteen members from among their own members or from outside, while the final fifteen members, chosen by the IOC President, are necessarily from outside the IOC, IFs, NOCs and the Association grouping them (art. 7). Before taking office, all the CAS members sign a solemn individual declaration worded as follows (art. 10):

'I solemnly declare upon my honour and in all conscience that I shall fulfil properly and faithfully my duties as an arbitrator, that I shall observe secrecy concerning the deliberations and votes and that I shall act in all objectivity and in all independence.'

For each case, the CAS sits in a 'Panel' composed of one or three arbitrators mandatorily chosen from among its members (art. 11). Each of the two parties appoints one arbitrator and the two parties then come to an agreement as to the appointment of the third arbitrator. Failing such agreement, the third arbitrator is appointed by the President of the Federal Tribunal of the Swiss Confederation. If the parties choose to have a Panel with one arbitrator, they nominate him by mutual agreement (art. 12). The arbitrators may be challenged by the parties, on account, in particular, of the links between them and one or other of them or because they have already been involved with the dispute in another capacity (art. 16). The CAS has its own judicial organization which is characterized by the existence of pleadings and an oral presentation, an ordinary procedure and a summary procedure (art. 27 et seq.). The deliberations of the Panel take place in camera (art. 58 para. 1). The CAS award is reasoned and notified to the parties (art. 61 and 63). It may be the subject of an application for interpretation (art. 64) and, on condition that such has been provided for in the arbitration agreement, a request for review based on the appearance of new facts (art. 66 et seq.). The operating costs of the CAS are borne by the IOC (art. 71). In cases of a pecuniary nature, the parties contribute to the costs entailed by the resolution of the dispute in a proportion established by an agreement made between them and the President of the Panel (art. 72; for a general description of this arbitral institution, cf. MBAYE, Une nouvelle institution d'arbitrage: Le Tribunal Arbitral du Sport, in: Annuaire Français de Droit International, 1984, p. 409 et seq., also published in: COLLOMB, Sport, droit et relations internationales, p. 95 et seq.).

The provisions governing the conduct of proceedings before the CAS are clearly aimed at the so called initial or originating procedure, in the manner of what is provided under art. 057 of the FEI statutes. However, numerous international sports associations have also made use of the possibility offered to them to appoint the CAS as a body of appeal charged to examine the validity of the penalties pronounced by their organs. Such is the case of the FEI which opened the means of appeal to the CAS against the decisions pronounced by its Judicial Committee in particular (art. 053). This legal instrument is supposed to exclude recourse to any other legal procedure before a state judge (art. 051 para. 4; on this question cf. SCHWAAR, Nouvelles du Tribunal Arbitral du Sport, in: Bulletin ASA, 1989, p. 369 et seq.), In the opinion of its founders and its representatives, the CAS is a true arbitral tribunal independent of the parties, which freely exercises complete juridical control over the decisions of the associations which are brought before it, in particular over the penalties prescribed by the regulations which have been imposed on the appellant (MBAYE, op. cit., p. 424; *passim,* in: Tribunal Arbitral du Sport, p. 33; SCHWAAR, Le Tribunal Arbitral du Sport, in: Pratique juridique actuelle (PJA), 1992, p. 396 et seq.; *passim* in: Bulletin ASA, 1990, p. 144; *passim,* Tribunal Arbitral du Sport, in: La législation sportive en Europe: évolution et harmonisation, 1er Séminaire juridique, Moscou 1991, p. 82/83; *passim,* in: Bulletin ASA, 1991, p. 201 et seq.; 'CARRARD, Au nom de la loi du sport, in: Revue Olympique, 1992, p. 614 et seq., this author nevertheless advocating more pronounced independence between the CAS and the IOC). Insofar as one can judge, this opinion is apparently unanimous in legal doctrine (SAMUEL/GERHART, Sporting Arbitration and the International Olympic Committee's Court of Arbitration for Sport, in: Journal of International Arbitration, 1989, p. 39 et seq.; NAFZIGER, International sports law: a replay of characteristics and trends, in: The American Journal of International Law, 1992, p. 489 et seq., 508; NETZLE, the Court of Arbitration for Sport, in: The Entertainment and Sports Lawyer, 1992, p. 1 et seq.; OSWALD, Le règlement des litiges et la répression des comportements illicites dans le domaine sportif, in: Mélanges en l'honneur de Jacques-Michel Grossen, p. 67 et seq., 80/81).

Such an opinion may be shared – not without hesitation, moreover, provided, at least, that it relates to proceedings conducted before the CAS in which the IOC does not appear as a party. This applies in this particular case. The CAS is not a body of the FEI; it does not receive instructions from this association and retains sufficient personal autonomy from the CAS insofar as it places at its disposal only three arbitrators of the maximum of sixty members of whom the CAS is composed (art. 053 eh. 3 of the FEI Statutes; from this point of view, the CAS can be distinguished from the sports tribunal of the Swiss Football Association (ASF), which the Vaud Cantonal Court refused to consider as a true arbitral tribunal, in: JT 1988 111 5 et seq.). Furthermore, art. 7 of the CAS Statute imposes the choice of at least fifteen members from outside the IOC, IFs and NOCs and the Association which regroups them, thereby offering the parties the possibility of designating as an arbitrator or umpire one of the fifteen persons belonging neither to the FEI nor to one of its sections. The guarantee of independence of the arbitrators in a concrete case is further assured by art. 16 of the CAS Statute relating to grounds for challenge. In these conditions, one may allow that the CAS offers the guarantees of independence upon which Swiss law makes conditional the valid exclusion of ordinary judicial recourse. His opinion is, moreover, corroborated by doctrinal opinion whereby the awards of the CAS may be the subject of international enforcement in conformity with the New York Convention on the subject (NAFZIGER, op. cit., p. 508). However, certain objections with regard to the independence of the CAS could not be set aside without another form of process, in particular those based on the organic and economic ties existing between the CAS and the IOC. In fact, the latter is competent to modify the CAS Statute; it also bears the operating costs of this court and plays a considerable role in the appointment of its members. The fact remains, however, that given, on the one hand, the possibility which exists of ensuring, by the remedy of challenge, the independence of the Panel called upon to hear a specific case and, on the other hand, the solemn declaration of independence signed by each CAS member before he takes office, such objections alone do not allow the CAS to be denied the quality of true arbitral tribunal (cf. JOLIDON, in: FS Kummer, p. 643 et seq.), even though it would be desirable for greater independence of the CAS from the IOC to be assured (CARRARD, Ibid.). Finally, the fact that the CAS is an institutionalized organization in no way prevents it from being considered as a true arbitral tribunal (ATF 107 la 152). Thus, from the procedural point of view, the decision contested is indeed an arbitral award of an international nature and may be the subject of a public law appeal in the meaning of art. 85 let. c OJ in conjunction with arts. 176 et seq. LDIR

c) The admissibility of the public law appeal presupposes, moreover, that the arbitral tribunal ruled on points of law and not solely on the application of games rules, which do not in principle lend themselves to juridical control (ATF 118 11 15 et seq. preamble 2,108 11 19 et seq. preamble 3, 103 la 412 preamble 3b). Such is indeed the case here. The withdrawal of prize money of the not inconsiderable sum of around 40,000 marks, in conjunction with the disqualification with retroactive effect from all competitions in which such prize money was won, together with the suspension from international equestrian competitions – a measure which indubitably affects the personal and economic sphere of a professional rider – go far beyond simple penalties intended to ensure the correct conduct of a game and constitute real penalties prescribed by the regulations which prejudice the juridical interests of the person whom they affect and which may, as a result, be subject to judicial control (ATF 108 11 21 preamble 3; KUMMER, Op. cit., p. 48 et seq.; JOLIDON, FS Kummer, p. 651 et *seq; passim,* Le droit du sport en Suisse, in: RSJ 86/1990, p. 389 et seq.; *passim,* Ordre sportif et ordre juridique, in: RJB 127/1991, p. 213 et seq., 231; OSWALD, op. cit., p. 71 et seq.).

d) Although the suspension imposed upon him has already ended, the appellant retains a current interest in it sufficient for the annulment of the contested award. Such is the unavoidable conclusion considering the personal and patrimonial effects which the penalty in question continues to produce. Moreover, the opposite conclusion would imply the impossibility of having suspensions of short duration examined by the appeals authority (ATF 118 la 53/54 preamble 3c).

e) Finally, seeing that the FEI has its headquarters in Switzerland, any exclusion prescribed by the regulations or fixed by contract of all recourse by the parties against the CAS award would be of no effect in the context of the present appeal procedure (art. 192 para. 1 LDIP).

This being so, it is appropriate to examine the subject matter.

4. (...)
5. Citing art. 190 para. 2 let. b LDIP, the appellant maintains that the CAS wrongly declared itself competent since the case at issue was not submissible to arbitration.

The plea of incompetence must be raised before the arbitral tribunal prior to any discussion of the merits (art. 186 paras. 1 and 2 LDIP). Failing this, it is no longer possible to claim lack of jurisdiction of the arbitral tribunal as a ground for appeal on the basis of art. 190 para. 2 let. b LDIP (LALIVE/POUDRET/REYMOND, Op. cit., no. 10 ad art. 186 LDIP). The plea of inarbitrability of the dispute observes the same rule (LALIVE/POUDRET/REYMOND, Op. cit., no. 6 ad art. 177 LDIP). The appellant does not claim to have raised these exceptions before the CAS; it is rather the opposite which emerges from the contested award where the CAS notes that its own jurisdiction is recognized by all the parties. This first ground is therefore inadmissible.

The argument in question in any case appears unfounded:

a) The appellant maintains, first of all, that the litigious penalty prescribed by the rules comes within the meaning of criminal law and is hence under the jurisdiction of state justice. This opinion is erroneous. It is generally accepted that the penalty prescribed by regulations represents one of the forms of penalty fixed by contract, is therefore based on the autonomy of the parties and may thus be the subject of an arbitral award (RIEMER, no. 205 et seq., part of no. 226 ad art. 70 CC with numerous references; SCHWAB/WALTER, Op. Cit., p. 281), on condition that, where international arbitration is concerned, it is of a patrimonial nature in the meaning of art. 177 para. 1 LDIP (on this point, cf. LALIVE/POUDRET/REYMOND, op. cit., no. 2 ad art. 177 LDIP). In other words, the penalty prescribed by regulations has nothing to do with the power to punish reserved by the criminal courts (HEINI, Op. cit., p. 60; CORBAT, Op. cit., p. 70), even if it is punishing behaviour which is also punished by the state (BGHZ 21 p. 374/5).

b) If one is to believe the appellant, Swiss work contract law would, moreover, exclude the possibility of having an arbitral tribunal settle the question of the validity of a litigious penalty prescribed by regulations. However, apart from the fact, according to prevailing opinion, art. 343 CO does not prohibit the submission of a dispute in matters of work to an arbitral tribunal (REHBINDER, no. 10/1 1 ad art. 343 CO; LALIVE/POUDRET/REYMOND, op. cit., no. 4 ad art 5 CIA), the appellant in no way demonstrates for what reason and to what extent the juridical relation in question would come within the meaning of the provisions of the Swiss law governing the work contract.

6. Citing art. 190 para. 2 let. a LDIP, the appellant further disputes that the arbitral tribunal which dealt with his case was properly appointed and composed. In support of this argument, he asserts that he was forced to choose an arbitrator from among the members of the CAS, and that, at least the two arbitrators designated by the parties and especially Mr Hans Ulrich Sutter, as President of the Swiss Equestrian Sports Federation, did not offer sufficient guarantees of independence to rule on his appeal.

It has already been indicated that the CAS in itself and the procedure for designating its members and arbitrators called upon to sit on a Panel fulfil the requirements which an arbitral tribunal must satisfy (cf. preamble 3 above). This state of affairs did not deprive the appellant of the right to lodge a motion challenging one or other, or even all the members of the Panel. However, for that he 'would have had to cite the ground for the challenge as soon as he knew of it, in accordance with the principle of good faith which also governs procedural law, under pain of being time-barred (ATF 113 la 67/68, 111 la 74/75 preamble 2b and 262 preamble 2b). Art. 180 para. 2 LDIP and art. 16 para. 3 of the CAS Statute furthermore give concrete form to the same idea. Consequently, the only grounds for challenge that may be cited, in the context of the argument provided under art. 190 para. 2 let. a LDIP – so long as they may be (Cf. JOLIDON, no. 41/42 ad art. 36 CIA) –, are those which a party was not in a position to raise before the pronouncement of the arbitral award (LALIVE/POUDRET/REYMOND, Op. cit., no. 5a ad art. 190 LDIP). lhis rule applies not only to the grounds for challenge which the interested party actually knew, but also to those which he could have known by showing the required attention. In this case, the appellant received, annexed to a letter from the CAS on 6th February 1992, the CAS booklet containing, among other texts, that of the Statute of the said court. From that moment, he could no longer be unaware that, of the sixty members of the CAS, only fifteen could not be part of a sports association affiliated to an IF or the IOC. Therefore, he should have informed himself, as soon as the Panel called upon to rule on his case was constituted, with regard to the identity of the arbitrators approached with a view to sitting and to any links they might have with an IF, so that he could immediately file a motion to challenge this. The abovementioned letter should have encouraged him all the more to take his investigations further, in that it expressly drew his attention to the fact that the arbitrators Klimke and Sutter, whose names were subsequently chosen, were specialists familiar with problems relating to equestrianism. Having omitted to seek some simple additional information on this subject at the time, the appellant is no longer entitled to cite today, with retroactive effect, the ground for challenge derived from the fact that two arbitrators belonged to associations or committees directly or indirectly linked with the FEI. As a result, the question of whether this latter circumstance would have sufficed to establish the appearance of bias of the interested parties may remain undecided.

7. According to the appellant, the CAS also violated his right to be heard (art. 190 para. 2 let. d LDIP) by imposing on the parties the obligation to bring their witnesses to the hearing, by not seeking the aid of the state judge to compel two defaulting witness to give evidence, by not of its own motion taking cognizance of the written report of one of the two witnesses and not adding to the file the photographs which had been produced.
   a) The rules of procedure of the CAS authorize the parties to bring witnesses and have them heard at their own expense (art. 49 of the Statute, art. 49 et seq. of the Regulations). These come within the framework of the sphere of autonomy which art. 182 para. 1 LDIP reserves for the parties concerning the arbitral procedure, and manifestly do not prejudice the minimum guarantees which art. 182 para. 3 LDIP requires to be respected, whatever the procedure chosen.
   b) If the aid of the state judiciary is necessary to the production of evidence, the arbitral tribunal, or the parties in agreement with it, may request the aid of the judge of the seat of the arbitral tribunal (art. 184 para. 2 LDIP). In order to be able to conclude that there was a violation of the parties' right to be heard, more precisely their right to collaborate in the production of evidence, it is not enough that the arbitral tribunal should not of its own motion seek the aid of the state judge without having been invited thereto by one of the parties; it is necessary rather that the tribunal should have refused without valid reason the request of one of the parties to obtain the aid of the state judiciary for the production of relevant evidence. lt appears from the non-contested minutes of the hearing held on 10th June 1992 that the agent of the appellant added to the file a written declaration by Professor Donike, one of the witnesses whom he had asked to be heard, and indicated to the arbitrators that another witness, Dr Cronau, would not appear. On this occasion, the aid of the judge with a view to a hearing was not requested. On the contrary, it is mentioned in the said minutes that 'no measure of examination proceedings was requested'. The CAS therefore did not violate the appellant's right to be heard for the above-mentioned reasons.
   c) The procedure applicable before the CAS is governed by the principle of hearings (art. 39 et seq. of the Statute, art. 41 et seq. of the Regulations). Also, by not of its own motion adducing evidence that the parties had not requested, in particular by not itself asking- the witness Cronau to provide it with a written declaration, the CAS did not further fail to recognize the right to produce evidence cited by the appellant, since such a guarantee applies only to evidence asked for within the prescribed time and within the prescribed form (ATF 106 II 171 preamble 6b).
   d) According to the non-contested minutes of the hearing of 9th September 1992, the CAS agreed, against the opinion of the opposing party, that the photographs produced by the agent of the appellant be added to the file and it listened to the comments made by this lawyer on them. The argument of violation is, on this point too, totally unfounded.
8. The appellant finally cites a violation of public policy (art. 190 para. 2 let. e LDIP).
   a) As the Federal Tribunal has already had occasion to observe on many occasions, whatever the conception that one accepts, there are in all cases two elements which characterize the notion of public policy of art. 190 LDIP: on the one hand, the ground relating to it is more restrictive and narrower than the argument of arbitrariness based on art. 4 Cst. or on art. 36 let. f CIA; in addition, the said notion covers only the fundamental principles of the legal order taken into consideration. Thus, the manifestly erroneous application of a rule of law or the clearly false establishment of a point of fact are not yet sufficient to justify the annulment of an award under international arbitration (ATF 117 11 606 and references; non published judgement of 25th July 1990 in the case society v., preamble 2, reproduced in: SJ 1991, p. 12 et seq.; KAUFMANN, in: Bulletin ASA 1992, p. 66 et seq.; POUDRET, in: Bulletin ASA 1992, p. 82183).
   b) Under these conditions, it is fruitless for the appellant to seek to call into question the outcome of the preliminary procedure by challenging the modalities of the anti-doping control and the assessment of the result of such control. As for the opinion of the CAS, whereby it is sufficient that the analyses performed reveal the presence of a banned product for there to be presumption of doping and, consequently, a reversal of the burden of proof, this relates not to public policy but to the burden of proof and the assessment of evidence, problems which cannot be resolved, in private law matters, in the light of notions proper to criminal

law, such as the presumption of innocence and the principle 'in dubio pro reo', and corresponding guarantees which feature in the European Convention on Human Rights. Nor is it contrary to public policy that the pertinent rules enacted by the FEI are characterized by great severity, in the opinion of the appellant, in that they prohibit products or amounts of a product which would not be likely to affect the performance of the horse. Indeed, whether they be appropriate or not, or even whether or not they stand up to the objection of arbitrariness, such rules do not in any case question the fundamental principles of the Swiss legal order in the area of relations of an international nature. In particular, there is no violation of public policy from the simple fact that the norms prescribed by the regulations relating to doping might be incompatible with certain statutory or legal provisions.

9. At the end of this examination, there is no alternative but to reject the appeal insofar as it is admissible.

Swiss Supreme Court, IInd Civil Court, December 4, 2000, 5P.427/2000 Raducan v. International Olympic Committee

Composition of the Court: Mr Bianchi, Chairman, Mr Raselli and Ms Nordmann, Justices.
Clerk: Mr Abrecht.

Ruling on the public law appeal lodged by

Andreea Raducan, domiciled in Rumania, represented with valid address for service by Messrs Jacques Michod and Olivier Rodondi, Attorneys-at-Law in Lausanne,

versus

the award rendered on September 28, 2000 by the ad hoc Division, constituted for the Sydney Olympic Games, of the Court of Arbitration for Sport, the seat of which is in Lausanne, in the cause opposing the appellant and the International Olympic Committee, in Lausanne, respondent;

(international arbitration in sports matters)
On the basis of the record, which evidences the following facts:

A. Andreea Raducan, a Romanian gymnast born on September 30, 1983, won the gold medal in the Gymnastics (Artistic) Women's Team Finals of the Sydney Olympics on September 19, 2000. She was not tested for doping at the end of that competition.
On September 20, 2000, Andreea Raducan complained of a headache and of a runny nose to the doctor of the Rumanian gymnastics team, Dr Oana. The latter gave her a pill of 'Nurofen Cold and Flu', that she absorbed in the doctor's presence.
On September 21, 2000, Andreea Raducan won the finals of the Gymnastics (Artistic) Women's Individual All-Around competition. Before the beginning of that competition, during her warm-up, she again complained to Dr Oana that she was not feeling well. This doctor thereupon gave her a second pill of 'Nurofen Cold and Flu', that she absorbed.

B. After the competition of September 21, 2000, Andreea Raducan was taken to the anti-doping control station, in accordance with the anti-doping procedures adopted for the Sydney Olympics. She delivered, in three urine samples, between 11:03 p.m. on September 21 and 12:20 a.m. on September 22, a total urine quantity of 62 milliliters (ml).
Analyzing this urine, divided into samples 'A' and 'B', the Australian Sports Drug Testing Laboratory detected therein the presence of pseudoephedrine. The concentration of this substance was between 88 and 90.6 micrograms per miltilitre in sarnple 'A', which contained 80 ml of urine, and between 90.8 and 93.71 micrograms per millilitre in sample 'B', which contained 20 ml of urine.

C. The Olympic Movement Anti-Doping Code (hereinafter the Anti-Doping Code), amended on January 1, 2000, provides as follows:

'Chapter II: The Offence of Doping and its Punishment
Article 1
1. Doping contravenes the fundamental principles of Olympism and sports and medical ethics.
2. Doping is forbidden.
Article 2
Doping is:
1. the use of an expedient (substance or method) which is potentially harmful to athletes' health and/or capable of enhancing their performance, or
2. the presence in the athlete's body of a Prohibited Substance or evidence of the use thereof or evidence of the use of a Prohibited Method.'

Appendix A of the Anti-Doping Code, amended on April 1, 2000, contains the following provisions:
'I. Prohibited Classes of Substances
A. Stimulants
Prohibited Substances in class (A) include the following examples:
(...) ephedrines**, (..)
** For ephedrine and methylephedrine, the definition of a positive is a concentration in urine greater that 10 micrograms per millilitre. For phenylpropanolamine and pseudoephedrine, the definition of a positive is a concentration in urine of greater than 25 micrograms per millilitre.'

D. A report prepared on September 27, 2000 by Dr Richard Day and filed by Andreea Raducan at the hearing of the same day before the arbitral tribunal (see letter F below) establishes that a pill of 'Nurofen Cold and Flu' contains 30 mg of pseudoephedrine and that the concentration of this substance found in samples 'A' and 'B' is consistent with the absorption by Andreea Raducan of a pill of 'Nurofen Cold and Flu' on the evening of the competition of September 21, 2000.

E. By decision of September 26, 2000, the International Olympic Committee (hereinafter the IOC) disqualified Andreea Raducan from the Gymnastics (Artistic) Women's Individual All-Around competition for 'use of prohibited substances (Chapter II, Article 2.2 of the Olympic Movement Anti-Doping Code)' and ordered the Romanian National Olympic Committee to withdraw and return the gold medal and the diploma awarded to Andreea Raducan for her first place in that competition.

F. On September 26, 2000, Andreea Raducan filed a request for arbitration with the Court of Arbitration for Sport (hereinafter the CAS), requesting that the IOC's decision be reversed and that she be reinstated as gold medalist.
By arbitral award, with reasons, of September 28, 2000, the CAS dismissed the request and confirmed the IOC's decision.

G. By way of a public law appeal before the Supreme Court, Andreca Raducan requests that this award be vacated, with costs.

Considering at Law:

1. The Supreme Court examines *ex officio* and with full scope of review the admissibility of appeals brought before it (ATF[160] 126 III 275, para. 1 and decisions referred to therein).
   a. The public law appeal against the CAS award is admissible only on the double condition that this ruling actually is an arbitral award rendered in international arbitration proceedings within the meaning of Articles 176 et seq. PIL Act[161] and that it pertains to legal issues, i.e. that it does not have as sole aim to decide on rules of the game, the application of which normally escapes all legal control (ATF 119 II 271 para. 3; 118 II 15, para. 2; 108 II 15; 103 Ia 410).
   b. The arbitral award, within the meaning of Article 189 PIL, is a judgment rendered on the basis of an arbitration agreement by a non-governmental tribunal which has been entrusted by the parties with the adjudication of a patrimonial matter (Article 177(1) PIL Act); a true award, equivalent to a judgment of a court, presupposes that the tribunal having rendered it offers all adequate guarantees of impartiality and independence, as these flow from Article 58 of the former Constitution and now from Article 30(1) of the Constitution (ATF 119 II

---

160 'ATF' is the French-language abbreviation for 'Supreme Court Decisions', i.e., the official report of Swiss Supreme Court decisions.

161 'PIL Act' is the English-language abbreviation for the Swiss Act on Private International Law of 1987.

271 para. 3; 117 la 168 para. 5a; 107 Ia 158 para. 2b). The Supreme Court has held that the CAS can be considered as a true arbitral tribunal regarding proceedings to which the IOC is not a party, and where the CAS is mandated by an international sports association to act as the appellate body entrusted with examining the validity of sanctions pronounced by the bodies of these associations (ATF 119 II 271 para. 3b).

c. The question whether the CAS can be considered as having rendered a true arbitral award within the meaning of Articles 176 *et seq* PIL Act when it has adjudicated a request for arbitration seeking the reversal of a decision of the IOC – the condition relating to the international connecting factor, set at Article 176(1) PIL Act, being met in this instance (see ATF 1 19 II 271 para. 3a) – does not need to be decided. Indeed, the public law appeal, supposing that it is admissible, would in any event be dismissed as will be seen below.

2. a. The Appellant argues firstly that Article 3.4 of the Anti-Doping Code, which prescribes a minimum urine quantity of 75 ml, has allegedly been breached in this instance. According to the appellant, the non-observation of this procedural rule allegedly violates the athlete's fundamental right to obtain a rigorous and infallible control of his or her physical condition and is allegedly contrary to public policy within the meaning of Article 190(2)(e) PIL Act. Indeed, in the context of anti-doping testing, the athlete is allegedly in a precarious situation, since the simple presence of a prohibited substance in his or her urine triggers a legal presumption of doping, which the athlete can rebut only by proving a malevolent act by a third party or an erroneous analysis result. The extreme rigor of this presumption of doping – which the Supreme Court has considered compatible with public policy (decision *in re* G. of March 15, 1993, para. 8b, not reported in ATF 119 II 271 but reproduced in ASA Bulletin 1993, p. 409) – should have as a corollary a very special rigor in the scrupulous application of the testing procedures issued by the sporting body.

b. The appellant also complains that her right to be heard in adversarial proceedings, within the meaning of Article 190(2)(d) PIL Act, has allegedly not been guaranteed. She alleges that, before the CAS, she argued that there was a 38 ml difference between the quantity of urine she delivered at the antidoping control station and that which arrived at the laboratory (80 ml in sample 'A' and 20 ml in sample 'B'). In its answer to this argument, the CAS stated that it was undisputed that the laboratory had received a sufficient volume of urine to undertake a valid analysis, and that the discrepancy between the quantity of urine delivered according to the report of the anti-doping control (62 ml) and that which results from the laboratory reports (100 ml) could not reasonably be considered to have had an impact on a correctly performed analysis (see award under appeal, para. 7.5 to 7.7, pp. 8-9). According to the appellant, the CAS allegedly did not answer her complaint, since the issue was not whether the laboratory had received a volume of urine that was sufficient to carry out the analysis of samples 'A' and 'B', but rather how and why a quantity of fluid that was greater than the 62 ml delivered by the appellant ended up in the laboratory.

c. Finally, the appellant argues that the award under appeal is contrary to public policy, within the meaning of Article 190(2)(e) PIL Act, to the extent that it violates the principles of good faith and equal treatment. Indeed, in an award rendered on June 25, 1992 in application of the General Regulations of the FEI *(Fédération Equestre Internationale),* the CAS had established that certain jars containing urine samples had not been closed in accordance with the General Regulations of the FEI; considering that it had thus become possible to open the caps slightly and that one could thus not rule out the possibility of a manipulation and therefore a contamination of the jars' contents by a foreign substance, the CAS admitted that there remained a doubt that should benefit the appellant (see Matthieu Reeb (ed.), Collection of CAS Awards 1986-1998, Bern 1998, p. 99 et seq.). To treat differently this case, in which the only plausible explanation to the excess of fluid that had been observed, would allegedly constitute flagrantly unequal treatment, violating the principle of good faith to a degree that is incompatible with public policy within the meaning of Article 190(2)(e) PIL Act.

3. a. In the totality of the arguments summarized above, the appellant loses sight of an essential factor. Indeed, the appellant was punished for 'use of Prohibited Substances (Chapter II, Article 2.2 of the Olympic Movement Anti-Doping Code)'. Pursuant to this provision, doping is defined not only as 'the presence in the athlete's body of a Prohibited Substance', but also as 'evidence of the use thereof '.

In this instance, the IOC's decision was not confirmed by the CAS on the sole basis of the urine analysis, which revealed a concentration of pseudoephedrine three times greater than the threshold as of which a result is deemed positive. Indeed, the appellant admitted to having taken a pill of 'Nurofen Cold and Flu' – which contains 30 mg of pseudoephedrine – during her warm-up for the finals of the Gymnastics (Artistic) Women's Individual All-Around competition and this clearly falls within the definition of doping as per Article 2.2 of the Anti-Doping Code. In fact, it results from the award under appeal (para. 7.8-7.19, pp. 9-11) that the CAS considered that the presence of pseudoephedrine in the appellant's body was actually due to the absorption – admitted by the appellant – of that pill, which is confirmed by Dr Day's report of September 27, 2000.

b. Since it is established that the appellant took a pill of 'Nurofen Cold and Flu' containing 30 mg of pseudoephedrine just before the competition and that this explains the concentration of pseudoephedrine in her urine that is three times greater than the threshold defining doping, the CAS did not violate the appellant's right to be heard by merely stating, in reply to the argument based on the discrepancy between the quantity of urine delivered according to the doping control report and that resulting from the laboratory reports, that this discrepancy could not reasonably be deemed to have had an impact of the results of the analysis (see para. 2b above).

   Again because it is established that the presence of pseudoephedrine in samples 'A' and 'B' in a concentration three times greater than the threshold set at Appendix A of the Anti-Doping Code is due to the absorption of a pill of 'Nurofen Cold and Flu' just before the competition, this case is totally different from that which was decided in the CAS award of June 25, 1992 to which the appellant refers, so that the complaint of unequal treatment in violation of public policy within the meaning of Article 190(2)(e) is ill-funded.

   Finally, under these circumstances, one cannot argue, as the appellant does (see para. 2a above), that the failure to comply with Article 3.4 of the Anti-Doping Code, which prescribes the delivery of a minimum urine quantity of 75 ml, amounts to a violation of procedural public policy within the meaning of Article 190(2)(d) PIL Act.

4. The appeal is thus obviously without merit assuming that it can be considered admissible and must therefore be dismissed to the extent that it is admissible. In application of Article 156(1) FJO,[162] the appellant shall bear the court costs. However, no legal costs will be awarded to the respondent, who was not invited to make a submission and who thus has not incurred any costs in connection with the proceedings before the Supreme Court (Articles 159(1) and (2) FJO; Poudret/Sandoz-Monod, Commentaire de la loi fédérale d'organisation judiciaire, vol. V, 1992, n. 2 re art. 159 FJO).

For these reasons
the Supreme Court:
in view of art. 36a FJO:

1. Dismisses the appeal to the extent that it is admissible;
2. Orders that the appellant shall bear court costs in the amount of 5,000 Fr.;
3. Serves a copy of this decision on the parties and on the ad hoe Division, constituted for the Sydney Olympic Games, of the Court of Arbitration for Sport.

[162] 'FJO' is the English-language abbreviation for 'Federal Act on Judicial Organization', i.e., the act governing appeal proceedings before the Swiss Supreme Court.

CHAPTER 10
MEDIATION IN SPORTS DISPUTES

10.1 Informal Survey on Sports Mediation by ISFs & NGBs

Dr Robert Siekmann, the Director of the International Sports Law Centre at the T.M.C. Asser Institute, The Hague, The Netherlands, conducted a few years ago an informal survey amongst several International Sports Federations and National Sports Governing Bodies on the use of Mediation in Sports Disputes.

Of such Bodies, i.e., national sports organizations (Olympic sports) in the European Union, 525 were sent a Questionnaire and 43 replied: that is 12 percent.

It appears from those Bodies, who did reply to the Questionnaire, that many of them do not have their own mediation rules, but rely on the arbitration and mediation rules of the CAS, to whom, in such cases, all disputes are exclusively referred.

For example, all disputes of the International Rowing Federation (FISA) are 'uniquely dealt with by the Court of Arbitration for Sport in Lausanne'.

Likewise the International Badminton Federation (IBF) does not have any specific rules on mediation but recognises the CAS under Rule 2.4 of its Statutes, which provides as follows:

> 'Members of the Federation shall not be permitted to bring disputes with the Federation before a Court of Justice and membership of the Federation shall involve members in renouncing the right to take a dispute before the Courts. Any such dispute shall be referred to the Court of Arbitration for Sport, unless agreed otherwise by the parties in dispute.'

Likewise, the International Federation of Associated Wrestling Styles (FILA) provides: 'In the event of a sport dispute with a National Federation or an athlete, it is the CAS who is in charge of the mediation and of the arbitration if necessary.'

The International Motorcycling Federation (FIM) in Article 9 of its Disciplinary and Arbitration Code (CDA) also provides for the mandatory reference of appeals to the CAS. The FIM also includes an unusual and interesting so-called 'Law of Mercy' provision (*Droit de Clémence*) – a kind of mediation clause – in Article 8 of its CDA.

This article provides as follows:

> 'The Management Council, after consultation with the CJI (International Judicial Panel) President or upon proposal of the latter, may mitigate or completely forgive the penalty of a person who has exhausted the appeal procedures.'

On the other hand, the International Ice Hockey Federation (IIHF) expressly recognises mediation as a first means of settling disputes within its own internal procedures, but also requires exclusive arbitration by the CAS in the event of any mediation proving to be unsuccessful. The IIHF Statutes provide as follows:

> '45. Subject Matter of the Arbitration
> Any dispute concerning the interpretation and/or application of the Statutes, Bylaws, Regulations and official rules or decisions of IIHF bodies or the decisions of any duly authorized representative of the IIHF and the appeal and/or the review processes within the IIHF having fully been exercised must be settled by arbitration – except of those specified in statutes 21 C. This also applies to disputes between and among the member national associations or between them and the IIHF bodies, if no amicable agreement has been reached.
>
> 46. Court of Arbitration for Sport
> Any dispute to be settled by arbitration must be submitted exclusively by way of appeal to the Court of Arbitration for Sport (CAS) in Lausanne, Switzerland, which will resolve the dispute definitively in accordance with the Code of Sports-related Arbitration. The time limit for appeal is twenty-one days after receipt of the decision concerning the appeal.'

So, also does the French Sailing Federation (FFV) and this is perhaps not so surprising since mediation of sports disputes is quite well established in France. Indeed, the FFV expressly recommends the use of mediation in major events 'to reduce the number of protests' pointing out that 'through the mediation system, disputes may be solved very shortly, resulting in a lighter penalty'. An interesting sidelight on the value of mediation.

Again, in Title VI (comprising Arts. 95-114) of the Statutes of the Spanish Basketball Federation, there is provision for 'extrajudicial conciliation' of sporting disputes between the clubs themselves and between clubs and the Federation in certain prescribed circumstances and under certain formal conditions.

Also, the Italian Olympic Committee (Comitato Olimpico Nazionale Italiano – 'CONI') on 28 December, 2000 approved the setting up of a special Chamber of Conciliation and Arbitration for Sport (Camera di Conciliazione e Arbitrato per lo Sport). Under Article 3.5 of the Rules (Regolamento) of this Body, it is obligatory for the parties in dispute to first attempt conciliation before instituting an arbitration procedure. Conciliation is expressed to be conducted on a 'without prejudice' basis (Art. 5.8, ibid.).

However, a number of Sports Bodies, for example, the British Triathlon Association, the Hellenic Table Tennis Federation, the Portuguese Judo Federation (FPJ), the Irish Football Association and the European Swimming League (LEN), do not have any specific arbitration or mediation rules nor do they make any particular provision for the settlement of sports disputes in their Constitutions.

Others in the same situation, however, are aware of the need to make such provision. For example, the International Mountaineering and Climbing Federation (UIAA), which is based in Zollikon-Zurich in Switzerland, does not have any special rules on international sports disputes, giving as a probable reason for this that they 'have never been involved in a dispute of this kind so that the urgency for regulations is low'. However, Dr Christoph Jezler, UIAA Attorney and Board Member, adds:

> 'We are aware that this might change, in particular in connection with lawsuits of athletes banned based on the doping regulations. We have not yet discussed this in the Board but my feeling is that we would refer to arbitration by the Court of Arbitration for Sport in Lausanne.'

And the Welsh Hockey Union commented:

> 'Whilst we have no definitive Arbitration and/or Mediation Rules at present (other than internal right of appeals etc) as we are members of the Welsh Sports Association, that organisation is presently [September 2001] formulating a new Arbitration system that we would utilise. They

will obviously be based on an independent based hearing and should be available to all National Governing Bodies in Wales within the next few months.'

The British Weightlifters' Association (BWLA) in its 2001 Disciplinary Code states in Article 1: 'This Code has the overriding objective of enabling the Disciplinary Committee to deal with cases justly and efficiently'. It goes on in Article 2 to elaborate on what, so far as is practical, dealing with a case justly involves as follows:

'2.1 Ensuring that the parties are on an equal footing;
2.2 Saving expense;
2.3 Dealing with a case that is proportionate
  2.3.1 To the importance of the case both to weightlifting and the world in general;
  2.3.2 To the complexity of the issues;
  2.3.3 To the financial resources of each party;
2.4 Ensuring it is dealt with expeditiously and fairly;
2.5 Allotting to it an appropriate share of resources while taking into account the need to allocate resources to other matters.'

Article 3 provides that: 'The Disciplinary Committee must seek to give effect to the overriding objectives when it exercises any powers given to it under this code or interprets any paragraph.'

And Article 4 requires the parties who come before a Disciplinary Committee 'to help the Committee to further the overriding objectives'.

Appeals from the BWLA Disciplinary Committee go to an independent arbitrator (Art. 67 of the Code). The arbitration is conducted according to English Law and expressly excludes the right of appeal, which is limited in any case, to the English High Court under Sections 1 and 2 of the Arbitration Act, 1979. Before appointing an arbitrator, the parties in dispute must agree in writing to these requirements (Art. 69, ibid.).

The International Cycling Union (UCI) has its own Disciplinary Commission for dealing with breaches of the UCI Regulations (Art. 12.2.013 of the UCI Cycling Regulations). Appeals from decisions of the Disciplinary Commission are referred to the UCI Appeals Board (Art. 12.2.022, ibid.).

As regards the Football Association of Ireland (FAI), under its Official Rule Book, effective from 6 June, 1998, the FAI operates an Appeal Board to deal with contested decisions made by League and Divisional Associations of the FAI National League, as well as rulings of the FAI National League itself (Art. 27A and B). When all such appeal procedures of the FAI have been exhausted, Article 28 provides for arbitration as follows:

'General

In pursuance of paragraphs 1 to 5 of Article 57 of the FIFA Statutes, members undertake not to refer disputes with other members, or the Association, to a court of law. Members agree to be bound by these rules and in the event of any differences or disputes under these rules the members agree to submit such disputes or differences to arbitration by a sole arbitrator to be appointed (in the absence of agreement between the members upon such appointment and on the application of either of them) by the President (or other Officer endowed with the functions of such President) for the time being of the Law Society of Ireland or (in the event of the President or other Officer as aforesaid being unable or unwilling to make such appointment) by the next Senior Officer of that Society who is so able and willing to make the appointment and such arbitration shall be governed by the Arbitration Acts 1954 and 1980.

> The decision of the Arbitrator in respect of any dispute or difference under these Rules shall be final and conclusive and heretofore binding on the members.'

Finally, the Royal Belgian Federation for Equestrian Sports (KBRSF – FRBSE) refers appeals against decisions of the Board and the Technical and Disciplinary Committees to arbitration by the Belgian Arbitration Commission for Sport (BAS) of the Belgian Olympic and Interfederal Committee, which is based in Brussels.

As the mediation service provided by the CAS becomes better known and used and the advantages of mediation become more widely appreciated, many International and National Sports Bodies can be expected to include specific provisions for mediation of appropriate sports disputes by the CAS in their Statutes and Constitutions.

Such a so-called CAS arbitration 'clause by reference' in the Statutes of the International Equestrian Federation has been held in a ruling by the Swiss Federal Tribunal of 31 October, 1996 in the case of *N.* v. *Federation Equestre Internationale (FEI)*[163] to be perfectly valid and legal. In that case, the appellant signed a model agreement which contained an undertaking to abide by the rules of the FEI, but did not mention the arbitration clause for settling disputes which is contained in those Rules. However, the confirmation of eligibility that the appellant received contained the following express reference to CAS arbitration in the section headed 'General rules, regulations and conditions':

> 'An arbitration procedure is provided for under the FEI Statutes and General Regulations as referred to above. In accordance with this procedure, any appeal against a decision rendered by the FEI or its official bodies is to be settled exclusively by the Court of Arbitration for Sport (CAS) in Lausanne, Switzerland.'

The question before the Court was whether the reference to arbitration by the CAS was, in all the circumstances of the particular case, a legally valid one, from the formal point of view. The Court decided in the affirmative and dismissed the appellant's challenge.

There is no reason to suppose that a similar CAS mediation 'clause by reference' would also not be legal. Again, in view of its importance, the English text of this ruling of the Swiss Federal Tribunal of 31 October, 1996 is now reproduced for ease of reference:

Extract of the judgement of 31st October 1996 delivered by the 1st Civil Division of the Swiss Federal Tribunal in the case N. versus Fédération Equestre Internationale (appeal) (translation)

A. N., a professional rider domiciled outside Switzerland, is a member of a local horse riding club attached to an equestrian association which comes under the control of a National Equestrian Federation, which is itself affiliated to the Fédération Equestre Internationale (FEI), whose headquarters are in Lausanne. On 18th September 1993, he took part in an international jumping event (CSIO) in San Marino.

On 30th May 1994, the Judicial Committee of the FEI, basing its action on the FEI statutes and general regulations, and considering that the analyses performed after the aforesaid competition revealed the presence of a prohibited substance in the urine and blood of the horse ridden by N., disqualified the rider and his horse, demanded the return of any trophy and prize money won at the event in question, suspended the rider for six months, ordered him to pay the costs of the procedure and ordered the publication of such sanctions.

---

[163] I Civil Division Swiss Fed Trib 31 October, 1996.

B. In his application of 24th June 1994, N. brought an action before the President of the Lausanne District Civil Court, within the meaning of art. 75 CC, seeking the setting aside of the sanctions. The FEI raised an objection of arbitration and submitted that the plaintiff's case be dismissed.
In his interlocutory order of 21st February 1995, the President of the Lausanne District Civil Court accepted the objection and instructed the plaintiff to take proceedings in the proper court. In an order dated 21st June 1995, the Appeals Division of the Vaud Cantonal Court rejected the appeal which N. had lodged against this judgement.

C. On appeal, the plaintiff invited the Federal Tribunal to annul the order of the cantonal court and reject the objection to jurisdiction. Subsidiarily, he called for the case to be referred to the cantonal authority for further inquiries into the facts and a new decision.
The defendant proposed that such appeal be rejected.

In Law

1. The present dispute relates to the punishments specified in the statutes which are imposed by an association whose headquarters are in Switzerland with a view to penalizing the behaviour of a non-Swiss participant in a competition held abroad; more precisely, it centres on establishing whether the jurisdiction of the state courts was validly excluded by an arbitration agreement, in which case the dispute should be settled pursuant to the procedure established by articles 176 et seq. LDIP (RS 291) which govern the area of international arbitration (art. 176 para. 1 LDIP). The international nature of the dispute, within the meaning of art. 1 para. 1 LDIP, is thus not in doubt. In consequence, the jurisdiction of the state court seized at the headquarters of the association in question must be examined in the light of the apposite provisions of the Swiss Code on private international law (art. 1 para. 1 letter a and para. 2 LDIP).
2. If the parties have concluded an arbitration agreement which applies to an arbitrable dispute, the Swiss court will decline to exercise jurisdiction, subject to any provisions to the contrary appearing in an international treaty (art. 1 para. 2 LDIP), unless it finds – this being the only reason taken into account in this particular case – that the arbitration agreement has lapsed, become ineffective or is not applicable (art. 7 letter b. LDIP). On this point, internal law coincides with art. II para. 3 of the New York Convention on the Recognition and Enforcement of Foreign Arbitral Awards (RS 0.277.12), which is not, however, applicable in this particular case since the court of arbitration which would have to have cognizance of the dispute has its seat in Switzerland (ATF 122 III 139 section 2a; Poudret, A propos de la validité d'une clause arbitrale – un arrêt pouvant prêter à confusion, in: JdT 1995 1 354 et seq., 355; Poudret/Cottier, Remarques sur l'application de l'article II de la Convention de New York, in: Bulletin de l'Association suisse de l'arbitrage [ASA] 1995, p. 383 et seq., 386 ch. 1).
   According to the case law of the Federal Tribunal, if an objection of arbitration is referred to the state judge and the court of arbitration has its seat in Switzerland, he must decline to exercise jurisdiction if the summary examination of the arbitration agreement does not permit him to find that such agreement has lapsed, become ineffective or is not applicable (ATF 122 III 139 section 2b). In principle, there is no reason to go back over this case law, at least when – as in the case which is the subject of the above-mentioned order – it is the material validity of the arbitration agreement which is at issue, given that the authority to rule on this point lies primarily, or even exclusively, with the arbitration court (art. 186 para. 1 LDIP). The same cannot be said, however, when the point at issue is the formal validity of an arbitration agreement, that is to say establishing essentially whether the jurisdiction of the ordinary court has been replaced by that of a court of arbitration by an extension agreement which respects the legal requirements in terms of form. The effects of the arbitration agreement, in the same way as those of the choice of jurisdiction clause, are generally characterized by the exclusion of a given decision-making jurisdiction and the extension of another decision-making power. The efficacy of the exclusion presupposes that the competent court pursuant to objective law has been validly excluded. Now, even in cases which lend themselves to this, such exclusion may, among other reasons, face obstacles drawn from the formal provisions of procedural law (H.R Walter, Derogation c. Prorogation – Kollisionen aus interkantonal oder international vereinbarter Zuständigkeit im Zivilprozess, in: Rechtskollisionen, Festschrift für A. Heini, p. 509 et seq., 510 and references). Consequently, the

court seized which is confronted with an incident raised in this connection, shall rule on the problem of form on the basis of its own jurisdiction, which the defendant intends to exclude, and not in terms of the extended competence of another jurisdiction. It should do this with full powers of examination, whether the extension agreement at issue seeks to establish the jurisdiction of another state court or that of a court of arbitration. Indeed, it alone has the power to pronounce a binding decision on the subject of the exclusion of its own jurisdiction, provided that a decision pronounced elsewhere which has the substantive force of *res judicata* has not already excluded such jurisdiction. The consequence of this is, *inter alia,* that a decision whereby a court (ordinary or arbitration) with extended jurisdiction declines jurisdiction is not alone sufficient to establish the jurisdiction of the court whose jurisdiction is supposed to have been excluded. Thus, once the state court before which the case has been brought is called upon to rule exclusively on the exclusion of its own jurisdiction and hence to pronounce a binding decision on this point, it must rule on the issue with full powers of examination, irrespective of whether it is the first or second court before which the objection to jurisdiction has been raised (in this sense, see also: POUDRET, op. cit., p. 356 et seq.; POUDRET/COTTIER, op. cit., p. 386 et seq.; for those holding the opposite opinion, see, lastly, C.U. MAYER, Die Überprüfung internationaler Schiedsvereinbarungen durch staatliche Gerichte. Überlegungen zu BGE 121 111 38 und BGE 122 III 139, in: Bull. ASA 1996, p. 331 et seq., 402/403 and 409 to 411, where the author argues in favour of a summary examination of the formal and material validity of arbitration agreements). Nor should one lose sight of the fact that formal provisions, where these perform a protective function, must ensure that waiving the legal protection provided by the state is not done lightly, but is the result of a well-established desire to do so (WENGER, Kommentar zum Schweizerischen Privatrecht, Internationales Privatrecht, Basle, n. 7 ad art. 178 LDIP and references). Consequently, the state court must make sure that only a validly agreed exemption excludes its effects.

3. According to the findings of the cantonal court, disputes such as the one which gave rise to the present action must be referred, pursuant to the provisions enacted by the FEI (statutes and regulations), to the Court of Arbitration for Sport (TAS; cf., in this connection, ATF 119 II 271) which the International Olympic Committee (IOC) made available to the federations affiliated to it, to the exclusion of state courts. In this case, the dispute concerns whether the plaintiff is subject to such jurisdiction by an arbitration agreement in the proper form.
The CAS, which is an institutionalized court of arbitration, has its seat in Lausanne (ATF 119 II 271 section 3a). This seat being in Switzerland, the formal validity of the arbitration agreement in dispute must be examined in the light of art. 178 LDIP, in accordance with what is today the majority opinion, and not on the basis of the stricter requirements (Cf. POUDRET Et POUDRET/COTTIER, ibid., who dispute the merits of the opinion expressed in ATF 121 III 38 section 2c p. 44) – laid down by art. II para. 2 of the New York Convention (see particularly LALIVE/POUDRET/REYMOND, Le droit de l'arbitrage interne et international en Suisse, n. 7 ad art. 178 LDIP; VOLKEN, in: IPRG-Kommentar, n. 9 et seq. ad art. 178 LDIP; WENGER, op. cit., n. 5 ad art. 178 LDIP; DUTOIT, Droit international privé suisse – Commentaire de la loi fédérale du 18 décembre 1987, n. 4 ad art. 178, and the references made by these authors, including the differing opinions of some of the legal authorities). In fact, even supposing the aforesaid convention had been applicable in this particular case, art. VII para. 1 thereof, which reserves the application of the more favourable national law would, in any case, have led to the application of art. 178 LDIP (VOLKEN, op. cit., n. 10 ad art. 178 LDIP; DUTOIT, ibid.; Lucius HUBER, Arbitration Clause 'By Reference', in: The Arbitration Agreement – Its Multifold Critical Aspects, ASA Special Series no 8, p. 78 et seq., 79).
   a) Pursuant to art. 178 para. 1 LDIP, the arbitration agreement is valid, with regard to form, if it is concluded in writing, by telegram, telex, fax or any other means of communication which allows the proof of this to be established by a text.
   b) The Appeals Division established finally (art. 63 para. 2 OJ) the following circumstances:
      - the plaintiff was already the subject of proceedings before the FEI Judicial Committee and himself lodged an appeal with the CAS against one of the decisions taken by such Committee;
      - when he was selected as a member of the national equestrian team, the plaintiff signed, on 25th January 1993, a model agreement under the terms of which he undertook, dur-

ing such time as he belonged to the national squad, to abide by the provisions of the FEI regulations;

- on 27th August 1993, the National Federation concerned confirmed to the plaintiff that he was entered for the San Marino CSIO and sent him a copy of the programma relating to it, which contained, under the heading 'General rules, regulations and conditions', a figure 6 worded as follows:

'An arbitration procedure is provided flor under the FEI Statutes and General Regulations as referred to above. In accordance with this procedure, any appeal against a decision rendered by the FEI or its official bodies is to be settled exclusively by the Court of Arbitration for Sport (CAS) in Lausanne, Switzerland.'

For the cantonal court, such circumstances and references are sufficient to establish the existence of an arbitration agreement valid with respect to form.

c) The model agreement signed by the plaintiff on 25th January 1993 refers to the FEI regulations, but without mentioning the arbitration clause which appears therein. The question of whether such a global reference satisfies the requirements as to form of art. 178 LDIP is disputed. In reality, it is not possible to answer this in any general way, only on the basis of the circumstances of the particular case (HUBER, op. cit., p. 81 and the authors referred to in footnote 11; WENGER, Op. cit., n. 54 ad art. 178 LDIP; DUTOIT, op. cit., n. 6 ad art. 178 LDIP). In this respect, the starting point must be the principle whereby the requirement of a specified form, alongside the probative function assigned to it, essentially seeks to protect the parties and avoid their concluding arbitration agreements inadvertently (cf. VOLKEN, Op. Cit., n. 14 ad art. 178 LDIP). In the global reference accepted in writing, the problem consequently moves from the form to the consent and thus brings into play the principle of confidence, which is also applicable when settling disputes relating either to the consent required for an arbitration agreement to achieve its purpose, or the interpretation of such an act (ATF 121 III 38 section 3; POUDRET, Op. Cit., p. 358 et seq.; *the same,* in: Bull. ASA 1992, p. 31 ch. 6 and the decisions cited; POUDRET/COTTIER, op. cit., p. 391 et seq.; HUBER, Op. Cit., p. 83 et seq.). Thus, it is not admissible to hold that an arbitration agreement resulting from a global reference does not bind the person who, already knowing the existence of the arbitration clause when he signs the document referring to it and thereby satisfies the requirement of the written form, makes no objection to such a clause and further demonstraties, through his subsequent behaviour, that he regards himself as bound by it (see also a decision of the Commercial Court of the Canton of Zurich published in: ZR 1992-1993, no 23 section 2). A similar demonstration may result, especially with respect to the principle of confidence, from the acceptance without argument of an arbitration clause, the detailed text of which is subsequently brought to the attention of the party concerned. Such behaviour indeed allows the author of the communication logically to deduce that the arbitration agreement corresponds to the actual wish of the person to whom it was addressed at the time when he accepted, in the specified form, the global reference.

When considered in the light of the principle of confidence as thus understood, the arbitration agreement at issue is binding on the plaintiff. Equally, it is established that the plaintiff already knew the arbitration clause inserted in the FEI regulations when he signed the model agreement, and he actuálly made use of it to have recourse to the CAS on the occasion of a previous dispute. Moreover, the clause in question was communicated to him verbatim on the occasion of his selection for the competition in San Marino, without his finding fault with it. In view of these circumstances, and interpreting objectively (or prescriptively) – in other words according to the principle of confidence – the intent that he expressed in this respect, one is forced to conclude that the plaintiff agreed to submit to the arbitration agreement, validly giving his consent in formal terms by signing the model agreement, and confirming it by his unreserved acceptance of the arbitration clause contained *expressis verbis* in the documents sent to him when he entered for the competition in San Marino. Against,this conclusion, it is futile for the plaintiff to cite the so-called rule of the unusual (cf ATF 119 II 443 section la p. 446). Ihis notion indeed presupposes that one is dealing with something unexpected, an element which the person to whom the manifestation of intent is addressed had not reckoned with (JÄGGI/GAUCH, Commentaire zurichois, n. 472 ad art. 18

CO; KRAMER, Commentaire bernois, n. 204 et seq. ad art. 1 CO). This could not be so when, as in this particular case, the plaintiff already knew, and had approved, the content of the contract to which the subsequent agreement referred. Consequently, the Cantonal Court did not violate federal law in arguing as to the formal validity of the arbitration agreement at issue.

4. From the material point of view, the plaintiff holds that the arbitration agreement violates art. 27 CC and provisions of the antitrust law.
   a) (...)
   b) In as much as they are admissible, the material grounds put forward by the plaintiff will be the subject only of a summary examination for the reasons indicated above (section 2). The fact that they are new certainly does not prevent the Federal Tribunal from taking them into account, as it applies the law at its own diseretion. However, only the facts established by the final cantonal authority may be taken into consideration in the framework of this analysis, since the plaintiff claims neither that they should be added to, owing to an allegedly incorrect application of the law by the previous judges, nor that he invoked, in this respect, before the cantonal authorities and in accordance with the formal requirements, relevant facts which were not recorded in the order being challenged (art. 64 OJ).
   It does not emerge from the unappealable findings of the cantonal judges that the plaintiff would not have obtained his licence, and hence would not have been able to take part in equestrian events such as the one in San Marino, if he had not accepted the arbitration agreement. On the basis of these findings alone, there is therefore no question of accepting the existence of an inadmissible restriction on the freedom of the plaintiff. There is consequently no need to decide whether an arbitration agreement can in itself constitutie such a restriction and thus fall within the ambit of art. 27 CC, nor whether the undertaking entered into, allegedly against his will, by the plaintiff should not be challenged exclusively by an action to set aside for vitiated consent. Be that as it may, it is appropriate to observe that, according to the case law of the Federal Tribunal, the CAS, even as initially organized, already enjoyed, generally speaking, sufficient independence for its awards to be treated as judgements by state courts (ATF 119 II 271), and that it has since been restructured, taking into account the reservations on this subject expressed in the above-mentioned order, so as now to be formally separated from the IOC and placed under the aegis of the International Council of Arbitration for Sport (ICAS), a body constituted as an autonomous foundation; it is moreover divided into two Divisions and has 150 arbitrators working for it, while it previously had only 60 (see, on this subject, STEPHAN NETZLE, Der Sportler – Subjekt oder Objekt, in: RDS 115 II 1 et seq., 72 s.). In these conditions, it is in all cases out of the question to treat as an excessive obligation, within the meaning of art. 27 CC, adoption by reference of the arbitration clause contained in the defendant's regulations.
   Nor do the findings of the cantonal court reveal the existence of an antitrust-type interference with the economic freedom of the plaintiff The claim that the arbitration clause violates art. 18 para. 1 aLCart, which was still in force at the time when the order being challenged was pronounced, is thus also seen to be without merit. In any case, the provision quoted could not be cited in the present case given both that art. 18 para. 3 aLCart excludes the application, on certain conditions, of objections brought before an international arbitration court, whether it has its seat in Switzerland or abroad and whatever the nationality of the arbitrators called upon to sit within it (for the interpretation of this Provision, Cf. SCHÜRMANN/SCHLUEP, Karteilgesetz – Preisüberwachungsgesetz, n. V ad art. 18 aLCart; HOMBERGER, Kommentar zum Schweizerischen Karteligesetz, n. 15 ad art. 18 aLCart), and that internal antitrust sanctions were not specified by the procedural provisions of art. 18 para. 1 aLCart (SCHÜRMANN/SCHLUEP, op. cit., n. VII ad art. 18 aLCart). Consequently, there could be no question of accepting, at least on the basis of a summary examination, that the arbitration agreement at issue violates antitrust law.

5. For all these reasons, the formal and material objections raised by the plaintiff with regard to the order being challenged are ill-founded, in as much as they can be taken into consideration. This finding implies the rejection of the present appeal, insofar as it is admissible, and affirmation of the decision appealed against.

In any case, there is nothing to stop *ad-hoc* mediations being arranged if the parties in dispute so desire and expressly agree.

As far as the handling and settlement of disputes (referred to as 'Protests') by the International Paralympic Committee (IPC) is concerned, there are fairly detailed rules and procedures laid down in the IPC Handbook.

Section II of Part I of the Handbook contains General Regulations on Protests about classification disputes. Whilst Protests concerning eligibility issues are dealt with in Section II of Part I of the IPC Handbook.

Section IV of Part II of the Handbook deals in individual chapters with Protests in the various Sports within the Paralympic Summer Games Programme. On the other hand, Protests in those Sports comprising the Paralympic Winter Games Programme are likewise dealt with in individual chapters but in Section V of Part III of the Handbook.

All the above Rules and Regulations of the IPC are set out for ease of reference in Appendix XVII to this book.

10.2 General Advantages of Sports Mediation

Perhaps the main advantage of using mediation to settle sports disputes is that the process preserves and even restores personal and business relationships.[164] It is well known that the sports world is a small one – everyone seems to know somebody – and relationships – and, indeed, reputations – are, therefore, more important and worth preserving. As Bernard Foucher, President of the French Board of Mediators, has put it: 'Mediation allows legal disputes to be resolved within "the family of sport".'[165]

As the process is not adversarial, there is no winner and, therefore, no loser. Or, at the very most, the parties share the 'pain'. Mediation reopens lines of communication, which have often broken down, requiring the parties to co-operate with one another in finding a solution to their problems. Mediation provides the opportunity for co-operative problem solving.

Through careful probing by the mediator, the actual underlying reasons for the particular dispute can be identified and addressed. This goes a long way towards finding an appropriate solution to the parties' problems.

Dispute settlement through the courts or arbitration is backward looking, the decision or award being reached on the basis of past facts and historical background. Mediation, on the other hand, is forward looking, having regard to the future and future possibilities. Mediation is not seeking to apportion blame or fault, but to reach a solution.

Mediation is more flexible than traditional forms of litigation and even arbitration, which has become rather technical and specialised. There are no set rules of procedure to get in the way. The approach is informal and flexible.

---

[164] See I. Blackshaw, 'Resolving Sports Disputes the Modern Way – by Mediation', 18/1 *Sport and the Law Journal* (2000); I. Blackshaw, 'Sporting Settlements' (2001) 145 (27) SJ; C. Newmark, 'Is Mediation Effective for Resolving Sports Disputes?', 5/6 *International Sports Law Journal* (2000) p. 37; W. Slate, 'The Growth of Mediation and Mediation in Sports Disputes in the US', Paper presented at the CAS Symposium on Mediation in Lausanne, Switzerland, 4 November 2000.

[165] B. Foucher, 'La Conciliation Comme Mode de Reglement des Conflits Sportifs en Droit Francais', Paper presented at the CAS Symposium on Mediation in Lausanne, Switzerland, 4 November 2000.

Mediation is swift, and this is a particular advantage to sports persons, who often have pressing event and other commitments and commercial deadlines.

This was one of the factors why a dispute in 1999 between Frank Warren, the well-known boxing promoter, and Richie Woodhall, the former WBO super middleweight world champion, was successfully resolved by mediation. The case also illustrates other reasons for opting to settle disputes by mediation.

10.3 Case Study: *The Woodhall/Warren* Case

In this case, in April 1999, Richie Woodhall sought to terminate his management and promotion agreements with Frank Warren, claiming that Warren was in breach of them and also that the agreements were unenforceable. Woodhall refused to fight for Warren, and also started approaches to other boxing promoters.

On the other hand, Warren refused to let Woodhall go, claiming that contracts were valid; that there was still some considerable time to run on them; and that he was not in breach of them. The parties were adamant in their respective positions.

Woodhall, therefore, started proceedings in the High Court in June, 1999. He requested an early hearing of the case to enable him to fight the defence of his world title by September, as required by the rules of the World Boxing organisation. As the agreements required that any disputes were to be referred to the British Boxing Board of Control, Warren, for his part, sought an order from the Court to that effect.

This dispute had all the makings of a full-blown legal fight in the Courts with lots of blood on the walls – and in the full glare of the media. As such, it would not only be time consuming and expensive to both parties, but also potentially damaging for their reputations. In addition, Woodhall was anxious to get back in the ring and, if he were to continue to be of any value to Warren, he needed to fight his mandatory defence to his world title within a short period of time. So, in all these circumstances, the question arose as to whether the Court was the best forum in which to resolve this bitter dispute. It was decided to refer the dispute to mediation. And the Court was prepared to adjourn the proceedings, for a short time, to enable the parties to see if they could, in fact, settle their differences by this method.

A hastily arranged mediation was set up and conducted by CEDR. Within 72 hours later, the dispute was resolved, and Woodhall signed a new deal with Warren and continues to box for him. Unfortunately, as mediation is confidential and there is no official record or transcript of the process, it is not possible to have a 'blow by blow' account of what was said, what arguments were adduced and exactly why a settlement was reached (e.g., what leverage the mediator was able to apply to reach a compromise) and what precisely were its actual terms. One thing can, however, be deduced from the brief facts and circumstances of this dispute, there were some sporting and commercial deadlines to concentrate the minds of the parties and act as a spur to reaching a compromise. There was also a pressing need for the parties not to 'wash their dirty linen in public'!

10.4 Other Sports Mediation Cases

For many years now, many labour disputes have been settled by mediation through private and official bodies, such as Arbitration and Conciliation Advisory Service (ACAS).

With more and more sports persons, especially footballers, being paid more and more for their services, more and more disputes are arising under their employment and service contracts. This is, therefore, a field in which many such disputes are capable of being successfully settled by mediation. This has certainly been the experience in the States where labour disputes in the sporting context are quite commonplace.

The Amateur Swimming Association (ASA) encourages 'informal mediation' in settling cases of alleged breaches of their Code of Ethics in 'suitable cases'. Also the ASA operates a 'Quick Justice' system (a kind of mediation) for charges of 'brutality' in water polo. Cases must be brought within thirty days.

A schedule of some other sports disputes mediated by CEDR in the last few years, giving brief details of the nature of the dispute, the parties and the amounts involved, as well as the outcomes, follows:

- Frank Warren boxing contract – GBP 3000,000 – settled in one day;
- golf club fees – GBP 20,000 – settled in one day;
- aircraft leasing in a parachute club – GBP 340,000 – settled in two days;
- rugby club contract and the Rugby Football League – GBP 340,000 – settled in one day;
- contract concerning a yachting club – GBP 1.5m – settled in one day;
- defamation case between an English Premier League football club and national broadsheet newspaper – settled in one day;
- land dispute with Formula One Company – GBP 350,000 – settled in one day;
- football club contract – GBP 400,000 – settled in one day;
- gliding club contract – GBP 50,000 – settled in one day;
- ground dispute between two rugby clubs – GBP 500,000 – settled in one day;
- shooting club and game (pheasant supplier) – GBP 120,000 – settled in one day.

Of course, not all disputes submitted to mediation have successful outcomes, but the majority of them do.

Likewise, brief details of some sports disputes and their outcomes mediated by the ADR Group during the last years:

- Personal injury claim against a sports body by a sportswoman injured in a track and field event, valued at around GBP 150,000, was referred to mediation, but did not proceed due to the parties reaching a settlement after mediation had been proposed.
- Personal injury claim in excess of GBP 200,000 brought by a female spectator at a sports event, who suffered severe back injury as a result of a seat collapsing, against a Trust responsible for the stadium was successfully settled within three weeks of being referred to mediation.
- Dispute, valued at around GBP 80,000, between a sports clothing manufacturer and a high street sports retailer under a sale and distribution agreement was referred to mediation, but did not settle on the day, but within a month afterwards. The parties chose mediation because they wanted to preserve their existing business relationship. The mediation helped the parties to narrow the issues in dispute.
- Claim for GBP 75,000 brought by a Premiership rugby football player against his club for breach of an employment contract was successfully mediated within one day.

- Claim of GBP 450,000 for breach of an architectural/engineering/construction contract relating to the building of a football stadium was also successfully settled by mediation within one day.

So, mediation was a great success in the *Woodhall/Warren* case and the majority of the other CEDR and ADR Group mediated sports disputes mentioned above. Even in those cases where mediation did not immediately result in the settlement of the dispute concerned, the process of mediation helped to bring the parties closer together on the issues and paved the way to an ultimate amicable settlement. But, it must be said, mediation does have some intrinsic limitations.

What are they?

10.5 Sports Mediation Limitations

Mediation, as a method of settling sports disputes, is not a panacea. Although it works in most cases, it does not work in all cases.

Mediation is not suitable in those cases in which a legal precedent or an injunction is required – it is not, as previously noted, a legally based process.

Neither is mediation appropriate where a sports body needs to make a public example of another party to the dispute in order to act as a deterrent to others. This point is illustrated by the banning on 10 October, 2000 by the English Football Association (FA) of the Arsenal manager, Arsene Wenger, from the touchline for four weeks for 'threatening behaviour and physical intimidation' of an official. He was also fined four weeks' wages amounting to GBP 100,000! This sort of case raises a point of principle on which the FA is unlikely to compromise in a mediation, especially as the FA wishes to enforce its new hard-hitting disciplinary code of conduct designed to preserve the integrity of the game of football.

Being a voluntary and non-binding process until a settlement is agreed, written down and signed by the parties, it is not suitable either in those cases where the parties are not interested in trying to find a settlement by mediation or extra-judicial means. For example, the Rugby Football Union (RFU) is attempting to resolve a major dispute between the two top divisions in English Rugby Union involving 26 professional clubs and has suggested mediation. The chairman of the RFU considers that appointing an independent third party with specialist skills in resolving difficult disputes is the right way forward, whilst the head of English First Division Rugby is reported in *The Guardian* on 20 October, 2000 as saying: 'It wouldn't make any difference if they brought the Queen in to arbitrate.'

The RFU may consider that mediation is a good idea, but if the teams in dispute do not, mediation will not work in such a case.

Again, if the full glare of publicity is important, mediation is not the kind of dispute resolution method to adopt. It is an entirely confidential process.

Neither is mediation suitable for resolving doping and other disciplinary cases. Indeed, as has previously been noted, the mediation procedure of the CAS is expressly excluded for dealing with such cases, and this is also the considered opinion of David Richbell, Training Director of CEDR. Mediation may, however, be useful for dealing with the commercial fall out from such cases – for example, claims for financial compensation for losses suffered as a result of a wrongful 'conviction'.

The well-known Dianne Modahl doping case would be a good example for mediation in relation to the financial claims and losses the athlete sought to recover through the Courts, as a result of having been exonerated from taking a banned performance enhancing substance, from her World Governing Body, the International Amateur Athletic Federation, that wrongly imposed the suspension from competition in the first place. Her claim for compensation of GBP 1 million against the British Athletic Federation for an unlawful doping ban imposed on her eventually ended in failure in the English Court of Appeal on 12 October, 2001.[166]

As Kenneth Kressel has pointed out in *The Handbook of Conflict Resolution: Theory and Practice*:[167]

> 'While mediation is generally useful in many types of conflicts, it is certainly no magic bullet. Even if mediation does not succeed in producing an agreement, parties still benefit when the process helps clarify issues, or "humanize" the disputants, or help reach a partial agreement. The following factors are key obstacles to a successful mediation:
> - High levels of Conflict. The measures of conflict intensity that correlate negatively with settlement include the severity of prior conflict between the parties; a perception that the other is untrustworthy, unreasonable, angry, or impossible to communicate with; and the existence of strong ideological or cultural differences.
> - Low Motivation to Reach Agreement.
> - Low Commitment to Mediation.
> - Shortage of Resources. Resource scarcity presumably limits the range of mutually acceptable solutions and may reduce the motivation of both the parties and the mediator.
> - Disputes Involving Fundamental Principles.
> - Parties of Unequal Power.'

10.6 Criteria for Mediating

In deciding, however, whether mediation is suitable or not, it is often said by protagonists of mediation, including David Richbell, Former Training Director of CEDR, that the question to be asked is not 'is mediation appropriate?', but rather 'why is mediation not appropriate?' Each case should be considered on its own particular merits.

However, in an insightful and practical article, entitled 'Ready ... Set ... Mediate'[168] Peter J. Comodeca, a Partner at Calfee, Halter & Griswold, Cleveland, Ohio, USA and a member of the American Arbitration Association Panel of Neutrals, identifies a number of key factors that disputants and their counsel must consider before pursuing mediation. The text of his article is as follows:

Peter J. Comodeca[169]
Ready ... Set ... Mediate

While it's no secret that more and more people are discovering the benefits of mediation, it is not always clear why some parties are more successful at it than others. This article by Peter Comodeca

[166] *Modahl* v. *British Athletic Federation* [2001] *All ER* (D) 181 (October). See also I. Blackshaw, 'Modahl Loses Appeal for Compensation', 4/6 *Sports Law Bulletin* (November/December 2001) pp. 1, 3 and 4.

[167] Edited by Morton Deutsch and Peter T. Coleman (San Francisco, Jossey-Bass 2000).

[168] *Dispute Resolution Journal* (November 2001/January 2002) at pp. 32-38.

[169] The author is a partner at Calfee, Halter & Griswold in Cleveland, Ohio. He serves on the AAA's roster of neutrals; his arbitration and mediation experience is primarily in the construction, commercial and international arenas. He is a member of several professional associations including the American Bar Association (Public Contract Law Section) and the International Bar Association.

identifies a number of key factors that disputants and their counsel must consider before pursuing mediation.

Regardless of one's position on mediation, it has become an integral part of the legal process in the United States. Given the crowded dockets most courts must contend with, the use of alternative dispute resolution methods, such as mediation, is only likely to increase in the future.

It is imperative that lawyers and clients be familiar with the fundamental aspects of mediation. They must be able to recognize when it may be in their best interest to mediate, or how to proceed when required to mediate by court order. Proper knowledge of mediation techniques can help an attorney avoid unnecessary surprises in the process.

This article will help attorneys identify issues to consider before agreeing to mediation.

Parties involved in a dispute participate in mediation either voluntarily or involuntarily. Often, parties recognize the benefits of mediation and choose to mediate voluntarily. The most common method used to commence mediation is by entering into a contract or agreement identifying mediation as a dispute resolution mechanism.

In the absence of a contract requirement, the parties may agree, after a dispute arises, to pursue mediation to resolve the dispute. However, mediation is not always chosen by the parties. It can be imposed involuntarily. Generally, this occurs pursuant to a court order or directive.

Involuntary mediation also occurs when the parties are subject to a governing policy or regulation requiring mediation of which they were unaware. For example, some standing court procedural rules require mediation as a preliminary step to either arbitration or litigation.

Appropriate Mediation Clause

Parties to a contract often choose to include a mediation clause applicable to any dispute that arises under the contract. Contractual mediation clauses are generally commingled with other dispute resolution procedures. Often, mediation is required as a precursor to arbitration or litigation. Also, mediation is commonly used in conjunction with nonbinding negotiations between the parties. Thus, many different issues must be considered in drafting the appropriate mediation clause for each individual contract.

First, a determination must be made whether the mediation should be binding or nonbinding. If the clause mandates binding mediation, a provision should be included in the contract permitting an entry of judgment by either party to enforce the mediation result. If the clause mandates nonbinding mediation, the clause should be clear as to whether or not mediation is required prior to the pursuit of arbitration or litigation.

Next, the parties must consider the scope of claims to be governed by the mediation. Mediation may not be appropriate for all claims that may arise related to the agreement. Thus, for various issues under the contract, the parties may wish to narrow the application of the mediation clause.

The clause may also limit mediation to certain categories of claims such as international, intellectual property, labor, or valuation issues. Additionally, mediation does not have to address the entire dispute. For example, mediation can be used as a method to resolve disputes and minimize costs of parallel proceedings by achieving agreements on discovery, stipulations, or protective orders.

The parties must also decide what types of damage claims may be considered by the mediator. Regardless, when attempting to limit the scope of the mediation clause the parties must clearly delineate the claims to which the mediation clause is applicable in order to avoid unnecessary confusion should a dispute arise.

Another issue to be considered by the parties is whether or not to extend the mediation clause to include disputes involving third parties. If the parties to a contract desire to include third parties in any mediation, it may be necessary to modify third-party contracts to require the third parties to participate in any mediation pursued by the parties to the core agreement.

An example of such a scenario would be a construction dispute between the project owner and the general contractor. A mediation clause could be drafted to require subcontractors to participate to the extent relevant to the dispute. The general contractor would then include this requirement in the subcontracts.

The parties must choose the manner in which the mediator will be selected. Mediation is often described as a process where the mediator functions as a neutral facilitator. To ensure fairness and neutrality, the mediation clause should include provisions describing how the mediator will be chosen.

The clause should provide, or refer to existing rules that provide, that the mediator shall be neutral and shall fully disclose any and all relationships he or she may have to the parties and/or to counsel involved in the mediation.

In some instances, it may be prudent to specifically identify in advance an agreed upon mediator by name. This could be done in the contract or by separate agreement referring to the contract.

Discovery in the United States under any alternative method of dispute resolution is generally less extensive than with litigation. However, some form of discovery, though limited, may be necessary to make a mediation effective. Thus, the mediation clause may also address what, if any, discovery will be required prior to conducting the actual mediation.

Generally, mediation clauses are silent on the scope of discovery. However, there are many situations where a requirement for the exchange of all related and relevant documents may be beneficial. This can he especially important in mediations involving international parties. For example, one party's legal system may provide for a full exchange of documents while the other party's legal system may not have a similar provision. In such situations, directly addressing discovery in the contract may help prevent ambiguity should a dispute arise, fostering a better climate for mediation.

There are many general issues to be considered in drafting a mediation clause. The parties may want to select which jurisdiction's law will govern the mediation. Additionally, the parties should select a mutually acceptable location for the mediation to take place. In an attempt to prevent unnecessary delay, the parties should also set forth a specific time frame for the mediation to commence and conclude relative to the acknowledgment of the dispute.

Mediation is generally a confidential process. However, to further protect against disclosure of statements or positions discussed during the mediation, the parties may wish to contractually define information exchanged and discussed during mediation as confidential. Such information would include presentations, statements, and positions advocated. Therefore, such information could not be used in any subsequent proceedings other than an action for breach of the mediation agreement.

For example, the parties could include a clause stating, 'The mediation process is confidential. Neither a party nor the mediator may disclose the existence, contents, or results of any mediation unless the parties agree in writing to such disclosure or unless such disclosure is required by law.'

When drafting a mediation clause, consideration should be given to the rules that will govern the mediation process. Many alternative dispute resolution organizations have developed their own rules governing mediation, such as the American Arbitration Association (AAA), the Center for Public Resources (CPR), and the International Chamber of Commerce (ICC). Choosing one of these organizations to conduct the mediation will save the parties from having to draft their own rules, while at the same time helping to ensure fairness and neutrality. Selecting the organization that will better suit the needs of the parties will depend upon the specific interests of the parties to the agreement.

Finding a Mediator

Generally, the agreement will establish a mechanism for selection of the mediator. If the parties have selected an alternative dispute resolution organization to conduct the mediation, such as the AAA, the CPR, or the ICC, then the clause may permit the selected organization to provide the parties with a roster of potential mediators. As mentioned above, the parties can also identify a particular mediator by name in the mediation clause.

If the mediation agreement remains silent as to the method of selecting a mediator, there are several ways that the mediator may be selected after a dispute arises. The parties may negotiate to select a mediator on their own. The parties may also agree to submit a request to an alternative dispute resolution organization for a proposed roster of mediators from which a selection will be made. From this list, the parties can negotiate a selection, or the selected organization may be asked to appoint a mediator.

The parties may also ask the ADR organization to provide a shortened roster of proposed mediators. Once this list is provided, the parties can rank the potential mediators in order from most desirable to least desirable. The intersection of the parties' respective rankings becomes the selected mediator. Or, the parties may choose, to strike names from the list in turn until only one mediator remains.

Often, if mediation is unsuccessful, the parties will proceed to arbitration. Thus, the parties must evaluate, should mediation fail, whether or not the chosen mediator can also later serve as the arbitrator. As a general rule, this is not advisable because of the structure and process of mediation, which necessitates frank and candid discussions between the parties. If the parties know that the same mediator will be used for any subsequent arbitration, it may have a chilling effect on the discussions between the parties during the mediation process.

The process of selecting a mediator is much more efficient if biographies are available to the parties for the potential mediators. Ideally, conflict disclosures by the potential mediators should be made prior to selection. Regardless, upon appointment of the mediator the parties should require him or her to fully disclose any potential conflicts which might affect his or her services as the mediator.

Factors to Consider in Mediator Selection

There are many factors to consider when selecting a mediator. Generally, a mediator must be skilled in dealing with people as well as the processes of mediation. It is also beneficial if a mediator has subject matter expertise regarding the issues involved in the dispute.

The ability to relate well with others is paramount to being a good mediator. Such abilities should be evaluated in light of the personalities of the parties, the requirement for overall fairness and integrity of the mediator, and the coercive factors that may be necessary to effectuate a successful mediation.

Needless to say, the mediator should be familiar with the process of mediation. The mediator must be able to facilitate sessions with the parties jointly, as well as private caucus sessions. A good mediator will be able to encourage innovative thought and compromise. Process skills must also include an overriding sense of fairness to each side with regard to their abilities to present argument and speak on the relevant issues.

While many people involved with mediation feel that subject matter expertise is an essential criteria for mediator selection, others argue that it is not. The need for subject matter expertise generally depends upon the theories argued in each individual case.

If the nature of the dispute hinges on the comprehension of a specific industry, subject matter expertise in that industry may be relevant to facilitating a successful mediation. If the dispute focuses on legal arguments, a mediator with expertise in the governing law would be more desirable. Since the parties will often argue different theories in a single case, they will frequently have a different conception of what qualities comprise the 'ideal' mediator.

Additionally, the nature of a dispute can be very different depending on whether the dispute is of a business nature or has emotional aspects. Thus, the parties would want to be careful to choose a mediator who is skilled at dealing with the specific type of dispute at issue.

Mediation has both an evaluative and facilitative function. The mediator must attempt to evaluate the dispute, and determine what a proper range of resolution might be. The mediator must also act as a facilitator, to guide the parties toward resolution.

These two criteria may be in conflict during the mediation. For example, there are times when a rational evaluation of the dispute results in favoring one party over the other. This may conflict with the facilitative role of the mediator. If this occurs, it should be handled tactfully by the mediator, avoiding the appearance of favoritism.

The style of mediation that the parties desire may also affect mediator selection. If the parties wish to have the mediator shuttle between them, they will want to choose a mediator that will be able to do this effectively. If the dispute requires a more forceful presence, that will also factor into the mediation selection process. Thus, the parties must consider whether they want a mediator that will aggressively push them towards compromise or one that will take a more relaxed approach.

Pre-Mediation Consideration

A mediator comes to the dispute with, at best, two-dimensional knowledge. While the mediator may have some level of subject matter expertise relating to the dispute, the mediator is unaware of the history and evolution of the dispute and the emotional implications that it may have on the parties.

Party advocates assume a different role in mediation than the roles adopted in other forums. The style of advocacy expected in arbitration or litigation is out of place in mediation.

In mediation, party advocates must take care to maintain credibility with the mediator at all times during the process. Advocates should view their roles as being partners to the process. They can enhance the process of mediation by presenting their client's case in a straightforward manner.

More importantly, party advocates can assist by presenting information to the mediator that may be helpful in persuading the opponent to believe that settlement will be more beneficial than proceeding to arbitration or litigation.

Party advocates should attempt to present the mediator with pre-mediation written submissions. The submissions should clearly include a statement of the facts of the case, as well as an argument that is based on those facts and supported by the governing law. At the very least, key documents as well as the text of relevant cases or statutes should be provided to the mediator prior to the mediation session.

Pre-mediation submissions are an important tool both for assisting the mediator in grasping the subtleties of the dispute at hand and for educating the opposing party. A compromise cannot be expected unless each party has a full understanding of the opposing arguments. The opportunity to evaluate and test the merit of the opposition's arguments is an essential facet of the mediation process.

Successful mediation requires the presence of a client representative with full settlement authority. This provides the best opportunity to take advantage of the dynamics, of mediation. It can be quite costly if an agreement is reached through mediation but is later vetoed by someone at a higher level who did not participate in the mediation.

Additionally, to ensure a knowledgeable response to the ebb and flow of mediation, the client should consider and prepare possible concessions in position as well as potential fallback positions prior to the mediation. Advance preparation for position movement allows for less stress and better understanding of the opposition's concerns during the mediation.

Basic Misconceptions

Mediation is not simply an opening statement followed by negotiation. Mediation is fundamentally different from arbitration/litigation. In mediation, the parties reach an agreement facilitated by the mediator. Conversely, in arbitration/litigation, the arbitrator, judge, or jury reaches the decision and imposes it upon the parries. Thus, the opening statement in mediation is not principally directed toward the mediator, hut rather to the opposing party.

Mediation is not the same as negotiation. Generally, mediation is commenced after an unsuccessful negotiation. Additionally, the distinction between mediation and negotiation is highlighted by the role of the mediator. The mediator's ultimate goal is to facilitate an agreement between the parties.

Preliminary steps towards reaching such an agreement involve minimizing the advocacy and posturing between the parties and focusing on the facts and law which are related to the dispute. In negotiation, party advocacy and posturing remain largely untempered, and may operate to aggravate the dispute.

Mediation is focused on achieving a settlement. In any dispute, an assessment of the risks and costs involved determine whether or not a party will settle. In mediation, an important goal is to encourage that such an assessment be done objectively. While counsel may initially advocate their client's position during a mediation, one goal of the mediator is to convert such advocacy to more objective counseling and advice to the client. Many party advocates hesitate to make this transition during mediation for fear of appearing to lack the appearance of zealously representing their client.

Mediation is not always the answer. In some cases, a party may steadfastly refuse to consider any position reflected in opposing arguments. Mediation is probably not appropriate in such scenarios. Also, because the results of mediation do not add to the common law, mediation is not appropriate if a party seeks to create legal precedent that will govern prospective or parallel disputes.

Conclusion

Mediation can be an effective tool for ensuring efficient, fair dispute resolution. Correctly drafted, a contractual mediation clause can help to protect the rights of the parties involved in the dispute by fully defining the scope of the process.

In order for mediation to be successful, however, the parties must be aware of the various concerns that need to be addressed prior to beginning the process. With careful consideration, the final result – a mutual agreement – will be acceptable, and even welcome, to all parties involved.

CHAPTER 11
SPORTS MEDIATION IN THE PEOPLE'S REPUBLIC OF CHINA

11.1 Background to the New Chinese Sports Law

Beijing put in a strong bid in Monaco in 1993 to host the Millennium Olympic Games of 2000, but was narrowly beaten by Sydney by two votes (45-43). The deciding factor seems to have been human rights and, in particular, the massacre in Tiananmen Square of June 1989. However, in Moscow on 16 July, 2001, the IOC accepted Beijing's bid – widely regarded objectively as being the best of the bids – to host the Summer Games of 2008, but not without controversy and active opposition from human rights' campaigners. The 2008 Beijing Games, as usual, were hailed by the President of the IOC, Dr Jacques Rogge, at the Closing Ceremony as 'the best games ever!' We will see what is said of the next Summer Olympic Games to be held in London in 2012.

China's profound disappointment in being rejected by the IOC in 1993 accelerated the completion of a new comprehensive Chinese Sports Law, which was published on 29 August, 1995 and took effect on 1 October, 1995.

An English translation of this important Law will be found in Appendix XVIII to this book.

In an article entitled, 'China's Sports Law',[170] Professor James Nafziger of Willamette University, USA and Li Wei, a former Assistant Professor of Law at Shanghai University, China, critically review – in some depth – this new Law, which they say 'reflects the complexity of a legal system in transition, giving new meaning to the concept of Market-Leninism'.

They add:

> 'On the one hand, the legislation confirms state control over sports by relying heavily on standard political ideology, centralized policy-making, and traditional administrative practice to help the national government achieve several major objectives. These objectives include gaining greater international prestige from the success of Chinese athletes; creating a structure of dynamic sports organizations; providing reliable sources of funding for sports; and deterring the use of banned drugs in sports activities, bribery of athletes and sports officials, and gambling on sports events. On the other hand, the Sports Law shifts much of the day-to-day control over sports to non-governmental initiatives. In particular, it has formalized the establishment of market-oriented, western-style sports associations to carry out national sports policy, develop new sources of funding, and impose sanctions against athletes for non-criminal violation of anti-doping and other organizational rules.'

En passant, it may be noted that the new Chinese Sports Law legalises the commercialisation of and investment in sports, including sports sponsorship (see Arts. 3 and 42), which

---

170 XLVI/3 *The American Journal of Comparative Law* (Summer 1998) pp. 453-483.

has become a popular marketing tool not only for major Chinese companies but also foreign ones doing business in or with China. Also, a National Sports Lottery to raise funds for sports has also been established pursuant to the provisions of the new Sports Law.

11.2 New Chinese Sports Mediation and Arbitration Body

The new Sports Law also provides for the establishment of a special body to mediate and arbitrate disputes arising in competitive sports. This, as the authors point out, is very much in line with the Chinese normal preference for mediation and arbitration over adjudication. This new body shares authority over dispute resolution with the non-governmental sports associations. And this very much reflects the growing trend internationally of settling sports disputes by a combination of administrative review by sports bodies and specialised arbitration and mediation.

Article 33 of the Chinese Sports Law provides that:

> 'Any disputes arising in competitive sports shall be subject to mediation and arbitration by a sports arbitration body.
>
> Rules governing the establishment of a sports arbitration body and the scope of its mandate shall be adopted by the State Council.'

This extra-judicial form of dispute resolution reflects traditional Chinese mechanisms of dispute resolution but, as James Nafziger and Li Wei also point out, it is also progressive 'in its reliance on a specialized process in which nongovernmental sports... will play a decisive role ... [and]... in line with official endorsement of nongovernmental (private) tribunals to arbitrate disputes'.

However, they also draw attention to a possible conflict of interest problem, namely: 'if dispute resolution is largely left up to the sports associations or bodies closely related to them, the body that applies sanctions might be the same as, or closely associated with, a party to a dispute'. In other words, one of the fundamental principles of 'natural justice', namely 'no person may be a judge in their own cause' (*nemo judex in causa sua potest*) – the so-called 'rule against bias' – may be breached.

11.3 Evaluation of Article 33 of the New Chinese Sports Law

Evaluating Article 33 of the new Chinese Sports Law, James Nafziger and Li Wei have this to say:

> 'it is noteworthy ... that the Sports Law rejects any recognition of the adjudicable rights of athletes, although it does entitle them to financial, educational and other privileges. In lieu of litigation, article 33 ... prescribes mediation and arbitration ... In this respect, China, doing what comes naturally, is in the vanguard of a global trend toward shunning the courtroom to resolve disputes involving athletes and sports activity. Taking an approach that is traditional for it but progressive for the global system, China may better avoid the risks and complexity of dispute avoidance and resolution that so beset the sports arena in other countries.'

And go on to conclude as follows:

'On the other hand, China's refusal to adjudicate any rights of individual athletes denies them an appropriate remedy for the most serious breaches of fairness and justice that more informal methods of dispute resolution do not always rectify. The Sports Law has accorded individual athletes many privileges and a measure of autonomy from the bureaucracy as members of the newly empowered sports associations, but their standing to vindicate fundamental rights remains doubtful. The legislation is thus a product of China's policy of Market-Leninism.'

CHAPTER 12
SPORTS OMBUDSMAN

For the sake of completeness, a word or two about a novel idea for settling sports disputes extra-judicially a la mediation: a Sports Ombudsman.

12.1 Background

This has been put forward by Philip Morris of the University of Stirling, who is an Associate Member of the British and Irish Ombudsman Association. He suggests that sports lawyers should think seriously about using the Ombudsman technique as a form of dispute resolution mechanism.

He points out:

> 'No longer confined to the province of government, Ombudsmen are now well entrenched in the professions and in the financial services sector in the UK and abroad. Indeed, this year has witnessed the creation of a "super" Financial Services Ombudsman scheme for the UK.'

And he goes on to say: 'In principle, there is no reason why, albeit on a self-regulatory and much smaller scale, this model could not be replicated by major UK sports governing bodies.'

12.2 Advantages

Whilst recognising that the arbitration and mediation services offered by the SDRP and CAS may make a Sports Ombudsman redundant, he mentions a number of advantages that an Ombudsman could offer in the sporting context. Amongst them are the following:

- An Ombudsman can draw on his/her own notions of fairness and good administration thus enhancing the protection of athletes.
- An Ombudsman in performing his/her conciliation functions can not only provide redress, but also use a complaint for improving practices within the sports 'industry'[the so-called 'quality control' dimension].
- An Ombudsman acts totally independently of any sports bodies or interests.

The author of this book, having had a good and wide professional experience of the work of Ombudsmen in the Scandinavian countries in settling consumer disputes in relation to advertising and marketing complaints, considers that the idea of a Sports Ombudsman is generally worth pursuing.

This is especially so if, as Morris also suggests, Ombudsman schemes are established in other sporting nations as part of what he calls 'an international extra-judicial resolution structure'. He goes on to propose that such schemes incorporate a final right of appeal to the CAS where the dispute 'involves important or novel issues of sports law or policy'. Such arrangements, he concludes, could 'extend and strengthen [the] role [of CAS] as a pivotal institution in the development of a coherent and sophisticated corpus of sports law jurisprudence'.

Certainly, as sport has become transnational, there is a need for a coherent international sports disputes structure, which relies on effective alternative forms of dispute resolution whenever and wherever appropriate. However, at the time of writing, it must be said that there would not appear to be any interest throughout the world in setting up Sports Ombudsmen as part of such an international network.

12.3 The Role of the Sports Ombudsman

Because of its novelty and interest, we reproduce the complete text, from which the above extracts are taken, of an article written by Morris and entitled, 'The Role of the Ombudsman in Sporting Disputes: Some Personal Thoughts'[171] in which he expounds his ideas for a Sports Ombudsman:

> The apparently relentless juridification of much professional sport both in the United Kingdom and abroad, which is an inevitable consequence of the massive commercial interests in the structures, processes and outcomes of modern sport, has prompted debate about the appropriate mechanisms for dispute resolution. The initial enthusiasm which accompanied increasing judicial intervention in sports administration has begun to wane, largely because of an increasing realisation that high profile, bitterly fought court battles between athletes and governing bodies do not necessarily serve the long term interests of sports governing bodies, athletes or indeed the sport itself. While academic and practising lawyers may view long running legal conflicts involving the likes of Jean- Marc Bosman, Butch Reynolds, Tonya Harding and Diane Modahl as providing fertile ground for research projects and fee income, these disputes leave significant problems in their wake.
>
> While I can accept that some sporting disputes may make a significant and lasting contribution to the development of national and international sports law jurisprudence as well as leading to structural changes in a particular sport for the enduring benefit of athletes (Bosman is perhaps the outstanding example of this) I would, on an objective cost-benefit analysis, express serious concerns about the utility of court involvement in most sporting disputes. The costs, antagonism, bad publicity and (all too frequently) ineffectual remedies awarded all make a compelling case for confining court intervention to disputes raising novel or crucial issues of sporting or legal policy where a clear, binding precedent is of overriding importance. To argue in favour of a shift toward a greater measure of self-regulation is of course not new. What is now urgently needed though is a balanced assessment of the various modes of alternative dispute resolution potentially on offer, the interaction between them and whether it might be possible to design an integrated national and international sports dispute resolution structure.
>
> Completion of this project requires sports lawyers to think seriously about the utility of the Ombudsman technique as a mechanism of redress. No longer confined to the province of government, Ombudsmen are now well entrenched both in the professions and in the financial services sector both in the United Kingdom and abroad. Indeed this year has witnessed the creation of a 'super' Financial Services Ombudsman scheme for the United Kingdom. The scheme is the largest Ombudsman institution in the world with 330 employees and an annual operating budget expected to exceed £20 million. In principle there is no reason why, albeit on a self -regulatory and much smaller basis, this model could not be replicated by major United Kingdom sports governing bodies. The obvious ob-

---

171 P. Morris, 'The Role of the Ombudsman in Sporting Disputes: Some Personal Thoughts', 3/4 *Sports Law Bulletin* (2000).

jection is that there is no room or need for the Ombudsman technique given the existence of distinct arbitration schemes operated by some governing bodies, the recent launch of the United Kingdom Sports Dispute Resolution Panel and, on the international plane, the increasingly important contribution of the Court of Arbitration for Sport.

Without wishing to understate the work of these bodies there are key advantages, I believe, offered by the Ombudsman model in the sporting context:

An Ombudsman, unlike arbitration techniques, is not confined to strict legal standards but can draw upon his/her own subjective notions of fairness and good administration which together furnish athletes with enhanced protection.

In performance of his/her adjudication and conciliation functions an Ombudsman does not characteristically focus on redress of individual grievance but may also use a complaint as a vehicle for improving administrative practices within the industry (the so-called 'quality control' dimension of an Ombudsman's work).

Arbitration mechanisms continue to suffer from the lingering suspicion by athletes (even one as prestigious and well established as the Court of Arbitration for Sport) that they are not truly independent of governing bodies whereas Ombudsmen schemes can be designed, as the United Kingdom financial services industry experience shows, in such a way as to allay any such fears.

Unlike arbitration, with its reliance on formal, court like hearings, Ombudsmen tend to prefer the use of inquisitorial, paper-based investigations which are user-friendly and more conducive to continuing harmonious relations between the athlete and the governing body

Where a dispute raises legal or policy issues more appropriately determined by a court it is possible, by use a 'test cases' clause in the Ombudsman's terms of reference, to provide for the timely transfer of the dispute to a court provided the complainant consents and with the sports governing body meeting the erstwhile complainant's legal costs.

If one accepts the case for United Kingdom Sports Ombudsman the next issue is to delineate its main features. It could, I think, be created on a self-regulatory basis using the same 'blue print' as existing private sector schemes, that is to say membership of a private company, an independent Ombudsman Council to perform a 'buffer' function between the sponsoring governing bodies and the Ombudsman and a separate Board, composed of a majority of sports' governing bodies representatives, raising the finance for the scheme which would take the form of a fixed levy and a case fee for every formal complaint lodged with the Ombudsman.

Given the self regulatory character of the scheme, achieving comprehensive membership by United Kingdom governing bodies would rest, ultimately, on persuading them of the benefits of membership in terms of cheapness, speed, informality and privacy compared with litigation and traditional arbitration. To avoid charges of ousting the athlete's 'constitutional' right of access to court for a determination as to his/her legal rights, use of the Ombudsman should be voluntary with a right to reject the Ombudsman's eventual recommendation and pursue the matter in court. I very much doubt whether many would opt to do so given that the Ombudsman unlike a court enjoys the capacity to transcend the parameters of legality by applying any relevant code of practice and his own subjective standards of fairness and good administrative practices.

Finally, if Ombudsman schemes along similar lines were established in other sporting nations an embryonic international extra-judicial dispute resolution structure could emerge by incorporating a final right of appeal for either party to the Court of Arbitration for Sport on the ground that the dispute involves important or novel issues of sports law or policy. The proliferation of national Sporting Ombudsmen and their integration with the Court in this manner could extend and strengthen its role as a pivotal institution in the development of a coherent and sophisticated corpus of sports law jurisprudence.

12.4 The Athletes Ombudsman

It should be added that the idea of a Sports Ombudsman as proposed by Morris is not entirely new. Under amendments passed in 1998 to the US Amateur Sports Act, an Ombudsman for Athletes has been established under the auspices of the United States Olympic Committee.

The Athletes Ombudsman has the two following functions:

'(A) to provide independent advice to athletes at no cost about the applicable provisions of [the Amateur Sports Act] ... and the constitution and bylaws of the corporation, national governing bodies, a paralympic sports organisations [sic], international sports federations, the International Olympic Committee, the International Paralympic Committee, and the Pan-American Sports Organization, and with respect to the resolution of any dispute involving the opportunity of an amateur athlete to participate in the Olympic Games, the Paralympic Games, the Pan-American Games, world championship competition as defined in the constitution and bylaws of the corporation; and (B) to assist in mediating any such disputes.'

CHAPTER 13
EVALUATION OF SPORTS MEDIATION

Although, as has been pointed out, it has certain limitations, mediation is generally proving itself to be a modern effective alternative method of resolving disputes in general. As the Woodhall/Warren and other sports cases show (e.g., the dispute between Ellery Hanley, the Rugby League coach, and his club's directors over some unflattering remarks he made publicly about them in 2000), mediation can also prove to be a most suitable way of settling sports disputes quickly, effectively and relatively cheaply.

The success of the mediation in the *Woodhall/Warren* case[172] is a clear sign that resort to the Courts is no longer the only and perhaps not the best way of resolving disputes. And it also shows that opting for mediation should no longer be regarded as a sign of weakness on the part of any of the parties. As Frank Warren remarked: 'It was important to all concerned to have brought this matter to a speedy conclusion. We have shaken hands and look forward to resuming our successful partnership.'

For Richie Woodhall, speed was also 'of the essence': 'I am pleased this episode has now come to an end. I can tell my fans that I will be back in the ring within the next few weeks.'

Mediation generally offers so many advantages over traditional dispute resolution methods. In the sports field, in particular, the attraction of mediation has been well summarised by Frank Warren's Lawyer, Dominic Bray, in the following terms:

> 'Mediation can have real benefits, not only in terms of savings of management time and money, but also, and perhaps more significantly, in the preservation of ongoing relationships between the parties. These relationships are fundamental to any business, but particularly so in the sporting context.'

Not only must the case be suitable for mediation, but the success of the mediation will also, to a large extent, depend upon the qualities and skills of the mediator. On this point, Richie Woodhall's Lawyer, Richard Cramer, remarked: 'The mediator proved to be a very positive feature and focused the parties' minds on settlement.'

He or she needs to have knowledge and understanding of sport as well as being a good mediator.

As Robert Barker, a former Senior International In-house Counsel of The Coca-Cola Company, one of the world's major sponsors of major international sports events, including the Summer and Winter Olympic Games, but now a partner in the Atlanta Office of the US Law Firm of Smith Helms Mulliss & Moore, has remarked in relation to the handling of sports disputes[173]: 'If mediation ... [is] required ... traditional mediators ... may not serve you well ... [t]hey are not skilled in the industry of sports ... .'

---

172 See CEDR Press Release of 21 July, 1999.

173 'Alternatives' Center for Public Resources/CPR Legal, May, 2000.

These remarks are made in an interesting article written for the Center for Public Resources (CPR) entitled, 'Resolving Sports Conflicts Centers on Rights' Analysis', in which Barker is in no doubt that: ' ... sport is a unique industry ... [and] ... produces a product – a sporting event – that excites emotion in the industry's consumers. Emotion is a contributing factor to its uniqueness'.

In view of sport's uniqueness, he points out that, if, for instance, an intellectual property issue arises in connection with a sports dispute:

> '... traditional mediators ... are not skilled in the finer issues of intellectual property ... [which] ... is its own law merchant, and it probably does little good to have a [mediator] who will not recognise an IP right just because it might not be recognised at law ... Like our judicial system today, traditional neutrals [i.e., mediators] tend to want to render equitable rulings, rather than enforcing the rights in a contract – particularly if those rights are hard fought and harsh.'

And on the subject of using ADR generally in sports matters, he adds rather perceptively:

> 'There is a need for a global solution to sport problems, not just solutions based on a case-by-case negotiation. If you are acting in a particular sector or sub-industry, encourage those in the industry to create a standard for mediation … Some sports lawyers are lucky enough today to be defining the rules for new leagues and sports for tomorrow. They should consider writing ADR into the governing documents of their leagues – and make it condition for all contracts with outsider parties.'

It is in the light of remarks such as these that suitably qualified mediators need to be chosen if the mediation is to be a successful one.

Reference was made earlier to the gender of the mediator and, according to the nature and circumstances of the particular dispute, this may also be a relevant consideration in choosing a suitable mediator to act in an individual case. Of course, much continues to depend on the skills and experience of the mediator generally and, in particular, his or her knowledge and understanding of the sports industry. In this connection, there are a number of women involved in the administration of sport and the practice of sports law internationally. In the author's experience, women generally do tend to have more patience and a better understanding of and insight into human nature than men! On the other hand, women, it is generally considered, also have a tendency to be swayed by emotion – to decide more according to their hearts than their heads! It is interesting to note that the UK Sports Solutions Panel of Mediators, contains only one woman. Beyond these brief remarks on the subject of women mediators, it is not prudent to venture any further into such a controversial minefield!

According to Maitre Paul Dahan, a leading French Sports Lawyer, based in Cannes, mediation is usually attempted in disputes between leading footballers (e.g., Anelka, Ginola and Vieira) and French and European Football Clubs, through the competent National Federations and/or FIFA, before invoking EU Law. In France, there is a special Law of 13 July, 1992 relating to the Settlement of Sports Disputes by Arbitration and Mediation. This Law has been strengthened by another Law of 6 July, 2000.

In Germany, according to Dr Markus Buchberger, a Sports Lawyer from Dortmund, who specialises in sports litigation, most of the German Sports Bodies, including the German Football Association, now include mediation in their Statutes as a dispute resolution procedure, although, to date, mediation has not been widely used in sports cases there. However, he expects the practice to grow in the future.

Surprisingly, in the States – the home of ADR – mediation in sports disputes is also still – relatively speaking – virgin territory, although because of its confidential nature, it is difficult to get a true picture of the actual extent of sports mediation. As Professor James A.R. Nafziger, Thomas B. Stoel Professor of Law at Willamette University College of Law, USA recently told the author:

> '... mediation merits much greater attention than it has had as an alternative to both forms of adjudication – arbitration and litigation. In fact, of course, much informal mediation does go on, but is seldom reported.'

However, in the States, a Uniform Mediation Act was approved in August, 2001 to replace the patchwork of State Laws on Mediation with a uniform code. In particular, the Act includes a new provision to prevent disclosure of communications during any subsequent legal procedures, which reads as follows:

> 'Unless subject to the [open meetings act/open records act], mediation communications are confidential to the extent agreed by the parties or provided by other laws or rules of this Sate.'

William K. Slate II, President and Chief Executive Officer of the American Arbitration Association has welcomed this new provision in the following terms: 'By protecting the confidentiality of mediator, party, and non-party communications, the Act meets the expectations of all participants to the mediation process.'

The New US Uniform Mediation Act will lead to more mediations.

Contrasting the apparent slow take up to date of mediation in sports-related disputes in the States, Professor Nafziger, in a joint article with Li Wie, on 'China's Sports Law'[174] points out that China, where a National Sports Policy is developing, is 'in the vanguard of the global trend' as far as the use of ADR, as a primary form of dispute resolution, is concerned (see previous chapter).

Mediation, as an alternative method of dispute resolution, has something valuable to offer to the world of sport in appropriate cases, including speed, confidentiality and cheapness. Many sports bodies and other organisations have recognised this and are offering – and also promoting – mediation services at the national and the international levels.

Much depends, as we have seen, on the personal skills and experience of the mediators, but the success of mediation equally depends on the willingness of the parties to settle their disputes amicably, if at all possible. Without such willingness, mediation is bound to fail!

One of the main advantages of mediation is that it is a 'without prejudice' process and so little, if anything, is lost if it fails. It is very much a case of: 'nothing ventured nothing gained!' For as David Richbell, former Director of Training at CEDR, has recently put it: 'Even if a settlement agreement is not reached, nothing is lost, as the parties are better informed, issues are narrowed down and the dispute is moved significantly towards resolution as a result.'

Mediation is not a universal solution for dispute settlement. It is very much, to use the sporting metaphor, a case of 'horses for courses'!

---

174 XLVI/3 *The American Journal of Comparative Law* (Summer 1998).

Neither is it cost-free. But savings in time are also saving in monetary terms and valuable management resources.

However, although mediation of sports disputes – both nationally and internationally – is still, in many respects, in its infancy, the cases, in which it has been used successfully to date, clearly demonstrate its potential and usefulness as an alternative dispute resolution method.

In the view of the author of this book, therefore, it is only a matter of time – and, hopefully, a short time at that – as well as education and training before sports mediation – in its widest sense – comes into its own; and is more widely and regularly practised and used and also recognised as an effective alternative dispute resolution mechanism for settling sports disputes around the world.

Part Two

Settling Sports Disputes by Arbitration Through the Court of Arbitration for Sport (CAS)

CHAPTER 14
CAS ARBITRATION

14.1 Introductory Remarks

In this chapter, we will describe the settlement of sports-related disputes by arbitration through the Court of Arbitration for Sport (CAS) under the 'ordinary' and 'appellate' procedures. We will also explain the functions of the Ad Hoc Division of CAS, which sits during the Summer and Winter Olympic Games, and also take a look at CAS Advisory Opinions under the so-called 'Consultation Procedure' and evaluate their relevance and usefulness in the alternative dispute resolution sphere.

However, to put the subject into context, we will begin with a brief history of the CAS, which was set up in 1983.

14.2 Brief History of the CAS

14.2.1 Origins

At the beginning of the 1980s, an increasing number of international sports disputes and the lack of any independent body to deal with them in a flexible, quick, inexpensive and binding manner prompted a number of international sports federations to look a this situation and see what could be done. Soon after assuming the Presidency of the International Olympic Committee (IOC) in 1981, Juan Antonio Samaranch had the idea of creating a sports court that would become 'the supreme court of world sport'. The following year at an IOC Meeting in Rome, Judge Keba Mbaye, from Senegal, an IOC member and at the time a Judge at the International Court of Justice in The Hague, was asked to chair a working party with the aim of preparing the Statutes of a sports dispute resolution body that, in time, would become known as the 'Court of Arbitration for Sport'.

In 1983, the IOC officially ratified the Statutes of the CAS, which came into force on 30 June, 1984. On the same date, the CAS became operational under Judge Mbaye as its President, a position he has occupied with distinction until his death in 2007.

14.2.2 The first ten years

The 1984 CAS Statutes were supplemented by a set of Procedural Regulations. Both were slightly modified in 1990. Under these Regulations, the CAS was composed of sixty members appointed by the IOC, the International Federations (IFs), the National Olympic Committees (NOCs) and the IOC President – fifteen members each. The IOC President had to choose members outside the other three groups. All the operating costs of the CAS were borne by the IOC. In general, the proceedings were free of charge, except for financial disputes, in which the parties could be required to pay a share of the costs. The CAS Statutes could be modified only by the IOC meeting in General Session, on the proposal of the IOC Executive Board.

The CAS Statutes and Regulations provided for only one kind of contentious procedure, irrespective of the nature of the dispute. In addition, there was also a 'consultation procedure' open to sports bodies or individuals. Through this procedure, which still exists, the CAS could give a legal opinion on any sports-related issue.

In 1991, the CAS published a 'Guide to Arbitration', which included several model arbitration clauses, including one for incorporation in the statutes or regulations of international sports federations. This clause foresaw the creation of special rules to settle disputes arising out of a decision taken by a sports federation (the 'Appeals Procedure'). The first such body to adopt this clause was the International Equestrian Federation (FEI).

The next significant development was in February 1992, when a horse rider, named Elmar Gundel, lodged an appeal for arbitration by the CAS, based on an arbitration clause in the FEI statutes, in which he challenged a decision rendered by the FEI. This decision, which followed a horse doping case, disqualified the rider, suspending and also fining him. The award rendered by CAS on 15 October, 1992 found partly in favour of the rider (the suspension was reduced from three months to one month). Dissatisfied with the CAS ruling, Gundel filed an appeal with the Swiss Federal Tribunal (Swiss Supreme Court). He disputed the validity of the award, on the grounds that it was rendered by a tribunal that did not meet the conditions of impartiality and independence need to be considered as a proper arbitration court. In its judgement of 15 March, 1993, the Tribunal recognised the CAS as a true court of arbitration. And noted, *inter alia*, that the CAS was not an organ of the FEI; that it did not receive instructions from this Federation; and that it retained sufficient autonomy with regard to it, in that it placed at the disposal of the CAS only three arbitrators out of the maximum of sixty members of which the CAS was composed. However, in its judgement, the Tribunal drew attention to numerous links between the CAS and the IOC: the fact that the CAS was financed almost exclusively by the IOC; the fact that the IOC was competent to modify the CAS Statutes; and the considerable power given to the IOC and its President to appoint CAS members. In the Tribunal's view, such links would be sufficiently serious to call into question the independence of the CAS if the IOC were a party to proceedings before it. As Matthieu Reeb, Secretary General of the CAS, has remarked: 'The Federal Tribunal's message was thus perfectly clear: the CAS had to be made more independent of the IOC both organizationally and financially.' So this decision led to some major reforms of the CAS in 1994.

14.2.3 The 1994 reforms

Firstly, the CAS Statutes and Regulations were completely revised to make them more efficient and to modify the structure of the institution to make it more independent of the IOC, which had sponsored it since its creation. The most important change resulting from these changes was the creation of an 'International Council of Arbitration for Sport' (ICAS) to deal with the running and financing of the CAS, thereby taking the place of the IOC (see below).

Another major change was the creation of two Arbitration Divisions of the CAS (the 'Ordinary Division' and the 'Appeals Division') in order to make a clear distinction between disputes of sole instance and those arising from a decision rendered by a sports body. And the CAS reforms were enshrined in a new Code of Sports-related Arbitration, which came into force on 22 November, 1994.

All these reforms were approved in Paris on 22 June, 1994 with the signing of the 'Agreement concerning the Constitution of the International Council of Arbitration for Sport' – known as the 'Paris Agreement'.

14.2.4 **Later developments**

The ICAS was responsible for the creation of the decentralised offices of the CAS (referred to below) and also the Ad Hoc Divisions (also referred to below); as well as the introduction of a 'Mediation Procedure' (see below).

More recently, the CAS has moved to new headquarters at the Chateau de Bethusy in Lausanne. This not only provides the CAS with the possibility to expand its personnel and facilities to cope with its ever increasing workload, but also represents a further – physical – separation and independence from the IOC.

14.3 The International Council of Arbitration for Sport (ICAS)

The ICAS is the supreme organ of the CAS. Its main function is to safeguard the independence of the CAS and the rights of the parties appearing before it.[175] Thus, it is responsible for the administration and financing of the CAS. The ICAS has twenty members, who, on appointment, must sign a declaration in which they undertake to exercise their functions in a personal capacity, with total objectivity and independence. The members comprise five sports persons; five independent persons, who are outside the Olympic Movement and sport generally; five persons from the IOC; five persons from the Association of Summer Olympics International Sports Federations (ASOIF) and the Association of Winter Olympics International Sports Federations (AIWF); and five persons from the Association of National Olympic Committees (ANOC). ICAS members are appointed for four-year renewable terms. ICAS, like CAS itself, is a Swiss Foundation based in Lausanne, Switzerland. The ICAS appoints the CAS arbitrators and mediators and approves the budget and the accounts of the CAS.[176]

The funding of CAS is shared between the constituents of CAS as follows:

- 4/12 by the IOC;
- 3/12 by the ASOIF;
- 1/12 by the AIWF; and
- 4/12 by the ANOC.

14.4 The Organisation of CAS

The CAS, also known by its French acronym TAS (*Tribunal Arbitral du Sport*) – the official languages are French and English – is based in Lausanne, Switzerland, and has two permanent branches in Sydney, Australia, and New York, USA, facilitating access to CAS

[175] For a complete list of the functions of ICAS, see Art. S6 of the Code of Sports-related Arbitration.
[176] See generally on the ICAS Arts. S4-S11, ibid.

for parties residing in Oceania and North America.[177] Because CAS is based in Switzerland, with its seat in Lausanne, the CAS is generally governed by Swiss Law. It has its legal seat in Lausanne for all purposes, even when it hears cases outside Switzerland.[178] The CAS Court Office, headed by the Secretary General and assisted by several Counsel and secretaries, supervises the arbitration and mediation procedures and acts as a Registry; it also organises the Ad Hoc Divisions (see below) and deals with other administrative matters.

During the Olympic Games, the CAS operates an Ad Hoc Division (AHD), which was first set up on September 28, 1995, for the Centennial Atlanta Summer Games of the Modern Era in 1996, resolving disputes relating to the Games within 24 hours and free of charge.[179] For example, the AHD established for the Athens Summer Olympics in 2004 handled ten cases on a variety of sporting issues in a variety of sports, including selection and doping matters.[180] The AHD was again in session for the 2008 Summer Games in Beijing. The AHD decides cases 'pursuant to the Olympic Charter, the applicable regulations, general principles of law and the rules of law, the application of which it deems appropriate'. All athletes participating in the Summer and Winter Olympic Games have to submit their disputes to the CAS AHD. The actual submission forms part of the Athlete's Entry Form to participate in the Olympics. The standard Arbitration Clause for the AHD is as follows:

> 'I agree that any dispute, controversy or claim arising out of, in connection with, or on the occasion of, the Olympic Games, not resolved after exhaustion of the legal remedies established by my NOC, the International Federation governing my sport, ATHOC and the IOC, shall be submitted exclusively to the Court of Arbitration for Sport (CAS) for final and binding arbitration in accordance with the "Arbitration Rules for the XXVIII Olympiad in Athens", which form part of the Code of Sports-related Arbitration.
>
> The CAS shall rule on its jurisdiction and has the exclusive power to order provisional and conservatory measures. The decisions of the CAS shall be final and binding. I shall not institute any claim, arbitration or litigation, or seek any other form of relief, in any other court of tribunal.
>
> The NOC confirms that all the relevant rules have been brought to the notice of the athlete/coach/trainer/official, and it has been authorised by the National Sports Federation concerned to sign this entry form on its behalf.'

The CAS now has a minimum of 150 arbitrators, who are specialists in arbitration and sports law.[181] They are appointed for four-year renewable terms and must sign a 'letter of independence' confirming that they will act impartially. In establishing the list of CAS arbitrators, the ICAS must, in principle, respect the following distribution of candidates:

---

177 See generally M. Reeb, 'The Role and Functions of the Court of Arbitration for Sport (CAS)', 2 *The International Sports Law Journal* (2002) pp. 21, 23-25.

178 For the legal and practical significance of this, see the Judgement of the New South Wales Court of Appeal of 1 September, 2000 in the case of *Angela Raguz* v. *Rebecca Sullivan* [2000] NSWCA 240. In that case, a legal challenge against a CAS arbitral award was dismissed on the ground of lack of jurisdiction because the Court upheld the choice of Lausanne, Switzerland as the seat (i.e., place) of arbitration under the CAS Code of Sports-related Arbitration.

179 See Ian Blackshaw, 'A Sporting Decision in Just 24 Hours', *The Times*, 23 July 2002.

180 See booklet 'CAS Awards – Salt Lake City & Athens 2004' published by ICAS in 2004.

181 At the time of writing, there are some 300 CAS arbitrators, from 87 countries, and around 200 cases are registered with CAS each year.

- 1/5 of the arbitrators selected from among the persons proposed by the IOC, chosen from within its membership or outside;
- 1/5 of the arbitrators selected from among the persons proposed by the IFs, chosen from within their membership or outside;
- 1/5 of the arbitrators selected from among the persons proposed by the NOCs, chosen from within their membership or outside;
- 1/5 of the arbitrators chosen, after appropriate consultations, with a view to safeguarding the interests of the athletes;
- 1/5 of the arbitrators chosen from among persons independent of the bodies responsible for proposing arbitrators in conformity with the present article.[182]

The CAS also has a permanent President, who is an Italian lawyer, Mino Auletta, who has recently been appointed as Interim President until 2010 in succession to the previous President and Founder Member of CAS, Judge Keba Mbaye, from Senegal, who died on 11 January, 2007. Mr Aulettta is also Acting President of ICAS until 2010.

CAS arbitrators, who sit on panels composed of one or three members, are not generally obliged to follow earlier decisions (*stare decisis*), but they usually do so in the interests of legal certainty.[183] Thus, a useful body of sports law (*lex sportiva*) is steadily being built up.[184] The extent to which this is happening continues to be the subject of academic debate.[185]

14.5 CAS Procedures

14.5.1 **Ordinary arbitration proceedings**

The procedure to be followed in CAS Arbitration cases is set out in the Code of Sports-related Arbitration, the latest edition of which dates from January 2004, and the text of which is set out in Appendix XIX to this book. Copies of the Code can be obtained from the CAS Court Office in Lausanne, Switzerland. And the applicable law for determining the dispute is Swiss law, unless the parties agree on another law. The parties may authorise the CAS to decide the dispute *ex aequo et bono*.[186]

To commence ordinary arbitration proceedings before CAS, it is necessary to file a written request, which must contain the following information:

- the name and address of the respondent;
- a brief statement of the facts and legal argument, including a statement of the issue to be submitted to the CAS for determination;

---

182 Art. S14 of the Code of Sports-related Arbitration.

183 See Case of *UCI* v. *J.*, 7 NCB, CAS 97/176 Award of 28 August, 1998, 14.

184 From time to time, the CAS publishes Digests of Cases, but respecting, as appropriate, the confidentiality of the parties. The latest Digest of CAS Awards Volume III covers the period the period 2001-2003 and was published in 2004 by Kluwer Law International, The Hague, The Netherlands. Previous Volumes I and II covered the periods 1986-1998 and 1998-2000 respectively and were published by Editions Staempfli SA Berne and Kluwer Law International/Editions Staempfli respectively.

185 See K. Foster, 'Is There a Global Sports Law?', 2/1 *Entertainment Law* (2003) pp. 1-18. Foster argues that the CAS as an institutional forum is not yet 'globally comprehensive'. And see also James A.R. Nafziger, *International Sports Law*, 2nd edn. (Ardsley, New York, Transnational Publishers 2004) pp. 48-61. Prof. Nafziger characterises the CAS *lex sportiva* as 'still incipient'.

186 Art. R45 of the Code of Sports-related Arbitration.

- the claimant's request for relief;
- a copy of the contract containing the arbitration agreement or of any document providing for arbitration in accordance with these procedural rules;
- any relevant information about the number and choice of the arbitrator(s), in particular if the arbitration agreement provides for three arbitrators, the name and address of the arbitrator chosen by the claimant from the CAS list of names.[187]

Upon filing the request, the claimant must pay the court office fee.[188]

If any of these requirements are not met, the CAS Court Office will grant a once only short deadline to comply, failing which the request for arbitration shall be 'deemed withdrawn'.[189]

The arbitration procedures generally fall into two different phases: a written procedure with exchange of written submissions; and an oral procedure, in which the parties present their cases and witnesses[190] in a hearing, which is usually held *in camera* at the CAS headquarters in Lausanne, Switzerland.[191] It should be added, however, that, pursuant to the provisions of Article R57 of the CAS Code of Sports-related Arbitration, the case may be decided without holding a hearing, but on the submission of documents alone, if the Panel of Arbitrators, after consulting the parties, 'deems itself sufficiently informed' to proceed without holding a hearing. But this may raise questions of 'due process', especially the right of a party to be heard (*audi alteram partem*), and may perhaps expose the CAS Award to a legal challenge in the Swiss Federal Tribunal (see later).

If the claimant fails to submit its statement of claim as required under the procedural rules, the request for arbitration shall be 'deemed withdrawn'.[192] Likewise, if the respondent fails to submit its response in accordance with the procedural rules, the Panel may proceed with the case and deliver an award.[193] And, finally, if any of the parties is duly summoned and fails to appear at the hearing, the Panel may nevertheless proceed with the hearing.[194] Again, this may raise questions of 'due process'.

14.5.2 Appeal proceedings

In appeal cases, it is interesting to note that, also pursuant to the provisions of Article R57 of the Code, 'The Panel shall have full power to review the facts and the law.' And 'it may issue a new decision which replaces the decision challenged or annul the decision and refer the case back to the previous instance.' In other words, the case is dealt with *de novo*. And, whilst on the subject of appeals, to commence the process the Appellant must file with CAS a Statement of Appeal, which must contain the following information:

---

187 Art. R38, ibid.

188 Ibid.

189 Ibid.

190 On the question of the rules on examination of witnesses and experts in CAS hearings, see comments of Stephan Netzle in I. Blackshaw, R.C.R. Siekmann and J. Soek, eds., *The Court of Arbitration for Sport 1984-2004* (The Hague, T.M.C. Asser Press 2006) pp. 210-215.

191 Under Art. R28 of the Code of Sports-related Arbitration, after consultation with all parties, the hearing may be held elsewhere.

192 Art. R44.5, ibid.

193 Ibid.

194 Ibid.

- the name and full address of the Respondent;
- a copy of the decision appealed against;
- the appellant's request for relief;
- the appointment of the arbitrator chosen by the Appellant from the CAS list, unless the parties have agreed to a Panel composed of a sole arbitrator;
- if applicable, an application to stay the execution of the decision appealed against, together with reasons;
- a copy of the provisions of the statutes or regulations or the specific agreement providing for appeal to the CAS.[195]

Upon filing the Statement of Appeal, the Claimant must pay the Court Office fee.[196]

If any of these requirements are not met, the CAS Court Office will grant a once only short deadline to comply, failing which the Appeal shall be 'deemed withdrawn'.[197]

There is a time limit for bringing an Appeal to CAS established in Article R49 of the CAS Code of Sports-related Arbitration, which provides as follows:

> 'In the absence of a time limit set in the statutes or regulations of the federation, association or sports-related body concerned, or of a previous agreement, the time limit for appeal shall be twenty-one days from the receipt of the decision appealed against. After having consulted the parties, the Division President may refuse to entertain an appeal if it is manifestly late.'

If the Appellant fails to submit its Appeal Brief as required under the procedural rules, the appeal shall be 'deemed withdrawn'.[198] If the Respondent fails to file an answer as required under the procedural rules, the Panel may nevertheless proceed with the case and deliver an award.[199] If any of the parties are summoned but fails to appear, the Panel may nevertheless proceed with the hearing.[200] Again, this may raise questions of 'due process'.

14.5.3 **Provisional or conservatory measures**

In appropriate cases, it is possible for the parties to apply to the CAS for so-called 'provisional or conservatory measures' under the procedural rules.[201] Such measures, if granted, may be made conditional on the provision of security.

Article R37 of the CAS Code of Sports-related Arbitration empowers the CAS to offer the parties in dispute certain protective measures within a very short timeframe.

This article does not specify or limit the kinds of preliminary measures that the CAS Arbitrators can issue in a given case. But traditionally in arbitral proceedings, these measures tend to fall into three categories:

- measures to facilitate the proceedings, such as orders to safeguard vital evidence;
- measures aimed at preserving the *status quo* during the proceedings, such as those that preserve the object of the proceedings; and

[195] Art. R48, ibid.
[196] Ibid.
[197] Ibid.
[198] Art. R51 of the Code of Sports-related Arbitration.
[199] Art. R55, ibid.
[200] Art. R57, ibid.
[201] Art. R37, ibid.

- measures that safeguard the future enforceability of the decision, such as those concerning property.

For example, in the infamous so-called *Skategate* case during the 2002 Salt Lake City Winter Games, an order was imposed on the judges not to leave the Olympic village before the CAS Ad Hoc Division had investigated the circumstances in which the disputed medal had been awarded. Again, orders have been made in doping cases to preserve samples taken during a disputed doping control. However, preliminary measures can never exceed the object of the dispute. Thus, such measures cannot be issued against anyone who is not a party to the dispute; or anyone else who is not bound by the arbitration agreement signed by the applicant seeking the preliminary measures.

Furthermore, under the terms of Article R37 of the Code, in appeal proceedings, the parties by agreeing to the CAS Procedural Rules 'waive their rights to request such measures from state authorities'. In other words from the local courts. However, such implied waiver does not apply to parties in cases under the CAS ordinary arbitration procedure (ibid.). Thus, in such proceedings, the parties can apply for similar measures from the competent local courts.

Again, under Article R37, provisional and conservatory measures may be made conditional on the provision of security by the party seeking them. Such security is often a financial guarantee to be given by the applicant seeking such measures against any possible loss suffered by the party subject to the restraining measures in case the applicant is not ultimately successful in the proceedings. This happens in civil litigation quite often when an interim injunction is awarded by the court.

The criteria for granting CAS preliminary measures are not stated in Article R37 of the Code, but are spelled out in the equivalent article dealing with the granting of such measures by the CAS Ad Hoc Division operating at the Olympic Games. This is Article 14 of the Arbitration Rules for the Olympic Games; and provides, in Paragraph 2, that, when deciding whether to award any preliminary relief, the following considerations shall be taken into account:

- whether the relief is necessary to protect the applicant from irreparable harm;
- the likelihood of success on the merits of the claim; and
- whether the interest of the applicant outweigh those of the opponent or other members of the Olympic Community.

It is not clear whether these considerations are cumulative or alternative, but, in practice, CAS Arbitrators have wide powers in relation to procedural matters. Also, reference may be made to the following view, with which the writer would entirely agree, expressed by an Ad Hoc Panel sitting at the Salt Lake City Winter Olympics: '... each of these considerations is relevant, but that any of them may be decisive on the facts of a particular case'.[202]

In other words, CAS Arbitrators should take all the circumstances of the particular case into account, including the above criteria, when deciding whether or not to grant any preliminary relief.

Another important issue that needs to be addressed is the extent to which any preliminary measures granted can be legally enforced either by the CAS Arbitrators themselves

---

[202] CAS JO-SLC 02/004, *COA* v. *ISU*, CAS Digest III, pp. 592-593.

or with the assistance of the 'state authorities'. This is a controversial subject that would merit a lengthy paper in its own right.[203] Suffice to say that, in practice, the measures carry a high degree of moral authority and, therefore, National and International Sports Federations tend to comply with them; and through their own internal regularity mechanisms also tend to ensure that sports persons under their jurisdiction also comply. Apart from this, failure to comply will weaken the position of the defaulting party in the subsequent proceedings. So it is in that party's interest to conform. As for enforcement by state courts, that is a matter of local law. For example, Swiss law provides for 'judicial assistance' under the provisions of Article 183(2) of the Swiss Private International Law Statute of 18 December, 1987, which states that, if the party concerned does not comply voluntarily, 'the arbitration tribunal may call upon the assistance of the competent judge'. This becomes more problematic when the provisional measures are to be enforced outside Switzerland. For example, in Germany, this is not a legal problem as German law allows German courts to authorise the enforcement of provisional measures ordered by an arbitral body with it seat outside Germany. But in Italy, it is a problem, because Italian law does not recognise the jurisdiction of arbitral bodies to grant provisional measures and will not, therefore, enforce them.

It is clear that the CAS is able to grant parties in dispute very valuable, relevant and generally effective kinds of interim protection and relief at an early stage in the proceedings; and these measures deserve to be better known and more widely used by the sporting community to ensure that fairness – an essential element in sport – and justice are duly served.

14.5.4 **Expedited proceedings**

Likewise, the CAS Panel may, with the consent of the parties, agree to expedite the proceedings, in respect of which it shall issue appropriate directions.[204] This, in practice, is a useful measure in sporting disputes, where athletes or teams/clubs are often subject to sporting deadlines and other time pressures. For example, a sports person or a team, who has been denied eligibility to compete in a particular sporting event, which is soon to take place, need to have their dispute settled very quickly, if the possibility of competing is to remain open and not lost through any delay. See the recent case of *Apollon Kalamarias FC* v. *Hellenic Football Federation & Olympiakos FC*,[205] the full text of which is set out in Appendix XIX to this book.[206]

Again, Article 48 of the Code also allows a party to obtain a 'stay of execution' of the decision appealed against, provided a request to that effect is made at the time of filing the statement of appeal with the CAS. This measure is particularly apposite in appeals against suspensions for doping offences. But it has also been invoked in a variety of other cases, including a decision to have a football match played on neutral territory to avoid a risk of terrorism in the host club's country. If the request is not made at the time of filing the

---

203 See Antonio Rigozzi 'Who Rules – The CAS or the Courts?', in I. Blackshaw, R.C.R. Siekmann and J. Soek, eds., *The Court of Arbitration for Sport 1984-2004* (The Hague, T.M.C. Asser Press 2006) pp. 217-224.

204 Under Art. R44.4, ibid.

205 CAS 2008/A/11525.

206 See also comments on this case in I. Blackshaw, 'The Court of Arbitration for Sport: Provisional and Conservatory Measures', 1/2 *ISLJ* (2008) pp. 103-104.

appeal, it is lost; the assumption being that there is no urgency; otherwise this would have been pleaded at the outset.

14.6 CAS 'Advisory Opinions'

The CAS also offers 'Advisory Opinions' (known as 'Consultation Proceedings' and the corresponding Rules will be found in Appendix XIX to this book) on potential disputes, similar to the concept of 'expert determination' in the business world, which has become a popular form of ADR for settling commercial and financial disputes. However, there is one important difference: CAS Advisory Opinions are not legally binding. However, this does detract from their usefulness, because, in practice, they are a quick and relatively inexpensive way of clarifying legal issues and thus, hopefully, avoiding lengthy and expensive litigation.

Such Opinions may be requested by the IOC, the International Sports Federations, National Olympic Committees, and certain other sports bodies, including the World Anti-Doping Agency on 'any legal issue with respect to the practice of sport or any activity related to sport'.[207] When a request for such an Opinion is filed, the CAS President shall

> 'review whether it may be the subject of an opinion. In the affirmative, he shall proceed with the formation of a Panel of one or three arbitrators from the CAS list and designate the President. He shall formulate, at his own discretion, the questions submitted to the Panel and forward these questions to the Panel.'[208]

The Opinion may be published with the consent of the party who requested it.[209] We will look at a couple of actual case examples of CAS Advisory Opinions, which illustrate how the CAS 'Consultation Procedure' works in practice: one relating to swimming; and the other relating to badminton.

We reproduce the following article entitled 'You Don't Win Silver – You Miss the Gold' by Janwillem Soek[210] on the CAS Advisory Opinion delivered by Professor Richard H. McLaren of Canada prior to the 2000 Sydney Summer Games in the case of the controversial FINA 'full body' swimsuits:

Janwillem Soek
You don't win silver – you miss the gold

Introduction

After the Olympic Games of Atlanta in 1996 swimwear manufacturer Speedo started the development of a fabric for a new generation of swimsuits. Scientists had discovered that the tiny ridges in the skins of sharks greatly reduced turbulence in the water caused by the shark's movements. In order to attain the same effect at swimming competitions the fabric of the new swimsuits had to bear a strong resemblance to sharkskin. Developing the fibre took two years. Not only was a swimsuit designed, made of the new fibre, but the suit was also divided into different panels connecting the muscle groups used in swimming. The seams between the panels acted like tendons. The fabric was

---

207 Art. R60 of the Code of Sports-related Arbitration.
208 Art. R61, ibid.
209 Art. R62, ibid.
210 September 2000 issue of *The International Sports Law Journal* at pp. 15-18.

highly elastic and felt like a second skin. It was a revolutionary swimsuit with which, according to the manufacturer, the top times in swimming could be set at even sharper levels. Not only would the new suit enable the swimmer to develop more speed, increase his endurance, reduce his resistance in the water, but the new suit would moreover give the swimmer more buoyancy. Competitor Adidas had, meanwhile, also developed a swimsuit bearing a strong resemblance to Speedo's. On 8 October 1999 the FINA Bureau in Kuwait dedicated a long meeting to the new swimsuits.

Representatives of both manufacturers submitted reports of their research, design and other aspects of the 'full body' swimsuits to FINA and they supplied background information concerning the technology behind the design of the 'full body' swimsuits, accompanied by video animations. The Bureau arrived at the conclusion that the use of the 'long john' swimsuits would not be in violation of existing FINA rules and approved the suits. It was left up to the swimmers whether they would actually use them.

On 16 March 2000 the new Speedo suit was introduced in Athens. The President of Speedo International told reporters of the British newspaper 'The Independent' at that occasion: 'independent testing shows this to be the fastest suit ever made. Some of our team swimmers have shown time savings enough to make a difference between winning and losing a race'. The shark suit was not only revolutionary, it was controversial right from the time of its introduction. British swimmers in March assumed that they would not be able to appear in shark suits at the Olympics, because the team was sponsored by Adidas. This manufacturer insisted that the swimmers would use its suits. Adidas had not yet launched its new swimsuit onto the market in mid-March. Various Australian top swimmers, among who Ian Thorpe, were under contract with Adidas and could not dispose of a 'long john'. John Coates, chairman of the Australian Olympic Committee (AOC) and member of the organizing committee SOCOG feared not only unfair competition, as the suit could not be worn by everybody, but also that a possible world record would not be recognized if it had been set using a banned swimsuit. Coates' fear was based on his judgement that the FINA had misinterpreted its own rules. The AOC had to select the Australian swimmers for participation in the Olympic Games on the basis of the results during the Open Australian championships from 13 to 20 May. It was of great interest to the AOC to know whether the use of the bodysuits really fell within the rules of the FINA. Could the AOC nominate swimmers, who would wear the bodysuits at the selection rounds, for the Olympics? In the background the question whether the results of the Australian swimmers at the Olympics, achieved by using the new swimsuits, might not become the subject of legal claims at a later stage also played a part.

Barely a week after the introduction of the Speedo suit the Australian swimmers O'Neil, Dunn and Klim said they considered not using the suits, because they feared that wearing them could perhaps cost them medals. The AOC requested an advisory opinion from the CAS in this controversial matter and submitted five questions to it for answering:

1. is wearing the new swimsuit not a violation of FINA rules because it helps swimmers with their speed, buoyancy and endurance during competitions?
2. is the FINA competent to approve the use of any device which could be in violation of FINA Swimming Rules (SW) 10.7?
3. if the FINA is so competent, what then is the effect of such approval?
4. if the FINA is not so competent, what then is the effect of the results achieved by swimmers in the new swimsuits?
5. did the FINA actually validly consent to the wearing of the new suits?

The advisory opinion

The President of the CAS, Judge Keba Mbaye, appointed Canadian Professor and solicitor Richard H. McLaren arbitrator. According to R61 of the CAS Procedural Rules it is at the discretion of the CAS President to decide whether a request for an advisory opinion will be granted. The Article also stipulates that the President has the right 'to formulate, in his own discretion, the questions submitted to the Panel ...'. Mbaye deemed it necessary to rephrase the AOC's questions. McLaren was presented with the following question:

1. may the swimsuits at issue be considered a 'device' in the sense of SW 10.7?
2. did the FINA approve the use of the swimsuits?
3. is the FINA competent to approve the use of swimsuits that are possibly in violation of SW 10.7?

4. if so, what is the effect of such approval?
5. if not, what is the effect on the results achieved by swimmers in the new swimsuits?

The AOC did not entirely agree with this rephrasal and requested the President of the CAS to include a question 1A: in case the answer to question 1 is in the affirmative, do the bodysuits contribute to the speed, the buoyancy and the endurance of the swimmer during a competition? The President denied the request, being of the opinion that question 1A was already included in his phrasing of question 1.

May the swimsuits at issue be considered a 'device' in the sense of SW 10.7?
This rule states:

> 'No swimmer shall be permitted to use or wear any device that may aid his speed, buoyancy or endurance during a competition (such as webbed gloves, flippers, fins, etc.) ...'

McLaren was of the opinion that this question was not for the CAS to be answered. Pursuant to Constitution C 14.11.2 and C 14.11.3[211] it was the task of the FINA Bureau to interpret the rule. The FINA had declared to the CAS that SW 10.7 'has never been interpreted as being applicable to swimming suits and certainly not to their dimensions and material. It had always been interpreted as concerning other elements ("devices") which are supplemental'. The question remained unanswered for reasons, which would be entered into in the answer to question 3.

Did the FINA approve the use of the swimsuits?
The Bureau had reviewed the shark suit within the framework of rules concerning the 'costume' of General Rules GR6[212] and not in the framework of the competition rules of SW 10.7. The Bureau – as the only institution entitled thereto under the FINA Constitution – had declared on the basis of the information submitted to it that using the suit would not be in violation of FINA rules. C 14.11.3 endowed the Bureau with the competence to review the swimsuits within the framework of the FINA rules. 'Once again under rule C14.11.3, the effect of reviewing the full bodysuits and determining them to be compliant with the Rules has caused FINA *in effect* to have granted its approval to the full bodysuit', McLaren found. The Bureau had the wide-ranging competence on the basis of C 14.11.3 to promulgate a rule with regard to the swimsuits but has chosen not to make use of this competence. Now that the Bureau failed to make us of its legislative competence the review of the swimsuits did not need to be submitted to the next congress for confirmation. The arbitrator found that the answer to question 2 should be in the affirmative.

Is the FINA competent to approve the use of swimsuits that are possibly in violation of SW 10.7?
The AOC wished for the CAS to give an advisory opinion concerning the proper interpretation of SW 10.7 and the application of that provision to the swimsuits. This should not be considered odd, given the provisions of R60 of the CAS Procedural Rules. Pursuant to that provision an OCOG, such as, in the present case, the AOC, may 'request an advisory opinion from the CAS about any legal issue with respect to the practice or development of sports or any activity related to sports'. So what did McLaren find? He found that 'this question (question 3) presupposes an issue as to the scope of the review to be made by CAS as the quasi-judicial authority overseeing disputes'. This is where the advisory opinion starts going astray. McLaren unjustifiably speaks of 'the scope of the

[211] C 14 Bureau
C 14.11 – Rights & Duties of the Bureau shall include the following:
C 14.11.2 – to interpret and enforce the Rules of FINA, subject to confirmation at the next meeting of the Congress,
C 14.11.3 – to decide and take action on any matter pertaining to the affairs of FINA, subject to confirmation at the next meeting of the Congress.

[212] GR 6 Costumes
GR 6.1 – The costumes of all competitors shall be in good moral taste and suitable for the individual sports discipline.
GR 6.2 – All costumes shall be non-transparent.
GR 6.3 – The referee of a competition has the authority to exclude any competitor whose costume does not comply with this Rule.

review' and 'disputes'. There was no dispute in the case at hand. Once having arrived at the wrong station, the next few cannot be right either. McLaren treats the request for an advisory opinion as if it concerns a dispute between the AOC and the FINA. He peruses the FINA rules for the mandate the FINA extends to the CAS in the case of disputes. He stumbles on rules C 10.8.3 and C 21 of the FINA Constitution, both concerning 'disputes'[213] and stipulating under which circumstances the CAS may be called in as arbitrator. For proper understanding it should be mentioned that C 10.8.3 is part of C 10, the subject of which is 'Sanctions'. According to C 10.8.3 judgments of, among others, the Bureau, which contain sanctions, may be appealed before the CAS. The AOC's request is hard to reconcile with the wording of C 10.8.3. Even harder is the link McLaren finds between C 21 and the AOC's request. Not only does that provision make mention of 'disputes', which are not at issue in the present case, it also speaks of 'disputes' between the FINA and its members and between the members themselves. The AOC cannot be considered a member of the FINA. Although he is playing his part supported by the wrong props, McLaren refuses to acknowledge it; he considers: 'for the purposes of this opinion it is presumed that the scope of the review discussed is in connection with a dispute arising under these two constitutional provisions, which dispute is before CAS for consideration'. Even though R60 of the CAS Procedural Rules gives the arbitrator every freedom to advise on every possible legal issue concerning the practice or development of sports, McLaren stubbornly maintains that the case at hand concerns a 'dispute', which is being appealed. 'CAS is the international adjudication body to whose jurisdiction FINA has attorned its disputes if they remain unresolved following exhaustion of FINA's procedures. The CAS conducts its appeals proceedings under the Code.' R58 of the CAS Procedural Rules[214], forming part of Section C 'Special provisions applicable to the appeal arbitration proceedings', is pointed at.

The arbitrator worked from the assumption that the CAS 'had discrete and limited review of IF decisions on certain specific grounds'. He went on to formulate the respective 'specific grounds' and proceeded to evaluate whether these had been met in the present case. The CAS can be petitioned to adjudge disputes concerning the interpretation of the Constitution, but this is not what is at stake in the present proceedings.

> 'The request for this opinion does not deal with the constitution of FINA. Therefore, there is no reason for a review of the decision of the Bureau by the CAS on the grounds that it would be interpreting the constating (*sic!*) instrument, the constitution.'

When an athlete violates the rules adopted or promulgated by a sports organization, the CAS may be petitioned when an institution has given a final judgment about such violation in disciplinary appellate proceedings. Such disciplinary proceedings have not taken place prior to the present request.

> 'The request for this opinion does not deal with the review of powers exercised over a particular individual pursuant to an IF's contractual arrangements which affect their (*sic!*) personality or property. Therefore, there is no basis for CAS to review the bodysuit decision of the Bureau on this jurisprudential theory.'

The grounds McLaren reviews that could enable the CAS to exercise jurisdiction are already placed in the incorrect framework of review of decisions of international federations. Now he finds that this situation does not occur in the present case. This conclusion should have put him on the right track;

---

[213] C 10.8.3 – An appeal against a decision by the Bureau or the FINA Doping Panel shall be referred to the Court of Arbitration for Sports ('CAS?), Lausanne, Switzerland, within the same terms as in C 10.8.2. The only appeal from a decision of the Doping Panel shall be to the CAS. The CAS shall also have exclusive jurisdiction over interlocutory orders and no other court or tribunal shall have authority to issue interlocutory orders relating to matters before the CAS. Decisions by the CAS shall be final and binding, subject only to the provisions of the Swiss Private International Law Act, section 190.
C 21 Disputes between FINA and any of its Members or individual members of its Members or between Members of FINA which are not resolved by a FINA Bureau decision may be referred for arbitration by either of the involved parties to the Court of Arbitration for Sports (CAS), Lausanne. Any decision made by the Arbitration Court shall be final and binding on the parties concerned.

[214] R58 The Panel shall decide the dispute according to the applicable regulations and the rules of law chosen by the panties or, in the absence of such a choice, according to the law of the country in which the federation, association or sports body is domiciled.

i.e. that the whole investigation into the grounds for 'discrete and limited review of IF decisions' should not have taken place.

SW 10.7 is a provision in Part III of the 'Swimming Rules'. The provisions of Part III describe how swimming competitions should be run, as opposed to the 'General Rules', which are applicable to all types of swimming sports, including diving, water polo, synchronized swimming, etc. General Rule GR6 is of the same character. The decision of the FINA Bureau concerning the shark suits was based on competition rules.

> 'Therefore, this Advisory Opinion is in connection with the rules of the sport as it is to be played; or, the basis upon which the swimming competition is to be held. Such rules are established by contract. They do not have the effect of defining the constitution, or, being used to affect directly individual rights of personality or property. They are the rules of the game sometimes referred to as the "game rule". There does not appear to be a consistent practice throughout the world in dealing with the review by judges of the "game rule".'

Had the decision of the Bureau violated the 'general principles of law or natural justice', the CAS would have had grounds for review of the decision, but in the present request such a claim was never presented. Therefore, the CAS is also unable to take any action on the basis of this third ?threshold value?. Nor has the CAS looked into this option of its own accord.

> 'While this would be a basis for a review by the CAS of the Bureau decision there is no indication that the Bureau acted without good faith in making its decision or otherwise acted contrary to general principles of contract law.'

According to McLaren, the CAS may also review the case if lack of procedural reasonableness and fairness may be shown. In this case, however, there is no indication whatsoever to suspect that the Bureau has acted in violation of the procedures when it took its decision of 8 October 1999.

> 'There would be no basis for reviewing the Bureau decision on this ground.'

There is another reason for review of a decision. If the decision of an IF is so unreasonable that no institution competent to take decisions could reasonably have arrived at it, the decision may be reviewed. But this was not the case here either.

> 'The Bureau in this matter is the appropriate body of the FINA who is in the best position to decide on the interpretation of the game rules and the application of them to the development of the bodysuit. In the Bureau's decision there are no sanctions arising from the application of the rules. Applying the above principles, it can be said that the Bureau in making its decision on the bodysuit, acted within the limits (i.e. did not act unreasonably) of the rules, which have been laid down by taking into consideration only those matters to which the rules applied. Consequently, CAS has no basis for a review of the FINA bureau decision on these grounds.'

The CAS was unable to answer the question whether the FINA, in approving the use of the new swimsuits, had acted in violation of SW 10.7.

> 'There is no review by CAS of a game rule in these circumstances. Therefore, it is not for CAS in the circumstances of this Advisory Opinion to offer an opinion on whether the bodysuit may contravene Rule SW 10.7. The Bureau decision had the effect of approving the bodysuit since in its view the suit did not contravene any rule.'

The arbitrator found question 4 to be no longer relevant and given the analysis he delivered in his answer to question 3, it has become unnecessary, in his opinion, to answer question 5.

The reaction to the advisory opinion

The advisory opinion of the CAS received worldwide attention. Headlines appeared in the papers reading 'Court supports FINA ruling', 'Court accepts FINA ruling on full-length bodysuits', 'Sportgericht erlaubt "Haihaut"'. Not everybody was convinced, however. 'Far from clarifying the legality of the Fastskin neck-to-ankle swimsuits, a Court of Arbitration for Sports ruling has further muddled the issue', The Independent cited John Coates on 2 May. In this the chairman of the AOC was absolutely right; the arbitrator had been unable to enter into the content of the decision of the FINA Bureau, because that decision concerned the interpretation of a competition rule and the interpretation of such rules is not subject to CAS judgment. The FINA Bureau could approve the 'long john' completely legitimately, because in doing so it stayed within the bounds of existing FINA rules. Even if the Bureau would have had to draft a new rule as basis for its approval, such approval would still have been legitimate, at least until the next congress would have given its verdict on that new rule. Given the fact that a swimsuit is not a 'device' in the sense of SW 10.7 and another rule does not prohibit it, a swimsuit may possess qualities, which have a positive effect on the speed, the endurance and the buoyancy of the swimmer wearing it.

The scope of the advisory opinion of the CAS

Pursuant to S12 sub c of the CAS Statutes it is part of the 'mission' of the CAS 'to give non-binding advisory opinions at the request of the IOC, the IFs, the NOCs, the associations recognized by the IOC and the Olympic Games Organizing Committees (OCOGs)'. Paragraph 3 of R27 stipulates that the Procedural Rules of the CAS also apply where the CAS is called upon to give an advisory opinion (consulting proceedings). In the *Digest of CAS Awards 1986-1998* Reeb remarked at the beginning of the part in which several advisory opinions are printed that 'of the requests for advisory opinions received, many have been for the interpretations of statutes or regulations'. Unfortunately, no examples of advisory opinions holding such interpretations are included in the Digest. Polvino[215] was of the opinion that the advisory opinions, 'which pertain to the relatively undeveloped area of international sports law, provide a cost-free benefit to those parties seeking to avail themselves of this institution of legal expertise. These advisory opinions are analogous to the submission of a dispute to an expert; a cheap non-jurisdictional form of conflict resolution found ... in the commercial world.' Simma[216], too, is very positive about the possibility of seeking advisory opinions. The relevant provisions of the Procedural Rules 'would allow the CAS to pronounce upon a far wider range of questions in its advisory function than in its arbitral role. Therefore, if its advisory potential actually came alive, the CAS could develop into an instrument of "constitutional" review and standard-setting in the realm of international sports law'. The advisory opinion is therefore an instrument for the interpretation of statutes and regulations (Reeb), it cheaply provides legal expertise (Polvino) and a far wider range of questions may be dealt with through it than is the case with arbitration (Simma). According to R60 of the Procedural Rules an advisory opinion may concern 'any legal issue with respect to the practice or development of sports or any activity related to sports'. All these advantages have not been brought to fruition in the present advisory opinion. The cause should not only be sought in the way in which the arbitrator interpreted his task (namely appeal of an IF decision); the way the AOC phrased its questions is also to blame. The Independent of 3 May reported the views of the head swimming coach of Australia, Don Talbot, who said: 'The Australian Olympic Committee was well meaning but has taken the wrong strategy by challenging the legality of full-length bodysuits'.

R61 of the CAS Procedural Rules accords a prominent role to the President of the CAS in requests for advisory opinions. Not only does he decide whether the request will be dealt with and does he appoint - if he so decides - the arbitrators from the list to act on the panel, but he is moreover competent to rephrase the questions posed. His freedom to decide whether the panel shall consist of one or three arbitrators may have consequences for the outcome of the advisory opinion. His discretionary power to submit the questions asked to the panel in a different form than the one in which they were originally submitted might also bear a strong influence on the outcome of the advisory opinion. Even a change in the order of the questions asked might influence the outcome. The Procedural Rules set no limits within which the President must exercise his discretionary powers. The requesting party cannot object to the changes the President makes to the questions; he can only ask the President to change the rephrasal, but again, the decision lies with the President. In 'normal' arbitrations the President's powers are not nearly as extensive. The question is why so much power rests with the President in the field of advisory opinions and what end this serves. The IOC's influence in the advisory practice is considerable, given the position accorded to the CAS President. Pursuant to

---

215 Anthony T. Polvino: 'Arbitration as preventative medicine for olympic ailments: the International Olympic Committee's Court of Arbitration for Sport and the future for the settlement of international sporting disputes', in 8 *Emory International Law Review* (1994), p. 370.

216 Bruno Simma: 'The Court of Arbitration for Sport', in K.-H. Böckstiegel et al., *Völkerrecht – Recht der Internationalen Organisationen – Weltwirtschaftsrecht / Law of Nations – Law of International Organizations – World's Economic Law, Festschrift für Ignaz Seidl-Hohenveldern* (Köln, Carl Heymans Verlag 1988), p. 579.

S6 of the CAS Statutes the ICAS appoints a President from among its members, who shall also be President of the CAS (S9), but who is 'proposed by the IOC'.

As an aside it should be mentioned here that Mbaye[217] wrote in 1984: 'par ailleurs, l'ensemble du contentieux relatif au sport peut être divisé en de rubriques: les "questions techniques" et les "questions non techniques" (du point de vue du sport, bien entendu). Les "questions techniques" relèvent des organes du sport'. He could have rejected the request for an advisory opinion as the questions of the AOC focused on the interpretation of FINA SW 10.7 and thus were 'questions techniques'.

Communication

Coates feared that the FINA's decision would result in an unfair balance during the qualifications between the swimmers who did and those who did not dispose of a shark suit. He feared even more that the lesser-endowed swimmers would at a certain moment legally challenge the results of the swimmers in shark suits. The reason why Coates did not take the principle of fair play as point of departure in phrasing his questions to the CAS may well be found in an aspect of the FINA decision that has not been dealt with yet. This aspect was left aside by the FINA itself in its publicity about the approval. The brief paragraph in the advisory opinion that makes mention of the approval of the swimsuits during the meeting of the FINA Bureau on 8 October in Kuwait is concluded by the arbitrator with the words 'that approval was based upon the provision that it would be available to every competitor'. This sentence, which plays no role of further importance in the advisory opinion, may be read thus that during competitions a 'long john suit' was not allowed to be worn by any participant, if not all participants could dispose of one. Whether the participants would actually use the suit would be irrelevant; what would matter is that they could dispose of one. We may well suspect that the AOC did not know of this condition.

From the previous issue of *Sportzaken Magazine,* in which Berry Bertels dedicated a few sentences to this advisory opinion on page 61, it appears that the CAS did not give permission to publish the advisory opinion *in extenso*. From the headlines quoted above it likewise appears that the press, too, has had to content itself with the announcements of the CAS concerning the advisory opinion. Pursuant to R62 of the Procedural Rules the advisory opinion can 'be published with the consent of the party who requested it'. We must therefore conclude that the AOC did not consent to the publishing of the advisory opinion. Stricter conditions apply to the publishing of advisory opinions than of arbitral awards of the CAS. With regard to arbitral awards, R59 paragraph 5 states that these 'shall be made public by the CAS, unless both parties agree that they should remain confidential'.

In conclusion

Since the approval of the 'long johns' by the FINA several new world records have been set by swimmers wearing the new swimsuits. It is impossible to decide whether the swimsuits have had any influence on these results. In the meantime, the swimwear manufacturers have taken care that all top swimmers have access to the new suits. With this, the fear of unfair competition has subsided. The CAS decision has in no way contributed towards the question whether these suits may be used in future competitions. The FINA allows it and the national federations, too, have given their approval. There will be swimmers who will not be using them, but there will also be those who wish to swim in as little fabric as possible. After a while, we will know whether the shark suits are really as revolutionary as the manufacturers claimed or whether this has been just another hype. Research at the faculty of motion studies of the *Vrije Universiteit* in Amsterdam has shown that some swimmers in Speedo suits actually experienced more resistance in the water than without those suits. The Russian Alexander Popov, who set the world record for the 100 metres free stroke without a shark suit, said in an interview: 'You don't win the silver – you miss the gold'. Of the CAS advisory opinion, neither can be said.

---

[217] Keba Mbaye: 'Une nouvelle institution d'arbitrage: le Tribunal Arbitral du Sport (T.A.S.)', in: XXX *Annuaire Français de Droit International* 1984), p. 411.

Regarding the CAS Advisory Opinion on the new scoring rules of the International Badminton Federation (IBF),[218] we reproduce below the remarks of Professor Richard McLaren in his chapter on CAS Advisory Opinions in the book *The Court of Arbitration for Sport 1984-2004* as follows:[219]

In the *Badminton Scoring Opinion*, the questions asked by the Canadian Olympic Committee (COC) as the requesting party of the Advisory Opinion were:

1) Has the IBF Council followed due process, acted within its jurisdiction and made a decision on the competition scoring system regulations as directed by the membetrship at the 2002 IBF general meeting?
2) If yes to #1, does the resulting scoring system distinction between men's and women's events constitute a sytem that is injurious to women (in terms of equitable opportunity) and is this decision contrary to social norms governing equitable conduct in sport?
3) If no to #1, would the CAS provide an opinion on an appropriate manner for the the IBF council to deal with the competition scoring system?
4) Is the IBF contravening the essence of natural justice and the democratic process by not including an internal neutral appeal procedure for the membership within its governing regulations?

The CAS President reformulated the questions to be submitted for consideration as follows:

1) Has the IBF council acted within its jurisdiction and within the published 'Rules of the International Badminton Federation' in making a decision on the competition scoring system regulations as directed by the membership at the 2002 IBF AGM?
2) In light of the fact that there does not exist an internal appeal procedure within the IBF regulations, did the IBF council, in making this decision, act in accordance with principles of natural justice?
3) Does the decision that was made by the IBF council constitute a kind of discrimination on grounds of sex in the meaning of the principles implemented by the Olympic Charter?

Although the broad-brush strokes of the COC request are certainly encompassed in the questions posed by the CAS President, certain significant changes are evident. Nevertheless, an Advisory Opinion on the questions posed by the CAS President can be expected to be substantially similar to one given on the questions posed by COC, had they been left unchanged. This is evidenced by the decision itself, in that it condemns the scoring changes as being unfair. There was a significant shift in the focus of the first two questions towards determining only if the IBF had acted within or outside of its authority, a matter that was also at the core of the *Long Johns Swimsuits Opinion*. The third reformulated question then went to the central reason for the application in the first place, which was the potential discriminatory effects of the scoring system as it rekated to the women's game of badminton.

Prof Ian Blackshaw, siting as the sole arbitrator in the *Badminton Scoring Opinion*, rendered an Advisory Opinion deeming that the new scoring rules decision produced the effect of baseless and unequal treatment between male and female competitiors. For that reason, it *could be* legally held to be discriminatory (*emphasis added*). Prof Blackshaw went on to suggest that the new scoring rules might also be regarded as being contrary to and incompatible with the principles against sex discrimination and the promotion of women in sport as enshrined in the IOC Charter, which the IBF, according to tis Rules, is legally obliged to respect and uphold. However, due to the non-binding nature of Advisory Opinions, no order was made to force compliance with his findings.

This was precisely the type of opinion being sought by the requesting parties. However, such a satisfactory resolution of contentious matters is not always the case, especially where significant changes have been made to the questions posed by the requesting party. In fact, the broad discretion

[218] See Advisory Opinion CAS 2003/C/445, Canadian Olympic Committee, 24 April 2003 rendered by Prof. Ian S. Blackshaw (United Kingdom) on the legality of the new scoring rules introduced by the International Badminton Federation on 23 May 2002.

[219] The Hague, T.M.C. Asser Press 2006, pp. 184-185.

of the CAS President to modify the questions of the requesting party, before submission to a panel for resolution, can yield peculiar and unsatisfactory results. The requesting party will not always agree with such changes, principally where the new questions do not address the issues over which resolution is sought. Regardless, this is left to the complete discretion of the CAS President.

It would seem that requests for Advisory Opinions, which are very much the product of the Civil Law tradition, are on the decline, possibly as a result of the anomalies and criticisms pointed out in the above extracts. This, in my view, is a pity, because, as pointed out at the beginning of this section, Advisory Opinions help to clarify legal issues, thereby perhaps avoiding legal proceedings in appropriate cases, or, if not, identifying such issues for resolution in subsequent arbitration or court proceedings.

On a general point, it may be noted, *en passant*, that a party may apply to the CAS for the interpretation of an award issued in an ordinary or appeals arbitration 'whenever the operative part of the award is unclear, incomplete, ambiguous or whenever its components are self-contradictory or contrary to the reasons, or whenever the award contains clerical mistakes or a miscalculation of figures'.[220] The Panel must rule on the request for interpretation within one month.[221] Again, this is a useful procedure in practice.

14.7 CAS *Ad Hoc* Division

Since the Centennial Games in Atlanta in 1996 – dubbed the 'Coca-Cola Games' – the CAS has operated a so-called *Ad Hoc* Division (AHD) to adjudicate on disputes arising during the Summer and Winter Games. The CAS AHD was again in session during the 2008 Summer Games in Beijing, dealing with the usual crop of doping cases.

The AHD operates under a special set of rules – Arbitration Rules for the Olympic Games – and its remit is to settle such cases within 24 hours[222] – it needs to act quickly because of sporting deadlines, especially in eligibility and selection disputes – and does so free of charge.[223] All athletes competing in the Games must agree in their entry forms to submit their disputes 'exclusively' to the jurisdiction of the CAS. The wording of this 'undertaking' is as follows: 'I shall not constitute any claim, arbitration or litigation, or seek any other form of relief in any other court or tribunal.'

The legal validity of such a clause – designed to 'oust the jurisdiction of the courts' – may be doubtful under various jurisdictions.[224]

Under the Special AHD Rules, the arbitrators selected to serve on the AHD Panels must decide cases in accordance with the principles of the Olympic Charter, the applicable sports regulations, general principles of law and the rules of law which they deem appropriate.[225] This gives them a wide scope to act fairly and provide just outcomes in the cases referred to them. The arbitrators also have full power to review the facts of the cases.[226]

---

220 Art. R63, ibid.

221 Ibid.

222 Art. 18 of the Rules.

223 Art. 22, ibid. However, the parties are required to pay their own costs of legal representation, experts, witnesses and interpreters (ibid.).

224 See the leading English case of *Scott* v. *Avery* [1856] 5 HL Cas 811.

225 Art. 17 of the Rules.

226 Art. 16, ibid.

The parties may be assisted or represented at AHD hearings by persons of their choice, including lawyers.[227]

The cases range from eligibility and selection issues to, sadly, doping issues. And there are an increasing number also of cases challenging the decisions of referees and judges. For example, at the last Winter Olympics in 2002 in Salt Lake City, one of the cases dealt with was the so-called 'skategate' scandal concerning the impartiality of the judges in one of the skating events. In that case, the CAS AHD imposed an order on the judges concerned not to leave the Olympic village before it had investigated the circumstances in which the disputed medal had been awarded, which illustrates the wide powers the members of the AHD have at their disposal.[228]

The CAS publishes a Digest of the cases dealt with by the AHD at each of the Games shortly afterwards, and these make interesting and informative reading.

The CAS also provides AHD proceedings at the Commonwealth Games and the Euro Football Championships.

One final but important legal and practical point. In AHD proceedings, the 'seat' of the CAS remains in Lausanne, Switzerland, where it is based. The case of *Angela Raguz*[229] well illustrates this point. In that case, the CAS AHD was asked just before the 2000 Sydney Summer Olympics to adjudicate in a selection dispute involving two Australian 'judokas'. The unsuccessful one, Angela Raguz, challenged the CAS award in the New South Wales Court of Appeal. The Court held that the CAS agreement for arbitration form signed by the parties was not a 'domestic arbitration agreement' within the Commercial Arbitration Act 1984, but a foreign one, and, therefore, outside the jurisdiction of the Australian Courts. Although the physical place of arbitration was Sydney, Australia, the legal place of arbitration, as expressly stipulated in the agreement, was Lausanne, Switzerland – the 'seat' of the CAS. The CAS award could only, therefore, be challenged in a Swiss Court under Swiss Law – in limited circumstances as explained later.

14.8 Sports Disputes

14.8.1 **Generally**

Parties involved in sports disputes have three possible ways of resolving them. They can appeal to the internal authorities of their sports federations – both national and international; they can take their disputes to the ordinary competent courts; or submit disputes to private arbitration or mediation. It is important to point out that the regulations of sports federations cannot exclude an appeal of a dissatisfied member to external judicial authorities. Such provisions designed to oust the jurisdiction of the courts are void.[230] However, they can provide in their regulations for parties involved in disputes to first exhaust all the internal remedies and appeal procedures before resorting to the ordinary courts.[231]

---

227 Art. 8, ibid.

228 As to the range of these powers to grant preliminary relief including stays of execution of sports bodies' rulings, see Art. 14, ibid.

229 *Angela Raguz* v. *Rebecca Sullivan & Ors*, 2000 NSECA 240; CAS Digest II, p. 783 – CAS Awards Sydney 2000, p. 185.

230 See *Baker* v. *Jones* [1954] 2 *All ER* 553.

231 See *Scott* v. *Avery* [1856] HL Cas 811.

The CAS is dedicated to hearing and settling any disputes directly or indirectly relating to sport.[232]

14.8.2 'On-field of play' disputes

However, it is well established in previous decisions that the CAS will not generally review so-called 'on-field of play' sporting decisions made on the playing field by judges, referees, umpires and other officials, who are responsible for applying the rules of a particular game. For example, in *Mendy* v. *International Amateur Boxing Association*, the Ad Hoc Division, sitting at the Atlanta Summer Games in 1996, dismissed the French boxer's appeal against disqualification for punching his opponent below the belt in violation of the rules.[233] In that case, the AHD held that '... the referee's decision, confirmed by the AIBA, is a purely technical one pertaining to the rules which are the responsibility of the federation concerned'. And added that the boxer had not provided any evidence that the competent sports authorities, in evaluating a technical rule specific to the sport concerned, had committed an error of law, a wrong or a malicious act against him.

Again, and more recently, the appeal during the Athens Summer Games in 2004 against the decision of the Appeal Committee of the International Equestrian Federation setting aside the Ground Jury ruling that a time penalty be imposed on the German equestrian athlete Bettina Hoy for failing to complete a jumping event within the required time limit was upheld. The Ad Hoc Division held, *inter alia*, that it was '... not necessary to deal with the merits or demerits of the Ground Jury's ruling, which was clearly a "on-field of play" decision made within its competence during the course of an event falling under its exclusive control'.[234]

But in cases in which such rules have been applied in bad faith, the CAS will exceptionally intervene in the interests of justice.[235] In doing so, there must be evidence, which generally must be direct evidence, of bad faith. This places a 'high hurdle' that must be cleared by anyone seeking to review a field of play decision: if the hurdle were to be lower, the flood-gates would be opened and any dissatisfied participant in a sporting event would be able to challenge such on field decisions.[236]

---

[232] Art. R27 of the Code of Sports-related Arbitration provides (in part) as follows: 'Such disputes may involve matters of principle relating to sport or matters of pecuniary or other interests brought into play in the practice or the development of sport and, generally speaking, any activity related or connected to sport.'

[233] See CAS Arbitration *Ad Hoc* Division (O.G. Atlanta 1996) 006, M./Association Internationale de Boxe Amateur (AIBA), Award of 1 August, 1996.

[234] See CAS *Ad Hoc* Division (OG Athens) 2004/007, Comite National Olympic et Sportif Francais (CNOSF), British Olympic Association (BOA), United States Olympic Committee (USOC)/Federation Equestre Internationale (FEI) and National Olympic Committee for Germany (NOCG), Award of 21 August, 2004.

[235] See CAS 2001/A/354, Irish Hockey Association (IHA)/Lithuanian Hockey Federation (LHF) and International Hockey Federation (FIH) and CAS 2001/A/355, Lithuanian Hockey Federation (LHF)/International Hockey Federation (FIH), Award of 15 April, 2002.

[236] See CAS *Ad Hoc* Division (OWG Salt Lake City 2002) 007, Korean Olympic Committee (KOC)/International Skating Union (ISU), Award of 23 February, 2002.

14.8.3 Sporting and commercial disputes

Sports disputes that the CAS hears may include purely sporting issues, such as selection and eligibility matters, as well as disciplinary matters, including doping;[237] and also commercial issues, which are on the increase in view of the mega sums now at stake in the promotion and marketing of professional sport and sports events, such as disputes over corporate sponsorship, merchandising and agency contracts. A sports person, body or a commercial company, such as a sports marketing company, may bring cases to CAS. The parties must agree to do so in writing. Cases can be referred to the CAS on an *ad hoc* basis at the time a particular dispute arises. But many sports bodies and sports marketing companies are now including an express CAS arbitration clause in their contracts.

The standard CAS clause for a sports body is as follows:

> 'Any decision made by....[insert the name of the disciplinary tribunal or similar court of the sports federation, association or sports body which constitutes the highest internal tribunal] may be submitted exclusively by way of appeal to the Court of Arbitration for Sport in Lausanne, Switzerland, which will resolve the dispute definitively in accordance with the Code of Sports-related Arbitration. The time limit for appeal is twenty-one days after the reception of the decision concerning the appeal.'

The standard CAS clause for a commercial dispute is as follows:

> '*Any dispute arising from or related to the present contract will be submitted exclusively to the Court of Arbitration for Sport in Lausanne, Switzerland, and resolved definitively in accordance with the Code of Sports-related Arbitration.*'

The parties may – and it is advisable to do so – include in this reference clause additional provisions regarding the number of CAS arbitrators (from one to three) and the language in which the CAS proceedings will be conducted (for example, English).

14.8.4 Sports-related commercial disputes: some examples

The CAS has dealt with a number of sports-related commercial disputes and mention will now be made of a few of them, which will give the reader a flavour of the range of sports-related commercial and financial disputes that may be referred to the CAS.

The CAS was brought in to deal with a dispute concerning the UEFA, the European Governing Body of Football, restrictions on common ownership of football clubs competing in their European competitions. The CAS held that these restrictions were not anti-competitive, as alleged by the English national Investment Company, which owned several clubs and wanted to acquire others, but could be justified on sporting grounds – the so-called 'sporting exception'.[238] These restrictions actually encouraged competition in a sporting sense. Incidentally, subsequently the EU Competition Commission agreed with this ruling in line with the legal distinction EU Law makes between the 'rules of the game' and commercial restrictions.

---

[237] Under Art. 13 of the World Anti-Doping Code of 2003, final appeals against doping decisions go exclusively to the CAS.

[238] See *AEK PAE and SK Slavia Praha* v. *UEFA*, CAS Case No. 98/2000, award dated August 20, 1999; *Digest of CAS Awards Vol. II 1998-2000* (Kluwer 2002) at p. 36.

In another case, the CAS was called upon to determine the legal nature of and interpret certain marketing contracts, including a sponsorship contract, entered into between a Sports Federation and a French company. *Inter alia*, the CAS held that where a contract's provisions concerning the payment of commission are unambiguous, there is no need to re-interpret them.[239]

Again, the CAS dealt with another sporting issue with significant commercial implications. Just before the 2000 Sydney Summer Games, the Australian Olympic Committee asked the CAS for an 'Advisory Opinion' on whether the introduction of the so-called 'full body' swimming costumes was lawful. Speedo and other sports apparel manufacturers had invested substantial sums of money in them. But did they give competitors, who wore them, an unfair advantage over those who did not and had the rules, allowing them, been properly passed by FINA, the World Governing Body of Swimming? The CAS, after a full review of the legal and sporting issues, held that they had been correctly introduced.[240]

In 2003, the author of this book was asked to give an 'Advisory Opinion', requested by the Canadian Olympic Committee, on whether controversial new scoring rules in Badminton introduced by the International Badminton Federation – introduced for marketing/commercial reasons with the intention of making the sport more telegenic and interesting for sponsors – discriminated against women players, who were subject to different playing rules. As there was no sporting reason for this difference, it was held that the new rules could be considered discriminatory.[241]

A number of commercial disputes have also been settled by CAS Mediation. These cases have included disputes with a sports management agency over the commercialisation of a cyclist's image rights and financial disputes between athletes and their advertising agencies in relation to substantial commission payments.

It should be added that, since FIFA joined the CAS in 2002, there have been many disputes referred to the CAS concerning the interpretation and application of the FIFA International Football Transfer Rules, especially the payment of compensation for the education and training costs of young players and disputes regarding the level of transfer fees payable in particular cases, on appeal from the FIFA Dispute Resolution Chamber. Many of these cases have involved well-known Football Clubs and players.[242] More recently, the decision of the FIFA Dispute Resolution Chamber in the case of the footballer Andrew Webster was appealed to the CAS.[243] In view of its importance, the full text of the corresponding CAS Award is set out in Appendix XXI to this book.

---

[239] See *X. Sarl and Federation Y*, CAS Case No. 319/2001, Award dated October 17, 2001; Digest of CAS Awards Vol III 2001-2003 (2004, Kluwer) at p. 10.

[240] See Advisory Opinion CAS 2000/C/267, Australian Olympic Committee (AOC), 1 May 2000 rendered by Prof. Richard H. McLaren (Canada) on the so-called 'Long John' swimsuits and their compliance with the FINA (International Amateur Swimming Federation) rules. For a critique of this Advisory Opinion, see the article by Janwillem Soek entitled, 'You don't win silver, you miss the gold', 2/2 *The International Sports Law Journal* (September) at pp. 15-18, quoted *in extensu* in Ian S. Blackshaw, *Mediating Sports Disputes: National and International Perspectives* (The Hague, T.M.C. Asser Press 2002).

[241] See Advisory Opinion CAS 2003/C/445, Canadian Olympic Committee, 24 April, 2003 rendered by Prof. Ian S. Blackshaw (United Kingdom) on the legality of the new scoring rules introduced by the International Badminton Federation on 23 May, 2002.

[242] For example, the dispute between Fulham Football Club and Olympique Lyonnais concerning the transfer of Steve Marlet: see Arbitration CAS 2003/O/486, Award of 15 September, 2003.

[243] Award of 30-01-2008, 2007/A/1298/1299/1300 Wigan Athletic FC/Heart of Midlothian/Webster.

14.9 Cost of CAS Proceedings

Challenges to decisions of international sports federations are dealt with by the Appeals Division of CAS. Where such disputes relates to disciplinary matters, including doping cases, apart from the payment of the Court fee of SFR 500, the proceedings are free of charge. However, in one case in which the parties settled their dispute prior to the hearing before CAS, but only informed CAS on the day of the actual hearing, resulting in the unnecessary attendance at CAS of the members of the CAS Panel, the CAS ordered the parties to pay the CAS costs.[244] In all other appeal cases, for example, an appeal relating to a football transfer dispute, costs are fixed in the same way as disputes dealt with in the Ordinary Division (see below).

Commercial disputes referred to the CAS are deal with under the Ordinary Jurisdiction. Apart from the payment of a Court fee of SFR 500, the CAS fixes the costs in accordance with a sliding scale based on the amount in dispute and before the case may proceed the parties are required to pay an advance of fees to the CAS Office.[245]

The CAS can award costs to the successful party in a CAS case or determine the proportion in which the parties are to share them; as a general rule, the prevailing party is granted a contribution towards its legal fees and other expenses, including the costs of witnesses and interpreters.[246]

14.10 *Lex Sportiva*

During its 25 years of existence, the CAS has dealt with a substantial number of cases covering a wide range of sports related legal issues. Although CAS arbitrators are not generally obliged to follow earlier decisions and obey the sacred Common Law principle of *stare decisis* (binding legal precedent),[247] in the interests of comity and legal certainty, they usually do so. As a result of this practice, a very useful body of sports law is steadily being built up.[248]

The extent to which the CAS is contributing to a discrete body of sports law (*lex sportiva*) is a complex and controversial subject and divides academics and practitioners alike. For a detailed review of the situation to date, see Chapter 15 below.

---

244 See CAS 2000/A/264.G, Federazione Italiana Sport Equestri, Order of 23 October, 2000.

245 Art. R64 of the Code of Sports-related Arbitration. See also Appendix II – Schedule of Arbitration Costs.

246 Art. R64.5 ibid., which provides (in full) as follows: 'The arbitral award shall determine which party shall bear the arbitration costs or in which proportion the parties shall share them. As a general rule, the award shall grant the prevailing party a contribution towards its legal fees and other expenses incurred in connection with the proceedings and, in particular, the costs of witnesses and interpreters. When granting such contribution, the Panel shall take into account the outcome of the proceedings, as well as the conduct and the financial resources of the parties.'

247 See *UCI* v. *J.* 7NCB, CAS 97/176 Award of 28 August 1998, 14.

248 See further on this, J. Nafziger, 'Arbitration of Rights and Obligations in the International Sports Arena', 35/2 *Valparaiso University Law Review* (2001) p. 57; James A.R. Nafziger, *International Sports Law*, 2nd edn. (Ardsley, NY, Transnational Publishers 2004) pp. 48-61 and I. Blackshaw, R.C.R. Siekmann and J. Soek, eds., *The Court of Arbitration for Sport 1984-2004*, (The Hague, T.M.C. Asser Press 2006) pp. 409-454.

14.11 The Legal Status of CAS Awards

Awards made by the CAS, like other international arbitral awards, are legally enforceable generally in accordance with the rules of International Private Law, and also specifically under the provisions of the New York Convention on the Recognition and Enforcement of Foreign Arbitral Awards of 10 June, 1958. The CAS is also recognised under the European Convention on the Recognition of the Legal Personality of International Non-Governmental Organizations.

So, the CAS decisions are legally effective and can be enforced internationally. This is particularly important in the case of disputes involving intellectual property rights, especially trademarks, which are generally of a territorial nature.

14.12 Legal Challenges to CAS Awards

The CAS awards can be legally challenged in the Swiss Federal Court, also based in Lausanne, by a dissatisfied party, but only in very limited circumstances, under the provisions of Article 190(2) of the Swiss Federal Code on Private International Law of December 18, 1987. This article reads (in translation) as follows:

> '[The Award] can be attacked only:
>
> – if a sole arbitrator was designated irregularly or the arbitral tribunal was constituted irregularly;
> – if the arbitral tribunal erroneously held that it had or did not have jurisdiction;
> – if the arbitral tribunal ruled on matters beyond the claims submitted to it or failed to rule on one of the claims;
> – if the equality of the parties or their right to be heard in an adversarial proceeding was not respected;
> – if the award is incompatible with Swiss public policy.'

In practice, perhaps ground (d) is the most important one, and the CAS bends over backwards in each case to ensure that the parties are properly heard and receive a fair hearing.[249]

In practice, there have been few legal challenges to CAS awards. In the latest challenge in 2003 concerning the independence of the CAS in view of its association with and partial funding by the IOC, the Swiss Federal Court held that the CAS offered all the guarantees of independence and impartiality to be regarded as a real court of arbitration, even where the IOC – as in that case – was a party in its proceedings.[250]

In that case, two Russian cross-country skiers, Larissa Lazutina and Olga Danilova unsuccessfully questioned the independence of CAS in the Swiss Federal Tribunal (TFS) in 2003. These skiers were disqualified by the IOC after the 2002 Winter Olympic Games in Salt Lake City for doping offences. The International Ski Federation (FIS) suspended both of them for two years. Their appeal to CAS, calling for the IOC and FIS decisions

---

[249] See the Judgement of 22 March, 2007 in the *ATP Tour Appeal* case brought before the Swiss Federal Court against a CAS Award of 23 May, 2006; Reference: 4P 172/2006, which was brought under either Para. (d) or Para. (e) of Art. 190(2) of the Swiss Federal Code on Private International Law of December 18, 1987.

[250] See Judgement of 27 May, 2003 of the First Civil Division of the Swiss Federal Tribunal in the case of *A. & B.* v. *International Olympic Committee and International Ski Federation* (4P.267/2002; 4P.268/2002; 4P.269/2002; and 4P.270/2002).

to be overruled was dismissed. Their legal challenge to the TFS on the grounds that CAS, because it is a creature of and receives some funding from the IOC, is not a truly independent body, was also dismissed. The TFS held that CAS offered all the guarantees of independence and impartiality to be regarded as a real court of arbitration, even where the IOC – as in the Russian skiers' case – is a party to its proceedings. On the question of the partial financing of the CAS by the IOC, the Court concluded as follows:

> 'To conclude our discussion of the financing of the CAS, it should be added that there is not necessarily any relationship of cause and effect between the way a judicial body is financed and its level of independence. This is illustrated, for example, by the fact that State courts in countries governed by the rule of law are often required to rule on disputes involving the State itself, without their judges' independence being questioned on the ground that they are financially linked to the State. Similarly, the CAS arbitrators should be presumed capable of treating the IOC on an equal footing with any other party, regardless of the fact that it partly finances the Court of which they are members and which pays their fees.'[251]

However, the TFS made the following observation/recommendation to make the list of arbitrators more transparent for the benefit of the parties selecting them:

> 'It would be preferable, if the published list were to indicate, alongside the name of each arbitrator, which of the five categories mentioned in Article S14 they belonged to (arbitrators chosen from those proposed by the IOC, the Ifs and the NOCs; arbitrators chosen to safeguard the interests of the athletes; arbitrators chosen from among persons independent of the three aforementioned bodies) and, for those in two of these categories, by which IF or NOC they were proposed). The parties would then be able to appoint their arbitrator with full knowledge of the facts. For example, it would prevent a party in dispute with the IOC, in the belief that he was choosing an arbitrator completely unconnected to the latter, from actually appointing a person who was proposed by that organisation but who is not an IOC member (see Art. S14 of the Code, which advocates this practice).'[252]

The TFS ruling of May 27, 2003 puts, I think, the question of the impartiality and independence of the CAS beyond any further doubt both now and in the future, although – it must be said – not all commentators would necessarily agree with this point of view.

14.13 Concluding Remarks

As the global sports industry continues to expand and sports-related disputes continue to rise, and ADR continues to find favour in the sporting and business communities, the services offered by the Court of Arbitration for Sport, as outlined in this paper, will continue to appeal to parties who wish to settle their disputes, fairly, quickly, effectively, confidentially and relatively inexpensively. The Court has distinguished itself and fulfilled the hopes and expectations of its founders, as well as withstanding a number of legal challenges to its independence and impartiality, during its first twenty-one years of operations.

As to the future, CAS would appear to have a bright and expanding one, by all accounts, and not least based on the following ringing endorsement by the Swiss Federal Tribunal given in the Russian cross-country skiers' case discussed above:

---

[251] Ibid. at Para. 3.3.3.1.
[252] Ibid. at Para. 3.3.3.2.

> 'The CAS is growing rapidly and continuing to develop. An important new step in its development was recently taken at the World Conference on Doping in Sport, held in Copenhagen at the beginning of March 2003. This Conference adopted the World Anti-Doping Code as the basis for the worldwide fight against doping in sport. Many States, including China Russia and the United States of America, have adopted the Copenhagen Declaration on Anti-Doping in Sport. Under the terms of Art. 13.2.1 of the new Code, the CAS is the appeals body for all doping-related disputes related to international sports events or international-level athletes. This is a tangible sign that States and all parties concerned by the fight against doping have confidence in the CAS. It is hard to imagine that they would have felt able to endorse the judicial powers of the CAS so resoundingly if they had thought it was controlled by the IOC. This new mark of recognition from the international community shows that the CAS is meeting a real need. There appears to be no viable alternative to this institution, which can resolve sports-related disputes quickly and inexpensively. Having gradually built up the trust of the sporting world, this institution which is now widely recognised remains one of the principal mainstays of organised sport.'[253]

CAS, as previously mentioned, was the brainchild of former IOC President, Juan Antonio Samaranch, whose aim was to set up a Supreme Court for World Sport. He seems to have succeeded, as CAS has become just that! With, in the words of the former ICAS/CAS President, the late Judge Keba Mbaye, 'a stature that inspires confidence and respect' to match.

---

[253] Ibid. at Para. 3.3.3.3.

CHAPTER 15
CAS AND AN EMERGING *LEX SPORTIVA*

15.1 Introductory

Is there such a thing as 'Sports Law'? Opinion on this subject is divided amongst academics and practitioners alike.[254]

According to Edward Grayson, the doyen of authors on sport and the law, jurisprudentially speaking, there is no such thing as 'sports law'. He argues that:

> 'As a soundbite headline, shorthand description, it has no juridical foundation; for common law and equity creates no concept of law exclusively relating to sport. Each area of law applicable to sport does not differ from how it is found in any other social or jurisprudential category... .'[255]

Likewise, Charles Woodhouse, CVO, the former legal adviser to the Commonwealth Games Foundation, a pioneer legal practitioner in the field of sport and a founder member of the British Association for Sport and the Law and the UK Sports Dispute Resolution Panel, is adamant that there is no such thing as 'sports law'. In a reflective valedictory article, he expresses his opinion as follows:

> 'I have often said there is no such thing as sports law. Instead it is the application to sport situations of disciplines such as contract law, administrative law (disciplinary procedures), competition law, intellectual property law, defamation and employment law.'

And adds in a slightly contradictory manner but then correcting himself: 'I hope the next generation of sports lawyers will enjoy it as much as I have over the past 25 years. But do remember there is no such thing as sports law.'[256]

Again, according to Hayden Opie, of the University of Melbourne, Australia, sports law is one of those fields of law which is applied law as opposed to pure theoretical law:

> 'Rather than being a discipline with a common legal theme such as criminal law, equity or contract law, sports law is concerned with how law in general interacts with the activity known as sport. Hence, the label applied is law. Yet there is an increasing body of law which is specific to sport. This produces debate among scholars over whether one should use the term sports law,

---

[254] See S. Gardiner, M. James, J. O'Leary, R. Welch, I. Blackshaw, S. Boyes and A. Caiger, *Sports Law*, 3rd edn. (London, Cavendish Publishing 2006) pp. 88-91 for a review of the arguments for and against a distinct/discrete body of law called 'sports law' (under the section title of 'Viva Sports Law – Sport and the Law RIP') and the general conclusion of the authors as follows: 'As an area of academic study and extensive practitioner involvement, the time is right to accept that a new legal area has been born and is thriving in the 'bloom of its youth' – Viva sports law.'

[255] Edward F.Grayson, *Sport and the Law* (London, Butterworths 1999) p. xxxvii.

[256] C. Woodhouse, 'The Lawyer in Sport: Some Reflections', 4/3 *Sport and the Law Journal* (1996) p. 14.

which indicates a legal discipline in its own right or "sport and law" which reflects the multifarious and applied nature of the field.'[257]

On the other hand, Beloff, Kerr and Demetriou, all practitioners, recognise the emergence and importance of sports law:

'... the law is now beginning to treat sporting activity, sporting bodies and the resolution of disputes in sport, differently from other activities or bodies. Discrete doctrines are gradually taking shape in the sporting field ... English courts are beginning to treat decisions of sporting bodies as subject to particular principles.'[258]

In other words, sport is 'special' and, as such, is deserving of 'special treatment' from a legal point of view. This is certainly true at the EU level reflecting the views of the European Commission and the European Court of Justice, where the term the 'specificity of sport' (also referred to, particularly by Sports Governing Bodies, as the 'sporting exception') has been coined and is widely used in various Commission rulings and Court decisions in sports cases.[259] This term refers to the special characteristics and dynamics of sport recognised in the EU Council of Ministers Nice Declaration on Sport of December 2000.[260]

Likewise, Lewis and Taylor, both academics and practitioners, have the following to say on the subject of 'sports law':

'... the editors share the belief of many writers in the field that in at least some areas, for example where international institutions such as the Court of Arbitration for Sport review the decisions of sports governing bodies, a separate and distinct body of law inspired by general principles of law common to all states is in the process of development'.[261]

So, leaving aside the argument whether there is such a thing as 'sports law' (a *lex sportiva*) – the author of this book, incidentally, takes the view that there is – which, Lewis and Taylor consider is a matter of academic rather than practical interest,[262] we turn now to consider the contribution of the Court of Arbitration for Sport to the development of a *lex sportiva.*

15.2 CAS AND A *LEX SPORTIVA*

During its 25 years of existence, the CAS has dealt with a substantial number of cases covering a wide range of sports related legal issues. For example, a contractual dispute concerning the organisation of a particular sport's world championships;[263] the equivalent

---

257 H. Opie, 'Sports Associations and Their Legal Environment', in M. McGregor-Lowndes, K. Fletcher and S. Sievers, eds., *Legal Issues for Non-Profit Associations* (Sydney, LBC 1996) pp. 74-94.

258 M. Beloff, T. Kerr and M. Demetriou, *Sports Law* (Oxford, Hart 1999) p. 3.

259 See the EU 'White Paper on Sport' published on 11 July, 2007 (COM(2007)391 final); see also the European Court of Justice Decision in *David Meca-Medina and Igor Majcen* v. *Commission* (C-519/04 P) defining the limits of the so-called 'sporting exception' to EU Law in general and EU Competition Law in particular. See also I. Blackshaw, 'The Specificity of Sport and the EU White Paper on Sport', 10 October 2007, at pp. 14-16.

260 'Declaration on the specific characteristics of sport and its social function in Europe', Presidency Conclusions, Nice European Council meeting, 7-9 December 2000.

261 Adam Lewis and Jonathan Taylor, *Sport: Law and Practice* (London, Butterworths 2003) p. vii.

262 Ibid.

263 *International Triathlon Union* v. *Pacific Sports Corpn*, CAS 96/161.

of a 'judicial review' of a decision of a particular sports governing body;[264] a challenge to the UEFA Rules restricting the multiple ownership of football clubs (the so-called *ENIC* case);[265] as well as an increasing number of football transfer cases on appeal from the FIFA Dispute Resolution Chamber, following the acceptance by FIFA in 2002 of the CAS as the final 'court of appeal', especially compensation disputes.[266] More recently, the CAS, on appeal from a ruling of the IAAF, dealt with the interesting case of Oscar Pistorius, the South African double leg amputee, and his claim to take part in the 2008 Beijing Olympics as if he were an able-bodied athlete. Although he won his appeal before CAS, in the event, he did not, in fact, qualify for a place in the Beijing Olympics. Again, in view of its importance, the full text of the corresponding CAS Award[267] is set out in Appendix XXII to this book.

Although CAS arbitrators are not generally obliged to follow earlier decisions and obey the sacred Common Law principle of *stare decisis* (binding legal precedent),[268] in the interests of comity and legal certainty, they usually do so. As a result of this practice, a very useful body of sports law is steadily being built up.[269]

The extent to which the CAS is contributing to a discrete body of sports law (*lex sportiva*) is a complex and controversial subject and also, as we have seen in relation to 'sports law', also divides academics and practitioners alike. For example, Ken Foster, who is generally credited with coining the term *lex sportiva*, argues that the CAS, as an institutional forum, is not yet: '...globally comprehensive...[but] has improved by becoming more independent of the International Olympic Committee and thus satisfying Teubner's criterion of externalisation'.[270]

And, according to Jim Nafziger, the CAS *lex sportiva* although 'still incipient', the general principles and rules derived from CAS Awards are becoming clearer on such issues as:

> '...the jurisdiction and review powers of the CAS; eligibility of athletes; and the scope of strict liability in doping cases ... A truly effective body of jurisprudence generated by CAS awards,

---

[264] *FFSA* v. *FISA*, CAS 97/168. In that case, the FFSA challenged the adoption by an Extraordinary Congress of the FISA to adopt a new by-law relating to 'Commercial Publicity, Sponsorship and Advertising'. The CAS rejected the arguments of the FFSA that the Extraordinary Congress did not have jurisdiction to make such a decision, but accepted that the procedure followed in adopting the amendment without allowing for a considered discussion of an important change to the by-laws was in breach of the FISA Statutes, and, accordingly, the CAS declared the decision void.

[265] *AEK Athens and Slavia Prague* v. *UEFA*, CAS 98/200.

[266] For a recent important example on compensation for unilateral premature termination by a football player, Andrew Webster, of his contract of employment with his Club, see *Wigan Athletic FC* v. *Heart of Midlothian*, CAS 2007/A/1298; *Heart of Midlothian* v. *Webster & Wigan Athletic FC*, CAS 2007/A/1299; *Webster* v. *Heart of Midlothian*, CAS 2007/A/1300.

[267] CAS 2008/A/1480.

[268] See *UCI* v. *J.* 7NCB, CAS 97/176 Award of 28 August 1998, 14.

[269] See further on this, J. Nafziger, 'Arbitration of Rights and Obligations in the International Sports Arena', 35/2 *Valparaiso University Law Review* (2001) p. 57; James A.R. Nafziger, *International Sports Law*, 2nd edn. (Ardsley, NY, Transnational Publishers 2004) pp. 48-61; and I. Blackshaw, R.C.R. Siekmann, and J. Soek, eds., *The Court of Arbitration for Sport 1984-2004* (The Hague, T.M.C. Asser Press 2006) pp. 409-454. See also I. Blackshaw, *Mediating Sports Disputes: National and International Perspectives* (The Hague: T.M.C. Asser Press 2002).

[270] K. Foster, 'Is there a Global Sports Law?', 2/2 *Entertainment and Sports Law Journal* (2003) p. 1. Teubner's criterion of externalisation applied to CAS is represented by an 'external arbitrator' who is able to make decisions amounting to 'official and organised' law.

however, will require more development before the emerging lex sportiva can become a truly effective regime of authority.'[271]

In Nafziger's view, if there is not yet a *lex sportiva* as a result of CAS Awards, which, as he also points out, in any case, like Arbitral Awards generally, are legally binding on and only have legal effects between the parties (*inter partes*), there is certainly, in his opinion, a *lex specialis* being established through CAS Decisions.

One area of sports law in which the CAS is developing a particular body of jurisprudence is, sadly, in doping cases. Indeed, in its Award in *Norwegian Olympic Committee and Confederation of Sports (NOCCS) & others* v. *International Olympic Committee (IOC)*,[272] a doping case, the CAS Panel held that the CAS has a distinct jurisprudence, expressed in the following terms:

> 'CAS jurisprudence has notably refined and developed a number of principles of sports law, such as the concepts of strict liability (in doping cases) and fairness, which might be deemed as part of an emerging "lex sportiva". Since CAS jurisprudence is largely based on a variety of sports regulations, the parties' reliance on CAS precedents in their pleadings amounts to the choice of that specific body of case law encompassing certain general principles derived from and applicable to sports regulations.'[273]

The legal challenges and limitations facing CAS in developing a consistent approach to such cases is well covered by Frank Oschutz, a German attorney, in his study entitled 'Doping Cases before the CAS and the World Anti-Doping Code'.[274] According to Oschutz:

> 'The Court of Arbitration for Sport offers a unique opportunity of international decision making in the world of sport ... The awards rendered by the various arbitrators prove that the CAS can provide effective protection for the rights of the accused athlete and is likewise able to ensure that the fight against doping will be upheld unremittingly ... the CAS has developed a quite impressive body of decisions which deal with all kinds of challenges.'[275]

Oschutz has some very interesting observations to make on certain disparities on the interpretation by CAS of the legal nature of the doping offence itself as follows:

> 'On the one hand, there are Panels which have stressed that the nature of a doping offence is one of pure strict liability, that is, a liability without fault. Consequently, there is no need to address the issue of intent or negligence at any stage of the proceedings. If an athlete is found with a forbidden substance he has to be sanctioned for a doping offence – period. However, some Panels, which applied the rules of strict liability, also felt the need to soften the harsh consequences of such a regime for athletes who committed the offence neither intentionally or negligently. In the eyes of these arbitrators, the athletes should enjoy the right to escape liability by providing evidence that the violation of the anti-doping rule was committed without their fault. So, the intentional element – that does not exist in a strict liability offence – sneaked in by the back door. On the other hand, there are more and more awards in which the Panels applied a rebuttable presumption of guilt if an athlete is found with a forbidden substance in his body. This athlete may adduce evidence that he or she did neither act intentionally, nor negligently.

[271] J. Nafziger, 'The Court of Arbitration for Sport: the Emerging Lex Sportiva', in I. Blackshaw, R.C.R. Siekmann and J. Soek, op. cit., pp. 409-419.

[272] CAS 02/O/372.

[273] Ibid., Para.65, n. 15.

[274] See Blackshaw, Siekmann and Soek, op. cit., pp. 246-265.

[275] Ibid. at p. 264.

> Consequently those Panels would not apply the concept of strict liability. However, one may also perceive a certain degree of misunderstanding of those two different legal concepts in some CAS decisions.'[276]

The strict liability principle – as such – is rarely criticised in the legal literature. The most prominent critic of the system was in fact the CAS itself as Janwillem Soek demonstrated in his PhD thesis 'The Strict Liability Principle and the Human Rights of Athletes in Doping Cases'.[277]

Janwillem Soek

In *Fritz Aanes v Fédération Internationale de Luttes Associées (FILA)*[278] the tribunal considered that:

> '[...] the Panel is of the opinion that as a matter of principle [...] an athlete cannot be banned from competition for having committed a doping offence unless he is guilty, i.e. he has acted with intent or negligence. Even if the rules and regulations of a sports federation do not expressly provide that the guilt of the athlete has to be taken into account the foregoing principle will have to be read into these rules to make them legally acceptable.'

In the view of the Panel in question an athlete could not be lawfully suspended under Swiss law[279] if no blame attached to him/her.[280] This shows a clear break with the views of previous Panels on this point. From the words 'an interpretation to the contrary would lead to the rules being void which would frustrate the objective of the fight against doping pursued by the entire sporting world' it may be derived that this Panel – which was composed of three civil law lawyers - based its reasoning on different starting points from Panels mainly composed of common law lawyers.

> 'It is obvious that it would be an important weapon in the fight against doping if the federations were able to impose sanctions on athletes who have tested positive, without having to establish any element of guilt on the part of the athlete. However, this argument, which is one of prevention and deterrence, loses sight of the general objective of doping sanctions, namely the punishment of the athlete for having violated the rules (Baddeley, L'association sportive face au droit (1994), p. 219).
>
> On the other hand, it has to be recognised that in professional sport doping sanctions have the effect of restraining the athlete from carrying out his chosen trade and thus from earning a living for a certain period of time. In addition, doping sanctions clearly affect the honour and social standing of the athlete concerned and are a stigma on his future.
>
> When weighing up the interests of both sides the Panel is of the view that the interests of the athlete take precedence over those of the federation to enforce a rule of "strict liability". The contrary view would only be acceptable if a strict liability rule were the only meaningful weapon in the fight against doping (see Baddeley in: Fritzweiler (ed.) *Doping Sanktionen, Beweise, Ansprüche* (2000), p. 9, 22; Scherrer in: Fritzweiler (ed), id. at p. 119, 127; see also CAS 95, 142, *L.* v. *FINA*, CAS Digest, p. 225, 231). [...].
>
> [...]
>
> The so-called strict liability-rule, i.e. a rule as advocated by the Respondent according to which the mere presence of a prohibited substance in an athlete's body justifies his suspension, does not, in the Panel's opinion, sufficiently respect the athlete's right of personality (Persönlichkeitsrecht) as established in Articles 20 and 27 et seq. of the Swiss Civil Code which CAS panels are required to apply (Art. 58 of the Code of Sports-related Arbitration).
>
> [...]

---

276 Ibid. at pp. 252-256.

277 T.M.C. Asser Press, The Hague, The Netherlands 2006, pp. 165-167.

278 CAS 2000/A/317, 9-7-2001, *F. Aanes v FILA*

279 According to Rule 45 of the Procedural Rules of the CAS 'the Panel shall decide the dispute according to the rules of law chosen by the parties or, in the absence of such a choice, according to Swiss law.'

280 Tribunal Fédéral, 15 May 1993, BGE 119 II 271.

> The Panel further notes that in a recent decision the Court of Appeals of Frankfurt/Main, Germany also held that liability without fault was incompatible with the rights of the athlete and German law (OLG Frankfurt/Main, judgement of May 18, 2000, 13W29/00 [*B.* v. *DLV*] p. 15).'[281]

The CAS Panel was aware of the fact that the strict liability paradigm as it had been developed by previous Panels was contrary to the prevailing legal opinion in Europe and especially in Germany and Switzerland. The lex sportiva[282] of which the CAS has been one of the most important authors could only find universal recognition if its main aspects did not meet with insurmountable resistance in the respective legal systems. The OLG Frankfurt had rejected the CAS's strict liability system and the Panel in the Aanes case used the judgment of the OLG as a whetting stone to reshape the position of the athlete in disciplinary doping proceedings in such a way as would be acceptable to the legal community – at least that in Europe.

The Panel held that suspension of an athlete for a doping offence required the athlete's guilt, but not in the way 'as is necessary in respect of a criminal act for which a presumption of innocence operates in favour of the accused'.[283] However, the sports organisation was not left in any doubt that it did have to prove the objective elements of the offence. As opposed in the case of presumed innocence, the Panel was of the opinion that with respect to the objective elements 'this follows from the general rule that a person who alleges a fact has the burden of proof'. Although this appears contradictory, it is still reasonable as '[...] it would put a definite end to any meaningful fight against doping if the federations were required to prove the necessary subjective elements of the offence, i.e. intent or negligence on the part of the athlete'. In weighing up the interests of the sports organisation in the fight against doping on the one hand and the interest of the athlete not to be punished when he/she is innocent, the scales in the Panel's view tipped in favour of the interests of the sports organisation. In principle the athlete was fully responsible for anything entering his body. 'In these circumstances it is appropriate to presume that the athlete has knowingly or at least negligently consumed the substance which has led to the positive doping test.' If the sports organisation has demonstrated the objective elements of the doping offence guilt on the part of the athlete must be presumed. The Panel followed this by an argument along the same lines as that of the OLG Frankfurt with respect to the *Anscheinsbeweis*.

> 'The principle of presumed fault on the part of the athlete does not, however, leave him without protection because he/she has the right to rebut the presumption, i.e. to establish that the presence of the prohibited substance in his/her body was not due to any intent or negligence on his/her part [...] The athlete may for example provide evidence that the presence of the forbidden substance is the result of an act of malicious intent by a third party.
> [...]
> [...] the Panel is conscious of the fact that there have been CAS decisions where the Panel was prepared to apply a strict liability standard with respect to suspensions and was not willing to take into account the subjective elements of the case in question [...]. However, it should be noted that all these decisions took account of the level of "guilt" on the part of the athlete when establishing the duration of the suspension. It can also

281 CAS 2000/A/317, 9-7-2001, F. Aanes v FILA, ground V.2.3.

282 James A.R. Nafziger, '*Lex Sportiva*', in *ISLJ* 2004/1-2, p. 3 *et seq*. (Nafziger 2004): 'The concept of a *lex sportiva*, as a coherent and influential corpus of practice, has been identified with the *lex mercatoria* or law merchant, a venerable source of law that is said to form the foundation of international commercial practice and commercial arbitration. [...] In practice [...] the awards and opinions of the CAS provide guidance in later cases, strongly influence later awards, and often function as precedent. Also, by reinforcing and helping elaborate established rules and principles of international sports law, the accretion of CAS awards and opinions is gradually forming a source of that body of law. This source has been called the *lex sportiva*.'

283 In the judgment of the DLV-Rechtsausschuß of 13-72000 (RA 1/00) in the *Baumann* case (*see also* CAS OG 00/006, 22-9-2000, *Dieter Baumann* v. *IOC, National Olympic Committee of Germany and IAAF*) it is considered that '[...] auf die Unschuldsvermutung gemäß strafrechtlicher Grundsätze [...] sich ein betroffener Athlet nicht berufen [kann]. Das Rechtsverhältnis zwischen Verband/Athlet ist auf vertragliche Basis gestützt. Im Vertragsrecht verteilt jedoch die Rechtsprechung aus praktischen Gründen der Billigkeit und eines gerechten Interessenausgleiches zunehmend die Beweislast nach Risikobereichen.' It is correct that the legal relationship between the athlete and the sports organisation is of a private law character. It is, however, not correct that private law-orientated concepts are reflected in the disciplinary procedure which is subject to the penal law of the sports organisation.

be taken from these awards that their reasoning was often based on arguments invoked to justify a simple disqualification. They did not consider the very purpose of suspensions as opposed to a mere disqualification and the differences between them. For these reasons the Panel is not prepared to follow these decisions.

The Panel recognises that the opinions of the courts and legal authorities differ as to whether the reversal of the burden of proof puts too much burden on the athlete. As an example the OLG Frankfurt in its decision of 18 May 2000 [...] is in favour of a rule pursuant to which the presence of a prohibited substance in an athlete's body provides prima facie evidence of guilt on the part of the athlete; this leaves the athlete with the burden of proving that, in his/her particular case, the facts were different from the normal sequence of events. In many cases the practical results of both scenarios - a reversal of the burden of proof or the rebuttal of prima facie evidence - will be the same, but the Panel does recognise that the burden on the athlete is slightly less in the latter case. The Panel does, however, believe that, as a matter of principle, the reversal of the burden of proof and thus the burden being on the athlete to provide full proof of the absence of intent or negligence, is adequate and appropriate when weighing the interests of both sides.

In the case in hand, in which none of the objective elements of the offence is in dispute, the Appellant is thus presumed do have intentionally or negligently committed the offence.'

Did this mean that the CAS had just executed an about turn where the strict liability rule was concerned or was this merely evidence of a difference of opinion within the CAS between common law and civil law lawyers? As opposed to previous Panels, this Panel was entirely composed of civil law lawyers.[284] Should the Aanes judgment be considered a rarity? Indeed: "Other CAS panels were not willing to follow this theory and Aanes remained unique in the history of the court", as Martens,[285] who presided over the Panel in Aanes, later observed.[286]

To a certain extent, the question of mitigation in doping cases has been clarified by the WADA Code and its recent revision, which comes into force on 1 January, 2009, and this should perhaps lead to a more consistent approach in CAS doping decisions in future.

In any case, as Oschutz further points out, the CAS is not in a position to create its own rules in the fight against doping but must interpret and apply the rules of the relevant sports governing body:

---

[284] CAS 96/149, 13-3-1997, *Cullwick* v. *FINA*, *Beloff* (United Kingdom), *Castle* (New Zealand), Carrard (Switzerland), Matthieu Reeb, ed., *Digest of CAS Awards 1986-1998* (Berne, Editions Stämpfli 1998) pp. 251-263. CAS 98/184, 25-9-1998, *Phoebe Hearst Cooke* v. *FEI*, *Beloff* (United Kingdom), *Young* (USA), Natter (Switzerland), Matthieu Reeb, ed., *Digest of CAS Awards II 1998-2000* (The Hague, Kluwer Law International 2002) pp. 197-204. CAS 98/211, 7-6-1999, *Smith-De Bruin* v. *FINA*, *Fortier* (Canada), *Beloff* (United Kingdom), Oswald (Switzerland), Matthieu Reeb, ed., *Digest of CAS Awards II 1998-2000* (The Hague, Kluwer Law International 2002) pp. 255-273. CAS 99/A/234 & CAS 99/A/235, 29-2-2000, *David Meca-Medina* v. *FINA* & *Igor Majcen* v. *FINA*, *Beloff* (United Kingdom), *McLaren* (Canada), Oswald (Switzerland). CAS OG 00/011, 28-9-2000, *Andreea Raducan* v. *IOC*, Matthieu Reeb, ed., *Digest of CAS Awards II 1998-2000* (The Hague, Kluwer Law International 2002) pp. 665-673, *Kavanagh* (Australia), Netzle (Switzerland), *Oliveau* (USA), Matthieu Reeb, ed., *Digest of CAS Awards II 1998-2000* (The Hague, Kluwer Law International 2002) pp. 665-673. CAS OG 00/015, 29-9-2000, *Mihaela Melinte* v. *IAAF*, *Young* (USA), Lee (Malaysia), *McLaren* (Canada), Matthieu Reeb, ed., *Digest of CAS Awards II 1998-2000* (The Hague, Kluwer Law International 2002) pp. 691-695. CAS 2000/A/270, 23-5-2001, *David Meca-Medina* v. *FINA* & *Igor Majcen* v. *FINA*, *Beloff* (United Kingdom), *McLaren* (Canada), Oswald (Switzerland). CAS 2000/A/274, 19-10-2000, *Susin* v. *FINA*, Matthieu Reeb, ed., *Digest of CAS Awards II 1998-2000* (The Hague, Kluwer Law International 2002) pp. 389-409, *Fortier* (Canada), Coccia (Italy), Oswald (Switzerland). CAS 2000/A/317, 9-7-2001, F. Aanes v FILA, Martens (Germany), Seim-Haugen (Norway), Rochat (Switzerland). The names in italics belong to common law panel members. In nine out ten cases a common law lawyer presided over the Panel.

[285] Dirk-Reiner Martens, 'Landmark decisions' in: *The Court of Arbitration for Sport 1984-2004* (Blackshaw, Siekmann, Soek, eds.), The Hague, T.M.C. Asser Press, 2005, p. 235 et seq.

[286] 'Despite a prevailing rule among IFs of strict liability for doping, CAS awards generally disclose an inclination to avoid unnecessarily harsh results', according to Nafziger (James A.R. Nafziger, 'Lex Sportiva', in *ISLJ* 2004/1-2, p. 3 *et seq.*). In a footnote to this statement he referred to the Aanes case to confirm this inclination; however, this is actually the sole exception in a series of CAS judgments on the issue of the strict liability rule.

> 'The CAS is a judicial authority, limited to the control of decisions, which are based on the rules of the sports governing bodies. The CAS is bound to apply existing bodies of rules and the law to certain facts, cf Art R58 of the Code. In doing so, the arbitrators may interpret these rules according to certain standards, but they must refrain from rewriting them.'[287]

To the author's knowledge, some CAS arbitrators consider – quite wrongly – that they can ignore the rules in doping cases and decide cases on the basis of fairness alone, justifying this point of view on the basis that in appeal cases they can deal with the case *de novo*, pursuant to the provisions of Article R57 of the CAS Code of Sports-related Arbitration, which provide that '[t]he Panel shall have full power to review the facts and the law ...' and also relying on the fact that the CAS has become the 'Supreme Court of World Sport'. In effect, such CAS Panel members are claiming to be free to rewrite the applicable legal rules in the interest of what they consider to be fairness in the circumstances of the particular case. This is a dangerous course of action and not conducive to legal certainty. Or put another way, is contrary to a so-called 'rule of sports law'. Fortunately, such CAS members tend to belong to the so-called 'old guard'of sports lawyers! The so-called *blaserattsi*. So, what are the general principles that CAS should and generally does follow?

15.3 General Principles of CAS Jurisprudence

Ken Foster, Emeritus Professor of Law at Warwick University, has identified the following general principles, which he considers to underscore the emerging jurisprudence of the CAS.[288] And they are worth setting out *in extensu* as follows:

> '... [these] principles [fall] into five main categories:
> *Lex ludica*: these are the rules of the game. There is a self-imposed reluctance on the Court of Arbitration for Sport to interfere with what it considers to be purely sporting matters. This covers not only the obvious refusal to reopen decisions made by match officials, but issues that are essentially about the nature of sport in a wider sense.
>
> Good governance: this covers the proper standards that are legally required of decision making within a private organisation that has disciplinary power over athletes. Specifically, it encompasses having clear authority in the rules to make a decision (the ultra vires principle); avoiding arbitrary decision making by decreeing that a sporting federation cannot be the sole arbiter of the interpretation of its rules; not acting in bad faith; not making such unreasonable decisions that no reasonable body could have reached them; and using transparent and objective criteria in reaching its decisions.
>
> Procedural fairness: these are a set of minimum standards that sporting federations must follow in hearing disciplinary matters.
>
> Harmonization of standards: as an international body, the Court of arbitration for Sport tries to ensure consistency. The general principles that it formulates should apply to all federations. So it harmonises standards. This policy also entails formulating the principle that international sporting federations have primacy over national federations, and exercising a supervisory function over the rulebooks of federations, suggesting amendments where necessary.
>
> Fairness and equitable treatment: the Court of Arbitration for Sport has a major function to achieve fairness in individual cases. This has been especially evident in its approach to penalties. It has disapproved of automatic fixed penalties; followed the principle of proportionality;

---

287 See n. 274 *supra*.

288 Ken Foster, '*Lex Sportiva* and *Lex Ludica*: The Court of Arbitration for Sport's Jurisprudence', in Blackshaw, Siekmann and Soek, op. cit., pp. 422-423.

and required sanctions to "fit the crime". It has also, where appropriate, followed the principles of legitimate expectation and of estoppel.'

All these principles identified and enunciated by Foster have been distilled from Decisions rendered over the years by the CAS, several of which he cites and discusses in his contribution to the *Court of Arbitration for Sport 1984-2004* book, of which the author of this book is one of the editors, and which principles continue to influence CAS Decisions at present and in the future. Thus, providing for all those involved in sports disputes a useful body of legal precedents. For example, a landmark CAS ruling on the application of the rules of the game/rules of law principle involving a boxer who challenged the referee's decision on a disqualification for a punch below the belt and whether such a dispute was arbitrable or not, the Panel limiting itself to the question whether the referee's decision violated the 'general principles of law'.[289]

As Allan Erbsen, of the University of Minnesota Law School, Minneapolis, USA, concludes in his contribution to the same book:[290]

'CAS's jurisprudence fills what until recently was a disturbing legal vacuum in international sports. Before the creation of CAS, the rights and obligations of athletes and officials were ill-defined and were enforceable – if at all – only through costly and lengthy litigation in national courts or in arbitration before tribunals staffed by the same sports federations whose actions the tribunals were asked to judge. Legal claims were thus difficult to frame, difficult to pursue, and, for political outsiders, difficult to win. CAS has thus made litigation a more viable remedy and deterrent ..., spotlighting legal norms on a stage where law previously played a more marginal role.'

15.4 *Lex Sportiva* Compared with *Lex Mercatoria*

In an endeavour to define the nature of sports law, the *lex sportiva* has been compared and contrasted by several academics and commentators on sports law with the *lex mercatoria* – the 'law merchant'. The body of rules developed in the Middle Ages and derived from the established customs of merchants in their dealings on a global basis and recognised and enforced in the ordinary civil courts.

According to Andrew Caiger and Simon Gardiner:

'The relative autonomy of sports is perhaps most closely mirrored by the Lex Mercatoria ... This analogy with the Lex Mercatoria allows sports law to develop distinctiveness and an incremental formation. It encourages sports organisations to reconsider their own rules and mode of governance in the light of dominant legal norms. This process of acculturation allows and promotes a convergence between the Lex Sportiva and the dominant legal norms.'[291]

Again, according to Gardiner:

'The analogy between lex mercatoria and a lex sportiva or sports law is germane: both respect a degree of autonomy, both acknowledge cultural specificities, both are part of a pluralist and

---

[289] CAS JO 96/006, *M* v. *AIBA*.

[290] Allan Erbsen, 'The Substance and Illusion of *Lex Sportiva*', in Blackshaw, Siekmann and Soek, op. cit., pp. 422-423.

[291] A. Caiger and S. Gardiner, eds., *Professional Sport in the European Union: Regulation and Re-regulation* (The Hague, T.M.C. Asser Press 2000) pp. 301-302.

> complex normative rule structure, and both acknowledge the need for international emphasis in terms of legal regulation. Lex mercatoria, or the Law Merchant, was the legal doctrine developed in the Middle Ages by special local courts in Britain and elsewhere. These Merchant Courts had judges and jury who were merchants themselves and would apply the lex mercatoria as opposed to local law. An analogy can be made with the Court of Arbitration for Sport and the view that it is developing a specific doctrine of international sports law.'[292]

Another similarity between the *law merchant* and the Court of Arbitration for Sport is that both bodies may settle disputes *ex aequo et bono*; in other words, applying a general principle of fairness or equity.

The CAS itself expressed the position well in 1998 in the so-called ENIC case, mentioned above, as follows:

> 'Sports law has developed and consolidated along the years, particularly through the arbitration settlement of disputes, a set of unwritten legal principles – a sort of lex mercatoria for sports or, so to speak, a lex ludica – to which national and international sports federations must conform, regardless of the presence of such principles with their own statutes and regulations or within any applicable national law.'[293]

An extensive and comparative review on the relationship between the *lex sportiva* and the *lex mercatoria* has recently been undertaken and published in *The International Sports Law Journal (ISLJ)* by Boris Kolev, co-chairman of the NGO Bulgarian Legal Society, which conducts research on the rights of sportsmen, and also a member of the Advisory Board of the ISLJ.[294] Although there are a number of similarities between the two legal systems, there are also several important and practical differences. Kolev writes:

> 'Sports law is highly potential to become a world law similar to mercantile law. The universally accepted rules of more than 200 games and universally accepted principles governing competitions at world level, significance of sport for demonstration of individual and national values, globalization of sport, are part of the conditions precedent for this to happen. However, the comparison with Lex Mercatoria reveals some important differences which might be relevant for the future development of sports law as a world law.
>
> A statement saying that the community of merchants is held together by common traditions and common trust does not seem to be applicable to contemporary sport, which, especially in recent years, departs from the Corinthian values of playing a game because of the love of that game. Nowadays, the result of the competition does not have only sporting implications but further determines who is going to get the better sponsor. Commercialization of sport invokes the need for protection of different and very often conflicting interests of the stakeholders in sport. Sports federations are often criticised for pursuing their own commercial interests without taking into account and sometimes even to the detriment of the interests of sportsmen.
>
> However, in view of the conflicting interests in sport, the role of CAS is very important and the consistent resolving of disputes might significantly contribute to the idea for the creation of an independent body of law capable of restoring and maintaining justice in sport. Evidence of the increasing role of CAS are the more frequent use of arbitration clauses in the contracts between sponsors, federations and clubs; the trend for increasing the volume of cases reaching CAS; and the number of sports federations admitting the authority of CAS to resolve the disputes in their particular sports.

---

[292] Gardiner, James, O'Leary, Welch, Blackshaw, Boyes and Caiger, *Sports Law*, 3rd edn. (London, Cavendish Publishing 2006) p. 93.

[293] CAS 98/200 *AEK Athens & SK Slavia Prague* v. *Union of European Football Associations (UEFA)*, p. 102.

[294] Boris Kolev, 'Lex Sportiva and Lex Mercatoria', 1/2 *ISLJ* (2008) pp. 57-62.

On the other hand, CAS is an institution for settlement of civil law disputes; it is not an administrative or constitutional court, before which provisions of sports regulations could be challenged on the ground of contradiction with acts staying higher in the hierarchy of the legal instruments. Furthermore, CAS is not entitled to review the substance of the decision-making process but only the procedure and the power of the particular bodies to pass the decision in issue. Although CAS has a lot of common characteristics with an international court it is not a court. An opinion has been expressed that CAS could develop into an instrument of "constitutional" review and standard-setting in the realm of international sports law; however, this is still not the case and the regulations of sports associations may be scrutinized on the basis of national laws. The incentive for clubs and sportsmen to refer their cases to the courts as well as their mistrust and suspicion of the federations will remain present until their interests are adequately safeguarded through their participation in the decision-making process especially as regards matters of primary concern for them. The lack of democratic rule-making process and credibility in respect of the actions of sport governing bodies further handicaps the possibilities for recognition of Lex Sportiva by the national laws of the States.

Another difference with Lex Mercatoria is the fact that CAS cannot apply Lex Sportiva through the application of the national law of a particular State as could be the case with Lex Mercatoria due to the fact that national laws usually have not incorporated Lex Sportiva. Very often, certain cases would have diametrically opposite outcomes under national laws in comparison with their potential outcomes under the law of international sports federations based on the principle of freedom of association due to conflicting provisions of national sports or employment laws. Lex Sportiva may apply to relations in sport also as an autonomous body of law, which is to be recognized as such by national laws; however, this is still not the case either. A review of modern court practices would show a third option for enforcement of Lex Sportiva – if the rules of Lex Sportiva constitute mandatory rules reflecting a public policy so commanding that they must be applied even if the general body of law to which they belong is not competent by application of the relevant rule of conflict of laws.'

Kolev concludes his review with the following pertinent remarks:

'However, being a private arbitration system and not a universally recognized court including by the EU Member States by virtue of an international treaty, the CAS awards will be subject to enforcement proceedings in the countries where the enforcement is sought and, therefore, their conformity with the public policy and mandatory rules in operation in such countries will be reviewed by the national courts.[295] In countries like Bulgaria and Hungary, for example, employment related disputes are not subject to arbitration at all and national courts have exclusive jurisdiction over employment disputes. It is true that FIFA ensures the compliance of the parties with the award not through the assistance of national courts but rather through threatening the parties with disciplinary sanctions. The latter, however, together with the already mentioned deficits of Lex Sportiva as a concept, as well as the mandatory reference to arbitration of players and clubs imposed through the by-laws of their federations, could threaten the recognition of CAS as a valid arbitration system and do not in any manner contribute to the idea of an objective, just, transparent, self-integrated and universally accepted international sports law or Lex Sportiva.'

The complete text of Kolev's interesting article is set out at Appendix XXIII to this book.

[295] It should perhaps be added here that 'exequatur' proceedings to enforce a CAS Award, which is considered to be an International Arbitral Award, will, generally speaking, only be required in those countries that have not acceded to the New York Convention of 1958.

15.5 Lack of Publicity

However, one of the difficulties faced by the CAS in developing a *lex sportiva* stems from the fact that, generally speaking, CAS proceedings and decisions are a matter of private law and confidential to the parties. CAS by its nature is a private arbitral body. And therein lies the paradox – the need, on the one hand, of the sporting community 'not to wash its dirty sports linen in public'; and, on the other hand, the need of a wider public to know how cases are being decided, including details of the evidence adduced to the CAS, particularly for future guidance and reference. Article R43 of the CAS Code of Sports-related Arbitration provides as follows:

> 'Proceedings under these procedural rules are confidential. The parties, the arbitrators and the CAS undertake not to disclose to any third party any facts or other information relating to the dispute or the proceedings.'

However, the last sentence of this article provides the following exceptions to the general rule of confidentiality: 'Awards shall not be made public unless the award itself so provides or all parties agree.'

But, in practice, more CAS Awards are being published,[296] especially on the CAS official website.[297] In fact, the CAS itself is interested in developing a Lex Sportiva as the following extract from Volume II of the CAS Digest of Awards makes clear:

> 'The "Digest of CAS Awards 1986-1998" recorded the emergence of a lex sportiva through the judicial decisions of the CAS. It is true that one of the interests of this court is to develop a jurisprudence that can be used as a reference by all the actors of world sport, thereby encouraging the harmonisation of the judicial rules and principles applied within the sports world.'

Furthermore, as the work of the CAS continues to expand and becomes more widely known and discussed, especially in press reports and articles, the need for such publicity also increases. In fact, a 'public interest' argument comes into play and needs to be satisfied in appropriate cases.[298] But, in this context, what interests the public is not necessarily the same as what is in the public interest![299]

15.6 Conclusions

It is clear from the above discussion that the CAS is in the process of developing a useful *lex sportiva* based on its many Awards rendered to date and the general principles derived

---

[296] The Secretary General of CAS, Matthieu Reeb, has edited and published three Digests of several CAS cases covering the periods 1986-1998; 1998-200; and 2001-2003. A further volume in the series is expected shortly.

[297] The CAS official website under the title 'Jursiprudence' contains a new section, entitled, 'Archive', which, at the time of writing is 'under construction'. Once this section is 'live', it will be interesting to see how comprehensive it is and what it covers.

[298] See, for example, the Decision in the Gaia Bassani Case (CAS 2003/O/468), where the author of this book was the sole arbitrator and, because of the particular circumstances of the case and the need for a wider audience to know about the case and its outcome, directed that the decision be published.

[299] On this point, see the discussion in the English case of *Lion Laboratories Ltd* v. *Evans* [1984] 2 *All ER* 417.

from them. And, with its increasing work load, this should lead to consistency and certainty in the future regarding such matters as the jurisdiction and review powers of the CAS and, in turn, lead to a timely, fair, effective and relatively inexpensive settlement of sports-related disputes for the benefit of the sporting world and its various stakeholders and constituents.

But, as Professor Nafziger points out: 'A truly effective body of jurisprudence generated by CAS awards, however, will require more development before the emerging lex sportiva can become a truly effective regime of authority.'[300]

Much will depend, however, as has been noted above, upon the transparency and availability of CAS Decisions and a willingness of CAS arbitrators to lay down clear principles and also follow them in future similar cases in a clear and consistent manner. Some inconsistencies have been observed in certain doping cases, for example, as noted above. Equally, the competence and independence of CAS arbitrators is a crucial ingredient in the process of achieving these laudable aims and results. With, in the words of the first ICAS/CAS President, the late Judge Keba Mbaye: 'a stature that inspires confidence and respect' to match.

---

300 James A.R. Nafziger, *International Sports Law*, 2nd edn. (Ardsley, NY, Transnational Publishers 2004) p. 61.

Part Three

Settling Sports Disputes Through the World Intellectual Property Organization

CHAPTER 16
INTRODUCTORY REMARKS AND OVERVIEW

In this part of the book, we will take a look at the different extra-judicial possibilities of resolving various kinds of sports-related disputes through the auspices of the Arbitration and Mediation Center of the World Intellectual Property Organization (WIPO), which is based in Geneva, Switzerland.

Before doing so and to set the scene, a brief description of WIPO, its history and its activities would not be out of place.

16.1 The World Intellectual Property Organization

16.1.1 **What is WIPO?**

The WIPO is a specialized agency of the United Nations. It is dedicated to developing a balanced and accessible international intellectual property (IP) system, which rewards creativity, stimulates innovation and contributes to economic development whilst, at the same time, safeguarding the public interest.

IP refers to creations of the mind: inventions, literary and artistic works, and symbols, names, images, and designs used in commerce. And IP is divided into two categories:

industrial property, which includes inventions (patents), trademarks, industrial designs, and geographic indications of source; and

copyright, which includes literary and artistic works such as novels, poems and plays, films, musical works, artistic works such as drawings, paintings, photographs and sculptures, and architectural designs.

Related rights to copyright include:

- those of performing artists in their performances;
- producers of phonograms in their recordings; and
- those of broadcasters in their radio and television programs.

WIPO publishes an *Intellectual Property Handbook* which offers a comprehensive introduction to the policy, law and use of IP. A summary of IP legislation in Member States, as well as contact information, is available in the *WIPO Guide to Intellectual Property Worldwide*. Further information about these WIPO publications – and, indeed, others – may be obtained from the WIPO official website at: <www.wipo.int>.

WIPO was established by the WIPO Convention, concluded in Stockholm on July 14, 1967, with a mandate from its Member States to promote the protection of IP throughout the world, through cooperation among states and in collaboration with other international organizations.

16.1.2 A brief history of WIPO

The origins of the WIPO go back to 1883, when Johannes Brahms was composing his Third Symphony; Robert Louis Stevenson was writing Treasure Island; and John and Emily Roebling were completing construction of New York's Brooklyn Bridge.

The need for international protection of intellectual property became evident when foreign exhibitors refused to attend the International Exhibition of Inventions in Vienna in 1873 because they were afraid their ideas would be stolen and exploited commercially in other countries.

1883 marked the birth of the Paris Convention for the Protection of Industrial Property, the first major international treaty designed to help the people of one country obtain protection in other countries for their intellectual creations in the form of industrial property rights, known as:

- inventions (patents);
- trademarks;
- industrial designs.

The Paris Convention entered into force in 1884 with fourteen Member States, which set up an International Bureau to carry out administrative tasks, such as organizing meetings of the Member States.

In 1886, copyright entered the international arena with the Berne Convention for the Protection of Literary and Artistic Works. The aim of this Convention was to help nationals of its Member States obtain international protection of their right to control, and receive payment for, the use of their creative works such as:

- novels, short stories, poems, plays;
- songs, operas, musicals, sonatas; and
- drawings, paintings, sculptures, architectural works.

Like the Paris Convention, the Berne Convention set up an International Bureau to carry out administrative tasks. In 1893, these two small bureaux united to form an international organisation called the United International Bureaux for the Protection of Intellectual Property (best known by its French acronym BIRPI). Based in Berne, Switzerland, with a staff of seven, this small organization was the precursor of the World Intellectual Property Organization of today – a dynamic entity with 184 Member States; a staff that now numbers some 938, from 95 countries around the world; and with a mission and a mandate that are constantly growing.

As the importance of intellectual property grew, the structure and form of the organization changed as well. In 1960, BIRPI moved from Berne to Geneva to be closer to the United Nations and other international organizations in that city. A decade later, following the entry into force of the Convention Establishing the World Intellectual Property Organization, BIRPI became WIPO, undergoing structural and administrative reforms and acquiring a secretariat answerable to the Member States.

In 1974, WIPO became a specialized agency of the United Nations system of organizations, with a mandate to administer intellectual property matters recognized by the Member States of the UN.

In 1978, the WIPO Secretariat moved into the headquarters building that has now become a Geneva landmark, with spectacular views of the surrounding Swiss and French countryside.

WIPO expanded its role and further demonstrated the importance of Intellectual Property rights in the management of globalized trade in 1996 by entering into a Cooperation Agreement with the World Trade Organization (WTO).

The impetus that led to the Paris and Berne Conventions – the desire to promote creativity by protecting the works of the mind – has continued to power the work of the Organization, and its predecessor, for some 120 years. But the scope of the protection and the services provided have developed and expanded radically during that time.

In 1898, BIRPI administered only four International Treaties. Today its successor, WIPO, administers 24 Treaties – 3 of those jointly with other international organizations – and carries out a rich and varied program of work, through its Member States and Secretariat, that seeks to:

- harmonize national intellectual property legislation and procedures;
- provide services for international applications for industrial property rights;
- exchange intellectual property information;
- provide legal and technical assistance to developing and other countries;
- facilitate the resolution of private intellectual property disputes; and
- marshal information technology as a tool for storing, accessing, and using valuable intellectual property information.

16.1.3 How WIPO works

The terms governing the mandate, functions, finances and procedures of WIPO are set out in the WIPO Convention of July 14, 1967.

16.1.4 Member States

The Member States of WIPO determine the strategic direction and activities of the Organization. They meet in the Assemblies, committees and working groups.

There are currently 184 Member States; in other words, over 90 percent of the countries of the world.

16.1.5 Secretariat

The WIPO Secretariat, or International Bureau, is based in Geneva. WIPO staff, who are drawn from more than ninety countries, include experts in diverse areas of IP law and practice, as well as specialists in public policy, economics, administration and, of course, IT.

16.1.6 Program and budget

Every two years, the Director General of WIPO presents a Program and Budget document to Member States for approval. This details objectives, performance measures and budgetary planning for all proposed program activities.

WIPO is unusual amongst the family of UN organizations in that it is largely self-financing. About 90 percent of the Organization's budgeted expenditure of SFR 531 million for the 2006-2007 biennium comes from earnings from the services, which WIPO provides to users of the international registration systems (PCT, Madrid system, The Hague System and so on). The remaining 10 percent will be made up mainly of revenue from the arbitration and mediation services of WIPO and sales of publications, plus contributions from its Member States. These contributions, however, are relatively small. The five largest contributing countries each donate about one-half percent of the organization's budget.

16.1.7 **Developing international IP laws and standards**

WIPO is responsible for promoting the progressive development and harmonization of IP legislation, standards and procedures among its Member States. This includes further development of international laws and treaties regarding patents; trademarks, industrial designs and geographical indications; and copyright and related rights.

WIPO handles the administration of 24 international treaties: 16 on industrial property; 7 on copyright; plus the convention creating WIPO.

16.1.8 **Delivering global IP protection services**

WIPO administers fee-based services, based on international agreements, which enable users in Member Countries to file international applications for patents (PCT); international registrations for trademarks (Madrid system); designs (Hague System); and appellations of origin (Lisbon System).

WIPO administers four IP classification systems, which organize the mass of information concerning inventions, trademarks, and industrial designs into indexed, manageable structures for easy retrieval.

The WIPO Arbitration and Mediation Center offers dispute resolution services to businesses and individuals, including the expanding area of Internet domain name disputes, which will be the main focus of this Part of this book.

16.2 WIPO Arbitration and Mediation Center

16.2.1 **Generally**

Also based in Geneva, Switzerland, the WIPO Arbitration and Mediation Center, is an independent and impartial body that forms part of the WIPO, and was established in 1994 to offer alternative dispute resolution (ADR) options for the resolution of international commercial disputes between private parties relating to intellectual property.

Developed by leading experts in cross-border dispute settlement, the arbitration, mediation and expert determination procedures offered by the Center are widely recognized as particularly appropriate for technology, entertainment (including sport) and other disputes involving intellectual property.

An increasing number of cases are being filed with the Center under the WIPO Arbitration, Expedited Arbitration, Mediation and Expert Determination Rules. The subject matter of these proceedings includes both contractual disputes (e.g., patent and software licenses, trademark coexistence agreements, distribution agreements for pharmaceutical products and research and development agreements) and non-contractual disputes (e.g., patent infringement). It should be noted that WIPO Arbitration and Mediation is available for all kinds of disputes in all kinds of industries, irrespective of whether the disputes are IP based or related. Such proceedings include sports disputes. And it should be further noted that, under the WIPO Mediation Rules, the 'without prejudice' nature of the mediation process is fully safeguarded and the process is completely confidential, including the existence and the outcome of the mediation itself. Thus, the parties to any WIPO mediation are able to negotiate freely and effectively, without having any concerns over publicity and also without harming or prejudicing their chances in any subsequent court or arbitration proceedings in the event of the mediation not being successful.

WIPO disputes have involved parties based in different jurisdictions including Austria, China, France, Germany, Hungary, Ireland, Israel, Italy, Japan, The Netherlands, Panama, Spain, Switzerland, the United Kingdom and the United States of America. The Center makes available a general overview of its caseload as well as descriptive examples of particular cases.

According to the Center, the quality and commitment of the neutrals are crucial to the satisfactory resolution of each case. The Center assists parties in the selection of mediators, arbitrators and experts from the Center's database of over a thousand neutrals with experience in dispute resolution and specialized knowledge in intellectual property disputes. Where necessary in individual cases, the Center will use its worldwide contacts to identify additional candidates with the required background. After appointment also, the Center monitors its cases in terms of their time and cost effectiveness.

One of the case administration facilities which the Center makes available for parties at their option is the WIPO Electronic Case Facility (WIPO ECAF). The WIPO ECAF allows for secure filing, storing and retrieval of case-related submissions in a web-based electronic docket, by parties, neutral(s) and the Center from anywhere in the world. It also facilitates case management by providing, in addition to the online docket, a case overview, time tracking and finance information.

Although the WIPO ECAF is available only to parties to a WIPO procedure, the Center, under certain circumstances, will make this facility available in non-WIPO procedures in certain cases. For example, the Center provided a customized version of WIPO ECAF for use in the Jury Procedure of the 32nd America's Cup, the international yachting competition, which commenced in 2004 and culminated in the final regattas in Valencia, Spain, in the summer of 2007.

The Center has also focused significant resources on establishing an operational and legal framework for the administration of disputes relating to the Internet and electronic commerce. In this connection, the Center is recognized as the leading dispute resolution service provider for disputes arising out of the abusive registration and use of Internet domain names (Internet addresses), commonly called 'cybersquatting'. The role of the Center in such disputes is to administer the proceedings, which includes verifying that the Complaint satisfies the formal requirements of the Uniform Domain Name Dispute Resolution Policy (UDRP) and Rules and WIPO Supplemental Rules; co-ordinating with the registrar(s) concerned to verify that the named Respondent is the actual registrant of the disputed domain name(s); checking the Respondent's contact details; notifying the Complaint to the Respondent; sending out case-related notifications; appointing the Administrative Panel; and otherwise ensuring that the administrative proceeding runs smoothly and expeditiously. The Center is independent and impartial. It does not decide the dispute between the parties. As an administrative body, it can provide general information on the procedural aspects of the UDRP Policy and Rules and WIPO Supplemental Rules, but cannot give any views about the strengths and weaknesses of any party's case.

Each year, the Center publishes a report on the 'cybersquatting' disputes that it has handled. In the latest report for 2007, sports-related and entertainment disputes (sport is now widely regarded as a form of home and out-of-home entertainment and sports persons as entertainers), both of which in the present age of the 'celebrity', are on the increase, accounted for 2.7 percent and 7 percent respectively of these cases.

The Center also publishes a Guide on the UDRP Administrative Procedure and any particular questions that are not covered in the Guide may be submitted by e-mail to the following address: arbiter.mail@wipo.int. It should be noted, however, that the Center does not provide any legal advice on the merits of a particular dispute or potential dispute to either Complainants or Respondents. Anyone requiring such advice regarding the strength of their case or any other advice other than purely procedural issues, should, of course, consult an independent lawyer specialised in the field. The Center does not recommend any such lawyers.

Information about the resolution of domain name disputes under the UDRP Administrative Procedure may also be obtained from the official website of the Internet Corporation for Assigned Names and Numbers (ICANN). ICANN is based in Marina del Rey, California, United States of America.

16.2.2 **WIPO neutrals**

As previously mentioned, effective dispute resolution procedures and mechanisms, to a large extent, depend on the quality, expertise and professionality of the so-called neutrals – the independent decision makers appointed to resolve the particular dispute. Intellectual Property disputes demand not only optimal procedural skills on the part of the decision-maker, but also specialized knowledge within the fields of patents, trademarks, copyright, designs and other forms of Intellectual Property that are the subject of the particular dispute.

Parties seeking to avail themselves of the wide range of WIPO dispute resolution services can draw upon a growing database of over a thousand independent WIPO arbitrators, mediators and experts from seventy countries. The candidates on the WIPO List of Neutrals range from experienced dispute resolution generalists to highly specialized practitioners and experts covering the entire legal and technical spectrum of Intellectual Property. Their geographical diversity suits the international character of many of the disputes that they are called upon to resolve.

The general WIPO List of Neutrals is not made available as such to the public. However, the WIPO Center does publish its specific list of WIPO Domain Name Panellists. Although the general WIPO List of Neutrals includes many more neutrals, who are specialized in other areas of Intellectual Property, the list of WIPO Domain Name Panellists may serve to give interested parties an indication of the kind of information which is maintained by the Center in relation to the candidates included on the general WIPO List of Neutrals and which is made available to parties in the circumstances mentioned below.

When the WIPO Center is called upon to appoint a neutral in the context of a pending procedure under the WIPO Rules, the WIPO Center, taking into account the specific characteristics of the dispute, makes available detailed database profiles of suitable candidates. These dispute characteristics include:

- method of resolving the dispute (i.e., arbitration, mediation, expert determination);
- governing law;
- nationality and/or identity of the parties and their representatives;
- area of Intellectual Property law;
- technical or business area;
- language of the proceedings; and
- venue of the proceedings.

16.2.3 **Independence and impartiality**

In view of the need for the neutral and the WIPO Center to preserve their impartiality and independence, the WIPO Center, in principle, does not make unilateral recommendations to only one party; that is, does not normally do so to one party without the other party's consent. The Center makes available detailed profiles to both parties when the 'list procedure' for the selection of a sole or presiding arbitrator, a mediator or an expert, as the case may be, is involved under the WIPO Rules.

The WIPO Center has a strong commitment to the time and cost effective conduct of all its cases. In its selection process, as well as in the administration of the cases themselves, the WIPO Center makes every effort to ensure that its appointed neutrals share this commitment. A very important and ongoing task!

As already mentioned and as their name suggests, neutrals must be independent and impartial in the cases they handle in compliance with the provisions of Paragraph 7 of the ICANN Rules, which provide as follows:

> '7. Impartiality and Independence
> A Panellist shall be impartial and independent and shall have, before accepting appointment, disclosed to the Provider any circumstances giving rise to justifiable doubt as to the Panellist's impartiality or independence. If, at any stage during the administrative proceeding, new circumstances arise that could give rise to justifiable doubt as to the impartiality or independence of the Panellist, that Panellist shall promptly disclose such circumstances to the Provider. In such event, the Provider shall have the discretion to appoint a substitute Panellist.'

For 'Provider' in the above quote, read 'WIPO' in the present context.

And, before being appointed by WIPO in Domain Name Disputes, Panellists, of which there at the time of writing 393, must sign a Statement of Acceptance and Declaration of Impartiality and Independence in the following terms:

ORGANISATION MONDIALE
DE LA PROPRIÉTÉ INTELLECTUELLE

Centre d'arbitrage et de médiation de l'OMPI

WORLD INTELLECTUAL
PROPERTY ORGANIZATION

WIPO Arbitration and Mediation Center

STATEMENT OF ACCEPTANCE
AND DECLARATION OF IMPARTIALITY AND INDEPENDENCE

Case Number:

I, the undersigned,

[ ] hereby declare that I accept to serve as a Panellist under the Uniform Domain Name Dispute Resolution Policy and the Rules for Uniform Domain Name Dispute Resolution Policy (the Rules), both approved by the Internet Corporation for Assigned Names and Numbers (ICANN) on October 24, 1999, and the WIPO Arbitration and Mediation Center's Supplemental Rules for Uniform Domain Name Dispute Resolution Policy (the Supplemental Rules), in effect as of December 1, 1999. By making this declaration, I confirm that I have familiarized myself with the principles, standards, requirements and fees set out in the aforementioned instruments and that I am available to serve as a Panellist in accordance therewith. I further declare that, by accepting to serve as a Panellist in this case, I shall execute my responsibilities honestly, fairly and within the time periods required by the Rules and Supplemental Rules.
Please check the appropriate box below, taking into consideration, inter alia, whether there exists any past or present relationship, direct or indirect, with either of the parties, whether financial, professional or of another kind and whether the nature of any such relationship is such that disclosure is called for. [Any doubt should be resolved in favour of disclosure].

   [ ] I am independent of each the parties. To the best of my knowledge and belief, there are no facts or circumstances, past or present, or that could arise in the foreseeable future, that need be disclosed as they might be of a such a nature as to call in to question my independence in the eyes of one or both of the parties.

   [ ] I am independent of each of the parties. However, I wish to disclose the circumstances described in the attachment hereto (attach separate sheet) as they might be of such a nature as to call in to question my independence in the eyes of one or both of the parties.

[ ] hereby declare that I decline to serve as a Panellist in the present case. (Disclosure of the reasons for declining to accept the appointment should be made on a separate sheet and attached hereto.)

Place: ____________________ Signature:______________________

Date: ______________

As will be seen from the above wording, full disclosure of any circumstances that might affect the Neutral's independence must be disclosed in full, to enable the Center to decide whether to use in the Neutral selected in the particular case. Equally, if the neutral selected declines to accept the appointment, full reasons should be given. One further point: the

Form has to be actually signed by the Neutral concerned and either faxed to the Center or scanned and e-mailed.

Indeed, to underscore the insistence on independence by the Center, when a Neutral is invited to be a Panellist in a case, the Invitation Letter contains the following warning:

> 'Our invitation to you is based on our understanding that there are no facts or circumstances, past or present, or that could arise in the foreseeable future, that might be of such a nature as to call into question your independence in the eyes of one or both of the parties identified above. Furthermore, taking into consideration the envisioned procedural schedule in this case, our invitation is made on the understanding that you will be able to commit the time required to discharge your duties as a panellist and within the required deadlines. Please note that pursuant to Paragraph 15(b) of the Rules for Uniform Domain Name Dispute Resolution Policy a decision on the Complaint is due within 14 days of the appointment of the Administrative Panel.'

As will be seen from this comprehensive wording, a high standard of impartiality and commitment is required from WIPO Neutrals in their appointment and in the exercise of their functions!

CHAPTER 17
ICANN UNIFORM DOMAIN NAME DISPUTE RESOLUTION POLICY

The ICANN Uniform Domain Name Dispute Resolution Policy (the UDRP Policy) sets out the legal framework for the resolution of disputes between a domain name registrant and a third party (i.e., a party other than the registrar) over the abusive registration and use of an Internet domain name ('cybersquatting') in the generic top level domains or gTLDs (e.g., .biz, .com, .info, .mobi, .name, .net, .org), and those country code top level domains or ccTLDs that have adopted the UDRP Policy on a voluntary basis.

At its meetings on August 25 and 26, 1999 in Santiago, Chile, the ICANN Board of Directors adopted the UDRP Policy, based largely on the recommendations contained in the Report of the WIPO Internet Domain Name Process, as well as comments submitted by registrars and other interested parties.

All ICANN-accredited registrars that are authorized to register names in the gTLDs and the ccTLDs that have adopted the Policy have agreed to abide by and implement it for those domains.

Any person or entity wishing to register a domain name in the gTLDs and ccTLDs in question is required to consent to the terms and conditions of the UDRP Policy.

On October 24, 1999, the ICANN Board adopted a set of Rules for Uniform Domain Name Dispute Resolution Policy (the UDRP Rules) setting out the procedures and other requirements for each stage of the Dispute Resolution Administrative Procedure. The WIPO Arbitration and Mediation Center (the WIPO Center) acted as technical advisors to the ICANN drafting committee charged with finalizing the UDRP Policy and Rules.

The WIPO Center has developed WIPO Supplemental Rules for Uniform Domain Name Dispute Resolution Policy which supplement the UDRP Policy and Rules, and these Rules additionally apply when a domain name dispute complaint is filed with and prosecuted through the Center. The WIPO UDRP Supplemental Rules are available on the WIPO official website.

The Dispute Resolution Administrative Procedure is administered by dispute resolution service providers accredited by ICANN. The WIPO Arbitration and Mediation Center is one such dispute resolution service provider and, in the professional experience of the author of this book as a WIPO Domain Name Panellist, a very important, prolific, efficient and effective one too!

The ICANN UDRP Policy and Rules are set out in Appendix XXIV to this book.

CHAPTER 18
THE UDRP ADMINISTRATIVE PROCEDURE

18.1 Advantages of the UDRP Administrative Procedure

The principal advantage of the UDRP Administrative Procedure is that it typically provides a faster and cheaper way to resolve a dispute regarding the registration and use of an Internet domain name (an Internet address – also often described as an 'electronic trademark') rather than going to court. In addition, the procedures are considerably more informal than litigation, in addition to which the decision-makers are experts in such areas as international trademark law; domain name issues; electronic commerce; the Internet; and dispute resolution.

The Procedure is also international in scope: it provides a single mechanism for resolving a domain name dispute regardless of where the registrar of the disputed domain name or the domain name registrant/holder or the complainant are located.

The Administrative Procedure is normally completed within sixty days of the date the Complaint is received by the WIPO Center.

A brief overview of the UDRP Administrative Procedure, which governs the filing, administration and resolution of WIPO domain name disputes, and related matters now follows.

For a case filed with the WIPO Center involving between one and five domain names that is to be decided by a single Panellist, the fee is USD 1500. For a case that is to be decided by three Panellists, the fee is USD 4000.

For a case involving between six and ten domain names that is to be decided by a single Panellist, the fee is USD 2000 and USD 5000 for a case that is to be decided by three Panellists.

It is the parties that decide whether the case is to proceed before one or three Panellists.

The Complainant is responsible for paying the total fees. The only time the Respondent has to share in the fees is when the Respondent chooses to have the case decided by three Panellists and the Complainant had chosen a single Panellist.

The fees described above do not include any payment that might have to be made to a lawyer representing a party in the administrative proceeding.

Further details may be found in the Schedule of Fees of the WIPO Center.

18.2 Overview

There are five basic stages in a UDRP Administrative Procedure as follows:

1. the filing of the Complaint with an ICANN-accredited dispute resolution service provider chosen by the Complainant, such as and usually the WIPO Center;
2. the filing of a Response by the person or entity against whom the Complaint has been made;

3. the appointment by the chosen dispute resolution service provider of an Administrative Panel consisting of one or three persons who will decide the dispute;
4. the issuance of the Administrative Panel's decision and the notification of all relevant parties; and
5. the implementation of the Administrative Panel's decision by the registrar(s) concerned where there is a decision that the disputed domain name(s) be cancelled or transferred.

18.3 Claimants under the UDRP Administrative Procedure

Any person or company in any part of the world can file a domain name complaint concerning a gTLD using the UDRP Administrative Procedure.

In case of a dispute involving a domain name registered in a ccTLD, the UDRP Administrative Procedure can also be used, provided that the concerned ccTLD registration authority adopted the UDRP Policy on a voluntary basis.

18.4 Kinds of Disputes Covered by the UDRP Administrative Procedure

Under the provisions of Paragraph 4(a) of the UDRP Policy, the UDRP Administrative Procedure is available only for disputes concerning an alleged abusive registration of a domain name ('cybersquatting') which satisfy the following requirements:

i. the domain name registered by the domain name registrant is identical or confusingly similar to a trademark or service mark in which the complainant (the person or entity bringing the complaint) has rights; and
ii. the domain name registrant has no rights or legitimate interests in respect of the domain name in question; and
iii. the domain name has been registered and is being used in bad faith

18.5 Bad Faith Requirement

Paragraph 4(b) of the UDRP Policy sets out the following examples of circumstances that will be considered by an Administrative Panel to be evidence of the bad faith registration and use of a domain name:

i. Circumstances indicating that the domain name was registered or acquired primarily for the purpose of selling, renting, or otherwise transferring the domain name registration to the complainant who is the owner of the trademark or service mark or to a competitor of that complainant, for valuable consideration in excess of the domain name registrant's out-of-pocket costs directly related to the domain name; or
ii. The domain name was registered in order to prevent the owner of the trademark or service mark from reflecting the mark in a corresponding domain name, provided that the domain name registrant has engaged in a pattern of such conduct; or
iii. The domain name was registered primarily for the purpose of disrupting the business of a competitor; or

iv. By using the domain name, the domain name registrant intentionally attempted to attract for financial gain, Internet users to the registrant's website or other on-line location, by creating a likelihood of confusion with the complainant's mark as to the source, sponsorship, affiliation, or endorsement of the registrant's website or location or of a product or service on the registrant's website or location.

The above examples are not exhaustive and other circumstances/situations may exist that tend to show that a domain name has been registered and used in bad faith.

One further point to note: the requirement that the disputed domain name has to be registered and used in bad faith is cumulative. In other words, both registration and use have to be shown. In practice, if it is clear from the Case File that the disputed domain name has been used in bad faith, then, according to the circumstances of the particular case, registration may be inferred to satisfy this requirement of the Policy.

18.6 Court Proceedings

Under the provisions of Paragraph 4(k) of the UDRP Policy the mandatory administrative proceeding requirement does not prevent either the domain name registrant (the Respondent) or the third party (the Complainant) from submitting the dispute to a Court of competent jurisdiction for independent resolution. It is possible for a party to start a lawsuit in court before an administrative proceeding is commenced. Equally a party can also commence a lawsuit after the administrative proceeding is concluded if it is not satisfied with the outcome.

Paragraph 18 of the UDRP Rules sets out what action an Administrative Panel may take if Court proceedings are initiated prior to or during an administrative proceeding.

18.7 Disputes Concerning Domain Names Registered in a Country Code Top Level Domain

The UDRP Administrative Procedure is available to resolve country code top level domain name disputes provided that the domain name Registration Agreement covering the domain name in issue specifically incorporates the UDRP Policy. This is the case for certain ccTLDs that have adopted the UDRP Policy on a voluntary basis.

18.8 Claims against the Registrar of the Disputed Domain Name and Others

The UDRP Administrative Procedure is only available to resolve disputes between a third party (the Complainant) alleging an abusive registration of a domain name (see above) and the domain name registrant (the Respondent) and may not, therefore, be used to make any claim against the Registrar of the dispute domain name.

Equally, a domain name holder may not use the UDRP Administrative Procedure to bring proceedings against someone who has threatened to sue and take away the domain name concerned.

18.9 Confidentiality

Following the formal commencement of an administrative proceeding, the WIPO Center publishes on its website the domain name(s) in issue; the date of the formal commencement of the administrative proceeding; and the status of the case. The WIPO Center also makes available on its website the decisions rendered under the UDRP Policy in accordance with Paragraph 16 of the UDRP Rules, by case number or by topic through a searchable Index.

The WIPO Center will normally not disclose any other information about the proceedings.

18.10 Language of the Proceedings

Under the provisions of Paragraph 11 of the UDRP Rules, unless the parties to an administrative proceeding agree otherwise, or the Registration Agreement that relates to the domain name in question specifies otherwise, the language of the administrative proceeding will normally be the language of the relevant Registration Agreement.

The Administrative Panel, however, has the discretion to designate a different language, taking into consideration the circumstances of the administrative proceeding (e.g., the nationality of the parties; and the language of the documentation). The Administrative Panel that is appointed to decide the dispute also has the authority to order parties to translate documents that are not in the language of the proceeding.

18.11 Hearings

Under the provisions of Paragraph 13 of the UDRP Rules, there shall be no in-person hearings (including hearings by teleconference, videoconference, and web conference), unless the Administrative Panel determines, only as an exceptional matter, that a hearing is necessary in order for it to make its decision.

18.12 Preparing and Filing a Complaint

The Complaint may be submitted to any accredited dispute resolution service provider. For the gTLDs, these providers are accredited by ICANN. For the ccTLDs to which the UDRP Policy applies, they are accredited by the administration of the ccTLD in question. Not only must the Complaint conform to the requirements specified in the UDRP Rules, but also to those specified in the chosen service provider's supplemental rules, if any.

The WIPO Center was the first provider to be accredited by ICANN and the first to receive cases under the UDRP Policy. Its expertise to administer domain name disputes stems from its involvement in the international process conducted by WIPO at the request of its Member States which led to the UDRP Policy and Rules. The WIPO Center also has specialist knowledge in intellectual property and considerable experience in dispute resolution administration generally.

18.13 Form of Complaint

There is no standard ICANN form of Complaint, but the WIPO Center has prepared a model Complaint and filing guidelines, which parties may wish to consult. This model has been prepared by the WIPO Center and is intended to serve as a guide for filing a Complaint under the UDRP Policy with the WIPO Center. Its use as a basis for the preparation of a party's complaint does not preclude the possibility of that Complaint being found deficient following the WIPO Center's formalities compliance review; nor, of course, does reliance on the model Complaint guarantee a Complainant's success on the merits.

18.14 Submission of the Complaint

Under the Rules, Complaints must be submitted in hard copy and in electronic format.

In order to facilitate electronic filing, the WIPO Center offers the following options:

- complete and submit directly online to the Center an electronic form of the model Complaint; or
- download and complete the model Complaint as a Word document to submit as an email attachment to domain.disputes@wipo.int.

The hard copies (signed original and four copies) including all annexes should be sent by postal or courier service with return receipt requested to:

WIPO Arbitration and Mediation Center
34 chemin des Colombettes
1211 Geneva 20
Switzerland
Further information may be obtained from the WIPO Center filing guidelines.

18.15 Language of the Complaint

Unless the Complainant and the Respondent agree otherwise, or if specified otherwise in the Domain Name Registration Agreement, the Complaint must normally be in the same language as the Registration Agreement. The Administrative Panel can order any attachments, not in the same language as the Registration Agreement, to be translated in full or in part by and at the cost of the submitting party.

18.16 Legal Representation

While the assistance of a lawyer may be helpful, there is no requirement that the Complaint be prepared or submitted by a lawyer.

18.17 Information to Be Included in the Complaint

The information that must be included in the Complaint is described in Paragraph 3 of the UDRP Rules. In addition, the WIPO Center has prepared a model Complaint and filing guidelines which serve as a checklist of elements to include in a Complaint. In order to assist parties in preparing their submissions, the WIPO Center also makes available an online Index of decisions rendered under the UDRP Policy, as well as a jurisprudential Overview.

18.18 Number of Domain Names that May Be Included in the Complaint

Under Paragraph 3(c) of the UDRP Rules, the Complaint may include more than one domain name, provided that the person or entity that is the registrant of the domain name(s) specified in the Complaint is one and the same.

18.19 Formalities of the Complaint

The Complainant does not have to be certified or notarised. However, an original version, together with four complete copies, signed by the Complainant or the Complainant's authorized representative must be submitted to the WIPO Center.

18.20 Payments on Filing the Complaint

The appropriate fee specified in the WIPO Center's Schedule of Fees must be submitted together with the Complaint, using one of the methods of payment specified.

18.21 Contact Details to Be Used When Sending the Complaint to the Respondent and Communication Methods to Be Used

In addition to submitting the Complaint to a dispute resolution service provider, the provisions of Paragraph 3(b)(xii) of the UDRP Rules require that a copy of the Complaint to be sent to the Respondent. For this purpose, unless the Respondent has indicated the method and contact details to be used for case-related communications, the Complaint may be sent by fax (with a confirmation of transmission); or postal or courier service (postage pre-paid and return receipt requested); or electronically via the Internet (provided a record of transmission is available); using the contact information available to the Complainant. See Rules, Paragraph 2(b).

18.22 Contact Details to Be Used When Sending the Complaint to the Registrar(s) Concerned and Communication Methods to Be Used

In addition to submitting the Complaint to the WIPO Center, the WIPO Supplemental Rules require that a copy of the Complaint to be sent to the registrar(s) concerned. The

Complainant should also notify the WIPO Center that the Complaint has, in fact, been sent to the registrar(s) concerned. Certain registrars have established specific contact details that should be used for these purposes, which may be obtained by contacting the registrar(s) in question.

18.23 Information as to the Registrant of a Domain Name

Certain registration information can be obtained for domain names registered in the gTLDs by conducting a 'Whois' search, in particular at <www.internic.net/whois.html>.

As for ccTLDs, or for additional information, the concerned registrar's 'Whois' service may be used, which is accessed through the registrar's website.

18.24 Preparing and Filing a Response

Under the provisions of Paragraph 5(a) of the UDRP Rules, the Respondent must file its Response within 20 days of the commencement of the administrative proceeding. An administrative proceeding is deemed to have formally commenced once the dispute resolution service provider has formally notified the Complaint in accordance with the provisions of Paragraph 2(a) of the UDRP Rules.

If the Respondent does not file its Response (including any payment that may be required) by the applicable deadline, the Respondent will be considered in default. Despite the Respondent's default, the WIPO Center will proceed to appoint the Administrative Panel. The Panel will be informed of the Respondent's default. It will decide the dispute based on the information available to it and may draw such inferences as it deems appropriate from the Respondent's failure to submit a timely or any Response.

18.25 Form of the Response

In addition to a Model Response, the WIPO Center has prepared filing guidelines, which parties may wish to consult for guidance. The use of the model form of Response and filing guidelines as a basis for the preparation of a party's Response does not, of course, guarantee a Respondent's success on the merits of the case.

18.26 Format of the Response

The electronic version of the text of a Response should preferably be submitted as an attachment to an e-mail in one of the following formats:

- word document;
- PDF file;
- text file; and
- RTF file.

Text annexes to the Response that are available in electronic form should also preferably be submitted in one of the formats mentioned above. If in doubt, the WIPO Center should be consulted.

18.27 Language of the Response

Unless the Complainant and the Respondent agree otherwise, or if specified otherwise in the Registration Agreement, the Response must normally be in the same language as the Registration Agreement. The Administrative Panel can order any attachments not in the same language as the Registration Agreement to be translated in full or in part by and at the expense of the party submitting them.

18.28 Legal Representation

Whilst the assistance of a lawyer may be helpful, there is no requirement for the Response to be prepared or submitted by a lawyer.

18.29 Information to Be Included in the Response

The information that must be included in the Response is described in Paragraph 5 of the UDRP Rules. In addition, the WIPO Center has prepared a model Response and filing guidelines, which serve as a checklist of the elements to include in the Response.

In order to assist the parties in preparing their submissions, the WIPO Center also makes available an online Index of decisions rendered under the UDRP Policy, as well as a jurisprudential Overview.

18.30 Demonstrating Rights to and Legitimate Interests in the Disputed Domain Name

Paragraph 4(c) of the UDRP Policy states that any of the following circumstances, in particular but without limitation, if found by the Administrative Panel to be proved, based on its evaluation of all evidence presented, shall demonstrate the domain name registrant's rights or legitimate interests to the disputed domain name for the purposes of Paragraph 4(a)(ii) of the Policy:

i. before any notice to the domain name registrant of the dispute, the registrant's use of, or demonstrable preparations to use, the domain name or a name corresponding to the domain name in connection with a bona fide offering of goods or services; or
ii. the domain name registrant (as an individual, business, or other organization) has been commonly known by the domain name, even if the registrant has acquired no trademark or service mark rights; or
iii. the domain name registrant is making a legitimate non-commercial or fair use of the domain name, without intent for commercial gain to misleadingly divert consumers or to tarnish the trademark or service mark at issue.

18.31 Formalities of the Response

The Response does not have to be certified or notarised. However, an original version, signed by the Respondent or the Respondent's authorized representative, must be submitted to the WIPO Center.

18.32 Payments on Filing the Response

The only time a fee has to be paid by the Respondent is when the Complainant chooses to have the case decided by a single Panellist, but the Respondent prefers to have the case decided by three Panellists. In such cases, the applicable fee is shared equally between the Complainant and the Respondent. The Respondent must submit its payment together with its Response. If the Respondent does not, the Respondent will be considered in default and the Center may disregard the Respondent's designation of the number of Panellists.

18.33 Submission of the Response

Under the UDRP Rules, a Response must be submitted electronically and in hardcopy: an original and four copies.

In order to facilitate filing, the WIPO Center offers the following options:

- complete and submit directly online to the Center as an electronic form of the model Response; or
- download and complete the model Response as a Word document to submit as an email attachment to: domain.disputes@wipo.int.

The hard copies – an original and four copies – should be sent by postal or courier service with return receipt requested to:

WIPO Arbitration and Mediation Center
34 chemin des Colombettes
1211 Geneva 20
Switzerland

18.34 Contact Details to Be Used when Sending the Response to the Complainant and Communication Methods to Be Used

The Response should be sent to the Complainant to the contact details and by the methods specified in the Complaint.

It is not necessary to send a copy of the Response to the registrar(s) concerned.

18.35 The Administrative Panel

An Administrative Panel is composed of one or three independent and impartial persons, who are appointed by the dispute resolution service provider selected to administer the dispute in accordance with the UDRP Policy and Rules. The Administrative Panel is independent of the dispute resolution service provider, ICANN, the registrar(s) concerned and, of course, the parties to the dispute.

18.36 The Panellists

The persons who appear on the WIPO Center's list of Domain Name Panellists have been selected on the basis of their well-established reputation for their impartiality, sound judgment and experience as decision-makers, as well as their substantive experience in the areas of international trademark law; electronic commerce; and Internet-related issues.

The WIPO Center's list is international, consisting of some 400 Panellists from over 50 countries, many of whom are multi-lingual.

18.37 Appointment of the Administrative Panel

The Administrative Panel is appointed after the filing of the Response, if one is made, or following the due date on which the Response should have been filed.

In the case of a Single Panellist administrative proceeding, the WIPO Center will work to appoint the Administrative Panel within five days of the filing of the Response or the Response due date.

In the case of a three-person Administrative Panel, normally the WIPO Center will appoint the Panel within fifteen days of the filing of the Response or the Response due date.

An Administrative Panel is appointed by the WIPO Center as follows:

i. If both the Complainant and Respondent indicate that they wish the dispute to be decided by a single Panellist, the Panellist will be appointed by the WIPO Center from its list of Domain Name Panellists.
ii. If the Complainant designates three Panellists and the Respondent designates 1 Panellist, or vice versa, then the WIPO Center will appoint a three-person Administrative Panel. In so doing, the WIPO Center will try to appoint one of the candidates nominated by the Complainant and one of the candidates nominated by the Respondent. If it is unable to do so, the Center will make an appropriate appointment from its list of Domain Name Panellists. The third Panellist, or Presiding Panellist, will be appointed on the basis of preferences indicated by the parties from among a list of five candidates that will have been provided to them by the WIPO Center. If the Respondent chooses a three-member Panel, the Respondent is required to pay half of the applicable fees; in all other situations, the fees are paid by the Complainant.
iii. If no Response is filed by the Respondent, then the WIPO Center will appoint the Administrative Panel in accordance with the number of Panellists designated by the Complainant (i.e., one or three). If the Complainant designated a three-member Panel, the Center will try to appoint one of the candidates nominated by the Complainant, failing which it will make the appointment from its published list. It will make the appointment of the other two Panellists from its list of Domain Name Panellists.

Notification of the Appointment of the Administrative Panel is formally communicated by the WIPO Center to the parties to the dispute and a reference is made in the Notification to the professional profile of the Panellist(s) appointed to resolve the case, which profile can be accessed at <www.wipo.int/amc/en/domains>. The Notification also includes the projected Decision date in accordance with Paragraph 15 of the Rules for the Uniform Domain Name Dispute Resolution Policy.

18.38 The Administrative Panel Decision

Only three types of decisions can be made by the Administrative Panel:

i. decide in favour of the person or entity that filed the Complaint and order that the disputed domain name(s) be transferred to that person or entity; or
ii. decide in favour of the person or entity that filed the Complaint and order that the disputed domain name(s) be cancelled; or
iii. decide in favour of the domain name registrant (i.e., deny the requested remedy).

In the latter case, if the Panel concludes that the dispute is not within the scope of Paragraph 4(a) of the UDRP Policy, it must specify this in its decision. Also, if after considering the submissions of the parties, the Panel finds that the Complaint was brought in bad faith, the Panel is required to declare in its decision that the Complaint was brought in bad faith and constitutes an abuse of the administrative proceeding.

The Administrative Panel cannot award any money judgments nor lawyers' costs.

Paragraph 15(b) of the UDRP Rules provides that, in the absence of exceptional circumstances, the Administrative Panel is required to forward its decision on the Complaint to the WIPO Center within fourteen natural days of its appointment.

The WIPO Center provides a Form of Model Administrative Panel Decision, together with the corresponding Formatting and Forwarding Guidelines to be used by Panellists.

18.39 Implementation of the Administrative Panel Decision

An Administrative Panel decision is implemented by the registrar with whom the disputed domain name is registered at the time the decision is rendered.

In accordance with the provisions of Paragraph 4(k) of the UDRP Policy, the registrar is required to implement the Panel's decision ten business days after it receives notification of the decision from the dispute resolution service provider, except if the registrar receives proper information from the domain name registrant (Respondent) in that ten-day period that it is challenging the decision in court (see below).

Each registrar establishes its own guidelines concerning the implementation of the transfer or cancellation of a domain name registration pursuant to the Administrative Panel's decision.

18.40 Challenging the Administrative Panel Decision

The provisions of Paragraph 4(k) of the Policy allows a domain name registrant that loses in the Administrative Proceeding to challenge the Administrative Panel's decision by filing a lawsuit in certain courts.

As noted above, the registrar(s) concerned will implement the Panel's decision ten business days after it receives notification of the decision from the dispute resolution service provider, unless it receives from the registrant during that ten-day period official documentation (such as a copy of a complaint, file-stamped by the clerk of the court) that the registrant has commenced a lawsuit against the Complainant in a jurisdiction to which the Complainant has submitted under Paragraph 3(b)(xiii) of the UDRP Rules, i.e., a 'Mutual Jurisdiction' (see below).

The registrar concerned will take no further action until it receives:

i. satisfactory evidence of a resolution of the dispute between the parties; or
ii. satisfactory evidence that the domain name registrant's lawsuit has been dismissed or withdrawn; or
iii. a copy of an order from the court in which the lawsuit was filed dismissing the lawsuit or ordering that the domain name registrant has no right to continue to use the domain name.

18.41 'Mutual Jurisdiction'

The 'Mutual Jurisdiction' is defined in the UDRP Rules as a court jurisdiction at the location of either

a. the principal office of the registrar (provided that the domain name registrant has submitted in the Registration Agreement to that jurisdiction for court adjudication of disputes concerning or arising from the use of the domain name); or
b. the domain name registrant's address as shown for the registration of the domain name in the 'WHOIS' database of the registrar concerned at the time the Complaint is submitted to a dispute resolution service provider.

18.42 Availability of Administrative Panel Decisions

Administrative Panel Decisions are available to the public. According to the provisions of Paragraph 16(b) of the Rules, except where an Administrative Panel decides otherwise in exceptional circumstances, a dispute resolution service provider is required to publish all decisions in full on the Internet.

WIPO Administrative Panel decisions can be accessed through the official website of the WIPO. An online Index of the decisions by domain name category, procedural or substantive issue is also available.

The WIPO Center also makes available a jurisprudential Overview.

18.43 Pre-Decision Settlement of the Dispute

If the parties come to a settlement agreement regarding their dispute, under the provisions of Paragraph 17 of the UDRP Rules, the administrative proceeding must be terminated.

18.44 The Role of the Registrar in the Administrative Proceeding

The role of the Registrar in the administrative proceeding is as follows:

i. to provide requested information to the WIPO Center, including confirming that the disputed domain name is registered with it; that it is registered by the person or entity identified as the Respondent in the Complaint; providing the Respondent's contact details; and, where necessary, the Registration Agreement and associated documents;
ii. to prevent the transfer to a third party of a domain name registration after an Administrative Proceeding has commenced; and
iii. to implement the Administrative Panel's decision.

18.45 The Role of the WIPO Case Administrator

The WIPO Case Administrator is principally responsible for managing the case procedures, including all administrative matters relating to the dispute and communications with the Administrative Panel. The Case Administrator may provide administrative assistance to the Panel, but has no substantive decision-making authority.

WIPO Case Administrators often have legal backgrounds; speak several languages; and are experienced in international dispute resolution and domain name issues.

18.46 The Formalities Compliance Review

The Formalities Compliance Review is a check by the WIPO Center of the Complaint to ensure that it satisfies all of the formal requirements set out in the UDRP Policy and Rules and also the WIPO Supplemental Rules.

Examples of the items checked by the Center include:

- whether the Complaint includes the Complaint Transmittal Coversheet;
- whether the hardcopy submission included the original and 4 copies;
- generally, whether the Complaint includes all of the items listed in Paragraph 3(b) of the UDRP Rules; and
- whether payment has been made in the correct amount.

18.47 WIPO Center Fees in Domain Name Disputes

The following fees are payable:

- For a case involving between one and five domain names, the fee for a case that is to be decided by a single Panellist is USD 1500; and USD 4000 for a case that is to be decided by three Panellists.
- For a case involving between six and ten domain names, the fee for a case that is to be decided by a single Panellist is USD 2000; and USD 5000 for a case that is to be decided by three Panellists.

The Complainant is responsible for paying the total fees. The only time the Respondent has to share in the fees is when the Respondent chooses to have the case decided by three Panellists and the Complainant had chosen a single Panellist.

In exceptional circumstances, either the Panel or the WIPO Center may ask the parties to make additional payments to defray the costs of the administrative procedure.

Further information may be obtained from the Schedule of Fees of the WIPO Center.

18.48 Additional Information about Domain Name Dispute Resolution

Additional information about domain name dispute resolution may be obtained by visiting the WIPO domain name dispute resources area or by logging on to: 'arbiter.mail@wipo.int'.

CHAPTER 19
SPORTS DOMAIN NAME DISPUTES

19.1 GENERALLY

From the launch of the Uniform Dispute Resolution Policy (UDRP) in December 1999 to December 2007, 12,334 UDRP or UDRP-based cases (gTLDs and ccTLDs) have been filed with the WIPO Arbitration and Mediation Center, covering 22,301 separate domain names.

In 2007 alone, named parties to WIPO cases represented over a hundred countries, with a significant increase in the number of Respondent countries represented. The growth in Respondent countries from 72 in the year 2000 to 96 in 2007, in part reflects the expansion of Internet access across regions of the world. The United States of America (USA), France and the United Kingdom remain the most frequent bases for Complainants, while the USA, the UK and China remain the most represented countries by Respondents.

In 2007, English remained the most common language for WIPO case proceedings (89.09 percent), reflecting the fact that the vast majority of domain names involved were registered with US-based registrars. Domain Name Dispute Cases were also handled in French, Spanish, German, Chinese, Korean, Italian, Dutch, Japanese, Romanian, Danish, Portuguese and Swedish (listed in order of frequency). The character set of the disputed domain names remained overwhelmingly ASCII (English alphabet), with a small number of names in Chinese, French, German, Japanese, Korean, Norwegian, Spanish, and Swedish.

During 2007, the .com gTLD also remained the solid leader in terms of the number of domain names included by complainants in cases filed with WIPO (73.62 percent), although, in comparison with 2006, .com ceded some ground to the .net, .info and .mobi domains.

Collectively, the number of disputed ccTLD domain names has been increasing over the years, having moved from less than 1 percent in the year 2000 to over 7 percent in 2007. During 2007, the number of ccTLD registries, which have designated WIPO to provide domain name dispute resolution services, has increased from 47 to 51 with the addition of Morocco (.ma), Nauru (.nr), Peru (.pe), and Saint Lucia (.lc).

WIPO parties have settled a quarter of all cases without an Administrative Panel decision. Of the remainder, 85 percent of Panel Decisions have ordered the transfer of the domain names in dispute to the Complainant; and 15 percent of the Complaints were denied, leaving the names in the possession of the registration holder. In 2007, domain name dispute cases were decided by 278 WIPO Panellists appointed from 42 countries. These are truly impressive statistics!

A very diverse mix of individuals and enterprises, foundations and institutions took advantage of the dispute resolution procedures of the WIPO Arbitration and Mediation Center in 2007. The top five sectors for Complainant business activity were as follows:

- biotechnology and pharmaceuticals;
- banking and Finance;
- internet and IT;
- retail; and
- entertainment.

Pharmaceutical manufacturers remained the top filers, due to numerous permutations of protected names registered for websites offering or linking to online sales of medications and drugs.

19.2 WIPO Overview of Panel Positions on Key UDRP Procedural and Substantive Issues

Decision-making authority under the Uniform Domain Name Dispute Resolution Policy and Rules (UDRP) lies exclusively with the appointed Panels. To facilitate awareness of their views on certain questions that commonly arise in proceedings under the UDRP, the WIPO Arbitration and Mediation Center has produced an informal Overview of Panel Positions on key procedural and substantive issues. Decision references supporting each line of opinion are included, with over a hundred decisions from over eighty different UDRP Panellists listed.

Whilst some of the listed issues in the Overview arise only infrequently, all of them are – or are perceived to be – relevant to the operation of the UDRP. On most of these issues, consensus or clear majority views have developed. Certain other questions continue to attract a diversity of views. The Center's identification of questions and evaluation of opinions is based on the 7,000 UDRP cases it has administered through February 2005. Broad information on all views is available from the Center's online Legal Index of WIPO UDRP Panel Decisions, which may be accessed on line at <www.wipo.int/amc/en/domains/search/>, as well as from the full posting of all Decisions, which may be accessed on line at <www.wipo.int/amc/en/domains/decisions.html>.

This Overview has been created in recognition of the need that has been expressed to identify, as much as possible, consensus among UDRP decisions, so as to maximize the consistency of the UDRP system. It should be understood that, with UDRP decisions covering a multitude of facts and arguments, genuine differences of opinion may be difficult to avoid on particular issues, all the more so where Panellists and parties come from a multitude of jurisdictions.

Whilst predictability remains a key element of any dispute resolution system, neither this informal Overview nor prior WIPO Administrative Panel Decisions are binding on WIPO Panellists, who will make their own judgments in the light of the particular circumstances of each individual case before them. In other words, strictly speaking, no principle of binding legal precedent (*stare decisis*) applies to previous WIPO Administrative Panel Decisions, but, with such a wealth of previous WIPO cases to draw on, inevitably WIPO Panellists tend to follow previous WIPO Decisions in similar subsequent cases. In practice, therefore, a body of WIPO Domain Name Dispute 'Law' is actually being built up and applied. The WIPO Center, in consultation with its Panellists, intends to update this Overview, from time to time in the future, based on subsequent relevant WIPO Administrative Panel Decisions, thus providing a very useful resource for all concerned in WIPO Domain Name Disputes!

It should also be noted that it is the responsibility of each party in a WIPO case to make its own independent assessment of previous WIPO Administrative Panel Decisions relevant to their own particular case. Thus, the WIPO Overview cannot be used by parties in Domain Name Disputes as a substitute for the fulfilment of their basic legal obligation to argue and establish their own particular cases/claims pursuant to the requirements of the Uniform Dispute Resolution Policy.

19.3 Sports Domain Name Disputes

19.3.1 **Introductory**

The new Director General of WIPO, Dr Francis Gurry, has recognised the commercial importance of sport and the corresponding increase in the number of Sports Domain Name Disputes being submitted to WIPO for adjudication under the Uniform Domain Name Dispute Resolution Policy and has well expressed this situation in the following terms:

> 'Reflecting the increasing commercial importance of sport, the number of sports-related WIPO UDRP complaints has been rising. In football, for example, WIPO complainants have included famous players, such as Ronaldinho and Totti, eminent managers, like Sir Alex Ferguson, and major clubs, like Real Madrid and Liverpool. In sport, as in other fields, there is need for continued vigilance by rights owners. The UDRP has proven to be a very effective instrument in combating predatory practices aimed at siphoning off the goodwill attached to major players and participants.'

19.3.2 **Unfair practices**

An example of such unfair practices occurred in a case involving the US Major Soccer League's most expensive player, Freddy Adu. In that case (see WIPO Case No. D2004-0682), the respondent registered the domain name 'freddyadu.com' and contacted Adu's representative, offering to create the official Freddy Adu fan site, in exchange for such benefits as a stake in advertising negotiations, access to the player and his sponsors and match tickets. The WIPO Panellist found that the Respondent had held Adu to ransom for the domain name by inappropriately seeking a long-term commercial relationship with him. As was pointed out by the Panellist in his Decision in that case:

> 'The most offensive act of a cybersquatter is to hold another's mark for ransom. Such conduct has earned its own subsection in Paragraph 4(b) of the Policy. The Policy was adopted specifically to provide an owner in these circumstances with a swift and inexpensive alternative to litigation to redeem his mark. Rather than a single payment for transfer of the Disputed Domain Name, Respondent's asked for continuing participation in Complainant's affairs and promotional activities, a majority interest in Complainant's official website, and ownership of media images featuring Complainant. The financial consequences to Respondent of such an arrangement would surely have exceeded his out of pocket costs for registering the Disputed Domain Name. Although Complainant initiated the possibility of transfer for money, it was Respondent who consistently pressed the Complainant for official status and participation in Complainant's marketing and financial activities. Paragraph 4(b)(i) specifically encompasses 'other consideration'. And it would defy common sense as well as the language and intent of the Policy to limit the scope of that paragraph to one-off cash transactions.'

The full text of this important Decision is set out in Appendix XXV to this book.

19.3.3 World Wrestling Federation case

Sports domain name disputes to date have involved a wide range of sports and constituents. It is interesting to note that the first domain name case handled through WIPO was a sporting one, involving the World Wrestling Federation (as it was then known) (WIPO Case No. D1999-0001) involving the domain name <www.worldwrestlingfederation.com>.

This Decision may be found at <http://arbiter.wipo.int/domains/decisions/html/1999/d1999-0001.html>.

19.3.4 Sports goods manufacturers cases

WIPO sports domain name disputes have also included high profile sports goods manufacturers, such as Nike, Inc. One of the early cases (WIPO Case No. D2000-1120) involving the famous sports ware NIKE brand involved the registration of the domain name 'nike.net'.

19.3.5 Sports personality cases

WIPO sports domain name disputes have also included such individual sports personalities as the well-known tennis players, Venus and Serena Williams (see WIPO Case No. D2000-1673 involving the domain name 'venusandserenawilliams.com'); the former Formula One racing champion, Damon Hill (see WIPO Case No. D2001-1362 involving the domain name 'damonhill.com'); and the famous footballer Ronaldinho (see WIPO Case No. D2004-0827 involving the domain name 'ronaldinhogaucho.com').

19.3.6 Football teams cases

WIPO Domain Name Disputes have also involved well-known football teams, including Real Madrid (see WIPO Case No. D2000-1805 involving the domain name 'realmadrid.org') and Bayern Munich (See WIPO Case No. D2003-0464 involving the domain name 'bayernmunchen.net'). Incidentally, the 5,000th case was a sporting one involving the leading English Football Club, Tottenham Hotspur, and the use of the domain name 'totenhamhotspur.com' (see WIPO Case No. D2003-0363).

19.3.7 Formula One teams cases

WIPO Domain Name Disputes have also involved well-known Formula One racing teams, including Jordan (See WIPO Case No. D2000-0233 involving the domain name 'jordanf1.com') and Ferrari (see WIPO Case No. D2003-0050 involving the domain names 'clubferrari.com' and 'clubferrari.net').

The Jordan case is particularly interesting, because in an earlier WIPO decision (see WIPO Case No. D2000-0193 involving the domain name 'f1.com'), a complaint made by a group of companies involved in the organization of the Formula One Grand Prix Motor Racing Championships, concerning the registration and use of the domain name 'f1.com', was disallowed. The Panel held that, because the trademark F1 consists of merely a single letter and a numeral, it was not sufficiently distinctive to justify the transfer of the domain name (see later concerning the use of the abbreviation for the FIFA World Cup of the letters 'wc'). In other words, the mark was generic and there was no evidence of considerable and widespread use of the mark for it to acquire a 'secondary meaning' – in other words a commercial association with the activities of Formula One – and thereby distinctiveness. Whereas, in the Jordan case, the Panel held that, because the name Jordan is so well-known as being associated with Formula One, there was a real danger of confusion in this case. Furthermore, there was also other evidence of bad faith, in that the respondent had offered to sell the disputed domain name to Jordan.

19.3.8 **Sports events cases**

The WIPO adjudication process has also been invoked in relation to the protection of sports event names. For example, the world governing body of football, FIFA, successfully challenged the use of its trade mark WORLD CUP in thirteen domain names by another party, who had used some of the domain names in the address of his website, which not only related to the FIFA event, but also included copyrighted content from the official website of FIFA (see WIPO Case No. D2000-0034). There was also evidence of bad faith, in that, prior to the WIPO proceedings, the other party offered to sell some of the domain names concerned to FIFA. However, in the same case, the Panel refused to order the transfer of two of the disputed domain names consisting of the letters 'wc', because they were not sufficiently distinctive to be unequivocally regarded by the public as being an abbreviation of the name 'world cup' designating the flagship event of FIFA.

The WIPO domain name dispute resolution process has also been used successfully to protect famous sporting leagues, including the UEFA Champions League (see WIPO Case No. D2000-0153 involving the domain name 'uefachampionsleague.com') and the English FA Premier League, a case in which the author of this book was the sole panellist (see WIPO Case D2005-0014 involving the domain name 'fapremierleague.com').

19.3.9 **Sports organisations**

WIPO Sports Domain Name Cases have also involved sports organisations, including the NBA (National Basketball Association) and the full text of one of their Decisions is as follows:

WIPO Arbitration and Mediation Center

ADMINISTRATIVE PANEL DECISION

NBA Properties, Inc., Rocket Ball, Ltd., New Jersey Basketball, LLC v. Rick Godwin

Case No. D2004-0983

1. The Parties

The Complainant is NBA Properties, Inc. of New York, New York, United States of America, Rocket Ball, Ltd. of Houston, Texas, United States of America, and New Jersey Basketball, LLC, of Brooklyn, New York, United States of America, represented by Ayala Deutsch, United States of America.

The Respondent is Rick Godwin of Whistler, British Columbia, Canada.

2. The Domain Names and Registrar

The disputed domain names are: <houstonrockets.com> and <newjerseynets.com>. The domain names were registered with Go Daddy Software.

3. Procedural History

The Complaint was filed with the WIPO Arbitration and Mediation Center (the 'Center') on November 23, 2004.

On November 25, 2004, the Center transmitted by email to Go Daddy Software a request for registrar verification in connection with the domain names at issue.

On November 29, 2004, Go Daddy Software transmitted by email to the Center its verification response confirming that the Respondent is listed as the registrant and providing the contact details for the administrative, billing, and technical contact.

The Center verified that the Complaint satisfied the formal requirements of the Uniform Domain Name Dispute Resolution Policy (the 'Policy'), the Rules for Uniform Domain Name Dispute Resolution Policy (the 'Rules'), and the WIPO Supplemental Rules for Uniform Domain Name Dispute Resolution Policy (the 'Supplemental Rules').

In accordance with the Rules, paragraphs 2(a) and 4(a), the Center formally notified the Respondent of the Complaint, and the proceedings commenced on November 30, 2004. In accordance with the Rules, paragraph 5(a), the due date for Response was December 20, 2004. The Respondent did not submit any response. Accordingly, the Center notified the Respondent's default on December 21, 2004.

The Center appointed Ada L. Redondo Aguilera as the sole panelist in this matter on December 28, 2004. The Panel finds that it was properly constituted.

The Panel has submitted the Statement of Acceptance and Declaration of Impartiality and Independence, as required by the Center to ensure compliance with the Rules, paragraph 7.

4. Factual Background

NBA Properties Inc. carries on the business of operating one of the most prominent professional basketball leagues in the world. The league is comprised of thirty teams, including the Houston Rockets and the New Jersey Nets, each of which is a member of the NBA. The NBA controls the activities of the league, including the holding of regular and exhibition basketball games between members of the league.

Complainant NBA Properties, Inc. ('NBAP') is the exclusive licensing and merchandising agent for the National Basketball Association ('NBA') and its member teams. NBA Properties, Inc. is the owner of several trademarks relating to the NBA and the exclusive licensee of certain other trademarks relating to the NBA member teams, including the HOUSTON ROCKETS and NEW JERSEY NETS trademarks, and therefore has sufficient rights in those trademarks and a sufficient common interest in the <houstonrockets.com> and <newjerseynets.com> domain names.

Complainant Rocket Ball, Ltd. ('RBL') is a limited partnership existing under the laws of the State of Texas. Complainant RBL is the owner and operator of the Houston Rockets basketball team, which is a member team of the NBA. RBL owns several United States trademark registrations for the 'HOUSTON ROCKETS' mark since 1971, and therefore has sufficient rights in that trademark and a sufficient common interest in the <houstonrockets.com> domain name for join in this dispute.

Complainant New Jersey Basketball, LLC ('NJB') is a limited liability company existing under the laws of the State of New Jersey. Complainant NJB is the owner and operator of the New Jersey Nets basketball team, which is a member team of the NBA. NJB owns several United States trademark registrations for the 'NEW JERSEY NETS' trademark since 1978, and therefore has sufficient rights in that trademark and a sufficient common interest in the <newjerseynets.com> domain name.

Complainant RBL has licensed to Complainant NBAP the exclusive right to exploit the 'HOUSTON ROCKETS' mark and relies upon NBAP to protect that mark. RBL has authorized NBAP to register and own domain names incorporating the 'HOUSTON ROCKETS' mark, and has expressly authorized NBAP to receive transfer of the <houstonrockets.com> domain name.

Correspondingly, Complainant NJB has licensed to Complainant NBAP the exclusive right to exploit the 'NEW JERSEY NETS' mark and relies upon NBAP to protect that mark. NJB has authorized NBAP to register and own domain names incorporating the 'NEW JERSEY NETS' mark, and has expressly authorized NBAP to receive transfer of the <newjerseynets.com> domain name.

Respondent, Rick Godwin registered the disputed domain names in1997. The <newjerseynets.com> domain name was registered on June 26, 1997, and <houstonrockets.com> on was registered on August 15, 1997, without authorization from the Complainants.

On July 23, 1997, attorneys for Complainant contacted Respondent in order to allege trademark infringement and to demand transfer of the disputed domain name to Complainant.

Respondent did not answer the July 23 letter and on August 6, 1997, NBAP sent a Letter to Networks Solutions Inc. ('NSI') requesting that pursuant to the Domain Name Dispute Policy in effect at that time, NSI place the domain name <newjerseynets.com> in hold status.

On August 13, 1997, Network Solutions Inc., sent Respondent a letter advising him that his <newjerseynets.com> domain name had become the subject of a complaint filed by NBAP and suggesting some alternative solutions. This letter also advised Respondent that, if he did not respond, the <newjerseynets.com> domain name would be placed on hold status at the end of thirty days.

On September 26, 1997, NSI sent Respondent a letter advising him that, because he had failed to respond to the August 13 NSI Letter, the <newjerseynets.com> domain name had been placed on hold status in accordance with the provisions of the Domain Name Dispute Resolution Policy then in effect.

Between 1997 and today Complainants have continued to attempt to contact Respondent in order to recover the domain names in dispute, receiving no direct answer or intention to discuss the matter from Respondent.

Also, during those years of requesting that Respondent answer to the communications that NBAP made, Complainant NBAP continued periodically to monitor Respondent's activities in connection with the <houstonrockets.com> and <newjerseynets.com> domain names, finding that these domain names were not being used to link to active pages. But, recently, Complainants have discovered that when a user types the <houstonrockets.com> domain name or the <newjerseynets.com> domain name into his/her Internet browser, the user is immediately redirected to a Web site called 'Snowboard.com', which is located at 'www.snowboard.com'. According to WHOIS, the <snowboard.com> domain name is registered to Respondent Rick Godwin. Complainants are not in any way affiliated with Respondent Rick Godwin or his 'Snowboard.com' Web site.

On November 22, 2004, after several years of unsuccessful attempts to resolve the dispute related to Respondent's unauthorized registration and infringing use of the <houstonrockets.com> and <newjerseynets.com> domain names, Complainants filed this proceeding in order to them bring back.

5. Parties' Contentions

A. Complainants

- The Houston Rockets and the New Jersey Nets are two, very popular basketball teams with sports fans and the general public, and the Houston Rockets and the New Jersey Nets are trademarks under the Laws of the United States and also under other countries and has become widely known through extensive advertising and media coverage.
- Complainant is the exclusive licensee of the federally registered trademarks HOUSTON ROCKETS and NEW JERSEY NETS.
- Complainant Rocket Ball, Ltd. is a limited partnership existing under the laws of the State of Texas. RBL owns several United States trademark registrations for the 'HOUSTON ROCKETS' mark since 1971, and therefore has sufficient rights in that trademark.
- Complainant New Jersey Basketball is a limited liability company existing under the laws of the State of New Jersey. Complainant NJB is the owner and operator of the New Jersey Nets basketball team, which is a member team of the NBA. NJB owns several United States trademark registrations for the 'NEW JERSEY NETS' trademark.

- Complainants has invested substantial financial resources that include time, labor, skill and expenses developing, advertising and promoting the Houston Rockets the New Jersey Nets trademarks to obtain the fame and prestige that these trademarks holds today.
- The disputed domain names are confusingly similar to Complainant's trademarks.
- Respondent has not been authorized to register or use the domain name for any legitimate purpose and thus has no rights or interests in it.
- The disputed domain name should be transferred to Complainant.

B. Respondent
The Respondent did not submit a response and is in default in this proceeding.

6. Discussion and Findings

In order for Complainant to prevail and have the disputed domain names <newjerseynets.com> and <houstonrockets.com> transferred to it, Complainant must prove the following (the Policy, paragraph 4(a)(i-iii):

- the domain names are identical or confusingly similar to the trademarks in which the Complainants has rights; and
- the Respondent has no rights or legitimate interests in respect of the domain names; and
- the domain names were registered and are being used in bad faith.

A. Identical or Confusingly Similar
Complainants have demonstrated their rights in the domain name as seen from the quotes (from the Complaint) extracted below.

'Complainant RBL is the owner and Complainant NBAP e the exclusive licensee of the U.S. federally registered trademark 'HOUSTON ROCKETS' in international class 41 (Reg. No. 976164) and the U.S. federally registered trademark 'HOUSTON ROCKETS and design' in international classes 24, 25, 28, and 41 (Reg. No. 1004459). (...)'

'The registrations for the 'HOUSTON ROCKETS' and 'HOUSTON ROCKETS and design' marks are in full force and effect, and the trademarks that are the subject thereof and the goodwill of the business in connection with which those marks are used never has been abandoned.'

'Complainant NJB is the owner and Complainant NBAP is the exclusive licensee of the U.S. federally registered trademark 'NEW JERSEY NETS' in international class 41 (Reg. No. 1209109) and the U.S. federally registered trademark 'NEW JERSEY NETS and design' in international class 41 (Reg. No. 1209110). (...) The registrations for the 'NEW JERSEY NETS' and 'NEW JERSEY NETS and design' marks are in full force and effect, and the trademarks that are the subject thereof and the goodwill of the business in connection with which those marks are used never has been abandoned.' For that reasons Complainant NJB and Complainant NBAP has legitimate interest of the nejerseynets.com domain name.'

The Complainants have provided evidence of their commercial activities on the Internet using the domain names <houstonrockets.biz>, <houstonrockets.cn>, <houston-rockets.com>, <houstonrockets.com.cn>, <houstonrockets.info>, <houstonrockets.net>, <houston-rockets.net>, <houstonrockets.org>, <newjerseynets.biz>, <newjerseynets.com>, <new-jersey-nets.com>, <newjerseynets.info>, <newjerseynets.net>, <njnets.com>, <nj-nets.com>, <njnets.net>, and <njnets.org>, among others. All of these domain names link to the Houston Rockets or New Jersey Nets home pages on 'www.nba.com', confirming their rights in the claimed marks.

There is no doubt that the <houstonrockets.com> domain name registered and used by Respondent is identical to the famous and distinctive trademark 'HOUSTON ROCKETS' owned by Complainant RBL, for which Complainant NBAP is the exclusive licensee. Also, there is no doubt that <newjerseynets.com> domain name is identical to the famous and distinctive trademark 'NEW JERSEY NETS' owned by Complainant NJB, for which Complainant NBAP is the exclusive licensee.

B. Rights or Legitimate Interests
Complainants have demonstrated their rights in the domain name as seen from the quotes below.

Complainants established in their Complaint that they in no way authorized the Respondent to use the trademarks: 'HOUSTON ROCKETS' and NEW JERSEY NETS' or to register the domain names in dispute.

The Respondent is in default in this proceeding and thus has made no attempt to demonstrate or prove any rights or interests in the disputed domain name. The Panel surmises from the copies of the disputed domain name website that Respondent has tried to use the domain name by *directing it to a website, either* 'www.digitalcameras.com' *or* 'www.snowboard.com'. This, however, is not a legitimate right or interest under the Policy.

The Panel finds the Respondent has no legitimate rights or interests in the disputed domain names: <houstonrockets.com> and <newjerseynets.com>.

C. Registered and Used in Bad Faith

The Panel is convinced that Respondent registered the <houstonrockets.com> and the <newjerseynets.com> domain names in order to prevent the owners of the trademarks reflecting their marks in corresponding domain names. Respondent was almost certainly aware of Complainant's marks at the time the disputed domain names were registered.

The Panel has found that Respondent has intentionally attempted to attract Internet users to its own web site or other on-line location, by creating a likelihood of confusion with the Complainant's trademarks as to the source, sponsorship, affiliation, or endorsement of Respondent own website or websites 'www.digitalcameras.com', 'www.snowboard.com' using the disputed domain names.

The Panel finds that Respondent registered and was using the disputed domain names <houstonrockets.com> and <newjerseynets.com> in bad faith. Respondent's conduct violates the Policy at Paragraph 4(b)(iv) (see similar cases such as *NBA Properties, Inc.* v. *Ituralde-Kasmir, Inc.*, WIPO Case No. D2000-1620; *NFL Properties, Inc. et al.* v. *BBC Ab*, WIPO Case No. D2000-0147 and *NFL Properties, Inc. et al.* v. *Rusty Rahe*, WIPO Case No. D2000-0128).

7. Decision

For all the foregoing reasons, in accordance with Paragraphs 4(i) of the Policy and 15 of the Rules, the Panel orders that the domain names <houstonrockets.com> and <newjerseynets.com> are transferred to the Complainant NBA Properties Inc.

Ada L. Redondo Aguilera
Sole Panelist
Dated: January 15, 2005

19.4 Two Case Studies

To illustrate the application of the ICANN UDRP to the resolution of sports domain disputes through the WIPO Arbitration and Mediation Center, we will take a look at the high profile domain name cases of the Manchester United and England footballer, Wayne Rooney, which was defended, and the famous Barcelona Football Club, which was not defended.

19.4.1 *Wayne Rooney* case

The well-known sports person, the Manchester United and England footballer, Wayne Rooney (the Complainant), who was born in Liverpool in 1985, has also been involved in WIPO Domain Name proceedings. The domain name in contention was <waynerooney.com> which was registered by the Respondent in the case, a busy actor and ardent fan of Everton Football Club, with whom Rooney started his career as a fifteen-year-old in 2000, turning professional with them in 2003 and then moving on to 'ManU' the following year.

In order to win, Rooney had to prove that, under the provisions of the ICANN DRP (the Policy), approved on October 24, 1999 and administered by the Center, this was a case of so-called 'cybersquatting' (the abusive registration and use of a domain name).

Under the Policy, Rooney, the Complainant, in order to obtain the transfer or cancellation of the offending domain name, the Complainant must prove each of the following basic elements of Paragraph 4(a) of the Policy, namely:

i. The disputed domain name is identical or confusingly similar to a trademark or service mark in which Complainant has rights. And
ii. Respondent has no rights or legitimate interests in respect of the domain name. And
iii. The disputed domain name has been registered and is being used in bad faith.

For the Complainant to succeed, all three of these conditions must be satisfied.

But, what, one may ask, is meant by the expression 'bad faith'? Paragraph 4(b) of the Policy lists four examples of acts, which *prima facie* constitute evidence of bad faith. They are as follows:

i. Offering to sell the domain name to the trademark owner or its competitor;
ii. An attempt to attract for financial gain Internet users by creating confusion with the trademark of another;
iii. Registration of a domain name in order to prevent the trademark owner from reflecting its mark in a corresponding domain name; and
iv. Registration of the domain name in order to disrupt the business of the competitor.

It should be noted that this list is not exhaustive, but merely illustrative of the kinds of situations that may fall within the concept of bad faith.

In practice, many of the disputes are not defended by the respondent to the Complaint, and this fact, along with a failure to respond to any 'cease and desist' letter from the complainant issued before the WIPO proceedings were commenced, may constitute further evidence of bad faith on the part of the respondent. Likewise, the respondent may have been previously involved in registering disputed domain names that have been the subject of previous WIPO cases, in which those names have been found to be without legal justification and ordered to be transferred to the complainants. Again, this would constitute evidence of bad faith.

As also would registering a fanciful or bizarre name, which happened in the so-called Pepsi case (*PepsiCo, Inc.* v. *PEPSI, SRL (a/k/a P.E.P.S.I.) and EMS COMPUTER INDUSTRY (a/k/a EMS)*, WIPO Case No. D2003-0696). In that case, an Italian Company, with the name of 'Partite Emozionanti Per Sportivi Italiani', which, in translation, stands for 'Leave the Histrionics for Italian Sports Fans', and known for short as 'P.E.P.S.I.', registered seventy domain names incorporating the famous soft drink trademark PEPSI in relation to an extensive range of sports, including 'pepsicricket.com', 'pepsigolf.com', 'pepsisoccer.com', 'pepsirugby.net', 'pepsisuperbike.net' and 'pepsivolleyball.net'. The sole panellist in this case held that there was 'opportunistic bad faith' because the domain names were so obviously connected with such a well-known product with which the respondent had no connection. See also *Veuve Cliquot Ponsardin, Maison Fondee en 1772* v. *The Polygenix Group Co.*, WIPO Case No. D2000-0163.

In the *Rooney* case, the domain name in contention had been registered before Rooney's trade mark rights in his name had 'matured' and this was one of the legal issues to be determined by the sole panellist appointed by the Center to decide the case. Likewise, in such circumstances, could the respondent be held to be acting in bad faith in registering and using the domain name? Irrespective of this, the other legal issue raised by the case was whether, at the time the respondent registered the disputed domain name, Rooney had already acquired a sufficient reputation, the 'goodwill' in which could be protected under the English Common Law Doctrine of 'Passing Off'(unfair competition in a legal sense).

The facts of the case, the contentions of the parties, and the discussion and findings of the panellist are set out in the decision itself, which is reproduced *in toto* in the text.

As will be seen from a reading of the decision itself, the particular facts and circumstances of the case play a crucial role in determining the outcome.

It is interesting to note that in the *Rooney* case the Panellist relies, to a large extent, on the 'WIPO Overview of WIPO Panel Views on Selected UDRP Questions' which are accessible on the WIPO official website (<www.wipo.int>). This is also a useful resource for parties contemplating bringing a domain name dispute before the Center in determining their arguments on various issues that may arise in their particular case.

As will also be seen from the decision in *Rooney*, certain procedural issues also needed to be addressed. And also, the decision, in accordance with the Policy, had to be rendered within 14 (natural) days of the date of the panel being constituted. Speed is particularly important in relation to sports disputes, where sporting deadlines often come into play.

As the Rooney case demonstrates, domain name disputes concerning well-known sports persons, with famous and valuable trademarks to protect, can be quickly and effectively resolved using the WIPO adjudication process under the terms of the ICANN Uniform Domain Name Dispute Resolution Policy. However, no damages or costs are awarded under the UDRP.

A further advantage of this process is that decisions to transfer or cancel disputed domain names must be enforced by the Registrar that originally registered them. However, following the ruling, the Respondent has ten days in which to file court proceedings challenging the decision, in an appropriate jurisdiction. This rarely happens in practice.

Again, the cost of using the WIPO process, which is user friendly, is relatively inexpensive. An undefended case costs a mere USD 1,500; whilst a defended one with a single member Panel costs USD 3,000.

19.4.2 *Barcelona FC* case

This case concerned a 'cyber squatter', who registered and tried to sell the domain names <fcbarcelona.net> and <fcbarcelona.org> (the disputed domain names) to the famous Barcelona Football Club.

Cyber squatting occurs where a party registers a domain name comprising the name and/or trademark of a third party, with a view to benefiting unfairly from the goodwill enjoyed by that name or mark. Barcelona FC, the Complainant in the case, already owns and has registered the domain names <fcbarcelona.es> and <fcbarcelona.com>. And also owns and has registered a number of trademarks covering various products and services, including a European Community trademark for FCBARCELONA, and also a Spanish trademark for FCBARCELONA.COM.

Not surprisingly, therefore, the Complainant sought to have the disputed domain names transferred to itself on the grounds that the other party (the Respondent) had acted unlawfully.

The Respondent, a company based nearby in Girona and in the same Autonomous Spanish Community as the Complainant, failed, without any justification, to file any response to the Complaint within the time allowed and, therefore, was held to be in default.

Again, under the ICANN UDRP, which is administered by the WIPO Center, in order to succeed, the Complainant must prove each of the following basic elements of Paragraph 4(a) of the Policy, namely:

i. The disputed domain name is identical or confusingly similar to a trademark or service mark in which Complainant has rights. And
ii. Respondent has no rights or legitimate interests in respect of the domain name. And
iii. The disputed domain name has been registered and is being used in bad faith.

If the Complainant fails to establish any of the above requirements, the Complaint fails.

As regards the bad faith requirement, Paragraph 4(b) of the Policy lists four examples of acts, which *prima facie* constitute evidence of bad faith. They are as follows:

i. offering to sell the domain name to the trademark owner or its competitor;
ii. an attempt to attract for financial gain Internet users by creating confusion with the trademark of another;
iii. registration of a domain name in order to prevent the trademark owner from reflecting its mark in a corresponding domain name; and
iv. registration of the domain name in order to disrupt the business of the competitor.

However, this list is not exhaustive, but merely illustrative. See *Nova Banka* v. *Iris*, WIPO Case No. D2003-0366. In many cases, the Respondent fails to reply to the Complainant's 'cease and desist' letter and also to answer the Complaint and participate in the proceedings. And these defaults have been held to constitute bad faith. And also, evidence of lack of rights or legitimate interests in the disputed domain name. Otherwise, if the Respondent had grounds for registering and using the disputed domain name, the Respondent would be ready to assert them in the proceedings. See *Patelco Credit Union* v. *Hong Kong Names LLC*, WIPO Case No. D2006-0202; and *Do the Hustle, LLC* v. *Tropic Web*, WIPO Case No. D2000-0624. In other words, the Respondent's silence is tantamount to admitting the Complainant's case. Again, in cases where the disputed domain name incorporates a well-known and notorious mark of the Complainant, the Respondent has been held to have acted in bad faith where the Respondent had actual or constructive knowledge of the mark at the time of registration. See *Exxon Mobil Corp.* v. *Fisher*, WIPO Case No. D2000-1412.

The cases are decided in accordance with the provisions of the Policy, the UDRP Rules (the 'Rules'), and the WIPO UDRP Supplemental Rules by either a three or single member Panel, appointed by the Center from amongst a list of Intellectual Property experts maintained by the Center. Such Panel members must be independent of the parties in dispute and make a signed declaration to that effect. The actual wording of this declaration is as follows:

> 'I am independent of the parties. To the best of my knowledge and belief, there are no facts or circumstances, past or present, or that could arise in the future, that need be disclosed as they

> might be of such a nature as to call in to question my independence in the eyes of one or both of the parties.'

In other words, there must be no 'conflict of interests' on the part of the member(s) of the Panel in the particular case. Even in those cases where the Panel member is independent of the parties, there may be certain circumstances which may call into question the independence of the member in the eyes of one or both of the parties to the dispute, in which case the Panel member must declare them in order for the Center to decide whether or not to confirm the appointment of the member concerned in the particular case.

In accordance with Paragraph 15(a) of the Rules, the Panel shall decide the Complaint on the basis of the statements and documents submitted and in accordance with the Policy, the Rules, and any rules and principles of law that it deems applicable. Furthermore, in the absence of exceptional circumstances, the Panel must decide the case within fourteen natural days of the date of the notification by the Center to the parties of its appointment.

In accordance with Paragraph 14(a) of the Rules, in the event that a party, in the absence of exceptional circumstances, does not comply with any of the time periods established by the Rules or the Panel, the Panel shall proceed to a decision on the complaint; and (b) if a party, in the absence of exceptional circumstances, does not comply with any provision of, or requirement under, the Rules or any request from the Panel, the Panel shall draw such inferences as it considers appropriate.

In accordance with Paragraph 10(d) of the Rules, the Panel shall determine the admissibility, relevance, materiality and weight of the evidence.

In previous UDRP cases in which the respondent failed to file a response, the Panel's decisions were based upon the complainant's assertions and evidence, as well as inferences drawn from the respondent's failure to reply. See *The Vanguard Group, Inc.* v. *Lorna Kang*, WIPO Case No. D2002-1064; and also *Köstritzer Schwarzbierbrauerei* v. *Macros-Telekom Corp*, WIPO Case No. D2001-0936.

Nevertheless, the Panel must not decide in the complainant's favour solely based on the respondent's default (*Cortefiel S.A.* v. *Miguel García Quintas*, WIPO Case No. D2000-0140). The Panel must decide whether the complainant has introduced elements of proof, which allow the Panel to conclude that its allegations are true.

In the Barcelona FC case, the single member Panel found that the disputed domain names were confusingly similar to the Complainant's trademarks FCBARCELONA and FCBARCELONA.COM, which had been registered and used by the Complainant prior to the registration by the Respondent of the disputed domain names; that the Respondent did not have any rights or legitimate interests in the disputed domain names, particularly because the Respondent must have been aware of the Complainant – a famous football club well-known both locally, where the Complainant and the Respondent are based, and internationally – when registering the disputed domain names containing the Complainant's well-known trademarks and could not, therefore, claim any such rights or interests; and that the Respondent had registered and was using the disputed domain names in bad faith, particularly as the Respondent had offered to sell the disputed domain names to the general public and its use of them prevented the owner of the trademarks, the Complainant, from registering the disputed domain names.

Thus, the domain names were ordered to be transferred from the Respondent to the Complainant.

The full text of this decision, which was rendered on April 11, 2006, is available on line at the Center's official web site, namely: <www.arbiter.wipo.int>. Please note, however, that the decision is in Spanish!

Incidentally, all previous WIPO UDRP decisions can also be accessed on line and thus provide a useful body of precedents.

In a Single Member Panel case, like the Barcelona FC case, where the Respondent does not reply to the Complaint or take any other part in the proceedings, the fee payable to the Center for the handling of the dispute amounts to USD 1,500.

Again, the Barcelona FC 'cybersquatting' case is another example of the service provided to the international sporting community by the WIPO Arbitration and Mediation Center in settling sports-related domain name disputes in a timely, inexpensive and effective manner.

19.5 Selected WIPO Sports Domain Name Decisions

It will be useful to provide some examples of WIPO sports domain name cases, and so the full texts of the decisions rendered in a selection of those cases are set out in Appendix XXVI to this book for the information of the reader.

19.6 Table of WIPO Sports Domain Name Cases

Likewise a list of WIPO Sports Domain Name Disputes Cases from 1999 (the beginning of the ICANN UDRP disputes procedures) to the end of 2007 is set out in Appendix XXVII, again for the convenience of the reader.

CHAPTER 20
'EXPERT DETERMINATION'

'Expert Determination' is an alternative dispute resolution process whereby a difference between parties in dispute is submitted, by agreement of the parties, to one (or more) experts who make a determination on the matter referred to it (them). The determination is legally binding on them, unless the parties agree otherwise.

Expert Determination enjoys the following characteristics:

20.1 Expert Determination is Consensual

Expert determination under the WIPO Expert Determination Rules can only be invoked if both parties have agreed to resolve their dispute in this way. In the case of future disputes/differences arising under a contract, the parties may include an 'expert determination clause' as part of the dispute resolution clause in the corresponding contract.

An existing dispute/difference can be referred to expert determination by means of a 'submission agreement' between the parties. In contrast to mediation, a party cannot unilaterally withdraw from expert determination.

20.2 The Parties Choose the Expert(s) with Relevant Expertise

Under the WIPO Expert Determination Rules, the parties can select an expert together. If the parties have not agreed on the expert or on a different procedure for appointing the expert, the expert will be appointed by the WIPO Center following consultation with the parties.

The WIPO Center has access to experts with specialized knowledge relevant to intellectual property issues in a broad range of technical and business areas. This allows the Center to propose and appoint the appropriate experts for the matter concerned.

20.3 Expert Determination is Neutral and Flexible

In addition to their selection of an expert with appropriate qualifications, the parties are able to choose such important matters as the language of the expert determination or the venue of any meeting.

20.4 Expert Determination is a Confidential Procedure

Subject to specifically defined exceptions, the WIPO Expert Determination Rules specifically protect the confidentiality of the existence of the expert determination; any disclosures made during the procedure; and the resulting determination. See Article 15 of the WIPO Expert Determination Rules for the details.

Confidentiality, as previously mentioned elsewhere in the book, is an important consideration for the sporting community when it comes to settling their disputes.

20.5 The Determination of an Expert is Binding, Unless the Parties Agree Otherwise

In principle, the determination of an expert is binding and, as such, produces contractual legal effects between the parties. Alternatively, by agreement between the parties, the determination may have effect as a recommendation to the parties, which, at their option, they are fee to follow or not, as the case may be.

Even in those cases where the expert determination is non-binding, the process often assists the parties in clarifying certain legal issues, which may well determine whether they go to law and engage in expensive and lengthy litigation or not.

Compare CAS Advisory Opinions which are not legally binding on the parties, but are often followed and acted on by the parties in practice.

20.6 Expert Determination Is a Flexible Procedure

Expert determination can operate on a more informal and expeditious basis than other broader dispute resolution processes, such as arbitration. Again, speed is often of the essence as far as sports disputes are concerned where deadlines come into play.

Expert determination may be used on a stand-alone basis, or in connection with an arbitration, mediation or an actual court case. For example, a specific technical issue involved in court proceedings may be referred for binding resolution by expert determination. In other words, it is not necessarily an 'all or nothing' method of resolving a dispute.

Obviously, the success of expert determination depends on the ability and expertise of the expert or experts appointed by the parties to resolve the dispute.

20.7 WIPO Recommended 'Expert Determination' Contract Clauses and Submission Agreements

WIPO offers some recommended contract clauses and submission agreements to be included as part of dispute resolution clauses in contracts to be used respectively in respect of future disputes or to be used where a dispute has already arisen and the parties wish to avail themselves of WIPO 'Expert Determination'.[301]

It is prudent to include such clauses in contracts before the fact of any dispute arising rather than after the fact when a dispute has actually arisen. Otherwise, if one party, in the event of a dispute arising, wishes to settle that dispute by WIPO 'Expert Determination', that party will only be able to do so if the other party to the dispute agrees.

---

[301] These clauses are accessible through the WIPO official website at <www.wipo.int>.

20.8 Expert Determination and Sports Disputes

For all the above reasons, 'expert determination' is an appropriate method of resolving sports disputes, especially those involving intellectual property issues, including trademarks, copyright and even patents relating to sports goods and equipment, arising under or in relation to various Sports Marketing and Merchandising Agreements, such as Event Mark Licences, Sponsorship Agreements, Sports Image Rights Agreements, to mention but a few of them. Also, WIPO 'expert determination' is particularly useful for resolving disputes with an international dimension, that is, which transcend national boundaries.

The WIPO Center is well able to handle such kinds of disputes under its 'expert determination' procedure; and has, in fact, done so on a number of previous occasions. Unfortunately, for reasons of confidentiality, we are not able to give any details or examples.

20.9 Costs of Expert Determination

Again, 'expert determination' through WIPO is a relatively inexpensive and cost-effective dispute resolution process.

WIPO has a Schedule of Fees and Costs for this kind of dispute resolution process, where it is stated in the preamble that 'in consultation with parties and neutrals, the Center ensures that fees charged in a WIPO procedure are appropriate in light of the circumstances of the matter'.

In other words, WIPO seeks to keep the fees payable as reasonable as possible taking in account the nature and circumstances of each particular case.

CHAPTER 21
WIPO ELECTRONIC CASE FACILITY

The WIPO Arbitration and Mediation Center aims to offer time and cost efficient mediation, arbitration and expert determination proceedings. To assist in this purpose, the Center makes available, at the parties' option, a very useful resource for parties involved in WIPO dispute resolution proceedings, known as the WIPO Electronic Case Facility (WIPO ECAF).

21.1 What Is the WIPO ECAF?

WIPO ECAF allows parties and all others involved in or with an interest in a case under the WIPO Mediation, Arbitration, Expedited Arbitration and Expert Determination Rules to submit communications electronically into an online docket. Parties receive e-mail alerts of any such submission being made and may view and search this docket at any time. The online docket may also be used to record the fact that a submission is being made in hardcopy outside the WIPO ECAF.

21.2 What Are the Other Functions of the WIPO ECAF?

In addition to facilitating online communication and storage, the WIPO ECAF can also provide:

- a summary of case information;
- an overview of timelines;
- contact information for all parties; and
- the finance status of the case.

21.3 Who May Use the WIPO ECAF?

Parties to a procedure under WIPO Rules may, by party agreement, opt to use the WIPO ECAF. At the stage of the appointment of the neutral(s), parties should also consult with the neutral(s) about the possible use of the WIPO ECAF facility.

WIPO ECAF is not available for cases under the Uniform Domain Name Dispute Resolution Policy (UDRP), in respect of which separate filing requirements apply.

Although the WIPO ECAF, as noted above, is generally available only to parties to a WIPO procedure, the Center, under certain circumstances, will make this facility available in non-WIPO procedures in certain cases. For example, the Center provided a customized version of WIPO ECAF for use in the Jury Procedure of the 32nd America's Cup, the international yachting competition, which commenced in 2004 and culminated in the final regattas in Valencia, Spain, in the Summer of 2007.

I.S. Blackshaw, Sport, Mediation and Arbitration

21.4 How to Access the WIPO ECAF?

Parties to a WIPO case may submit to the Center a request to obtain access to the WIPO ECAF either:

- by e-mail; or
- by fax to +41 22 740 3700.

Such requests, which should contain the contact information of all the parties, may be made prior to the formal submission of the case or at any time thereafter.

21.5 What Security Does the WIPO ECAF Offer?

Every time a party accesses the WIPO ECAF, it will be authenticated through its user-name, password and a changing passcode delivered by RSA SecurID card, a hand-held device that furnishes changing passcodes.

All information stored in the WIPO ECAF is 'firewall' protected and 'encrypted' by using the modern Secure Socket Layer (SSL) technology.

21.6 Further Information on the WIPO ECAF

Information requests concerning the use of the WIPO ECAF may be sent to the WIPO Center either:

- by e-mail; or
- by telephone on +41 22 338 8247.

For example, the Center provided a customized version of WIPO ECAF for use in the Jury Procedure of the 32nd America's Cup, the international yachting competition, which commenced in 2004 and culminated in the final regattas in Valencia, Spain, in the summer of 2007.

CHAPTER 22
CONCLUDING REMARKS

The WIPO Arbitration and Mediation Center offers parties in IP-related and other kinds of disputes a wide range of alternative dispute resolution (ADR) services, which are user-friendly, well structured, organised and administered, as well as being relatively speedy, inexpensive and cost-effective.

Such services are of particular interest to the international sporting community, which prefers, generally speaking, to settle their disputes, including IP-related ones, outside the ordinary Courts system and, generally, in private. And also in a more informal and flexible manner, both of which needs are fully reflected in the WIPO dispute resolution services that are on offer and that have been described in this Part of this book.

These services are becoming better known and used amongst sports persons, bodies, organisations and their administrators and professional advisers and are likely to be more widely used in the future.

Of course, the sporting world, it has to be acknowledged, already has its own so-called 'Supreme Court of World Sport' in the form of the Court of Arbitration for Sport (CAS), which is also based in Switzerland and a provider of ADR services, which have been described in Part Two of this book. However, the services of WIPO and the CAS are by no means overlapping or in conflict with one another, which might at first sight appear to be the case, as there is room for both bodies to co-exist in serving the alternative dispute resolution needs and interests of a wide range of sports' constituents. This is particularly true now that sport – as noted at the beginning of this book – has become such a significant global industry, with a corresponding and impressive financial footprint to boot.

To use a sporting metaphor, it is very much a case, therefore, of 'horses for courses'. In other words, the sporting world is given the choice of *fora* – the courts or alternative dispute resolution processes and services offered by sports' and non-sports' bodies alike all of which have been covered in this book – and it will always be a case of finding and using the most appropriate one on a case-by-case basis. Choice of legal services is, of course, the hallmark of an advanced and democratic society in which sport is an important player and stakeholder.

WIPO, like the CAS and several other organisations providing a wide range of ADR services at a national and international level, which have been described in this book, have one very important characteristic in common: they offer a highly professional and entirely independent and impartial resource to all those who call upon them for their assistance in settling their disputes, including sporting ones of various kinds, a growing number of them involving IP issues, not least relating to sports image and broadcasting rights,[302] in relation

[302] See I.S. Blackshaw and R.C.R. Siekmann, *Sports Image Rights in Europe* (The Hague, T.M.C. Asser Press 2005) and I.S. Blackshaw, R.C.R. Siekmann and J. Soek, *TV Right and Sport* (The Hague, T.M.C. Asser Press 2008).

to which the particular expertise and experience of WIPO, particularly in settling domain name disputes, has a part to play.

Despite the considerable number of sports domain name disputes that have been settled through the WIPO Arbitration and Mediation Center over the years, individuals, companies and organisations are still 'trying it on' and engaging in 'cybersquatting' – something which never ceases to amaze the author of this Book!

I am sure, therefore, that sports disputes of all kinds will not abate and that sports bodies, sports administrators, sports persons, sports marketers and merchandisers, sports broadcasters and all others engaged in one way or another in the organisation, promotion and delivery of sport and sports events and their professional advisers, including their lawyers, will continue to have much work to do in the future in protecting and safeguarding their legal rights and interests. And I very much hope that this Book will prove to be of guidance and assistance to them in pursuing the appropriate dispute resolution processes and remedies – whatever form they may take!

Appendices

APPENDIX I

SPEECH BY LORD PHILLIPS OF WORTH MATRAVERS LORD CHIEF JUSTICE OF ENGLAND AND WALES

ALTERNATIVE DISPUTE RESOLUTION: AN ENGLISH VIEWPOINT GIVEN IN INDIA ON 29 MARCH 2008

My professional life in the law started as a barrister 46 years ago. In England a young barrister in those days cut his teeth on small criminal prosecutions, such as infringements of road traffic legislation and small civil cases in the County Court, such as disputes between landlord and tenant. Actions in the High Court normally went to barristers of experience. One such action was down for trial in which a senior member of my chambers was instructed for the plaintiff. Then, at the last minute, he was unable to appear because a previous action in which he was appearing had overrun. Our clerk persuaded the solicitor to transfer the brief to me instead. This was my first High Court action, producing mixed emotions of excitement and terror. I read the papers with great care.

My client was an elderly lady who had slipped and fallen in a vegetable shop, sustaining a nasty broken ankle. She alleged that she had slipped on a squashed plum that had been left on the floor, and that the shop was in breach of its duty to her under the Occupiers' Liability Act. The shop denied this and suggested that the old lady must have tripped over her own shopping bag.

None the less, the shop's liability insurers had made an offer to settle on the basis of paying 50% of the damages. My client had refused this offer. There were no witnesses. The result of the action was going to depend on whether the judge accepted my client's version of the accident.

I met my client for the first time in the corridor outside the court on the day that the Action was due to begin. She was obviously very nervous. The first thing that she said to me was "I won't have to give evidence will I?"

I explained to her that her evidence was absolutely critical. She said that she was too frightened to go into the witness box. Try as I might I could not persuade her to change her mind. What a disaster for my first High Court case. I saw my opponent at the opposite end of the corridor. He was a very experience counsel who regularly acted for the insurance company involved. I went up to him and explained that I had only just come into the case. I said that my view was that my client had been foolish to reject the 50% offer (so it was, but I did not tell him why). I asked whether the offer was still open for acceptance. Experienced as he was he viewed my question with some suspicion. "Is your client actually here?" he asked? I assured him that she was and pointed her out to him.

He then took instructions and returned to say that the insurance company would still settle for 50%, so I quickly clinched the deal on that basis.

She was relieved to miss her day in court, but I was very disappointed to miss mine.

That was my first lesson in the merits of alternative dispute resolution. It avoids the trauma of court proceedings. If, like my client, you are not prepared to undergo that trauma at any price, then there is no alternative to alternative dispute resolution, and in the first thirty years of my life in the law, the only form of ADR was negotiation. Any sensible person who finds himself party to a dispute will wish to resolve it, if possible, by negotiation. Over 90% of actions that are commenced in England end in a negotiated settlement before trial. One reason for this is the cost of litigating under the adversarial process. Resolving a dispute by adversarial litigation usually involves a solicitor on each side, a barrister on each side and the judge, whose cost is covered by the court fees that the claimant has to pay.

Add to this, very often, the cost of professional expert witnesses on each side and it is no wonder that the cost of litigation is frequently disproportionate to what is at stake.

Under the English procedure, there is a principle that 'costs follow the event'. This means that the party who loses has to pay not only his own legal costs, but the costs of the successful party. So the detriment of losing an action is immeasurably greater than the benefit of winning. This added to the incentive to negotiate a settlement, and this used to be the only realistic form of dispute resolution that provided an alternative to litigation or arbitration. If a plaintiff refused to accept the best offer that the defendant was prepared to make, there was one way that he could attempt to protect himself against the costs of the litigation. That was to pay into court the sum that he was prepared to pay in settlement.

If the plaintiff did not accept the money paid into court, but recovered less than this, he would have to bear the costs of the litigation from the time that the money was paid into court. This was a protective measure that the defendant could only take once an action had been commenced by the plaintiff.

The risk of a disproportionate liability to pay costs has been significantly increased, for defendants at least, by the legalisation of conditional fee agreements, or CFAs, under the Access to Justice Act 1999. These were introduced by the Government as an alternative to providing claimants with free legal aid. Under a CFA the claimant agrees with his lawyers that if his claim fails he will pay no legal fees, but that if it succeeds his lawyers will receive a mark-up of up to 100% on top of what they would otherwise have charged.

This mark-up is known as a 'success fee'. Where the claim is successful the unsuccessful defendant is liable to reimburse the claimant both for his costs and for the success fee. Indeed the defendant's position may be even worse, because a CFA only protects the claimant from having to pay his own legal expenses if his claim fails. He remains liable to pay the defendant's costs in that event. But he can insure against the risk of his claim failing and thus of having to pay the defendant's costs. The premium for such insurance is often very large. If the claimant's claim succeeds, he can recover not only his own legal costs and the success fee from the defendant but also the premium he had to pay for insuring against his potential liability in costs to the defendant. So in addition to losing the action the defendant is faced with a huge bill for the claimant's costs and insurance.

So the desire to avoid the risk of liability for all these costs is an additional cogent reason why a defendant may want to seek an alternative means of dispute resolution that does not involve litigation.

In this lecture I propose to concentrate on that form of ADR that is described as mediation. In 2004 the Centre for Effective Dispute Resolution, known as CEDR, published a revised definition of mediation as follows:

> "*A flexible process conducted confidentially in which a neutral person assists the parties in working towards a negotiated agreement of a dispute or difference, with the parties in ultimate control of the decision to settle and the terms of resolution.*"

Mediation offers many attractions in addition to that of avoiding the cost and trauma of litigation.

In India it may well be that it is not so much the cost of litigation as the delay involved that makes the parties anxious to find an alternative way of solving their disputes. Before this audience I suspect that there is no need to labour the other attractions of mediation. It is a private and confidential way of resolving a dispute. It is informal. It is voluntary. It is a process that those involved can understand.

Once you are in the hands of professional litigants they take charge of you, willy-nilly, and you find that you have embarked on a course that has no turning back and the incidents of which you cannot even understand. Mediation is not like that. You can always turn back and you have explained to you precisely what is going on. You are in control of what is happening to you.

You can preserve, or restore, good relationships with the other party to the dispute – you can come to feel that you are partners in a common endeavour rather than antagonists. And the resolution of the dispute can involve a much wider range of remedies than the court can offer.

There are of course down sides to mediation. If what you are after is your just rights according to the law, then mediation is not the place for you – but you need to consider carefully the cost of seeking those rights. Above all, so it seems to me, mediation is really suited for two parties who are in genuine dispute.

Sometimes it is necessary for a defendant to stand his ground and challenge the claimant to prove his case in court, because if he does not do so, he will find himself facing claims that are not made in good faith but are brought be fraudsters, relying on the fact that the defendant may think that it is cheaper to reach a settlement agreement than to fight the action, even if successful.

I started this talk with an account of a claim by an old lady who had slipped over in a shop and who was undoubtedly a *bona fide* claimant. But local authorities in England are familiar with claims from people claiming to have injured themselves by tripping over uneven paving stones, some of whom are not genuine claimants but fraudsters "tripping and slipping". There was one local authority, Knowsley Council, that almost always settled such claims on the grounds that this was a desirable alternative to litigation.

In 1998 they dealt with 600 claims. By 2002 the number of claims had risen to 1800. They then had a change of policy and rigorously investigated and defended claims, with the result that by 2006 the annual number of claims had reduced to below 400.

Mediation is a relatively recent arrival on the legal scene – having its origin in the United States in the latter half of the C 20. In the United States there are different reasons for resolving disputes without recourse to litigation. In litigation in the States the successful claimant does not recover his costs from the defendant, but has often agreed that his lawyer will receive a substantial percentage of any recovery he makes under a contingency fee agreement. The defendant is often faced with the fact that if he loses the action the damages will be assessed by a jury and the sky will be the limit.

Mediation has been enthusiastically embraced by a number of States, often making it a mandatory stage of the court process. I have seen a judge conducting mediation in California – admittedly some years ago now, and it was very robust indeed. In England the court's enthusiasm for mediation had been much more muted and the growth of what I might term 'court induced mediation' has been attributable in large measure to the enthusiasm of a comparatively small number of judges.

I shall start with the greatest and most influential of these – Lord Woolf, who preceded me in the offices of both the Master of the Rolls and the Lord Chief Justice. He will be known personally to many of you. In the early 1990s there was an awful lot wrong with the civil justice system in England and Wales.

Cases moved very slowly, they were beset by complex and costly interlocutory battles and, in part for this reason, they were inordinately expensive. Lord Woolf was asked to examine our civil system and to recommend reforms to it. He did so very comprehensively, tearing up and re-writing from scratch our rules of civil procedure. But, for present purposes the interest of his reforms lies in their approach to mediation. Some urged him to follow the America example and make ADR compulsory.

In his *Interim Access to Justice Report in* 1995 he declined to follow this course. He did not recommend court annexed mediation. He saw the role of the court as being no more than to encourage the parties to consider ADR, without suggesting any sanction if they declined to respond to such encouragement.

As so often in the file of English civil law, the English Commercial Court was ahead of the game. The Commercial Court, of which I was a member when I was a puisne judge, is drawn from barristers who practice in commercial work, much of which is international, and they tend to be more forward looking than some of their colleagues. In 1994 the Commercial Court had published a Practice Note requiring legal advisers in all cases:

(a) to consider with their clients and the other parties concerned the possibility of attempting to resolve the particular dispute or particular issues by mediation, conciliation or otherwise; and
(b) to ensure that parties are fully informed as to the most cost-effective means of resolving the particular dispute.

This Practice Note may not sound very significant – but it was none the less valuable.

One problem with mediation had been that neither side wanted to be the first to propose it, fearing that this would be taken for a sign of weakness. Now the court had made it mandatory for the parties to at least consider ADR. I shall be returning to the support given to mediation by the Commercial Court in due course. But first I want to return to Lord Woolf.

In his final *Access to Justice Report* Lord Woolf recommended that, when a judge was considering how to award costs at the end of an action he should take into account an unreasonable refusal of a court's proposal that the parties should attempt to resolve their differences by ADR. When the new Civil Procedure Rules were drawn up in 1998 they contained a number of express provisions designed to promote ADR.

The very first Rule laid down an overriding objective of the civil procedure rules, namely that of 'enabling the court to deal with cases justly'. This includes 'saving expense' and 'dealing with the case in ways which are proportionate…' Instead of leaving it to the litigants to make the running, the new Rules placed a duty of 'active case management' on the court, and this includes:

> "*1.4(e) encouraging the parties to use an alternative dispute resolution procedure if the court considers that appropriate and facilitating the use of such procedure.*"

This was the first time that ADR was officially recognised by the rules of court.

Under the old rules, when the court was considering awards of costs, it was only entitled to have regard to how the parties behaved after the action had been commenced. The new rules radically change the position.

Rule 44.5 now provides that the court must have regard to the conduct of the parties, including conduct before as well as during the proceedings and, in particular, the efforts made, if any, before and during the proceedings in order to try to resolve the dispute.

Here then is a Rule that permits the court to use liability in costs as a sanction against a party who unreasonably refuses to attempt alternative dispute resolution before the action begins. We shall see in due course what use the English court has made of that power. First, though, I want to draw attention to another novelty of civil procedure consequent upon Lord Woolf's Reports, and that is the 'pre-action protocol'. These are protocols, prepared individually, for different types of litigation, that direct the manner in which the parties ought to behave before the litigation is commenced.

They are endorsed by Practice Directions issued by the Master of the Rolls as my nominee. Since 2006 these have directed that every pre-action protocol shall contain the following clause:

> "*The parties should consider whether some form of alternative dispute resolution procedure would be more suitable than litigation and, if so, endeavour to agree which form to adopt. Both the Claimant and Defendant may be required by the court to provide evidence that alternative means of resolving their dispute were considered. The Courts take the view that litigation should be a last resort, and that claims should not be issued prematurely when a settlement is still being actively explored. Parties are warned that if the protocol is not followed (including this paragraph) then the Court must have regard to such conduct when determining costs.*"

We shall see, in due course, to what extent the courts have made use of the costs sanction to encourage parties to resort to ADR. First let me draw attention to provisions in the Rules that enable the court to encourage ADR while the action is in progress.

Early on in an action there is a stage called allocation, when the court decides on the manner in which the action is to be tried.

The Rules provide that at that stage the court may, on the application of the parties or on its own initiative, stay the proceedings to enable the parties to explore ADR and the court may, where appropriate, extend that stay.

A more powerful weapon is given to the court by a Practice Direction (Part 29 PD 4.10(9), introduced in 2005, as follows "in such cases as the court thinks appropriate, the court may give directions requiring the parties to consider ADR". Such directions may be, for example, in the following terms:

> "*The parties shall by [the date determined by the court] consider whether the case is capable of resolution by ADR. If any party considers that the case is unsuitable for resolution by ADR, that party shall be prepared to justify that decision at the conclusion of the trial, should the judge consider that such means of resolution were appropriate, when he is considering the appropriate costs order to make.*
>
> *The party considering the case unsuitable for ADR shall, not less than 28 days before the commencement of the trial, file with the court a witness statement without prejudice, save as to costs, giving reasons upon which they rely for saying that the case was unsuitable.*"

That order was invented by a Queen's Bench Master, Master Ungley. It stops short of ordering the parties to resort to ADR, but it certainly concentrates the mind and fires a warning shot across the bows of any litigant disinclined to resort to ADR.

Master Ungley deals with a lot of personal injury litigation and, as you can see, he is an enthusiast for ADR. Another enthusiast who has recently retired from the Commercial Court is Mr Justice Colman. Some of you may know him, for he is not only an enthusiast of ADR but also an enthusiast of India.

He it is who must take most, or perhaps all, the credit for what has come to be known as 'the Commercial Court ADR Order'. This takes, more or less, the following form:

> "(1) *On or before [Date 1] the parties shall exchange lists of 3 neutrals or identifying one or more panels of individuals who are available to conduct ADR procedures in the case prior to [Date 4]*
>
> (2) *On or before [Date 2] the parties shall in good faith endeavour to agree a neutral individual or panel from the lists so exchanged or provided.*
>
> (3) *Failing such agreement by [Date 3] the court will facilitate agreement on a neutral individual or panel.*

(4) the parties shall take such serious steps as they may be advised to resolve their disputes by ADR procedures before the individual or panel so chosen not later than [Date 4].
(5) If the case is not settled, the parties shall inform the court what steps towards ADR have been taken and why such steps have failed."

This is a pretty robust order. So far as I know, litigants have not objected to it and it quite often results in a mediated settlement.

We have now seen how, over the last 12 years – and it is only 12 years Rules of Court, which are statutory instruments, give the court the powers to encourage ADR but fall short of entitling the court to direct that the parties actually engage in this. The Rules also expressly impose on the court the duty to have regard to any unreasonable refusal to take part in ADR when considering awards of costs. In his final Report on *Access to Justice* Lord Woolf had gone further and recommended that the court should have regard when awarding costs to unreasonable conduct in the course of ADR. That recommendation was not adopted and, indeed, it would be difficult to reconcile with the confidential nature of the mediation process.

I am now going to turn to see how the English courts have responded to the Woolf Reports and to the powers that they have been given by the new Rules. The first case that I wish to refer to is one in which Lord Woolf was presiding as Master of the Rolls. It is particularly significant because it was not a dispute between two private parties but a public law dispute. The case is *Cowl and others v Plymouth City Council* [2001] All ER (D) 206. The claimants were elderly people (the oldest was 92) who lived in an old people's home run by the Council. The Council had decided to close down their home and they were understandably upset. Some said that Council officials had assured them that they could live out the rest of their days in the home. The claimants sought judicial review to quash the closure decision. The Council made a sensible suggestion under which the claimants' complaints would be dealt with by an informal process before an independent panel, but the claimants insisted on going to court.

There were proceedings that lasted several days at first instance in which psychiatric evidence was called as to the effect that closure might have on some of the claimants. The judge decided that the Council had acted lawfully and expressed the view that it was a pity that that the Council's offer had not been taken up. He observed that the offer was still open. The claimants did not, however, take advantage of it. Instead they had a lengthy and expensive visit to the Court of Appeal, where they got Lord Woolf.

He was characteristically gentle to the claimants, but he made it plain that they had been mistaken in resisting the overtures of the Council to an alternative to litigation. He observed at the outset of his judgment:

"The importance of this appeal is that it illustrates that, even in disputes between public authorities and the members of the public for whom they are responsible, insufficient attention is paid to the paramount importance of avoiding litigation whenever this is possible."

Later on he added:

"Without the need for the vast costs which must have been incurred in this case already, the parties should have been able to come to a sensible conclusion as to how to dispose of the issues that divided them."

In fact, earlier in the year, the Lord Chancellor published a pledge on behalf of all Government Departments and Agencies that ADR would be considered and used in all suitable cases whenever the other party accepted it. The Government regularly publishes figures that purport to show that it is honouring this pledge.

Lord Woolf's judgment in *Cowl* was given in December 2001. Two months later Lord Justice Brooke gave the only judgment of the Court of Appeal dealing with costs in *Dunnett v Railtrack* [2002] 2 All ER 850.

Sir Henry Brooke is a great jurist and I made him my deputy as President of the Civil Division of the Court of Appeal when I was Master of the Rolls. He was and is a great enthusiast for mediation. He retired from the Bench 18 months ago and has since conducted 30 mediations with a 75 to 80 % success rate. His enthusiasm for ADR is apparent from his decision in *Dunnett.* It was a sad case. Mrs Dunnett kept horses in a field that abutted a railway line. Railtrack installed a new gate between her field and the line and she requested them to keep it padlocked. They declined to do so. Strangers left the gate open and three of her horses wandered onto the line and were killed by the Swansea to London express. She sued Railtrack in negligence, claiming both for the value of her horses and for psychiatric injury that she said she had suffered as a result of the accident. She lost at first instance but was given permission to appeal. At that point the Court of Appeal offered a free mediation service. The judge who gave permission to appeal urged the parties to take advantage of this. Mrs Dunnett was prepared to do so but Railtrack turned the suggestion down flat. They offered £2,500 in settlement but Mrs Dunnett turned the offer down. She lost her appeal and Railtrack applied for an order that she pay their costs. They argued that she should have accepted their offer. Lord Justice Brooke was not sympathetic. He refused to award them their costs. He observed:

> "*...this was a case in which, at any rate before the trial, a real effort ought to have been made by way of alternative dispute resolution to see if the matter could be resolved by an experienced mediator, with out the parties having to incur the no doubt heavy legal costs of contesting the matter at trial*".

So far as the appeal was concerned, he held that Railtrack had been wrong to turn down the offer of mediation.

He said:

> "*Mr Lord, when asked by the court why his clients were not willing to contemplate alternative dispute resolution, said that this would be necessarily involve the payment of money, which his clients were not willing to contemplate, over and above what they had already offered. This appears to be a misunderstanding of the purpose of alternative dispute resolution. Skilled mediators are now able to achieve results satisfactory to both parties in many cases which are quite beyond the power of lawyers and courts to achieve. The court has knowledge of cases where intense feelings have arisen, for instance in relation to clinical negligence claims. But when the parties are brought together on neutral soil with a skilled mediator to help them resolve their differences, it may very well be that the mediator is able to achieve a result by which the parties shake hands at the end and feel that they have gone away having settled the dispute on terms with which they are happy to live. A mediator may be able to provide solutions which are beyond the powers of the court to provide. Occasions are known to the court in claims against the police, which can give rise to as much passion as a claim of this kind where a claimant's precious horses are killed on a railway line, by which an apology from a very senior officer is all that the claimant is really seeking and the money side of the matter falls away.*"

He added:

> "*It is to be hoped that any publicity given to this part of the judgment of the court will draw the attention of lawyers to their duties to further the overriding objective in the way that is set out in CPR Pt 1 and to the possibility that, if they turn down out of hand the chance of alternative dispute resolution when suggested by the court, as happened on this occasion, they may have to face uncomfortable costs consequences.*"

Practitioners certainly did take this judgment to heart. They were shocked by a decision that robbed the successful party of costs even though an offer of settlement made by that party had been refused. CEDR (the 'Centre for Effective Dispute Resolution') keeps statistics.

Those statistics showed that mediations increase at the rate of 25% per annum in the two years that followed the decision in *Dunnett.* CEDR say '*post hoc ergo propter hoc*' and I am inclined to think that they are right.

The Courts adopted the approach in *Dunnett* in a number of other cases. In *Leicester Circuits Limited v Coats* [2003] EWCA Civ 333 the parties had actually agreed to mediate and appointed a mediator. The defendants then pulled out of the mediation the day before it was due to take place. Their solicitors had, apparently, insisted that they do so. The claim failed but the Court of Appeal subsequently denied the defendants the costs that they had incurred after pulling out of the mediation. This was on the basis that the mediation might have been successful and saved incurring these costs.

Royal Bank of Canada v Ministry of Defence [2003] EWHC 1479 was a landlord and tenant dispute.

The Ministry of Defence was successful on most of the issues, but had several times refused an offer of mediation. The court ruled that this was contrary to the Government's pledge to make use of ADR and refused to award the Ministry of Defence its costs.

Another enthusiast for mediation is Sir Gavin Lightman, who has recently retired from the Chancery Division. He has been an outspoken critic of the high cost of civil litigation and in *Hurst v*

Leeming [2001] EWHC 1051 he ruled that a number of reasons that were given by the defendant for refusing an offer of mediation were without validity. These included that heavy costs had already been incurred, that the claimant was alleging that the defendant had committed serious professional negligence and that the defendant was confident that he had a watertight defence. He held, however, that it was reasonable to reject the request for mediation because mediation would have been doomed to failure.

The facts of that case were extreme. The claimant was an obsessive litigant who was suing everyone in sight on charges of professional negligence and I do not think that it would have been reasonable to expect anyone to sit down with him at the mediation table. In general, however, it does not seem right to me to entertain an argument that the mediation would not have succeeded as justification for a refusal to mediate. Usually it is impossible to know whether a mediation may succeed until you try it.

These were all cases in which the Court made, or considered making, adverse costs orders against parties who declined to attempt mediation, usually in circumstances where this had been urged by the court. There were, however, a number of early cases in which the court actually directed the parties to mediate. I have referred to the standard Commercial Court order, which comes very close to that.

In one unreported case Mrs Justice Arden, now Lady Justice Arden, sitting in the Chancery Division, directed that a particularly complex web of disputes be referred to mediation, over the objections of some of the parties. Mr Justice Blackburne, also sitting in the Chancery Division, followed her example in making an ADR order in the face of strenuous opposition from the claimant. Whether it was appropriate for the court to act in this way came under review in what has, to date, been by far the most important English judgment about ADR. This is the judgment of the Court of Appeal delivered by Lord Justice Dyson in two appeals that were heard together: *Halsey v Milton Keynes General NHS Trust* and *Steel v Joy and Halliday* [2004] EWCA Civ 576; [2004] 4 All ER 920.

In each case the relevant issue was whether it was right to deprive a successful party of an award of costs on he ground that the party had refused an invitation from the opposing party to take part in alternative dispute resolution. Lord Justice Dyson used the appeals, however, as a vehicle for some general observations on ADR. First he dealt with the question of whether the court had power to order ADR and, if so, whether it was a power that the court should exercise. He said:

> "We heard argument on the question whether the court has power to order parties to submit their disputes to mediation against their will. It is one thing to encourage the parties to agree to mediation, even to encourage them in the strongest terms. It is another to order them to do so. It seems to us that to oblige truly unwilling parties to refer their disputes to mediation would be to impose an unacceptable obstruction on their right of access to the court.
>
> The court in Strasbourg has said in relation to article 6 of the European Convention on Human Rights that the right of access to a court may be waived, for example by means of an arbitration agreement, but such waiver should be subjected to 'particularly careful review' to ensure that the claimant is not subject to 'constraint'. See *Deweer v Belgium* (1980) 2 EHRR 439, para 49. If that is the approach of the ECtHR to an *agreement* to arbitrate, it seems to us likely that *compulsion* of ADR would be regarded as an unacceptable constraint on the right of access to the court and, therefore, a violation of article 6. Even if (contrary to our view) the court does have jurisdiction to order unwilling parties to refer their disputes to mediation, we find it difficult to conceive of circumstances in which it would be appropriate to exercise it.
>
> We would adopt what the editors of Volume 1 of the White Book (2003) say at para 1.4.11:
>
> "*The hallmark of ADR procedures, and perhaps the key to their effectiveness in individual cases, is that they are processes voluntarily entered into by the parties in dispute with outcomes, if the parties so wish, which are non-binding. Consequently the court cannot direct that such methods be used but may merely encourage and facilitate.*"
>
> If the court were to compel parties to enter into a mediation to which they objected, that would achieve nothing except to add to the costs to be borne by the parties, possibly postpone the time when the court determines the dispute and damage the perceived effectiveness of the ADR process. If a judge takes the view that the case is suitable for ADR, then he or she is not, of course, obliged to take at face value the expressed opposition of the parties. In such a case, the judge should explore the reasons for any resistance to ADR.
>
> But if the parties (or at least one of them) remain intransigently opposed to ADR, then it would be wrong for the court to compel them to embrace it.
>
> Parties sometimes need to be encouraged by the court to embark on an ADR. The need for such encouragement should diminish in time if the virtue of ADR in suitable cases is demonstrated even more convincingly than it has been thus far. The value and importance of ADR have been established within a remarkably short

> time. All members of the legal profession who conduct litigation should now routinely consider with their clients whether their disputes are suitable for ADR. But we reiterate that the court's role is to encourage, not compel. The form of encouragement may be robust."

Later in his judgment Lord Justice Dyson commented on the Commercial Court ADR Order.

He commented that this was the strongest form of encouragement but that it stopped short of actually compelling the parties to undertake an ADR.

He then referred to the Order devised by Master Ungley, commenting:

> "*This form of order has the merit that (a) it recognises the importance of encouraging the parties to consider whether the case is suitable for ADR, and (b) it is calculated to bring home to them that, if they refuse even to consider that question, they may be at risk on costs even if they are ultimately held by the court to be the successful party. We can see no reason why such an order should not also routinely be made at least in general personal injury litigation, and perhaps in other litigation too. A party who refuses even to consider whether a case is suitable for ADR is always at risk of an adverse finding at the costs stage of litigation, and particularly so where the court has made an order requiring the parties to consider ADR.*"

These comments were strictly *obiter dicta.*

The same is not true of the comments that Lord Justice Dyson made in relation to the use of adverse costs orders as a sanction for an unreasonable failure to resort to ADR. He said:

> "*In deciding whether to deprive a successful party of some or all of his costs on the grounds that he has refused to agree to ADR, it must be borne in mind that such an order is an exception to the general rule that costs should follow the event. In our view, the burden is on the unsuccessful party to show why there should be a departure from the general rule. The fundamental principle is that such departure is not justified unless it is shown (the burden being on the successful party) that the successful party acted unreasonably in refusing to agree to ADR. We shall endeavour in this judgment to provide some guidance as to the factors that should be considered by the court in deciding whether a refusal to agree to ADR is unreasonable.*"

Lord Justice Dyson identified the following factors as being relevant to whether it was reasonable to refuse an invitation to mediate:

> "*(a) The nature of the dispute. Some disputes are not suitable to mediation – for instance a dispute where the parties want the court to set a binding precedent on a point of law.*
> *(b) The merits of the case. Lord Justice Dyson said that it could be reasonable to refuse mediation where one reasonably believes that one has a strong case. He rejected the view to the contrary expressed by Lightman J in* Hurst.
> *(c) Failure of other settlement methods may make it reasonable to decline ADR.*
> *(d) The cost of ADR may be disproportionately high.*
> *(e) ADR may threaten to involve unacceptable delay.*
> *(f) Lord Justice Dyson agreed with Mr Justice Lightman that it was not unreasonable to refuse mediation if, by reason of the intransigence of the other party, mediation had no prospect of success. He held, however, that the burden was on the party seeking to avoid paying costs to show that mediation would have had a reasonable prospect of success, not on the party refusing mediation to show that mediation would not have had a reasonable prospect of success.*"

Lord Justice Dyson's judgment has been controversial. Those who support ADR say that it has had a dampening effect on the willingness of parties to agree to mediation. They suggest that in some respects, Lord Justice Dyson's analysis was wrong. In his judgment Lord Justice Dyson differed in some respects from the judgment of Mr Justice Lightman in *Hurst.*

Mr Justice Lightman got his own back at a summer reception given by solicitors called SJ Berwin for mediators and mediation users. The reception was enlivened by a jazz and blues band, but I doubt if this was any more lively than the critique Mr Justice Lightman made of Lord Justice Dyson's judgment in a talk entitled 'Mediation: An approximation to justice'.

In that talk Mr Justice Lightman drew attention to the fact that the cost of litigation and the withdrawal of legal aid have left many disadvantaged citizens without realistic access to justice in the courts. He argued that for this mediation was a necessary palliative. It could provide an approximation to justice. But if it was to do so, it required the removal of two obstacles placed in its path by the decision in *Halsey.*

The first was the finding that the court could not require a party to proceed to mediation against his will, because this would defeat his right of access to a court under Article 6 of the European

Convention on Human Rights. The second was the finding that the burden of proving an unreasonable refusal to proceed to mediation lay on the party seeking a costs sanction. Mr Justice Lightman described these findings not merely as unfortunate but, in his opinion as "clearly wrong and unreasonable". As to the first proposition, Mr Justice Lightman said this:

> *"(1) the court appears to have been unfamiliar with the mediation process and to have confused an order for mediation with an order for arbitration or some other order which places a permanent stay on proceedings. An order for mediation does not interfere with the right to a trial: at most it merely imposes a short delay to afford an opportunity for settlement and indeed the order for mediation may not even do that, for the order for mediation may require or allow the parties to proceed with preparation for trial; and (2) the Court of Appeal appears to have been unaware that the practice of ordering parties to proceed to mediation regardless of their wishes is prevalent elsewhere throughout the Commonwealth, the USA and the world at large, and indeed at home in matrimonial property disputes in the Family Division. The Court of Appeal refers to the fact that a party compelled to proceed to mediation may be less likely to agree a settlement than one who willingly proceeds to mediation. But that fact is not to the point.*
> *For it is a fact: (1) that by reason of the nature and impact on the parties of the mediation process parties who enter the mediation process unwillingly often can and do become infected with the conciliatory spirit and settle; and (2) that, whatever the percentage of those who against their will are ordered to give mediation a chance do settle, that percentage must be greater than the number to settle of those not so ordered and who accordingly do not give it a chance."*

Turning to the question of the burden of proof on the issue of whether it was unreasonable not to agree to mediation he said:

> *"The decision as to onus must be guided by consideration of three factors: (1) the importance that those otherwise deprived of access to justice should be given a chance of an approximation to it in this way;*
> *(2) the commonsense proposition that the party who has decided not to proceed to mediation and knows the reasons for his decision should be required to give, explain and justify his decision; and (3) the explicit duty of the court to encourage the use of mediation and the implicit duty to discourage unjustified refusals to do so and this must involve disclosing, explaining and justifying the reasons for the refusal. All these factors point in the opposite direction to that taken by the Court of Appeal."*

Mr Justice Lightman ended with this conclusion:

> *"no thinking person can but be disturbed by the imposition of the twin hurdles to mediation which the decision in Halsey creates to achieving the approximation to justice which the institution of the mediation process may afford".*

This is pretty punchy stuff by way of commentary on the decision of a superior court, but Gavin Lightman is not one to pull his punches. Is his criticism of these parts of *Halsey* well founded?

Let me first deal with the suggestion that Lord Justice Dyson was wrong to express the view that it would infringe Article 6 of the European Convention on Human Rights for the court to order the parties to submit to mediation.

Article 6 provides, in so far as relevant:

> *"In the determination of his civil rights and obligations ... everyone is entitled to a fair and public hearing within a reasonable time by an independent and impartial tribunal established by law. Judgments shall be pronounced publicly... ."*

Lord Justice Dyson referred to the decision of the European Court in the case of *Deweer*.

He did so, however, only as supporting the proposition that any waiver of the Article 6 right to a public trial must be subjected to careful review to ensure that it was not induced by "constraint" – ie that it really was voluntary. Some have attributed considerable significance to this reference to *Deweer*. The authors of the useful ADR Practice Guide, now in its Third Edition, describe it as the leading case on this topic.

So let us see what the European Court had to say. In *Deweer* a Belgian butcher was facing a criminal prosecution for over-charging for pork. The Belgian authorities threatened a provisional closure of his business until the conclusion of the criminal proceedings, which might be for a period of months. Alternatively they offered the butcher what they described as 'a friendly settlement', which involved payment of the relatively modest sum of 10,000 Belgian francs.

Not surprisingly he chose the 'friendly settlement', but he complained to the European Court of Human Rights at Strasbourg that he had been constrained to do so and thus was in reality denied the fair trial to which he was entitled. The Strasbourg Court agreed. It held that while there was nothing wrong in principle with a party waiving his right to either a civil or a criminal trial by entering into an agreed settlement, on the facts of the case the settlement had been procured by constraint, so that it was not voluntary. The consequences of having his business closed down for months were so severe that the butcher had no practical alternative but to agree to pay the 10,000 francs. What in effect had happened was that the state had inflicted a penalty on the butcher without a trial.

The facts of *Deweer* are a long way away from the imposition of a mediation order. That case demonstrates that a coerced agreement that involves waiving the right to trial will infringe Article 6.

Does if follow from *Deweer* that it is contrary to the citizen's right to have his dispute resolved by a court to compel him first to try to reach an agreement by mediation? I think that it depends what you men by 'compel'. This involves considering the sanctions if the litigant does not comply with the court order to attempt mediation. It is of the essence of mediation that the parties are prepared to consider forgoing their strict legal rights. What of the litigant who simply refuses to contemplate this. Who when the court orders him to attempt mediation simply says 'no I won't'. If you commit him to prison for contempt of court then you can truly say that you are compelling him to mediate. What if you say – unless you attempt mediation you cannot continue with your court action. In quite a lot of jurisdictions mediation is ordered by the court on this basis.

I think that if a litigant in Europe was subjected to such an order, refused to comply with it and was consequently refused the right to continue with the litigation, the European Court of Human Rights at Strasbourg might well say that that he had been denied his right to a trial in contravention of Article 6. The European Commission has shown support for mediation, but not compulsory mediation. Whether such a scenario is a very likely is another matter. Experience shows that where a court directs the parties to attempt mediation they usually comply.

Lord Justice Dyson approved of the practice of the English courts of penalising a party in costs for unreasonably refusing to attempt mediation, so he plainly did not consider that the use of a costs sanction was tantamount to compelling a party to litigate.

But Lord Justice Dyson significantly weakened the costs sanction by saying that the burden was on the party seeking costs to show that the other party had *unreasonably* refused to resort to mediation, rather holding that it was on the party refusing mediation to justify his conduct. I think that there is little doubt that this finding significantly reduced the pressure on English litigants to attempt mediation. After all, parties usually resort to litigation because they believe that they are going to win and, if you win, it can be quite difficult for the loser to show that you acted unreasonably on insisting on your full legal rights. At the time that Lord Justice Dyson gave his judgment in *Halsey* I agreed with it, but with hindsight I tend to agree with Gavin Lightman that it is a pity that he said what he did about burden of proof. There is much to be said for the robust attitude that a party who refuses to attempt mediation should have to justify his refusal.

I referred to the support given to mediation by the European Commission. Let me tell you about that. In 2002 the European Commission circulated a Green Paper seeking the views of Member States on ADR in civil and commercial disputes. The answers led the Commission to extol the virtues of mediation and to comment:

> *"The Commission believes that mediation holds an untapped potential as a dispute resolution mechanism and as a means of providing access to justice for individuals and businesses."*

In 2004 the Commission published a draft Directive designed to encourage mediation. The most significant Article of this, Article 3, provides:

> "*1. A court before which an action is brought may, when appropriate and having regard to all the circumstances of the case, invite the parties to use mediation in order to settle the dispute. The court may in any event require the parties to attend an information session on the use of mediation.*
> *2. This directive is without prejudice to national legislation making the use of mediation compulsory or subject to incentives or sanctions, whether before or after judicial proceedings have started, provided that such legislation does not impede on the right of access to the judicial system, in particular in situations where one of the parties is resident in a Member State other than that of the court.*"

That Article does not explain how a court can make mediation compulsory without 'impeding the right of access to the judicial system'. On the face of it this is something of a contradiction in terms.

Whatever European law says, the fact remains that in a number of jurisdictions the courts make orders which, on their face, compel the parties to resort to ADR, and these, as I understand it, include India.

What are the pros and cons of compulsory mediation? Strong views are expressed about this on both sides. Those opposed argue that compulsion is the very antithesis of mediation. The whole point of mediation is that it is voluntary. How can you *compel* parties to indulge in a voluntary activity? 'You can take a horse to water, but you cannot make it drink'. To which those in favour of compulsory mediation reply, 'yes, but if you take a horse to water it usually does drink'. Statistics show that settlement rates in relation to parties who have been compelled to mediate are just about as high as they are in the case of those who resort to mediation of their own volition.

Let me end by nailing my colours firmly to the mast. I number myself with Sir Anthony Colman and Sir Gavin Lightman as an enthusiastic supporter of ADR.

It is madness to incur the considerable expense of litigation – in England usually disproportionate to the amount at stake – without making a determined attempt to reach an amicable settlement. The idea that there is only one just result of every dispute, which only the court can deliver is, I believe, often illusory. Litigation has a cost, not only for the litigants but for society, because judicial resources are limited and their cost is usually born – at least in part – by the state. Parties should be given strong encouragement to attempt mediation before resorting to litigation. And if they commence litigation, there should be built into the process a stage at which the court can require them to attempt mediation – perhaps with the assistance of a mediator supplied by the court.

I believe that we are moving in that direction in England. In family law disputes about property there is now a requirement for the parties to attempt mediation and this has I believe, an 80% success rate.

The government has established a National Mediation Helpline which currently receives 7,800 calls a month. Through this mediation can be arranged for civil law disputes on fixed fees. For those who qualify legal aid is available for this. For this service there is a 15% year on year growth rate planned. At the end of last year there was at Cobham an important meeting sponsored by the Ministry of Justice, the Civil Justice Council and the Civil Mediation Council, in which the Master of the Rolls took part. It was agreed to form a Proportionate Dispute Resolution Team to consider possible reforms of the law and practice of ADR. Suggestions included a Mediation Code, an appropriate practice direction, mediation training for judges and lawyers, the mandatory inclusion of mediation as part of legal professional training and legislation to alter the effect of the decision in *Halsey*.

In this field, as in others, India is ahead of us.

I was aware before this visit of the amendment made to your procedural code by the famous Section 89 and of Chief Justice Sabharwal's support of mediation in *Salem Advocate Bar Association, Tamil Nadu v Union of India* (2003) 1 SCC 49. On this visit I have been learning with admiration of the progress made in instilling a culture of ADR in this jurisdiction. I hope very much that we shall follow where India is leading.

APPENDIX II

ADR GROUP CODE OF PRACTICE FOR SOLICITORS

All ADR Group accredited mediators are lawyers and subscribe to The Law Society's code of practice ('Code of Practice') for civil/commercial mediation (Annex 22A). The Law Society recommends that all solicitors who offer ADR services (including mediation) comply with a code of practice.

1. Objectives of Civil/Commercial Mediation
   Civil commercial mediation is a process in which:
   1.1 two or more parties in dispute
   1.2 whether or not they are legally represented
   1.3 and at any time, whether or not there are or have been legal proceedings
   1.4 agree to the appointment of a neutral third party (the mediator)
   1.5 who is impartial
   1.6 who has no authority to make any decisions with regard to their issues
   1.7 which may relate to all or any part of a dispute of a civil or commercial nature
   1.8 but who helps them reach their own decisions
   1.9 by negotiation
   1.10 without adjudication.

2. Qualifications and Appointment of mediator
   2.1 Every mediator must comply with the criteria and requirements for mediators stipulated from time to time by the Law Society, including those relating to training, consultancy, accreditation and regulation.
   2.2 Save where appointed by or through the court, a mediator may only accept appointment if both or all the parties to the mediation so request, or agree.
   2.3 Whether a mediator is appointed by the parties or through the court or through any other agency, he or she may only continue to act as such so long as both or all parties to the mediation wish him or her to do so. If any party does not wish to continue with the mediation, the mediator must discontinue the process as regards that party and may discontinue the process as regards all parties. Also, if the mediator considers that it would be inappropriate to continue the mediation, the mediator shall bring it to an end, and may, subject to the terms of the mediation agreement, decline to give reasons.

3. Conflicts of interest, confidential information and the impartiality of the mediator
   3.1 The impartiality of mediator is a fundamental principle of mediation.
   3.2 Impartiality means that:
      3.2.1 the mediator does not have any significant personal interest in the outcome of the mediation;
      3.2.2 the mediator will conduct the process fairly and even-handedly, and will not favour any party over another
   3.3 Save as set out in 3.2 above, a mediator with an insignificant interest in the personal outcome of the mediation may act if, full disclosure is made to all of the parties as soon as it is known, and they consent.
   3.4 The mediator must not act, or, having started to do so, continue to act:
      3.4.1 in relation to issues on which he or she or a member of his firm has any act for any party;
      3.4.2 if any of the circumstances exist which may constitute an actual or potential conflict of interest

3.4.3 if the mediator or a member of his or her firm has acted for any of the parties in issues not relating to the mediation, unless that has been disclosed to the parties as soon as it is known and they consent.

3.5 Where a mediator has acted as such in relation to a dispute, neither he or she nor any member of his or her firm may subsequently for any party in relation to the subject matter of the mediation.

4. Mediation Procedures

4.1 The mediator must ensure that the parties agree the terms and conditions regulating the mediation before dealing with the substantive issues. This should be in written agreement which should reflect the main principles of this code. Such agreement should also contain the remuneration of the mediator.

4.2 The procedure for the conduct of the mediation is a matter for the decision of the mediator. Insofar as the mediator establishes an agenda of matters to be covered in the mediation, the mediator shall be guided by the needs, wishes and priorities of the parties in doing so.

4.3 In establishing any procedures for the conduct of the mediation, the mediator must be guided by a commitment to procedural fairness and a high quality of process.

5. The decision making process

5.1 The primary aim of the mediation is to help the parties to arrive at their own decisions regarding the disputed issues.

5.2 The parties should be helped to reach such resolution of such issues which they feel are appropriate to their particular circumstances. Such resolution may not necessarily be the same as that which may be arrived at in the event of adjudication by the court. That allows the parties to explore and agree upon a wider range of options for settlement that might otherwise be the case.

5.3 The mediator may meet the parties individually and/or together. Solicitors, barristers or other professional advisers acting for the individual parties may, but need not necessarily, participate in the mediation process if the parties so wish. Such solicitors and/or advisers may take part in discussions and meetings, with or without the parties, and in other communication and representation, in such manner as the mediator may consider useful and appropriate.

5.4 Parties are free to consult with the individual professional advisers as the mediation progresses. The mediator may make suggestions to the parties as to the appropriateness of seeking further assistance from professional advisers such as lawyers, accountants, expert valuers or others.

5.5 The mediator must not seek to impose his or her preferred outcome on the parties.

5.6 The mediator shall be free to make management decisions with regard to the conduct of the mediation process.

5.7 The mediator may suggest possible solutions and help the parties to explore these, where he or she thinks this would be helpful to them.

5.8 The mediator must recognise that the parties can reach decisions on any issues at any stage of the mediation.

5.9 Agreements reached in mediation fall into three categories:

5.9.1 non-binding agreement

5.9.2 binding agreements (which would be enforceable by a court)

5.9.3 binding agreements enshrined in a court or arbitration order

The mediator should ascertain how the parties wish their agreement to be treated. Where the parties do not wish to have a legally binding solution (for example where they have resolved personal rather than legal issues), their wishes should be respected.

5.10 At the end of the mediation or at any interim stage, the mediator and/or the parties or their representatives may prepare a written memorandum or summary or any agreements reached by the parties, which may, where considered by the mediator to be appropriate, compromise draft heads of such agreements for formalisation by the legal advisers acting for the parties.

5.11 If the parties wish to consult their respective individual legal advisers before entering into any binding agreement, then any terms which they may provisionally propose as the basis for resolution will not be binding on them until they have each had the opportunity of taking advise form such legal advisers and have thereafter agreed, in writing, to be bound.

5.12 Mediation does not provide for the disclosure and inspection of documents in the same way or to the same extent as required by court rules. The parties may voluntarily agree to provide such documentation, or any lesser form of disclosure considered by them to be sufficient. This should be considered in advance of the mediation. The mediator may indicate any particular documents that he or she considers should be bought to the mediation.

5.13 The mediator may assist the parties, so far as appropriate and practicable, to identify what information and documents will help the resolution of any issue(s), and how best such information and documents should be obtained. However, the mediator has no obligation to make independent enquiries or undertake verification in relation to any information or documents sought or provided in the mediation.

5.14 If, in cases where one or more parties is unrepresented at the mediation and the parties are proposing a resolution which appears to the mediator to be unconscionable, having regard to the circumstances, then the mediator must inform the parties accordingly and may terminate the mediation and/or refer the parties to their legal advisers.

6. Dealing with power imbalances

6.1 The mediator should be alive to power imbalances existing between the parties. If the such imbalances seem likely to cause the mediation process to become unfair or ineffective, the mediator must take reasonable steps to try to prevent this.

6.2 The mediator must seek, in particular, to prevent abusive or intimidating behaviour by any of the parties.

6.3 If the mediator believes that, because of power imbalances, the mediation would not be able to be fairly and effectively conducted, he or she may discuss this with the parties, recognising that the mediation may have been bought to any end and/or the parties referred to their lawyers.

7. Confidentiality and privilege

7.1 Before the mediation commences, the parties should agree in writing as to the provisions concerning confidentiality and privilege that will apply to the mediation process itself and any resultant mediation agreement, save as otherwise agreed in the mediation settlement agreement.

7.2 The mediator must maintain confidentiality in relation to all matters dealt with in the mediation. The mediator may disclose:

7.2.1 matter which the parties and the mediator agree may be disclosed;

7.2.2 matters which are already public;

7.2.3 matter which the mediator considers appropriate where he or she believes that if the life or safety of any person is or may be at serious risk;

7.2.4 matters where the law imposes an overriding obligation of disclosure on the mediator.

7.2.5 Subject to paragraph 7.2 above, where the mediator meets the parties separately and obtains information from any party which is confidential to that party, the mediator must maintain the confidentiality of that information from all other parties, except to the extent that the mediator has be authorised to disclose any such information.

7.3 Mediators should note that the mediation privilege will not ordinarily apply in relation to communications indicating that a person is suffering or likely to suffer serious bodily harm, or where other public policy considerations prevail, or where for any other reason, the rules of evidence render privilege inapplicable.

7.4 The mediator should remind the parties that (unless the mediation agreement provides otherwise) the confidentiality and privilege attaching to the mediation process may not extend to the provisions of any settlement agreement which results. The mediator should suggest to the parties that they consider the extent to which they wish the terms of the resulting settlement to be discloseable – and to provide accordingly in the agreement itself.

8. Professional indemnity cover

8.1 All solicitor mediators must carry professional indemnity cover in respect of their acting as mediators.

8.1.1 Solicitors who practise as mediators will be covered by the Solicitor's Indemnity Fund in respect of their acting as a mediator, provided they are doing so in their capacity as a member of their firm.

8.1.2 If a solicitor is acting as a mediator as a separate activity outside his or her legal practise, separate indemnity insurance must be obtained.

9. Promotion of mediation

9.1 Solicitor mediators may promote their practice as such, but must always do so in a professional, truthful and dignified way. They may reflect their qualification as a mediator and their membership of any other relevant mediation organisation.

9.2 Solicitor mediators must comply with the Solicitors' Publicity Code 1990.

APPENDIX III

CEDR CODE OF CONDUCT

April 2008
CODE OF CONDUCT FOR THIRD PARTY NEUTRALS

1 Introduction
This Code of Conduct ("the Code") applies to any person who acts as a Mediator or other neutral third party ("the Neutral") in any dispute resolution procedure ("the Process") conducted under the auspices of the Centre for Effective Dispute Resolution ("CEDR Solve") in relation to an attempt to resolve a dispute or difference ("the Dispute") between all the parties ("the Parties") to the Dispute under the terms of a written agreement signed by the Parties the Neutral and CEDR Solve ("the Process Agreement") to seek resolution of the Dispute.

2 Competence and availability
The Neutral assures the Parties that he or she:
2.1 possesses the necessary competence and knowledge about the Process to deal with the Dispute, based on proper training and updating of education and practice in the necessary skills; and
2.2 has sufficient time to prepare properly for and conduct the Process expeditiously and efficiently.

3 Fees and expenses
The Neutral undertakes:
3.1 to make clear either directly to the Parties or through CEDR Solve the basis for charging fees and expenses as between CEDR Solve and the Parties for the conduct of the Process before the Process starts; and
3.2 not to prolong the Process unnecessarily where there is, in the Neutral's opinion, no reasonable likelihood of progress being made towards settlement of the Dispute through the Process.

4 Independence and neutrality
The Neutral:
4.1 will at all times act, and endeavour to be seen to act fairly, independently and with complete impartiality towards the Parties in the Process, without any bias in favour of, or discrimination against, any of the Parties;
4.2 will ensure that the Parties and their representatives all have adequate opportunities to be involved in the Process;
4.3 will disclose to the Parties any matter of which the Neutral is or at any time becomes aware which could be regarded as being or creating a conflict of interest (whether apparent, potential or real) in relation to the Dispute or any of the Parties involved in the Process, and, having done so, will not act or continue to act as Neutral in relation to the Dispute unless the Parties specifically acknowledge such disclosure and agree to the Neutral's continuing to act in the Process: such matters include but are not limited to:
- any personal or business relationship with any of the Parties;
- any financial or other interest in the outcome of the Mediation;
- having acted (either personally or through the Neutral's own firm or business) in any capacity other than as a Neutral in another Process for any of the Parties;
- being in prior possession of any confidential information about any of the Parties or about the subject-matter of the Dispute (but excluding any confidential information given to the Neutral by one of the Parties while acting as Neutral in relation to the Dispute);

- any such matters involving a close member of the Neutral's family.

4.4 will not (nor will any member of the Neutral's own firm or business or close family) act for any of the Parties individually in relation to the Dispute either while acting as Neutral or at any time thereafter, without the written consent of all the Parties.

5 Conduct of the Process
The Neutral will observe all the terms of the Process Agreement (especially as regards confidentiality) and will conduct the Process consistent with any relevant CEDR Model Procedure.

6 Professional Indemnity Insurance
The Neutral will take out professional indemnity insurance in an adequate amount with a responsible insurer against such risks as may arise in the performance of the Neutral's duties in relation to the Dispute before acting as a Neutral.

7 Withdrawing from any Process
7.1 The Neutral will withdraw from the Process and cease to act as such in relation to the Dispute if the Neutral:

- is requested to do so by one of the Parties, except where the Parties have agreed to a procedure involving a binding decision by the Neutral to conclude the Mediation;
- would be in breach of the Code if continuing to act as the Neutral; or
- is required by one or more of the Parties to act or refrain from acting in a way which would be in material breach of the Code or in breach of the law.

7.2 The Neutral may withdraw from the Process at the Neutral's own discretion and after such consultation with the Parties as the Neutral deems necessary and appropriate (and always subject to the Neutral's obligations as to confidentiality) if:

- any of the Parties is acting in material breach of the Process Agreement;
- any of the Parties is acting in an unconscionable or criminal manner;
- the Neutral decides that continuing the Process is unlikely to result in a settlement;
- any of the Parties alleges that the Neutral is in material breach of the Code.

8 Complaints
The Neutral will respond to, and co-operate with, any complaints procedure initiated by a party through CEDR Solve in relation to the Process in which the Neutral acted, including attending (without charging a fee or claiming any expenses for attending) any meeting convened by CEDR Solve as part of that complaints procedure.

APPENDIX IV

THE EUROPEAN UNION AND ALTERNATIVE DISPUTE RESOLUTION

In April 2002, the European Commission published a discussion paper on alternative dispute resolution. In July 2004 the Commission organised the launch of a Code of Conduct for Mediators which was approved and adopted by a large number of Mediation experts and in October 2004 the Commission adopted and submitted to the European Parliament and the Council a proposal for a Directive on certain aspects of mediation in civil and commercial matters. The Directive was adopted on 21 May 2008.

The Green Paper, the Code of Conduct and the Directive on mediation all form part of the European Community's current work on establishing an area of freedom, security and justice, and particularly on improving access to justice. It is the Commission's view that encouraging the use of Mediation and other forms of ADR assists in the resolution of disputes and helps to avoid the worry, time and cost associated with court-based litigation and so assists citizens in a real way to secure their legal rights.

Following on from the Vienna Action Plan in 1998 and the Conclusions of the Tampere European Council in 1999, the Council of Justice and Home Affairs Ministers called on the Commission to present a Green Paper on alternative dispute resolution in civil and commercial law other than arbitration, taking stock of the current situation and launching broad consultations on the measures to be taken. Priority was given to the possibility of laying down basic principles, either in general or in specific fields, which would offer the requisite guarantees that out-of-court dispute resolution will ensure the proper degree of security in the administration of justice.

In its Green Paper the Commission recalled that the development of these forms of dispute settlement was not to be regarded as a means of remedying deficiencies in the operation of the courts but as an alternative, more consensus-based form of social peace-keeping and conflict and dispute resolution which in many cases would be more appropriate than the resolution of disputes by a third party as through the courts or by arbitration.

Alternative dispute resolution techniques such as mediation allow the parties to resume dialogue and come to a real solution to their dispute through negotiation instead of getting locked into a logic of conflict and confrontation with a winner and a loser at the end. The importance of this is highly obvious, for instance, in family disputes, but it is potentially very valuable in many other types of dispute.

It is used increasingly in complex commercial disputes where the parties, whilst wishing to resolve a conflict, also wish to retain as far as possible a continuing commercial relationship. It is becoming increasingly common in disputes arising out of medical accidents where Mediation can lead to the adoption of an innovative resolution of what are often very sensitive conflicts and provide creative remedies which may be beyond the powers of the courts.

The Green Paper also provided a host of information and considered a wide range of questions, thereby setting out to familiarise the largest possible number of people with these alternative, often new, forms of dispute settlement. It was directed in particular towards litigants, the judiciary and the legal profession.

The main purpose of the Green Paper was to come up with answers to the delicate question of the balance to be achieved between the need for flexibility and the need to guarantee quality of results, and the harmonious relationship with court procedures. It also highlighted the existing achievements and initiatives in this area both in the Member States and in the Community.

Lastly, by publishing this Green Paper, the Commission contributed to the continuing debates in the Member States and internationally on the best way of ensuring that the best possible environment was available for the development of alternative dispute resolution.

The 21 questions put in the Green Paper concerned the decisive elements of the different forms of alternative dispute resolution, such as clauses providing agreements to go to ADR, the problem of periods of prescription and limitation, the need for confidentiality, the validity of consent, the effect of resulting agreements particularly for enforcement, training for mediators and other third parties, their accreditation and the rules governing their liability.

The Code of Conduct
The Code of Conduct sets out a series of norms which can be applied to the practice of Mediation and which can be adhered to by Mediation organisations. It was elaborated in co-operation with a large number of organisations and individuals among whom are skilled practitioners of Mediation and others who are interested in seeing Mediation develop in the European Union. The Code was adopted by a meeting involving these experts in July 2004 and the Commission was very pleased to be involved in and to have the opportunity to assist this process.

The Directive on Mediation
The Directive seeks to further the use of Mediation by making certain legal rules available within the legal systems of the Member States. These rules cover the areas of confidentiality of the mediation process and of mediators as witnesses, enforcement of agreements for settling disputes as a result of mediation, the suspension of the running of periods of prescription and limitation of actions while mediation is in progress thus removing one potential disincentive to the use of mediation. The Directive also encourages the training of mediators and the adoption of codes of conduct to ensure the quality of mediation throughout the European Union.

The Green Paper also made reference to a number of existing achievements
Alternative dispute resolution has already been recommended, directly or indirectly, in a number of Community instruments and proposals. Many of these encourage the Member States are recommended to introduce, or at least to promote the introduction and operation of ADR.

A few examples are shown here:

The Commission is interested in the financial aspects of ADR in general. Following a Commission proposal, on 27 January 2003 the Council adopted a Directive on legal aid, which provides for legal aid to be available for extra-judicial proceedings in certain circumstances, to help less well-off people enjoy access to alternative dispute resolution.

As regards family relationships, the Commission has endeavoured to promote alternative dispute resolution in the Regulation (EC) 2201/2003 of 27 November 2003 concerning jurisdiction and the recognition and enforcement of judgments in matrimonial matters and in matters of parental responsibility.

Regarding consumer disputes in e-commerce, the role of alternative dispute resolution is stressed both in Directive 2000/31/EC on electronic commerce and in a Joint Declaration by the Council and the Commission made when the "Brussels I" Regulation on jurisdiction and the recognition and enforcement of judgments in civil and commercial matters was adopted.

Directive 98/10/EC on the application of open network provision (ONP) to voice telephony and on universal service for telecommunications in a competitive environment provides that "easily accessible and in principle inexpensive procedures shall be available at a national level to resolve such disputes in a fair, transparent and timely manner" in the Member States.

Directive 2002/21/EC (Framework Directive) on a common regulatory framework for electronic communications networks and services provides for non-judicial structures to settle disputes between professionals.

In some areas the Commission has gone further than simply encouraging the establishment of alternative dispute resolution. It has sought to promote the quality and effectiveness of alternative dispute resolution in consumer disputes.

The quality of alternative dispute resolution
Care is taken in the C ommunity to distinguish two major categories of alternative dispute resolution available to help consumers settle their disputes with tradespeople:

Processes in which third parties help the parties come to an agreement without actually formally expressing an opinion on the different possible solutions to the dispute.

The Commission has taken an initiative to ensure that non-judicial consumer dispute settlement procedures respect a certain number of principles. On 4 April 2001 it published a Recommendation concerning procedures in which the third party does not express an opinion on the solution but simply helps the parties find the solution that suits them best. The Recommendation sets out four principles: impartiality, transparency, effectiveness and fairness.

Procedures in which the third party finds the solution and puts it to the parties:

The Commission has taken an initiative to ensure that these procedures respect a certain number of principles.

On 30 March 1998, it published a Recommendation concerning procedures in which the third party actually settles the dispute between the parties in a manner which may or may not be binding on them. This Recommendation also covers arbitration in consumer disputes. It contains seven basic principles: independence, transparency, the adversarial principle, effectiveness, legality, liberty and representation. Member States are asked to produce an inventory of bodies responsible for the out-of-court resolution of consumer disputes that they regard as compliant with the Commission Recommendation. The Commission has been notified of the national lists, which can be consulted on the website of the Directorate-General for Health and Consumer Protection (DG SANCO).

The effectiveness of alternative dispute resolution

The Commission is behind the establishment of two European networks of judicial bodies sharing the objective of facilitating consumer access to non-judicial procedures for the settlement of cross-border disputes in cases where the tradesperson is established in a Member State other than the one where the consumer resides. They pursue the same objective but work in different ways:

The European extra-judicial network "ECC- Net" is a structure to provide assistance and information for consumers, consisting of national contact points in each Member State and in Norway and Iceland. Each of the contact points acts as an information relay for the 400 bodies regarded by the Member States as meeting the demands of the two Commission Recommendations concerning the principles applicable to bodies responsible for the out-of-court settlement of consumer disputes.

The out-of-court complaints network for financial services "FIN-NET" links thirty or so national bodies responsible for the out-of-court resolution of disputes falling under the first Commission Recommendation. FIN-NET offers consumers facing a problem relating to financial services (banking, insurance, investments) direct access to an out-of-court dispute resolution facility.

SOLVIT is an on-line problem solving network in which EU Member States work together to solve without legal proceedings cross-border problems caused by the misapplication of Internal Market law by public authorities. Using SOLVIT is free of charge.

Encouragement for practical initiatives

In parallel with all this quasi-legislative activity, the European Union provides financial support for certain initiatives, in particular in the on-line settlement of consumer disputes. The Commission was financially involved in the launching of ECODIR (Electronic COnsumer DIspute Resolution Platform), an electronic dispute resolution platform.

Reference documents

Directive 2008/52/EC on certain aspects of mediation in civil and commercial matters

Green Paper on alternative dispute resolution in civil and commercial law

Council Directive 2002/8/EC of 27 January 2003 to improve access to justice in cross-border disputes by establishing minimum common rules relating to legal aid and other financial aspects of civil proceedings

Council Regulation (EC) 2201/203 of 27 November 2003 concerning jurisdiction and the recognition and enforcement of judgments in matrimonial matters and in matters of parental responsibility repealing Regulation (EC) No 1347/2000

Joint Declaration by the Council and the Commission on jurisdiction and the recognition and enforcement of judgments in civil and commercial matters

Commission Recommendation of 4 April 2001 on the principles for out-of-court bodies involved in the consensual resolution of consumer disputes

Commission Recommendation of 30 March 1998 on the principles applicable to the bodies responsible for out-of-court settlement of consumer disputes

APPENDIX V

CPR INSTITUTE FOR DISPUTE RESOLUTION: MODEL MEDIATION AGREEMENT: EUROPE

Agreement made ____________________, 19__
Between ________ A Company ____
represented by ____
and ___________ B Company________________________________
[and ________ C Company represented by ____________________]
represented by ____
and
(the Mediator) ____
(the Trainee) ____

A dispute has arisen between the parties (the "Dispute") [sentence(s) describing Dispute]. The parties have agreed to participate in a mediation proceeding (the "Proceeding") under the [CPR Model Procedure for Mediation of Business Disputes in Europe], [as modified by mutual agreement] (the "Procedure"). The parties have chosen the Mediator for the Proceeding. The parties and the Mediator agree as follows:

A. Duties and Obligations
1. The Mediator and [the Trainee] and each of the parties agree to be bound by and to comply faithfully with the Procedure, including without limitation the provisions regarding confidentiality.
2. The Mediator and [the Trainee] have no previous commitments that may significantly delay the expeditious conduct of the proceeding and will not make any such commitments.
3. The Mediator and [the Trainee], the CPR Institute for Dispute Resolution ("CPR") and their employees, agents and partners shall not be liable for any act or omission in connection with the Proceeding, other than as a result of its/his/her own willful misconduct or gross negligence. Neither party shall seek to require the mediator to give evidence in any subsequent litigation about the dispute except in the case of an allegation of misconduct during the mediation proceedings.

B. Disclosure of Prior Relationships
1. The Mediator [and the Trainee] have made a reasonable effort to learn and has/have disclosed to the parties in writing (a) all business or professional relationships the Mediator's and/or the Trainee's firm has/have had with the parties or their lawyers within the past five years, including all instances in which the Mediator [or the Trainee] or the Mediator's [or the Trainee's firm] served as a lawyer for any party or adverse to any party; (b) any financial interest the Mediator [and the Trainee] has in any party; (c) any significant social, business or professional relationship the Mediator [or the Trainee] has/have had with an officer or employee of a party or with an individual representing a party in the Proceeding; and (d) any other circumstances that may create doubt regarding the Mediator's [and the Trainee's] impartiality in the Proceeding.
2. Each party and its lawyer has made a reasonable effort to learn and has disclosed to every other party and the Mediator [and the Trainee] in writing any relationships of a nature described in paragraph B.1. not previously identified and disclosed by the Mediator [and the Trainee].
3. The parties and the Mediator [and the Trainee] are satisfied that any relationships disclosed pursuant to paragraphs B.1. and B.2. will not affect the Mediator's [or the Trainee] independence or impartiality. Notwithstanding such relationships or others which the Mediator [and the

Trainee] and the parties did not discover despite good faith efforts, the parties wish the Mediator [and the Trainee] to serve in the Proceeding, waiving any claim based on said relationships, and the Mediator [and the Trainee] agrees to so serve.

4. The disclosure obligations in paragraphs B.1. and B.2. are continuing until the Proceeding is concluded. The ability of the Mediator [and the Trainee] to continue serving in this capacity shall be explored with each such disclosure.

C. Future Relationships

1. The Mediator, [the Trainee,] the Mediator's firm [and the Trainee's firm] shall not undertake any work for or against a party regarding the Dispute, and pending the mediation proceedings, any other matter.
2. Neither the Mediator [or the Trainee] nor any person assisting the Mediator [or the Trainee] with this Proceeding shall personally work on any matter for or against a party, regardless of specific subject matter, prior to [six] months following cessation of the Mediator's [and the Trainee's] services in the Proceeding without the consent of both (all) parties.

D. Remuneration

The Mediator shall be remunerated for time expended in connection with the Proceeding at the rate of ___________, plus reasonable travel and other out-of pocket expenses. The Mediator's fee shall be shared equally by the parties. No part of such fee shall accrue to CPR. No fee is payable to the Trainee.

E. Governing Law and Jurisdiction

This agreement is governed by appropriate law and shall be subject to the [non exclusive] jurisdiction of the appropriate country's courts.

____
Party
by ___________________________
Party's Lawyer

____
Party
by ___________________________
Party's Lawyer

____
by Mediator

____
Trainee

APPENDIX VI

CPR INSTITUTE FOR DISPUTE RESOLUTION: MODEL MEDIATION PROCEDURE FOR BUSINESS DISPUTES IN EUROPE

1. Proposing Mediation

Mediation can be used in disputes including those where numerous parties are involved. Any party to a business dispute may propose the use of mediation to the other party or parties. If the parties have made a contractual commitment to mediate disputes between them, or if they have subscribed to another commitment to engage in alternative dispute resolutions (ADR), that commitment or policy may be invoked. Sometimes a neutral organisation may help persuade a party to engage in mediation. CPR may be requested to play that role.

2. Selecting the Mediator

Unless the parties promptly, as part of their agreement to mediate, agree on a mediator, they will notify CPR of their need for assistance in selecting a mediator, informing CPR of any preferences as to matters such as candidates' mediation style, technical and/or legal expertise, competence in certain languages or geographic location. In international disputes, CPR will endeavour to appoint a mediator from a country other than that of either of the parties, unless the parties agree otherwise.

CPR will convene the parties, in person or by telephone, to attempt to select a mediator by agreement. If the parties do not promptly reach agreement, CPR will submit to the parties the names of not less than three candidates, with their resumes and hourly rates. If the parties are unable to agree on a candidate from the list within seven days following receipt of the list, each party will, within 10 days following receipt of the list, send to CPR the list of candidates ranked in descending order of preference. The candidate with the lowest combined score will be appointed as the mediator by CPR. CPR will break any tie.

Before proposing any mediator candidate, CPR will request the candidate to disclose any circumstances known to him or her that would cause reasonable doubt regarding the candidate's impartiality. If a clear conflict is disclosed, the individual will not be proposed and CPR will promptly propose another candidate. Other circumstances a candidate discloses to CPR will be disclosed to the parties. A party may challenge a mediator candidate if it knows of any circumstances giving rise to reasonable doubt regarding the candidate's impartiality.

The mediator's fees will be determined before appointment. Those fees, and any other costs of the process, will be shared equally by the parties unless they otherwise agree. If a party withdraws from a multiparty mediation but the procedure continues, the withdrawing party will not be responsible for any costs incurred after it has notified the mediator and the other parties of its withdrawal. Shared costs will not include costs that each party incurs in preparing its own case, attending meetings and instructing representatives. The parties will bear these costs themselves.

Before appointment, the mediator will assure the parties of his or her availability to conduct the proceeding expeditiously. It is strongly advised that the parties and the mediator enter into a mediation agreement. A model agreement is attached.

3. Ground Rules of Proceeding

The following ground rules will apply, subject to any changes on which the parties and the mediator agree.

- *3.1* The process is voluntary and depends on the co-operation of the parties. The mediator does not issue a binding decision.
- *3.2* Each party may withdraw at any time by written notice to the mediator and the other party or parties.
- *3.3* The mediator is neutral, independent and impartial.
- *3.4* The mediator controls the procedural aspects of the mediation. The parties cooperate fully with the mediator.

(a) The mediator is free to meet and communicate separately with each party.
(b) The mediator decides when to hold joint meetings with the parties and when to hold separate meetings. The mediator fixes the time and place of each session and its agenda in consultation with the parties. There is no formal written, audio or video record of any meeting. Formal rules of evidence or procedure do not apply.
(c) Unless otherwise agreed by the parties, the mediator decides, if necessary, the language in which the mediation is to be conducted and whether any documents should be translated.

3.5 Each party is represented at each mediation conference by a business executive authorized to negotiate a resolution of the dispute and to execute a settlement agreement. Each party may be represented by more than one person, e.g. a business executive and a lawyer. The mediator may limit the number of persons representing each party.

3.6 The process is to be conducted expeditiously. Each representative undertakes to make every effort to be available for meetings.

3.7 The mediator does not transmit information received in confidence from any party to any other party or any third party, unless authorised to do so by the party transmitting the information, or unless ordered to do so by a court of competent jurisdiction.

3.8 The mediator and any persons assisting the mediator is disqualified as a witness, consultant or expert in any pending or future investigation, action or proceeding relating to the subject matter of the mediation (including any investigation, action or proceeding which involves persons not party to this mediation).

3.9 If the dispute goes into arbitration, the mediator will not serve as an arbitrator.

3.10 The mediator may obtain assistance and independent expert advice, with the prior agreement of and at the expense of the parties. Any candidate proposed as an independent expert will also be required to disclose any circumstances known to him or her that would cause reasonable doubt regarding the candidate's impartiality.

3.11 Neither CPR nor the mediator is liable for any act or omission in connection with the mediation, except for its/his/her own wilful misconduct or gross negligence.

3.12 The mediator may withdraw at any time by written notice to the parties. Either party may seek assistance from CPR in such a situation.

3.13 At the inception of the mediation process, each party and representative agrees in writing to all provisions of this Model Procedure, as modified by agreement of the parties. A model mediation agreement is attached.

3.14 With the approval of the parties, the mediator may sit with a trainee mediator, who may observe the process, but takes no active part in it and charges no fee. The trainee will be bound by the same obligations of confidentiality as the mediator.

4. *Exchange of Information*

Each party shall produce the documents it relies on in the mediation and may, but shall not be obliged to, produce any further documents requested by the mediator or the other party.

At the conclusion of the mediation process, upon the request of a party which provided documents or other material to one or more other parties, the recipients undertake to return them to the originating party without retaining copies thereof. All documents and other information provided to a party, in the course of a mediation, shall be used by that party exclusively for the purposes of the mediation.

5. *Presentation to the Mediator*

Before dealing with the substance of the dispute, the parties and the mediator discuss preliminary matters, such as possible modification of the ground rules, place and time of meetings, and each party's need for documents or other information in the possession of the other.

At least five business days before the first substantive mediation conference, unless otherwise agreed, each party submits to the mediator a written statement summarising the background and present status of the dispute and such other material and information as it deems helpful to familiarise the mediator with the dispute. The parties may agree to submit jointly certain other materials. The mediator may request any party to provide clarification and additional information. The mediator may limit the length of written statements and supporting material. The mediator may direct the parties to exchange concise written statements and other materials they submit to the mediator to further each party's understanding of the other party's viewpoints. Except as the parties otherwise agree, the mediator keeps confidential any written materials or information that are submitted to him or her. The parties and their representatives are not entitled to receive or review any materials or information submitted to the mediator by another party or representative without the concurrence of the latter. At the conclusion of the mediation process, upon request of a party, the mediator without retaining copies returns to that party all written materials and information which that party had provided to the mediator.

6. *Negotiation of Terms*
The mediator may promote settlement in any manner the mediator believes is appropriate. The mediator helps the parties focus on their underlying interests and concerns, explore resolution alternatives and develop settlement options. The mediator decides when to hold joint meetings, and when to confer separately with each party.
The mediator expects the parties to make settlement proposals.
Finally, if the parties fail to develop mutually acceptable settlement terms, before terminating the procedure, and only with the consent of the parties, (a) the mediator may submit to the parties a final settlement proposal which the mediator considers fair and equitable to all parties; and (b) if the mediator believes he/she is qualified to do so, the mediator may give the parties an evaluation (which if the parties choose will be in writing) of the likely outcome of the case if it were tried to final judgment. Thereupon, the mediator may suggest further discussions to explore whether the mediator's evaluation or proposal may lead to a resolution.
Efforts to reach a settlement continue until (a) a written settlement is reached, or (b) the mediator concludes and informs the parties that further efforts would not be useful, or (c) one of the parties or the mediator withdraws from the process. However, if there are more than two parties, the remaining parties may elect to continue following the withdrawal of a party.

7. *Settlement*
If a settlement is reached, the representatives of the parties draft a written settlement document incorporating all settlement terms, which may include mutual general releases from or discharges of all liability relating to the subject matter of the dispute. This draft will be circulated among the parties and the mediator, amended as necessary, and formally executed. Initially, a preliminary memorandum of understanding may be prepared at the mediation and executed by the parties; the memorandum should make it expressly clear whether it is intended to be binding or not.
If litigation is pending, the settlement may provide that the parties will request the court to make an appropriate order disposing of the case promptly upon execution of the settlement agreement. The settlement agreement may also be entered as a consent judgment.

8. *Failure to Agree*
If a resolution is not reached, the mediator discusses with the parties the possibility of their agreeing on arbitration or another form of ADR. If the parties agree in principle, the mediator may offer to assist them in structuring a procedure designed to result in a prompt, economical process.

9. *Confidentiality*
For, Austrian, Belgian, Dutch, English, French, German, Italian, Scottish, Spanish, Swedish and Swiss mediations: The parties agree that the mediation process, and all negotiations, statements and documents expressly prepared for the purposes of the mediation shall be 'without prejudice'. The entire mediation process is confidential. Unless agreed among all the parties or required by law or ordered by the Court, the parties and the mediator may not disclose to any person any information regarding the process (including pre-process exchanges and agreements), contents (including written and oral information), settlement terms or outcome of the proceeding. If litigation is pending, the participants may, however, inform the court of the schedule and overall status of the mediation for purposes of litigation management.

APPENDIX VII

ADR GROUP MEDIATION PROCEDURE

ADR Group mediations shall be governed by the following procedure ('the Mediation Procedure'), as amended by ADR Group from time to time) and the parties shall be taken to have agreed that the mediation shall be conducted in accordance with the Mediation Procedure.

1. Mediation Procedure
   - 1.1 The parties to a dispute or negotiation in question will attempt to settle it by mediation. Representatives of the parties including their advisers (legal representatives) and the mediator will attend the mediation sessions. Any and all communications relating to, and at, the mediation are private & confidential and will be without prejudice.
   - 1.2 The representatives of the parties must have the necessary authority to settle the dispute. If a party is a natural person, that person must attend the mediation session. If a party is not a natural person it must be represented at the mediation session by an officer or employee with full authority to make binding agreements settling the dispute. If that person comes with 'limited' authority, that is, authority up to a certain amount, he or she must disclose this information to the mediator prior to the mediation.
   - 1.3 The procedure at the mediation will be determined by the mediator.
   - 1.4 The parties will agree to the appointment of an ADR Group accredited mediator. ADR Group will provide to the parties, in advance of the mediation, details of recommended mediators drawn from ADR Net Limited's panel of mediators. If the parties are unable to agree to the appointment of a mediator, ADR Group will appoint a mediator if requested to do so.

2. Mediation Agreement
   - 2.1 The parties and ADR Group will enter into and sign an agreement ('Agreement to Mediate') in advance of the mediation and which agreement shall govern the relationship between the parties before, during and after the mediation.
   - 2.2 Each party, in signing the Agreement to Mediate, will be deemed to be agreeing on behalf of both itself and all such other persons to be bound by the confidentiality provisions of the Mediation Procedure.

3. The Mediator
   - 3.1 The mediator will:
     - (a) attend any meetings with any or all of the parties preceding the mediation, if requested to do so, or if the mediator decides it is appropriate;
     - (b) prior to the commencement of the mediation read and familiarise him/herself with each party's Position Statement and any documents provided in accordance with paragraph 6.1 below;
     - (c) determine the procedure (see paragraph 1.3 above);
     - (d) assist the parties in drawing up any written settlement agreement;
     - (e) abide by the terms of the Mediation Procedure, the Agreement to Mediate and the Solicitors Code of Practice (as amended from time to time) ('Code of Practice').
   - 3.2 The mediator will not:
     - (a) impose a settlement on the parties;
     - (b) offer legal advice or act as legal adviser to any party;
     - (c) analyse an party's legal position or rights.
   - 3.3 The parties and mediator acknowledge that the mediator is an independent contractor and is not appointed as an agent or employee of any of the parties or ADR Group. Neither the mediator nor a member of his or her firm will act, or have acted, as a profes-

sional adviser, or in any other capacity, for any of the parties individually in connection with the dispute either during the currency of the mediation or at any time thereafter.

4. Mediation arrangements
   4.1 ADR Group, will in consultation with the parties and the mediator, make the necessary arrangements for the mediation including, as appropriate:
      (a) recommend mediators with regard to, inter alia, nature of the dispute, degree of complexity, location of parties etc and drawing up the Agreement to Mediate;
      (b) liaise between the parties to agree suitable date and venue;
      (c) assist the parties in preparing their Position Statement (see paragraph 6) and supporting documentation;
      (d) discuss or meet with any or all of the parties or their representatives (and the mediator if appropriate), either together or separately, on any matter pursuant to the proposed mediation;
      (e) general administration in relation to the mediation.

5. Representation
   5.1 Parties do not require legal representation to attend the mediation.
   5.2 Where a party is un-represented, ADR Group encourages such party to obtain independent legal advice pursuant to the mediation.
   5.3 Each party is required to notify ADR Group and other parties involved in the mediation of the names of those people intended to be present on its behalf at the mediation.

6. Position Statements & Documentation
   6.1 Each party will be required to prepare and deliver to the mediator, within seven (7) days of the mediation, a concise summary ('Position Statement') of the case in dispute and copies of any and all documents referred to in the Position Statement and which it will be seeking to refer to during the mediation.
   6.2 ADR Group do not impose any obligation on the parties to exchange Position Statements, but parties are free to agree to the simultaneous exchange of the Position Statements, if so agreed or if considered appropriate.
   6.3 The Position Statement is private and confidential and will not be disclosed (by the mediator) to any other third party unless expressly authorised to do so. ADR Group will provide to the parties, upon request, a guide to position statement preparation.
   6.4 Parties are encouraged to prepare and agree a joint bundle of documents where appropriate.

7. The Mediation
   7.1 No formal record or transcript of the mediation will be made.
   7.2 The mediation session is for the purpose of attempting to achieve a negotiated settlement and all information provided during the mediation session is without prejudice and will be inadmissible in any litigation or arbitration of the dispute. Evidence, which is otherwise admissible, shall not be rendered inadmissible as a result of its use in the mediation session.
   7.3 If the parties are unable to reach a settlement during the mediation, the mediator may, if requested to do so, facilitate further negotiation after the mediation session itself has ended.

8. Settlement Agreement
   Any settlement reached in the mediation will not be legally binding until it has been recorded in writing and signed by, or on behalf of, the parties.

9. Termination
   9.1 Any of the parties may withdraw from the mediation at any time and shall immediately inform the mediator and the other representatives either orally or in writing. The mediation will terminate when:

(a) a party voluntarily withdraws from the mediation; or
(b) a written settlement agreement is concluded; or
(c) the mediator elects, in his/her sole discretion, that continuing the mediation is unlikely to result in a settlement; or
(d) the mediator decides that he/she should retire for any of the reasons set out in the Code of Practice.

10. Effect on legal proceedings
Where the dispute has been referred to mediation by the Court or where the Court has ordered that the parties consider mediation (under the current civil procedure legislation (as amended from time to time)), and the mediation does not achieve settlement, the current litigation or arbitration in relation to the dispute may be commenced or continued, notwithstanding the mediation, unless the parties agree otherwise.

11. Confidentiality
11.1 Every person involved in the mediation will keep confidential and not use for any collateral or ulterior purpose:
(a) the fact that the mediation is to take place or has taken place; and
(b) all information, (whether given orally or in writing or otherwise), produced for, or arising pursuant to, the mediation including the settlement agreement (if any) arising out of it except in so far as is necessary to implement and enforce any such settlement agreement.
11.2 All documents (which include anything upon which evidence is recorded including tapes or computer discs) or other information produced for, or arising in relation to, the mediation will be privileged and not admissible as evidence or discoverable in any litigation or arbitration connected with the dispute (see paragraph 11.1 (b) above). This does not apply to any information, which would in any event have been admissible or discloseable in any such proceedings.
11.3 The parties will not subpoena or otherwise require the mediator, ADR Group (or any employee, consultant, director or representative of ADR Group) or any other person attending the mediation under the auspices of ADR Group to testify or produce records, notes or any other information or material whatsoever in any future or continuing proceedings.

12. Mediation Costs
12.1 It is usual that the costs of the mediation are borne equally between the parties.
12.2 Payment of these costs will be made to ADR Group in accordance with its fee schedule and terms and conditions of business (as amended from time to time).
12.3 Each party attending the mediation is to bear its own costs and expenses of its participation in the mediation (including legal representative costs) and unless agreed otherwise, such costs will be costs in the cause.

13. Waiver of Liability
Neither the mediator nor ADR Group shall be liable to the parties for any act or omission in connection with the services provided by them in, or in relation to, the mediation, unless the act or omission is fraudulent or involves wilful misconduct.

14. Human Rights
The referral of a dispute to mediation does not affect any rights that may exist under Article 6 of the European Convention of Human Rights. Should the dispute not settle through the process of mediation, the parties' right to a fair trial shall remain unaffected.

APPENDIX VIII

THE CAS MEDIATION RULES

Pursuant to Articles S2 and S6 paragraph 10 of the Code of Sports-related Arbitration, the International Council of Arbitration for Sport adopts the present Mediation Rules.

A. Definitions

Article 1
CAS mediation is a non binding and informal procedure, based on a mediation agreement in which each party undertakes to attempt in good faith to negotiate with the other party, and with the assistance of a CAS mediator, with a view to settling a sports-related dispute.

CAS mediation is provided solely for the resolution of disputes related to the CAS ordinary procedure. A decision passed by the organ of a sports organization cannot be the subject of mediation proceedings before the CAS. All disputes related to disciplinary matters, as well as doping issues, are expressly excluded from CAS mediation.

Article 2
A mediation agreement is one whereby the parties agree to submit to mediation a sports-related dispute which has arisen or which may arise between them.

A mediation agreement may take the form of a mediation clause inserted in a contract or that of a separate agreement.

B. Scope of application of rules

Article 3
Where a mediation agreement provides for mediation under the CAS Mediation Rules, these Rules shall be deemed to form an integral part of such mediation agreement. Unless the parties have agreed otherwise, the version of these Rules in force on the date when the mediation request is filed shall apply.

The parties may however agree to apply other rules of procedure.

C. Commencement of the mediation

Article 4
A party wishing to institute mediation proceedings shall address a request to that effect in writing to the CAS Court Office, and at the same time send a copy of this to the other party.

The request shall contain: the identity of the parties and their representatives (name, address, telephone and fax numbers), a copy of the mediation agreement and a brief description of the dispute.

Upon filing its request, the party shall pay the administrative fee stipulated in Article 14 of the present Rules.

The day on which the mediation request is received by the CAS Court Office shall be considered as the date on which the mediation proceedings commence.

The CAS Court Office shall immediately inform the parties of the date on which the mediation commences, and shall fix the time limit by which the other party shall pay its share of the administrative costs pursuant to Article 14 of the present Rules.

D. Appointment of the mediator

Article 5
The ICAS draws up the list of mediators chosen from the list of CAS arbitrators or from outside.

The personalities whom the ICAS chooses appear on the list of mediators for a four-year period, and are thereafter eligible for reselection.

Article 6

Unless the parties have agreed between themselves on who the mediator will be, he shall be chosen by the CAS President from among the list of CAS mediators and appointed after consultation with the parties.

In accepting such appointment, the mediator undertakes to devote sufficient time to the mediation proceedings as will allow these to be conducted expeditiously.

The mediator shall be and must remain independent of the parties, and is bound to disclose any circumstances likely to compromise his independence with respect to any of the parties.

Having duly been informed thereof, the parties may however authorize the mediator to continue his mandate, by means of a signed separate or joint declaration.

In the event of an objection by any of the parties, or at his own discretion if he deems himself unable to bring the mediation to a successful conclusion, the mediator shall cease his mandate and inform the CAS President accordingly, whereupon the latter will make arrangements to replace him, after consulting the parties.

E. Representation of parties

Article 7

The parties may be represented or assisted in their meetings with the mediator.

If a party is being represented, the other party and the CAS must be informed beforehand as to the identity of such representative.

The representative must have full authority to settle the dispute alone, without consulting the party he is representing.

F. Conduct of mediation

Article 8

The mediation shall be conducted in the manner agreed by the parties. Failing such agreement between the parties, the mediator shall determine the manner in which the mediation will be conducted.

As soon as possible, the mediator shall establish the terms and timetable for submission by each party to the mediator and to the other party of a statement summarizing the dispute, including the following details:

1. a brief description of the facts and points of law, including a list of the issues submitted to the mediator with a view to resolution;
2. a copy of the mediation agreement.

Each party shall cooperate in good faith with the mediator and shall guarantee him the freedom to perform his mandate to advance the mediation as expeditiously as possible. The mediator may make any suggestions he deems appropriate in this regard. He may meet with separately with one of the parties, if he deems it necessary to do so.

G. Role of the mediator

Article 9

The mediator shall promote the settlement of the issues in dispute in any manner that he believes to be appropriate. To achieve this, he will:

a. identify the issues in dispute;
b. facilitate discussion of the issues by the parties;
c. propose solutions.

However, the mediator may not impose a solution of the dispute on either party.

H. Confidentiality

Article 10

The mediator, the parties, their representatives and advisers, experts and any other persons present during the meetings between the parties may not disclose to any third party any information given to them during the mediation, unless required by law to do so.

Under their own responsibility, the parties undertake not to compel the mediator to divulge records, reports or other documents, or to testify in regard to the mediation in any arbitral or judicial proceedings.

Any information given by one party may be disclosed by the mediator to the other party only with the consent of the former.

No record of any kind shall be made of the meetings. All the written documents shall be returned to the party providing these upon termination of the mediation, and no copy thereof shall be retained.

The parties shall not rely on, or introduce as evidence in any arbitral or judicial proceedings:

- views expressed or suggestions made by a party with respect to a possible settlement of the dispute;
- admissions made by a party in the course of the mediation proceedings;
- documents, notes or other information obtained during the mediation proceedings;
- proposals made or views expressed by the mediator; or
- the fact that a party had or had not indicated willingness to accept a proposal.

I. Termination

Article 11

Either party or the mediator may terminate the mediation at any time.

The mediation shall be terminated:

- by the signing of a settlement by the parties;
- by a written declaration of the mediator to the effect that further efforts at mediation are no longer worthwhile; or
- by a written declaration of a party or the parties to the effect that the mediation proceedings are terminated.

J. Settlement

Article 12

The settlement is drawn up by the mediator and signed by the mediator and the parties.

Each party shall receive a copy thereof. In the event of any breach, a party may rely on such copy before an arbitral or judicial authority.

A copy of the settlement is submitted for inclusion in the records of the CAS Court Office.

K. Failure to settle

Article 13

The parties may have recourse to arbitration when a dispute has not been resolved by mediation, provided that an arbitration agreement or clause exists between the parties.

The arbitration clause may be included in the mediation agreement. In such a case, the expedited procedure provided for under Article 44, paragraph 4 of the Code of Sports-related Arbitration may be applied.

In the event of failure to resolve a dispute by mediation, the mediator shall not accept an appointment as an arbitrator in any arbitral proceedings concerning the parties involved in the same dispute.

L. Costs

Article 14
Each party shall pay the CAS Court Office the administrative fees fixed by the Court within the time limit provided in Article 4 of the present Rules. In the absence of such payment, the mediation proceedings will not be not set in motion.

The parties will pay their own mediation costs.

Unless otherwise agreed between the parties, the final costs of the mediation, which include the CAS fee, the fees of the mediator calculated on the basis of the CAS fee scale, a contribution towards the costs of the CAS, and the costs of witnesses, experts and interpreters, will be borne by the parties in equal measure.

The CAS Court Office may require the parties to deposit an equal amount as an advance towards the costs of the mediation.

Recommended clause for CAS mediation to be inserted in a contract

> *"Any dispute, any controversy or claim arising under, out of or relating to this contract and any subsequent amendments of or in relation to this contract, including, but not limited to, its formation, validity, binding effect, interpretation, performance, breach or termination, as well as noncontractual claims, shall be submitted to mediation in accordance with the CAS Mediation Rules. The language to be used in the mediation shall be ... ."*

Additional clause in the absence of settlement of the dispute

> *"If, and to the extent that, any such dispute has not been settled within 90 days of the commencement of the mediation, or if, before the expiration of the said period, either party fails to participate or continue to participate in the mediation, the dispute shall, upon the filing of a Request for Arbitration by either party, be referred to and finally settled by CAS arbitration pursuant to the Code of Sports-related Arbitration. When the circumstances so require, the mediator may, at his own discretion or at the request of a party, seek an extension of the time limit from the CAS President."*

APPENDIX IX

UK SPORT RESOLUTIONS MEDIATION PROCEDURE

MEDIATION PROCEDURE

The following procedure ("the Mediation Procedure") (as amended by Sport Resolutions from time to time) shall govern the mediation of any dispute and the Parties shall be taken to have agreed that the mediation shall be conducted in accordance with the Mediation Procedure.

1. Mediation Procedure
1.1 Mediation is, in general terms, a negotiation assisted by an independent third party ("the Mediator"). The process is flexible and determined by the Mediator in consultation with the Parties and normally comprises a series of confidential joint and private meetings. Except as noted in clause 11 all communications relating to, and at, the mediation are confidential and without prejudice.
1.2 The representatives of the Parties must have the necessary authority to settle the dispute.

2. Mediation Agreement
2.1 The Parties, the Mediator and Sport Resolutions will enter into an `agreement based on Sport Resolutions Mediation Agreement ("the Mediation Agreement").

3. The Mediator
3.1 The Parties will agree a Mediator from the list of mediators provided by Sport Resolutions. If they cannot agree as to who should be appointed, the Mediator shall be appointed by the Executive Director of Sport Resolutions.
3.2 The Mediator will:
 (a) attend any meetings with any or all of the parties preceding the mediation, if requested or if the mediator decides this is appropriate;
 (b) read before the mediation each Summary and all the Documents sent to him/her in accordance with paragraphs 6.1 and 6.2 below;
 (c) determine the procedure (see paragraph 1.1 above);
 (d) assist the Parties in drawing up any written settlement agreement;
 (e) abide by the terms of the Mediation Procedure, the Mediation Agreement and any Code of Conduct adopted from time to time ("the Code of Conduct).
3.3 The Mediator will not at any time advise a party or offer an opinion. The Mediator's independence and impartiality is to be maintained throughout the Mediation.
3.4 The Mediator and any member of a firm or company associated with the Mediator will not act for any of the Parties individually in connection with the dispute in any capacity during the currency of the Mediation Agreement.
3.5 The Parties accept that in relation to the dispute neither the Mediator nor Sport Resolutions is an agent of, or acting in any capacity for, any of the Parties. The Parties and the Mediator accept that the Mediator is acting as an independent contractor and not as agent or employee of Sport Resolutions.
3.6 None of the Parties to the Mediation Agreement will call the Mediator or Sport Resolutions (or any employee, consultant, officer or representative of Sport Resolutions) as a witness, consultant, arbitrator or expert in any litigation or arbitration in relation to the dispute and the Mediator and Sport Resolutions will not voluntarily act in any such capacity without the written agreement of all the parties.

3.7 An Assistant Mediator may accompany the Mediator. The Assistant is present to gain experience and assist the Mediator as appropriate and attends without cost to the Parties. All references to 'Mediator' in this Procedure also apply to the Assistant Mediator.

4. Sport Resolutions

4.1 Sport Resolutions, in conjunction with the Mediator, will make the necessary arrangements for the mediation including, as necessary:

a) assisting the Parties in appointing the Mediator and in drawing up the Mediation Agreement;
b) organising a suitable venue and dates;
c) organising exchange of the Summaries and Documents;
d) meeting with any or all of the representatives of both Parties (and the Mediator if he/she has been appointed) either together or separately, to discuss any matters or concerns relating to the mediation;
e) general administration in relation to the mediation including post-mediation follow-up.

5. Other Participants

5.1 Each Party will notify the other Party or Parties, through Sport Resolutions, of the names of those people that it intends will be present on its behalf at the mediation.

6. Exchange of Information

6.1 Each Party will, simultaneously through Sport Resolutions, exchange with the other and send to the Mediator at least two weeks before the mediation or such other date as may be agreed between the Parties:

(a) a concise summary ("the Summary") stating its case in the dispute;
(b) copies of all key documents to which it refers in the Summary and to which it may want to refer in the mediation ("the Documents").

6.2 In addition, each Party may send to the Mediator (through Sport Resolutions) and/or bring to the mediation further documentation which it wishes to disclose in confidence to the Mediator but not to any other Party, clearly stating in writing that such documentation is confidential to the Mediator and Sport Resolutions.

6.3 The Parties will, through Sport Resolutions, agree the maximum number of pages of each Summary and of the Documents and try to agree a joint set of documents from their respective Documents.

7. Records

7.1 No formal record or transcript of the mediation will be made.

8. Settlement

8.1 Any settlement reached in the mediation will not be legally binding until it has been reduced to writing and signed by, or on behalf of, the parties.

9. Law and Jurisdiction

9.1 Except where the parties have otherwise agreed, this Agreement shall be governed by, be construed and take effect in accordance with English law, and the courts of England and Wales shall have exclusive jurisdiction to settle any claim, dispute or matter of difference which may arise out of or in connection with the mediation.

9.2 The referral of the dispute to mediation does not affect any rights that may exist under Article 6 of the European Convention on Human Rights. If the dispute is not settled by mediation, the Parties rights to a fair trial are unaffected.

9.3 The mediation will terminate when:

(a) a written Settlement Agreement is concluded; or
(b) a Party withdraws from the mediation; or
(c) the Mediator decides to retire where he/she deems it to be professional to do so.

10. Proceedings
10.1 Any litigation or arbitration in relation to the dispute may be commenced or continued notwithstanding the mediation unless the Parties agree otherwise.

11. Confidentiality
11.1 Every person involved in the mediation will keep confidential and not use for any collateral or ulterior purpose all information, (whether given orally, in writing or otherwise), produced for, or arising in relation to, the mediation including the Settlement Agreement (if any) arising out of it except insofar as is necessary to implement and enforce any such Settlement Agreement.
11.2 All documents (which include anything upon which evidence is recorded including tapes and computer discs) or other information produced for, or arising in relation to, the mediation will be privileged and not be admissible as evidence or discoverable in any litigation or arbitration connected with the dispute except any documents or other information which would in any event have been admissible or discoverable in any such litigation or arbitration.

12. Fees, Expenses and Costs
12.1 Unless otherwise agreed, Sport Resolutions' fees (which include the Mediator's fees) and the other expenses of the mediation will be borne equally by the Parties. Payment of these fees and expenses will be made to Sport Resolutions in accordance with its Fee Schedule and Terms of Business.
12.2 Unless otherwise agreed, each Party will bear its own costs and expenses of its participation in the mediation.

APPENDIX X

UK SPORT RESOLUTIONS **DRAFT MEDIATION AGREEMENT**

Date:

Parties

1:	<<Name>>, <<full address including postcode>>	("Party A")
2:	<<Name>>, <<full address including postcode>> (jointly "the Parties")	("Party B")
3:	c/o Sport Resolutions (UK), 107-111 Fleet Street, London EC4A 2AB	("the Mediator")
4:	Sport Resolutions (UK), the trading name of the Sports Dispute Resolution Panel Ltd, 107-111 Fleet Street, London EC4A 2AB	("SR")

Dispute ("the Dispute")

[A dispute has arisen between Party A and Party B concerning <<the brief outline of the matter>>.]

Participation in the Mediation

The Parties will attempt to settle the Dispute by mediation ("the Mediation"). The SR Mediation Procedure ("the Mediation Procedure") as varied by this agreement will determine the conduct of the Mediation and is incorporated into, and forms part of, this agreement.

The Mediator

The Mediator will be <<full name of mediator>>.

The Representatives

The representatives for each of the Parties at the Mediation will be:

Party A:	<<Full Name>>	<<Job Title if relevant>>
Party B:	<<Full Name>>	<<Job Title if relevant>>

(jointly "the Representatives")

A Party will immediately notify the other Party, SR and the Mediator of any change to the above.

Each Representative in signing this agreement is deemed to be agreeing to the provisions of this agreement on behalf of the Party he/she represents and all other persons present on that Party's behalf at the Mediation.

Other Participants

The following, in addition to the Representatives, will be present on behalf of each of the Parties at the Mediation:

Party A:	<<Full Name>>	<<Job Title if relevant>>
Party B:	<<Full Name>>	<<Job Title if relevant>>

A Party will immediately notify the other Party, SR and the Mediator of any change to the above.

Place and Time

The Mediation will take place on <<Day dd Month yyyy>> at <<time>> at <<full address of venue including postcode>>.

Confidentiality

Each Representative in signing this agreement is deemed to be agreeing to the confidentiality provisions of the Mediation Procedure (set out in paragraphs 1.1 and 11) on behalf of the Party he/she represents and all other persons present on behalf of that Party at the Mediation.

Amendments to Mediation Procedure

8. As required.

Law and Jurisdiction

9. This agreement shall be governed by, construed and take effect in accordance with English law. The courts of England and Wales shall have exclusive jurisdiction to settle any claim, dispute or matter of difference which may arise out of or in connection with the mediation.

Signed

______________________	______________________
(On behalf of Party A)	(On behalf of Party B)
______________________	______________________
(The Mediator)	(On behalf of SR)

APPENDIX XI

UK SPORT RESOLUTIONS RULES FOR AN ADVISORY OPINION

The following Rules (as amended by Sport Resolutions from time to time) shall govern the giving of an advisory opinion ("the Opinion") and the party or parties shall be taken to have agreed that the Opinion shall be given in accordance with these Rules.

1. The party or parties who wish to submit a request for an Opinion must sign an agreement with Sport Resolutions in relation to costs before Sport Resolutions will consider a request for an Opinion.

2. The request for an Opinion shall be in Sport Resolutions' standard form and shall include:
   (a) the name of the party or parties requesting the Opinion;
   (b) copies of any documents which may be relevant to or have a bearing on the Opinion; and
   (c) a brief statement describing the nature and circumstances and background to the request and why it is requested.

3. The party or parties shall decide how many and which of the Arbitrators shall consider the request and give the Opinion and, if they fail to do so or in the absence of agreement, the Chairman of Sport Resolutions shall so decide and shall notify the party or parties who made the request of his choice.

4. The Arbitrator(s) selected shall have absolute discretion to decide what documents and further information shall be supplied to the Arbitrator(s) and may consult with the party making the request or with any other party or relevant person or body before issuing an Opinion.

5. Any costs relating to the Opinion as agreed with Sport Resolutions, must be paid in full to Sport Resolutions before the Opinion will be issued.

6. The Arbitrator(s) selected to give the Opinion shall have absolute discretion as to the form, length and content of the Opinion.

7. The Opinion shall not constitute a binding arbitral award.

APPENDIX XII

UK SPORT RESOLUTIONS CODE OF CONDUCT FOR PANEL MEMBERS

1. INTRODUCTION
   1.1 This Code sets down general principles that apply to Members of the Sport Resolutions Panel.
   1.2 The term Member shall be taken to include members of the Panel of Arbitrators, the Panel of Mediators, and any other Panel(s) operated from time to time by Sport Resolutions (UK).
   1.3 The Code shall apply to all aspects of a Member's involvement with Sport Resolutions.

2. DUTIES OF THE PANEL MEMBER
   2.1 Sport Resolutions is committed to providing an independent service for the fair, speedy and effective resolution of sports disputes in the United Kingdom at an affordable cost. In supporting this aim, Members shall uphold the principles of honesty, openness (subject to clause 2.2 below), independence, impartiality and even-handedness.
   2.2 Save as may be: i) required by law; ii) provided for under Sport Resolutions, or any other applicable, rules; iii) otherwise agreed between the parties, Members shall maintain confidentiality of all matters concerning any dispute to which they are appointed.
   2.3 Members shall disclose at the earliest possible time anything which might be perceived as a conflict of interest.
   2.4 Members shall not act on behalf of any party in connection with a dispute to which they have been appointed.
   2.5 Save for any agreed fee and expenses, a Member shall not seek to gain in any way from any dispute to which the Member is appointed.
   2.6 Members shall carry out their duties expeditiously and professionally.
   2.7 Save where expressly agreed otherwise with Sport Resolutions, it is the responsibility of professional Members to maintain adequate Professional Indemnity insurance to cover work undertaken under the auspices of Sport Resolutions. If requested to do so, Members shall provide evidence of the agreed level of cover.
   Members shall observe the highest standards of conduct at all times and, in particular, shall not act in any way which is liable to bring Sport Resolutions into disrepute.

3. RELATIONSHIP WITH SPORT RESOLUTIONS (UK)
   3.1 Members shall act in a manner which is consistent with the aims and interests of Sport Resolutions and shall seek to enhance its reputation and influence as the specialist dispute resolution provider to Sport in the United Kingdom.
   3.2 The relationship of trust between Sport Resolutions and its Members is paramount. Members shall at all time act so as to preserve this relationship of trust and confidence. In keeping with this, Members shall not misrepresent the nature of their involvement with Sport Resolutions nor shall they use Sport Resolutions appointments to promote themselves in a manner which is detrimental to Sport Resolutions.
   3.3 Any breach of this Code may result in action being taken against the Member concerned including but not limited to Sport Resolutions absolute discretion to withdraw membership of the Panel.

APPENDIX XIII

THE FIFA REGULATIONS FOR THE STATUS AND TRANSFER OF PLAYERS

Contents

Annex 3: Administrative procedure governing the transfer of players between associations
Annex 4: Training compensation
Annex 5: Solidarity mechanism

REGULATIONS ON THE STATUS AND TRANSFER OF PLAYERS

Based on article 5 of the FIFA Statutes of 19 October 2003, the Executive Committee has issued the following regulations and annexes, which form an integral part of the basic text.

DEFINITIONS
For the purpose of these regulations, the terms set out below are defined as follows:

Former association: the association to which the former club is affiliated.
Former club: the club that the player is leaving.
New association: the association to which the new club is affiliated.
New club: the club that the player is joining.
Official matches: matches played within the framework of organised football, such as national league championships, national cups and international championships for clubs, but not including friendly and trial matches.
Organised football: association football organised under the auspices of FIFA, the confederations and the associations, or authorised by them.
Protected period: a period of three entire seasons or three years, whichever comes first, following the entry into force of a contract, where such contract is concluded prior to the 28th birthday of the professional, or two entire seasons or two years, whichever comes first, following the entry into force of a contract, where such contract is concluded after the 28th birthday of the professional.
Registration period: a period fixed by the relevant association in accordance with article 6.
Season: the period starting with the first official match of the relevant national league championship and ending with the last official match of the relevant national league championship.
Training compensation: the payments made in accordance with Annex 4 to cover the development of young players.

Reference is also made to the Definitions section in the FIFA Statutes.
NB: Terms referring to natural persons are applicable to both genders. Any term in the singular applies to the plural and vice-versa.

I. INTRODUCTORY PROVISION

Article 1 Scope
These regulations lay down global and binding rules concerning the status of players, their eligibility to participate in organised football, and their transfer between clubs belonging to different associations.

The transfer of players between clubs belonging to the same association is governed by specific regulations issued by the association concerned in accordance with article 1 paragraph 3 below, which must be approved by FIFA. Such regulations shall lay down rules for the settlement of disputes between clubs and players, in accordance with the principles stipulated in these regulations. Such regulations should also provide for a system to reward clubs investing in the training and education of young players.

a) The following provisions are binding at national level and must be included without modification in the association's regulations: articles 2-8, 10, 11, 18 and 18bis.
b) Each association shall include in its regulations appropriate means to protect contractual stability, paying due respect to mandatory national law and collective bargaining agreements. In particular, the following principles must be considered:
   - article 13: the principle that contracts must be respected;
   - article 14: the principle that contracts may be terminated by either party without consequences where there is just cause;

- article 15: the principle that contracts may be terminated by professionals with sporting just cause;
- article 16: the principle that contracts cannot be terminated during the course of the season;
- article 17 paragraphs 1 and 2: the principle that in the event of termination of contract without just cause, compensation shall be payable and that such compensation may be stipulated in the contract;
- article 17 paragraphs 3-5: the principle that in the event of termination of contract without just cause, sporting sanctions shall be imposed on the party in breach.

These regulations also govern the release of players to association teams and players' eligibility to play for such teams in accordance with the provisions of Annexes 1 and 2 respectively. These provisions are binding for all associations and clubs.

II. STATUS OF PLAYERS

Article 2 Status of players: amateur and professional players

Players participating in organised football are either amateurs or professionals.

A professional is a player who has a written contract with a club and is paid more for his footballing activity than the expenses he effectively incurs. All other players are considered to be amateurs.

Article 3 Reacquisition of amateur status

A player registered as a professional may not re-register as an amateur until at least 30 days after his last match as a professional.

No compensation is payable upon reacquisition of amateur status. If a player re-registers as a professional within 30 months of being reinstated as an amateur, his new club shall pay training compensation in accordance with article 20.

Article 4 Termination of activity

Professionals who end their careers upon expiry of their contracts and amateurs who terminate their activity shall remain registered at the association of their last club for a period of 30 months.

This period begins on the day the player made his last appearance for the club in an official match.

III. REGISTRATION OF PLAYERS

Article 5 Registration

A player must be registered at an association to play for a club as either a professional or an amateur in accordance with the provisions of article 2. Only registered players are eligible to participate in organised football. By the act of registering, a player agrees to abide by the statutes and regulations of FIFA, the confederations and the associations.

A player may only be registered with one club at a time.

Players may be registered with a maximum of three clubs during one season. During this period, the player is only eligible to play official matches for two clubs. As an exception to this rule, a player moving between two clubs belonging to associations with overlapping seasons (i.e. start of the season in summer/autumn as opposed to winter/spring) may be eligible to play in official matches for a third club during the relevant season, provided he has fully complied with his contractual obligations towards his previous clubs. Equally, the provisions relating to the registration periods (article 6) as well as to the minimum length of a contract (article 18 paragraph 2) must be respected.

Under all circumstances, due consideration must be given to the sporting integrity of the competition. In particular, a player may not play official matches for more than two clubs competing in the same national championship or cup during the same season, subject to stricter individual competition regulations of member associations.

Article 6 Registration periods

1. Players may only be registered during one of the two annual registration periods fixed by the relevant association. As an exception to this rule, a professional whose contract has expired prior to the end of a registration period may be registered outside that registration period. As-

sociations are authorised to register such professionals provided due consideration is given to the sporting integrity of the relevant competition. Where a contract has been terminated with just cause, FIFA may take provisional measures in order to avoid abuse, subject to article 22.
The first registration period shall begin after the completion of the season and shall normally end before the new season starts. This period may not exceed twelve weeks. The second registration period shall normally occur in the middle of the season and may not exceed four weeks. The two registration periods for the season shall be communicated to FIFA at least 12 months before they come into force. FIFA shall determine the dates for any association that fails to communicate them on time.
Players may only be registered – subject to the exception provided for in article 6 paragraph 1 – upon submission of a valid application from the club to the relevant association during a registration period.
The provisions concerning registration periods do not apply to competitions in which only amateurs participate. The relevant association shall specify the periods when players may be registered for such competitions provided that due consideration is given to sporting integrity of the relevant competition.

Article 7 Player passport
The registering association is obliged to provide the club with which the player is registered with a player passport containing the relevant details of the player. The player passport shall indicate the club(s) with which the player has been registered since the season of his 12th birthday. If a birthday falls between seasons, the player passport shall indicate the club with which he was registered during the season following his birthday.

Article 8 Application for registration
The application for registration of a professional must be submitted together with a copy of the player's contract. The relevant decision-making body has discretion to take account of any contractual amendments or additional agreements that have not been duly submitted to it.

Article 9 International Transfer Certificate
1. Players registered at one association may only be registered at a new association once the latter has received an International Transfer Certificate (hereinafter: ITC) from the former association. The ITC shall be issued free of charge without any conditions or time limit. Any provisions to the contrary shall be null and void. The association issuing the ITC shall lodge a copy with FIFA. The administrative procedures for issuing the ITC are contained in Annex 3 of these regulations.
2. An ITC is not required for a player under the age of 12 years.

Article 10 Loan of professionals
A professional may be loaned to another club on the basis of a written agreement between him and the clubs concerned. Any such loan is subject to the same rules as apply to the transfer of players, including the provisions on training compensation and the solidarity mechanism.

Subject to article 5 paragraph 3, the minimum loan period shall be the time between two registration periods.

The club that has accepted a player on a loan basis is not entitled to transfer him to a third club without the written authorisation of the club that released the player on loan and the player concerned.

Article 11 Unregistered players
Any player not registered at an association who appears for a club in any official match shall be considered to have played illegitimately. Without prejudice to any measure required to rectify the sporting consequences of such an appearance, sanctions may also be imposed on the player and/or the club. The right to impose such sanctions lies in principle with the association or the organiser of the competition concerned.

Article 12 Enforcement of disciplinary suspensions
Any disciplinary suspension imposed on a player prior to a transfer must be enforced or applied by the new association at which the player is registered. The former association is obliged to notify the new association of any sanction in writing and upon issuing the ITC.

IV. MAINTENANCE OF CONTRACTUAL STABILITY BETWEEN PLAYERS AND CLUBS

Article 13 Respect of contract
A contract between a professional and a club may only be terminated upon expiry of the term of the contract or by mutual agreement.

Article 14 Terminating a contract with just cause
A contract may be terminated by either party without consequences of any kind (either payment of compensation or imposition of sporting sanctions) where there is just cause.

Article 15 Terminating a contract with sporting just cause
An established professional who has, in the course of the season, appeared in fewer than ten per cent of the official matches in which his club has been involved may terminate his contract prematurely on the ground of sporting just cause. Due consideration shall be given to the player's circumstances in the appraisal of such cases. The existence of a sporting just cause shall be established on a case-by-case basis. In such a case, sporting sanctions shall not be imposed, though compensation may be payable. A professional may only terminate his contract on this basis in the 15 days following the last official match of the season of the club with which he is registered.

Article 16 Restriction on terminating a contract during the season
A contract cannot be unilaterally terminated during the course of a season.

Article 17 Consequences of terminating a contract without just cause
The following provisions apply if a contract is terminated without just cause:

In all cases, the party in breach shall pay compensation. Subject to the provisions of article 20 and Annex 4 in relation to training compensation, and unless otherwise provided for in the contract, compensation for the breach shall be calculated with due consideration for the law of the country concerned, the specificity of sport, and any other objective criteria. These criteria shall include, in particular, the remuneration and other benefi ts due to the player under the existing contract and/or the new contract, the time remaining on the existing contract up to a maximum of five years, the fees and expenses paid or incurred by the former club (amortised over the term of the contract) and whether the contractual breach falls within a protected period.

Entitlement to compensation cannot be assigned to a third party. If a professional is required to pay compensation, the professional and his new club shall be jointly and severally liable for its payment. The amount may be stipulated in the contract or agreed between the parties.

In addition to the obligation to pay compensation, sporting sanctions shall also be imposed on any player found to be in breach of contract during the protected period. This sanction shall be a four-month restriction on playing in official matches. In the case of aggravating circumstances, the restriction shall last six months. In all cases, these sporting sanctions shall take effect from the start of the following season at the new club. Unilateral breach without just cause or sporting just cause after the protected period shall not result in sporting sanctions. Disciplinary measures may, however, be imposed outside the protected period for failure to give notice of termination within 15 days of the last official match of the season (including national cups) of the club with which the player is registered. The protected period starts again when, while renewing the contract, the duration of the previous contract is extended.

In addition to the obligation to pay compensation, sporting sanctions shall be imposed on any club found to be in breach of contract or found to be inducing a breach of contract during the protected period. It shall be presumed, unless established to the contrary, that any club signing a professional who has terminated his contract without just cause has induced that professional to commit a breach.

The club shall be banned from registering any new players, either nationally or internationally, for two registration periods.

Any person subject to the FIFA Statutes and regulations (club officials, players' agents, players, etc.) who acts in a manner designed to induce a breach of contract between a professional and a club in order to facilitate the transfer of the player shall be sanctioned.

Article 18 Special provisions relating to contracts between professionals and clubs

If an agent is involved in the negotiation of a contract, he shall be named in that contract.

The minimum length of a contract shall be from its effective date until the end of the season, while the maximum length of a contract shall be five years. Contracts of any other length shall only be permitted if consistent with national laws. Players under the age of 18 may not sign a professional contract for a term longer than three years. Any clause referring to a longer period shall not be recognised.

A club intending to conclude a contract with a professional must inform the player's current club in writing before entering into negotiations with him. A professional shall only be free to conclude a contract with another club if his contract with his present club has expired or is due to expire within six months. Any breach of this provision shall be subject to appropriate sanctions.

The validity of a contract may not be made subject to a successful medical examination and/or the grant of a work permit.

If a professional enters into more than one contract covering the same period, the provisions set forth in Chapter IV shall apply.

V. THIRD-PARTY INFLUENCE

Article 18bis Third-party influence on clubs

No club shall enter into a contract which enables any other party to that contract or any third party to acquire the ability to influence in employment and transfer-related matters its independence, its policies or the performance of its teams.

The FIFA Disciplinary Committee may impose disciplinary measures on clubs that do not observe the obligations set out in this article.

VI. INTERNATIONAL TRANSFERS INVOLVING MINORS

Article 19 Protection of minors

International transfers of players are only permitted if the player is over the age of 18.

The following three exceptions to this rule apply:

a) The player's parents move to the country in which the new club is located for reasons not linked to football;
b) The transfer takes place within the territory of the European Union (EU) or European Economic Area (EEA) and the player is aged between 16 and 18. In this case, the new club must fulfil the following minimum obligations:
   i) It shall provide the player with an adequate football education and/or training in line with the highest national standards.
   ii) It shall guarantee the player an academic and/or school and/or vocational education and/or training, in addition to his football education and/or training, which will allow the player to pursue a career other than football should he cease playing professional football.
   iii) It shall make all necessary arrangements to ensure that the player is looked after in the best possible way (optimum living standards with a host family or in club accommodation, appointment of a mentor at the club, etc.).
   iv) It shall, on registration of such a player, provide the relevant association with proof that it is complying with the aforementioned obligations;
c) The player lives no further than 50km from a national border and the club with which the player wishes to be registered in the neighbouring association is also within 50km of that border. The maximum distance between the player's domicile and the club's headquarters shall be 100km.

In such cases, the player must continue to live at home and the two associations concerned must give their explicit consent.

The conditions of this article shall also apply to any player who has never previously been registered with a club and is not a national of the country in which he wishes to be registered for the first time.

Each association shall ensure the respect of this provision by its clubs.

The Players' Status Committee shall be competent to decide on any dispute arising in relation to these matters and shall impose appropriate sanctions in the event of violations of this provision.

VII. TRAINING COMPENSATION AND SOLIDARITY MECHANISM

Article 20 Training compensation

Training compensation shall be paid to a player's training club(s): (1) when a player signs his first contract as a professional and (2) each time a professional is transferred until the end of the season of his 23rd birthday. The obligation to pay training compensation arises whether the transfer takes place during or at the end of the player's contract. The provisions concerning training compensation are set out in Annexe 4 of these regulations.

Article 21 Solidarity mechanism

If a professional is transferred before the expiry of his contract, any club that has contributed to his education and training shall receive a proportion of the compensation paid to his former club (solidarity contribution). The provisions concerning solidarity contributions are set out in Annex 5 of these regulations.

VIII. JURISDICTION

Article 22 Competence of FIFA

Without prejudice to the right of any player or club to seek redress before a civil court for employment-related disputes, FIFA is competent to hear:

a) disputes between clubs and players in relation to the maintenance of contractual stability (articles 13-18) where there has been an ITC request and a claim from an interested party in relation to said ITC request, in particular regarding the issue of the ITC, sporting sanctions or compensation for breach of contract;
b) employment-related disputes between a club and a player of an international dimension, unless an independent arbitration tribunal guaranteeing fair proceedings and respecting the principle of equal representation of players and clubs has been established at national level within the framework of the association and/or a collective bargaining agreement;
c) employment-related disputes between a club or an association and a coach of an international dimension, unless an independent arbitration tribunal guaranteeing fair proceedings exists at national level;
d) disputes relating to training compensation (article 20) and the solidarity mechanism (article 21) between clubs belonging to different associations;
e) disputes relating to the solidarity mechanism (article 21) between clubs belonging to the same association provided that the transfer of a player at the basis of the dispute occurs between clubs belonging to different associations;
f) disputes between clubs belonging to different associations that do not fall within the cases provided for in a), d) and e).

Article 23 Players' Status Committee

The Players' Status Committee shall adjudicate on any of the cases described under article 22 c) and f) as well as on all other disputes arising from the application of these regulations, subject to article 24.

In case of uncertainty as to the jurisdiction of the Players' Status Committee or the Dispute Resolution Chamber, the chairman of the Players' Status Committee shall decide which body has jurisdiction.

The Players' Status Committee shall adjudicate in the presence of at least three members, including the chairman or the deputy chairman, unless the case is of such a nature that it may be settled by a single judge. In cases that are urgent or raise no difficult factual or legal issues, and for decisions on the issue of a provisional ITC in accordance with Annex 3, the chairman or a person appointed by him, who must be a member of the committee, may adjudicate as a single judge. Each party shall be heard once during the proceedings. Decisions reached by the single judge or the Players' Status Committee may be appealed before the Court of Arbitration for Sport (CAS).

Article 24 Dispute Resolution Chamber (DRC)
The DRC shall adjudicate on any of the cases described under article 22 a), b), d) and e) with the exception of disputes concerning the issue of an ITC.

The DRC shall adjudicate in the presence of at least three members, including the chairman or the deputy chairman, unless the case is of a nature that may be settled by a DRC judge. The members of the DRC shall designate a DRC judge for the clubs and one for the players from among its members. The DRC judge may adjudicate in the following cases:

i) all disputes up to a litigious value of CHF 100,000;
ii) disputes relating to the calculation of training compensation;
iii) disputes relating to the calculation of solidarity contributions.

The DRC judge is obliged to refer cases concerning fundamental issues to the chamber. The chamber shall consist of equal numbers of club and player representatives, except in those cases that may be settled by a DRC judge. Each party shall be heard once during the proceedings. Decisions reached by the Dispute Resolution Chamber or the DRC judge may be appealed before the Court of Arbitration for Sport (CAS).

Article 25 Procedural guidelines
As a rule, the single judge and the DRC judge shall adjudicate within 30 days of receipt of a valid request and the Players' Status Committee or the Dispute Resolution Chamber shall adjudicate within 60 days. The proceedings shall be governed by the FIFA General Procedural Rules.

The maximum cost of proceedings before the Players' Status Committee, including the single judge, shall be set at CHF 25,000 and shall normally be paid by the unsuccessful party. The allocation of costs shall be explained in the decision. Proceedings before the DRC and the DRC judge are free of charge.

Disciplinary proceedings for violation of these regulations shall, unless otherwise stipulated herein, conform to the FIFA Disciplinary Code.

If there is reason to believe that a case raises a disciplinary issue, the Players' Status Committee, the Dispute Resolution Chamber, the single judge or the DRC judge (as the case may be) shall submit the file to the Disciplinary Committee together with a request for the commencement of disciplinary proceedings in accordance with the FIFA Disciplinary Code.

The Players' Status Committee, the Dispute Resolution Chamber, the single judge or the DRC judge (as the case may be) shall not hear any case subject to these regulations if more than two years have elapsed since the event giving rise to the dispute. Application of this time limit shall be examined *ex officio* in each individual case.

The Players' Status Committee, the Dispute Resolution Chamber, the single judge or the DRC judge (as the case may be) shall, when taking their decisions, apply these regulations whilst taking into account all relevant arrangements, laws and/or collective bargaining agreements that exist at national level, as well as the specificity of sport.

The detailed procedure for the resolution of disputes arising from the application of these regulations shall be further outlined in the FIFA General Procedural Rules.

IX. FINAL PROVISIONS

Article 26 Transitional measures
Any case that has been brought to FIFA before these regulations come into force shall be assessed according to the previous regulations.

As a general rule, all other cases shall be assessed according to these regulations with the exception of the following:

a) disputes regarding training compensation;
b) disputes regarding the solidarity mechanism;
c) labour disputes relating to contracts signed before 1 September 2001.

Any cases not subject to this general rule shall be assessed according to the regulations that were in force when the contract at the centre of the dispute was signed, or when the disputed facts arose.

Member associations shall amend their regulations in accordance with article 1 to ensure that they comply with these regulations and shall submit them to FIFA for approval by 30 June 2007. Notwithstanding the foregoing, each member association shall implement article 1 paragraph 3 a) as from 1 July 2005.

Article 27 Matters not provided for
Matters not provided for in these regulations and cases of *force majeure* shall be decided by the FIFA Executive Committee, whose decisions are final.

Article 28 Official languages
In the case of any discrepancy in the interpretation of the English, French, Spanish or German texts of these regulations, the English text shall be authoritative.

Article 29 Annulment, enforcement
These regulations shall replace the special regulations governing players' eligibility to play for association teams dated 4 December 2003 and the Regulations for the Status and Transfer of Players of 5 July 2001 as well as all subsequent amendments, including all relevant circular letters issued before the effective date of these regulations.

These regulations were approved by the FIFA Executive Committee on 18 December 2004 and come into force on 1 July 2005. Article 1 paragraph 3 a); article 5 paragraphs 3 and 4; article 17 paragraph 3; article 18bis; article 22 e) and f); Annex 1 article 1 paragraph 4 d) and e); Annex 1 article 3 paragraph 2; Annex 3 article 1 paragraphs 2, 3 and 4 and Annex 3 article 2 paragraph 2 were supplemented or amended by the FIFA Executive Committee on 29 October 2007. These amendments come into force on 1 January 2008.

Zurich, December 2004/October 2007
For the FIFA Executive Committee
President General Secretary Joseph S. Blatter Jérôme Valcke

ANNEX 1
RELEASE OF PLAYERS TO ASSOCIATION TEAMS

Article 1 Principles
Clubs are obliged to release their registered players to the representative teams of the country for which the player is eligible to play on the basis of his nationality if they are called up by the association concerned. Any agreement between a player and a club to the contrary is prohibited.

The release of players under the terms of paragraph 1 of this article is mandatory for matches on dates listed in the coordinated international match calendar and for all matches for which a duty to release players exists on the basis of a special decision by the FIFA Executive Committee.

It is not compulsory to release players for matches scheduled on dates not listed in the coordinated international match calendar.

Players must also be released for the period of preparation before the match, which is laid down as follows:

a) friendly matches: 48 hours;
b) qualifying matches for an international tournament: four days (including the day of the match). The release period shall be extended to five days if the match concerned is held in a different confederation to the one in which the player's club is registered;

c) qualifying matches for an international tournament that are staged on a date reserved for friendly matches: 48 hours;
d) friendly matches that are staged on a date reserved for qualifying matches for an international tournament: 48 hours;
e) the final competition of an international tournament: 14 days before the fi rst match in the competition.

Players shall join the association team no later than 48 hours before kick-off.

The players of associations that have automatically qualified for the final competition of the FIFA World Cup™ or for continental championships for national "A" teams shall be released for friendly matches on dates reserved for official qualifying matches in accordance with the directives that would apply for official matches staged on those dates.

The clubs and associations concerned may agree a longer period of release.

Players complying with a call-up from their association under the terms of this article shall resume duty with their clubs no later than 24 hours after the end of the match for which they were called up. This period shall be extended to 48 hours if the match concerned took place in a different confederation to the one in which the player's club is registered. Clubs shall be informed in writing of a player's outbound and return schedule ten days before the match. Associations shall ensure that players are able to return to their clubs on time after the match.

If a player does not resume duty with his club by the deadline stipulated in this article, the next time the player is called up by his association, the period of release shall be shortened as follows:

a) friendly matches: 24 hours;
b) qualifying matches: three days;
c) the final competition of an international tournament: ten days.

Should an association repeatedly breach these provisions, the FIFA Players' Status Committee may impose appropriate sanctions, including but not limited to:

a) fines;
b) a reduction of the period of release;
c) a ban on calling up a player(s) for subsequent match(es).

Article 2 Financial provisions and insurance

Clubs releasing a player in accordance with the provisions of this annex are not entitled to financial compensation.

The association calling up a player shall bear the costs of travel incurred by the player as a result of the call-up.

The club with which the player concerned is registered shall be responsible for his insurance cover against illness and accident during the entire period of his release. This cover must also extend to any injuries sustained by the player during the international match(es) for which he was released.

Article 3 Calling up players

As a general rule, every player registered with a club is obliged to respond affirmatively when called up by the association he is eligible to represent on the basis of his nationality to play for one of its representative teams.

Associations wishing to call up a player who is playing abroad must notify the player in writing at least 15 days before the day of the match for which he is required. Associations wishing to call up a player for the final competition of an international tournament must notify the player in writing at least 15 days before the beginning of the 14-day preparation period (cf. Annexe 1 article 1 paragraph 4 e)). The player's club shall also be informed in writing at the same time. The club must confirm the release of the player within the following six days.

Associations that request FIFA's help to obtain the release of a player playing abroad may only do so under the following two conditions:

a) The association at which the player is registered has been asked to intervene without success.
b) The case is submitted to FIFA at least five days before the day of the match for which the player is needed.

Article 4 Injured players
A player who due to injury or illness is unable to comply with a call-up from the association that he is eligible to represent on the basis of his nationality shall, if the association so requires, agree to undergo a medical examination by a doctor of that association's choice. If the player so wishes, such medical examination shall take place on the territory of the association at which he is registered.

Article 5 Restrictions on playing
A player who has been called up by his association for one of its representative teams is, unless otherwise agreed by the relevant association, not entitled to play for the club with which he is registered during the period for which he has been released or should have been released pursuant to the provisions of this annex. This restriction on playing for the club shall, moreover, be prolonged by five days in the event that the player, for whatsoever reason, did not wish to or was unable to comply with the call-up.

Article 6 Disciplinary measures
Violations of any of the provisions set forth in this annex shall result in the imposition of disciplinary measures.

If a club refuses to release a player or neglects to do so despite the provisions of this annexe, the FIFA Players' Status Committee shall furthermore request the association to which the club belongs to declare any match(es) in which the player took part to have been lost by the club concerned. Any points thus gained by the club in question shall be forfeited. Any match contested according to the cup system shall be regarded as having been won by the opposing team, irrespective of the score.

If a player reports late for duty with his club more than once after being called up by an association, the FIFA Players' Status Committee may, at the request of the player's club, impose additional sanctions on the player and/or his association.

ANNEX 2
ELIGIBILITY TO PLAY FOR ASSOCIATION TEAMS OF PLAYERS WHOSE NATIONALITY ENTITLES THEM TO REPRESENT MORE THAN ONE ASSOCIATION ADMINISTRATIVE PROCEDURE GOVERNING THE TRANSFER OF PLAYERS BETWEEN ASSOCIATIONS

Article 1 Conditions
1. A player who, under the terms of article 15 of the Regulations Governing the Application of the FIFA Statutes, is eligible to represent more than one association on account of his nationality, may play in an international match for one of these associations only if, in addition to having the relevant nationality, he fulfils at least one of the following conditions:
   a) he was born on the territory of the relevant association;
   b) his biological mother or biological father was born on the territory of the relevant association;
   c) His grandmother or grandfather was born on the territory of the relevant association;
   d) he has lived on the territory of the relevant association for at least two years without interruption.
2. Notwithstanding paragraph 1 of this article, associations sharing a common nationality may make an agreement under which item d) of paragraph 1 of this article is deleted completely or amended to specify a longer time limit. Such agreements must be lodged with and approved by FIFA.

ANNEX 3

Article 1 Principles
Any player who is registered with a club that is affiliated to one association shall not be eligible to play for a club affiliated to a different association unless an ITC has been issued by the former association and received by the new association in accordance with the provisions of this annex. Special forms provided by FIFA for this purpose or forms with similar wording shall be used.

At the very latest, the ITC must be requested on the last day of the registration period of the new association.

The association issuing the ITC shall also attach a copy of the player passport to it.

The new association shall inform the association(s) of the club(s) that trained and educated the player between the ages of 12 and 23 (cf. Article 7 – Player passport) in writing of the registration of the player as a professional after receipt of the ITC.

Article 2 Issue of an ITC for a professional

All applications to register a professional must be submitted by the new club to the new association during one of the registration periods established by that association. All applications shall be accompanied by a copy of the contract between the new club and the professional. A professional is not eligible to play in official matches for his new club until an ITC has been issued by the former association and received by the new association.

Upon receipt of the application, the new association shall immediately request the former association to issue an ITC for the professional ("ITC request"). An association that receives an unsolicited ITC from another association is not entitled to register the professional concerned with one of its clubs.

Upon receipt of the ITC request, the former association shall immediately request the former club and the professional to confirm whether the professional's contract has expired, whether early termination was mutually agreed or whether a contractual dispute exists.

Within seven days of receiving the ITC request, the former association shall either:

a) issue the ITC to the new association; or
b) inform the new association that the ITC cannot be issued because the contract between the former club and the professional has not expired or that there has been no mutual agreement regarding its early termination.

If the new association does not receive a response to the ITC request within 30 days of the ITC request being made, it shall immediately register the professional with the new club on a provisional basis ("provisional registration"). A provisional registration shall become permanent one year after the ITC request. The Players' Status Committee may withdraw a provisional registration, if, during this one-year period, the former association presents valid reasons explaining why it did not respond to the ITC request.

The former association shall not issue an ITC if a contractual dispute has arisen between the former club and the professional. In such a case, the professional, the former club and/or the new club are entitled to lodge a claim with FIFA in accordance with article 22. FIFA shall then decide on the issue of the ITC and on sporting sanctions within 60 days. In any case, the decision on sporting sanctions shall be taken before the issue of the ITC. The issue of the ITC shall be without prejudice to compensation for breach of contract. FIFA may take provisional measures in exceptional circumstances.

The new association may grant a player temporary eligibility to play until the end of the season that is underway on the basis of an ITC sent by fax. If the original ITC is not received by that time, the player's eligibility to play shall be considered definitive.

Associations are forbidden from requesting the issue of an ITC in order to allow a player to participate in trial matches.

The foregoing rules and procedures also apply to professionals who, upon moving to their new club, acquire amateur status.

Article 3 Issue of an ITC for an amateur

All applications to register an amateur player must be submitted by the new club to the new association during one of the registration periods established by that association.

Upon receipt of the application, the new association shall immediately request the former association to issue an ITC for the player ("ITC request").

The former association shall, within seven days of receiving the ITC request, issue the ITC to the new association.

If the new association does not receive a response to the ITC request within 30 days, it shall immediately register the amateur with the new club on a provisional basis ("provisional registration"). A provisional registration shall become permanent one year after the ITC request. The Players' Status Committee may withdraw a provisional registration, if, during this one-year period, the former association presents valid reasons explaining why it did not respond to the ITC request.

The foregoing rules and procedures also apply for amateurs who, upon moving to their new club, acquire professional status.

Article 4 Loan of players
The rules set out above also apply to the loan of a professional from a club affiliated to one association to a club affiliated to another association.
The terms of the loan agreement shall be enclosed with the ITC request.
Upon expiry of the loan period, the ITC shall be returned, upon request, to the association of the club that released the player on loan.

ANNEX 4
TRAINING COMPENSATION

Article 1 Objective
A player's training and education takes place between the ages of 12 and 23. Training compensation shall be payable, as a general rule, up to the age of 23 for training incurred up to the age of 21, unless it is evident that a player has already terminated his training period before the age of 21. In the latter case, training compensation shall be payable until the end of the season in which the player reaches the age of 23, but the calculation of the amount payable shall be based on the years between the age of 12 and the age when it is established that the player actually completed his training.

The obligation to pay training compensation is without prejudice to any obligation to pay compensation for breach of contract.

Article 2 Payment of training compensation
1. Training compensation is due when: i) a player is registered for the fi rst time as a professional; or ii) a professional is transferred between clubs of two different associations (whether during or at the end of his contract) before the end of the season of his 23rd birthday.
2. Training compensation is not due if: i) the former club terminates the player's contract without just cause (without prejudice to the rights of the previous clubs); or ii) the player is transferred to a category 4 club; or iii) a professional reacquires amateur status on being transferred.

Article 3 Responsibility to pay training compensation
On registering as a professional for the first time, the club with which the player is registered is responsible for paying training compensation within 30 days of registration to every club with which the player has previously been registered (in accordance with the players' career history as provided in the player passport) and that has contributed to his training starting from the season of his 12th birthday. The amount payable is calculated on a *pro rata* basis according to the period of training that the player spent with each club. In the case of subsequent transfers of the professional, training compensation will only be owed to his former club for the time he was effectively trained by that club.

In both of the above cases, the deadline for payment of training compensation is 30 days following the registration of the professional with the new association.

If a link between the professional and any of the clubs that trained him cannot be established, or if those clubs do not make themselves known within 18 months of the player's first registration as a professional, the training compensation shall be paid to the association(s) of the country (or countries) where the professional was trained. This compensation shall be reserved for youth football development programmes at the association(s) in question.

Article 4 Training costs
In order to calculate the compensation due for training and education costs, associations are instructed to divide their clubs into a maximum of four categories in accordance with the clubs' fi-

nancial investment in training players. The training costs are set for each category and correspond to the amount needed to train one player for one year multiplied by an average "player factor", which is the ratio of players who need to be trained to produce one professional player.

The training costs, which are established on a confederation basis for each category of club, as well as the categorisation of clubs for each association, are published on the FIFA website (www.FIFA.com). They are updated at the end of every calendar year.

Article 5 Calculation of training compensation

As a general rule, to calculate the training compensation due to a player's former club(s), it is necessary to take the costs that would have been incurred by the new club if it had trained the player itself.

Accordingly, the first time a player registers as a professional, the training compensation payable is calculated by taking the training costs of the new club multiplied by the number of years of training, in principle from the season of the player's 12th birthday to the season of his 21st birthday. In the case of subsequent transfers, training compensation is calculated based on the training costs of the new club multiplied by the number of years of training with the former club.

To ensure that training compensation for very young players is not set at unreasonably high levels, the training costs for players for the seasons between their 12th and 15th birthdays (i.e. four seasons) shall be based on the training and education costs of category 4 clubs.

The Dispute Resolution Chamber may review disputes concerning the amount of training compensation payable and shall have discretion to adjust this amount if it is clearly disproportionate to the case under review.

Article 6 Special provisions for the EU/EEA

1. For players moving from one association to another inside the territory of the EU/EEA, the amount of training compensation payable shall be established based on the following:
   a) If the player moves from a lower to a higher category club, the calculation shall be based on the average training costs of the two clubs;
   b) If the player moves from a higher to a lower category, the calculation shall be based on the training costs of the lower-category club.

   Inside the EU/EEA, the final season of training may occur before the season of the player's 21st birthday if it is established that the player completed his training before that time.

   If the former club does not offer the player a contract, no training compensation is payable unless the former club can justify that it is entitled to such compensation. The former club must offer the player a contract in writing via registered post at least 60 days before the expiry of his current contract. Such an offer shall furthermore be at least of an equivalent value to the current contract. This provision is without prejudice to the right to training compensation of the player's previous club(s).

Article 7 Disciplinary measures

The FIFA Disciplinary Committee may impose disciplinary measures on clubs or players that do not observe the obligations set out in this annex.

ANNEX 5
SOLIDARITY MECHANISM

Article 1 Solidarity contribution

If a professional moves during the course of a contract, 5% of any compensation, not including training compensation paid to his former club, shall be deducted from the total amount of this compensation and distributed by the new club as a solidarity contribution to the club(s) involved in his training and education over the years. This solidarity contribution reflects the number of years (calculated *pro rata* if less than one year) he was registered with the relevant club(s) between the seasons of his 12th and 23rd birthdays, as follows:

- Season of 12th birthday: 5% (i.e. 0.25% of total compensation);
- Season of 13th birthday: 5% (i.e. 0.25% of total compensation);
- Season of 14th birthday: 5% (i.e. 0.25% of total compensation);

- Season of 15th birthday: 5% (i.e. 0.25% of total compensation);
- Season of 16th birthday: 10% (i.e. 0.5% of total compensation);
- Season of 17th birthday: 10% (i.e. 0.5% of total compensation);
- Season of 18th birthday: 10% (i.e. 0.5% of total compensation);
- Season of 19th birthday: 10% (i.e. 0.5% of total compensation);
- Season of 20th birthday: 10% (i.e. 0.5% of total compensation);
- Season of 21st birthday: 10% (i.e. 0.5% of total compensation);
- Season of 22nd birthday: 10% (i.e. 0.5% of total compensation);
- Season of 23rd birthday: 10% (i.e. 0.5% of total compensation).

Article 2 Payment procedure

The new club shall pay the solidarity contribution to the training club(s) pursuant to the above provisions no later than 30 days after the player's registration or, in case of contingent payments, 30 days after the date of such payments.

It is the responsibility of the new club to calculate the amount of the solidarity contribution and to distribute it in accordance with the player's career history as provided in the player passport. The player shall, if necessary, assist the new club in discharging this obligation.

If a link between the professional and any of the clubs that trained him cannot be established within 18 months of his transfer, the solidarity contribution shall be paid to the association(s) of the country (or countries) where the professional was trained. This solidarity contribution shall be reserved for youth football development programmes in the association(s) in question.

The Disciplinary Committee may impose disciplinary measures on clubs that do not observe the obligations set out in this annex.

APPENDIX XIV

THE FIFA DISPUTE RESOLUTION CHAMBER DECISION IN WEBSTER

47936
DECISION OF THE DISPUTE RESOLUTION CHAMBER
passed in Zurich, Switzerland, on 4 April 2007,
in the following composition:
Slim Aloulou (Tunisia), Chairman
Mario Gallavotti (Italy), Member
Ivan Gazidis (USA), Member
Theo van Seggelen (Netherlands), Member
Carlos Soto (Chile), Member
on the claim presented by
the club, B, as Claimant
against
the player, Webster, and the club, C as Respondents
regarding compensation for contractual breach and inducement to contractual breach

I. FACTS OF THE CASE

1. The player Webster, born on 23 April 1982, signed an employment contract with the club B on 31 March 2001 and due to expire on 30 June 2005 which, on 1 July 2003, was renewed until 30 June 2007.
2. The above-mentioned employment contract also provides, inter alia, that in the event of an intentional failure of the club to fulfil the terms of the contract, the player is entitled to give 14 days written notice to the club to terminate the agreement.
3. A transfer compensation of 75,000 had been paid by B to the club Arbroath for Webster's transfer.
4. On 9 August 2006 Webster signed a three-year employment contract with the club, C, whereby a basic weekly wage of 10,000 is foreseen in favour of the player for the season 2006/2007. A bonus of 3,000 or 1,500 would be paid to the player in case he was named in the starting eleven or as a substitute, respectively.
5. The weekly salary would rise up to 11,000 in case the player was named in the starting eleven in 12 league games. Should this be the case, a bonus of 4,000 or 2,000 would be paid to the player in case he was named in the starting eleven or as a substitute, respectively.
6. If the player was named in the starting eleven in 20 league games, a bonus of 5,000 or 2,000 would be paid to him in case he was named in the starting eleven or as a substitute, respectively.
7. The weekly salary would rise up to 12,000 as of 1 July 2007 in case the player was named in the starting eleven in 25 league games.
8. On 9 August 2006 the C Football Association requested the international transfer certificate (ITC) from the B Football Association for the player in question.
9. The Football Association replied in writing to this request stating that they cannot issue the requested ITC since Webster is still under contract with their affiliated club, B.
10. On 18 August 2006 the C Football Association turned to FIFA asking for the authorisation to provisionally register the player concerned for its member club, C.
11. On 28 August 2006, at the request of FIFA, the B Football Association stated that it was not in a position to comply with the ITC request, since Webster was still under contract with their affiliated club, B.
12. On 31 August 2006 the Single Judge of the Players' Status Committee authorised the C Football Association to provisionally register A with its affiliated club C with immediate effect.
13. Whereas the matter of the player's provisional registration has been decided upon, the dispute at stake lies on the substance of the contractual dispute between the player and the club and, in particular, on the conditions of the contractual termination.

14. In January 2007 A was transferred to the club Y on a loan basis until the end of the season.

B's position:

15. In November 2006 B contacted FIFA claiming compensation for breach of contract in the amount of 5,037,311 against Mr Webster as well as against C, for having induced the aforementioned breach.
16. The claimant also asks for the player to be ineligible to take part in any official matches for a period of two months, in compliance with Article 17.3 of the FIFA Regulations for the Status and Transfer of Players (hereafter, the Regulations), and for C to be banned from registering any new player for one registration period, in compliance with Article 17.4 of the FIFA Regulations.
17. According to the club, the relationship with A, until then one of the team's bedrocks, deteriorated when the player refused to extend the contract eighteen months before its expiry. It is clear, in the club's view, that Mr Webster was already then seeking a more lucrative contract and, to this effect, planning to walk out of his contract.
18. Subsequently, Mr Webster first notified B that lie would terminate his contract for just cause with a 14-day notice from 4 May 2006 under clause 18 of the employment contract. Such termination notice would then be withdrawn by the player on 7 July 2006.
19. Then, the player notified the club in writing on 26 May 2006 of his intention to terminate the employment contract in accordance with the provision contained in Article 17.3 of the Regulations, i.e. allegedly outside of the Protected Period and within 15 days following the last match of the Season.
20. After having rejected B's proposals for an extension of the contract, Mr Webster addressed, through his agent, Mr ..., a fax to approximately fifty clubs, stating that the player had terminated his contract with the club, that no sanctions would apply as a result of this termination and that compensation would be fixed by FIFA at 200,000.
21. It is clear that Mr Webster breached the contract without just cause utterly disregarding the principles set out in the Regulations for the maintenance of the contractual stability, but whereas the first notice of termination will not be taken into account, the second notice of termination raises the most relevant issues.
22. To this effect, the club asserts that, according to point 9) of the Definitions of the Regulations, the Season ends with the last Official Match of the relevant national league championship. As the last match of the national league championship, i.e. the Premier League, for the Season 2005/2006 was on 7 May 2006, the notice of termination dated 26 May 2006 was not issued within 15 days following the last match of the Season under the purpose of Article 17.3 of the Regulations.
23. In all cases, as the player breached the employment contract without just cause, he shall pay compensation. The latter should be calculated in accordance with the criteria established by Article 17 of the Regulations, yet bearing in mind that the relevant list is not exhaustive, as already pointed out by the Dispute Resolution Chamber itself in its previous decisions.
24. In particular, national law, in casu National Law, should also assist in the calculation of the amount due as compensation by the player and/or the new club. This is confirmed by the parties' intention, expressed in clause 26 of the employment contract, to have the rules of the Football Association and of the Premier League govern any issue pertaining to the suspension and termination of the contract. The rules of the Football Association and of the Premier League are governed by the law of, where the contract was performed and where both parties were domiciled.
25. According to National Law, remedies for the breach of contract are based on the restitutio in integrum, which attempts to return the injured party to the same position it would have been in had the breach not occurred. Hence, B request to be awarded an amount, which would return the club in the position it would have been in had A not committed breach of contract without just cause.
26. According to National Law, it should also be taken into account the lucrum cessans suffered by the club, insomuch as Mr Webster and C should be condemned to pay 1% default interest until such time as B receive the full payment of the amount due as compensation.
27. As regards the loss of opportunity to receive a transfer compensation (lucrum cessans) for the transfer of the player, the claimant requests that the Chamber apply the same principle that it

applied in one of their precedents (Auxerre Football Club, France v Player Philippe Mexes, France and AS Roma, Italy), the damage suffered by the club being analogous to the one for which the French dub was appropriately restored.

28. Mr Webster was in fact one of the best players for the club, and a leading player for the national team. B would have received at least 3 million for the player's transfer, had he not unilaterally terminated the contract. The second division club X made an offer of 1.5 million on 21 June 2006, which was rejected since it was deemed considerably below the player's real value. A number of top division clubs would have been ready to pay significantly more for the player's transfer and some of them, Blackburn Rovers among the others, expressed their genuine interest in the player.
29. This would be corroborated by the fact that in the top division the amount paid for the transfer of a player of a similar pedigree to A would have been between 3 million and 5 million. The claimant further resorts to an expertise according to which, in comparison with a number of players sharing the same age and ability with A, the latter's market value at the last transfer window would be of 5 million.
30. The club invested a lot of money and resources in the player's training and education. Between salary, appearance bonuses, other bonuses and sign-on fee, B as from 1 July 2003 invested on A the amount total of 709,137, also taking into account the amount that the player would have earned for the last season of contract.
31. By means of a further submission received by FIFA after the investigation was officially closed, B amended the above-mentioned figure, through the witness statement of the club's secretary, whereby the total amount paid to the player in the five years spent with the club as from 31 March 2001 is of 1,004,346.
32. On account of the fact that the compensation should also take into consideration the remuneration and other benefits due to the player under the new contract, the claimant reckons that the difference between the bast season of contract with them and the first season of contract with C amounts to 717,335.
33. The costs of a replacement player to be paid by the claimant should also be taken into account by the Chamber, in accordance with its previous jurisprudence. Yet again, the price for a player of A's calibre would be between 3 million and 5 million.
34. Mr Webster's unilateral termination of contract deprived the claimant of a very valuable player and, as a consequence, the club suffered a competitive and commercial loss, the player being very popular among the supporters. The shirt sales and other commercial revenues, which could have been generated are quantified by the claimant in 70,000.
35. B further maintain that they should 5e entitled to receive a reimbursement of 50,000 incurred in as legal expenses.
36. The claimant, B, request the Dispute Resolution Chamber to condemn Mr Webster and C to pay the total amount of 5,037,311 corresponding to 4 million as loss of opportunity to receive a transfer compensation (lucrum cessans) for the transfer of the player, 199,976 as the remaining value of the player's employment contract with the claimant, 717,335 as the difference between the last season of contract with the claimant and the first season of contract with C, 50,000 as legal expenses, 70,000 as commercial loss following the player's unilateral termination.
37. Finally, B request that Mr Webster be declared ineligible to take part in any official matches for a period of two months, in compliance with Article 17.3 of the Regulations, for having breached the contract without just cause and failed to give notice in due time. The fact that the player attempted to breach the contract twice should be taken into account by the Chamber as an aggravating circumstance.
38. B also request that C be banned from registering any new player for one registration period, in compliance with Article 17.4 of the Regulations, for having induced the contractual breach and failed to contact the claimant with regard to the player's contractual position before signing him.

Mr Webster's position:

39. Mr Webster firstly states that he was an ever present in the B's first team in seasons 2003/04, 2004/05 and until 7 February 2006 of the 2005/06 season. He was widely acknowledged as one of B's best and most consistent players. Despite having approximately one and a half years left

to run on the contract, he was being pressured by B into entering into a new playing contract to extend his term at the club, on terms that were not acceptable to him. Following his refusal to enter into a new playing contract on such terms, on 7 February 2006, he was dropped from the side for which he had featured in every minute of every match from the start of the 2005/06 season. This began a course of non-selection by B of Mr Webster.

40. Mr Webster considers that he was dropped from the B's team due to his refusal to sign a new contract and that the decision taken to consistently drop him was based on non-sporting reasons, and taken by the majority shareholder, Vladimir Romanov, rather than by the manager of B.
41. Mr Webster sought legal advice from the Professional Footballers Association ('sPFA'), which advised him that the course of unfair treatment, culminating in the very public and unwarranted criticism of him and his family constituted a complete breakdown of mutual trust and confidence and thus gave him a legal right to terminate the contract for just cause.
42. It was also considered that Mr Webster could terminate the contract under the Regulations on the grounds of sporting just cause due to his sudden non-selection from the team after having been an ever present for purely non-sporting reasons. This non-selection also resulted in him losing his place in the national team. The SPFA considered that such a situation should fail within the definition of sporting just cause under Article 15 of the Regulations, particularly as Mr Webster had been told that he would not play again for the remainder of the contract (i.e. that this non-selection would continue throughout the 2006/07 season).
43. Mr Webster therefore served notice on B to terminate his contract for just cause with a 14-day notice from 4 May 2006 under clause 18 of the employment contract. The SPFA advised Mr Webster that this process may take some time as the procedure and possible appeals process that may follow, could be lengthy This could damage his prospects of securing a contract with another club before the end of the next registration period in August. The SPFA therefore also advised Mr Webster of his rights to terminate the contract under Article 17.3 of the Regulations which would present a more expedient route.
44. Mr Webster resolved to proceed with a termination under Article 173 of the Regulations and served a notice on B to this effect on 26 May 2006. This decision was based on procedural reasons to ensure a swift resolution to his contractual relationship with the club and was not an acceptance that he did not have grounds to terminate for just cause.
45. Mr Webster therefore reiterates his right to terminate the contract for just cause and sporting just cause as well as under Article 17.3 of the Regulations and requests that the Dispute Resolution Chamber make a pronouncement on these grounds before considering the termination under Article 17.3 and the issues of compensation and sanctions.
46. Mr Webster contends that he should not be liable for any sanctions or compensation in this case as he had just cause and sporting just cause to terminate the contract. If this is not accepted, then Mr Webster makes the following points with regard to any sanctions and compensation that the Dispute Resolution Chamber decides to award.
47. Mr Webster, unlike B, has acted properly throughout this process and in principle, It is the club that should be liable to pay damages to Mr Webster. Mr Webster was badly treated due to the simple fact that he would not extend his contract with B. He was dropped from the team for non playing reasons and then suffered the ultimate punishment when lie was left out of the team for the Cup Final.
48. However, to reduce the damages that B would have otherwise been liable to pay, Mr Webster did his utmost to find a new club in due time. As he was successful in obtaining a new job at C, there is no direct financial damage for the player and there was no need for him to claim damages from B.
49. The misconduct of B leading to this conflict could instead justify a referral to the FIFA Disciplinary Committee.
50. The contract was terminated in accordance with Article 17.3 of the Regulations outside of the Protected Period by the unilateral action of the player. Mr Webster signed the contract at the age of 21 and served 3 full seasons under it and was thus entitled to utilise 'the Article 17.3 procedure'. The fact that Mr Webster has been allowed to play for his new club underlines this, and no sporting sanctions can be applied to Mr Webster in this case.
51. Mr Webster wants to emphasise that it was his own decision to terminate the contract. There was no club involved that induced this termination, nor did his agent. Mr Webster refers the

Dispute Resolution Chamber to the witness statement of the agent which confirms that Mr Webster's new club, C, only became involved in this case on 10 July 2006 following receipt of a fax from Mr Webster's agent. C therefore had no involvement in the contract termination. As such, there is no justifiable reason to hold his new club, C, responsible for the consequences of his termination.

52. Mr Webster also wishes to state that he terminated the contract within 15 days of the last game of the season that his club played, i.e. the Cup Final on 13 May 2006 which is the premier cup competition in and is organised and controlled by the Football Association. The winner of this trophy gains automatic entry into the UEFA Cup for the following season.
53. Mr Webster notes that the Cup Final is an 'Official Match' under the Regulations and he therefore understood that the 15 day notice period would run from this game. In this respect, it is noted that under Article 15 of the Regulations when terminating for sporting just cause, the notice is to be sent within 15 days of the last 'Official Match'.
54. It is therefore contended that Mr Webster's actions of sending the letter under Article 17.3 of the Regulations, which was aimed at avoiding disruption to B before the Cup Final, are justifiable and in line with the principle behind the notice period of Article 17.3 of the Regulations.
55. Even if the Dispute Resolution Chamber does not accept that the end of the season was the Cup Final on 13 May 2006, then Mr Webster would state that his notice to terminate on 26 May 2006 was only 4 days outside the 15-day period after the last league fixture (7 May 2006) and therefore caused no prejudice to B.
56. In the circumstances, and for the reasons set out, Mr Webster respectfully requests that he should not face any disciplinary measures under Article 17.3 of the Regulations. It is also dear that there can be no 'sporting sanctions' in this case as the termination came outside the Protected Period.
57. In this regard, Mr Webster would request the Dispute Resolution Chamber to note that lie has already been out of football for some time due to his non-selection at B and subsequent lack of match fitness whereby lie did not play during the period from April to October 2006 at either club or international level.
58. In the event that Mr Webster is held liable for damages to B he would like to point out that these damages must be limited to the residual value of the contract.
59. As the termination of contract occurred outside of the Protected Period there is no factor available to increase the amount of this residual value although B uses a lot of paperwork to state otherwise. In the view of the player It is not possible that the breach of a contract between two parties with a certain value (the salary of the player) would lead to a compensation that exceeds this amount many times. In previous Dispute Resolution Chamber cases the residual value of the contract has been the guideline for the settlement of the compensation. In this case there is no justified reason to deviate from that guideline.
60. The residual value of the contract is in fact the only applicable factor for calculating the compensation as it is obvious that the said value represents the value of the contract between the two parties. The fact that the termination of the contract took place outside of the stability period is a mitigating factor.
61. In the Regulations and Dispute Resolution Chamber's jurisprudence there is no foundation for the position of B that the compensation shall be calculated on the basis of an alleged 'market value' of a player. In any case B failed to substantiate this.
62. Of course it is possible that parties come to a mutual agreement that exceeds the residual value of the contract, but this is not the position here.
63. Moreover, from the submission of B can be learnt that an offer of 1.5 million (10 times the residual value of the contract) was turned down. It should be noted that this bid came after A had terminated the contract. So even if B were minded to accept the bid it was not in a position to do so as A had already terminated the contract.
64. Furthermore, B seem to forget that at the end of the contract on 1 July 2007 – if It were not terminated – A could have left the club without any compensation at all.
65. To this effect, Mr Webster has also noted the details response of C to B's claim for compensation and confirms that he fully concurs with these submissions and requests that the Dispute Resolution Chamber also take them into account when assessing any compensation that may be payable by him in this case.

66. Finally, and as far as B's latest submission is concerned, whereby they propose a calculation of the amount paid to the player during the course of his contract, Mr Webster maintains that the club has had two previous opportunities to submit any evidence regarding this case. Therefore, according to the procedures set Out by FIFA to govern the manner in which these proceedings are conducted, any evidence produced by the club within its latest submission is out of time and cannot be relied upon. In any case the evidence produced does not offer any new insight into the case and is not relevant to the facts of the case.
67. However, if the Dispute Resolution Chamber does choose to allow this new evidence, Mr Webster would like to state that the club has chosen to outline salary figures it maintains were paid to him for a period of five seasons from 2001 until 2006. These figures cannot contribute to the calculation of any compensation that may be payable to B, as it can only be the residual value of the contract that can be taken into consideration by the Chamber.
68. Furthermore, within the club's own schedule of payments the amounts for the seasons 2001/02 and 2002/03 relate to a previous contract concluded between the parties and are therefore completely irrelevant, whereas for the seasons 2003/04, 2004/05 and 2005/06 the club has of course had a return for these payments by way of having Mr Webster play for them during this period. Again these figures are irrelevant to the case.
69. It is interesting however to note that B, in submitting this as evidence, are clearly acknowledging that the player's contract is indeed the only relevant factor with regard to the calculation of any compensation. This is a change from the club's previous submissions where its position was based around purely subjective views of the player's transfer market value.
70. A would like to stress once more that it can only be the residual value of the final year of his contract that can be taken as relevant, and the club appears indeed to agree with this view by means of its latest submission. The new evidence does not in any case contribute to the facts of the matter.
71. For the reasons set out above, Mr Webster hereby request the dismissal of the claims of B against him. Mr Webster submits he had just cause and sporting just cause to terminate the contract. Furthermore, the player acted entirely properly in terminating the contract under Article 17.3 of the Regulations and no sporting sanctions or disciplinary measures can be imposed against him. Finally, any compensation deemed payable to B, must be limited to the residual value of the contract.

C's position:

72. C's recollection of the facts reflect that of the player.
73. C maintain in their position that the employment contract between the player, Mr Webster, and B was unilaterally terminated by the earlier outside the Protected Period. The employment contract at stake was in fact concluded on 1 July 2003 and is due to expire on 30 June 2007. Therefore, the Protected Period has come to an end with the end of the third season, i.e. on 7 May 2006.
74. To this effect, C are eager to point out that the player gave the club even two notices of termination, one on 4 May 2006 on the grounds of just cause, and the second on 26 May 2006, in compliance with the provision contained in Article 17 of the Regulations, i.e. outside of the Protected Period and within 15 days following the last match of the Season. This second notice was not, however, a withdrawal of the underlying allegations that support the player's right to terminate the contract for just cause.
75. According to the club, the first contact between Mr Webster and C occurred on 10 July 2006, i.e. six weeks after the termination of contract performed by the player. As a matter of law, there is no causative link between C and the termination of the contract, as a consequence of which, the club cannot be deemed liable for any damage arising from such a breach.
76. As regards B's request to be awarded an amount, which would return the club in the position it would have been in had A not committed breach of contract without just cause, It is not so obvious that the club is the damaged party in this case, especially taking into account that their behaviour led the player to terminate the contract.
77. Furthermore, the club appears to request a 'transfer fee' which not only is not provided for in the Regulations, but what is more is not included in the criteria listed in Article 17 of the Regulations to assess the amount of compensation due for breach of contract.

78. The club also points out that the offer made by X occurred after the player had terminated the contract and, therefore, cannot be taken into consideration as loss of opportunity, apart from the fact that the evaluation X give of the player is subjective and cannot be regarded as a proof of the player's actual value. In fact, all the club's allegation with respect to the player's value are entirely arbitrary and hypothetical.
79. As regards B's calculation of the compensation due, when it comes to the remaining value of the contract, only the salary and sign-on fee and no other bonuses should be taken into account. Therefore, the residual value of Mr Webster's contract with B should not exceed 149,976.
80. Also the projection for the player's future salary made by the claimant is totally ungrounded, since no sign-on fee is provided for under the new contract and, taking into account that the player earns 10,000 per week, a likely figure as yearly salary is 450,000 plus approximately 33,000 as appearance bonus.
81. For the record, the player only featured in a small number of matches for C and is now on ban to the club Y.
82. As far as B's request for A to be imposed disciplinary sanctions is concerned, C's position reflects that of the player.
83. Finally, and as far as B's latest submission concerning the player's salaries is concerned, C's position again reflects that of the player, especially under the procedural point of view, i.e. the latest evidence was produced out of time and should not be taken into consideration.
84. However, It the Dispute Resolution Chamber does choose to allow this new evidence, it has to be noted that the amounts for the seasons 2001/02 and 2002/03 are completely irrelevant, since they relate to a previous different contract, which was superseded by the one signed on 1 July 2003.
85. In any case, Article 17.1 of the Regulations refers to 'benefits due to the player under the existing contract', i.e. the sums that have not yet been paid to him. Therefore, what has been paid by the club is totally irrelevant. Plus, that club has largely benefited from the services of the player, who played 239 games with them.
86. It is also worth emphasising that the figures of the latest submission are greater than those presented by means of the claimant's submission.
87. To conclude with, C request the Dispute Resolution Chamber that all requests filed by B be rejected.
88. The Dispute Resolution Chamber is asked to rule upon the breach of contract, as well as on the possible consequences.

Players' Agent:

89. The Dispute Resolution Chamber is also asked to pronounce itself on the relevance of the role played by Mr Webster's agent in the affair at stake.

II. CONSIDERATIONS OF THE DISPUTE RESOLUTION CHAMBER

1. First of all, the Dispute Resolution Chamber analysed whether It was competent to deal with the matter at stake. In this respect, it referred to art. 18 par. 2 and 3 of the Rules Governing the Procedures of the Players' Status Committee and the Dispute Resolution Chamber. The present matter was submitted to FIFA in November 2006, as a consequence the Chamber concluded that the revised Rules Governing Procedures (edition 2005) on matters pending before the decision making bodies of FIFA apply to the matter at hand.
2. With regard to the competence of the Chamber, art. 3 par. 1 of the abovementioned Rules states that the Dispute Resolution Chamber shall examine its jurisdiction in the light of articles 22 to 24 of the current version of the Regulations (edition 2005). In accordance with art. 24 par. 1 in connection with art. 22 (a) of the aforementioned Regulations, the Dispute Resolution Chamber shall adjudicate on employment-related disputes between a club and a player in relation to the maintenance of contractual stability if there has been an ITC request and if there is a claim trom an interested party in relation to such ITC request, in particular regarding its issuance, regarding sporting sanctions or regarding compensation for breach of contract.
3. As a consequence, the Dispute Resolution Chamber is the competent body to decide on the present litigation regarding a dispute in relation to the maintenance of contractual stability arisen following the issuance of an ITC regarding compensation for breach of contract.

4. Subsequently, the members of the Chamber analysed which edition of the Regulations should be applicable as to the substance of the matter. In this respect, the Chamber referred, on the one hand, to art. 26 par. 1 and 2 of the Regulations (edition 2005) and, on the other hand, to the fact that the relevant contract at the basis of this dispute was signed on 1 July 2003 and that this claim was lodged at FIFA by B in November 2006. In view of the aforementioned circumstances, the Chamber concluded that the current FIFA Regulations for the Status and Transfer of Players apply to the case at hand as to the substance.
5. Before entering the substance of the matter, the Chairman of the Dispute Resolution Chamber addressed the issue raised by B, that challenged one of the members, Mr Theo van Seggelen, and asked the Chamber to reconsider the constitution of the panel.
6. In this context, B drew FIFA's attention to the article that appeared on the website of FIFPro, the General Secretary of which is Mr Theo van Seggelen himself, under the title: 'A case, step forwards in the freedom of players'. This report contained some statements suggestive of the decision that the Dispute Resolution Chamber would have reached in the case at hand.
7. The club therefore questioned the presence of a FIFPro member (what is more, its General Secretary) in the case at stake and, in particular, challenged Mr Theo van Seggelen and sought its replacement on the grounds of lack of impartiality.
8. In this respect, Mr Theo van Seggelen pointed out that the above-said article represents an independent opinion expressed by an individual operating outside FIFPro and that, either in this one or in any other case in which he has been involved in his quality of member of the Dispute Resolution Chamber, he has never made any comment either before or after a decision, abways abiding by the duty of confidentiality.
9. The Chairman was then eager to emphasise that the Chamber is an impartial deciding authority composed by an equal number of members chosen amongst representatives of clubs and representatives of players, of which FIFPro is the leading organisation at international level. It was also underlined that the aforementioned composition has always allowed a fair resolution of the football-related disputes.
10. None of the members, the Chairman assured, has ever represented the interests of either the players or the clubs, but always taken care of the exclusive interest of the Dispute Resolution Chamber itself.
11. Consequently, and in view of the concerned person's above explanations, the Chairman along with all the remaining members concluded that the request for the dismissal of Mr Theo van Seggelen shall be rejected.
12. In continuation, and entering into the substance of the matter, the Chamber acknowledged the documentation contained in the file and focussed its attention on the fact that Webster and the club B signed an employment contract on 31 March 2001 due to expire on 30 June 2005 which, on 1 July 2003, was renewed until 30 June 2007.
13. The Chamber also noted that, on 9 August 2006, A signed a three-year employment contract with the club, C and that, whereas the subsequent matter of the player's provisional registration had been decided upon by the FIFA competent authority, the dispute at stake lay on the substance of the contractual dispute between the player and the club and, in particular, on the conditions of the contractual termination.
14. To this effect, the Chamber took note of the fact that, on 26 May 2006, Mr Webster served notice of termination on B and, in this regard, the members had to ascertain whether or not the said notice of termination, and the subsequent unilateral termination of the contract, occurred in compliance with the provisions established under Article 17.3 of the Regulations, i.e. outside of the Protected Period and within 15 days following the last match of the Season.
15. It was observed that, on account of the fact that the employment contract between the player and the club was concluded on 1 July 2003 and due to expire on 30 June 2007, the unilateral termination undeniably occurred after three seasons, i.e. outside of the Protected Period, as indicated under point 7) of the Definitions section of the Regulations.
16. This being established, the Chamber stated that it had to assess the unavoidable consequences of this unilateral termination, in accordance with the provisions provided for by Articles 13 ff. of the Regulations.
17. The deciding authority incidentally noticed that Mr Webster had firstly served notice on B to terminate his contract for just cause with a 14-day notice from 4 May 2006 under clause 18 of

the employment contract whereby, in the event of an intentional failure of the club to fulfil the terms of the contract, the player would be entitled to give a 14-day written notice to the club to terminate the agreement.

18. However, it was also noted that Mr Webster had been advised that this process may have taken some time as the procedure and possible appeals process that may have followed, could have been lengthy and that this could have damaged his prospects of securing a contract with another club before the end of the next registration period in August. Mr Webster then resolved to proceed with a termination under Article 17.3 of the Regulations and served a further notice on B to this effect on 26 May 2006. This decision was based on procedural reasons to ensure a swift resolution to his contractual relationship with the club and, according to the player, was not an acceptance that he did not have grounds to terminate for just cause.
19. In this context, and whilst not discounting the difficulties that the player and the club may have been faced with in the final part of their contractual relationship, the Chamber was left with no other choice than to regard the termination that the player actually performed on 26 May 2006, on the basis of Article 17.3 of the Regulations as the only valid one, for the purpose of this procedure.
20. In continuation, and for the sake of good order, the Chamber deemed it essential to state that also the termination of the contract for sporting just cause, which the player appears to invoke, at least on a subsidiary basis, could not be further considered. In fact, a player intending to make use of this possibility, would have to proceed by serving notice on the club that he is registered with and call upon the relevant sporting just cause in the fifteen days following the last Official Match of the Season (cf. Article 15 of the Regulations). Undisputedly, the player had never served such a notice. Yet, on 7 July 2006 the player withdrew his first termination notice.
21. However, as far as the timeliness of the notice of termination of 26 May 2006 is concerned, It has to be noted that according to point 9) of the Definitions section of the Regulations, the Season ends with the last Official Match of the relevant national league championship. As the last match of the national league championship, i.e. the Premier League, for the Season 2005/2006 occurred on 7 May 2006, the notice of termination dated 26 May 2006 does not appear to have been issued within 15 days following the last match of the Season for the purpose of Article 17.3 of the Regulations.
22. In this respect, the members of the Chamber understood that Mr Webster terminated the contract within 15 days of the last game of the season that his club actually played, i.e. the Cup Final on 13 May 2006, and that such a match is to be regarded as an Official Match' under the FIFA Statutes and Regulations (cf., in particular, point 5) of the Definitions section of the Regulations) and he therefore understood that the 15-day notice period would run from this game.
23. However, point 9) of the Definitions section of the Regulations is unambiguous in stating that the Season ends with the last Official Match of the relevant national league championship and, therefore, any notice of termination served after fifteen days of the last Official Match of the Season may result in the application of disciplinary measures, in accordance with Article 17.3 of the Regulations.
24. The deciding authority emphasised the relevance of the strict implementation of this rule, and of the consequent adoption of disciplinary measures, so as to enhance the legal certainty in the contractual relationships between players and clubs.
25. Nonetheless, the Chamber took also into consideration that, in any case, the notice was notified nineteen days after the last Official Match of the Season, i.e. four days only beyond the fifteen days required by Article 17.3 of the Regulations.
26. In light of the above, the Dispute Resolution Chamber decided that Mr Webster failed to give B due notice of termination on time as provided for under Article 17.3 of the Regulations, and, as a consequence, the player will not be eligible to participate in any official football match for a period of two weeks as from the beginning of the next national league championship of the club for which he will be registered.
27. After the consequences of the failure to give B due notice of termination on time were thus established, the Chamber went on to consider the consequences of terminating the employment contract without just cause.
28. In this respect, the deciding body first and foremost laid emphasis on the primacy of the principle of the maintenance of contractual stability, which represents the backbone of the agreement

between FIFA/UEFA and the European Commission signed in March 2001. This agreement and its pillars represent the core of the former (edition 2001) as well as of the current version of the Regulations.

29. In particular, the Chamber was eager to point out that the measures provided for by the above Regulations concerning compensation for breach of contract without just cause serve as a deterrent and that a back of a firm response by the competent deciding authorities would represent an inappropriate example towards all the football actors, especially in view of the particular attention that this case arouses in the world of football.
30. Above all, it was underscored that the criteria contained in Article 17 of the Regulations are applied on the principle of reciprocity for clubs and players, signifying that both clubs and professionals who are seen to have committed a breach of contract without just cause will in all cases be subject to pay compensation and, under specific circumstances, also subject to the imposition of sporting sanctions.
31. In this respect, awarding compensation in favour of the damaged party (either the player or the club, as the case may be) has proven to be an efficient means and has always found a widespread acceptance since it guarantees that the fundamental principle of the respect of the contracts is duly taken care of.
32. As it was observed, Article 17 of the Regulations, far from stipulating the right of a contractual party to terminate the employment contract, affirms that in all cases the party in breach of contract shall pay compensation.
33. This notwithstanding, the members of the Chamber were also unanimously keen to emphasise that the breach of contract without just cause committed by Mr Webster outside of the Protected Period cannot result in the imposition of sporting sanctions, in compliance with the applicable Regulations (cf. Article 17 of the Regulations).
34. Consistently with the above, and in conformity with the relevant Regulations, the player's new club, the C, shall not suffer sporting sanctions for inducing the contractual breach and its responsibility shall be limited to being jointly and severally liable for the payment of any amount of compensation for breach of contract that Mr Webster will be ordered to pay (cf. Article 17.3 and 17.2 of the Regulations). In this respect, the Chamber was eager to point out that the joint liability of the player's new club is independent from the question of a possible inducement to contractual breach.
35. Moreover, and with respect to a possible responsibility of the club for having entered into negotiations with A during the course of his contract and for having failed to inform B in writing in accordance with Article 18.3 of the Regulations, the Dispute Resolution Chamber underlined that there is no evidence in support of the fact that the club contacted the player any time before the unilateral termination of the contract with the club.
36. On the contrary, the time elapsed between the notice of termination, dated 26 May 2006, and the conclusion of the contract between C and A on 9 August 2006 led the Chamber to conclude that there is no causative link between C and the termination of the contract by the player and, therefore, to rule out any wrongdoing by the club.
37. In continuation, according to the members of the Chamber a careful reading of the applicable provision, i.e. Article 17.1 of the Regulations, provides the key to assess the amount of compensation due by the player to the club.
38. The Chamber stated that the criteria listed therein are, however, not exhaustive and that each request for compensation for breach of contract has to be assessed on a case-by-case basis, leaving to the deciding body the faculty to decide ex aequo et bono, where appropriate.
39. The members thus stated that it falls under their responsibility to estimate the prejudice suffered by B in the case at hand, not only in accordance with the above-stated criteria, but also with their specific knowledge of the world of football, as well as with the experience the Chamber itself has gained throughout the years.
40. In the calculation of the amount of compensation due by A, at first the Chamber turned its attention on the remuneration and other benefits due to the player under the existing contract and under the new contract.
41. According to the documentation provided by B to FIFA, it appears that the remaining value of the player's employment contract with the club can be calculated in the amount of 199,976.

42. As regards the financial conditions of the employment contract concluded between A and C, the Chamber acknowledged the fact that the player would receive a basic weekly wage of 10,000 for the season 2006/2007, plus a number of appearance bonuses.
43. In addition to that, transfer compensation of 75,000 had also been paid by B to the club Arbroath for A's transfer. According to Article 17.1 of the Regulations, this amount shall be amortised over the term of the relevant employment contract.
44. The deciding body concluded its analysis of the objective criteria listed in Article 17.1 of the Regulations, by recalling that the contractual breach occurred outside the Protected Period and pointing out that, at the time when the contract was breached, A was still bound to B by one further year of contract only.
45. As a matter of fact, the five seasons A spent with B shall also play a chief role in determining the amount of compensation due for contractual breach.
46. Likewise, the deciding authority observed that another crucial factor to be taken into account is the way B have greatly contributed to the steady improvement of a player, A, who joined the club at the age of nineteen and, throughout the course of his spell with the side, has become a high-profile footballer, deserving a constant presence in the national team and arousing the interest of top-flight clubs both in the and in the Premiership, as the events revealed. According to the Chamber, such a stance demonstrates the real interest the club had always had in the services of the player.
47. Once again, emphasis was placed on the tact that Article 17.1, while listing certain factors to be included in the Chamber's consideration in the calculation of the amount of compensation payable, does not purport to limit the factors that may be considered by the Chamber in any individual case. These factors may include, in addition to local law and the specificity of sport, 'any other objective criteria', including those specifically listed in Article 17.1.
48. The aforementioned considerations led the deciding authority to the conclusion that limiting the compensation for breach of contract to the residual value of the contract not only is not in line with the jurisprudence of the Dispute Resolution Chamber, but would also undermine the principle of maintenance of contractual stability, reducing to a mere formula the legitimate right of the damaged party to receive compensation.
49. In this respect, it was declared that as a general rule, a player cannot, at any time and under any circumstances, 'buy out' an employment contract by simply paying to his club the remaining value of his contract.
50. In light of all the above-exposed circumstances, and after a careful analysis of the documentation at its disposal, the specificities of the case at hand, as well as of all the parties' respective positions, the Chamber decided that A must pay the amount of 625,000 to B as compensation for breach of contract.
51. To conclude with, the members of the Dispute Resolution Chamber were of the unanimous opinion that, under the light of the facts of this dispute, the role played by the players' agent in the breach of contract requires further investigation by the competent authorities.
52. Therefore, in compliance with Article 21.1 in connection with Article 14 c) of the Players' Agents Regulations and 17.5 of the Regulations, the matter will be forwarded to the Players' Status Committee for investigation and decision.

III. DECISION OF THE DISPUTE RESOLUTION CHAMBER

1. The claim of the club, B, is partially accepted.
2. The player, A, has unilaterally breached the employment contract with S without just cause outside the Protected Period.
3. Mr Webster has to pay the amount of 625,000 to B within 30 days of notification of this decision.
4. If this amount is not paid within the aforementioned deadline, a 5% interest rate per annum as from the expiry of the aforementioned deadline will apply, and the present matter will be submitted to the FIFA's Disciplinary Committee, so that the necessary disciplinary sanctions may be imposed.
5. The club C is jointly and severally liable for the aforementioned payment.
6. Any other request filed by B is rejected.

7. B is directed to inform Mr Webster and C immediately of the account number to which the remittance is to be made, and to notify the Dispute Resolution Chamber of any payment received.
8. Mr Webster failed to give B due notice of termination.
9. Mr Webster is not eligible to participate in any official football match for a period of two weeks as from the beginning of the next national league championship for which he will be registered.
10. The matter concerning the role played by the players' agent in the breach of contract, will be forwarded to the Players' Status Committee for investigation and decision.
11. According to art. 61 par. 1 of the FIFA Statutes, this decision may be appealed against before the Court of Arbitration for Sport (CAS). The statement of appeal must be sent to the CAS directly within 21 days of receipt of notification of this decision and shall contain all the elements in accordance with point 2 of the directives issued by the CAS, a copy of which we enclose hereto. Within another 10 days following the expiry of the time limit for filing the statement of appeal, the appellant shall file a brief stating the facts and legal arguments giving rise to the appeal with the CAS (cf. point 4 of the directives).

APPENDIX XV

AMERICAN ARBITRATION ASSOCIATION INTERNATIONAL ARBITRATION AND MEDIATION RULES

Commercial Arbitration Rules and Mediation PROCEDURES
(Including Procedures for Large, Complex Commercial Disputes)
Amended and Effective September 1, 2007
Summary of Changes

TABLE OF CONTENTS

IMPORTANT NOTICE

These rules and any amendment of them shall apply in the form in effect at the time the administrative filing requirements are met for a demand for arbitration or submission agreement received by the AAA. To ensure that you have the most current information, see our Web Site at www.adr.org.

INTRODUCTION

Each year, many millions of business transactions take place. Occasionally, disagreements develop over these business transactions. Many of these disputes are resolved by arbitration, the voluntary submission of a dispute to an impartial person or persons for final and binding determination. Arbitration has proven to be an effective way to resolve these disputes privately, promptly, and economically.

The American Arbitration Association (AAA), a not-for-profit, public service organization, offers a broad range of dispute resolution services to business executives, attorneys, individuals, trade associations, unions, management, consumers, families, communities, and all levels of government. Services are available through AAA headquarters in New York and through offices located in major cities throughout the United States. Hearings may be held at locations convenient for the parties and are not limited to cities with AAA offices. In addition, the AAA serves as a center for education and training, issues specialized publications, and conducts research on all forms of out-of-court dispute settlement.

Standard Arbitration Clause

The parties can provide for arbitration of future disputes by inserting the following clause into their contracts:

> *"Any controversy or claim arising out of or relating to this contract, or the breach thereof, shall be settled by arbitration administered by the American Arbitration Association under its Commercial Arbitration Rules, and judgment on the award rendered by the arbitrator(s) may be entered in any court having jurisdiction thereof."*

Arbitration of existing disputes may be accomplished by use of the following:

> *"We, the undersigned parties, hereby agree to submit to arbitration administered by the American Arbitration Association under its Commercial Arbitration Rules the following controversy: (describe briefly) We further agree that the above controversy be submitted to (one) (three) arbitrator(s). We further agree that we will faithfully observe this agreement and the rules, that we will abide by and perform any award rendered by the arbitrator(s), and that a judgment of any court having jurisdiction may be entered on the award."*

In transactions likely to require emergency interim relief, the parties may wish to add to their clause the following language:

> *"The parties also agree that the AAA Optional Rules for Emergency Measures of Protection shall apply to the proceedings."*

These Optional Rules may be found below.

The services of the AAA are generally concluded with the transmittal of the award. Although there is voluntary compliance with the majority of awards, judgment on the award can be entered in a court having appropriate jurisdiction if necessary.

Administrative Fees

The AAA charges a filing fee based on the amount of the claim or counterclaim. This fee information, which is included with these rules, allows the parties to exercise control over their administrative fees.

The fees cover AAA administrative services; they do not cover arbitrator compensation or expenses, if any, reporting services, or any post-award charges incurred by the parties in enforcing the award.

Mediation

The parties might wish to submit their dispute to mediation prior to arbitration. In mediation, the neutral mediator assists the parties in reaching a settlement but does not have the authority to make a binding decision or award. Mediation is administered by the AAA in accordance with its Commercial Mediation Procedures. There is no additional administrative fee where parties to a pending arbitration attempt to mediate their dispute under the AAA's auspices.

If the parties want to adopt mediation as a part of their contractual dispute settlement procedure, they can insert the following mediation clause into their contract in conjunction with a standard arbitration provision:

> "*If a dispute arises out of or relates to this contract, or the breach thereof, and if the dispute cannot be settled through negotiation, the parties agree first to try in good faith to settle the dispute by mediation administered by the American Arbitration Association under its Commercial Mediation Procedures before resorting to arbitration, litigation, or some other dispute resolution procedure.*"

If the parties want to use a mediator to resolve an existing dispute, they can enter into the following submission:

> "*The parties hereby submit the following dispute to mediation administered by the American Arbitration Association under its Commercial Mediation Procedures. (The clause may also provide for the qualifications of the mediator(s), method of payment, locale of meetings, and any other item of concern to the parties.)*"

Large, Complex Cases

Unless the parties agree otherwise, the procedures for Large, Complex Commercial Disputes, which appear in this pamphlet, will be applied to all cases administered by the AAA under the Commercial Arbitration Rules in which the disclosed claim or counterclaim of any party is at least $500,000 exclusive of claimed interest, arbitration fees and costs.

The key features of these procedures include:

- a highly qualified, trained Roster of Neutrals;
- a mandatory preliminary hearing with the arbitrators, which may be conducted by teleconference;
- broad arbitrator authority to order and control discovery, including depositions;
- presumption that hearings will proceed on a consecutive or block basis.

COMMERCIAL MEDIATION PROCEDURES

M-1. Agreement of Parties

Whenever, by stipulation or in their contract, the parties have provided for mediation or conciliation of existing or future disputes under the auspices of the American Arbitration Association (AAA) or under these procedures, the parties and their representatives, unless agreed otherwise in writing, shall be deemed to have made these procedural guidelines, as amended and in effect as of the date of filing of a request for mediation, a part of their agreement and designate the AAA as the administrator of their mediation.

The parties by mutual agreement may vary any part of these procedures including, but not limited to, agreeing to conduct the mediation via telephone or other electronic or technical means.

M-2. Initiation of Mediation

Any party or parties to a dispute may initiate mediation under the AAA's auspices by making a request for mediation to any of the AAA's regional offices or case management centers via telephone, email, regular mail or fax. Requests for mediation may also be filed online via WebFile at www.adr.org.

The party initiating the mediation shall simultaneously notify the other party or parties of the request. The initiating party shall provide the following information to the AAA and the other party or parties as applicable:

A copy of the mediation provision of the parties' contract or the parties' stipulation to mediate.

The names, regular mail addresses, email addresses, and telephone numbers of all parties to the dispute and representatives, if any, in the mediation.

A brief statement of the nature of the dispute and the relief requested.

Any specific qualifications the mediator should possess.

Where there is no preexisting stipulation or contract by which the parties have provided for mediation of existing or future disputes under the auspices of the AAA, a party may request the AAA to invite another party to participate in "mediation by voluntary submission". Upon receipt of such a request, the AAA will contact the other party or parties involved in the dispute and attempt to obtain a submission to mediation.

M-3. Representation

Subject to any applicable law, any party may be represented by persons of the party's choice. The names and addresses of such persons shall be communicated in writing to all parties and to the AAA.

M-4. Appointment of the Mediator

Parties may search the online profiles of the AAA's Panel of Mediators at www.aaamediation.com in an effort to agree on a mediator. If the parties have not agreed to the appointment of a mediator and have not provided any other method of appointment, the mediator shall be appointed in the following manner:

Upon receipt of a request for mediation, the AAA will send to each party a list of mediators from the AAA's Panel of Mediators. The parties are encouraged to agree to a mediator from the submitted list and to advise the AAA of their agreement.

If the parties are unable to agree upon a mediator, each party shall strike unacceptable names from the list, number the remaining names in order of preference, and return the list to the AAA. If a party does not return the list within the time specified, all mediators on the list shall be deemed acceptable. From among the mediators who have been mutually approved by the parties, and in accordance with the designated order of mutual preference, the AAA shall invite a mediator to serve.

If the parties fail to agree on any of the mediators listed, or if acceptable mediators are unable to serve, or if for any other reason the appointment cannot be made from the submitted list, the AAA shall have the authority to make the appointment from among other members of the Panel of Mediators without the submission of additional lists.

M-5. Mediator's Impartiality and Duty to Disclose

AAA mediators are required to abide by the Model Standards of Conduct for Mediators in effect at the time a mediator is appointed to a case. Where there is a conflict between the Model Standards and any provision of these Mediation Procedures, these Mediation Procedures shall govern. The Standards require mediators to (i) decline a mediation if the mediator cannot conduct it in an impartial manner, and (ii) disclose, as soon as practicable, all actual and potential conflicts of interest that are reasonably known to the mediator and could reasonably be seen as raising a question about the mediator's impartiality.

Prior to accepting an appointment, AAA mediators are required to make a reasonable inquiry to determine whether there are any facts that a reasonable individual would consider likely to create a potential or actual conflict of interest for the mediator. AAA mediators are required to disclose any circumstance likely to create a presumption of bias or prevent a resolution of the parties' dispute within the time-frame desired by the parties. Upon receipt of such disclosures, the AAA shall immediately communicate the disclosures to the parties for their comments.

The parties may, upon receiving disclosure of actual or potential conflicts of interest of the mediator, waive such conflicts and proceed with the mediation. In the event that a party disagrees as to whether the mediator shall serve, or in the event that the mediator's conflict of interest might reasonably be viewed as undermining the integrity of the mediation, the mediator shall be replaced.

M-6. Vacancies
If any mediator shall become unwilling or unable to serve, the AAA will appoint another mediator, unless the parties agree otherwise, in accordance with section M-4.

M-7. Duties and Responsibilities of the Mediator
The mediator shall conduct the mediation based on the principle of party self-determination. Self-determination is the act of coming to a voluntary, uncoerced decision in which each party makes free and informed choices as to process and outcome.

The mediator is authorized to conduct separate or ex parte meetings and other communications with the parties and/or their representatives, before, during, and after any scheduled mediation conference. Such communications may be conducted via telephone, in writing, via email, online, in person or otherwise.

The parties are encouraged to exchange all documents pertinent to the relief requested. The mediator may request the exchange of memoranda on issues, including the underlying interests and the history of the parties' negotiations. Information that a party wishes to keep confidential may be sent to the mediator, as necessary, in a separate communication with the mediator.

The mediator does not have the authority to impose a settlement on the parties but will attempt to help them reach a satisfactory resolution of their dispute. Subject to the discretion of the mediator, the mediator may make oral or written recommendations for settlement to a party privately or, if the parties agree, to all parties jointly.

In the event a complete settlement of all or some issues in dispute is not achieved within the scheduled mediation session(s), the mediator may continue to communicate with the parties, for a period of time, in an ongoing effort to facilitate a complete settlement.

The mediator is not a legal representative of any party and has no fiduciary duty to any party.

M-8. Responsibilities of the Parties
The parties shall ensure that appropriate representatives of each party, having authority to consummate a settlement, attend the mediation conference.

Prior to and during the scheduled mediation conference session(s) the parties and their representatives shall, as appropriate to each party's circumstances, exercise their best efforts to prepare for and engage in a meaningful and productive mediation.

M-9. Privacy
Mediation sessions and related mediation communications are private proceedings. The parties and their representatives may attend mediation sessions. Other persons may attend only with the permission of the parties and with the consent of the mediator.

M-10. Confidentiality
Subject to applicable law or the parties' agreement, confidential information disclosed to a mediator by the parties or by other participants (witnesses) in the course of the mediation shall not be divulged by the mediator. The mediator shall maintain the confidentiality of all information obtained in the mediation, and all records, reports, or other documents received by a mediator while serving in that capacity shall be confidential.

The mediator shall not be compelled to divulge such records or to testify in regard to the mediation in any adversary proceeding or judicial forum.

The parties shall maintain the confidentiality of the mediation and shall not rely on, or introduce as evidence in any arbitral, judicial, or other proceeding the following, unless agreed to by the parties or required by applicable law:

Views expressed or suggestions made by a party or other participant with respect to a possible settlement of the dispute;

Admissions made by a party or other participant in the course of the mediation proceedings;
Proposals made or views expressed by the mediator; or
The fact that a party had or had not indicated willingness to accept a proposal for settlement made by the mediator.

M-11. No Stenographic Record
There shall be no stenographic record of the mediation process.

M-12. Termination of Mediation
The mediation shall be terminated:

By the execution of a settlement agreement by the parties; or
By a written or verbal declaration of the mediator to the effect that further efforts at mediation would not contribute to a resolution of the parties' dispute; or
By a written or verbal declaration of all parties to the effect that the mediation proceedings are terminated; or
When there has been no communication between the mediator and any party or party's representative for 21 days following the conclusion of the mediation conference.

M-13. Exclusion of Liability
Neither the AAA nor any mediator is a necessary party in judicial proceedings relating to the mediation. Neither the AAA nor any mediator shall be liable to any party for any error, act or omission in connection with any mediation conducted under these procedures.

M-14. Interpretation and Application of Procedures
The mediator shall interpret and apply these procedures insofar as they relate to the mediator's duties and responsibilities. All other procedures shall be interpreted and applied by the AAA.

M-15. Deposits
Unless otherwise directed by the mediator, the AAA will require the parties to deposit in advance of the mediation conference such sums of money as it, in consultation with the mediator, deems necessary to cover the costs and expenses of the mediation and shall render an accounting to the parties and return any unexpended balance at the conclusion of the mediation.

M-16. Expenses
All expenses of the mediation, including required traveling and other expenses or charges of the mediator, shall be borne equally by the parties unless they agree otherwise. The expenses of participants for either side shall be paid by the party requesting the attendance of such participants.

M-17. Cost of the Mediation
There is no filing fee to initiate a mediation or a fee to request the AAA to invite parties to mediate.

The cost of mediation is based on the hourly mediation rate published on the mediator's AAA profile. This rate covers both mediator compensation and an allocated portion for the AAA's services. There is a four-hour minimum charge for a mediation conference. Expenses referenced in Section M-16 may also apply.

If a matter submitted for mediation is withdrawn or cancelled or results in a settlement after the agreement to mediate is filed but prior to the mediation conference the cost is $250 plus any mediator time and charges incurred.

The parties will be billed equally for all costs unless they agree otherwise.

If you have questions about mediation costs or services visit our website at www.adr.org or contact your local AAA office.

Conference Room Rental
The costs described above do not include the use of AAA conference rooms. Conference rooms are available on a rental basis. Please contact your local AAA office for availability and rates.

COMMERCIAL ARBITRATION RULES

R-1. Agreement of Parties*+

(a) The parties shall be deemed to have made these rules a part of their arbitration agreement whenever they have provided for arbitration by the American Arbitration Association (hereinafter AAA) under its Commercial Arbitration Rules or for arbitration by the AAA of a domestic commercial dispute without specifying particular rules. These rules and any amendment of them shall apply in the form in effect at the time the administrative requirements are met for a demand for arbitration or submission agreement received by the AAA. The parties, by written agreement, may vary the procedures set forth in these rules. After appointment of the arbitrator, such modifications may be made only with the consent of the arbitrator.

(b) Unless the parties or the AAA determines otherwise, the Expedited Procedures shall apply in any case in which no disclosed claim or counterclaim exceeds $75,000, exclusive of interest and arbitration fees and costs. Parties may also agree to use these procedures in larger cases. Unless the parties agree otherwise, these procedures will not apply in cases involving more than two parties. The Expedited Procedures shall be applied as described in Sections E-1 through E-10 of these rules, in addition to any other portion of these rules that is not in conflict with the Expedited Procedures.

(c) Unless the parties agree otherwise, the Procedures for Large, Complex Commercial Disputes shall apply to all cases in which the disclosed claim or counterclaim of any party is at least $500,000, exclusive of claimed interest, arbitration fees and costs. Parties may also agree to use the Procedures in cases involving claims or counterclaims under $500,000, or in nonmonetary cases. The Procedures for Large, Complex Commercial Disputes shall be applied as described in Sections L-1 through L-4 of these rules, in addition to any other portion of these rules that is not in conflict with the Procedures for Large, Complex Commercial Disputes.

(d) All other cases shall be administered in accordance with Sections R-1 through R-54 of these rules.

* The AAA applies the *Supplementary Procedures for Consumer-Related Disputes* to arbitration clauses in agreements between individual consumers and businesses where the business has a standardized, systematic application of arbitration clauses with customers and where the terms and conditions of the purchase of standardized, consumable goods or services are nonnegotiable or primarily non-negotiable in most or all of its terms, conditions, features, or choices. The product or service must be for personal or household use. The AAA will have the discretion to apply or not to apply the Supplementary Procedures and the parties will be able to bring any disputes concerning the application or non-application to the attention of the arbitrator. Consumers are not prohibited from seeking relief in a small claims court for disputes or claims within the scope of its jurisdiction, even in consumer arbitration cases filed by the business.

+ A dispute arising out of an employer promulgated plan will be administered under the AAA's National Rules for the Resolution of Employment Disputes.

R-2. AAA and Delegation of Duties

When parties agree to arbitrate under these rules, or when they provide for arbitration by the AAA and an arbitration is initiated under these rules, they thereby authorize the AAA to administer the arbitration. The authority and duties of the AAA are prescribed in the agreement of the parties and in these rules, and may be carried out through such of the AAA's representatives as it may direct. The AAA may, in its discretion, assign the administration of an arbitration to any of its offices.

R-3. National Roster of Arbitrators

The AAA shall establish and maintain a National Roster of Commercial Arbitrators ("National Roster") and shall appoint arbitrators as provided in these rules. The term "arbitrator" in these rules refers to the arbitration panel, constituted for a particular case, whether composed of one or more arbitrators, or to an individual arbitrator, as the context requires.

R-4. Initiation under an Arbitration Provision in a Contract

(a) Arbitration under an arbitration provision in a contract shall be initiated in the following manner:

(i) The initiating party (the "claimant") shall, within the time period, if any, specified in the contract(s), give to the other party (the "respondent") written notice of its intention to arbitrate (the "demand"), which demand shall contain a statement setting forth the nature of the dispute, the names and addresses of all other parties, the amount involved, if any, the remedy sought, and the hearing locale requested.

(ii) The claimant shall file at any office of the AAA two copies of the demand and two copies of the arbitration provisions of the contract, together with the appropriate filing fee as provided in the schedule included with these rules.

(iii) The AAA shall confirm notice of such filing to the parties.

(b) A respondent may file an answering statement in duplicate with the AAA within 15 days after confirmation of notice of filing of the demand is sent by the AAA. The respondent shall, at the time of any such filing, send a copy of the answering statement to the claimant. If a counterclaim is asserted, it shall contain a statement setting forth the nature of the counterclaim, the amount involved, if any, and the remedy sought. If a counterclaim is made, the party making the counterclaim shall forward to the AAA with the answering statement the appropriate fee provided in the schedule included with these rules.

(c) If no answering statement is filed within the stated time, respondent will be deemed to deny the claim. Failure to file an answering statement shall not operate to delay the arbitration.

(d) When filing any statement pursuant to this section, the parties are encouraged to provide descriptions of their claims in sufficient detail to make the circumstances of the dispute clear to the arbitrator.

R-5. Initiation under a Submission

Parties to any existing dispute may commence an arbitration under these rules by filing at any office of the AAA two copies of a written submission to arbitrate under these rules, signed by the parties. It shall contain a statement of the nature of the dispute, the names and addresses of all parties, any claims and counterclaims, the amount involved, if any, the remedy sought, and the hearing locale requested, together with the appropriate filing fee as provided in the schedule included with these rules. Unless the parties state otherwise in the submission, all claims and counterclaims will be deemed to be denied by the other party.

R-6. Changes of Claim

After filing of a claim, if either party desires to make any new or different claim or counterclaim, it shall be made in writing and filed with the AAA. The party asserting such a claim or counterclaim shall provide a copy to the other party, who shall have 15 days from the date of such transmission within which to file an answering statement with the AAA. After the arbitrator is appointed, however, no new or different claim may be submitted except with the arbitrator's consent.

R-7. Jurisdiction

(a) The arbitrator shall have the power to rule on his or her own jurisdiction, including any objections with respect to the existence, scope or validity of the arbitration agreement.

(b) The arbitrator shall have the power to determine the existence or validity of a contract of which an arbitration clause forms a part. Such an arbitration clause shall be treated as an agreement independent of the other terms of the contract. A decision by the arbitrator that the contract is null and void shall not for that reason alone render invalid the arbitration clause.

(c) A party must object to the jurisdiction of the arbitrator or to the arbitrability of a claim or counterclaim no later than the filing of the answering statement to the claim or counterclaim that gives rise to the objection. The arbitrator may rule on such objections as a preliminary matter or as part of the final award.

R-8. Mediation

At any stage of the proceedings, the parties may agree to conduct a mediation conference under the Commercial Mediation Procedures in order to facilitate settlement. The mediator shall not be an arbitrator appointed to the case. Where the parties to a pending arbitration agree to mediate under the AAA's rules, no additional administrative fee is required to initiate the mediation.

R-9. Administrative Conference
At the request of any party or upon the AAA's own initiative, the AAA may conduct an administrative conference, in person or by telephone, with the parties and/or their representatives. The conference may address such issues as arbitrator selection, potential mediation of the dispute, potential exchange of information, a timetable for hearings and any other administrative matters.

R-10. Fixing of Locale
The parties may mutually agree on the locale where the arbitration is to be held. If any party requests that the hearing be held in a specific locale and the other party files no objection thereto within 15 days after notice of the request has been sent to it by the AAA, the locale shall be the one requested. If a party objects to the locale requested by the other party, the AAA shall have the power to determine the locale, and its decision shall be final and binding.

R-11. Appointment from National Roster
If the parties have not appointed an arbitrator and have not provided any other method of appointment, the arbitrator shall be appointed in the following manner:
(a) Immediately after the filing of the submission or the answering statement or the expiration of the time within which the answering statement is to be filed, the AAA shall send simultaneously to each party to the dispute an identical list of 10 (unless the AAA decides that a different number is appropriate) names of persons chosen from the National Roster. The parties are encouraged to agree to an arbitrator from the submitted list and to advise the AAA of their agreement.
(b) If the parties are unable to agree upon an arbitrator, each party to the dispute shall have 15 days from the transmittal date in which to strike names objected to, number the remaining names in order of preference, and return the list to the AAA. If a party does not return the list within the time specified, all persons named therein shall be deemed acceptable. From among the persons who have been approved on both lists, and in accordance with the designated order of mutual preference, the AAA shall invite the acceptance of an arbitrator to serve. If the parties fail to agree on any of the persons named, or if acceptable arbitrators are unable to act, or if for any other reason the appointment cannot be made from the submitted lists, the AAA shall have the power to make the appointment from among other members of the National Roster without the submission of additional lists.
(c) Unless the parties agree otherwise when there are two or more claimants or two or more respondents, the AAA may appoint all the arbitrators.

R-12. Direct Appointment by a Party
(a) If the agreement of the parties names an arbitrator or specifies a method of appointing an arbitrator, that designation or method shall be followed. The notice of appointment, with the name and address of the arbitrator, shall be filed with the AAA by the appointing party. Upon the request of any appointing party, the AAA shall submit a list of members of the National Roster from which the party may, if it so desired, make the appointment
(b) Where the parties have agreed that each party is to name one arbitrator, the arbitrators so named must meet the standards of Section R-17 with respect to impartiality and independence unless the parties have specifically agreed pursuant to Section R-17(a) that the party-appointed arbitrators are to be non-neutral and need not meet those standards.
(c) If the agreement specifies a period of time within which an arbitrator shall be appointed and any party fails to make the appointment within that period, the AAA shall make the appointment.
(d) If no period of time is specified in the agreement, the AAA shall notify the party to make the appointment. If within 15 days after such notice has been sent, an arbitrator has not been appointed by a party, the AAA shall make the appointment.

R-13. Appointment of Chairperson by Party-Appointed Arbitrators or Parties
(a) If, pursuant to Section R-12, either the parties have directly appointed arbitrators, or the arbitrators have been appointed by the AAA, and the parties have authorized them to appoint a chairperson within a specified time and no appointment is made within that time or any agreed extension, the AAA may appoint the chairperson.

(b) If no period of time is specified for appointment of the chairperson and the party-appointed arbitrators or the parties do not make the appointment within 15 days from the date of the appointment of the last party-appointed arbitrator, the AAA may appoint the chairperson.
(c) If the parties have agreed that their party-appointed arbitrators shall appoint the chairperson from the National Roster, the AAA shall furnish to the party-appointed arbitrators, in the manner provided in Section R-11, a list selected from the National Roster, and the appointment of the chairperson shall be made as provided in that Section.

R-14. Nationality of Arbitrator
Where the parties are nationals of different countries, the AAA, at the request of any party or on its own initiative, may appoint as arbitrator a national of a country other than that of any of the parties. The request must be made before the time set for the appointment of the arbitrator as agreed by the parties or set by these rules.

R-15. Number of Arbitrators
If the arbitration agreement does not specify the number of arbitrators, the dispute shall be heard and determined by one arbitrator, unless the AAA, in its discretion, directs that three arbitrators be appointed. A party may request three arbitrators in the demand or answer, which request the AAA will consider in exercising its discretion regarding the number of arbitrators appointed to the dispute.

R-16. Disclosure
(a) Any person appointed or to be appointed as an arbitrator shall disclose to the AAA any circumstance likely to give rise to justifiable doubt as to the arbitrator's impartiality or independence, including any bias or any financial or personal interest in the result of the arbitration or any past or present relationship with the parties or their representatives. Such obligation shall remain in effect throughout the arbitration.
(b) Upon receipt of such information from the arbitrator or another source, the AAA shall communicate the information to the parties and, if it deems it appropriate to do so, to the arbitrator and others.
(c) In order to encourage disclosure by arbitrators, disclosure of information pursuant to this Section R-16 is not to be construed as an indication that the arbitrator considers that the disclosed circumstance is likely to affect impartiality or independence.

R-17. Disqualification of Arbitrator
(a) Any arbitrator shall be impartial and independent and shall perform his or her duties with diligence and in good faith, and shall be subject to disqualification for
   (i) partiality or lack of independence,
   (ii) inability or refusal to perform his or her duties with diligence and in good faith, and
   (iii) any grounds for disqualification provided by applicable law. The parties may agree in writing, however, that arbitrators directly appointed by a party pursuant to Section R-12 shall be nonneutral, in which case such arbitrators need not be impartial or independent and shall not be subject to disqualification for partiality or lack of independence.
(b) Upon objection of a party to the continued service of an arbitrator, or on its own initiative, the AAA shall determine whether the arbitrator should be disqualified under the grounds set out above, and shall inform the parties of its decision, which decision shall be conclusive.

R-18. Communication with Arbitrator
(a) No party and no one acting on behalf of any party shall communicate ex parte with an arbitrator or a candidate for arbitrator concerning the arbitration, except that a party, or someone acting on behalf of a party, may communicate ex parte with a candidate for direct appointment pursuant to Section R-12 in order to advise the candidate of the general nature of the controversy and of the anticipated proceedings and to discuss the candidate's qualifications, availability, or independence in relation to the parties or to discuss the suitability of candidates for selection as a third arbitrator where the parties or party-designated arbitrators are to participate in that selection.
(b) Section R-18(a) does not apply to arbitrators directly appointed by the parties who, pursuant to Section R-17(a), the parties have agreed in writing are non-neutral. Where the parties have so

agreed under Section R-17(a), the AAA shall as an administrative practice suggest to the parties that they agree further that Section R-18(a) should nonetheless apply prospectively.

R-19. Vacancies

(a) If for any reason an arbitrator is unable to perform the duties of the office, the AAA may, on proof satisfactory to it, declare the office vacant. Vacancies shall be filled in accordance with the applicable provisions of these rules.

(b) In the event of a vacancy in a panel of neutral arbitrators after the hearings have commenced, the remaining arbitrator or arbitrators may continue with the hearing and determination of the controversy, unless the parties agree otherwise.

(c) In the event of the appointment of a substitute arbitrator, the panel of arbitrators shall determine in its sole discretion whether it is necessary to repeat all or part of any prior hearings.

R-20. Preliminary Hearing

(a) At the request of any party or at the discretion of the arbitrator or the AAA, the arbitrator may schedule as soon as practicable a preliminary hearing with the parties and/or their representatives. The preliminary hearing may be conducted by telephone at the arbitrator's discretion.

(b) During the preliminary hearing, the parties and the arbitrator should discuss the future conduct of the case, including clarification of the issues and claims, a schedule for the hearings and any other preliminary matters.

R-21. Exchange of Information

(a) At the request of any party or at the discretion of the arbitrator, consistent with the expedited nature of arbitration, the arbitrator may direct
   i) the production of documents and other information, and
   ii) the identification of any witnesses to be called.

(b) At least five business days prior to the hearing, the parties shall exchange copies of all exhibits they intend to submit at the hearing.

(c) The arbitrator is authorized to resolve any disputes concerning the exchange of information.

R-22. Date, Time, and Place of Hearing

The arbitrator shall set the date, time, and place for each hearing. The parties shall respond to requests for hearing dates in a timely manner, be cooperative in scheduling the earliest practicable date, and adhere to the established hearing schedule. The AAA shall send a notice of hearing to the parties at least 10 days in advance of the hearing date, unless otherwise agreed by the parties.

R-23. Attendance at Hearings

The arbitrator and the AAA shall maintain the privacy of the hearings unless the law provides to the contrary. Any person having a direct interest in the arbitration is entitled to attend hearings. The arbitrator shall otherwise have the power to require the exclusion of any witness, other than a party or other essential person, during the testimony of any other witness. It shall be discretionary with the arbitrator to determine the propriety of the attendance of any other person other than a party and its representatives.

R-24. Representation

Any party may be represented by counsel or other authorized representative. A party intending to be so represented shall notify the other party and the AAA of the name and address of the representative at least three days prior to the date set for the hearing at which that person is first to appear. When such a representative initiates an arbitration or responds for a party, notice is deemed to have been given.

R-25. Oaths

Before proceeding with the first hearing, each arbitrator may take an oath of office and, if required by law, shall do so. The arbitrator may require witnesses to testify under oath administered by any duly qualified person and, if it is required by law or requested by any party, shall do so.

R-26. Stenographic Record
Any party desiring a stenographic record shall make arrangements directly with a stenographer and shall notify the other parties of these arrangements at least three days in advance of the hearing. The requesting party or parties shall pay the cost of the record. If the transcript is agreed by the parties, or determined by the arbitrator to be the official record of the proceeding, it must be provided to the arbitrator and made available to the other parties for inspection, at a date, time, and place determined by the arbitrator.

R-27. Interpreters
Any party wishing an interpreter shall make all arrangements directly with the interpreter and shall assume the costs of the service.

R-28. Postponements
The arbitrator may postpone any hearing upon agreement of the parties, upon request of a party for good cause shown, or upon the arbitrator's own initiative.

R-29. Arbitration in the Absence of a Party or Representative
Unless the law provides to the contrary, the arbitration may proceed in the absence of any party or representative who, after due notice, fails to be present or fails to obtain a postponement. An award shall not be made solely on the default of a party. The arbitrator shall require the party who is present to submit such evidence as the arbitrator may require for the making of an award.

R-30. Conduct of Proceedings
(a) The claimant shall present evidence to support its claim. The respondent shall then present evidence to support its defense. Witnesses for each party shall also submit to questions from the arbitrator and the adverse party. The arbitrator has the discretion to vary this procedure, provided that the parties are treated with equality and that each party has the right to be heard and is given a fair opportunity to present its case.
(b) The arbitrator, exercising his or her discretion, shall conduct the proceedings with a view to expediting the resolution of the dispute and may direct the order of proof, bifurcate proceedings and direct the parties to focus their presentations on issues the decision of which could dispose of all or part of the case.
(c) The parties may agree to waive oral hearings in any case.

R-31. Evidence
(a) The parties may offer such evidence as is relevant and material to the dispute and shall produce such evidence as the arbitrator may deem necessary to an understanding and determination of the dispute. Conformity to legal rules of evidence shall not be necessary. All evidence shall be taken in the presence of all of the arbitrators and all of the parties, except where any of the parties is absent, in default or has waived the right to be present.
(b) The arbitrator shall determine the admissibility, relevance, and materiality of the evidence offered and may exclude evidence deemed by the arbitrator to be cumulative or irrelevant.
(c) The arbitrator shall take into account applicable principles of legal privilege, such as those involving the confidentiality of communications between a lawyer and client.
(d) An arbitrator or other person authorized by law to subpoena witnesses or documents may do so upon the request of any party or independently.

R-32. Evidence by Affidavit and Post-hearing Filing of Documents or Other Evidence
(a) The arbitrator may receive and consider the evidence of witnesses by declaration or affidavit, but shall give it only such weight as the arbitrator deems it entitled to after consideration of any objection made to its admission.
(b) If the parties agree or the arbitrator directs that documents or other evidence be submitted to the arbitrator after the hearing, the documents or other evidence shall be filed with the AAA for transmission to the arbitrator. All parties shall be afforded an opportunity to examine and respond to such documents or other evidence.

R-33. Inspection or Investigation

An arbitrator finding it necessary to make an inspection or investigation in connection with the arbitration shall direct the AAA to so advise the parties. The arbitrator shall set the date and time and the AAA shall notify the parties. Any party who so desires may be present at such an inspection or investigation. In the event that one or all parties are not present at the inspection or investigation, the arbitrator shall make an oral or written report to the parties and afford them an opportunity to comment.

R-34. Interim Measures**

(a) The arbitrator may take whatever interim measures he or she deems necessary, including injunctive relief and measures for the protection or conservation of property and disposition of perishable goods.
(b) Such interim measures may take the form of an interim award, and the arbitrator may require security for the costs of such measures.
(c) A request for interim measures addressed by a party to a judicial authority shall not be deemed incompatible with the agreement to arbitrate or a waiver of the right to arbitrate.

** The Optional Rules may be found below.

R-35. Closing of Hearing

The arbitrator shall specifically inquire of all parties whether they have any further proofs to offer or witnesses to be heard. Upon receiving negative replies or if satisfied that the record is complete, the arbitrator shall declare the hearing closed. If briefs are to be filed, the hearing shall b e declared closed as of the final date set by the arbitrator for the receipt of briefs. If documents are to be filed as provided in Section R-32 and the date set for their receipt is later than that set for the receipt of briefs, the later date shall be the closing date of the hearing. The time limit within which the arbitrator is required to make the award shall commence, in the absence of other agreements by the parties, upon the closing of the hearing.

R-36. Reopening of Hearing

The hearing may be reopened on the arbitrator's initiative, or upon application of a party, at any time before the award is made. If reopening the hearing would prevent the making of the award within the specific time agreed on by the parties in the contract(s) out of which the controversy has arisen, the matter may not be reopened unless the parties agree on an extension of time. When no specific date is fixed in the contract, the arbitrator may reopen the hearing and shall have 30 days from the closing of the reopened hearing within which to make an award.

R-37. Waiver of Rules

Any party who proceeds with the arbitration after knowledge that any provision or requirement of these rules has not been complied with and who fails to state an objection in writing shall be deemed to have waived the right to object.

R-38. Extensions of Time

The parties may modify any period of time by mutual agreement. The AAA or the arbitrator may for good cause extend any period of time established by these rules, except the time for making the award. The AAA shall notify the parties of any extension.

R-39. Serving of Notice

(a) Any papers, notices, or process necessary or proper for the initiation or continuation of an arbitration under these rules, for any court action in connection therewith, or for the entry of judgment on any award made under these rules may be served on a party by mail addressed to the party, or its representative at the last known address or by personal service, in or outside the state where the arbitration is to be held, provided that reasonable opportunity to be heard with regard to the dispute is or has been granted to the party.
(b) The AAA, the arbitrator and the parties may also use overnight delivery or electronic facsimile transmission (fax), to give the notices required by these rules. Where all parties and the arbitra-

tor agree, notices may be transmitted by electronic mail (E-mail), or other methods of communication.

(c) Unless otherwise instructed by the AAA or by the arbitrator, any documents submitted by any party to the AAA or to the arbitrator shall simultaneously be provided to the other party or parties to the arbitration.

R-40. Majority Decision

When the panel consists of more than one arbitrator, unless required by law or by the arbitration agreement, a majority of the arbitrators must make all decisions.

R-41. Time of Award

The award shall be made promptly by the arbitrator and, unless otherwise agreed by the parties or specified by law, no later than 30 days from the date of closing the hearing, or, if oral hearings have been waived, from the date of the AAA's transmittal of the final statements and proofs to the arbitrator.

R-42. Form of Award

(a) Any award shall be in writing and signed by a majority of the arbitrators. It shall be executed in the manner required by law.

(b) The arbitrator need not render a reasoned award unless the parties request such an award in writing prior to appointment of the arbitrator or unless the arbitrator determines that a reasoned award is appropriate.

R-43. Scope of Award

(a) The arbitrator may grant any remedy or relief that the arbitrator deems just and equitable and within the scope of the agreement of the parties, including, but not limited to, specific performance of a contract.

(b) In addition to a final award, the arbitrator may make other decisions, including interim, interlocutory, or partial rulings, orders, and awards. In any interim, interlocutory, or partial award, the arbitrator may assess and apportion the fees, expenses, and compensation related to such award as the arbitrator determines is appropriate.

(c) In the final award, the arbitrator shall assess the fees, expenses, and compensation provided in Sections R-49, R-50, and R-51. The arbitrator may apportion such fees, expenses, and compensation among the parties in such amounts as the arbitrator determines is appropriate.

(d) The award of the arbitrator(s) may include:

   (i) interest at such rate and from such date as the arbitrator(s) may deem appropriate; and

   (ii) an award of attorneys' fees if all parties have requested such an award or it is authorized by law or their arbitration agreement.

R-44. Award upon Settlement

If the parties settle their dispute during the course of the arbitration and if the parties so request, the arbitrator may set forth the terms of the settlement in a "consent award." A consent award must include an allocation of arbitration costs, including administrative fees and expenses as well as arbitrator fees and expenses.

R-45. Delivery of Award to Parties

Parties shall accept as notice and delivery of the award the placing of the award or a true copy thereof in the mail addressed to the parties or their representatives at the last known addresses, personal or electronic service of the award, or the filing of the award in any other manner that is permitted by law.

R-46. Modification of Award

Within 20 days after the transmittal of an award, any party, upon notice to the other parties, may request the arbitrator, through the AAA, to correct any clerical, typographical, or computational errors in the award. The arbitrator is not empowered to redetermine the merits of any claim already decided. The other parties shall be given 10 days to respond to the request. The arbitrator shall dispose of the request within 20 days after transmittal by the AAA to the arbitrator of the request and any response thereto.

R-47. Release of Documents for Judicial Proceedings
The AAA shall, upon the written request of a party, furnish to the party, at the party's expense, certified copies of any papers in the AAA's possession that may be required in judicial proceedings relating to the arbitration.

R-48. Applications to Court and Exclusion of Liability
(a) No judicial proceeding by a party relating to the subject matter of the arbitration shall be deemed a waiver of the party's right to arbitrate.
(b) Neither the AAA nor any arbitrator in a proceeding under these rules is a necessary or proper party in judicial proceedings relating to the arbitration.
(c) Parties to an arbitration under these rules shall be deemed to have consented that judgment upon the arbitration award may be entered in any federal or state court having jurisdiction thereof.
(d) Parties to an arbitration under these rules shall be deemed to have consented that neither the AAA nor any arbitrator shall be liable to any party in any action for damages or injunctive relief for any act or omission in connection with any arbitration under these rules.

R-49. Administrative Fees
As a not-for-profit organization, the AAA shall prescribe an initial filing fee and a case service fee to compensate it for the cost of providing administrative services. The fees in effect when the fee or charge is incurred shall be applicable. The filing fee shall be advanced by the party or parties making a claim or counterclaim, subject to final apportionment by the arbitrator in the award. The AAA may, in the event of extreme hardship on the part of any party, defer or reduce the administrative fees.

R-50. Expenses
The expenses of witnesses for either side shall be paid by the party producing such witnesses. All other expenses of the arbitration, including required travel and other expenses of the arbitrator, AAA representatives, and any witness and the cost of any proof produced at the direct request of the arbitrator, shall be borne equally by the parties, unless they agree otherwise or unless the arbitrator in the award assesses such expenses or any part thereof against any specified party or parties.

R-51. Neutral Arbitrator's Compensation
(a) Arbitrators shall be compensated at a rate consistent with the arbitrator's stated rate of compensation.
(b) If there is disagreement concerning the terms of compensation, an appropriate rate shall be established with the arbitrator by the AAA and confirmed to the parties.
(c) Any arrangement for the compensation of a neutral arbitrator shall be made through the AAA and not directly between the parties and the arbitrator.

R-52. Deposits
The AAA may require the parties to deposit in advance of any hearings such sums of money as it deems necessary to cover the expense of the arbitration, including the arbitrator's fee, if any, and shall render an accounting to the parties and return any unexpended balance at the conclusion of the case.

R-53. Interpretation and Application of Rules
The arbitrator shall interpret and apply these rules insofar as they relate to the arbitrator's powers and duties. When there is more than one arbitrator and a difference arises among them concerning the meaning or application of these rules, it shall be decided by a majority vote. If that is not possible, either an arbitrator or a party may refer the question to the AAA for final decision. All other rules shall be interpreted and applied by the AAA.

R-54. Suspension for Nonpayment
If arbitrator compensation or administrative charges have not been paid in full, the AAA may so inform the parties in order that one of them may advance the required payment. If such payments are not made, the arbitrator may order the suspension or termination of the proceedings. If no arbitrator has yet been appointed, the AAA may suspend the proceedings.

EXPEDITED PROCEDURES

E-1. Limitation on Extensions
Except in extraordinary circumstances, the AAA or the arbitrator may grant a party no more than one seven-day extension of time to respond to the demand for arbitration or counterclaim as provided in Section R-4.

E-2. Changes of Claim or Counterclaim
A claim or counterclaim may be increased in amount, or a new or different claim or counterclaim added, upon the agreement of the other party, or the consent of the arbitrator. After the arbitrator is appointed, however, no new or different claim or counterclaim may be submitted except with the arbitrator's consent. If an increased claim or counterclaim exceeds $75,000, the case will be administered under the regular procedures unless all parties and the arbitrator agree that the case may continue to be processed under the Expedited Procedures.

E-3. Serving of Notices
In addition to notice provided by Section R-39(b), the parties shall also accept notice by telephone. Telephonic notices by the AAA shall subsequently be confirmed in writing to the parties. Should there be a failure to confirm in writing any such oral notice, the proceeding shall nevertheless be valid if notice has, in fact, been given by telephone.

E-4. Appointment and Qualifications of Arbitrator
(a) The AAA shall simultaneously submit to each party an identical list of five proposed arbitrators drawn from its National Roster from which one arbitrator shall be appointed.
(b) The parties are encouraged to agree to an arbitrator from this list and to advise the AAA of their agreement. If the parties are unable to agree upon an arbitrator, each party may strike two names from the list and return it to the AAA within seven days from the date of the AAA's mailing to the parties. If for any reason the appointment of an arbitrator cannot be made from the list, the AAA may make the appointment from other members of the panel without the submission of additional lists.
(c) The parties will be given notice by the AAA of the appointment of the arbitrator, who shall be subject to disqualification for the reasons specified in Section R-17. The parties shall notify the AAA within seven days of any objection to the arbitrator appointed. Any such objection shall be for cause and shall be confirmed in writing to the AAA with a copy to the other party or parties.

E-5. Exchange of Exhibits
At least two business days prior to the hearing, the parties shall exchange copies of all exhibits they intend to submit at the hearing. The arbitrator shall resolve disputes concerning the exchange of exhibits.

E-6. Proceedings on Documents
Where no party's claim exceeds $10,000, exclusive of interest and arbitration costs, and other cases in which the parties agree, the dispute shall be resolved by submission of documents, unless any party requests an oral hearing, or the arbitrator determines that an oral hearing is necessary. The arbitrator shall establish a fair and equitable procedure for the submission of documents.

E-7. Date, Time, and Place of Hearing
In cases in which a hearing is to be held, the arbitrator shall set the date, time, and place of the hearing, to be scheduled to take place within 30 days of confirmation of the arbitrator's appointment. The AAA will notify the parties in advance of the hearing date.

E-8. The Hearing

(a) Generally, the hearing shall not exceed one day. Each party shall have equal opportunity to submit its proofs and complete its case. The arbitrator shall determine the order of the hearing, and may require further submission of documents within two days after the hearing. For good cause shown, the arbitrator may schedule additional hearings within seven business days after the initial day of hearings.
(b) Generally, there will be no stenographic record. Any party desiring a stenographic record may arrange for one pursuant to the provisions of Section R-26.

E-9. Time of Award

Unless otherwise agreed by the parties, the award shall be rendered not later than 14 days from the date of the closing of the hearing or, if oral hearings have been waived, from the date of the AAA's transmittal of the final statements and proofs to the arbitrator.

E-10. Arbitrator's Compensation

Arbitrators will receive compensation at a rate to be suggested by the AAA regional office.

PROCEDURES FOR LARGE, COMPLEX COMMERCIAL DISPUTES

L-1. Administrative Conference

Prior to the dissemination of a list of potential arbitrators, the AAA shall, unless the parties agree otherwise, conduct an administrative conference with the parties and/or their attorneys or other representatives by conference call. The conference will take place within 14 days after the commencement of the arbitration. In the event the parties are unable to agree on a mutually acceptable time for the conference, the AAA may contact the parties individually to discuss the issues contemplated herein. Such administrative conference shall be conducted for the following purposes and for such additional purposes as the parties or the AAA may deem appropriate:

(a) to obtain additional information about the nature and magnitude of the dispute and the anticipated length of hearing and scheduling;
(b) to discuss the views of the parties about the technical and other qualifications of the arbitrators;
(c) to obtain conflicts statements from the parties; and
(d) to consider, with the parties, whether mediation or other non-adjudicative methods of dispute resolution might be appropriate.

L-2. Arbitrators

(a) Large, Complex Commercial Cases shall be heard and determined by either one or three arbitrators, as may be agreed upon by the parties. If the parties are unable to agree upon the number of arbitrators and a claim or counterclaim involves at least $1,000,000, then three arbitrator(s) shall hear and determine the case. If the parties are unable to agree on the number of arbitrators and each claim and counterclaim is less than $1,000,000, then one arbitrator shall hear and determine the case.
(b) The AAA shall appoint arbitrator(s) as agreed by the parties. If they are unable to agree on a method of appointment, the AAA shall appoint arbitrators from the Large, Complex Commercial Case Panel, in the manner provided in the Regular Commercial Arbitration Rules. Absent agreement of the parties, the arbitrator(s) shall not have served as the mediator in the mediation phase of the instant proceeding.

L-3. Preliminary Hearing

As promptly as practicable after the selection of the arbitrator(s), a preliminary hearing shall be held among the parties and/or their attorneys or other representatives and the arbitrator(s). Unless the parties agree otherwise, the preliminary hearing will be conducted by telephone conference call rather than in person. At the preliminary hearing the matters to be considered shall include, without limitation:

(a) service of a detailed statement of claims, damages and defenses, a statement of the issues asserted by each party and positions with respect thereto, and any legal authorities the parties may wish to bring to the attention of the arbitrator(s);
(b) stipulations to uncontested facts;
(c) the extent to which discovery shall be conducted;
(d) exchange and premarking of those documents which each party believes may be offered at the hearing;
(e) the identification and availability of witnesses, including experts, and such matters with respect to witnesses including their biographies and expected testimony as may be appropriate;
(f) whether, and the extent to which, any sworn statements and/or depositions may be introduced;
(g) the extent to which hearings will proceed on consecutive days;
(h) whether a stenographic or other official record of the proceedings shall be maintained;
(i) the possibility of utilizing mediation or other non-adjudicative methods of dispute resolution; and
(j) the procedure for the issuance of subpoenas.

By agreement of the parties and/or order of the arbitrator(s), the pre-hearing activities and the hearing procedures that will govern the arbitration will be memorialized in a Scheduling and Procedure Order.

L-4. Management of Proceedings
(a) Arbitrator(s) shall take such steps as they may deem necessary or desirable to avoid delay and to achieve a just, speedy and cost-effective resolution of Large, Complex Commercial Cases.
(b) Parties shall cooperate in the exchange of documents, exhibits and information within such party's control if the arbitrator(s) consider such production to be consistent with the goal of achieving a just, speedy and cost-effective resolution of a Large, Complex Commercial Case.
(c) The parties may conduct such discovery as may be agreed to by all the parties provided, however, that the arbitrator(s) may place such limitations on the conduct of such discovery as the arbitrator(s) shall deem appropriate. If the parties cannot agree on production of documents and other information, the arbitrator(s), consistent with the expedited nature of arbitration, may establish the extent of the discovery.
(d) At the discretion of the arbitrator(s), upon good cause shown and consistent with the expedited nature of arbitration, the arbitrator(s) may order depositions of, or the propounding of interrogatories to, such persons who may possess information determined by the arbitrator(s) to be necessary to determination of the matter.
(e) The parties shall exchange copies of all exhibits they intend to submit at the hearing 10 business days prior to the hearing unless the arbitrator(s) determine otherwise.
(f) The exchange of information pursuant to this rule, as agreed by the parties and/or directed by the arbitrator(s), shall be included within the Scheduling and Procedure Order.
(g) The arbitrator is authorized to resolve any disputes concerning the exchange of information.
(h) Generally hearings will be scheduled on consecutive days or in blocks of consecutive days in order to maximize efficiency and minimize costs.

OPTIONAL RULES FOR EMERGENCY MEASURES OF PROTECTION

O-1. Applicability
Where parties by special agreement or in their arbitration clause have adopted these rules for emergency measures of protection, a party in need of emergency relief prior to the constitution of the panel shall notify the AAA and all other parties in writing of the nature of the relief sought and the reasons why such relief is required on an emergency basis. The application shall also set forth the reasons why the party is entitled to such relief. Such notice may be given by facsimile transmission, or other reliable means, but must include a statement certifying that all other parties have been notified or an explanation of the steps taken in good faith to notify other parties.

O-2. Appointment of Emergency Arbitrator
Within one business day of receipt of notice as provided in Section O-1, the AAA shall appoint a single emergency arbitrator from a special AAA panel of emergency arbitrators designated to rule on emergency applications. The emergency arbitrator shall immediately disclose any circumstance likely, on the basis of the facts disclosed in the application, to affect such arbitrator's impartiality or independence. Any challenge to the appointment of the emergency arbitrator must be made within one business day of the communication by the AAA to the parties of the appointment of the emergency arbitrator and the circumstances disclosed.

O-3. Schedule
The emergency arbitrator shall as soon as possible, but in any event within two business days of appointment, establish a schedule for consideration of the application for emergency relief. Such schedule shall provide a reasonable opportunity to all parties to be heard, but may provide for proceeding by telephone conference or on written submissions as alternatives to a formal hearing.

O-4. Interim Award
If after consideration the emergency arbitrator is satisfied that the party seeking the emergency relief has shown that immediate and irreparable loss or damage will result in the absence of emergency relief, and that such party is entitled to such relief, the emergency arbitrator may enter an interim award granting the relief and stating the reasons therefore.

O-5. Constitution of the Panel
Any application to modify an interim award of emergency relief must be based on changed circumstances and may be made to the emergency arbitrator until the panel is constituted; thereafter such a request shall be addressed to the panel. The emergency arbitrator shall have no further power to act after the panel is constituted unless the parties agree that the emergency arbitrator is named as a member of the panel.

O-6. Security
Any interim award of emergency relief may be conditioned on provision by the party seeking such relief of appropriate security.

O-7. Special Master
A request for interim measures addressed by a party to a judicial authority shall not be deemed incompatible with the agreement to arbitrate or a waiver of the right to arbitrate. If the AAA is directed by a judicial authority to nominate a special master to consider and report on an application for emergency relief, the AAA shall proceed as provided in Section O-1 of this article and the references to the emergency arbitrator shall be read to mean the special master, except that the special master shall issue a report rather than an interim award.

O-8. Costs
The costs associated with applications for emergency relief shall initially be apportioned by the emergency arbitrator or special master, subject to the power of the panel to determine finally the apportionment of such costs.

ADMINISTRATIVE FEES

The administrative fees of the AAA are based on the amount of the claim or counterclaim. Arbitrator compensation is not included in this schedule. Unless the parties agree otherwise, arbitrator compensation and administrative fees are subject to allocation by the arbitrator in the award.

In an effort to make arbitration costs reasonable for consumers, the AAA has a separate fee schedule for consumer-related disputes. Please refer to Section C-8 of the *Supplementary Procedures for Consumer-Related Disputes* when filing a consumer-related claim.

The AAA applies the *Supplementary Procedures for Consumer-Related Disputes* to arbitration clauses in agreements between individual consumers and businesses where the business has a standardized, systematic application of arbitration clauses with customers and where the terms and conditions of the purchase of standardized, consumable goods or services are non-negotiable or primarily non-negotiable in most or all of its terms, conditions, features, or choices. The product or service must be for personal or household use. The AAA will have the discretion to apply or not to apply the Supplementary Procedures and the parties will be able to bring any disputes concerning the application or non-application to the attention of the arbitrator. Consumers are not prohibited from seeking relief in a small claims court for disputes or claims within the scope of its jurisdiction, even in consumer arbitration cases filed by the business.

Fees

An initial filing fee is payable in full by a filing party when a claim, counterclaim or additional claim is filed. A case service fee will be incurred for all cases that proceed to their first hearing. This fee will be payable in advance at the time that the first hearing is scheduled. This fee will be refunded at the conclusion of the case if no hearings have occurred. However, if the Association is not notified at least 24 hours before the time of the scheduled hearing, the case service fee will remain due and will not be refunded.

These fees will be billed in accordance with

Amount of Claim	Initial Filing Fee	Case Service Fee
Above $0 to $10,000	$750	$200
Above $10,000 to $75,000	$950	$300
Above $75,000 to $150,000	$1,800	$750
Above $150,000 to $300,000	$2,750	$1,250
Above $300,000 to $500,000	$4,250	$1,750
Above $500,000 to $1,000,000	$6,000	$2,500
Above $1,000,000 to $5,000,000	$8,000	$3,250
Above $5,000,000 to $10,000,000	$10,000	$4,000
Above $10,000,000	*	*
Nonmonetary Claims**	$3,250	$1,250

Fee Schedule for Claims in Excess of $10 Million.

The following is the fee schedule for use in disputes involving claims in excess of $10 million. If you have any questions, please consult your local AAA office or case management center.

Claim Size	Fee	Case Service Fee
$10 million and above	Base fee of $ 12,500 plus .01% of the amount of claim above $ 10 million.	$6,000
	Filing fees capped at $65,000	

** This fee is applicable only when a claim or counterclaim is not for a monetary amount. Where a monetary claim amount is not known, parties will be required to state a range of claims or be subject to the highest possible filing fee.

Fees are subject to increase if the amount of a claim or counterclaim is modified after the initial filing date. Fees are subject to decrease if the amount of a claim or counterclaim is modified before the first hearing.

The minimum fees for any case having three or more arbitrators are $2,750 for the filing fee, plus a $1,250 case service fee. Expedited Procedures are applied in any case where no disclosed claim or counterclaim exceeds $75,000, exclusive of interest and arbitration costs.

Parties on cases held in abeyance for one year by agreement, will be assessed an annual abeyance fee of $300. If a party refuses to pay the assessed fee, the other party or parties may pay the entire fee on behalf of all parties, otherwise the matter will be closed.

Refund Schedule

The AAA offers a refund schedule on filing fees. For cases with claims up to $75,000, a minimum filing fee of $300 will not be refunded. For all other cases, a minimum fee of $500 will not be refunded. Subject to the minimum fee requirements, refunds will be calculated as follows:

100% of the filing fee, above the minimum fee, will be refunded if the case is settled or withdrawn within five calendar days of filing.
50% of the filing fee will be refunded if the case is settled or withdrawn between six and 30 calendar days of filing.
25% of the filing fee will be refunded if the case is settled or withdrawn between 31 and 60 calendar days of filing.

No refund will be made once an arbitrator has been appointed (this includes one arbitrator on a three-arbitrator panel). No refunds will be granted on awarded cases.

Note: the date of receipt of the demand for arbitration with the AAA will be used to calculate refunds of filing fees for both claims and counterclaims.

Hearing Room Rental

The fees described above do not cover the rental of hearing rooms, which are available on a rental basis. Check with the AAA for availability and rates.

APPENDIX XVI

ADR RULES OF THE INTERNATIONAL CHAMBER OF COMMERCE

FOREWORD

ICC has almost eight decades of experience in devising rules to govern and facilitate the conduct of international business. These include those designed to resolve the conflicts that inevitably arise in trading relations. The present ADR Rules represent ICC's most recent initiative in this field.

The ICC-ADR Rules are the result of discussions between dispute resolution experts and representatives of the business community from 75 countries. Their purpose is to offer business partners a means of resolving disputes amicably, in the way best suited to their needs. A distinctive feature of the Rules is the freedom the parties are given to choose the technique they consider most conducive to settlement. Failing agreement on the method to be adopted, the fallback shall be mediation.

As an amicable method of dispute resolution, ICC ADR should be distinguished from ICC arbitration. They are two alternative means of resolving disputes, although in certain circumstances they may be complementary. For instance, it is possible for parties to provide for ICC arbitration in the event of failure to reach an amicable settlement. Similarly, parties engaged in an arbitration may turn to ICC ADR if their dispute seems to warrant a different, more consensual approach. The two services remain distinct, however, each administered by a separate secretariat based at ICC headquarters in Paris.

The ICC ADR Rules replace the 1988 ICC Rules of Optional Conciliation and join the Rules of Arbitration, the Rules for Expertise and the Docdex Rules as an important component in ICC's range of dispute resolution services.

The ICC ADR Rules, which are effective as of 1 July 2001, may be used in domestic as well as international contexts.

June 2001

SUGGESTED ICC ADR CLAUSES
OPTIONAL ADR

'The parties may at any time, without prejudice to any other proceedings, seek to settle any dispute arising out of or in connection with the present contract in accordance with the ICC -ADR Rules.'

OBLIGATION TO CONSIDER ADR

'In the event of any dispute arising out of or in connection with the present contract, the parties agree in the first instance to discuss and consider submitting the matter to settlement proceedings under the ICC ADR Rules.'

OBLIGATION TO SUBMIT DISPUTE TO ADR WITH AN AUTOMATIC EXPIRATION MECHANISM

'In the event of any dispute arising out of or in connection with the present contract, the parties agree to submit the matter to settlement proceedings under the ICC ADR Rules. If the dispute has not been settled pursuant to the said Rules within 45 days following the filing of a Request for ADR or within such other period as the parties may agree in writing, the parties shall have no further obligations under this paragraph.'

OBLIGATION TO SUBMIT DISPUTE TO ADR, FOLLOWED BY ICC ARBITRATION AS REQUIRED

'In the event of any dispute arising out of or in connection with the present contract, the parties agree to submit the matter to settlement proceedings under the ICC ADR Rules. If the dispute has not been settled pursuant to the said Rules within 45 days following the filing of a Request for ADR or within such other period as the parties may agree in writing, such dispute shall be finally settled under the Rules of Arbitration of the international Chamber of Commerce by one or more arbitrators appointed in accordance with the said Rules of Arbitration.'

ADR RULES OF THE INTERNATIONAL CHAMBER OF COMMERCE

Preamble

Amiable settlement is a desirable solution for business disputes and differences. It can occur before or during the litigation or arbitration of a dispute and can often be facilitated through the aid of a third party (the 'Neutral') acting in accordance with simple rules. The parties can agree to submit to such rules in their underlying contract or at any other time.

The International Chamber of Commerce ('ICC') sets out these amicable dispute resolution rules, en titled the ICC ADR Rules (the 'Rules'), which permit the parties to agree upon whatever settlement technique they believe to be appropriate to help them settle their dispute. In the absence of an agreement of the parties on a settlement technique, mediation shall be the settlement technique used under the Rules. The Guide to ICC ADR, which does not form part of the Rules, provides an explanation of the Rules and of various settlement techniques which can be used pursuant to the Rules.

Article 1
Scope of the ICC ADR Rules

All business disputes, whether or not of an international character, may be referred to ADR proceedings pursuant to these Rules. The provisions of these Rules may be modified by agreement of all of the parties, subject to the approval of ICC.

Article 2
Commencement of the ADR Proceedings

A Where there is an agreement to refer to the Rules

1 Where there is an agreement between the parties to refer their dispute to the ICC ADR Rules, any party or parties wishing to commence ADR proceedings pursuant to the Rules shall send to ICC a written Request for ADP, which shall include:
   a) the names, addresses, telephone and facsimile numbers and e-mail addresses of the parties to the dispute and their authorized representatives, if any;
   b) a description of the dispute including, if possible, an assessment of its value;
   c) any joint designation by all of the parties of a Neutral or any agreement of all of the parties upon the qualifications of a Neutral to be appointed by ICC where no joint designation has been made;
   d) a copy of any written agreement under which the Request for ADR is made; and
   e) the registration fee of the ADR proceedings, as set out in the Appendix hereto.

2 Where the Request for ADR is not filed jointly by all of the parties, the party or parties filing the Request shall simultaneously send the Request to the other party or parties. Such Request may include any proposal regarding the qualifications of a Neutral or any proposal of one or more Neutrals to be designated by all of the parties. Thereafter, all of the parties may jointly designate a Neutral or may agree upon the qualifications of a Neutral to be appointed by ICC. In either case, the parties shall promptly notify ICC thereof

3 ICC shall promptly acknowledge receipt of the Request for ADR in writing to the parties.

B Where there is no agreement to refer to the Rules

1 Where there is no agreement between the parties to refer their dispute to the ICC ADR Rules, any party or parties wishing to commence ADR proceedings pursuant to the Rules shall send to ICC a written Request for ADP, which shall include:
   a) the names, addresses, telephone and facsimile numbers and e-mail addresses of the parties to the dispute and their authorized representatives, if any;
   b) a description of the dispute including, if possible, an assessment of its value; and
   c) the registration fee of the ADR proceedings, as set out in the Appendix hereto.

   The Request for ADR may also include any proposal regarding the qualifications of a Neutral or any proposal of one or more Neutrals to be designated by all of the parties.

2 ICC shall promptly inform the other party or parties in writing of the Request for ADR. Such party or parties shall be asked to inform ICC in writing, within 15 days of receipt of the Request for ADR, as to whether they agree or decline to participate in the ADR proceedings. In the former case, they may provide any proposal regarding the qualifications of a Neutral and may propose one or more Neutrals to be designated by the parties. Thereafter, all of the parties may jointly designate a Neutral or may agree upon the qualifications of a Neutral to be appointed by ICC. In either case, the parties shall promptly notify ICC thereof.
In the absence of any reply within such 15-day period, or in the case of a negative reply, the Request for ADR shall be deemed to have been declined and ADR proceedings shall not be commenced. ICC shall promptly so inform in writing the party or parties which filed the Request for ADR.

Article 3
Selection of the Neutral

1 Where all of the parties have jointly designated a Neutral, ICC shall take note of that designation, and such person, upon notifying ICC of his or her agreement to serve, shall act as the Neutral in the ADR proceedings. Where a Neutral has not been designated by all of the parties, or where the designated Neutral does not agree to serve, ICC shall promptly appoint a Neutral, either through an ICC National Committee or otherwise, and notify the parties thereof. ICC shall make all reasonable efforts to appoint a Neutral having the qualifications, if any, which have been agreed upon by all of the parties.

2 Every prospective Neutral shall promptly provide ICC with a *curriculum vitae* and a statement of independence, both duly signed and dated. The prospective Neutral shall disclose to ICC in the statement of independence any facts or circumstances which might be of such nature as to call into question his or her independence in the eyes of the parties. ICC shall provide such information to the parties in writing.

3 If any party objects to the Neutral appointed by ICC and notifies ICC and the other party or parties thereof in writing, stating the reasons for such objection, within 15 days of receipt of notification of the appointment, ICC shall promptly appoint another Neutral.

4 Upon agreement of all of the parties, the parties may designate more than one Neutral or request ICC to appoint more than one Neutral, in accordance with the provisions of these Rules. In appropriate circumstances, ICC may propose the appointment of more than one Neutral to the parties.

Article 4
Fees and Costs

1 The party or parties filing a Request for ADR shall include with the Request a non-refundable registration fee, as set out in the Appendix hereto. No Request for ADR shall be processed unless accompanied by the requisite payment.

2 Following the receipt of a Request for ADR, ICC shall request the parties to pay a deposit in an amount likely to cover the administrative expenses of ICC and the fees and expenses of the Neutral for the ADR proceedings, as set out in the Appendix hereto. The ADR proceedings shall not go forward until payment of such deposit has been received by ICC.

3 In any case where ICC considers that the deposit is not likely to cover the total costs of the ADR proceedings, the amount of such deposit may be subject to readjustment. ICC may stay the ADR proceedings until the corresponding payments are made by the parties.

4 Upon termination of the ADR proceedings, ICC shall settle the total costs of the proceedings and shall, as the case may be, reimburse the parties for any excess payment or bill the parties for any balance required pursuant to these Rules.

5 All above deposits and costs shall be borne in equal shares by the parties, unless they agree otherwise in writing. However, any party shall be free to pay the unpaid balance of such deposits and costs should another party fail to pay its share.

6 A party's other expenditure shall remain the responsibility of that party.

Article 5
Conduct of the ADR Procedure

1 The Neutral and the parties shall promptly discuss, and seek to reach agreement upon, the settlement technique to be used, and shall discuss the specific ADR procedure to be followed.
2 In the absence of an agreement of the parties on the settlement technique to be used, mediation shall be used.
3 The Neutral shall conduct the procedure in such manner as the Neutral sees fit. In all cases the Neutral shall be guided by the principles of fairness and impartiality and by the wishes of the parties.
4 In the absence of an agreement of the parties, the Neutral shall determine the language or languages of the proceedings and the place of any meetings to be held.
5 Each party shall cooperate in good faith with the Neutral.

Article 6
Termination of the ADR Proceedings

1 ADR proceedings which have been commenced pursuant to these Rules shall terminate upon the earlier of:
  a) the signing by the parties of a settlement agreement;
  b) the notification in writing to the Neutral by one or more parties, at any time after the discussion referred to in Article 5(1) has occurred, of a decision no longer to pursue the ADR proceedings;
  c) the completion of the procedure established pursuant to Article 5 and the notification in writing thereof by the Neutral to the parties;
  d) the notification in writing by the Neutral to the parties that the ADR proceedings will not, in the Neutral's opinion, resolve the dispute between the parties;
  e) the expiration of any time limit set for the ADR proceedings, if not extended by all of the parties, such expiration to be notified in writing by the Neutral to the parties;
  f) the notification in writing by ICC to the parties and the Neutral, not less than 15 days after the due date for any payment by one or more parties pursuant to these Rules, stating that such payment has not been made; or
  g) the notification in writing by ICC to the parties stating, in the judgment of ICC, that there has been a failure to designate a Neutral or that it has not been reasonably possible to appoint a Neutral.
2 The Neutral, upon any termination of the ADR proceedings pursuant to Article 6(1), (a)-(c), shall promptly notify ICC of the termination of the ADR proceedings and shall provide ICC with a copy of any notification referred to in Article 6(1), (b)-(c). In all cases ICC shall confirm in writing the termination of the ADR proceedings to the parties and the Neutral, if a Neutral has already been designated or appointed.

Article 7
General Provisions

1 In the absence of any agreement of the parties to the contrary and unless prohibited by applicable law, the ADR proceedings, including their outcome, are private and confidential. Any settlement agreement between the parties shall similarly be kept confidential except that a party shall have the right to disclose it to the extent that such disclosure is required by applicable law or necessary for purposes of its implementation or enforcement.
2 Unless required to do so by applicable law and in the absence of any agreement of the parties to the contrary, a party shall not in any manner produce as evidence in any judicial, arbitration or similar proceedings:
  a) any documents, statements or communications which are submitted by another party or by the Neutral in the ADR proceedings, unless they can be obtained independently by the party seeking to produce them in the judicial, arbitration or similar proceedings;
  b) any views expressed or suggestions made by any party within the ADR proceedings with regard to the possible settlement of the dispute;
  c) any admissions made by another party within the ADR proceedings;
  d) any views or proposals put forward by the Neutral; or

e) the fact that any party had indicated within the ADR proceedings that it was ready to accept a proposal for a settlement.

3 Unless all of the parties agree otherwise in writing, a Neutral shall not act nor shall have acted in any judicial, arbitration or similar proceedings relating to the dispute which is or was the subject of the ADR proceedings, whether as a judge, as an arbitrator, as an expert or as a representative or advisor of a party.

4 The Neutral, unless required by applicable law or unless all of the parties agree otherwise in writing, shall not give testimony in any judicial, arbitration or similar proceedings concerning any aspect of the ADR proceedings.

5 Neither the Neutral, nor ICC and its employees, nor the ICC National Committees shall be liable to any person for any act or omission in connection with the ADR proceedings.

APPENDIX
SCHEDULE OF ADR COSTS

A The party or parties filing a Request for ADR shall include with the Request a non-refundable registration fee of US$ 1,500 to cover the costs of processing the Request for ADR. No Request for ADR shall be processed unless accompanied by the requisite payment.

B The administrative expenses of ICC for the ADR proceedings shall be fixed at ICC's discretion depending en the tasks carried out by ICC. Such administrative expenses shall not exceed the maximum sum of US$ 10,000.

C The fees of the Neutral shall be calculated en the basis of the time reasonably spent by the Neutral in the ADR proceedings, at an hourly rate fixed for such proceedings by ICC in consultation with the Neutral and the parties. Such hourly rate shall be reasonable in amount and shall be determined in light of the complexity of the dispute and any other relevant circumstances. The amount of reasonable expenses of the Neutral shall be fixed by ICC.

D Amounts paid to the Neutral do not include any possible value added taxes (VAT) or other taxes or charges and imposts applicable to the Neutral's fees. Parties are required to pay any such taxes or charges; however, the recovery of any such taxes or charges is a matter solely between the Neutral and the parties.

APPENDIX XVII

INTERNATIONAL PARALYMPIC COMMITTEE
PROTEST RULES

HANDBOOK PART I
SECTION II – GENERAL REGULATIONS

CHAPTER 5 – CLASSIFICATION

9. Classification (Protests)

Protests, although in and of themselves a right of athletes and classifiers, should not be used in a manner that would unfairly affect the outcome of the competition. 'Tactical protests' are a breach of the principles of fair play.

9.1 The SAEC's[1] are responsible for the selection of Sports Classification Juries.

9.2 A member of the Sports Classification Jury should normally be exempted from dealing with a protest concerning a classification that he/she bas been involved with him/herself.

9.3 The decision of the Sports Classification Jury is final and without appeal.

9.4 Classification Protest Procedure

The following regulations for classification protests shall apply:

9.4.1 All protests must be made on the official IPC Protest Form and handed to the respective Chairman of the Sports Classification Jury. The protest must be accompanied by a protest fee which will be refunded if the protest is upheid, otherwise it remains with the SAEC.

In accordance with 7.4 the Classification Committee may protest a competitors classification following observation during competition. Such a protest shall be without fee.

9.4.2 Protest on own classification

Such protests must be handed in not later than six (6) hours after classification.

9.4.3 Protest on another competitor

Only the Chef de Mission (or his/her representative) or relevant classification committee can make such protests.

9.4.4 Protest in Team Sports

Only the Head of Delegation (or his/her representative) or relevant classification committee can make such protests.

9.4.5 Classification protests shall be dealt with as soon as possible after the protest has been received. The head of classification shall decide the time of the hearing.

9.4.6 At re-classification tests the competitor may be accompanied by a person of his/her choice.

9.4.7 If a competitor refuses to attend a protest re-classification test he/she will be banned from further participation.

9.4.8 The final decision will be written on the official form. The original will be kept by the SAEC concerned and copies will be distributed to the athlete concerned, his/her NSO and the Organising Committee.

9.4.9 Following any re-classification the implementation of the change shall be according to the rules of the SAEC'S.

9.4.10 Any records set by an athlete who was reclassified will not be ratified.

9.4.11 If it can be shown that the IPC Code of Ethics for Classification has not been followed during a classificafion, the competitor shall be reciassified by a different classification panel.

---

[1] SAEC = Sports Assembly Executive Committee.

CHAPTER 6 – REGULATIONS FOR OFFICIAL AND SANCTIONED IPC COMPETITIONS

11. Protests

11.1 Classification Protests
See Section II – Chapter 5.

11.2 Sports Technical Protests
Protest concerning the conduct of competition shall follow the procedures of the specific sports rules (see Sections III and IV).

11.3 General Protests

11.3.1 All protests dealing with IPC General Regulations and By Laws including matters of discipline must be made in writing and handed over to the Chairperson of the Protest Jury of three (3) persons appointed by the IPC Executive Committee for each official competition.
The Protest must be accompanied by a protest fee of 100 USD. The fee will be refunded if the protest is upheld, if not it remains with IPC.

11.3.2 The Protest Jury shall deal with the protest without delay.

11.3.3 A person, a committee or a team accused must be given the opportunity to be heard.

11.3.4 Protest Jury decisions shall be in writing and handed over to the protesting party.

11.3.5 The Protest Jury may invoke penalties in the form of:

- Disqualification
- Suspension
- Rebuke

HANDBOOK PART II
SECTION IV – SUMMER SPORTS

CHAPTER 2 – ATHLETICS
APPENDIX V – CLASSIFICATION PROTEST RULES

It is the policy of IPC Athletics to allow classification protests during the Games, under specific circumstances. It is the aim of IPC Athletics that all classification issues will be settled before the Games commence but it is also recognised that in certain circumstances, this is not possible. The following are the classification and classification protest rules.

IPC Athletic Classification

(...)

8. The protest system is clearly defined and takes into account the designation of the athlete, i.e., whether the classification is permanent (P), review (R), or new (N). It also takes into account who can protest and when the protest has to be made.
There are four (4) categories:

Category A

Protests on athletes who have a permanent classification (P) must be made by the Team Manager or Chef de Mission of a country at the Games. These protests can be made up to 72 hours before the first competition event of the Games.
Athletes with a permanent classification (P) cannot change or have their classification changed during the Games.
If, in the view of the Classification Committee, a permanent athlete's class needs to be reviewed as a result of performances during the Games, that review can only take place after the individual athlete's last competition event at the Games.

Category B

Athletes who have a review (R) classification are usually athletes who are on the borderline of two classes. Their classification is being reviewed because the classification committee is concerned. The classification committee can make this decision up to 72 hours before the first competition event of the Games.

The classification procedure of a review athlete includes a medical examination, functional assessment prior to the Games and review during the athlete's first event at the Games. The final decision must be made within 30 minutes of the announcement of the official results of that event.

Category C
Athletes who are new (N), have never been classified at an international Games. After the performance of their first event, the classification of a new (N) athlete may be protested by the chef de mission or team manager or the chief athletic coach of a country. This protest must be made within 30 minutes of the announcement of the official results of the event.
The classification procedure for a new athlete includes a medical examination, functional assessment prior to the Games and review during the athlete's first event at the Games. The final decision must be made within 30 minutes of the announcement of the official results of the event.

Category D
If a review (R) athlete or a new (N) athlete is subsequently observed, during the Games, to show more function than they did at the time of the initial assessment during the Games, then the only people allowed to make a classification protest are members of the classification committee. The basis of the protest will be that the athlete has cheated during the classification process.
If the athlete is found to have cheated after the appropriate assessment has been undertaken, then the penalty will be disqualification from the Games. Any medals that have been won, will be returned.

Note: If the Classification Committee believes that the athlete was co-operative at the times of assessment, and that the classification is an error on their behalf, then the initial classification (the classification confirmed after the first competition event) will stand for the particular Games. At the end of the Games, the classification Committee may review the athlete's classification and either allocate the category (P) or (R) for future competitions.

9. The Chairman of the IPC Athletic Classification Committee will appoint a protest panel where necessary. This protest panel should not include (where possible) people who were involved in the initial assessment.
   Prior to the Games commencing, any protest should be heard as soon as practicable for the people involved, including the athlete.
   A protest during the Games requires an immediate hearing because the results of the event will be held up, pending the result of the protest (if the particular athlete is involved in the results).
10. The athletic program will, as far as is possible, be organised such that if an athlete shifts from a more disabled class to a less disabled class, then the athlete will not miss out on his or her competition. It has been our experience, after 8 international Games that 90% of changes involve an athlete going from a more disabled class to a less disabled class. Those athletes that do the reverse, obviously will miss out on the particular event. If an athlete's classification is changed after assessing their performance during their first event, they are not entitled to medals that their performance may have merited in that event or in any other events, i.e., the result cannot be transferred to another event.
11. A fee will be charged for a protest made by the chef de mission or the team manager or the team athletic coach. The classification committee do not have to pay a fee to make a protest. The actual fee will be determined by the IPC Athletic Executive and may very from Games to Games. If the protest is successful, i.e., the decision is in favour of those people making the protest, then the fee will be refunded in full. The classification committee will have the right to dismiss any protest it considers frivolous without holding a review of the athlete's classification. In these circumstance, the fee tended with the protest will be kept by IPC Athletics.

CHAPTER 3 – BOCCIA

14. Clarification and Protest

14.1 During a match a side may feel that the referee has overlooked an event or made an incorrect decision which effects the resuit of the match. At that time, the side may draw the referee's attention to this situation and seek clarification.

14.2 During the match a player/captain may request a ruling from the Head Referee, whose decision is final.

14.3 If a side feels that the referee has not acted in accordance with the rules then they must not sign the referee's result sheet. Within 30 minutes, a watten protest must be presented to the Competition Secretariat for consideration and action. If no written protest is received then the result stands. (ref-17.)

19. The Captain's Responsibility

19.1 In Team and Pairs Division, each side is led by a captain. The captain should be clearly identified to the referee. The referee will act as the executive of the team and assume the following responsibilities:

(...)

– Submitting a protest.

CHAPTER 8 – LAWN BOWLS

12. Protest procedure

12.1 When a game is in progress the Umpires decision shall be final.

12.2 All other protests come under the jurisdiction of the Sports Technical Committee who shall adhere to the WBB and the IPC rules.

CHAPTER 9 – POWERLIFTING
Powerlifting Classification Rules

5. Sport Classification Juries (Protest Committees).

1. Sports Classification Juries shall comprise at least 2 medical persons (at least one Medical Doctor) and one technical person.
2. The medical Officer shall in cooperation with the Powerlifting Classifier appoint a Classification Jury Chairperson.
3. Whenever possible, a member of the Powerlifting Classification Juries should be exempted from dealing with a protest concerning a classification that he/she has been involved with him/herself. In such cases the Chief Classifier shall appoint a temporary substitute for the jury.
4. The decision of the Sports Classification Jury is final and without appeal.
5. The Sports Section shall keep alt protest forms filed.

6. Classification protest

1. Protest on own classification:
   Such protest must be made in writing on the official protest form and handed to the chairman of the Sports Classification Jury, not later than 6 hours after classification. The protest must be accompanied by a protest fee of $ US 100 which will be refunded, if the protest is upheld. lf it is not, the protest fee remains with the Powerlifting Committee.
   Reclassification wilt take place as soon as practicable.
   The athlete shall present him/herself to the protest committee with the classification form.
2. Protest on another competitor:
   Such protest must be made in writing on the official protest form and handed to the Chairman of the Powerlifting Classification Jury and accompanied by a protest fee of $ US 100. This fee will be returned if the protest is upheld, otherwise it remains with the Powerlifting Committee. Only the chief of delegation (or his/her representative) or chairman of any of the Sports Sections can make such protests. Reclassification will take place immediately.

CHAPTER 11 – SHOOTING

1. General Rules Shooting

1.1. Basic Rules

The U.I.T. rules shall be enforced in al cases except where they are modified by these rules of the International Shooting Committee for the Disabled (hereafter called ISCD).

The U.I.T. Rules are re-enforced and not inserted or restated here and the rules in this book must be read in conjunction with the U.I.T Rules.
The International Paralympic Committee (hereafter called the IPC) Rules are not inserted or restated here and the Rules in the ISCD Shooting Rulebook must be read in conjunction with the IPC Rules if applicable.
(...)
1.1.7 All protests, appeals inclusive, regarding technical matters must be handled as per U.I.T. Rules (General Technical Rules, chapter 13), however the protest fees are set in the rulebook of the ISCO. Protest fee (US $50) must be delivered by hand to the Organising Committee. Appeals must be accompanied by a fee of US $100. If the protest is upheld, the protest fee must be returned by the Organising Committee. If the protest is denied the protest fee will be retained by the ISCD. The decision of the Jury d'Appeal is final. (Model of protest form appendix G).
(...)

4. Functional classification

4.1 Basic rules

(...)

4.1.8 Protests, regarding the functional classification, must be made to the functional classification panel of the ISCD. The classification protest fee ($US 100) must be paid to the head of the protest jury of the functional classification panel. Protest fee must be returned if the protest is upheld and will be retained by the ISCD if the protest is denied.

4.1.9 A protest, made by the competitor against his/her classification, must be lodged within 30 minutes after classification.

4.1.10 A protest, made by others, which is todged 24 hours prior to the start of the competition which results in re-classification, then the new class will be applied in that competition. When re-classification takes place during competition, the new class will be applied in the next competition.

4.1.11 The decision of the classification panel that handles the protest is final.

CHAPTER 13 – SWIMMING
SAEC-SW SWIMMING RULES
Section 2 GN General Rules

GN 4 Disqualification

(...)

GN 4.2 If a competitor does not attend a classification protest when requested they may be disqualified from further competition.

GN 7 Paralympic Games, World Championships, SAEC-SW Championships and General Rules for SAEC-SW

(...)

GN 7.4 Protests

GN 7.4.1 Protests are possible

(...)

e. against decisions of the referee; however, no protest shall be allowed against decisions of fact.

GN 7.4.2 Protests must be submitted

a. to the referee for technical protests or to the head of classification for classification protests
b. in writing on the SAEC-SW official forms [Appendix V]. These forms wilt be made available, on site, by the Organising Committee.
c. by the responsible team leader only
d. together with a deposit of one hundred US dollars [$100] or the fee agreed upon by the SAEC-SW and the Organising Committee.

e. within thirty [30] minutes following the conclusion of the respective event,

f. in case of a classification protest prior to the first day of competition the protest shall be submitted six [6] hours after the completion of the classification of all swimmers. If this time expires between 2200 and 0800 hours, the classification protest wilt be delivered by 0800 hours on the following day.
lf conditions causing a potential protest are noted prior to the competition, a protest must be lodged before the signal to start is given,

GN 7.4.3 All protests shall be considered by the referee and/or the head of classification. lf they reject the protest, they must state the reasons for their decision. The team leader may appeal the rejection to the Jury of Appeal whose decision shall be final. The final decision shall be in writing on the SAEC-SW official form [Appendix V]. A copy for the team leader concerned shall be distributed.

GN 7.4.4 A FCS classification protest panel at IPC competition will consist of three [3] authorised classifiers appointed by the head of classification. The protest panel must consist of at least one medical and one technical classifier who has not previously classified the swimmer within a two [2] year period.

GN 7.4.5 If a technical or classification protest is rejected, the fee shall be forfeited to SAEC-SW. lf the protest is upheld the deposit shall be returned.

GN 7.4.6 For FCS classification and reclassification procedures refer to the classification manual.

GN 7.5 Jury of Appeal

GN 7.5.1 The decision of the Jury is final.

GN 7.5.2 A technical Jury will consist of the technical delegate/assistant technical delegate, technical adviser, referee and head of classification.

GN 7.5.3 A classification Jury for the FCS wilt consist of the technical delegate, head of classification and at least two authorised classifiers appointed by the head of classification. The Jury must consist of at least one medical and one technical classifier.

GN 7.5.4 A classification Jury for the visually impaired will be appointed by the Chief IBSA Ophthalmologist.

GN 7.5.5 A classification Jury for swimmers with mental handicap/intellectual disability will be conducted according to the INAS-FMH ruling.

GN 7.6 Organising Committee

(...)

GN 7.6.3 The Organising Committee, in conjunction with the appointed technical delegate and the assistant technical delegate, shall be responsible for the entire management of the contest, including the arrangement of the programma of events, arrangement for the classification of swimmers, all technical equipment and installation prior to and during competition, appointment of officials and adjudication of protests.

CHAPTER 14 – TABLE TENNIS

3. Regulations for international championships

(...)

3.13 The draw and playing system in the team and class events

(...)

Protests

All protests must be made through the Referee with the appropriate fee, set by the Organising Committee.

- The Referee will resolve the matter on subjects within his jurisdiction.
- The Referee will refer all matters not within his jurisdiction to the international Jury selected by the International Table Tennis Committee.
- The protest fee will only be refunded if the protest is upheld.
- A classifier may re-classify a competitor at any time during a championships.
- If a player is re-classified after a protest or by a classifier during a championships he/she will transfer to the new class in the next event and the draw will be altered. Example: if a player during the team event is re-classified from class 6 to class 7 he will for the individual event be transferred to class 7 and the draw for class 7 will be altered.
- If it is deemed that a player has deliberately misled the classifiers he shall be immediately disqualified at the discretion of the Referee.

HANDBOOK PART III
SECTION IV – SUMMER SPORTS

CHAPTER 1 – WINTER SPORTS CLASSIFICATION

1. Generalities

(...)

1.4 Protests

For classification protest rules see IPC Handbook, Section 11 – Chapter 5.
Special regulations:
(...)

CHAPTER 5-5.1 – RULES COMMON TO CROSS COUNTRY EVENTS

903 The jury and its duties

903.3 The Jury must ensure that the competition is organized and carried out according to the FIS and IPC rules.

903.3.1 The Jury must clarify and decide:

(...)

- whether protests should be accepted and disqualifications announced.

(...)

904 The FIS and IPC Technical Delegates (TD) and their duties

(...)

904.4 Duties after the Competition

(...)

– Subsequently they meet with the Jury and deal with any infractions and protests,

(...)

931 Disqualification, protests and appeals

(...)

933 Protests

933.1 A protest shall be considered by a Jury or higher tribunal provided that:

933.1.1 The protest has been delivered within the time limit specified.

933.1.2 The protest has not been deliberately delayed to obtain an advantage.

933.1.3 The protest is accompanied by 100 Swiss Francs, or an equivalent value.

933.2 Protests against the admission of a competitor must be delivered in writing to the Competition Secretary before the competition begins.

933.3 Protests against the conduct of another competitor or of an official must be delivered in writing to the Competition Secretary within one hour after the publication of the unofficial rest list.

933.4 Protest concerning timekeeping must be delivered in writing to the Competition Secretary within one hour after the publication of the unofficial result list.

933.5 Protests concerning erroneous and clerical errors, or contraventions of the IPC Rules only established after the competition, will be considered if sent by registered post through the competitor's National Association to the IPC Nordic SAEC (through its Chairperson) within one month of the competition. These protests must be dealt with within a month.

933.6 If an error is proved, the corrected results must be published and the prizes redistributed.

CHAPTER 5-5.2 – PARTICULAR RULES OF RELAY COMPETITIONS

957 Protests

For protests, art. 933.

APPENDIX XVIII

SPORTS LAW OF THE PEOPLE'S REPUBLIC OF CHINA OF 29 AUGUST 1995

Law of the People's Republic of China on Physical Culture and Sports

(Adopted at the 15th Meeting of the Standing Committee of the Eighth National People's Congress on August 29,1995, promulgated by Order No. 55 of the President of the People's Republic of China on August 29, 1995 and effective as of October 1, 1995)

Chapter I
General Provisions

Article 1
This Law is formulated in accordance with the Constitution for the purpose of developing undertakings of physical culture and sports, building up the people's physique, raising sports performance level and promoting the socialist material, ideological and cultural development.

Article 2
The State promotes development of undertakings of physical culture and sports and carries out mass sports activities to improve physical fitness of the whole nation. The work of physical culture and sports shall adhere to the principle of combining popularization with the raising of standards based on the unfolding of the national fitness campaign so as to promote coordinated development of various sports.

Article 3
The State adheres to the principle that physical culture and sports should serve economic, construction, national defense and social development. Undertakings of physical culture and sports shall be incorporated into the plan for national economy and social development.

The State promotes reform in the sports administration system. The State encourages enterprises, institutions, public organizations and citizens to run and support undertakings of physical culture and sports.

Article 4
The administrative department for physical culture and sports under the State Council shall be in charge of the work of physical culture and sports throughout the country. Other relevant departments under the State Council shall administer the work of physical culture and sports within their respective functions and powers.

The administrative departments for physical culture and sports of the local people's governments at or above the county level or the organs authorized by the people's governments at the corresponding levels shall be in charge of the work of physical culture and sports within their administrative areas.

Article 5
The State provides special guarantee to physical activities of children, juveniles and young people to improve their physical and mental health.

Article 6
The State helps ethnic minority areas develop undertakings of physical culture and sports and cultivates sport talents of ethnic minorities.

Article 7
The State promotes education and scientific research in physical culture and sports, popularizes advanced and practical achievements in sports science and technology, and develops undertakings of physical culture and sports by relying on science and technology.

Article 8
The State awards the organizations and individuals that have made contributions to the cause of physical culture and sports.

Article 9
The State encourages international exchanges in sports. In conducting international exchanges in sports, the principles of independence, equality, mutual benefit and mutual respect shall be adhered to, the State sovereignty and dignity defended and the international treaties the People's Republic of China has concluded or acceded to shall be observed.

Chapter II
Social Sports

Article 10
The State advocates citizens' participation in social sports activities so as to improve their physical and mental health. Social sports activities shall be carried out in spare time and en a voluntary, small-scale and diversified basis, following the principle of suiting such activities to the local conditions and conducting them in a scientific and civilized way.

Article 11
The State implements the National Fitness Program, carries out the Physical Training Qualification Standards and conducts monitoring of the people's physique.

The State practices a skill-grading system for social sports instructors, who shall guide social sports activities.

Article 12
The local people's governments at various levels shall create necessary conditions for citizens' participation in social sports activities, support and help the development of mass sports activities.

In urban areas the role of the residents' committees and other community organizations at the grass-roots level shall be brought into play in organizing residents to carry out sports activities.

In rural areas the role of the villagers' committees and cultural and sports organizations at the grass-roots level shall be brought into play in carrying out sports activities suitable to rural conditions.

Article 13
State organs, enterprises and institutions shall carry out various kinds of sports activities and organize athletic competitions of mass character.

Article 14
Trade unions and other public organizations shall organize sports activities in light of their own characteristics.

Article 15
The State encourages and supports the exploration, consolidation and improvement of national and folk traditional sports.

Article 16
The whole society should be concerned about and support the aged and disabled people to participate in physical activities. People's governments at various levels shall take measures to provide conditions for the aged and disabled people to participate in physical activities.

Chapter III
School Sports

Article 17
Departments of education administration and schools shall take physical culture and sports as a component part of school education and cultivate talents with all-round development in moral, intellectual and physical qualities.

Article 18
Schools must offer Physical Education and make ir a subject for assessing students' academic performance.
Schools shall create conditions for organizing sports activities suitable to the special features of students who are in poor health or disabled.

Article 19
Schools must implement the National Physical Training Qualification Standards and ensure that the students have time for sports activities every day at school.

Article 20
Schools shall organize various kinds of after-class sports activities, carry out after-class athletic training and competitions, and in light of specific conditions hold a school-wide sports meet every school year.

Article 21
Schools shall, according to relevant regulations of the State, have qualified physical education teachers and ensure that they enjoy the privileges commensurate with the nature of their work.

Article 22
Schools shall, according to the criteria set by the department of education administration under the State Council, have sports fields, sports installations and facilities and sports apparatus.
Sports fields in schools must be used for sports activities and may not be used for any other purposes.

Article 23
Schools shall institute a system of medical examination for students. The administrative departments for education, physical culture and sports and public health shall strengthen the monitoring of students' physique.

Chapter IV
Competitive Sports

Article 24
The State promotes the development of competitive sports, encourages athletes to raise their athletic performance level and achieve excellent results in sports competitions so as to win honors for the country.

Article 25
The State encourages and supports spare time athletic training to foster reserve sports talents.

Article 26
Athletes and teams that participate in major national and international sports competitions shall be selected and formed on the principle of fairness and according to qualifications Specific measures shall be formulated by the administrative department for physical culture and sports under the State Council.

Article 27
In nurturing athletes, training and management must be carried out in a strict, scientific and civilized way. Athletes shall be educated in patriotism, collectivism and socialism as well as in morality and discipline.

Article 28
The State grants preferential treatment to outstanding athletes in their employment and enrollment for schools.

Article 29

The national sports association of an individual sport shall manage the registration of athlctes of such sport. A registered athlete may, in accordance with the regulations of the administrative department for physical culture and sports under thc State Council, participatie in relevant sports competitions and flow from one team to another.

Article 30

The State practices a skill-grading system for athletics and referees, and a grading system of professional and technical titles for coaches.

Article 31

The State practices classified administration of sports competitions at different levels.

Comprehensive national games shall be administered by the administrative department for physical culture and sports under the State Council or by the administrative department for physical culture and sports under the State Council in conjunction with other relevant organizations.

National competition of an individual sport shall be administered by the national association of the said sport.

Measures for the administration of local comprehensive sports games and local individual sport competitions shall be formulated by the local people's governments.

Article 32

The State practices an examination and approval system for national sports records. National sports records shall be confirmed by the administrative department for physical culture and sports under the State Council.

Article 33

Disputes arising in competitive sports activities shall be mediated and arbitrated by sports arbitration institutions. Measures for the establishment of sports arbitration institutions and the scope of arbitration shall be prescribed separately by the State Council.

Article 34

The principle of fair competition shall be followed in sports competitions. Organizers of competitions, athletes, coaches and referees shall abide by sportsmanship, and may not practice fraud or engage in malpractice for selfish ends.

Use of banned drugs and methods is strictly prohibited in sports activities. Institutions in charge of testing banned drugs shall conduct strict examination of the banned drugs and methods. It is strictly forbidden for any organization or individual to engage in gambling activities through sports competitions.

Article 35

Symbols such as titles, emblems, flags and mascots of major sports competitions to be held within the territory of the People's Republic of China shall be protected in accordance with the relevant regulations of the State.

Chapter V
Public Sports Organizations

Article 36

The State encourages and supports publie sports organizations to organizc and conduct sports activities in accordancc with their articles of association to promote the development of undertakings of, physical culture and sports.

Article 37

Sports federations at various levels are mass sports organizations that link and rally athletes and sports personnel and shall fully play their roles in the development of undertakings of physical culture and sports.

Article 38
The Chinese Olympic Committee, as a sports organization whose chief task is to develop and promote the Olympic movement. shall represent China to participate in international Olympic affairs.

Article 39
Public organizations of sports science are academic mass organizations of personnel engaged in sports science and technology, which shall fully play their roles in promoting the development of sports science and technology.

Article 40
The national sports association of an individual sport shall be in charge of the popularization and enhancement of such sport, and shall represent China in the corresponding international sports organization.

Chapter VI
Conditions of Guarantee

Article 41
The people's governments at or above the county level shall include sports expenditure and funds for sports capital construction in financial budgets and plans for capital construction investment at the corresponding levels and along with the development of national economy gradually increase their input to undertakings of physical culture and sports.

Article 42
The State encourages enterprises, institutions and public organizations to raise funds on their own for the development of undertakings of physical culture and sports and encourages organizations and individuals to donate to and sponsor. undertakings of physical culture and sports.

Article 43
Relevant departments of the State shall strengthen the management of sports funds. No organization or individual may misappropriate or intercept sports funds.

Article 44
The administrative departments for physical culture and sports of the local people's governments at or above the county level shall, in accordance with the relevant regulations of the State, strengthen the management of and supervision over business operations in sports activities such as body-building and competitive sports.

Article 45
The local people's governments at or above the county level shall. In accordance with the regulations of the State governing land allotment for public sports installations and facilities in urban areas, incorporate the construction of public sports installations and facilities into urban construction plans and general plans for land utilization so as to achieve rational distribution and overall arrangement.

In planning the layout of enterprises, schools, streets and residential quarters, sports installations and facilities shall be incorporated into the construction plan.

Townships, nationality townships and towns shall build and improve sports installations and facilities along with the economic development.

Article 46
Public sports installations and facilities shall be open to the public and be easily accessible to them for sports activities. Students, the aged and disabled people shall be given preferential treatment in this regard, and sports installations and facilities shall be fully utilized.

No organization or individual may seize or damage public sports installations and facilities. Where temporary occupation of sports installations and facilities is necessitated by special circumstances, it shall be subject to the approval of the administrative department for physical culture and sports and the department of construction planning and such installations and facilities shall be returned without delay. If any sports field is to be used for other purposes according to urban planning, new sports field shall, in accordance with the relevant regulations of the State, be constructed beforehand for replacement.

Article 47
Sports equipment and apparatus to be used for national and international sports competitions must be subjected to examination and approval of institutions designated by the administrative department for physical culture and sports under the State Council.

Article 48
The State promotes physical culture and sports education, establishes various types of colleges, schools, departments and specialities of physical culture and sports to nurture professional personnel in such fields as sports, training and coaching, Physical Education teaching, scientific research, management and mass sports.

The State encouragcs enterprises, institutions, public organizations and citizens to operate professional institutions for physical culture and sports education in accordance with law.

Chapter VII
Legal Liability

Article 49
Whoever commits fraud or other acts violating the discipline or sports rules in competitive sports shall be punished by the relevant public sports organization in accordance with the provisions of its articles of association. State functionaries who are held directly responsible shall be subject to administrative sanctions in accordance with law.

Article 50
Whoever resorts to banned drugs or methods in sports activities shall be punished by the relevant public sports organization in accordance with the provisions of its articles of association; State functionaries who are held directly responsible shall be subject to administrative sanctions in accordance with law.

Article 51
Whoever engages in gambling activities through competitive sports shall be ordered to stop the illegal practice by the public security organ in conjunction with the administrative department for physical culture and sports and shall be punished by the public security organ in accordance with the provisions of the Regulations on Administrative Penalties for Public Security. Whoever commits bribery, fraud, or the organizing of gambling shall, if the case constitutes a crime, be investigated for criminal responsibility in accordance with law.

Article 52
Whoever seizes or damages public sports installations or facilities shall be ordered by the administrative department for physical culture and sports to make corrections within a time limit and shall bear civil liability according to law. Whoever commits any of the acts specified in the preceding paragraph and violates the administration of public security shall be punished by the public security organ in accordance with the relevant provisions of the Regulations on Administrative Penalties for Public Security; if the case constitutes a crime, the offender shall be investigated for criminal responsibility according to law.

Article 53
Whoever creates disturbances or disturbs public order in sports activities shall be criticized and educated and such act shall be stopped; if the case violates the administration of public security, the offender shall be punished by the public security organ in accordance with the provisions of the Regulations on Administrative Penalties for Public Security; if the case constitutes a crime, the offender shall be investigated for criminal responsibility according to law.

Article 54
Whoever, in violation of the State financial or accounting rules, misappropriates or intercepts sports funds shall be ordered by the authorities at higher levels to return the misappropriated or intercepted funds within a time limit; the responsible persons directly in charge and other persons directly responsible for the offense shall be subject to administrative sanctions in accordance with law; if the case constitutes a crime. The offender shall be investigated for criminal responsibility in accordance with law.

Chapter VIII
Supplementary Provisions

Article 55
Specific measures for the administration of sports activities in the Army shall be formulated by the Central Military Commission in accordance with this Law.

Article 56
This Law shall be effective from October 1, 1995.

APPENDIX XIX

THE CAS CODE OF SPORTS-RELATED ARBITRATION

PROCEDURAL RULES

A – GENERAL PROVISIONS

R27 – Application of the rules

1. These Procedural Rules apply whenever the parties have agreed to refer a sports-related dispute to the CAS. Such disputes may arise out of a contract containing an arbitration clause or be the subject of a later arbitration agreement (ordinary arbitration proceedings) or involve an appeal against a decision given by the disciplinary tribunals or similar bodies of a federation, association or sports body where the statutes or regulations of such bodies, or a specific agreement provides for an appeal to the CAS (appeal arbitration proceedings).
2. Such disputes may involve matters of principle relating to sport or matters of pecuniary or other interests brought into play in the practice or the development of sport and, generally speaking, any activity related or connected to sport.
3. These Procedural Rules also apply where the CAS is called upon to give an advisory opinion (consultation proceedings).

R28 – Seat

The seat of the CAS and of each Arbitration Panel ('Panel') is in Lausanne, Switzerland. However, should circumstances so warrant, and after consultation with all parties, the President of the Panel or, failing him, the President of the relevant Division may decide to hold a hearing in another place.

R29 – Language

1. The CAS working languages are French and English. In the absence of agreement between the parties, and taking into account all pertinent circumstances, the President of the Panel shall select one of these two languages as the language of the arbitration at the start of the proceedings before the Panel.
2. The parties may choose another language provided that the Arbitration Panel agrees. The parties shall advise the CAS of such a choice. In the event of such a choice, the Panel may order that the parties bear all or part of the translation and interpreting costs.

R30 – Representation and assistance

The parties may be represented or assisted by persons of their choice. The names, addresses, telephone and facsimile numbers of the persons representing the parties shall be communicated to the Court Office, the other party and the Panel after its formation.

R31 – Notifications and communications

1. All notifications and communications that the CAS or the Panel intend for the parties shall be made through the Court Office. The notifications and communications shall be written in French or in English and sent to the address shown in the arbitration request, statement of appeal or application for an opinion, or to any other address specified at a later date.
2. All arbitration awards, orders, and other decisions made by the CAS and the Panel shall be notified by any means permitting proof of receipt.
3. All communications from the parties intended for the CAS or the Panel, including the arbitration request, statement of appeal, application for an opinion and request for participation of a third party, as well as the reply shall be sent to the CAS in as many copies as there are parties, counsel and arbitrators, together with one additional copy for the CAS itself.

R32 – Time-limit
Upon application on justified grounds, either the President of the Panel or, failing him, the President of the relevant Division, may extend the time-limits provided in these Procedural Rules, if the circumstances so warrant.

R33 – independence and qualifications of arbitrators
1. Every arbitrator shall be and remain independent of the parties and shall immediately disclose any circumstances likely to affect independence with respect to any of the parties.
2. Every arbitrator shall appear on the list drawn up by the ICAS in accordance with the Statutes which are part of this Code and shall have the availability required to expeditiously complete the arbitration.

R34 – Challenge
1. An arbitrator may be challenged if the circumstances give rise to legitimate doubts over his independence. The challenge shall be brought immediately after the ground for the challenge has become known.
2. Challenges are in the exclusive power of the ICAS which may exercise such power through its Board in accordance with the Statutes which are part of this Code. The challenge shall be brought by way of a petition setting forth the facts giving rise to the challenge. The ICAS or its Board shall rule on the challenge after the other parties, the challenged arbitrator and the other arbitrators have been invited to submit written comments. It shall give brief reasons for its decision.

R35 – Removal
An arbitrator may be removed by the ICAS if he refuses to or is prevented from carrying out his duties. The ICAS may delegate this function to its Board. The Board shall invite the parties, the arbitrator in question and the other arbitrators to submit written comments and shall render a brief reasoned decision.

R36 – Replacement
In the event of resignation, death, challenge or removal of an arbitrator, such arbitrator shall be replaced in accordance with the provisions applicable to his appointment. Unless otherwise agreed by the parties or otherwise decided by the Panel, the proceedings shall continue without repetition of the procedure which took place prior to the replacement.

R37 – Provisional and conservatory measures
1. No party may apply for provisional or conservatory measures under these Procedural Rules before the request for arbitration or the statement of appeal, which implies the exhaustion of internal remedies, has been filed with the CAS.
2. The President of the relevant Division, prior to the transfer of the file to the Panel, or thereafter the Panel may, upon application by one of the parties, make an order for provisional or conservatory measures. In agreeing to submit to these Procedural Rules any dispute subject to appeal arbitration proceedings, the parties expressly waive their rights to request such measures from state authorities. This waiver does not apply to provisional or conservatory measures in connection with disputes subject to ordinary arbitration proceedings.
3. If an application for provisional measures is filed, the President of the relevant Division or the Panel invites the opponent to express his position within fifteen days or within a shorter time-limit if circumstances so require. The President of the relevant Division or the Panel shall issue an order within a short time. In case of utmost urgency, the President of the relevant Division prior to the transfer of the file to the Panel, or thereafter the President of the Panel may issue an order upon mere presentation of the application, provided that the opponent shall be heard subsequently.
4. Temporary and conservatory measures may be made conditional upon the provision of security.

B – SPECIAL PROVISIONS APPLICABLE TO THE ORDINARY ARBITRATION PROCEEDINGS

R38 – Request for Arbitration

1. The party intending to submit a reference to arbitration under these Procedural Rules shall file a request with the CAS containing:
   * a brief statement of the facts and legal argument, including a statement of the issue to be submitted to the CAS for determination;
   * the claimant's request for relief;
   * a copy of the contract containing the arbitration agreement or of any document providing for arbitration in accordance with these Procedural Rules;
   * any relevant information about the number and choice of the arbitrator(s), in particular if the arbitration agreement provides for three arbitrators, the name and address of the arbitrator chosen by the claimant from the CAS list of names.
2. Upon filing its request, the claimant shall pay the fee provided in Article R64.1.

R39 – Initiation of the arbitration by the CAS and answer

Unless it is apparent from the outset that there is manifestly no agreement to arbitrate referring to the CAS, the Court Office shall take all appropriate actions to set the arbitration in motion. To this effect, it in particular communicates the request to the respondent, calls upon the parties to express themselves on the law applicable to the merits of the dispute and sets time-limits for the respondent to submit any relevant information about the number and choice of the arbitrator(s), in particular to appoint an arbitrator from the CAS list, as well as to file an answer to the request for arbitration. The answer shall contain:

* a brief statement of the defence;
* any defence of lack of jurisdiction;
* any counterclaim.

R40 – Formation of the Panel

R40.1 – Number of arbitrators

The Panel is composed of one or three arbitrators. If the arbitration agreement does not specify the number of arbitrators, the President of the Division shall determine the number taking into account the amount in litigation and the complexity of the dispute.

R40.2 – Appointment of the arbitrators

1. The parties may agree on the method of appointment of the arbitrators. In the absence of an agreement, the arbitrators shall be appointed in accordance with the following paragraphs.
2. If, by virtue of the arbitration agreement or a decision of the President of the Division, a sole arbitrator is to be appointed, the parties may select him by mutual agreement within a time-limit of twenty days set by the Court Office upon receipt of the request. In the absence of an agreement within such time-limit, the President of the Division shall proceed with the appointment.
3. If, by virtue of the arbitration agreement or of a decision of the President of the Division, three arbitrators are to be appointed, the claimant shall appoint its arbitrator in the request or within the time-limit set in the decision on the number of arbitrators and the respondent shall appoint its arbitrator within the time-limit set by the Court Office upon receipt of the request. In the absence of such appointment, the President of the Division shall proceed with the appointment in lieu of the parties. The two arbitrators so appointed shall select the President of the Panel by mutual agreement within a time-limit set by the Court Office. In the absence of an agreement within such time-limit, the President of the Division shall appoint the President of the Panel in lieu of the two arbitrators.

R40.3 – Confirmation of the arbitrators and transfer of the file

1. Any arbitrator selected by the parties or by other arbitrators shall only be deemed appointed after confirmation by the President of the Division. Before proceeding with such confirmation, the latter shall ascertain that the arbitrator fulfils the requirements of Article R33.
2. Once-the Panel is formed, the Court Office takes notice of the formation and transfers the file to the arbitrators.

R41 – Multiparty arbitration

R41.1 – Plurality of claimants / respondents

1. If the request for arbitration names several claimants and/or respondents, the CAS shall proceed with the formation of the Panel in accordance with the number of arbitrators and the method of appointment agreed by all parties. In the absence of such an agreement, the President of the Division shall decide on the number of arbitrators in accordance with Article R40.1.
2. If a sole arbitrator is to be appointed, Article R40.2 shall apply. If three arbitrators are to be appointed and there are several claimants, the claimants shall jointly appoint an arbitrator. If three arbitrators are to be appointed and there are several respondents, the respondents shall jointly appoint an arbitrator. In the absence of such a joint appointment, the President of the Division shall proceed with the appointment in lieu of the claimants/respondents. If (i) three arbitrators are to be appointed, (ii) there are several claimants and several respondents, and (iii) either the claimants or the respondents fail to jointly appoint an arbitrator, then both co-arbitrators shall be appointed by the President of the Division in accordance with Article R40.2. In all cases, the co-arbitrators shall select the President of the Panel in accordance with Article R40.2.

R41.2 – Joinder

If a respondent intends to cause a third party to participate in the arbitration, it shall so state in its answer, together with the reasons therefore, and file an additional copy of its answer. The Court Office shall communicate this copy to the person the participation of which is requested and set such person a time-limit to state its position on its participation and to submit a response pursuant to Article R39. It shall also set a time-limit for the claimant to express its position on the participation of the third party.

R41.3 – Intervention

If a third party intends to participate as a party in the arbitration, it shall file with the CAS an application to this effect, together with the reasons therefore within the time-limit set for the respondent's answer to the request for arbitration. To the extent applicable, such application shall have the same contents as a request for arbitration. The Court Office shall communicate a copy of this application to the parties and set a time-limit for them to express their position on the participation of the third party and to file, to the extent applicable, an answer pursuant to Article R39.

R41.4 – Joint provisions on joinder and intervention

1. A third party may only participate in the arbitration if it is bound by the arbitration agreement or if itself and the other parties agree in writing.
2. Upon expiration of the time-limit set in Articles R41.2 and R41.3, the President of the Division shall decide on the participation of the third party, taking into account, in particular, the prima facie existence of an arbitration agreement as referred to in Article R39 above. Such decision shall be without prejudice to the decision of the Panel on the same matter.
3. If the President of the Division accepts the participation of the third party, the CAS shall proceed with the formation of the Panel in accordance with the number of arbitrators and the method of appointment agreed by all parties. In the absence of such an agreement, the President of the Division shall decide on the number of arbitrators in accordance with Article R40.1. If a sole arbitrator is to be appointed, Article R40.2 shall apply. If three arbitrators are to be appointed, the co-arbitrators shall be appointed by the President of the Division and shall choose the President of the Panel in accordance with Article R40.2.
4. Regardless of the decision of the Panel on the participation of the third party, the formation of the Panel cannot be challenged. In the event that the Panel accepts the participation, it shall, if required, issue related procedural directions.

R42 – Conciliation

The President of the Division, before the transfer of the file to the Panel, and thereafter the Panel may at any time seek to resolve the dispute by conciliation. Any settlement may be embodied in an arbitral award rendered by consent of the parties.

R43 – Confidentiality

Proceedings under these Procedural Rules are confidential. The parties, the arbitrators and the CAS undertake not to disclose to any third party any facts or other information relating to the dispute or the proceedings. Awards shall not be made public unless the award itself so provides or all parties agree.

R44 – Procedure before the Panel

R44.1 – Written submissions

1. The procedure before the Panel comprises written submissions, if the Panel deems it appropriate, and an oral hearing. Upon the receipt of the file, the President of the Panel, if appropriate, shall issue directions in connection with the written submissions. As a general rule, there shall be one statement of claim, one response and, if the circumstances so require, one reply and one second response. The parties may, in the statement of claim and in the response, raise claims not contained in the request for arbitration and in the answer to the request. Thereafter, no party may raise any new claim without the consent of the other party.
2. Together with their written submissions, the parties shall produce all written evidence upon which they intend to rely. After the exchange of the written submissions, the parties shall not be authorized to produce further written evidence, except by mutual agreement or if the Panel so permits on the basis of exceptional circumstances.
3. In their written submissions, the parties shall specify any witnesses and experts which they intend to call and state any other evidentiary measure which they request.

R44.2 – Hearing

1. Once the exchange of pleadings is closed, the President of the Panel shall issue directions with respect to the hearing and in particular set the hearing date. As a general rule, there shall be one hearing during which the Panel hears the parties, the witnesses and the expert as well as the parties' final oral arguments, for which the respondent has the floor last.
2. The President of the Panel shall conduct the hearing and ascertain that the statements made are concise and limited to the subject of the written presentations, to the extent that these presentations are relevant. Except if the parties agree otherwise, the hearings are not public. There shall be minutes of the hearing. Any person heard by the Panel may be assisted by an interpreter at the cost of the party which called such upon.
3. The parties may call to be heard by the Panel such witnesses and experts which they have specified in their written submissions.
4. Before hearing any witness, expert or interpreter, the Panel shall solemnly invite such persons to tell the truth, subject to the sanctions of perjury.
5. Once the hearing is closed, the parties shall not be authorized to produce further written pleadings, except if the Panel so orders.

R44.3 – Evidentiary proceedings ordered by the Panel

1. A party may request the Panel to issue an order that the other party produces documents in its custody or under its control. The party seeking such production shall demonstrate that the documents are likely to exist and to be relevant.
2. If it deems it appropriate to supplement the presentations of the parties, the Panel may at any time order the production of additional documents or the examination of witnesses, appoint and hear experts, and proceed with any other procedural act.
3. The Panel shall consult the parties with respect to the appointment and terms of reference of such expert. The expert appointed by the Panel shall be and remain independent of the parties and shall immediately disclose any circumstances likely to affect independence with respect to any of the parties.

R44.4 – Expedited procedure

With the consent of the parties, the Panel may proceed in an expedited manner for which it shall issue appropriate directions.

R45 – Law applicable to the merits

The Panel shall decide the dispute according to the rules of law chosen by the parties or, in the absence of such a choice, according to Swiss law. The parties may authorize the Panel to decide ex aequo et bono.

R46 – Award

1. The award shall be made by a majority decision, or, in the absence of a majority, by the President alone. The award shall be written, dated and signed. Unless the parties agree otherwise, it shall briefly state reasons. The signature of the President of the Panel shall suffice.
2. The award shall be final and binding upon the parties. It may not be challenged by way of an action for setting aside to the extent that the parties have no domicile, habitual residence, or business establishment in Switzerland and that they have expressly excluded all setting aside proceedings in the arbitration agreement or in an agreement entered into subsequently, in particular at the outset of the arbitration.

C – SPECIAL PROVISIONS APPLICABLE TO THE APPEAL ARBITRATION PROCEEDINGS

R47 – Appeal

A party may appeal from the decision of a disciplinary tribunal or similar body of a federation, association or sports body, insofar as the statutes or regulations of the said body so provide or as the parties have conclude a specific arbitration agreement and insofar as the appellant has exhausted the legal remedies available to him prior to the appeal, in accordance with the statutes or regulations of the said sports body.

R48 – Statement of appeal

1. The appellant shall submit to the CAS a statement of appeal containing:
   * a copy of the decision appealed from;
   * the appellant's request for relief;
   * the appointment of the arbitrator chosen by the appellant from the CAS list, unless the parties have agreed to the Panel composed of a sole arbitrator;
   * if applicable, an application to stay the execution of the decision appealed from, together with reasons;
   * a copy of the provisions of the statutes or regulations or the specific agreement providing for appeal to the CAS.
2. Upon filing the statement, the appellant shall pay the fee provided for under Article R65.2.

R49 – Time-limit for appeal

In the absence of a time-limit set in the statutes or regulations of the federation, association, sports body concerned, or of a previous agreement, the time-limit for appeal shall be twenty-one days from the communication of the decision which is appealed from.

R50 – Number of arbitrators

The appeal shall be submitted to a Panel of three arbitrators, except if the appellant establishes at the time of the statement of appeal that the parties have agreed to a Panel composed of a sole arbitrator or if the President of the Division considers that the matter is an emergency and the appeal should be submitted to a sole arbitrator.

R51 – Appeal brief

Within ten days following the expiration of the time-limit for the appeal, the appellant shall file with the CAS a brief stating the facts and legal arguments giving rise to the appeal, together with all exhibits and specification of other evidence upon which he intends to rely, failing which the appeal shall be deemed withdrawn.

R52 – Initiation of the arbitration by the CAS

Unless it is apparent from the outset that there is manifestly no agreement to arbitrate referring to the CAS, the CAS Shall take all appropriate actions to set the arbitration in motion. To this effect, the Court Office shall, in particular, communicate the statement of appeal to the respondent, and the President of the Division shall proceed with the formation of the Panel in accordance with Articles R53 and R54. If applicable, he shall also decide promptly on an application for a stay.

R53 – Appointment of arbitrator by respondent
Unless the parties have agreed to a Panel composed of a sole arbitrator or the President of the Division considers that the appeal is an emergency and must be submitted to a sole arbitrator, the respondent shall appoint an arbitrator within ten days after the receipt of the statement of appeal. In the absence of an appointment within such time-limit, the President of the Division shall proceed with the appointment in lieu of the respondent.

R54 – Appointment of the sole arbitrator or of the President and confirmation of the arbitrators by the CAS
1. If, by virtue of the parties' agreement or of a decision of the President of a Division, a sole arbitrator is to be appointed, the President of the Division shall appoint the sole arbitrator upon receipt of the motion for appeal.
2. If three arbitrators are to be appointed, the President of the Division shall appoint the President of the Panel upon appointment of the arbitrator by the respondent. The arbitrators selected by the parties shall only be deemed appointed after confirmation by the President of the Division. Before proceedings with such confirmation, the President of the Division shall ascertain that the arbitrators fulfil the requirements of Article R33.
3. Once the Panel is formed, the Court Office takes notice of the formation of the Panel and transfers the file to the arbitrators.

R55 – Answer of respondent
Within twenty days from the receipt of the grounds for the appeal, the respondent shall submit to the CAS an answer containing:
* a statement of defence;
* any defence of lack of jurisdiction;
* any exhibits or specification of other evidence upon which the respondent intends to rely.

R56 – Statement of appeal and answer complete
Unless the parties agree otherwise or the President of the Panel orders otherwise on the basis of exceptional circumstances, the parties shall not be authorized to supplement their argumentation, nor to produce new exhibits, nor to specify further evidence on which they intend to rely after the submission of the grounds for the appeal and of the answer.

R57 – Scope of Panel's review, hearing
The Panel shall have full power to review the facts and the law. Upon transfer of the file, the President of the Panel shall issue directions in connection with the hearing for the examination of the parties, the witnesses and the experts, as well as for the oral arguments. He may also request communication of the file of the disciplinary tribunal or similar body, the decision of which is subject to appeal. Articles R44.2 and R44.3 shall apply.

R58 – Law applicable
The Panel shall decide the dispute according to the applicable regulations and the rules of law chosen by the parties or, in the absence of such a choice, according to the law of the country in which the federation, association or sports body is domiciled.

R59 – Award
1. The award shall be rendered by a majority decision, or in the absence of a majority, by the President alone. It shall be written, dated and signed. The award shall state brief reasons. The signature of the President shall suffice.
2. The Panel may decide to communicate the holding of the award to the parties, prior to the reasons.
3. The award shall be final from such written communication. The award shall be final and binding upon the parties. It may not be challenged by way of an action for setting aside to the extent that the parties have no domicile, habitual residence, or business establishment in Switzerland and that they have expressly excluded all setting aside proceedings in the arbitration agreement or in an agreement entered into subsequently in particular at the outset of the arbitration.

4. The holding of the award shall be communicated to the parties within four months after the filing of the statement of appeal. Such time-limit may be extended by the President of the Appeals Arbitration Division upon a motivated request from the President of the Panel.
5. The award or a summary setting forth the results of the proceedings shall be made public by the CAS, unless both parties agree that they should remain confidential.

D – SPECIAL PROVISIONS APPLICABLE TO THE CONSULTATION PROCEEDINGS

R60 – Request for opinion

The IOC, the IFs, the N0Cs, the associations recognized by the IOC, the OCOGS, may request an advisory opinion from the CAS about any legal issue with respect to the practice or development of sports or any activity related to sports. The request for an opinion shall be addressed to the CAS and accompanied by any document likely to assist the Panel entrusted with giving the opinion.

R61 – Initiation by the CAS

When a request is filed, the CAS President shall review whether it may be the subject of an opinion. In the affirmative, he shall proceed with the formation of a Panel of one or three arbitrators from the CAS list and designate the President. He shall formulate, in his own discretion, the questions submitted to the Panel and forward these questions to the Panel.

R62 – Opinion

Before rendering its opinion, the Panel may request additional information. The opinion may be published with the consent of the party which requested it. It does not constitute a binding arbitral award.

E – INTERPRETATION

R63

1. A party may apply to the CAS for the interpretation of an award issued in an ordinary or appeals arbitration, whenever the holding of the award is unclear, incomplete, ambiguous or whenever its components are contradictory among themselves or contrary to the reasons, or whenever it contains clerical mistakes or a miscalculation of figures.
2. When an application for interpretation is filed, the President of the relevant Division shall review whether there is ground for interpretation. If there is ground, he shall submit the request to the Panel which has rendered the award for interpretation. The arbitrators of the Panel who are unable to act shall be replaced in accordance with Article R36. The Panel shall rule on the request within one month following the submission of the request to the Panel.

F – COSTS OF THE PROCEEDINGS

R64 – Ordinary arbitration

R64.1

Upon filing of the request, the claimant shall pay a minimum fee of Swiss-francs 500.–, without which the CAS shall not proceed. The CAS shall in any event keep this fee. The Panel shall take it into account when assessing the final amount of the fees.

R64.2

1. Upon formation of the Panel, the Court Office shall fix, subject to later changes, the amount and the method of payment of the advance of costs. The filing of a counterclaim or a new claim shall result in the determination of separate advances.
2. To determine the amount of the advance, the Court Office shall fix an estimate of the costs of arbitration, which shall be borne by the parties in accordance with Article R64.4. The advance shall be paid in equal shares by the claimant and the respondent. If a party fails to pay its share, the other may substitute for it; in the absence of substitution, the claim to which the unpaid share relates shall be deemed withdrawn.

R64.3

1. Each party shall advance the cost of its own witnesses, experts and interpreters.
2. If the Panel appoints an expert, retains an interpreter or orders the examination of a witness, it shall issue directions with respect to an advance of costs, if appropriate.

R64.4

At the end of the proceedings, the Court Office shall determine the final amount of the cost of arbitration, which shall include the fee of the CAS, the costs and fees of the arbitrators computed in accordance with the CAS fee scale, the contribution towards the costs and expenses of the CAS, and the costs of witnesses, experts and interpreters.

R64.5

The foregoing costs shall be stated in the arbitral award, which shall also determine which party shall bear such costs or in which portion the parties shall share them. As a general rule, the award shall grant the prevailing party a contribution towards its legal fees and other expenses incurred in connection with the proceedings and, in particular, the costs of witnesses and interpreters. When granting such contribution, the Panel shall take into account the outcome of the proceedings, as well as the conduct and the financial resources of the parties.

R65 – Appeals arbitration

R65.1

1. Subject to Articles R65.2 and R65.4, the proceedings shall be free.
2. The fees and costs of the arbitrators, calculated in accordance with the CAS fee scale, together with the costs of the CAS are borne by the CAS.

R65.2

Upon submission of the statement of appeal, the appellant shall pay a minimum fee of Swiss francs 500.- without which the CAS shall not proceed and the appeal shall be deemed withdrawn. The CAS shall in any event keep this fee.

R65.3

The costs of the parties, witnesses, experts and interpreters shall be advanced by the parties. In the award, the Panel shall decide which party shall bear them or in what proportion the parties shall share them, taking into account the outcome of the proceeding, as well as the conduct and financial resources of the parties.

R65.4

If all circumstances so warrant, the President of the Appeals Arbitration Division may decide to apply Articles R64.4 and R64.5 to an appeals arbitration.

R66 – Consultation proceedings

The Court Office shall determine, after consultation with the person requesting the opinion, to what extent and upon what terms such person shall contribute towards the costs of the consultation procedure.

G – MISCELLANEOUS PROVISIONS

R67

The arbitration agreements entered into prior to November 22, 1994 shall be deemed to refer to the present Rules, unless both parties request the application of the Rules in force prior to November 22, 1994.

R68

The French text and the English text are authentic. In the event of any discrepancy, the French text shall prevail.

R69

The Procedural Rules may be amended by the decision of the Council, in conformity with Article S8.

APPENDIX XX

APOLLON KALAMARIAS FC v/ HELENIC FOOTBALL FEDERATION & OLYMPIACOS FC CAS AWARD

CAS 2008/A/11525 Apollon Kalamarias FC v/ HFF & Olympiacos FC
DECISION ON PROVISIONAL AND CONSERVATORY MEASURES
Pronounced by the
COURT OF ARBITRATION FOR SPORT
Sitting in the following composition:
President: Mr Efraim **Barak,** Attorney-at-law, Tel Aviv, Israel
Arbitrators: Mr Mark Hoven. Solicitor, Manchester, United Kingdom Dr Chris Georghiades, Attorney-at-law, Limassol, Cyprus
Ad hoc Clerk: Mr Fabrizio La Spada, Attorney-at-law, Geneva, Switzerland in the arbitration between
Apollon Kalamarias FC, Kalamaria Thessaloniki, Greece
Represented by Dr Gregory Ioannidis and Mrs Maria Ioannidis, Nicosia, Cyprus
as Appellant and
Hellenic Football Federation (HFF), N. **Smyrni, Greece**
Represented by Mr Theodoros Kouridis, legal counsel of the HFF, N. Smyrni, Greece
and
Olympiacos FC, Piraeus, Greece
Represented by Mr Gianpaolo Moteneri, Zurich, Switzerland and Mr. Theodore Giannikos, Piraeus, Greece
as Respondents
Panathinaikos, Athens, Greece
Represented by Mr George C. Stratos, Athens, Greece
and
AEK Athens, Athens, Greece
Represented by Mr Theocharis Grigoriou, Athens, Greece
as Intervening Parties

Tribunal Arbitral du Sport Court of Arbitration for Sport

1. THE PARTIES

1. Apollon Kalamarias ("the Appellant" or "Apollon") is a Greek football club based in Kalamaria Thessaloniki, Greece.
2. The Hellenic Football Federation ("the HFF" or "Respondent 2") is the Greek national football federation. It is based in Athens, Greece.
3. Olympiacos FC ("Olympiacos" or "Respondent 1") is a Greek football club based in Piraeus, Greece.
4. Panathinaikos ("Panathinaikos") is a Greek football club based in Athens, Greece.
5. AEK Athens ("AEK") is a Greek football club based in Athens, Greece.
6. Apollon, Olympiacos, Panathinaikos and AEK are all members of the HFF and participate in the Greek Super League Championship.

2. THE FACTS

7. On 3 February 2008, Apollon played an official football match against Olympiacos, during which it fielded the player Roman Wallner ("the Player").
8. Following this match, Olympiacos filed a complaint, claiming that the Player was ineligible to play in the match, because he had already played in official matches for two other football

clubs during the same season, namely for Falkirk FC (in Scotland's Premier League) and Hamilton Academical FC (in Scotland's First Division).

9. Following the complaint filed by Olympiacos, the Disciplinary Committee of the Super League decided that the Player had been indeed ineligible to play, annulled the result of the match, and ordered that the match be replayed.

10. Apollon and Olympiacos bath appealed the decision before the Appeal Committee of the HFF ("the Appeal Committee").

11. On 5 March 2008, the Appeal Committee issued a decision ("the Decision") whereby it dismissed Apollon's appeal, decided that the result of the match should be 3-0 in favour of Olympiacos and deducted one point from Apollon's standing. The Decision, without the reasons, was notified to the Appellant on 6 March 2008.

12. On 20 March 2008, Apollon appealed against this decision before the Court of Arbitration for Sport.

3. THE APPEAL TO THE CAS AND THE REQUEST FOR PROVISIONAL AND CONSERVATORY MEASURES

13. On 20 March 2008, Apollon lodged a statement of appeal with the Court of Arbitration for Sports ("CAS"), pursuant to the Code of Sports-related Arbitration ("the Code"). In its statement of appeal, it made the following prayer for relief:

> "*WE REQUEST FROM YOUR COURT*
> *To accept this recourse.*
> *To annul and reverse the number 57/5-3-2008 decision by the Hellenic Federation Appeal Committee.*
> *To reject the objection of the club of Olympiacos Piraeus against the validil), of the match played between our teams on 2-3-2008 for irregular participation of the prayer ROMAN WALLNER on the above grounds.*"

14. On 31 March 2008, the Appellant filed a request for provisional and conservatory measures (the "Request").

15. In the Request, the Appellant pointed out that the Decision was attracting media attention. It also stressed that the HFF had not yet provided the reasons for the Decision and submitted that such delay was a breach of established principles of natural justice and due process.

16. According to the Appellant, the Decision is "*erroneous or procedurally incorrect*". In this respect, the Appellant contends that the HFF "*failed to consider in an appropriate manner the current regulatory framework, with the result to misdirect itself and reach an erroneous and unfair result*". In addition, the Appellant stated that information and documents were "*missing from the investigation, or there was a blatant omission, on behalf of Respondent 2, to consider them*".

17. In the Request, the Appellant made the three following separate requests.

3.1 Request for Order for Disclosure

18. The Appellant requested the Panel to order the disclosure of the following documents and information:
    - The reason(s) for the Decision;
    - The transcripts of the minutes of the proceedings before the Disciplinary Committee of the Super League and the Appeal Committee of the HFF;
    - The document identifying receipt of the International Transfer Certificate ("ITC") of the Player;
    - A witten explanation by the HFF outlining the reasons for submitting the ITC late and allowing at the same time the Player to participate in the match which gave rise to this arbitration;
    - The ITC and the Player' s passport.

19. The Appellant explained that these documents and this information are in the direct control of the HFF, or could become available to it. In addition, the Appellant contended that they are relevant to the issues in dispute

3.2 Request for Interim Measures

20. The Appellant requested the Panel to "*order Respondent 2 and the Organising Body of the Hellenic League, called 'Super League', to restore the 4 point deficit back to the Appellant, and construe the Super League Standings Table accordingly and with immediate effect*". In addition, the Appellant requested the Panel to order the HFF to comply with paragraph 20.3 of the Regulations of Professional Matches of the HFF and, as a consequence, to order the HFF and the Super League not to validate the Super League Standings Table pending the outcome of these proceedings.

21. In support of these requests, the Appellant explained that because of the erroneous Decision, it is facing imminent relegation from the Hellenic Super League. It further submitted that Respondent 2, when considering the issue through its competent body (the Appeal Committee) "*ought to have considered*" Article 5.4 and 10.2 of the FIFA Regulations on the Status and Transfer of Players. The appellant further contested that "*according to the rules and aids of interpretation, a proper and literal interpretation of the above would clearly indicate that the Appellant, correctly and properly, used his employee Roman Wallner, during the game...*".

3.3 Request for an extension of the time limit for the service of the Appellant's brief

22. The Appellant requested the Panel to extend the time limit for the service of Apollon's appeal brief. The Appellant did not specify to what extent this time limit should be postponed.

23. On 14 April 2008, the HFF filed its answer to the Appellant's Request, in which it disputed all of Apollon's statements and opposed the measures requested. The HFF's position can be summarized as follows:
    - The HFF fully recognises the jurisdiction of CAS, in accordance with its Statutes and Regulations, and with the Statutes of FIFA and UEFA.
    - In accordance with Article 35.4 of the Football Matches Regulations of Professional Championships, the recourse before the CAS must be made pursuant to the terms and conditions set out **in the Statutes of the HFF and UEFA.**
    - Article 62.2 of the UEFA Statutes provides that "*Only panties directly affected by a decision may appeal to the CAS.*" In the present case, Apollon is not directly affected by the Decision: its position would not change as a result of the appeal, since it would in any event be relegated. In addition, in accordance with this provision, no third party could legally intervene in this case.
    - In accordance with Article 62.3 of the UEFA Statutes, the time limit for the appeal is of ten days from the receipt of the decision in question. In the present case, the appeal was late.
    - Article 62.4 of the UEFA Statutes provides that an appeal before CAS may only be brought after UEFA's internal procedures and remedies have been exhausted. This is not the case in the matter at hand, since the Player has filed a motion for review of the Decision.
    - In accordance with Article 63.1 of the UEFA Statutes, the CAS is not competent to deal with matters related to the application of ***a purely sporting rule,*** such as the Laws of the Game or the technical modalities of a competition. According to the HFF, this case comes under this provision, since it concerns a matter that is purely procedural (participation or not in a match).
    - In order to issue provisional and conservatory measures, the following conditions must be fulfilled: (a) there must be a case of emergency or imminent risk which must be averted; (b) it must be necessary to secure or preserve a right or regulate a condition. These conditions are directly related to the legal interest of the party seeking the measures. In the present case, these conditions are not fulfilled. Even if the Appellant obtained a ruling restoring the points that were deducted, ***it would stilt be relegated,*** regardless of the outcome of the last championship match.
    - In addition, the measures requested would cause more damage to a large number of clubs and to the championship itself, as it would be impossible to complete the playoffs scheduled to start on 20 April 2008. They would also adversely affect the preparations of the Greek National team for the EURO 2008 competition.

24. On 14 April 2008, Olympiacos filed its answer to the Appellant's request. It made the following prayers for relief:

> *"Primarily,*
> *1) to not consider the Appellant's request for provisional and conservatory measures on the ground that it is inadmissible;*
> *2) to condemn the Appellant to the payment in the favour of the Second Respondent of the legal expenses incurred;*
> *Subsidiarily, only in the case that the above is rejected:*
> *1) to reject the Appellant's request for provisional and conservatory measures;*
> *2) to condemn the Appellant to the payment in the favour of the Second Respondent of the legai expenses incurred;*
> *3) to establish that the casts of the present procedure shall be borne by the Appellant;"*

25. Olympiacos' position can be summarized as follows:

- The Respondents lack standing to be sued. Indeed, in its Request, Apollon requested the Panel to order the HFF and the Super League not to validate the Super League Standings Table. However, the HFF is not the organizer of the first division championship in Greece, which falls exclusively in the domain of the Super League, which is not a party to this arbitration. In accordance with Article 20.3 of the Regulations of Professional Matches of the HFF, the validation of the Standings Table is made by means of a decision of the Board of Directors of the Super League. Therefore, the Appellant's request should have been directed exclusively against the Super League. The HFF and Olympiacos lack standing to be sued and, as a consequence, the Request is inadmissible.
- Assuming the Panel was to entertain the Request, the conditions for granting provisional and conservatory measures are not fulfilled and, therefore, the Request must be rejected. The three conditions that must be met are the following: (a) usefulness of the measure to protect the Appellant from irreparable harm; (b) likelihood of success on the merits of the appeal; (c) balance of convenience or interests.
  a) The Appellant stands on the 16th and last position of the table with only one more match to play and is already mathematically relegated. It would be relegated to the Second division even if it were successful on the merits of its appeal. Therefore, the Appellant cannot claim that it would suffer irreparable harm. In addition, according to Olympiacos, the Appellant has put itself in its current situation and can therefore not benefit from its own wrongdoing. Finally, granting the measures requested by Apollon would put the Super League competition in a situation of both legal and sporting uncertainty, which would cause more damage than the Appellant may suffer.
  b) Olympiacos submits that the Appellant must make at least plausible that the facts relied upon and the rights which it seeks to enforce exist and that the material conditions for a legal action are fulfilled. According to Olympiacos, these conditions are not met. In this respect, Olympiacos argues that Article 5(3) of the FIFA Regulations on the Status and Transfer of Players ("the FIFA Regulations") and 5(4) of the HFF Regulations for the Status and Transfer of Players clearly state that players are only eligible to play in official matches for two clubs during the period from 1 July until 30 June of the following year. Therefore, a player that has played in official matches for three different clubs, as is the case of the Player who played for Falkirk FC, Hamilton Academial FC and the Appellant, is undoubtedly violating these provisions. The conditions for an exception to this rule, as provided by Article 5(3) of the FIFA Regulations, are not met. In particular: the football seasons of the different clubs for which the Player has played are the same and therefore do not overlap; the Player has not complied with the rules concerning transfer periods; the Player has not complied with the rules concerning the minimum duration of the employment contracts (as a loaned player). Olympiacos submits that in accordance with the foregoing, the Decision is correct.
  c) Olympiacos contends that the Appellant clearly violated Article 5(3) of the FIFA Regulations and committed this violation at least by gross negligence, by not having applied the usual care in its business activity. According to Olympiacos,

the negligence of the Appellant shall not produce any negative effect on the Respondents or on the normal activity of the Super League and its competing clubs. Hence, the interests of the Respondents outweigh these of the Appellant.

26. On 11 April 2008, Panathinaikos wrote to the CAS requesting to participate in the proceedings by way of an intervention, pursuant to R41.3 of the Code. In support of this request, Panathinaikos stated, in brief and general terms, that the Decision was negligent, erroneous and without legal substance, precludes Panathinaikos from participating in the Super League championship with equal means, and gives Olympiacos an unfair advantage.

27. On 14 April 2008, AEK also requested to participate in the proceedings in accordance with R41.3 of the Code. AEK submitted that it has an unquestionable legal interest in the case. It contended that the Decision is invalid and not legally binding, that the composition of the Appeal Committee was illegal, and that the Decision is "*without substance and based on the wrong interpretation and application of the regulations*". AEK considers that as a result of the Decision, it is in a position of a disadvantage towards fulfilling its legal interest of participating in the Super League, and being given an equal opportunity to gain the first place on the Table.

28. On 14 April 2008, subject to an extension granted by the Deputy President of the Appeals Arbitration Division due to the delay by the HFF in providing the reasons for the decision to the Appellant, the Appellant filed its Appeal Brief, together with supporting exhibits.

29. On 17 April 2008, the Panel held a hearing at the CAS premises. In addition to the Panel, the Ad hoc Clerk and the CAS Counsel, all parties were present and assisted by their respective legal counsel. Panathinaikos and AEK were also invited to attend the hearing in order to present their request for intervention in the proceedings.

30. All parties, including the intervening parties, presented their case.

4. ISSUES

- Based on the written submissions of the parties, including the intervening parties, and their statements and pleadings during the hearing, the Panel has identified the following issues that should be decided at this stage:
- Does CAS have jurisdiction to deal with the Appeal, and as a consequence, with the Request (see below, section 5)?
- Do the Respondents have standing to be sued (see below, section 6)?
- Are the intervening parties entitled to participate in the proceedings (see below, section 7)?
- Should the provisional remedies, all of them or any one of them, be granted or not (see below, section 8)?

5. CAS JURISDICTION AND APPLICABLE LAW

32. Article R47, first paragraph, of the Code provides as follows:

> "*An appeal against the decision of a federation, association or sports-related body may be filed with the CAS insofar as the statutes or regulations of the said body so provide or as the parties have concluded a specific arbitration agreement and insofar as the Appellant has exhausted the legal remedies available to him prior to the appeal, in accordance with the statutes or regulations of the said sports-related body.*"

33. In the present case, the parties have not concluded any specific arbitration agreement. However, The Appellant, as all the other clubs participating in the championship organized by the I-IFF or the Super League signed a declaration, stating, inter alia, the following:

> "*That it promises to abide by the statutes, the regulations and the decisions of FIFA, UEFA, HFF and all its members, as well as it recognizes the jurisdiction of CAS Lausanne, as prescribed in articles 59 and 63 of the statutes of UEFA.*"

34. Article 60 of the FIFA Statutes provides as following:

> "*(1) FIFA recognises the independent Court of Arbitration for Sport (CAS) with headquarters in Lausanne (Switzerland) to resolve disputes between FIFA, Members, Confederations, Leagues, clubs, Players, Officials and licensed match agents and players' agents.*

(2) *The provisions of the CAS Code of Sports-Related Arbitration shall apply to the proceedings. CAS shall primarily apply the various regulations of FIFA and, additionally, Swiss law.*"

35. Article 61(1) of the FIFA Statutes provides the following:

"*Appeals against final decisions passed by FIFA's legal bodies and against decisions passed by Confederations, Members or Leagues shall be lodged with CAS within 21 days of notification of the decision in question.*"

36. In accordance with CAS jurisprudence, Article 61(1) of the FIFA Statutes does not **by itself** grant jurisdiction to CAS over appeals against decisions passed by Confederations, Members or Leagues (see, e.g., CAS 2005/A/952; CAS 2004/A1676; CAS 2002/0/422). On the contrary, in order for the CAS to have jurisdiction to hear an appeal, the statutes or regulations of the sports-related body from whose decision the appeal is being made must expressly recognise the CAS as an arbitral body. In this respect, Article 62(1) of the FIFA Statutes confirms the following:

"*The Confederations, Members and Leagues shall agree to recognise CAS as an independent judicial authority and to ensure that their members, affiliated Players and Officials comply with the decisions passed by CAS. The same obligation shall apply to licensed match and players' agents.*"

37. In the present case, Article 35(4) of the Greek Football Matches Regulations, Professional competition (ed. 2007) approved by the HFF and which describe the rules for holding professional football competitions, provides the following:

"*The reference to the Court for Arbitration of Sports (CAS) is permitted past the conclusion of all levels of jurisdiction of the Hellenic Football Bodies, under the terms and conditions stated in the Statutes of the HFF and UEFA.*"

38. In addition, Article 53(2)(a) of the HFF Statutes reads as follows: "*Any natural person or legal entity involved in football by any way, is obligated to:*

a) ***to recognise the jurisdiction*** *and observe the* ***decisions of the Court for Arbitration for Sport (CAS) in Lausanne (Switzerland), as specified in the relevant provisions of the FIFA*** *and UEFA Statutes;*

39. Article 2(3)(k) of the HFF Statutes contains the following similar rule:

"*The Hellenic Football Federation (H.F.F.) as a member of FIFA and UEFA is obligated:*
a) to recognise the jurisdiction and observe the decisions of the Court for Arbitration for Sport (CAS) in Lausanne (Switzerland), as specified in the relevant provisions of the FIFA and UEFA Statutes;"

40. During the hearing, the Panel asked the HFF to comment on the interpretation of the aforementioned provisions and to explain its position on the jurisdiction of CAS. The HFF stated that as a general mie. and as also clearly stated in its written submission: "*the Hellenic Football Federation with its statutes and regulations fullv recognises the Jurisdiction of CAS*". However, in the eyes of the HFF, the question whether CAS had jurisdiction to entertain appeals against decisions passed by the HFF Appeals Committee bas to be decided on a case-by-case basis; the HFF provided examples of cases where it considered that CAS would not have jurisdiction. Nevertheless, the HFF did not provide any explanation why in a case as the matter at hand, in which a club member of the HFF appeals a decision such as the Decision issued by the HFF Appeal Committee, there is no jurisdiction to CAS and why this case does not fall within the general reference of the HFF regulations to the FIFA regulations regarding the jurisdiction of CAS.

41. In addition, the objections to jurisdiction raised by the HFF in its written submission of 14 April 2008 were based on the rules set out in the **UEFA Statutes.** These rules are inapplicable in this case, as the Decision is based on provisions contained in FIFA Regulations, namely Article 5(3) of the FIFA Regulations on the Status and Transfer of Players. Furthermore the UEFA regulations to which the HFF referred are irrelevant to this case since those regulations deal with appeals on decision of "UEFA organs". The HFF and its competent bodies are not

UEFA Organs. The Panel has examined these objections and has indeed found them inapplicable to the present matter.

42. The Panel considers that Articles 2(3)(k) and 53(2)(a) of the HFF Statutes, as well as article 35(4) of the Professional Football Matches regulations, which refers to the Statutes of the HFF, do constitute provisions that grant jurisdiction to the CAS to entertain an appeal against the Decision. As a consequence, the Panel rules that CAS has jurisdiction to decide upon **this dispute,** in accordance with Articles 35(4) of the Football Matches Regulations, Articles 2(3)(k) and 53(2)(a) of the HFF Statutes, and Articles 60, 61, 62 ff. of the FIFA Statutes.

43. Concerning the Request, the Panel further notes that Article R37 of the Code allows the Appellant to request provisional or conservatory measures. The Panel, if formed as in this case, has the jurisdiction to decide on such requests.

44. Finally, the Panel notes that the Appellant filed its statement of appeal within the 21-day time limit provided in Article 60 of the FIFA Statutes.

45. Concerning the law applicable to the resolution of the dispute, according to Article R58 of the Code, the Panel is required to decide the dispute:

> "*according to the applicable regulations and the rules of law chosen by the parties or, in the absence of such a choice, according to the law of the country in which the federation, association or sports-related body which has issued the challenged decision is domiciled or according to the rules of law, the application of which the Panel deems appropriate. In the latter case, the Panel shall give reasons for its decision.*"

46. Article 60 paragraph 2 of the FIFA Statutes reads as follows:

> "*The provisions of the CAS Code of Sports-related Arbitration shall apply to the proceedings. CAS shall primarily apply the various regulations of FIFA and, additionally, Swiss law.*"

47. In the present matter, the partjes have not agreed on the application of any particular law. Therefore, the rules and regulations of FIFA and of the HFF shall apply primarily and Greek law, as the law of the country where the HFF has its Beat, shall apply subsidiarily.

6. STANDING TO BE SUED

48. As set out above, Olympiacos has argued that the Respondents lack standing to be sued as far as it concerns the remedies requested in this appeal, since they are not the organizers of the Greek championship and do not have the power to validate the Super League Standings Table.

49. On the basis of the evidence produced by the parties and undisputed statements made during the hearing, it appears that the Super League is not a body or organ of the HFF, but a separate legal entity, and a **member of the HFF,** with powers and authority to organize the Greek professional football championship with respect to 16 Greek professional teams (including the Appellant, Olympiacos, Panathinaikos and AEK) constituting the Super League Championship.

50. In accordance with Article 20(2) of the Football Matches Regulations, the organising authority of each championship is obligated to maintain a classification list and ratify the final classification of the clubs on the basis thereof. Article 20(3) of the Football Matches Regulations specifies that "*the ratification of the aforementioned list is made by the Board of the organising authority*".

51. Based on these provisions, and as acknowledged by the parties during the hearing, **the Panel finds that it is the Board of Directors of the Super League that has the power and authority to ratify the final standings of the Super League championship,** in accordance with the terms and conditions proclaimed at the beginning of the relevant season.

52. Based on the applicable regulations. the HFF has no authority to interfere with the decision of the Board of Directors of the Super League or to instruct such body to modify the list of standings. No evidence was produced that would lead the Panel to find otherwise.

53. The Super League is not a party to these proceedings. The Appellant has not directed its Request against the Super League and has taken no other steps to join the Super League in the proceedings. As a consequence, even if the Panel came to the conclusion that the provisional and conservatory measures should be granted (which is not the case – see below, section

8), the Panel could not issue an order against the Super League which is not a party to the proceedings nor against the HFF which is not the competent body to validate and rectify the standings of the championship organised by the Super League.

7. INTERVENTION

54. By applications dated 11 and 14 April 2008, Panathinaikos and AEK requested to intervene in the proceedings. In accordance with their applications, and as confirmed during the hearing, these two clubs adopted the argumentation presented by the Appellant and supported the latter' s prayers for relief.

55. Article R41.3 of the Code provides the following concerning intervention:

> "*If a third party intends to participate as a party in the arbitration, it shall file with the CAS an application to this effect, together with the reasons therefor within the time limit set for the Respondent's answer to the request for arbitration. To the extent applicable, such application shall have the same contents as a request for arbitration. The Court Office shall communicate a copy of this application to the parties and set a time limit for them to express their position on the participation of the third party and to file, to the extent applicable, an answer pursuant to Article R39.*"

56. In the present case, Panathinaikos and AEK each filed its application within the time limit set for the Respondents to produce their answers. In their application, and during the hearing, they highlighted their specific interest in connection with the matter. In particular, they explained that the outcome of the dispute would have an incidence on their standing in the championship and, possibly, on their participation to the next UEFA Champions League.

57. Nevertheless, the Panel notes that neither Panathinaikos nor AEK sought to intervene in any manner in the course of the proceedings that have led to the Decision, but waited until this late stage of the proceedings before CAS to intervene.

58. In addition, the applications filed by Panathinaikos and AEK do not contain the elements that should be contained in a request for arbitration, respectively an appeal. In particular, they do not contain factual and legal argumentation, nor specific prayers for relief. On the contrary, AEK's submission expressly states that AEK "*shall be able to substantiate the above with evidence and well constructed arguments, should you kindly give us the opportunity to do so*". The Panel therefore finds that the applications filed on 11 and 14 April 2008 does not comply with the requirements of Article R41.3 of the Code.

59. The Panel therefore rules that the applications for an intervention filed by Panathinaikos and AEK must be dismissed and that these two clubs must not be allowed to participate in the proceedings. The Panel furthermore notes that even if the request for intervention would have been granted, this would not change the result on the merits in light of the reasons detailed in section 8 of this award.

8. REQUEST FOR PROVISIONAL AND CONSERVATORY MEASURES

60. Appellant's Request is based on Article R37 of the Code, which reads as follows:

> "*No party may apply for provisional or conservatory measures under these Procedural Rules before the request for arbitration or the statement of appeal, which implies the exhaustion of internal remedies, has been filed with the CAS.*
>
> *The President of the relevant Division, prior to the transfer of the file to the Panel, or thereafter the Panel may, upon application by one of the parties, make an order for provisional or conservatory measures. In agreeing to submit to these Procedural Rules any dispute subject to appeal arbitration proceedings, the parties expressly waive their rights to request such measures from state authorities. This waiver does not apply to provisional or conservatory measures in connection with disputes subject to ordinary arbitration proceedings.*
>
> *If an application for provisional measures is filed, the President of the relevant Division or the Panel invites the opponent to express his position within ten days or within a shorter time limit if circumstances so require. The President of the relevant Division or the Panel shall issue an order within a short time, In case of utmost urgency, the President of the relevant Division, prior to the transfer of the file to the Panel, or thereafter the President of the Panel may issue an order upon mere presentation of the application, provided that the opponent is heard subsequently.*
>
> *Provisional and conservatory measures may be made conditional upon the provision of security.*"

61. Before coming to the detailed discussion on the criteria applicable when such a request is considered, the Panel would like to point out that the reasoned decision (exhibit 16) was submitted by the Appellant only in the Greek language whilst the language of the proceeding are English. This was made in spite of the fact that pursuant to R29 of the Code, the counsel to the CAS wrote to the Appellant already on 31 March 2008 that "*as English has been chosen as the language of the present arbitration, all written submissions shall be in English and all exhibits submitted in any other language shall be accompanied by a translation into English*". The fact that the Appellant did not comply with this order, especially with respect the reasoned Decision, is more than questionable and could by itself create sufficient grounds for the rejection of the Request. Nevertheless, and without undermining the importance of the compliance with the Code and the procedural orders, the Panel decided to deal with the matter as to the merits, of the application for provisional or conservatory measures.

62. According to the CAS jurisprudence, when deciding whether to stay the execution of the decision appealed against, it is necessary to consider (a) whether the appeal has a *prima facie* likelihood of success on the merits; (b) whether the Appellant is likely to suffer serious and irreparable harm as a result of the decision; and (c) the balance of interests between the parties. The appellant must make at least a plausible case that the facts it relies upon and the rights it seeks to enforce exist, and that the material conditions for a legal action are all fulfilled (CAS 2000/A/274, published in the Digest of CAS Awards II, p. 757; CAS 20041A1678; CAS 2004/A1780; see also A. Rigozzi, L'arbitrage international en matière sportive, Helbing & Lichtenhahn, Basic 2005, n. 1142 ff., pp. 582 ff.).

(a) Likelihood of success on the merits

63. As set out above, the Respondents contend that the Appellant has no likelihood to prevail in its appeal. According to the Respondents, the Decision is correct, as the application of Article 5(3) of the FIFA Regulations and Article 5(4) of the HFF Regulations for the Status and Transfer of Players, did indeed prevent the Player from playing in official matches for the Appellant during the current season. In addition, according to the Respondents, the conditions set out in Article 5(3) of the Regulations that must be fulfilled to allow for an exception to the general rule are not met in the present case.

64. It is normally difficult to conclude, at the stage of the provisional measures and on a *prima facie* basis, that the Appellant is unlikely to succeed on the merits. Most of the time indeed, the resolution of the issues raised by the appeal depends upon the assessment of all the evidence, which can only sensibly be undertaken by the Panel at the full hearing of the case (see CAS 2000/A/274; CAS 2004/A/678; CAS 2004/A/780).

65. However, based on the undisputed facts of the matter, the Panel is of the opinion that, on a *prima facie* basis, the Appellant did not succeed to satisfy the o^p^us required by the Panel that there exists a reasonable possibility that the appeal has sufficient likelihood of success, to warrant the issuance of the provisional and conservatory measures that have been requested.

66. Article 5(3) of the Regulations provides as follows:

> "*Players may he registered with a maximum of three clubs during one season. During this period, the player is only eligible to play official matches for two clubs. As an exception to this rule, a player moving between two clubs belonging to associations with overlapping seasons (Le. start of the season in summer/autumn as opposed to winter/spring) may be eligible to play in official matches for a third club during the relevant season, provided he has fully complied with his contractual obligations towards his previous clubs. Equally, the provisions relating to the registration periods (article 6) as well as to the minimum length of a contract (article 18 paragraph 2) must be respected.*"

67. As a matter of fact, it is undisputed that the Player has played in official matches with the Scottish club Falkirk FC after 1 June 2007. It is also undisputed that he has played in official matches with the Scottish club Hamilton Academial FC after 1 June 2007. As a consequence, *prima facie* and in accordance with the wording of Article 5(3), the Player was not eligible to play for the Appellant before the end of the relevant season. In particular, he was not eligible to play for the Appellant on 3 February 2008.

68. The Panel notes that the fact that the Player was on loan from Falkirk FC when he played for Hamilton Academial FC and considered the allegations of the Appellant regarding the facts

that the loan was made out of the transfer window period stipulated in Article 6 of the FIFA Regulations, and that the period of the loan was less than the minimum loan period stipulated in Article 10.2 of the same Regulations, as well as the requirement of Article 3 (a) of the same Regulations which provide that those provisions are "*binding at national level*". However, and at this preliminary stage, the reliance on these articles is irrelevant. Even if those facts would, after a full and comprehensive consideration during the hearing, lead to the conclusion that the conduct of the Scottish Clubs in making "emergency" or short loans, does not fully comply with the FIFA Regulations by the previous clubs in which the player played, stilt Article 5(3) of the regulations does not provide for an exception in such circumstances.

69. The Panel further considers that the exception set out in Article 5(3), the second sentence of the Regulations is not applicable in the present case. In particular, since the Scottish and Greek championships both have seasons that run from 1 July to 30 June each year and which are therefore not overlapping under the meaning of this provision.

70. Since the first of the three cumulative conditions that must be met in order to obtain provisional and conservatory measures is not fulfilled, the Request must be dismissed. Nevertheless, the Panel will briefly address below the two other conditions.

(b) Risk of irreparable harm

71. According to CAS jurisprudence (see CAS 2003/0/541), the applicant for the stay of a decision must at least allege and bring *prima facie* evidence of the risk of incurring irreparable harm.

79. In this respect, the Appellant has acknowledged during the hearing that in view of the current list of standings, the outcome of the present dispute would have no incidence on whether or not Apollon will be relegated. Indeed, Apollon would be relegated even if successful in these proceedings. The learned counsel for the Appellant during the hearing endeavoured to explain that there is a possibility in which the return of four points to the Appellant may "save" the Appellant from being relegated, in case that other clubs will be punished and suffer deductions of points, as a consequence of hypothetic circumstances, such as the conduct of their supporters during the last match of the season etc. However, a request for provisional measures, especially in light of the other elements that are mentioned in sections 8 (a) and 8 (c) of this award cannot rely on such remote hypotheses.

80. The Appellant has nevertheless submitted that it kept a legal interest in obtaining the requested measures, since the addition of the four disputed points would allow it not to finish last in the season's standings.

81. The Panel understands that a club may have an interest not to finish the national championship as the last team. However, the Appellant bas not produced evidence or provided convincing explanations demonstrating that it would suffer irreparable harm if the provisional and conservatory measures it has requested were not granted but it would succeed on the merits.

82. Based on elements of the matter, and in particular the undisputed fact that the Apollon would be relegated even if the measures requested were granted, the Panel considers that the Appellant has not brought *prima facie* evidence of a risk of irreparable harm.

(c) Balance of interests

83. According to CAS jurisprudence, the potential harm to which the Appellant would be subject if the provisional measures are not granted must appear to outweigh the interest of the Respondents or third partjes to the *status qua.*

84. The Appellant did not specifically address this issue in its Request.

85. The Panel considers that the risk of harm caused to the Appellant if the measures are not granted is limited (see above, section 8(b)). On the contrary, ordering a modification of the Super League standings as a provisional and conservatory measure might harm Olympiacos, as well the HFF and other Greek teams, since this could directly affect their capacity to play in next years European competitions.

86. As a consequence, the interest of the Appellant in obtaining the measures (which, as already set out above, would not change the Appellant's position regarding relegation) does not outweigh the interests of the Respondents.

(d) Conclusion

87. In view of the foregoing, the Panel finds that the conditions for granting the measures requested by the Appellant are not met. Therefore, the Appellant's application is rejected.

9. COSTS

88. Article R64 para. 4 of the Code provides the following:

> *"At the end of the proceedings, the Court Office shall determine the final amount of the cast of arbitration, which shall include the CAS Court Office fee, the administrative costs of the CAS calculated in accordance with the CAS scale, the costs and fees of the arbitrators calculated in accordance with the CAS fee scale, a contribution towards the expenses of the CAS, and the casts of witnesses, experts and interpreters. The final account of the arbitration casts may either be included in the award or communicated separately to the parties."*

89. Article R64 para. 5 of the Code provides:

> *"The arbitral award shall determine which party shall bear the arbitration costs or in which proportion the parties shall share them. As a general Tule, the award shall grant the prevailing party a contribution towards its legal fees and other expenses incurred in connection with the proceedings and, in particular, the costs of witnesses and interpreters. When granting such contribution, the Panel shall take into account the outcome of the proceedings, as well as the conduct and the financial resources of the parties."*

Court of Arbitration For Sport
by the Panel in the framework of the final award.

ON THESE GROUNDS

The Court of Arbitration for Sport rules:

1. The request for provisional and conservatory measures filed by Apollon Kalamarias on 31 March 2008 is rejected.
2. The costs of the present order shall be determined in the final award. Thus done in Lausanne, on 21 April 2008.

THE COURT OF ARBITRATION FOR SPORT
President of the Panel
Mr. Efraim Barak

APPENDIX XXI

ANDREW WEBSTER CAS AWARD

CAS 2007/A/1298 Wigan Athletic FC v/ Heart of Midlothian
CAS 2007/A/1299 Heart of Midlothian v/ Webster & Wigan Athletic FC
CAS 2007/A/1300 Webster v/ Heart of Midlothian

ARBITRAL AWARD
delivered by the
COURT OF ARBITRATION FOR SPORT
sitting in the following composition:
President: Mr Quentin Byrne-Sutton, Attorney-at-law in Geneva, Switzerland
Arbitrators: Mr Jean-Jacques Bertrand, Attorney-at-law in Paris, France
The Hon. Michael Beloff QC MA, Barrister in London, United Kingdom

CAS 2007/A/1298:
between
Wigan Athletic AFC Limited, Wigan, United Kingdom
Represented by Mr Matthew Bennett, Brabners Chaffe Street LLP, Manchester, United Kingdom
As Appellant
and
Heart of Midlothian PLC, Edinburgh, United Kingdom
Represented by Mr Peter Limbert, Hammonds, London, United Kingdom
As Respondent

CAS 2007/A/1299:
between
Heart of Midlothian PLC, Edinburgh, United Kingdom
Represented by Mr Peter Limbert, Hammonds, London, United Kingdom
As Appellant
and
Mr Andrew Webster, Glasgow, United Kingdom
Represented by Mr Fraser Wishart, Chief Executive, PFA Scotland, Glasgow, United Kingdom and Mr Juan de Dios Crespo, Valencia, Spain
and
Wigan Athletic AFC Limited, Wigan, United Kingdom
Represented by Mr Matthew Bennett, Brabners Chaffe Street LLP, Manchester, United Kingdom
As Respondents

CAS 2007/A/1300:
between
Mr Andrew Webster, Glasgow, United Kingdom
Represented by Mr Fraser Wishart, Chief Executive, PFA Scotland, Glasgow, United Kingdom and Mr Juan de Dios Crespo, Valencia, Spain
As Appellant
and
Heart of Midlothian PLC, Edinburgh, United Kingdom
Represented by Mr Peter Limbert, Hammonds, London, United Kingdom
As Respondent

I. THE PARTIES AND THE ORIGIN OF THE DISPUTE

A. CAS 2007/A/1298

a) The Appellant

1. Wigan Athletic AFC Limited (the Appellant, hereinafter referred to as "Wigan") is a football club with its registered office in United Kingdom. It is a member of the English Football Federation, which is affiliated to FIFA.

b) The Respondent

2. Heart of Midlothian PLC (the Respondent, hereinafter referred to as "Hearts" or the "Club") is a Scottish football club with its registered office in the United Kingdom. It is a member of the Scottish Football Association, which is affiliated to FIFA.

B. CAS 2007/A/1299

a) The Appellant

3. Heart of Midlothian PLC (the Appellant, hereinafter referred to as "Hearts" or the "Club").

b) The Respondents

4. Mr Andrew Webster (the First Respondent, hereinafter referred to as "Andrew Webster" or the "Player") was born on 23 April 1982 and is of English nationality. He is a professional football player currently on loan to the Glasgow Rangers, a Scottish football club, after having been transferred from Hearts to Wigan.
5. Wigan Athletic AFC Limited (the Second Respondent, hereinafter referred to as "Wigan").

C. CAS 2007/A/1300

a) The Appellant

6. Mr Andrew Webster (the Appellant, hereinafter referred to as "Andrew Webster").

b) The Respondent

7. Heart of Midlothian PLC (the Respondent, hereinafter referred to as "Hearts" or the "Club").

D. The Origin of the Dispute

8. On 31 March 2001, shortly before the Player's 19th birthday, Hearts and Andrew Webster signed an employment contract that was due to expire on 30 June 2005.
9. Upon engaging Andrew Webster, Hearts paid a transfer fee of £75,000 to the Scottish football club Arbroath.
10. On 31 July 2003, two years before the expiry of the initial contract and following a renegotiation of its terms, Hearts and Andrew Webster entered into a new employment contract, which provided for the Player's employment for a term of four years until 30 June 2007 (the "employment contract").
11. While employed by Hearts, Andrew Webster became an important member of the first team and enjoyed significant national and international success. He made his debut for Scotland in 2003 and went on to gain twenty two international caps by the age of 24.
Hearts also enjoyed a number of sporting successes during the period of his employment.
12. Consequently, Hearts became interested in retaining the Player for a longer period of time.
13. Thus, in April 2005, more than two years before the end of the employment contract, Hearts wrote to the Player's agent, Charles Duddy, offering to extend the contract for a further two seasons, on improved terms. However, no agreement was reached.
14. In January 2006, with approximately 18 months to run under the employment contract, discussions resumed regarding its re-negotiation. Through his agent, Andrew Webster turned down an initial offer from Hearts.
15. Between January and April 2006, Hearts made several other offers to Andrew Webster but none of them were accepted because the terms did not match his expectations.
16. During the same period, Andrew Webster was not selected by Hearts for several games.

Due to the timing and circumstances of the decisions, he formed the impression that this was a tactic designed by Hearts to compel accepting a new employment contract.

17. Matters came to a head between April and May 2006, when the majority shareholder of Hearts, Mr Vladimir Romanov, made various statements in the media to the effect that Andrew Webster's commitment to the club was uncertain and that he would therefore be put on the transfer list. Mr Romanov was also quoted as having declared that "Unfortunately in football there are agents, but the most negative influence is the parents – they shouldn't interfere in matters."
18. Upset by these statements, Andrew Webster decided to seek advice from the Scottish Professional Footballer's Association ("SPFA").
19. During a meeting with representatives of SPFA in early May 2006, Andrew Webster explained his feelings about the situation. He was advised that if there was a complete mutual breakdown in trust he had the legal right to terminate his contract by invoking clause 18 of his employment contract, whereby: "If the Club intentionally fails to fulfil the terms and conditions of this Agreement the Player may, on giving fourteen days' written notice to the Club, terminate this Agreement".
20. In light of the discussions with SPFA, Andrew Webster resolved to terminate his contract for just cause. On 4 May 2006, he wrote to Hearts indicating he was terminating his contract with 14 days notice. In the letter, Mr Webster explained that he believed the club had failed in its duties towards him and that a fundamental breakdown in trust justified his action.
21. Hearts replied by stating it had lodged an appeal with the Scottish Premier League Board.
22. In the light of this development, SPFA further advised Andrew Webster that, in addition to the termination for just cause, he could unilaterally terminate his contract without cause in accordance with article 17 of the FIFA Regulations for the Status and Transfer of Players (the "FIFA Status Regulations"), since his termination would occur outside a Protected Period of three years commencing from the date when he was employed by Hearts.
23. Realizing that the appeal procedure triggered by Hearts could result in a protracted dispute that might prevent him from securing a contract with another club in time for the 2006/2007 season, Andrew Webster decided to follow the alternative route suggested to him by SPFA.
24. As a result, on 26 May 2006, Andrew Webster notified Hearts that he was also unilaterally terminating his contract on the basis of article 17 of the FIFA Status Regulations, i.e. irrespective of the existence or otherwise of a just cause.
25. On 28 June 2006, Hearts wrote to Andrew Webster asking him to clarify whether he was relying on the notice of 4 May 2007 or on the subsequent notice of unilateral termination.
26. On 7 July 2006, Andrew Webster replied to the effect that he was no longer relying on the grounds invoked in his notice of 4 May 2007 but was maintaining his unilateral termination with reference to article 17 of the FIFA Status Regulations.
27. Meanwhile, in the final weeks of June 2006, Hearts had rejected an offer of £1.5 million from Southampton Football Club for the transfer of Andrew Webster, in the belief that Player's market value was higher.
28. On 9 and 10 July 2006, Andrew Webster's agent sent a fax to approximately fifty clubs, stating that the player had terminated his contract with Hearts, that no sanctions would apply as a result of this termination, and that compensation would be fixed by FIFA in the region of £200,000.
29. On 4 August 2006, Blackburn Rovers, a Premier League club, wrote to Hearts to indicate its interest in signing the Player and to enquire about his contractual status.
30. On 9 August 2006, Andrew Webster signed a three-year employment contract with Wigan.
31. Neither the Player nor Wigan offered Hearts any compensation upon his departure.
32. In November 2006, Hearts filed a claim against Andrew Webster and Wigan in front of the FIFA Dispute Resolution Chamber ("DRC"). It claimed compensation for breach of contract in the amount of £5,037,311 against Mr Andrew Webster, and against Wigan as jointly and severally liable for having induced the breach.
33. Hearts also requested that the Andrew Webster be declared ineligible to take part in any official matches for a period of two months, in application of article 17.3 of the FIFA Status Regulations and that Wigan be banned from registering any new player for one registration period, in application of article 17.4.

34. The DRC heard the case and, on 4 April 2007, handed down the following decision (the "DRC decision"):
    1. The claim of the Scottish club, Heart of Midlothian, is partially accepted.
    2. The Scottish player, Andrew Webster, has unilaterally breached the employment contract with Heart of Midlothian without just cause outside the Protected Period.
    3. Mr Andrew Webster has to pay the amount of GBP 625,000 to Heart of Midlothian within 30 days of notification of this decision.
    4. If this amount is not paid within the aforementioned deadline, a 5% interest rate per annum as for the expiry of the aforementioned deadline will apply, and the present matter will be submitted to the FIFA's Disciplinary Committee, so that the necessary disciplinaiy sanctions may be imposed.
    5. The English club Wigan Athletic is jointly and severally liable for the aforementioned payment.
    6. Any other request filed by Heart of Midlothian is rejected.
    7. Heart of Midlothian is directed to inform Mr Andrew Webster and Wigan Athletic immediately of the account number to which the remittance is to be made, and to notify the Dispute Resolution Chamber of any payment received.
    8. Mr Andrew Webster failed to give Heart of Midlothian due notice of termination.
    9. Mr Andrew Webster is not eligible to participate in any official football match for a period of two weeks as from the beginning of the next national league championship for which he will be registered.
    10. The matter concerning the role played by the Scottish player's agent, Mr Charles Duddy, in the breach of contract, will be forwarded to the Players' Status Committee for investigation and decision.

35. Each party disagreed for different reasons with the finding of the DRC and, therefore, each decided to file an Appeal in front of the Court of Arbitration for Sport ("CAS").

36. In January 2007, Andrew Webster was loaned by Wigan to the Glasgow Rangers until the end of the season.

II. SUMMARY OF THE ARBITRATION PROCEEDINGS

37. On 24 May 2007, Wigan filed its Statement of Appeal with the CAS against the DRC decision, requesting the following relief:
    "1) The Appellant requests that the CAS annuls Section III paragraph 3 of the DRC Decision relating to compensation and replaces the sum £625,000 with a sum representing no more than the residual value of the Contract; or in the alternative
    2) In the event that the CAS upholds the DRC decision to award a sum of compensation in excess of the residual value of the Contract, the Appellant shall in any event request the CAS to annul Section III paragraph 3 of the DRC Decision relating to compensation and replace it with a new decision as it is unclear how the DRC has arrived at the figure of £625,000 and furthermore, this amount of compensation is excessive. In particular, the Appellant requests that the compensation awarded to the Respondent by the DRC be reduced for a number of reasons including, but without limitation as follows:
        (i) the DRC Decision is procedurally flawed due to the way in which the DRC Decision was reached in breach of Article 13.4 of the Rules Governing the Procedures of the Players' Status Committee and the Dispute Resolution Chamber (ed June 2005) ("Procedural Rules") which provides that decisions of the DRC must contain "reasons for the findings". Although the DRC refers to a number of factors that is considered relevant to the calculation of compensation due to the Respondent, it fails to adequately explain the significance of each of the factors and how the final award has been calculated; and/or in the alternative
        (ii) the DRC in the DRC Decision has failed to follow its own settled jurisprudence, in accordance with Swiss Law and in particular, Article 44(1) of the Swiss Civil Code of Obligations, that contributory fault of the "injured party" (i.e. the Respondent) is a material factor to consider when calculating the sums of calculation due in the case of a contractual termination without just cause. It is the Appellant's case that

the Respondent treated the Player unfairly in the 2005/06 season and this is a material factor to be considered by the CAS when determining the sum of compensation due to the Respondent; and/or in the alternative

(iii) the DRC in the DRC Decision appears to place reliance in the Respondent's favour on the fact that the Player had spent five seasons with the Respondent. Furthermore, the DRC incorrectly observes that the Respondent had a real interest in retaining the services of the Player, however, the manner in which the contractual negotiations were conducted between the Respondent and the Player and the Respondent's subsequent unfair treatment of the Player are clear evidence to the contrary; and/or in the alternative

(iv) the DRC in the DRC Decision wrongly considers that the amortised transfer fee paid by the Respondent to Arbroath for the acquisition of the Player in 2001 is relevant to the determination of the sum of compensation payable in this case (given that the original playing contract the Player entered into in March 2001 was replaced by the Contract in July 2003);

and/or in the alternative

(v) the DRC in the DRC Decision has incorrectly placed reliance on the weekly wage that the Player was due to earn under his new employment contract with the Appellant. The Appellant submits that this contract is irrelevant to the calculation of compensation, given that it has no bearing on the loss suffered by the Respondent.

3) The DRC at Section II, paragraph 36 of the DRC Decision has itself acknowledged that the Appellant is not guilty of any wrongdoing, nor has it induced the Player to breach the Contract. The Appellant submits that it should therefore not be held to be jointly and severally liable to compensate the Respondent, nor should it be deprived of the Player's playing services for the two week period in which the DRC has ordered a playing ban to take effect.

Thus, the Appellant further requests that the CAS respectively annuls Section III paragraph 5 and 9 on the following grounds:

(i) the DRC has determined that the Appellant is not guilty of any wrongdoing and did not induce the Player to terminate the Contract and therefore it should not be held liable to pay compensation for such breach. Contrary to the DRC's reasoning, the liability for breach of contract and the liability pay compensation flowing from such a breach are inextricably linked;and/or in the alternative

(ii) the DRC in the DRC Decision wrongly imposed a two week playing ban on the Player as it incorrectly concluded that the 15 day time period within which the Player must have served his notice to terminate the Contract in accordance with Article 17(3) of the FIFA Regulations for the Status and Transfer of Players (ed Dec 2004) commenced on the last league match and did not include the Scottish FA Cup Final. In the alternative, if the DRC interpretation is upheld, the two week playing ban imposed by the DRC is disproportionate to the 4 day delay in the service of the notice by the Player. Furthermore and in any event, given that the DRC has decided that the Appellant is not guilty of any wrongdoing in this matter, these "disciplinary measures" adversely impact on the Appellant and its own sporting performance as it is deprived of the Player's playing services during this period and are not therefore sustainable.

4) The Appellant therefore requests that in accordance with Article R 57 of the CAS Code, the Panel reviews the facts and the law relevant to above points, annuls the specified sections of the DRC Decision and replaces them with a new decision. In addition to the above requests, and in the event that they are successful, the Appellant shall request the Panel to grant an order that the Respondent shall be liable for all costs and expenses incurred by the Appellant in bringing this appeal, including the costs and expenses of the CAS."

38. On the same date, Andrew Webster filed an appeal with the CAS against the DRC decision, requesting the following relief:

"27.(1) The Appellant requests that the CAS annuls Section III paragraph 3 of the DRC Decision relating to compensation and replaces it with a new decision as it is un-

clear how the DRC has arrived at this decision and in any event, the amount of compensation awarded to the Respondent is excessive. In particular, the Appellant requests that the compensation payable to the Respondent be reduced for a number of reasons including, but without limitation as follows:
(i) to (iii) same as Wigan's (2) (i) to (iii))
(iv) the DRC in the DRC Decision wrongly considers that the amortised transfer fee paid by the Respondent to Arbroath for the acquisition of the Player in 2001 is relevant to the determination of the sum of compensation.
(v) the DRC in the DRC Decision has incorrectly took into account the weekly wage of the new contract. The Appellant submits that this contract is irrelevant to the calculation of compensation. Also the guidelines indicate that this way of calculation is only possible for players transferring from outside the EU/EEA zone of from this zone.

(2) the DRC wrongly imposed a two week playing ban on the Player as it incorrectly concluded that the 15 day time period within which the Player must have served his notice to terminate his playing contract with the Respondent in accordance with Article 17(3) of the FIFA Regulations for the Status and Transfer of Players (ed Dec 2004) commenced on the last league match and did not include the Scottish FA Cup Final. In the alternative, if the DRC interpretation is upheld, the two week playing ban imposed by the DRC is disproportionate to the 4 day delay in the service of the notice by the Player.

(3) The Appellant therefore requests that in accordance with Article R 57 of the CAS Code, the Panel reviews the facts and the law relevant to above points, annuls the specified sections of the DRC Decision and replaces them with a new decision. In addition to the above requests, and in the event that they are successful, the Appellant shall request the Panel to grant an order that the Respondent shall be liable for all costs and expenses incurred by the Appellant in bringing this appeal, including the costs and expenses of the CAS. ((same as 4. of Wigan))."

39. In their Statements of Appeal, Wigan and Andrew Webster jointly appointed Mr Jean-Jacques Bertrand as arbitrator.

40. On 25 May 2007, Hearts filed its Statement of Appeal with the CAS against the DRC decision, requesting the following relief:
"4.1 The relief sought on the Appeal is, pursuant to R57 and R65.4, that CAS:
(a) Accepts this Appeal against the Decision;
(b) Replaces the Decision of the FIFA DRC and issues a new decision, which:
  (i) Confirms that the FIFA DRC failed to assess the level of compensation payable in accordance with Article 17(1) of the FIFA Regulations, either adequately, or at all;
  (ii) Specifies the level of compensation for which the First and Second Respondents should be liable to the Appellant pursuant to Article 17(1) of the FIFA Regulations, in an amount to be determined in accordance with Article 17(1). (In the Appeal Brief the Appellant will make submissions as to the amount.);
  (iii) Orders that the Respondents pay the amount so assessed; and
  (iv) Orders the Respondents to pay costs before the DRC and CAS in an amount to be assessed by the CAS."

41. In its Statement of Appeal, Hearts appointed The Hon. Michael Beloff QC MA as arbitrator.

42. On 31 May 2007, the CAS invited the parties to indicate whether the same Panel should be appointed in the cases CAS 2007/A/1298, CAS 2007/A/1299 and CAS 2007/A/1300 and whether they would agree that the three appeals proceedings be joined.

43. On 31 May 2007, Wigan indicated its agreement to the appointment of the same Panel and to the joinder of the three proceedings.

44. On 1 June 2007, Andrew Webster indicated his agreement to the appointment of the same Panel and to the joinder of the three proceedings.

45. On 4 June 2007, Hearts indicated its agreement to the appointment of the same Panel and to the joinder of the three proceedings.

46. On 4 June 2007, all three parties filed their appeal briefs and Andrew Webster indicated that he would be relying on the arguments and evidence submitted by Wigan.

47. On 6 June 2007, following the agreement of the Parties, the CAS confirmed that the same Panel would be appointed to decide the three appeals in a single arbitral award.

48. On 26 June 2007, Wigan filed its Answer, which contained the following prayers for relief:

"98. The Respondent requests that the Panel dismisses the Appellant's claim for compensation in the sum of approximately £4,680,508.96.

99. In particular, in respect of each head of loss claimed at paragraph 11.2 of the Appeal Brief, the Respondent responds as follows:

(i) loss of opportunity to receive a transfer fee / or the replacement value of the Player – £4 million: the Respondent rejects this head in its entirety and refers the CAS to its arguments set out above and in particular, to paragraphs 41 to 61;

(ii) the residual value of the final year of the Contract – £199,976: the Respondent accepts that this is the only head of potential recovery for the Appellant but submits that the residual value of the Contract should be calculated in accordance with its arguments as set out in more detail in the Respondent's Appeal Brief (and summarised below at paragraph 100) so that the sum due to the Appellant is limited to £132,585.24;

(iii) the profit that the Player will make from the New Contract – £330,524: the Respondent rejects this head in its entirety and refers the Panel to its arguments set out above and in particular, to paragraphs 82 to 84;

(iv) the fees and expenses incurred by the Appellant to date – £80,008.96 (plus further legal expenses pursuant to the proceedings before the CAS): the Respondent rejects this head in its entirety and refers the Panel to its arguments set out above and in particular, to paragraph 86;

(v) the sporting and commercial losses suffered by the Appellant – £70,000: the Respondent rejects this head in its entirety and refers the Panel to its arguments set out above and in particular, to paragraphs 94 to 95.

100. Furthermore, the Respondent refers to its Appeal Brief which it submits must be read in conjunction with this Answer. In the Appeal Brief, the Respondent sets out its own interpretation of the relevant provisions of the Regulations and its request for relief which, in summary, is that the CAS annuls the DRC Decision and replaces it with its own decision which orders that:

(i) the compensation due to the Appellant is limited to the residual value of the Contract, given that this is a termination which occurred outside the Protected Period. On the facts of this case, given that the Appellant had informed the Player that he would not play again until he signed a new playing contract, only the guaranteed sums payable under the Contract can be taken into account and no appearance or performance bonuses are relevant. Furthermore, the outstanding bonus payment due to the Player should also be deducted so the Respondent calculates the maximum residual value of the Contract in the sum of £132,585.24. Furthermore, in accordance with Article 44(1) of the Swiss Civil Code of Obligations, the compensation should be also reduced to reflect the fact that the Appellant, by treating the Player unfairly during the period February to May 2006, had contributed to its own loss; or in the alternative

(ii) a figure of compensation that is less than the £625,000 is payable to the Appellant, which it considers to be reasonable in the circumstances, giving due regard to the objective criteria under Article 17(1) as detailed in the Respondent's Appeal Brief, the most important of which is that the termination occurred outside the Protected Period, so that the most severe aggravating factor of a termination inside the Protected Period is absent in this case. Furthermore, the Respondent requests that the compensation in any event should be further reduced as the Appellant has contributed to its own losses by its treatment of the Player during the period of February to May 2006; and

(iii) the Respondent is not to be held jointly and severally liable to pay compensation for the Player's termination as the DRC has determined that the Respondent was not guilty of any wrongdoing and did not induce the Player to terminate the Contract. Contrary to the DRC's reasoning, the Respondent avers that the liability for breach of contract and the liability to pay compensation flowing from such a breach are inextricably linked; and

(iv) the DRC in the DRC Decision wrongly imposed "disciplinary measures" in the form of a two week playing ban on the Player as it incorrectly calculated the 15 day time period within which the Player must have served his notice to terminate the Contract, or in the alternative, if it has corrected calculated this 15 day time frame, that the two week playing ban is in any event excessive."

49. On 27 June 2007, Hearts filed its Answer, which contained the following prayers for relief: "6.1 In light of the arguments made in this Response, Hearts respectfully requests that the Appellants' appeal be dismissed."

50. On 27 June 2007, Andrew Webster filed his Answer.

51. On 28 June 2007, FIFA informed the CAS that it was renouncing its right to intervene in the proceedings.

52. On 3 July 2007, Hearts filed additional exhibits.

53. On 3 July 2007, the CAS confirmed the constitution of the Panel as follows: Mr Quentin Byrne-Sutton, as President, Mr Jean-Jacques Bertrand and The Hon. Michael Beloff QC MA, as arbitrators.

54. On 24 July 2007, the Panel issued three procedural orders containing the following decisions:

"1. The two additional exhibits filed by Hearts are admitted on record.
2. Wigan and the Player are entitled to file any rebuttal documents (affidavits and/or other documents) by 24 August 2007.
3. CAS will make arrangements for a hearing to be held in September at a date which is convenient.
4. The costs of the present order shall be determined in the final award.

and

1. A hearing shall take place as soon as possible after 1 September 2007 at a convenient date to be found between the parties and CAS.
2. If the parties cannot agree on a reasonable date of hearing, it shall be fixed by the Panel.
3. The costs of the present order shall be determined in the final award.

and

1. CAS has no jurisdiction to entertain an appeal against that part of FIFA's decision of 4 April 2007 imposing two-weeks of ineligibility on the player Andrew Webster as a disciplinary measure.
2. The costs of the present order shall be determined in the final award."

55. On 21 August 2007, Andrew Webster filed additional exhibits.

56. On 7 September 2007, the CAS informed the parties that the hearing would take place over a period of two days and that it would be held on 17 and 18 October 2007 at the CAS Court Office in Lausanne.

57. On 12 September 2007, the CAS informed the parties that the additional exhibits submitted by Andrew Webster had been admitted on record.

58. On 15 October 2007, the Lega Nazionale Professionisti filed a non-solicited letter with the CAS purporting to comment on certain aspects of the dispute between the parties.

59. On 15 October CAS issued a general procedural order, which was subsequently countersigned by the parties for acceptance, indicating, among others, that the CAS had jurisdiction and that the parties confirmed their acceptance of the joint appeal proceedings for the three cases and of the issuance of a single award.

60. The hearing took place in front of the Panel on 17 and 18 October 2007 in Lausanne, Switzerland, with the Counsel of CAS (Mr David Casserly) in attendance. The following participants were present:

a) Hearts
Ian Mill QC, counsel
Peter Limbert, counsel
Stephen Sampson, counsel
Jane Mulcahy, counsel
Dr Stephan Netzle, counsel
Simon Di Rollo QC, counsel

Pedro Lopez, witness
Frank Clark, witness
Vilma Venslovaitienne, observer
Donaldas Urniezius, observer

b) Andrew Webster
Juan de Dios Crespo Perez, counsel
Andrew Webster, player

c) Wigan
Brenda Spencer, Chief Executive
John Benson, General Manager
Jim Sturman QC, counsel
Carol Couse, counsel
Fraser Wishart, witness
Charles Duddy, witness
Graham Rix, witness
Philippe Piat, witness

61. At the beginning of the hearing three outstanding procedural issues were addressed. The Panel informed the parties that the letter submitted by the Lega Nazionale Professionisti was not admitted into the record, due to the latter not being a party to the proceedings. Furthermore, with the parties' agreement, it was decided that an additional witness statement submitted by Hearts would be admitted into the record and that the Panel's determination as to the applicable law would be included in the final award after hearing the parties' pleadings on that issue, together with expert testimony on Scottish and Swiss law.

62. The hearing continued with opening statements by the parties, followed by the examination of the witnesses and of Andrew Webster and, finally, the parties' closing arguments.

III. THE PARTIES' CONTENTIONS

A. Hearts

63. Hearts in summary submits the following:

- The relationship with Andrew Webster deteriorated when he refused to extend the employment contract.
- It is clear the Player was already then seeking a more lucrative contract and, to this end, would not hesitate to terminate his employment with Hearts.
- Only the second termination, without just cause, is relevant in determining what compensation Andrew Webster must pay to Hearts as a result.
- In that respect, it is not disputed that the Player is liable to Hearts for compensation. Rather, the appeal relates only to the amount of compensation awarded by the DRC decision.
- This is the first case concerning a player breaching his contract without just cause outside the "Protected Period" as defined in the FIFA Status Regulations.
- In front of the DRC, Hearts claimed approximately £4.9 million in compensation, however the DRC awarded the Club just £625,000, thus falling into error by assessing the amount of compensation at far too low a level.
- Moreover, the FIFA DRC failed to explain how it arrived at the figure of £625,000 for compensation.
- That figure of compensation does not compensate Hearts as required by the FIFA Status Regulations.
- The dispute forming the subject of this appeal must be viewed in the light of the purpose underlying Article 17 of the FIFA Status Regulations, namely the maintenance of contractual stability. This is of paramount importance to the football world. Indeed the importance of the maintenance of contractual stability underpins the entirety of section IV of the FIFA Status Regulations.
- In order to ensure the maintenance of contractual stability the FIFA Status Regulations provide for deterrents in the form of sporting sanctions (i.e. a ban on a player from play-

ing for four months or more) and the payment of compensation to the injured party by the player and his new club.

- The sanction to act to deter a player breaching his contract outside of the Protected Period is the payment of compensation.
- Compensation assessed in accordance with the Status Regulations has two purposes: (i) to act as a deterrent, especially where the breach is outside of the Protected Period – as an injured club does not benefit from the player being subject to a ban – and (ii) to compensate the injured club for the loss it has suffered.
- The deterrent element is particularly necessary as the FIFA Player's Status Committee will not permit a club to prevent a player who has terminated in breach of contract without just cause from playing for his new club.
- In this case, the contract did not provide for any assessment of compensation in the event of a breach by either party.
- Thus, the compensation must be calculated in accordance with Article 17(1) of the FIFA Status Regulations, whereby the assessment should be undertaken by establishing and giving due consideration (i) to the relevant national law, (ii) the specificity of sport, (iii) if relevant, the examples of objective criteria as set out in the Article, (iv) whether the breach occurred within a Protected Period, and (v) any other objective criteria which is relevant.
- This approach was also confirmed in several prior decisions of the DRC and in CAS award Mexes & AS Roma vs. AJ Auxerre (TAS 2005/A/902, dated 5 December 2005) ("Mexes"). In that case, the CAS confirmed that the three principal criteria established by Article 22 of the 2001 edition of the Status Regulations for assessing compensation for breach of contract are: (i) the principles used in the applicable national law to establish and quantify losses recoverable for breach of contract, (ii) the specificity of the sport, and (iii) "any other objective criteria relevant to the case", including those objective criteria specified in Article 22 itself.
- In Mexes, the club Auxerre had not signed the player as a professional from another club and therefore did not have unamortised acquisition costs to take into account. The CAS instead calculated the compensation payable (–7 million) by reference to (among other things) the amounts payable to the player under the contract he had breached (including the commission paid by the club to the player's agent), as well as the losses that Auxerre suffered as a result of losing the possibility to receiving a transfer fee for the player's registration.
- Mexes is a particularly apposite case. It dealt with a central defensive player (like Webster); whom the former club had acquired without a transfer fee (the fee for Webster was the de minimis sum of £75,000); whom the club had trained and developed for nearly six years, four of those as a professional (Hearts trained and developed Webster for five years as a professional); where the player was 22 at the time of his unilateral breach of contract (Webster was 24); and was of some significant reputation and potential (like Webster), although with only a handful of international appearances for his country, France (whereas Webster had 22, for Scotland).
- In this case, to the extent that the Panel is required to construe the meaning of the relevant parts of the FIFA Status Regulations (which Hearts' asserts are clear), the Panel must do so in accordance with Swiss Law, as the law of the domicile of FIFA and the law governing the FIFA Statutes. That is the limit to which Swiss Law is relevant to this dispute.
- Indeed, pursuant to Article 17 (1) "compensation for breach shall be calculated with due consideration for the law of the country concerned".
- In this case the "law of the country concerned" under Article 17(1) of the FIFA Status Regulations is Scots Law.
- Consequently, the FIFA Status Regulations, as governed by Swiss Law, require that the DRC and now the CAS give due consideration to Scots Law when assessing the compensation due to the Club. To apply any other national law would be contrary to article 17(1).

- The particular remedies which exist under Scots law for breach of contract are based on the principle of restitutio in integrum which attempts to return the injured party to the position he would have been in had the breach not occurred.
  In other words, Hearts' remedy for the Player's unilateral termination without just cause should be the award of damages in an amount which would return the Club to the position it would have been in had the Player not terminated the Contract.
- It is also well established that, under Scots law, damages for loss of profit pursuant to breach of contract are recoverable. Therefore the DRC should have had regard to Hearts' loss of opportunity to agree the transfer of the Player's registration to another football club and profit consequent thereon.
- Similarly, the DRC should have had regard to the costs that would be incurred by Hearts had it purchased a replacement player of a similar age, experience and ability to the Player.
- In addition, the DRC should have had regard to the costs which were wasted in the acquisition, training and development of the Player, and for which it did not receive the expected return of a transfer fee.
- Another basic axiom of Scots law is that interest is recoverable on contractual damages. As such, the DRC should have imposed upon the Player and/or Wigan, interest on the compensation payable from the date of the Player's termination.
- Alternatively, and in the event that the CAS decides Swiss law principles should be applied in establishing the measure of the compensation to be paid, the CAS should arrive at broadly the same position as exists under Scots law as the steps set out below are similarly consistent with the application of Swiss law.
- In order to assess the amount that it would cost Hearts to obtain a replacement player of similar age, experience and quality to the Player, or the loss of the opportunity to receive a transfer fee, it is necessary for the CAS to consider the market value of the Player or his replacement by reference to the following three factors: (a) whether there were existing or pre-existing bids from other football clubs for the Player; (b) the transfer fees recently paid for players of similar value to the Player; and (c) the assessment of the Player's market value by an independent expert witness, in this case Mr Frank Clark.
- In respect of the first criterion, on 21 June 2006 Hearts received an official written offer of £1.5million GBP for the Player from Southampton.
- However, Hearts refused this offer since it was considerably below the market value of the Player.
- Other clubs, including Blackburn Rovers Football Club, also expressed interest in the Player.
- In respect of the second criterion, the cost to a club in the English Premier League for a player of a similar pedigree to the Player would have been between £3-5 million. This is evidenced by the transfer fees paid by or to English Premier League clubs during the transfer window in Summer 2006 for players of a similar age, position, calibre, and contractual status as the Player.
- In respect of the third criterion, the CAS is invited to consider the evidence of Mr Frank Clark, who is an independent expert in assessing a player's value in the football market, particularly in the UK.
- As set out in full in his report, Mr Clark's view of the market value of the Player at the time of his unilateral termination without just cause was approximately £5 million.
- Hearts submits that this would also form the basis of a sum to obtain a replacement player of the same standing. In practice, Hearts has not obtained a player of similar age, ability and experience chiefly because the Club has not had the financial resources to enter the transfer market at the necessary level. Instead, the Club has been compelled to replace the Player with Christophe Berra, a former academy player.
- The CAS must also have regard to characteristics of the Player's employment at the Club. In particular, it is relevant to establish the training and educational role played by Hearts, and its approach to the maintenance of contractual stability.
- It is recognised by the DRC decision that Hearts played a fundamental role in the vast improvement of the Player during the time he spent with Club from the ages of 19 to 24.

- The improvement in the Player, which Hearts facilitated and cultivated, was itself duly recognised by Hearts. Hearts attempted over a period of one year to agree the terms of a new and substantially improved contract, but its offers were rejected.
- Further, the CAS should recognise that it cannot be for the good of the game for a breach of contract in these circumstances to be compensated inadequately.
- The residual value of the Player's Contract should also be considered as an element informing the assessment of compensation due to Hearts.
- The CAS should also have regard to the profit the Player will make on his contract with Wigan, which was obtained as a direct result of his unilateral termination without just cause.
- With regard to the fees and expenses incurred by Hearts, it signed the Player on a 4-year contract in 2001 for £75,000 from Arbroath Football Club. In 2003, the Club and the Player agreed to re-negotiate the Player's employment terms and entered into the Contract.
- In view of the above, the amortisation of the transfer fee paid for the Player should be considered, but not to the detriment of other factors, as to do so would result in Hearts not being compensated for the unilateral termination. Rather, what is relevant to this calculation is the sporting and financial investment Hearts has made in training and developing the Player during the last 5 years.
- Hearts (a) has also incurred legal fees in dealing with the Player's unilateral termination and pursuing its claim for compensation and sanctions before the FIFA DRC, amounting to £80,008.96 and (b) will incur additional costs in relation to this appeal, none of which would have been incurred but for the Player's unilateral termination.
- When calculating the level of compensation which should be awarded to Hearts, the CAS should take into account the following criteria are: (i) whether there are any terms in the Contract which provide for compensation in the event that the Player terminates his contract or is transferred; (ii) the circumstances surrounding the Player's unilateral termination of the Contract and his disregard for contractual stability; and (iii) the playing and commercial losses suffered by Hearts as a result of the Player's unilateral termination of the Contract.
- In that relation, Clause 21 of the contract states, inter alia: ".the Player shall not be registered for any other club without payment of a compensation fee (fixed in manner provided by the Rules of The Scottish Premier League) by that other club to the club which previously held the Player's Scottish Premier League Registration.'
- In this case, the Player deliberately sought to circumvent Hearts' contractual right to compensation in the event of the Player's transfer to another club. The actions of the Player have been reprehensible from the outset. The Player has sought to exploit the good faith of Hearts and his actions to date as evidenced by his consistent aim to secure a significant financial gain directly at the expense of, and without regard for, Hearts, the maintenance of contractual stability, his National Association or FIFA regulations.
- The Player's actions in this matter are an aggravating factor which must be taken into accounted.
- With respect to sporting and commercial losses suffered by Hearts, had the Player honoured the terms of the Contract as the parties intended, Hearts would not have been deprived of the services and positive impact for its image of one of its most important players.
- For all the foregoing reasons, pursuant to the proper assessment of compensation under Article 17(1) of the FIFA Status Regulations, Hearts should be compensated in a sum in the region of £4,680,508.96 broken down as follows: (i) for Hearts' loss of opportunity to receive a transfer fee for the Player / or the replacement value of the Player (calculated reasonably by reference to the schedule of players transferred in the last transfer window, the offers received for the Player from other clubs, and the estimated market value for the Player given by Frank Clark) – £4 million; (ii) for the residual value of the last year of the Player's Contract (calculated in accordance with the salary of the Player for the last 12 months of the Contract) – £199,976; (iii) for the profit the Player will make from the New Contract – calculated by reference to the difference between the

value of the last year of the Contract and the first year of the New Contract – (subject to clarification by Wigan) approximately £330,524; (iv) for the fees and expenses incurred by Hearts to date – £80,008.96 (plus further legal expenses pursuant to the proceedings before the CAS to be provided); (v) for the sporting and commercial losses suffered by Hearts – £70,000 (which is an estimated sum at this stage).

B. Andrew Webster and Wigan

64. Although the Player's newly appointed counsel added some points during his closing arguments, the Player's submissions of both fact and law throughout the proceedings have largely incorporated or reflected those of Wigan. Consequently, except for the specific argument made by Wigan in relation to the issue of its joint liability, the following summary reflects the substance of both the Player's and Wigan's submissions:

- The DRC decision is procedurally flawed due to the way in which the DRC Decision was reached in breach of Article 13.4 of the Rules Governing the Procedures of the Players' Status Committee and the Dispute Resolution Chamber (ed June 2005), which provides that decisions of the DRC must contain "reasons for the findings". Although the DRC refers to a number of factors that it considered relevant to the calculation of compensation due to the Respondent, it fails to adequately explain the significance of each of the factors and how the final award has been calculated.
- The DRC decision fails to follow its own settled jurisprudence, in accordance with Swiss Law and in particular, Article 44(1) of the Swiss Civil Code of Obligations, that contributory fault of the 'injured party' (i.e. Hearts) is a material factor to consider when calculating the sums of calculation due in the case of a contractual termination without just cause. Hearts having treated the Player unfairly during the 2005/06 season this is a material factor to be considered when determining the sum of compensation.
- The DRC decision appears to place reliance in the Club's favour on the fact that the Player had spent five seasons with the Club. Furthermore, the DRC incorrectly considers that Hearts had a general interest in retaining the services of the Player.

  The manner in which the contractual negotiations were conducted and the Club's subsequent unfair treatment of the Player are clear evidence to the contrary.
- The DRC decision wrongly considers that the amortised transfer fee paid by Hearts for the acquisition of the Player in 2001 is relevant to the determination of the sum of compensation payable in this case (given that the original playing contract the Player entered into in March 2001 was replaced by the contract in July 2003).
- The DRC decision incorrectly places reliance on the weekly wage that the Player was due to earn under his new employment contract with Wigan. That contract is irrelevant to the calculation of compensation, given that it has no bearing on the loss suffered by Hearts.
- The DRC decision recognizes that Wigan is not guilty of any wrongdoing, nor has it induced the Player to breach the contract. Wigan should therefore not be held jointly and severally liable to compensate Hearts.
- The employment contract is not expressed to be governed by Scottish law, but rather the contract provides at clause 26 that it is subject to the 'Articles of the Scottish Football Association and the Rules of the Scottish Premier League'.

  These Articles and Rules have made themselves expressly subject to the statutes and regulations of FIFA, including, in particular, the Regulations themselves.

  Furthermore, the Appellant has expressly accepted the relevance of the Regulations by submitting the resolution of the dispute to both FIFA and the CAS.
- In this respect, it is to be noted that according to article 17(1) and article 25 (6) of the FIFA Status Regulations, national law is not binding upon the DRC or, therefore, the CAS in these appeal proceedings.
- Given the international nature of this dispute, it is appropriate that the Regulations should apply to this dispute as far as possible unfettered by the idiosyncrasies of individual national laws.
- This principle is confirmed in the CAS Case 2005/A/983 & 984 Club Atletico Penarol v Carlos Heber Bueno Suarez and Christian Gabriel Rodriguez Barotti & Paris Saint Ger-

main, in which the CAS held: "Sport is, by its nature a phenomenon which transcends borders. It is not only desirable, but essential that the rules governing sport on an international level have a uniform and broadly consistent nature throughout the world. To ensure its respect on a world level, such regulations cannot be applied differently from one country to another, particularly because of the interferences between state law and sports regulations. The principle of the universal application of FIFA rules – or any other international federation – meets the requirements of rationality, safety and legal predictability. The uniformity which results tends to guarantee equality of treatment between all destinees of these standards whatsoever country they are in."

- However, Swiss law is also relevant to determine the crux of this matter, i.e. the sum of compensation due to the Appellant.
- In the Mexes case the CAS held that in the context of the dispute regarding the premature termination of a French employment contract, which expressly referred to the 'Professional Football Charter' (which governs football employment relations in France) French law was relevant, but only to 'the limited angle of the interpretation and/or assessment of Mr Philippe Mexes' employment contract'. It went on to hold that the substance of the dispute should be determined in accordance with Swiss law: 'as all the parties to these proceedings agreed to submit to the FIFA statutes and the Code of Arbitration...., the Unit considered that Swiss law must govern determining the loss'.
- EC law is also applicable in this case as all three parties reside and engage in economic activities in Member States of the EU. Furthermore, the Regulations themselves actually govern the movement of players between EU Member States and therefore they affect trade between Member States.
- Therefore the activities of Hearts, Wigan and the Player are subject to EC law and EC law is applicable in this case so far as the DRC decision and the Panel's own determination must be in compliance with EC law to be legal and prima facie enforceable.
- That said, it is clear that the resolution of the issues at the centre of this appeal will turn on an interpretation of Article 17 of the FIFA Status Regulations.
- Hearts seeks to place reliance on the importance of contractual stability, which it asserts is a justifying factor for the level of compensation sought by Hearts as a suitable 'deterrent' for the Player having terminated his contract. It fails to acknowledge, however, that another fundamental concept, developed with the goal of striking a right balance between the respective interests of clubs and players was the so called 'Protected Period'. Whilst a player may be required to compensate his former club for a unilateral termination of contract which has occurred, if this termination occurred outside the Protected Period, then the sum of compensation awarded cannot constitute a restriction upon that player's right of freedom of movement within the EU, as he has already complied with the stipulated period of contractual stability.
- Imposition of compensation in excess of the residual value of the employment contract would constitute such a restriction. The imposition of any amount in the region of £4,680,508.96 as requested by Hearts, which effectively comprises the imposition of an arbitrary transfer fee, would undoubtedly create a barrier to the free movement of the Player, contrary to the principles of EC Law.
- There is a vital distinction between the treatment of a termination, dependent upon whether this has occurred inside or outside the Protected Period. It is evident that the Player has observed the terms of the contract during the agreed stability period, a concept which had been expressly approved by clubs and thus Hearts.
- Given that under article 17 of he FIFA Status Regulations there is a sliding scale of sanctions in place that is referable to whether the termination took place inside or outside the Protected Period, by analogy, the issue of whether the termination occurred inside or outside the Protected Period must therefore be of major significance when determining the level of compensation payable.
- Indeed, whether the termination occurred inside or outside the Protected Period is expressly stated as being one of the objective criteria for calculating compensation under Article 17(1) of the FIFA Status Regulations. Therefore whilst it accepts that compensation is due to Hearts in accordance with the provisions set out in Article 17(1) of the

Regulations, such sums must not be punitive in nature, so as to restrict the Player's free movement rights, contrary to the rights enshrined in Article 39 of the EC Treaty, as the Player has fully respected the required contractual stability period of three years.

- Whilst it is accepted that the article 17 objective criteria may not be exhaustive, it is the particular criteria Hearts seeks to introduce that are unacceptable. The two considerations upon which Hearts' whole case for compensation hinges are the alleged criteria for the replacement costs of acquiring a new player and/or the loss of opportunity to receive a transfer fee.
- It is noteworthy that two such purportedly significant factors, which are likely to form part of the factual matrix of any termination and which Hearts values in this case at £4 million are not expressly included in the article 17 objective criteria. If these factors were intended to be included, they would have been listed in article 17(1).
- Even if the CAS accepted that the principle of 'restitutio in integrum' was applicable, then the position that Hearts be in had the Player not utilised the article 17(3) mechanism would be to have had the Player contractually bound to it under the contract for a further year. This position is a wholly different position from the one put forward by Hearts that it has in fact lost the opportunity to sell the Player for a profit.
- Furthermore, Hearts cannot claim that it would have sold the Player had he not terminated the contract as any such transfer would have required his consent.

  Consequently, Hearts has not proven that had the Player not terminated the contract, it would have transferred him for a profit. Indeed, it is very likely that the Player would have left Hearts upon the expiry of the contract without any compensation being payable to Hearts. Hearts accepts this at paragraph 9.10 of the Appeal Brief as it states that 'upon expiry of the contract, the Player would be able to move to another club without payment of a transfer fee'. Hearts cannot therefore prove that it has lost a transfer fee in respect of the Player. Its claim for loss of a transfer fee must therefore be rejected.
- In its argument for loss of a transfer fee, Hearts attempts to construct a claim based upon an arbitrary and subjective 'market value' of the Player by reference to three factors. This whole argument for a transfer fee is rejected as a matter of principle: however the relevance of the evidence adduced by Hearts as to the market value is also rejected.
- Hearts adduces evidence of transfer fees paid by or to English Premier League clubs during the summer 2006 Registration Period for 'players of a similar age, position, calibre and contractual status as the Player'. Such an approach is flawed as it fails to recognise the fact that each of these transfers was a mutually agreed transfer between the selling club, player and the buying club of a player under contract and thus has no resemblance to the situation where a player has legitimately terminated his contract in accordance with Article 17(3). The comparisons which Hearts seeks to make cannot be made.
- Moreover, the CAS was critical of a similar approach by Auxerre in the Mexes case, holding that 'AJ Auxerre's argument is based on a hypothetical transfer price contingent on transfers completed for other players. The amount claimed is therefore unfounded because it is hypothetical and based solely on estimates'.
- Although Hearts relies on the Mexes case, the present case is clearly distinguishable since the unilateral termination occurred outside the Protected Period. It is, however, also vital to note the basis upon which the conclusion in the Mexes case was reached: the player's former club Auxerre and his new club, AS Roma, had been in negotiations over a possible transfer of the player's registration which had not proven to be successful, in which Roma had made a definite offer of £4.5m for the transfer of the player. The CAS therefore concluded that '(I)t is therefore quite clear that Mr Mexes' violation of his contract resulted in the French club being deprived of a transfer fee which had been the object of a concrete offer from AS Roma in the region of £4,500,000.'
- Thus clearly the calculation of damages in Mexes has to be considered within the context of a negotiation between two clubs both where the buying club made an offer for the transfer of the player's registration and whilst the player was inside the Protected Period. Therefore the situation constituted what CAS refers to as a 'failed transfer'.

This was the only reason that the CAS concluded that Auxerre had suffered a loss in not receiving a transfer fee from AS Roma.

- The evidence of Mr Frank Clark relied on by Hearts is irrelevant. Mr Clark has evidently been requested to provide a subjective opinion on a perceived transfer market value of the Player during the Summer 2006 transfer Registration Period.
- Furthermore, Hearts rejected the offer from Southampton FC on 21 June 2006 and was thus prepared to wait for other offers into July and August 2006, i.e. during the last 12 months of the Contract. As such, the evidence of Mr Clark that "the general rule is that the value of a player reduces when he is coming towards the end of his contract – i.e. when he is within the last 12 months of it" actually undermines Heart's argument for a transfer fee in excess of the level of Southampton's offer.
- Hearts asserts that the DRC should have had regard to the costs that would be incurred by Hearts had it purchased a replacement player of a similar age, experience and ability to the Player. However, it is clear that by the Appellant's own admission, this is a hypothetical head of loss that has not been proven as the Appellant has not demonstrated what its loss actually is. Indeed, Hearts states 'in practice, Hearts has not obtained a player of a similar age, ability and experience.' The Panel must therefore reject this argument.
- Furthermore, on the basis of the Swiss law principle that contributory fault of the injured party should be taken into account when assessing damages, given that it was Hearts that chose not to select the Player and transfer listed him, Hearts must be held solely responsible for the situation it finds itself in, or in the alternative to have made a major contribution in this regard.
- Hearts states that the DRC should have had regard to the costs which were allegedly wasted in the acquisition, training and development of the Player and for which it did not receive the expected return of a transfer fee. However no transfer fee was guaranteed in respect of this Player.
- Moreover, any credit attributable to Hearts for the Player's development can only be by reference to the seasons between the ages of nineteen and twenty one, i.e. until his training period ended, and in this case no Training Compensation is payable under Article 20, Annex 4 of the FIFA Status Regulations as the Player was twenty four when he terminated the contract.
- In any event, the costs of acquisition of the Player were not 'wasted' since Hearts benefited from what it has acknowledged as the performances of a player who became 'integral to the first team' over a course of over 5 years in return for what it has itself acknowledged to be 'a de minimis sum of £75,000' transfer fee to Arbroath in March 2001.
- On the basis of established jurisprudence of the DRC, interest is only payable on contractual damages awarded by the DRC if payment of the said sum has not been paid within thirty days of the decision to this effect, (unless, of course, an appeal is made). Furthermore until a final and binding determination is reached, neither party is aware of the exact sum of compensation due to Hearts, so interest cannot yet run.
- The principle of the specificity of sport is a factor which is to be considered within the context of assessing compensation under Article 17(1) as the said Article makes express reference to it.
- In that relation, credit must be attributed to the Player's development to his own abilities, commitment and professionalism. The CAS itself ratified such approach in Mexes, where it held that when assessing compensation, credit should be given to the player for his own effort in progressing his career.
- In addition, insofar as Hearts seeks an increase in the compensation due to the development role it played, it must also therefore accept its role in the relative decline of the Player during the period of February 2006 to October 2006 during which time his appearances in both first team club football and international football were greatly diminished. This negative impact on the Player must also be considered under the head of the 'specificity of sport' in reducing the sum of damages payable Hearts.

- Hearts refers to the CAS case of Ariel Ortega v Fenerbahce SK & FIFA (2003/O/482) ('Ortega case'), in which the DRC calculated the sum of USD 11,000,000 as compensation due to Ortega's previous club, Fenerbahce SK in consideration of: (i) the transfer fee paid to the player's previous club, Parma AC; (ii) payments to the Argentine Football Association pursuant to the terms of a collective bargaining agreement; (iii) payments in respect of the acquisition of the image rights of the player; and (iv) the residual value of the player's playing contract.
- The Ortega Case should, however, be considered on its own facts as this case related to Mr Ortega's unilateral termination of his contract inside the Protected Period and after only 9 months of service to Fenerbahce. The question of when the termination occurs is fundamental to the calculation of compensation. In any event, even if the Panel were to apply the reasoning behind the Ortega case to the facts of this case, given that the transfer fee of £75,000 paid by the Appellant to Arbroath in 2001 is not relevant, and in the absence of image right payments and/or payments to any football association, the only factor of relevance is the residual value of the contract (which on the facts of this appeal is £132,585.24).
- Hearts also refers to the DRC case of Club A v Player B dated 15 January 2004. However that case does not support its claim. The sum of compensation awarded was based on the proportion of a signing on fee which had been paid to the player up front, and for which the club had not received a benefit, as the player prematurely terminated his contract. The player was therefore required to reimburse the club the proportion of the signing on fee which related to the unexpired portion of the playing contract. This decision is therefore not directly relevant.
- The residual remuneration due to the Player under the Contract is the sole factor, or in the alternative the principal factor to consider when assessing the compensation that is payable to Hearts.
- In the case in hand, the residual value of the contract can only comprise the guaranteed sums of salary and signing-on fee that the Player was due to receive under the contract, rather than estimated bonuses based on previous seasons when the Player was an ever present member of the team.
- Hearts reliance on the DRC case of Player X v Club Y of 22 November 2005 is both surprising and misconceived since that case concerns a breach of contract by a club and not by a player. The club was therefore liable to pay damages to the player which must of course be calculated by reference to the sums payable to the player under his new contract to facilitate the principle of the 'mitigation' i.e. so that the player is required to give credit for any sums he receives under a new contract to reduce his losses as a result of the breach of contract by the club. This is the only situation when the value of the new contract can be relevant.
- Hearts has failed to adduce any other jurisprudence to support its argument that remuneration and benefits under the New Contract are relevant. Moreover the exact wording of Article 17(1) i.e. 'and/or the new contract' is indicative of the fact that the terms of any new contract are clearly not applicable in all circumstances.
- Although Hearts seeks to recoup the legal costs in the sum of £80,008.96 that it has incurred to date, in accordance with established DRC jurisprudence, such fees are not recoverable in DRC proceedings. In respect of the legal fees incurred by Hearts, the Panel must determine this issue in accordance with article R 64.5 of the CAS Code.
- Hearts' submission that it had an absolute right to a compensation fee in reliance on clause 21 of the contract is self-serving as the Appellant has selectively quoted from this clause.
- In that relation and as a preliminary matter it is noteworthy that Scottish Premier League Rules referred to in clause 21 must be limited in scope to national transfers and therefore this clause is irrelevant in this case which is governed by the Regulations.

65. Furthermore, clause 21 must be examined in its true context by accounting for the fact that this provision cross refers to the compensation procedure set out in detail at Rule D 11 of the Rules of the Scottish Premier League, which expressly provides at Rule D 11.2 that 'a club

shall not be entitled to Compensation in the event that Registration to another Club occurs after the Professional Player concerned reaches the age of 24'.
Given that the Player was over twenty four when his registration was transferred, this provision is in any event irrelevant.

IV. DISCUSSION OF THE CLAIMS

A. Jurisdiction

66. The appeals are admissible as they were filed within the deadline stipulated in article 61 of the FIFA Statutes and in the appealed decision.
67. The jurisdiction of CAS, which is not disputed, derives from articles 60 and 61 of the FIFA Statutes and art. R47 of the Code of Sports-related Arbitration ('CAS Code').
68. The scope of the Panel's jurisdiction is defined in art. R57 of the CAS Code, which provides that: 'The Panel shall have full power to review the facts and the law. It may issue a new decision which replaces the decision challenged or annul the decision and refer the case back to the previous instance'.

B. Applicable Law

69. The rules of law applicable to the dispute between the Player and Hearts, on the one hand, and between the latter and Wigan, on the other hand, could in theory be different, since the parties are not the same and the clubs are not contractually bound to one another as the Player was with Hearts.
70. However, for the reasons now examined, the Panel finds that the same set of regulations and same national law are applicable to all three of the proceedings having been joined and to all aspects of the dispute between the parties.
71. Since chapter 12 of the Swiss Private International Law Act ('PILact') governs all international arbitrations with their seat in Switzerland and this arbitration constitutes an international arbitration with its seat in Switzerland as defined by article 176 of the PILact, article 187 PILact is the underlying conflict-of-law rule which is applicable in determining the governing rules of law.
72. According to article 187 of the PILact (free translation): 'The Arbitral tribunal shall decide the dispute according to the rules of law chosen by the parties or, in the absence of such a choice, according to the rules of law with which the case has the closest connection.'
73. Article 187 of the PILact gives the parties a large degree of autonomy in selecting the applicable rules of law – including the possibility of choosing conflict-of-law rules (to determine the governing substantive law), a national law or private regulations.
Moreover, the parties' choice can be tacit, e.g. result from their conduct during the proceedings.
74. In the present case, the applicable regulations and national law result from a combination of choices and references by the parties.
75. With respect to the Player and Hearts, the primary source of choice of law would be the employment contract. That said the employment contract contains no choice-of-law clause. With regard to the applicable regulations, clause 10 provides that:
"The Player and the Club shall observe and be subject to the Rules, Regulations and Bye-Laws of The Scottish Football Association, The Scottish Premier League and such other organisations of which these bodies or the Club is a member and in the case of any conflict between this Agreement and such Rules, Regulations or Bye-Laws then such Rules, Regulations or Bye-Laws shall take precedence. The Player shall also at all times observe the reasonable Rules of the Club."
76. Since the Scottish Football Association is a member of FIFA, the FIFA regulations and by-laws are applicable and take precedence in accordance with the reference in clause 10.
77. The FIFA regulations and bylaws in turn contain a main choice-of-law clause under article 60§2 of the FIFA Statutes, whereby: 'The provisions of the CAS Code of Sports- Related Arbitration shall apply to the proceedings. CAS shall primarily apply the various regulations of FIFA and, additionally, Swiss law.'

78. The foregoing choice-of-law clause underlines the primary application of the various FIFA regulations, while referring to the CAS Code and Swiss law.

79. In the present case, the reference to the CAS Code simply has the effect of re-confirming the primary application of the FIFA regulations and the additional application of Swiss law since art. R58 of the CAS Code provides that: 'The Panel shall decide the dispute according to the applicable regulations and the rules of law chosen by the parties or, in the absence of such a choice, according to the law of the country in which the federation, association or sports-related body is domiciled or according to the rules of law, the application of which the Panel deems appropriate. In the latter case, the Panel shall give reasons for its decision.'

80. Furthermore, all the parties in all three cases are basing their contentions in part on the FIFA regulations, notably on the FIFA Status Regulations.

81. For the above reasons, the Panel finds that all three parties have chosen the primary application of the FIFA regulations to the matters in dispute in all three cases.

82. That said, a question remains concerning the scope of application of Swiss law in addition to the FIFA regulations, in light of the fact that according to article 17(1) of the FIFA Status Regulations, "compensation for breach shall be calculated with due consideration for the law of the country concerned" and that according to article 25 (6) the DRC shall when making its decisions," apply these Regulations whilst taking into account all relevant arrangements, laws and/or collective bargaining agreements that exist at national level, as well as the specificity of sport'.

83. The Panel considers that the reference in article 17(1) of the FIFA Status Regulations to 'the law of the country concerned' does not detract from the fact that according to the clear wording of article 60§2 of the FIFA Statutes, the FIFA intended the interpretation and validity of its regulations and decisions to be governed by a single law corresponding to its law of domicile, i.e. Swiss law.

84. Thus, the Panel finds that the interpretation of the FIFA regulations and the validity of the DRC decision under appeal must be determined in application of Swiss law.

85. Moreover, the Panel finds that article 25(6) of the FIFA Status Regulations and the reference in article 17(1) to the 'law of the country concerned' are not, properly speaking, choice-of-law clauses.

86. Given its formulation, article 25(6) must be deemed a general reminder to the decisionmaking bodies of FIFA (PSC, DRC, Single Judge and DRC Judge) that in making their decisions under the FIFA regulations they must not apply those regulations in a vacuum but must account for the applicable contractual arrangements, collective agreements and national law. Article 25(6) does not purport to specify what national law is relevant.

87. As to article 17(1) of the FIFA Status Regulations, it is clear from its wording that the reference to the 'law of the country concerned' is not a choice-of-law clause, since it merely stipulates that such law is among the different elements to be taken into consideration in assessing the level of compensation.

88. In other words, article 17(1) does not require that compensation be determined in application of a national law or that the rules on contractual damage contained in the law of the country concerned have any sort of priority over the other elements and criteria listed in article 17(1). It simply means that the decision-making body shall take into consideration the law of the country concerned while remaining free to determine what weight, if any, is to be given to the provisions thereof in light of the content of such law, the criteria for compensation laid down in article 17(1) itself and any other criteria deemed relevant in the circumstances of the case.

89. In the present case, the law of the country concerned is Scottish law, since Scotland has the closest connection with the contractual dispute; being at once the country where the employment contract was signed and performed and where the club claiming compensation (Hearts) and the Player were domiciled at the time of signature and termination.

90. In sum and for the above reasons, the Panel considers the applicable law and regulations to be as follows:

- The FIFA regulations in determining the amount of compensation due to Hearts as a result of the Player's unilateral termination of his employment contract.
- Swiss law in interpreting the FIFA regulations and the validity of the DRC's decision under appeal.

– Scottish law, if the Panel deems any provisions are relevant to apply in conjuction with the FIFA Status Regulations in determining the level of compensation due to Hearts.

91. For reasons that will be explained below when discussing the claims, the Panel considers that the provisions of Scottish law invoked by Hearts should not be applied.

92. Finally, with respect to EC law invoked by the Player and Wigan, the Panel shall examine its scope of application if it becomes necessary in relation to the type of compensation decided.

C. Merits of the Appeals

93. The central provision of the FIFA Status Regulations invoked by the parties is article 17, which provides as follows:

"Article 17 Consequences of Terminating a Contract Without Just Cause The following provisions apply if a contract is terminated without just cause:

1. In all cases, the party in breach shall pay compensation. Subject to the provisions of Art.20 and annex 4 in relation to Training Compensation, and unless otherwise provided for in the contract, compensation for breach shall be calculated with due consideration for the law of the country concerned, the specificity of sport, and any other objective criteria. These criteria shall include, in particular, the remuneration and other benefits due to the player under the existing contract and/or the new contract, the time remaining on the existing contract up to a maximum of five years, the fees and expenses paid or incurred by the Former Club (amortised over the term of the contract) and whether the breach falls within a Protected Period.

2. Entitlement to compensation cannot be assigned to a third party if a Professional is required to pay compensation, the Professional and his New Club shall be jointly and severally liable for its payment. The amount may be stipulated in the contract or agreed between the parties.

3. In addition to the obligation to pay compensation, sporting sanctions shall also be imposed on any player found to be in breach of contract during the Protected Period.

This sanction shall be a restriction of four months on his eligibility to play in Official Matches. In the case of aggravating circumstances, the restriction shall be six months. In all cases, these sporting sanctions shall take effect from the start of the following Season of the New Club. Unilateral breach without just cause or sporting just cause after the Protected Period will not result in sporting sanctions.

Disciplinary measure may, however, be imposed outside of the Protected Period for failure to give due notice of termination (i.e. within fifteen days following the last match of the Season). The Protected Period starts again when, while renewing the contract, the duration of the previous contract is extended."

94. The parties are at one in arguing that the DRC misapplied article 17 of the FIFA Status Regulations and in doing so violated procedural requirements of FIFA regulations by failing to explain how it arrived at the figure of £625'000 in compensation.

95. The parties however disagree as to how the criteria laid down in article 17(1) should be applied and therefore as to the amount of compensation owed to Hearts.

96. Consequently, the Panel shall (a) begin by examining whether the DRC decision can be deemed in violation of the FIFA regulations and, if so, shall (b) make a new determination as to the amount of compensation owed to Hearts in application of article 17 of the FIFA Status Regulations. Since the parties also disagree as to the joint and several liability of Wigan to pay compensation, this point shall be addressed thereafter (c).

a) The Validity of the DRC's Decision

97. The Panel shall begin by determining whether the DRC breached any formal and procedural requirements of the FIFA regulations and/or any mandatory principles of Swiss law of associations.

98. In that relation, the Panel finds that Wigan rightly invokes article 13.4 of the FIFA Rules Governing the Procedures of the Players' Status Committee and the Dispute Resolution Chamber (the 'FIFA Rules'), which provides that decisions of the DRC must contain " reasons for its findings'.

99. The relevance and importance of article 13.4 is confirmed by several mandatory principles of Swiss law that limit the regulatory and decisional freedom of an association in order to protect its members. One such principle is that an association must correctly apply its own

regulations, another being that its regulations must be applied and its decisions made in a predictable and cognisable manner, notably to ensure equality of treatment and due process.

100. The Panel finds that in this case the DRC has failed to meet the requirements of article 13.4 of the FIFA Rules, since although the DRC decision does discuss some of the criteria listed in article 17 of the FIFA Status Regulations for determining the level of compensation owed, in the final analysis it is impossible to understand from reading the decision what weight was given to what criteria in determining the quantum, i.e. there is no indication of the method and figures used by the DRC to arrive at the amount of £625'000, or in other words what the figure consists of.

101. For the above reasons, the Panel finds that the DRC's decision is invalid for having failed to meet the formal requirements laid down in the FIFA regulations.

102. Therefore and given the prayers of all three parties that the Panel directly renders a new decision, as well as the Panel's authority to do so in accordance with art. R57 of the CAS Code, the Panel shall issue a new decision and now turns to the determination of the level of compensation to be awarded on the basis of article 17 of the FIFA Status Regulations.

b) Level of Compensation Owed by Hearts

103. In determining the level of compensation owned, the Panel shall begin, as a preliminary matter, by (i) listing a certain number of undisputed facts, and (ii) examining the disputed existence of any aggravating factors and contributory negligence. The Panel shall then (iii) turn to the interpretation and application of article 17 of the FIFA Status Regulations.

i. Undisputed Facts

104. The Panel notes that the following circumstances relating to the issue of compensation are undisputed:

- Although the Player initially purported to terminate his contract by relying on just cause, he finally renounced such approach, retracted his initial notice and unilaterally terminated his employment contract without cause as defined in article 17 of the FIFA Status Regulations.
- Consequently, the only matter to assess is one of compensation and article 17 of the FIFA Status Regulations applies in that respect.
- The rounded-off figure of £150'000 is accepted by all parties as the residual value of the Player's employment contract remaining after its termination (this figure was agreed at the hearing).

ii. Existence of Aggravating Factors or Contributory Negligence

105. With respect to the reasons which led to the unilateral termination, Hearts is contending in essence that it was a matter of greed on the Player's part who, knowing the end of his contract was approaching, unfairly refused to negotiate a further prolongation of his employment contract despite having received several offers from Hearts, and then made a deliberate attempt to circumvent the requirement of a transfer fee. Hearts views this as an aggravating factor.

106. The Player is essentially arguing the contrary, i.e. that due to the not-too-distant prospect of the end of his employment contract and the likely fast-diminishing value of his transfer value beyond the upcoming 2006 Summer transfer window, Hearts attempted to pressure him into signing a new contract with Hearts on terms that suited the Club.

107. According to the Player, this pressure was applied by the President of the Club, Mr. Romanov, inappropriately giving instructions to the managers not to select him for certain games despite the Player being willing and able to play and having been consistently a leading and respected member of the team.

108. The Player confirmed at the hearing that perception of the reasons for his non-selection led to a breakdown in his confidence in the Club's intentions, which was increased by disparaging comments being made in the media, attributed to Mr. Romanov, about the Player's commitment to Hearts and about the role of his parents behind the scene. It is in this context that he ultimately decided to terminate his contract, without having had any contacts or offers from Wigan or any other clubs beforehand.

109. To the extend he is required to pay compensation to the Club, the Player contends that the above circumstances constitute a form of contributory negligence on the part of Hearts that should have the effect of diminishing any amount of compensation allowed.

110. Although the Panel is not convinced that the concept of aggravating factors or of contributory negligence are legally relevant or applicable to the calculation of compensation under the criteria of article 17 (1) of the FIFA Status Regulations, the legal question can be left open because the Panel finds there is no sufficient evidence that either party (Hearts or the Player) in fact had ill intentions or misbehaved in their attitude with regard to each other; whatever may have been the contrary perception of each.
Neither is there any evidence that Wigan or any other club intervened in the relationship between Hearts and the Player in a manner which would sour it, or incited the Player to leave Hearts by means of an offer prior to the Player's notice of termination.

111. Rather it would appear that through an unfortunate combination of circumstances, probably fuelled in part by a lack of direct communication between Mr Romanov and the Player, the relationship of confidence between Hearts and the Player gradually broke down.

112. Having carefully listened to the Player as well as several of the Club's managers and bearing in mind the other evidence on record, the Panel is convinced that the Player's confidence in the Club and desire to continue playing for the Club was broken; his sensitivity to the fact of not being selected for certain games and to various statements in the media in all likelihood being exacerbated by a sentimental attachment to a club in which he began his professional career as a young player and in which he was originally recognized as a player upon whose motivation the club could confidently count.

113. At the same time, given the realities of the transfer market combined with the Player's incontestable right to leave the Club free of charge at the end of his contract, the Panel finds it is more likely than not that Hearts felt under some pressure to secure a new contract with the Player, in order to leave time to place him on the 2006 Summer transfer list if such contract was not signed. Indeed, the manager and experts who testified on the subject were unanimous in declaring that with 18 months left to run on the contract, the Player's value on the market would rapidly decline, if not become in practice extinguished, after the Summer transfer period.

114. For the above reasons, whether or not the question is legally relevant, the Panel does not find that any aggravating factors on part of the Player or contributory negligence on part of the Club have been clearly established. Accordingly, the Panel will take account of neither in determining the level of compensation owed to Hearts in application of article 17 of the FIFA Status Regulations.

iii. The Interpretation and Application of Article 17 of the FIFA Status Regulations

115. In keeping with the practice under Swiss law relating to the interpretation of the bylaws of an association, the Panel shall have regard first for the wording of article 17, i.e. its literal meaning, and if this is unclear shall have regard to the provision's internal logic, its relationship with other provisions of the FIFA Status Regulations as well as its purpose revealed by the history of its adoption.

116. As a starting point, it is noteworthy that according to the first sentence of article 17, in case of unilateral termination without cause: 'In all cases, the party in breach shall pay compensation'. This comes as a logical consequence of article 13 of the FIFA Status Regulations which underlines the principle pacta sunt servanda, by stating 'A contract between a Professional and a club may only be terminated on expiry of the term of contract or by mutual agreement'; such provision being further reinforced by article 16 whereby 'A contract cannot be unilaterally terminated during the course of a Season'.

117. In other words, article 17 is not a provision that allows a club or a Player unilaterally to terminate an employment contract without cause. On the contrary, within the framework of section IV of the FIFA Status Regulations – entitled 'Maintenance of Contractual Stability Between Professionals and Clubs' and covering articles 13-18, any such termination is clearly deemed a breach of contract.

118. Thus, unilateral termination must be viewed as a breach of contract even outside the Protected Period and the position expressed by the Player's counsel in his closing arguments that

no compensation at all should be due is not sustainable; the only possible question in this case being how much is due under the system designed by article 17 to deal with the consequences of unilateral termination without cause.

119. A second preliminary point is that according to the wording of its first paragraph article 17 is not intended to deal directly with Training Compensation – such compensation being specially regulated in detail by other provisions of the FIFA Status Regulations.

120. The Panel finds therefore that in determining the level of compensation payable to Hearts under article 17 of the FIFA Status Regulations as a result of the Player's unilateral termination without cause, the amounts having been invested by the Club in training and developing the Player are irrelevant, i.e. are not factors that come into consideration under article 17. Consequently, the Panel disagrees with Heart's submission that among the relevant circumstances in calculating compensation for unilateral termination under article 17 "is the sporting and financial investment Hearts has made in training and developing the Player during the last 5 years".

121. A third preliminary point is that article 17 gives primacy to the parties' contractual agreement in terms of stipulating types and amounts of compensation, since according to article 17(1) the criteria for calculating compensation only apply if not "otherwise provided for in the contract" and article 17(2) provides that the amount of compensation "may be stipulated in the contract or agreed between the parties".

122. In the present case, the parties have not invoked any provisions of the Player's employment contract with respect to the assessment of the level of compensation, except Hearts' reference to clause 21 of the contract, whereby "The Club may offer the Player a further period of engagement under the Rules of The Scottish Premier League and the Player shall not be registered for any other club without payment of a compensation fee (fixed in manner provided by the Rules of The Scottish Premier League) by that other club to the club which previously held the Player's Scottish Premier League registration if and so long as the Club has offered to engage the Player on terms which are in the opinion of the Board not less favourable in all monetary respects that those applicable hereunder."

123. However, Hearts has neither indicated the relevance of clause 21 with respect to the specific case of compensation for unilateral termination without cause nor established any amount of compensation that would allegedly be owed according to such clause. Instead, Hearts has chosen to invoke compensation criteria it deems relevant in application of the FIFA Status Regulations and Scottish law and has based its calculations thereon. In addition, Hearts' foregoing reference to clause 21 of the employment contract is partly contradictory to its written submission that the contract did not provide for any assessment of compensation in the event of breach by either party.

124. For the above reasons, the Panel finds that Hearts has failed to allege or prove that any amount of compensation for unilateral termination or criteria for calculating it is contractually specified in the Player's employment contract.

125. Having dealt with the foregoing preliminary points, the Panel shall now analyse the factors to be taken into consideration according to the wording of article 17 of the FIFA Status Regulations when determining the level of compensation. Article 17(1) refers to three categories of factor, which the Panel shall examine in turn: the law of the country concerned, the specificity of sport and any other objective criteria (followed by a list of examples).

126. With respect to the law of the country concerned and as indicated earlier, the Panel considers that it is Scottish law but that the Panel has the discretion to decide whether or not any provisions of Scottish law should be applied in determining the level of compensation.

127. The Panel finds there are several reasons not to apply the rules of Scottish law invoked by Hearts.

128. One reason is that Hearts is relying on general rules and principles of Scottish law on damages for breach of contract, i.e. on provisions of Scottish law that are neither specific to the termination of employment contracts nor to sport or football, while article 17 of the FIFA Status Regulations was adopted precisely with the goal of finding in particular special solutions for the determination of compensation payable by football players and clubs who unilaterally terminate their contracts without cause. In other words, it is important to bear in mind that it is because employment contracts for football players are atypical, i.e. require that

the particularities of the football labour market and the organization of the sport be accounted for, that article 17 was adopted. At the same time, footballers' contracts remain more akin to employment contracts (and are generally characterized as such under national laws), than to some form of commercial contract to which general rules on damage are applicable.

129. The Panel therefore sees no reason to renounce application of the specific solutions and criteria laid down in article 17 of the FIFA Status Regulations in favour of general rules on contract damages. On the contrary, the fact that several of the applicable choice-of-law rules (article 60§2 of the FIFA Statutes and art. R58 of the CAS Code) underline the primary application of the regulations chosen by the parties, that article 17(1) itself refers to the specificity of sport and that it is in the interest of football that solutions to compensation be based on uniform criteria rather than on provisions of national law that may vary considerably from country to country, are all factors that reinforce the Panel's opinion that in this case it is not appropriate to apply the general principles of Scottish law on damages for breach of contract invoked by Hearts.

130. Consequently, in determining the level of compensation, the Panel will not rely on Scottish law.

131. With respect to the 'specificity of sport', article 17(1) of the FIFA Status Regulations stipulates that it shall be taken into consideration, without however providing any indication as to the content of such concept.

132. In light of the history of article 17, the Panel finds that the specificity of sport is a reference to the goal of finding particular solutions for the football world which enable those applying the provision to strike a reasonable balance between the needs of contractual stability, on the one hand, and the needs of free movement of players, on the other hand, i.e. to find solutions that foster the good of football by reconciling in a fair manner the various and sometimes contradictory interests of clubs and players.

133. Therefore the Panel shall bear that balance in mind when proceeding to an examination of the other criteria for compensation listed in article 17.

134. With regard to the other criteria for determining compensation, article 17(1) leaves a substantial degree of discretion to the deciding authority to account for the circumstances of the case, since after stipulating that compensation may be calculated on the basis of 'any other objective criteria', it provides that 'These criteria shall include, in particular, the remuneration and other benefits due to the player under the existing contract and/or the new contract, the time remaining on the existing contract up to a maximum of five years, the fees and expenses paid or incurred by the Former Club (amortised over the term of the contract) and whether the breach falls within a Protected Period'.

135. In that relation is it noteworthy that independently from the specificities of a given case, the criteria listed in article 17 need to cope with a number of categories of cases, notably those where unilateral termination occurs inside the protected period as distinct from those where it occurs outside such period and those cases where unilateral termination is by the Player as distinct from those where termination is by the Club. It is therefore logical that article 17(1) includes a broad range of criteria, many of which cannot in good sense be combined, and some of which may be appropriate to apply to one category of case and inappropriate to apply in another.

136. Furthermore, in seeking to balance appropriately the interests of clubs and players for the good of the game, it is necessary to bear in mind that because article 17 of the FIFA Status Regulations applies to the unilateral termination of contracts both by players and by clubs, the system of compensation provided by article 17 must be interpreted and applied in a manner which avoids favouring clubs over players or vice versa.

137. In the foregoing context, the Panel finds it appropriate to consider that the clubs particular need for contract stability is specifically and adequately addressed by means of the Protected Period and the provisions designed to enforce it, which comprise the basic period of protection as defined in paragraph 7 of the 'Definitions' contained in the FIFA Status Regulations, the automatic renewal of that period upon the contract being extended (article 17(3), last sentence) and the relatively severe sanctions that can be imposed in case of disrespect for the Protected Period (article 17(3)); such stability being further enhanced for clubs and players

alike by article 16 of the FIFA Status Regulations, which entirely prohibits unilateral termination during the course of a Season.

138. The clubs' special interest having been recognized and protected in such regulatory manner, the Panel finds that, beyond the Protected Period and subject to the parties' contractual stipulations, compensation for unilateral termination without cause should not be punitive or lead to enrichment and should be calculated on the basis of criteria that tend to ensure clubs and players are put on equal footing in terms of the compensation they can claim or are required to pay. In addition, it is in the interest of the football world that the criteria applicable in a given type of situation and therefore the method of calculation of the compensation be as predictable as possible.

139. Accordingly, the Panel deems that in the present case the alleged estimated value of the Player on the transfer market, upon which Heart's is basing its main claim (£4 million), by alternatively claiming such amount as lost profit or as the replacement value of the Player, cannot come into consideration when determining compensation on the basis of article 17(1) of the FIFA Status Regulations because any such form of compensation was clearly not agreed upon contractually and to impose it by regulation would simultaneously cause the Club to be enriched and be punitive vis à vis the Player.

140. Indeed, in this case the Player was initially purchased by the Club for an amount of £75'000 whereas it is today claiming a market value of £4 million. This means that independently from the question of amortization of the initial purchase amount, that the Panel shall deal with below, the Club is claiming to be entitled to a profit of at least £3.9 million on the sole premise that it trained and educated the Player.

141. In any event, subject to it being validly agreed by an enforceable contract, the Panel finds there is no economic, moral or legal justification for a club to be able to claim the market value of a player as lost profit.

142. From an economic perspective there in no reason to believe that a player's value on the market owes more to training by a club than to a player's own efforts, discipline and natural talent. An empirical study might even demonstrate the contrary, i.e. that a talented and hard-working player tends to fare well, stand out and succeed independently from the exact type of training he receives, whereas an untalented and/or lazy player will be less successful no matter what the environment. Also market value could stem in part from charisma and personal marketing. In any case, it is clear that a club cannot simply assume it is the only source of success of a player and thus claim his entire market value, particularly without bringing any proof (which would be very difficult) of its paramount role in the player's success leading to his market value. In this case, Hearts have underlined the Player's success and alleged his market value but have brought no evidence that the Club entirely or even predominantly generated the alleged market value in question through its training and education.

143. In addition from an economic and moral point of view, it would be difficult to assume a club could be deemed the source of appreciation in market value of a player while never be deemed responsible for the depreciation in value. Consequently, if the approach relied on by Hearts were followed, players should be entitled to claim for example that they are owed compensation for their alleged decrease in market value caused by such matters as being kept on the bench for too long or having an incompetent trainer, etc. Obviously, such a system would be unworkable and would not serve the good of the football.

144. From a regulatory standpoint, to allow clubs to claim the market value of players as lost profit under article 17 of the FIFA Status Regulations would not make sense and would amount to double counting, since, as mentioned earlier, article 20 and annex already provide for a system of compensation to clubs for the training and education of players, and it is not by chance that such compensation is not based on the player's market value but on demonstrable investment made and costs incurred by the club.

145. Moreover, since a club's possible entitlement to the transfer or market value of players is entirely absent from the criteria of compensation listed in article 17(1) and there is no reference to any such form of compensation in favour of Hearts in the Player's employment contract, to apply such criteria and thereby imply it into the contract would contradict both the principle of fairness and the principle of certainty.

146. Finally, because of the potentially high amounts of compensation involved, giving clubs a regulatory right to the market value of players and allowing lost profits to be claimed in such manner would in effect bring the system partially back to the pre-Bosman days when players' freedom of movement was unduly hindered by transfer fees and their careers and well-being could be seriously effected by them becoming pawns in the hands of their clubs and a vector through which clubs could reap considerable benefits without sharing the profit or taking corresponding risks. In view of the text and the history of article 17(1) of the FIFA Status Regulations, allowing any form of compensation that could have such an effect would clearly be anachronistic and legally unsound.

147. For the above reasons, the Panel finds that Hearts is not entitled to claim any part of the Player's alleged market value as lost profit or on any other ground and that as a result its corresponding claim for £4 million must be rejected.

148. Neither can Hearts claim the right to reimbursement of any portion of the fee of £75'000 initially paid by it to purchase the Player from his former club, since according to the criteria laid down in article 17(1) in this respect, which the Panel finds reasonable, that fee must be deemed amortised over the term of the contract, and in this case the Player remained with the club for a longer period in total than the initially agreed fixed term of four years.

149. In addition, the Panel is not convinced that beyond the Protected Period it is admissible for a club to reclaim a portion of the engagement fee as compensation for unilateral termination unless such form of compensation is stipulated in the employment contract, since contractual fairness would tend to require that upon accepting his employment a player be fully aware of the financial engagements he has undertaken and the way in which they can affect his future movements. In other words, if a club expects an engagement fee to be proportionately reimbursable beyond the Protected Period – which is a matter that cannot be implied – there should be a negotiation and a meeting of the minds on the subject.

150. Among the other criteria of compensation referred to in article 17(1), the Panel considers that the remuneration and benefits due to the Player under his new contract is not the most appropriate criterion on which to rely in cases involving unilateral termination by the Player beyond the Protected Period, because rather than focusing on the content of the employment contract which has been breached, it is linked to the Player's future financial situation and is potentially punitive.

151. Instead the Panel finds it more appropriate to take account of the fact that under a fixedterm employment contract of this nature both parties (club and player) have a similar interest and expectation that the term of the contract will be respected, subject to termination by mutual consent. Thus, just as the Player would be entitled in principle to the outstanding remuneration due until expiry of the term of the contract in case of unilateral termination by the club [subject it may be, to mitigation of loss], the club should be entitled to receive an equivalent amount in case of termination by the Player.
This criterion also has the advantage of indirectly accounting for the value of the Player, since the level of his remuneration will normally bear some correlation to his value as a Player. Thus a Player receiving very high remuneration (and thereby being able to expect high remuneration in case of a change of club) will have a correspondingly high amount of compensation to pay even if he terminates his contract outside the Protected Period, and the earlier such termination occurs the higher will be the total amount of compensation owed.

152. For the above reasons, the Panel finds that Heart's claim of £330,524 based on the difference between the value of the old and new contract must be rejected and that the most appropriate criteria of article 17(1) to apply in determining the level of compensation owed to Hearts by the Player is the remuneration remaining due to the Player under the employment contact upon its date of termination, which the parties have referred to as the residual value of the contract.

153. Consequently and because the parties have agreed that such residual value represents an amount of £150,000, the Panel considers the foregoing amount to be due to Hearts as full compensation under article 17(1) of the FIFA Status Regulations for the Player's termination of his contract.

154. Having determined that Hearts is entitled to such amount as fair and adequate compensation for the Player's unilateral termination of his employment contract and since the criteria listed

in article 17(1) are not designed to be cumulative per se, the Panel sees no reason to award any other amount as an additional head of damage.

155. For sake of good order, the Panel nevertheless points out that with respect to Heart's claim of £70,000 for alleged sporting and commercial losses, the Club has established neither the causality of the Player's termination nor the existence of the damage; and that with respect to Heart's claim for £80,008.96 for costs linked to the proceeding in front of the DRC, there is no reason to award such amount because according to the DRC's practice such proceedings do not give rise to awards of costs and because in any event Hearts has lost the present appeal resulting from the DRC proceeding.

156. Finally, with respect to the amount of £150,000 being awarded, the Panel considers that it shall carry interest from the first day following the effective termination of the contract, since within the logic of the system of compensation instituted by article 17(1) such is the date when the compensation became due. Because none of the parties have contested the rate of interest of 5% used by the DRC, that rate shall apply from the date in question.

157. According to the Player's final letter of termination of 26 May 2006, the notice of termination was to take effect on 30 June 2006 given the Player's statement that he would not be honouring the last 12 months of his employment contract. Thus interest is awarded from 1 July 2006.

D. Several and Joint Liability of Wigan

158. Article 17(2) of the FIFA Status Regulations stipulates that:
"Entitlement to compensation cannot be assigned to a third party. If a professional player is required to pay compensation, the Professional and his New Club shall be jointly and severally liable for its payment. The amount may be stipulated in the contract or agreed between the parties."

159. Wigan contends that it should not be held jointly liable on the basis of the foregoing provision because it took no part in inciting the Player to leave Hearts and that it had not made him any offer or even made contact with him at the time he decided to leave Hearts and gave the Club his final notice of termination.

160. In light of the evidence on record, the Panel has no reason to doubt Wigan's assertion in this respect or therefore to conclude that Wigan had any causal role in the Player's decision to terminate his contract with Hearts.

161. That said, according to its wording the application of article 17(2) is not conditional on fault and Wigan offered no evidence that article 17(2) should be given any other meaning than its literal sense.

162. Consequently, the Panel considers that the joint and several liability provided under 17(2) must be deemed a form of strict liability, which is aimed at avoiding any debate and difficulties of proof regarding the possible involvement of the new club in a player's decision to terminate his former contract, and as better guaranteeing the payment of whatever amount of compensation the player is required to pay to his former club on the basis of article 17.

163. The Panel finds therefore that Wigan is jointly and severally liable with the Player for the payment of £150,000 in compensation to Hearts.

V. COSTS

164. Pursuant to article R64.4 of the Code, the Court Office shall, upon conclusion of the proceedings, determine the final amount of the costs of the arbitration, which shall include the CAS Court Office fee, the costs and fees of the arbitrators computed in accordance with the CAS fee scale, the contribution towards the costs and expenses of the CAS, and the costs of witnesses, experts and interpreters. In accordance with the consistent practice of CAS, the award states only how these costs must be apportioned between the parties. Such costs are later determined and notified to the parties by separate communication from the Secretary General of CAS.

165. Considering that the absence of any indication provided in the DRC decision as to the manner of calculation of the amount of compensation caused all the parties to remain in doubt as to the correctness of the decision and to legitimately require a clarification by means of an

appeal, the Panel finds that the costs of the arbitration shall be shared equally between the parties, i.e. that each party shall bear one third thereof.

166. For the same reasons, the Panel finds it fair that each party bears its own costs and expenses irrespective of which party prevailed in its claims.

ON THESE GROUNDS

The Court of Arbitration for Sport pronounces, jointly, with respect to the three proceedings:

1. The appealed decision of 4 April 2007 of the FIFA Dispute Resolution Chamber is set aside.
2. Mr Andrew Webster shall pay Heart of Midlothian an amount of £150,000 (one hundred and fifty thousand Pounds Sterling) as compensation, with interest at 5% from 1 July 2006.
3. Wigan Athletic FC is jointly and severally liable with Mr Andrew Webster to pay Heart of Midlothian the amount of £150,000 (one hundred and fifty thousand Pounds Sterling), with interest at 5% from 1 July 2006.
4. Each party shall bear one third of the total costs of the three proceedings, to be determined and served on the parties by the CAS Court Office.
5. Each party shall bear its own legal costs.
6. Any and all other prayers for relief are dismissed.

Lausanne, 30 January 2008
THE COURT OF ARBITRATION FOR SPORT
Quentin Byrne-Sutton
President of the Panel
Jean-Jacques Bertrand
Arbitrator
Michael Beloff
Arbitrator

APPENDIX XXII

OSCAR PISTORIUS CAS AWARD

CAS 2008/A/1480 Pistorius v/IAAF
ARBITRAL AWARD
delivered by the
THE COURT OF ARBITRATION FOR SPORT
(the "CAS")
sitting in the following composition:
Professor Martin **Hunter**, Barrister, London, England
Mr David W. **Rivkin,** Attorney, New-York, USA.

Me Jean Philippe **Rochat**, Avocat, Lausanne, Switzerland
Ad Hoc Clerk: Mr Alexandre **Vagenheim,** London, England
in the arbitration between:

MR OSCAR PISTORIUS, represented by Mr Marco Consonni, Jeffrey L. Kessler and David G. Feher, Attorneys, of Dewey & Leboeuf LLP, Milan, Italy, and New York, USA.
Appellant v/
INTERNATIONAL ASSOCIATION OF ATHLETICS FEDERATIONS (IAAF), represented by Mr Mark Gay, Mr Huw Roberts, Solicitors of DLA Piper, London, England, and Me Habib Cisse, Avocat, Paris, France.
Respondent

A. INTRODUCTION

The Parties and the Dispute

1. The Appellant, Oscar Pistorius (hereafter "Mr Pistorius") is a citizen of, and resident in, the Republic of South Africa. He is a professional athlete competing in 100, 200 and 400 meter sprints.
2. The Respondent, the International Association of Athletics Federations (the "IAAF" or the "Federation"), governs the sport of athletics throughout the world and recognized as such by the International Olympic Committee. The IAAF has its seat in the Principality of Monaco.
3. In this arbitration, Mr Pistorius appeals Decision No. 2008/01 of the IAAF Council on 14 January 2008 (the "IAAF Decision") that the "Cheetah" prosthetic legs worn by Mr. Pistorius, who has been a double amputee since he was eleven months old, constituted a technical device and provided him with an advantage over an able-bodied athlete in violation of IAAF Competition Rule 144.2(e).
4. The IAAF Decision was based on a report prepared for the IAAF by Professor Brüggemann and his colleagues at the German Sport University in Cologne (the "Cologne Report"). As a result of the IAAF Decision, Mr Pistorius is banned from competing against able-bodied athletes in IAAF-sanctioned events.

The Arbitration Agreement and Jurisdiction of the CAS

5. The Arbitration Agreement is contained in Rule 60.11 of the IAAF Competition Rules:
In cases involving International-Level athletes (or their athlete support personnel), or involving the sanction of a Member by the Council for a breach of the Rules, whether doping or non-doping related, the decision of the relevant body of the Member may (unless Rule 60.17 applies) be appealed exclusively to CAS in accordance with the provisions set out in Rules 60.25 to 60.30.
6. Pursuant to Rule 60.25 of the IAAF Competition Rules (the "IAAF Rules"), an athlete may give notice of an appeal from a final decision of the IAAF within 30 days from the date of

communication of its written reasons. The IAAF sent the IAAF Decision to Mr Pistorius on 16 January 2008. He filed this appeal with the CAS on 13 February 2008. Neither party has challenged the jurisdiction of the CAS, and the appeal has been held admissible by the CAS.

7. The IAAF Rules state that such an appeal shall take the form of a de novo review and rehearing:

All appeals before CAS shall take the form of a re-hearing de novo of the issues raised by the case and the CAS Panel shall be able to substitute its decision for the decision of the relevant Tribunal of the Member of the IAAF where it considers the decision of the relevant tribunal of the Member or the IAAF to be erroneous or procedurally unsound.

8. It follows that this CAS Appellate Panel is mandated to review *de novo* the facts as well as the provisions of the relevant Rules and the applicable law (CAS Code, Article R57).

B. THE APPELLATE PROCESS

The Statement of Appeal and Request for an extension of time

9. In his Statement of Appeal filed on 13 February 2008, Mr Pistorius requested the annulment of the IAAF Decision. Mr Pistorius also requested an extension of the 15 day time limit to deliver his appeal brief provided for in IAAF Rule 60.25.

10. On 14 February 2008, the CAS invited the parties to submit their observations regarding the applicable procedural rules because the IAAF Competition Rules, IAAF Constitution and the CAS Code provide different deadlines for the filing of the statement for appeal.

11. The IAAF Constitution Article 15.1 states:

"*All disputes arising under this Constitution shall be [...] subject to appeal to the [CAS].*"

"*The appeal shall be in accordance with the Rules of CAS currently in force, provided [...] the appellant shall submit its statement of appeal within sixty days of the date of communication of the decision that is to be appealed.*"

12. The CAS Code, Article R51 provides that the Appellant shall have "*ten days following the expiry of the time limit for the appeal*" in which to file his or her appeal brief.

13. The IAAF Rule 15.5 provides that disputes arising under the IAAF Rules and Regulations shall be resolved in accordance with their provisions. With respect to all decisions subject to appeal under the IAAF Competition Rules "*.... the appellant shall have 30 days from the date of communication of the written reasons of the decision to be appealed [..] in which to file his statement of appeal with CAS.*" The IAAF Rule 60.25 further provides that "within 15 *days of the deadline for filing the statement of appeal the appellant shall file its appeal brief with CAS [...]*"

14. On 20 February 2008, the IAAF agreed to Mr Pistorius' request for an extension of time and proposed a procedural timetable, which was in turn accepted by Mr Pistorius on 22 February 2008.

Request for a stay

15. In his Statement of Appeal, Mr Pistorius also requested a stay of the execution of the IAAF Decision, so that he would be able to compete in IAAF-sanctioned events pending a decision in the appeal.

16. On 28 February 2008, the IAAF submitted its observations in reply to Mr Pistorius' request.

17. On 10 March 2008, the Deputy-President of the Appeals Arbitration Division of the CAS denied Mr Pistorius' request for stay of the IAAF Decision on the basis that his harm in being prevented from participating in IAAF events was not irreparable, and that at the time of the request no evidence had been presented to contradict the Cologne Report.

Request for Relief

18. In his Statement of Appeal, Mr Pistorius requested the CAS to vacate the IAAF Decision, and to determine that he may participate in competitions held under the IAAF Rules using his *Cheetah* prosthetic limbs.

The Proceedings

19. The pre-hearing activity was organised, by agreement between the Parties, on a timetable that took account of the necessarily expedited nature of the process.
20. On 25 March 2008, Mr Pistorius delivered his Brief, accompanied by witness statements and exhibits.
21. On 25 April 2008, the IAAF delivered its Reply Brief, accompanied by witness statements and exhibits
22. On 29 and 30 April 2008, the Panel held a witness hearing in Lausanne at the premises of the CAS.
23. At the hearing, both Parties were represented by the counsel identified on the title page of this Award. The following fact witnesses were heard:
    For the Appellant, Mr Oscar Pistorius and Mr Peet Van Zyl
    For the Respondent, Mr Nick Davies and Dr Elio Locatelli
24. The following experts were heard:
    For the Appellant, Dr Hugh Herr and Dr Rodger Kram
    For the Respondent, Professor Piet Brüggemann and Dr Wolfgang Potthast
25. By agreement between the Panel and the Parties, the following procedure was adopted and followed:
    - Counsel for each Party made an opening statement of approximately 30 minutes.
    - The fact witnesses for both Parties were heard.
    - Meanwhile, the experts for both sides held a conference in another room, with a mission to make two lists: (a) the matters on which they agreed, and (b) the matters on which they were not agreed.
    - The fact witnesses' testimony was completed before the first lunch break.
    - After lunch on the first day the experts returned to the hearing room and presented the two lists, as requested.[2]
    - Most of the remaining hearing time was devoted to hearing the experts, partly in conferencing format in the presence of the Panel, and partly in traditional common law style examination-in-chief, cross-examination and re-examination format.
    - The hearing concluded with closing statements by the Parties' counsel, and a personal statement by Mr Pistorius.
    - At the end of the hearing, the Parties confirmed that they had no objections to raise regarding their right to be heard and to be treated equally in the arbitration proceedings.
26. The hearing ended at approximately 6.00 pm on Wednesday 30 April.
27. Thereafter the Panel held deliberations, partly in person and partly by telephone, before agreeing unanimously on the reasons and decisions given in this Award.

C. THE FACTUAL BACKGROUND

Introduction

28. The history of this matter is remarkable, and possibly without precedent. It is necessary to recount it in some detail, in order that the reader may understand the extraordinary nature of the disputed issues and the complexity of the related scientific aspects.
29. Mr Oscar Pistorius is a South African citizen, born on 22 November 1986 without fibula bones in his legs. At the age of eleven months his legs were amputated below his knees. Since then Mr Pistorius has run, walked and undertaken many other physical activities using prosthetic lower limbs, and he will continue to do so for the rest of his life.
30. Nevertheless, sport has dominated his life. During his time at school, Mr Pistorius competed in a number of different sports, including rugby, water polo, tennis and wrestling. During the hearing he stated that he had never thought of himself as being "disabled". He has no recollection of having his own natural legs. At the hearing, the IAAF's counsel described him as *a great athlete, an inspiring athlete.*

---

[2] In fact the title of the second list was Issues to be discussed.

31. Mr Pistorius began running competitively in January 2004 when, after seriously injuring his knee on the rugby field, he took up sprinting as part of his rehabilitation programme.
32. For participation in sporting activities Mr Pistorius uses a prosthesis known as the *Cheetah Flex-Foot,* supplied by a company headquartered in Iceland, Ossur HF ("Ossur"). The *Cheetah Flex-Foot* is designed for single and double transtibial (below-the-knee) and transfemoral (above-the-knee) amputees who intend to run at recreational and/or competitive levels. It has been used by many single and double amputees, almost unchanged, since 1997.
33. In 2004, only a few months after he started running competitively, Mr Pistorius competed in the Athens Paralympics, where he won the Gold Medal in the 200-metre event and the Bronze medal in the 100-metre event. At the time of this appeal process he is the paralympic world-record holder at 100, 200 and 400 metres.
34. In 2004 Mr Pistorius also began to compete in IAAF-sanctioned events in South Africa alongside able-bodied athletes. He won a 100-metre open competition in Pretoria with a time of 11.51. In the following year he competed alongside able-bodied athletes in the South African Championship, in which he finished sixth in the 400 metre event.
35. In 2005 Mr Pistorius began to receive invitations to participate in IAAF international track events overseas. He was invited to compete in an IAAF-sanctioned international event in Helsinki in that year. However, he decided not to participate in that event, preferring to finish his secondary education and to train further before participating in IAAF international level competitions. For approximately a couple of years he concentrated on completing his education and continuing with his training in athletics.
36. In early 2007 Mr Pistorius returned to competitive sprinting, and in March of that year he finished in second place in the South African Championships 400-metre event with a time of 46.56.
37. On 26 March 2007, the IAAF Council met in Mombassa, Kenya and decided to introduce an amendment to IAAF Rule 144.2 for the purpose of regulating the use of technical devices. The new rule prohibits:
(e) Use of any technical device that incorporates springs, wheels or any other element that provides the user with an advantage over another athlete not using such a device.
38. In the Spring of 2007 Mr Pistorius received an invitation to participate in the Norwich Union Glasgow Grand Prix, which was to be held on 3 June 2007. However, this invitation was subsequently withdrawn following intervention by the IAAF.
39. On 15 June 2007, at a press conference during the first 2007 Golden League meeting in Oslo, the IAAF President, when asked about the eligibility of Mr Pistorius, stated that he would not be excluded unless the IAAF received scientific evidence demonstrating that his prosthesis gave him an advantage. He was therefore considered eligible to compete at that time.

The Rome Observations

40. On 25 June 2007, Mr Pistorius received an invitation to participate in the Golden Gala event in Rome on 13 July 2007, where he ran in a specially staged "B" race which the IAAF arranged to be videotaped by an Italian sports laboratory using several high-definition cameras from different angles. He finished in second place, and the video subsequently became an exhibit in this appeal.
41. For a non-scientific observer, the video appears to show that Mr Pistorius was slower than other runners off the starting blocks, during the acceleration phase (approximately the first 50 metres) and running around the first bend, but faster over the "back straight". The split times of the race provided by the IAAF confirmed this observation. The able-bodied sprinters ran their fastest 100 metre splits in the first and second 100 metres, but Mr Pistorius ran his fastest 100 metre splits in the second and third 100 metres.
42. The initial scientific analysis of the videotapes by the Italian laboratory indicated that neither Mr Pistorius' stride-length, nor the length of time that his prosthesis was in contact with the ground, was significantly different from those of the other runners.

The Cologne Tests

43. The IAAF official who had been given responsibility by the President of the IAAF to evaluate whether Mr Pistorius' prostheses contravened the new Rule 144.2(e) was Dr Elio Locatelli,whose testimony was heard by the Panel. As noted above the Rome observations, and the subsequent analysis of them, produced some results that were unexpected by Dr Locatelli and were, overall, inconclusive.

44. In order to take the evaluation further Dr Locatelli asked Professor Peter Brüggemann at the Institute of Biomechanics and Orthopaedics at the German Sport University in Cologne if he could conduct a biomechanical study to demonstrate whether or not Mr Pistorius' prosthetic limbs gave him an advantage over other athletes. Prof. Brüggemann confirmed that he could undertake such a study, and on 24 July 2007 Mr Pistorius agreed to participate in the tests.

45. Prof. Brüggemann prepared a "testing protocol" based on instructions given to him by the IAAF in email correspondence, and conversations primarily by telephone. In summary, the tests were designed to evaluate Mr Pistorius' sprint movement using an inverse dynamic approach and also to study Mr Pistorius' oxygen intake and blood lactate metabolism over a 400-metre race simulation.

46. On 31 October 2007 Prof Brüggemann contacted the IAAF to propose some revisions to the testing protocol. Essentially, these were to replace his initial proposal to carry out certain tests on a treadmill with other tests on a static exercise bicycle, because he had been informed that running fast on a treadmill, even with handrails, might be dangerous for Mr Pistorius.

47. The tests were conducted in Cologne over two days, on 12 and 13 November 2007. Mr Pistorius was accompanied by his agent, Mr Peet van Zyl, and Mr Knut Lechler, who was associated with Ossur.

48. On 12 November 2007 Mr Pistorius and five "control" athletes of similar sprinting ability to him ran a sub-maximal 400-metre race on an outdoor track, followed by a series of maximal and sub-maximal sprints on a 100-metre track at the laboratory of the Institute. VO2 consumption measurements were taken and blood lactate levels were recorded.

49. On 13 November 2007, anthropometric measures were conducted on all the participants using a 3D body scanner. The prostheses were measured using a materials testing machine. Two further tests were carried out, on an exercise bicycle, to measure the metabolic capacity of the athletes.

The Cologne Report

50. Prof Brüggemann and his colleagues Messrs Arampatzis and Emrich issued the Cologne Report on 15 December 2007. The abstract of the Report contained the following conclusory passage:

The hypothesis that the transtibial amputee's metabolic capacity is higher than that of the healthy counterparts was rejected. The metabolic tests indicated a lower aerobic capacity of the amputee than of the controls. In the 400 m race the handicapped athlete's VO2 uptake was 25% lower than the oxygen consumption of the sound controls, which achieved about the same final time. The joint kinetics of the ankle joints of the sound legs and the "artificial ankle joint" of the prosthesis were found to be significantly decent. Energy return was clearly higher in the prostheses than in the human ankle joints, The kinetics of knee and hip joints were also affected by the prostheses during stance. The swing phase did not demonstrate any advantages for the natural legs in relation with artificial limbs. In total the double transtibial amputee received significant biomechanical advantages by the prosthesis in comparison to sprinting with natural human legs. The hypothesis that the prostheses lead to biomechanical disadvantages was rejected. Finally it was shown that fast running with the dedicated Cheetah prosthesis is a different kind of locomotion than sprinting with natural human legs. The "bouncing" locomotion is related to lower metabolic cost.

The IAAF Council's Decision no. 2008/01

51. On 14 January 2008, the IAAF Council issued a Decision which included the following findings:

"*a. running with these prostheses requires a less-important vertical movement associated with a lesser mechanical effort to raise the body,*" and

"*b. the energy loss resulting from the use of these prostheses is significantly lower than that resulting from a human ankle joint at a maximal sprint speed.*"

Based on these findings the IAAF ruled that the *Cheetah Flex-Foot* prosthetics used by Mr Pistorius were to be considered as a *technical device that incorporates springs,* wheels or any other element that provides the user with an advantage over valid athletes, and therefore contravened Rule 144.2(e).

52. Mr Pistorius was thus declared ineligible to compete in IAAF-sanctioned events with immediate effect. He delivered his Statement of Appeal to the CAS on 13 February 2008.

C. THE ISSUES TO BE DETERMINED

53. The issues raised by Mr Pistorius in his appeal may be categorised under four general headings:

i. Did the IAAF Council exceed its jurisdiction in taking the IAAF Decision?
ii. Was the process leading to the IAAF Decision procedurally unsound?
iii. Was the IAAF Decision unlawfully discriminatory?
iv. Was the IAAF Decision wrong in determining that Mr Pistorius' use of the *Cheetah Flex-Foot* device contravenes Rule 144.2(e)?

D. THE PANEL'S ANALYSIS

54. The Panel considers that there is no need to set out the submissions of the Parties *in extenso,* or to quote long extracts *verbatim.* They are contained in the Parties' Briefs and can be read in those documents. The Panel also considers that it would be inappropriate to attempt to summarise the Parties' submissions, since many of them comprise complex scientific material that is not susceptible to reduction to summary form. Instead, the Panel provides references to the Parties' submissions by using footnotes where appropriate.

55. Mr Pistorius' counsel abandoned the jurisdictional objection (Issue (i)) at a late stage in the hearing. The Panel now considers issues (ii), (iii) and (iv) in turn.

Issue (ii). Was the process leading to the IAAF Council's Decision no. 2008/01 procedurally unsound?

56. The events leading to the IAAF Decision began with the Council's adoption of the new Rule 144.2(e) on 26 March 2007 at its meeting in Mombasa, Kenya. The Panel found unconvincing Mr Davies' testimony that the introduction of this new Rule was aimed primarily at the use of spring technology in running shoes. There was evidence that the problems with running shoes had been around for some time, and were dealt with both before and after March 2007 without any need for a new Rule. Indeed, as the IAAF pointed out at the hearing, Rule 143.2 prohibits shoes that gives an athlete any unfair additional assistance including by the incorporation of any technology which will give the wearer an "unfair advantage".

57. The Panel considers it likely that the new Rule was introduced with Mr Pistorius in mind, and that it started the process that led to IAAF declaring him ineligible to compete in IAAF-sanctioned events in January 2008.

58. The next significant event was the filming of Mr Pistorius during the staged "B" race in Rome on 13 July 2007. The Panel finds nothing wrong with this. It appears to have been a *bona fide* exercise primarily designed to check whether Mr Pistorius' stride-length was greater than that of other athletes who ran comparable times in competition.

59. Then the IAAF decided to investigate further by retaining the Cologne Institute to carry out biomechanical and metabolic tests, and to submit a report on whether Mr Pistorius' prostheses gave him an advantage over other athletes. As stated above, Mr Pistorius agreed to participate in these tests.

60. At this stage, in the Panel's view, the process began to go "off the rails". The correspondence between the IAAF and Prof. Brüggemann shows that his instructions were to carry out the testing only when Mr Pistorius was running in a straight line after the acceleration phase. By the time that the IAAF commissioned the Cologne tests it was known that this was the part of the race in which Mr Pistorius usually ran at his fastest.

61. Having viewed the Rome Observations, including the videotape that was shown to the Panel, the IAAF's officials must have known that, by excluding the start and the acceleration phase, the results would create a distorted view of Mr Pistorius' advantages and/or disadvantages by not considering the effect of the device on the performance of Mr Pistorius over the entire race. The Panel considers that this factor calls into question the validity and relevance of the test results on which the Cologne Report was based. The Panel emphasises that there is no reason to believe that this was Prof. Brüggemann's responsibility. At the hearing, Prof. Brüggemann made it clear that he did not believe that his mandate was to determine all of the advantages and disadvantages of running with the *Cheetah Flex-Foot* prosthesis. It was to determine whether or not it provided an advantage on the measures he was asked to undertake. It follows, in the view of the Panel, that the Cologne Report does not answer the question that the Panel is required to decide. This is not the fault of Prof. Brüggemann, whom the Panel regards as a scientist having expertise and integrity. It originates from the mission he was given by the IAAF.

62. The story is not enhanced by the fact that Dr. Robert Gailey, the scientist nominated by Mr Pistorius, and Ossur, to participate in the Cologne testing,[3] was effectively "frozen out" to such an extent that he declined to attend the Cologne tests. He was informed that he would be allowed to attend only as an observer, with no input on the testing protocol or on the analysis that would be made subsequently by Prof. Brüggemann's team.

63. In fact, Dr Gailey's electronic letter of 29 October 2007 to Dr Locatelli, in which he set out a number of questions and suggestions directly relating to the testing protocol, was not only ignored by the IAAF, but was also not shown to Prof. Brüggemann.[4] Indeed, Prof. Brüggemann testified that he was not aware of Dr Galley's potential involvement, or the questions and suggestions that he had made in relation to the testing protocol.

64. Other elements of the process also give rise to concern. Following receipt of the Cologne Report, Mr Pistorius was given less than a month to respond to its findings. On 11 January 2008, the IAAF provided to its Council a summary of the Cologne Report prepared by the IAAF's own officials, and Mr Pistorius' letter in reply to the Report, which in effect stated that it would take time to produce a considered scientific response. The IAAF Council members were not sent any potentially relevant scientific studies, or indeed any of the other materials that had been produced during the IAAF investigation concerning Mr Pistorius.

65. Even more troubling, it emerged during the hearing that the IAAF's brief summary of the Cologne Report as communicated to its Council members was not approved by Prof. Brüggemann. When the Panel showed Prof. Brüggemann the summary during his testimony, he stated that he had not seen it before, and he was invited to take it away and comment on it later during the hearing. He later acknowledged that the summary as presented to Council members was not wholly accurate; in particular, certain percentages were stated incorrectly.

66. Further more, the Panel was not impressed by the fact that, on an important issue such as the eligibility of an athlete to compete in international events, the voting procedure, and the subsequent announcement of the result, can only be described as less than perfect. The document sent to Council members over the IAAF President's signature was despatched on a Friday (11 January 2008) with a request that the votes should be returned by the following Monday morning (14 January 2008). It comes as no great surprise that only 14 of the 27 Council members had returned their votes by the initial deadline, which was then extended.

---

[3] Dr Robert Gailey, University of Miami School of Medicine, who stated in his letter: "..... *where we feel our combined 30 years of experience with amputee track athletes would be of service is in the analysis and interpretation of the data after it is processed. As you know, motion analysis data interpretation can be somewhat subjective and knowledge of extraneous variables can assist with reaching informed conclusions.*"

[4] Brüggemann testimony 30 April 2008 at about 5.30pm.

67. The Panel also considers the technique specified by the IAAF in the voting papers, which stated that abstentions would be counted as positive votes to declare Mr Pistorius ineligible, was not a satisfactory method of justifying the FIAA's press statement to the effect that the decision was made by the Council *unanimously.*

68. The impression of prejudgment is also enhanced by the fact that Dr Locatelli and other IAAF officials told the press *before the vote was taken* that Mr Pistorius would be banned from IAAF-sanctioned events.

69. In summary, the Panel's impression is that, notwithstanding the IAAF's dignified and appropriate press statement in the Summer of 2007 from the highest levels of the Federation, by November of that year at least some IAAF officials had determined that they did not want Mr Pistorius to be acknowledged as eligible to compete in international IAAF-sanctioned events, regardless of the results that properly conducted scientific studies might demonstrate.

70. In the Panel's view, the manner in which the IAAF handled the situation of Mr Pistorius in the period from July 2007 to January 2008 fell short of the high standards that the international sporting community is entitled to expect from a federation such as the IAAF.

71. However, this conclusion makes little difference, if any, to the outcome of the appeal. As the IAAF's counsel rightly pointed out, this appeal is a *de novo* process. The merits of the issues are to be investigated, in a judicial manner, on the evidence and submissions presented to the Panel during the appellate process.

Issue (iii). Was the IAAF Council's Decision unlawfully discriminatory?

72. Mr Pistorius claims that the IAAF Decision is in breach of its obligation of nondiscrimination, because it did not search for an appropriate accommodation as required by law. He claims that, in finding Mr Pistorius ineligible in all IAAF-sanctioned events without attempting to seek any alternative solution, modification or adjustment that might permit him to participate in such events on an equal basis with all able-bodied athletes, the IAAF has denied Mr Pistorius his fundamental human rights, including equal access to Olympic principles and values.

73. Disputes arising under the IAAF Rules shall be resolved in accordance with the provisions of the Rules. The Parties agree that the law applicable to substantive issues is the law of Monaco, as the law governing the IAAF Constitution pursuant to its Article 16.

74. The Convention on the Rights of Persons with Disabilities and its Optional Protocol (the "Convention") was adopted on 13 December 2006 at the UN Headquarters in New York, and was opened for signature on 30 March 2007. It came into force according to its terms (Art.45), thirty days after the twentieth ratification was deposited, on 3 May 2008.

75. Signing a Convention may create an obligation, in the period between signing and ratification, to refrain from acts that would defeat the object and purpose of the treaty. Ratification is an action taken by States that signal an intention to undertake legal rights and obligations contained in the Convention or the Optional Protocol. None of these actions have been taken by the Principality of Monaco, and the UN Convention has not been enacted in its Law.

76. Furthermore, the Convention would not be engaged in the circumstances of this appeal. By way of example, Article 30.5 provides that Contracting State shall encourage and promote the participation of persons with disabilities in mainstream sporting activities at all levels with a view to enabling them to participate on an *equal basis* to sporting activities.

77. In other words, disability laws only require that an athlete such as Mr Pistorius be permitted to compete on the same footing as others. This is precisely the issue to be decided by this Panel: that is, whether or not Mr Pistorius is competing on an equal basis with other athletes not using *Cheetah Flex-Foot* prostheses. As counsel for the IAAF rightly mentioned, if this Panel finds that Mr Pistorius' Cheetah Flex-Foot prostheses provide no advantage to Mr Pistorius, he will be able to compete on an equal basis with other athletes. If the Panel concludes that Mr Pistorius does gain an advantage, the Convention would not assist his case.

78. Mr Pistorius' submission based on unlawful discrimination is accordingly rejected.

Issue (iv). Was the IAAF Council's Decision wrong in determining that Mr Pistorius' use of the Cheetah Flex-Foot device contravenes Rule 144.2(e)?

79. The Panel's point of departure for this part of the analysis is Rule 144.2(e), adopted by the IAAF's Council at its meeting in Mombasa, Kenya on 26 March 2007. As stated above, it reads as follows:

"*For the purposes of this Rule, the following shall be considered assistance, and are therefore not allowed:*

[...]

(e) Use of any technical device that incorporates springs, wheels, or any other element that provides the user with an advantage over another athlete not using such a device."

80. Without implying any criticism of the draftsman, who faced an extraordinarily difficult task, the Panel considers that this provision is a masterpiece of ambiguity. What constitutes a *technical device?* For the purposes of the present enquiry, the Panel is prepared to assume that a passive prosthetic such as the *Cheetah Flex-Foot* is to be considered as a "technical device", even though this proposition may not be wholly free from doubt.

81. What constitutes a device that *incorporates springs?* Technically, almost every non-brittle material object is a "spring" in the sense that it has elasticity. Certainly the *Cheetah Flex-Foot* is a "spring", but does it *incorporate* a "spring"? A natural human leg is itself a "spring".

82. Then there is the critical question of the meaning of an *advantage ... over another athlete. It* was urged on the Panel by the IAAF's counsel that the ordinary and natural meaning of the word *advantage* is absolute, in the sense that if a *technical device* is used, and is determined (presumably by an appropriate and fair process) to provide an athlete with any *advantage,* however small, in any part of a competition, that device must render that athlete ineligible to compete regardless of any compensating disadvantages.

83. The Panel does not accept this proposition. Of course, athletes should not be forced to compete against persons who use powered aids such as motors, wheels, springs (as in "pogo sticks", for example), or other active propulsive devices. This is not in doubt, and interpreted in this way the new Rule 144.2(e) is a sensible and appropriate rule. But to propose that a passive device such as the *Cheetah Flex-Foot* as used by Mr Pistorius should be classified as contravening that Rule without convincing scientific proof that it provides him with *an overall net advantage* over other athletes flies in the face of both legal principle and commonsense. The rule specifically prohibits a technical device that ... *provides the user with an advantage over an athlete not using that device.* If the use of the device provides more disadvantages than advantages, then it cannot reasonably be said to provide an advantage over other athletes, because the user is actually at a competitive disadvantage. That is the only sensible reading of the teems of Rule 144.2(e).

84. The Panel notes that this interpretation of Rule 144.2(e) was effectively adopted by Dr Locatelli of the IAAF in his testimony at the hearing, when he said that the rule would not prohibit Mr Pistorius from running in 100-metre or 200-metre races. Dr Locatelli said that such distances did not allow Mr Pistorius to catch up from his slower start. Thus, Dr Locatelli focused on the overall effect of the prosthesis and not on whether Mr Pistorius had an advantage at only one point in the race.

85. Unfortunately, as Prof. Brüggemann made clear during the hearing, the IAAF did not ask him to determine whether or not Mr Pistorius' use of the *Cheetah Flex-Foot* prosthesis provided him with an overall net advantage or disadvantage. The Cologne Report therefore does not address the central question that the Panel is required to answer in this appeal.

Burden and Standard of Proof

86. This leads the analysis into the question of proof. The IAAF rightly accepted the *burden* of proof. No further discussion of this aspect is required. However, the Parties were not agreed on the *standard* of proof to be applied. It clearly is not the "beyond reasonable doubt" standard applicable in criminal cases in most jurisdictions; nor, in the Panel's view, can it be any of the possible intermediate standards that are discussed from time to time in connection with the disciplinary processes of, for example, professional bodies or regulatory bodies.

87. It is to be emphasised that this appeal does not concern any disciplinary element. No-one involved in the matter has suggested at any time that the predicament of Mr Pistorius is a disciplinary matter. The Panel agrees with the IAAF that the applicable standard is the "balance of probability".

The Panel's Assessment of the Evidence

88. The Panel took away from this proceeding a feeling of great respect for all the experts, and appreciated their efforts to educate its members on matters of considerable scientific complexity. The Panel particularly appreciates the spirit of co-operation and mutual respect with which they entered into the expert conferencing procedure proposed by the Panel and accepted by the Parties. The opening paragraph of the Points of Agreement by Drs Brüggemann, Potthast, Herr and Kram is instructive in this connection:
In general the scientific teams from both Cologne and Houston have a mutual trust in the scientific integrity of each other.

89. There were areas of genuine agreement, and areas of genuine disagreement. As noted above, the Panel should not here try to summarise here all of the extensive scientific evidence presented by these experts. However, it is useful to understand their basic findings and the contentions of the Parties that are based on them.

90. As shown in the quotation above from the abstract to the Cologne Report, and as stated in the IAAF Decision, the finding of an advantage in using the *Cheetah Flex-Foot* prosthesis comes principally from two elements of the Cologne Report: First, Mr Pistorius, in using the device, does not have as much vertical force with each step; in other words, he runs in a flatter manner than able-bodied runners. All the experts agreed that these measurements were valid. Second, Mr Pistorius uses less metabolic energy in running, perhaps as a result of that flatter running. These test results were challenged.

91. The experts presented by Mr Pistorius conducted their own tests on him and on able-bodied athletes as controls at a laboratory in Houston in February 2008 (the "Houston Report"). Among other things, tests set out in the Houston Report found that Mr Pistorius used the same oxygen amounts as able-bodied runners at a sub-maximal running speed, and thus did not have a metabolic advantage. Other tests also showed that Mr. Pistorius fatigued normally. Again, the experts agreed that these test results were valid. The Houston Report also tested the amount of energy loss from the *Cheetah Flex-Foot* prosthesis against the intact human leg, which includes tendons and other elements that generate positive energy (and which, for obvious reasons, an amputated athlete would not have). It is common ground that the Cologne Report did not measure any of these elements.

92. In summary, the Panel determines that the IAAF has not met its "on the balance of probability" burden of proof that Rule 144.2(e) is contravened by Mr Pistorius' use of the *Cheetah Flex Foot* prosthesis for several reasons. First, as noted above, a violation would only occur if the user of the prosthesis gained an *overall net advantage* over other runners, and the IAAF did not ask Prof. Brüggemann and his colleagues to make that determination. The terms of reference put to Prof. Brüggemann and his team by the IAAF did not propose the appropriate question.

93. The testing protocol that he prepared for the purposes of writing the Cologne Report, on the basis of his instructions from the IAAF, was not designed to provide a scientific opinion as to whether Mr Pistorius' *Cheetah Flex-Foot* prosthesis provided him with an overall net advantage over other athletes not using such devices. The point was stated clearly by Dr Locatelli in one of his press interviews, when he said "*... we are looking for advantages, not for disadvantages*". The experts also agreed at the hearing that "*neither the Cologne nor Houston studies have quantified all of the possible advantages or disadvantages of Mr Pistorius in a 400m race*".

94. Secondly, the Panel is not persuaded that there is sufficient evidence of any metabolic advantage in favour of a double amputee using the *Cheetah Flex-Foot.* Certainly, the evidence presented in the Cologne Report is not capable of satisfying the burden of proof that is acknowledged by the IAAF. The IAAF seemed to recognize this fact at the hearing as it focused on the biomechanical aspects of the Cologne Report, and it

acknowledged that most of the metabolic findings, including its blood lactate measurements, were not conclusive.

95. Similarly, the IAAF has not proven the other basis of the IAAF Decision: namely that the biomechanical effects of using the particular prosthetic device give Mr Pistorius an advantage over other athletes not using the device. In the last conferencing session among the experts and the Panel, the experts accepted that comparisons between the effective energy that can be used to increase the speed of sprinters using natural legs and prosthetic legs cannot be treated as providing definitive conclusions in the light of current scientific knowledge. They could not opine with certainty that the conflicting hypotheses they were advancing were indeed more than unprovable hypotheses. In particular, the scientists do not know if the fact that able-bodied runners create more vertical force than Mr. Pistorius is an advantage or disadvantage. There is at least some scientific evidence that sprinters, including 400m runners, train themselves to bounce more (ie, to use more vertical force) because it creates more speed. Thus, the Cologne Report's finding, on which the IAAF Decision relied, that Mr Pistorius uses less vertical force and runs in a flatter manner may be a *disadvantage* rather than *an advantage.*

96. In addition, while the Cologne Report found less energy loss in the *Cheetah Flex-Foot* prosthesis than in the human ankle, the scientific experts all agreed that the energy "lost" in the ankle could be transferred elsewhere in the body, through tendons, ligaments and muscles etc, because the human body does not like to lose energy. They agreed that that such a transfer cannot be properly measured or currently understood. Thus, based on current scientific knowledge, it appears to be impracticable to assess definitively whether the *Cheetah Flex-Foot* prosthesis acts as more than, or less than, the human ankle and lower leg, in terms of "spring-like" quality.

97. Moreover, the scientific experts agreed that a "*mechanical advantage provided by a prosthetic leg would be expected to lead to a metabolic advantage for a runner*". As noted above, neither the Cologne Report nor the Houston Report showed such a metabolic advantage.

98. In the light of the Panel's analysis of the facts, the scientific expert opinions and the legal principles involved, the Panel has no doubt in finding that the IAAF has failed to satisfy the burden of proof that it accepts. It follows that Mr Pistorius' appeal must be upheld.

99. The Panel is re-inforced in reaching this conclusion by the fact that the *Cheetah Flex-Foot* prosthesis has been in use for a decade, and yet no other runner using them – either a single amputee or a double amputee – has run times fast enough to compete effectively against able-bodied runners until Mr Pistorius has done so. In effect, these prior performances by other runners using the prosthesis act as a control for study of the benefits of the prosthesis and demonstrate that even if the prosthesis provided an advantage, and as noted none has been proven, it may be quite limited.

100. The consequence of this ruling by the Panel is that the IAAF Council's Decision 2008/O 1 of 14 January 2008 is revoked with immediate effect, and Mr Pistorius is currently eligible to compete in IAAF-sanctioned events.

101. However, it is important to clarify what the result of this appeal does *not* decide.

102. First, the Panel's decision applies to Mr Pistorius while using the particular model of Cheetah Flex-Foot prosthesis that was the subject of the Cologne tests and shown to the Panel as exhibits during the hearing in Lausanne. It is not a general licence for Mr Pistorius to use any further developments of the *Cheetah Flex-Foot* that might be found to provide him with an overall net advantage.

103. Secondly, the Panel does not exclude the possibility that, with future advances in scientific knowledge, and a testing regime designed and carried out to the satisfaction of both Parties, the IAAF might in the future be in a position to prove that the existing *Cheetah Flex-Foot* model provides Mr Pistorius with an overall net advantage over other athletes.

104. Thirdly, the Panel's decision in this appeal has absolutely no application to any other athlete, or other type of prosthetic limb. Each case must be considered by the IAAF on its own merits. The ruling does not grant a blanket licence to other single or double amputees to compete in IAAF-sanctioned events using *Cheetah Flex-Foot* prosthetics, or indeed any other type of prosthesis. Each amputee athlete must collaborate with the IAAF

to have his or her eligibility under Rule 144.2(e), as interpreted by this Panel, established on an individual basis. The Panel hopes that this will not impose a substantial new burden on the IAAF, because of the unique nature of Mr Pistorius' case. However, if it does create an additional burden, it must be viewed as just one of the challenges of 21st Century life.

F. COSTS

105. The CAS Code, Article R64.5 provides that the award should determine which party shall bear the arbitration costs, or in which proportion the Parties should share the costs. As a general rule, the award grants to the prevailing party a contribution towards its legal fees and other expenses incurred in connection with the proceedings, and, in particular, the costs of witnesses, interpreters and other similar expenses. The Panel takes into account both the outcome of the proceedings as well as the conduct and financial resources of the parties in making an order for contribution.

106. However, in this case neither party seeks an order for costs. Therefore, the Panel decides to make no order. Each party will bear its own costs. The CAS Court Office shall retain the CH 500 registration fee paid by Mr Pistorius.

ON THESE GROUNDS
The Court of Arbitration for Sport rules that:

1. The IAAF having failed to satisfy the applicable burden of proof that it expressly acknowledged, the appeal filed by Oscar Pistorius on 13 February 2008 must be upheld.
2. Accordingly, the IAAF Council's Decision no. 2008/1 of 14 January 2008 is revoked with immediate effect, and the athlete is currently eligible to compete in IAAF-sanctioned events while wearing the Ossur *Cheetah Flex-Foot* prosthesis model as used in the Cologne tests and presented as an exhibit at the Hearing of this appeal.
3. It is emphasised that the scope of application of this Ruling is limited to the eligibility of Mr Pistorius only and, also, only to his use of the specific prostheses in issue in this appeal.
4. It follows that this Ruling has no application to the eligibility of any other amputee athletes, or to any other model of prosthetic limb; and it is the IAAF's responsibility to review the circumstances on a case-by-case basis, impartially, in the context of up-to-date scientific knowledge at the time of such review.
5. No order is made as to costs, except that the CAS shall retain the Court Office fee of CHF 500 paid by the Appellant at the outset of this arbitration.

THE COURT OF ARBITRATION FOR SPORT
President: Professor Martin Hunter
Done at Lausanne, Switzerland on 4 May 2008.

APPENDIX XXIII

LEX SPORTIVA AND *LEX MERCATORIA*[5]

Boris Kolev[6]

The idea about the emergence of "world law" is recently gaining popularity within the legal science. A definition of the term "world law" is given by Harold Berman – a prominent professor from Harward University and currently a chairman of the World Law Institute of the Emory University in Atlanta, Georgia. According to Berman by "world law" is meant the common features of the legal systems of the world, and especially the body of customary law that is gradually being created by the people of the world in their transnational interrelationships. Included are many aspects of world economic law, such as bankers' letters of credit, negotiable instruments, and documentary trade terms. Included also inter alia is the world sports law enforced by the Court of Arbitration of Sport in Lausanne, Switzerland, and emerged in result of the uniform application and interpretation of legal rules in sport due to the activity of CAS.[7]

The world sports law, currently referred to as *Lex Sportiva,* is deemed to be an autonomous body of rules having anational character. The concept of *Lex Sportiva* draws an analogy with the concept of *Lex Mercatoria* (the law merchant) as an anational legal system. This article makes a comparison between the historical developments of *Lex Mercatoria* as presented in the book of Harold J. Berman, Law and Revolution: The Formation of the Western Legal Tradition, on the one hand, and *Lex Sportiva*, on the other hand. This comparison is considered, in author's opinion, very useful for illustration of the legal situation, in which sport has found itself to be nowadays, could provide some clues for the future of the sport governance and could be helpful for the analysis of the alternative models of the future legal development in sport.

Some similarities in the genesis of *Lex Mercatoria* and *Lex Sportiva* may be outlined:

1. The formative period of *Lex Mercatoria* was according to Berman the late eleventh and twelfth centuries[8]. Necessary condition precedent for its development was the formation of a merchant class, a community of merchants, which number significantly grew during the said centuries. *From the second half of 20th century onward due to factors like development of television and other broadcasting means and the followed commercialization of sport, the latter was transformed from one purely leisure and recreational activity into professional activity capable to provide enough funds for the living of its practitioners. In result, a large number of professional sportsmen emerged and is still growing. Consolidation of the sport movement worldwide made for the formation of a community – the world community of sportsmen.*
2. "Initial development of law merchant was left largely, though not entirely, to the merchant themselves, who organized international fairs and markets, formed mercantile courts, and established mercantile offices in the new urban communities that were springing up throughout western Europe."[9] *The initial development of international sports law is also attributed to the rules created by sport federations, formed by sportsmen and sport clubs and enjoying the autonomy of sport. Member associations of FIFA, for instance, are more than member of the United Nations as FIFA officials usually boast. The consolidated sport movement established in 1984 their own institution to settle the sport related disputes – the based in Luisanna, Switzerland*

[5] Kolev, Boris, 'Lex Sportiva and Lex Mercatoria', ISLJ 2008-1/2, at pp. 57-62.

[6] The author is Co-chairman of the NGO Bulgarian Legal Society, which conduct research on the rights of sportsmen, Member of the Advisory Board of the ISLJ.

[7] Harold J. Berman, Epilogue: An Ecumenical Christian Jurisprudence, Internet Publication, available at the time of writing at http://www.argobooks.org/berman/ecumenical-christian-jurisprudence.html, abstract.

[8] Harold J. Berman, Law and Revolution: *The Formation of the Western Legal Tradition*, Harvard University Press 1983, p. 332.

[9] Id., at p. 340.

Court of Arbitration for Sport. However, with the commercialization of sport, sport was necessary to fall within some form of legal scrutiny to guarantee the fair result of the application of sporting rules in the cases where these rules trigger economic implications.

3. Uniformity of *Lex Mercatoria* across the countries was not achieved at once but was part of a gradual process. As Berman put it, however, "the differences among countries and localities in the law and custom applicable to mercantile transactions were differences of detail or in the words of William Mitchell citing also by Berman "everywhere the leading principles and the most important rules were the same, or tended to become the same"[10]. *The current situation in football within the EU very much resembles the process towards uniformity of Lex Mercatoria across the then countries. Number of states adopted interventionist approach sometimes complying and sometimes conflicting the sport rules developed by FIFA and national associations. Whether the differences are of detail should be judged on a case by case basis.*
4. In addition to the discriminatory treatment under local laws Berman indicates as a fear experienced by the merchants at that time the "rapacity" of local taxing authorities towards them[11]. *Nowadays, the right of the states to levy taxes at their discretion is undisputable and its limits are specified through bilateral or multilateral agreements between states. Fear of heavy taxation of the income from sporting activity is still among the considerations, which players take into account while choosing their clubs.*
5. In the formative era of *Lex Mercatoria* the system of law merchant co-existed with the system of canon law, the law of the church. Cannon law provided for ecclesiastical jurisdiction in certain matters including mercantile cases, which met the opposition of merchants. As an example of this resistance was the decree issued in 1369 by the Doge and Council of Alderman of the city of Genoa imposing a substantial fine on any person who had recourse to an ecclesiastical or other court claiming incompatibility of certain conduct with canon law. Despite of the claims of the church to have jurisdiction over mercantile cases it did not deny merchants their relative autonomy[12]. *Likewise, the system of Lex Sportiva coexists with the system of the EU law. The EU law claims its right to intervene in sport when matters such as mobility and competition are involved. During long period of time sport world was resisting any involvement of the EU law and the law in general in sport issues and athletes used to be threaten with punishment if decide to refer to the ordinary courts. Recently in football, although officially recourse to court system was not denied, in practice the same result was achieved through influence over players. After starting the battle against the transfer system in football, neither club wanted to establish any contacts with Jean-Marc Bosman, who was for the whole world of football at that time a sort of "persona non grata"*[13]. *If similar measures of influence do not produce the desired effect, there is still an option available – football officials could buy off the interest in the potential lawsuit so that the claim is never tried before a court. Football rulers further rely on their own dispute settlement mechanisms including recourse to CAS in order to keep the relationships in football beyond the scope of any publicly made law either national or supranational. Recently, after failure of the idea to establish a court of arbitration for football, UEFA decided to accept the jurisdiction of CAS on civil law disputes and to avoid recourse to ordinary courts of law this way.*[14]
6. Principles and concepts of the cannon law supported by the new at that time Romanist legal science were taken over with some modifications by the mercantile law[15]. *Similarly nowadays, CAS relies on the principles and concepts developed by the European Court of Justice in sport related cases as well as on the general principles and concepts developed by the contemporary legal science.*

---

[10] Id., at p. 343.

[11] Harold J. Berman, Law and Revolution: *The Formation of the Western Legal Tradition*, Harvard University Press 1983, p. 343.

[12] Id., at p. 345.

[13] Judgment in Bosman concludes in para. 37 that Mr. Bosman has been boycotted by all the European clubs which might have engaged him.

[14] Article 56 (2) UEFA Statutes.

[15] Id., at p. 339.

7. Merchants as members of the church were subject to the canon law, but as members of the mercantile community they were further subject to the law merchant. In case of conflict between the two bodies of law it was not clear which would prevail and only time could mediate the conflict[16]. *Nowadays, sportsmen are subject to the EU law while moving from one Member state to another and sport associations and clubs as undertakings are subject to competition rules. At the same time they are subject to Lex Sportiva represented by the regulations and jurisprudence of sporting governing and dispute settlement bodies. It is still not clear in case of conflict which rules will prevail. Especially as regards the rules of competition certain exemption is given for the rules of purely sport interest but the borderline with the economic rule is still vague and only time will show which rules will pass successfully the EU law scrutiny.*
8. Commercial courts included special courts of markets and fairs consisted of judges elected among the members of the market or fair. The procedure was marked by speed and informality and justice was to be done while the merchants' feet were still dusty. Further, the court was to be ruled by equity with giving a right of a merchant to be heard, professional lawyers were generally excluded and also technical legal argumentation was frowned upon[17]. *During the modern Olympic Games a special ad hoc division of CAS operates, which is obliged to decide the disputes in extremely short time limits like, for instance, before the next stage of the competition or in other words from day to day. Members of this division of CAS might be also persons with high reputation in the sport world and sportsmen involved can be heard. The need for timely recovery of justice in sport is in paradoxical discrepancy vis-vis the duration of the procedure before the Court of Justice where sometimes the issuance of the decision takes around two years.*[18]
9. The participation of merchants in the resolution of mercantile disputes was seen by Berman not only as reflection of the principle of abstract justice, a legal ideal, contributing to the equitable solution of individual commercial cases, but also in negative aspect since it "helped to insulate commercial law from ecclesiastical, royal and even urban control and to preserve mercantile privileges"[19]. *Participatory adjudication of contemporary individual sport cases reveals the same negative aspect since it prevents sportsmen from having their disputes decided by national courts and thus preserves the privileged status of sport as occupation in comparison with other professions. On the other hand, exactly as in the case of mercantile law, this is also aspect of the relative autonomy of sport.*

The parallel between the formations of *Lex Mercatoria* and *Lex Sportiva* further shows some very important differences, as set out below:

1. The most important such difference lays in the moral, in the conscience of the then merchants and the present football rulers. As Berman stated "from the church's point of view, the law developed by the merchants to regulate their own interrelationships, the *Lex Mercatoria*, was supposed to reflect, not contradict, the canon law"[20]. Although merchants did disagree with that position of the church it was also indisputable from merchant's point of view that merchants were subordinated to the church in matters of moral. No such moral and conscience could be found in the rulers of the contemporary football as the most illustrative example of the contemporary sport. These rulers consider themselves to be above law and they do not respect any influence including such coming from judges.
2. Merchants were independent individuals united in a guild to protect their common interests. In the commercialized sport today and in particular in football, such common interest cannot be found. On the contrary, different and conflicting interests do exist – these are the interests of sport governing bodies, sponsors, media and broadcasters, sporting clubs and sportsmen.

---

[16] Id., at p. 345.

[17] Id., at p. 346-347.

[18] For instance the judgment of ECJ on the claim lodged by the Belgian club Sharleroi challenging the FIFA system for releasing players for participation in international matches is expected in 20 months starting at the time of writing of this paper.

[19] Harold J. Berman, Law and Revolution: *The Formation of the Western Legal Tradition*, Harvard University Press, p. 348

[20] Id, at p. 339.

Such areas of conflicts are, for example: release of the players for international matches – between the clubs and UEFA and FIFA; transfer system – between the clubs and the players; overburdened calendar of international and domestic football matches – between the players, on the one hand, and the governing bodies and sponsors, on the other hand; blocked hours for football transmissions – between national federations and TV broadcasters etc. In this complex situation rules in sport have to be drafted by an independent organization without financial interests, however, such organization does not exist in practice for the time being. That is why football players and clubs do not have any other remedies against the governing bodies in case of a conflicting rule affecting pervasively their interests instead of resorting to the national and supranational laws. With respect to *Lex Mercatoria* Berman stressed that "the integrity of the new system of mercantile law, that is, the structural coherence of its principles, concepts, rules, and procedures, derived primarily from the integrity and structural coherence of the mercantile community whose law it was"[21]. Although sportsmen formed a community, in fact, their voice is still not heard in the rule-making process. In other words *Lex Sportiva* cannot achieve the structural coherence, of which Berman spoke in the context of *Lex Mercatoria*, unless the rule-making in sport becomes a result of a transparent and democratic process representing, safeguarding and balancing the interests of all stakeholders.

3. *Lex Mercatoria* was a customary law "approved by the authority of all kingdoms and commonweals and not a law established by the sovereignty of any prince."[22] *Lex Sportiva* is a transnational law which is not approved by national states similarly to the EU law in order to have supremacy over national laws. From the point of view of national laws the rules of international sport organizations are rules established on the basis of freedom of association and therefore, constitute association law subordinated to the national law. This is the basic reason why national football authorities have found themselves in a "legal jungle" as to which acts they have to apply – the law of international federations, national law or the EU law.[23] CAS is not internationally recognized court, but simply arbitration system for dispute settlement, which awards are subject to the conditions for recognition and enforcement of arbitral awards. The matter is further complicated when the state apply interventionist approach and regulate sport in a diverse way.
4. One particularly important aspect of *Lex Sportiva* is vested in the fact that sportsmen are in most of the cases employees. Many national laws preclude labour disputes from being resolved by way of arbitration. The reason is that employees as the weaker party would not be at equal footing with the other party to the arbitration proceedings. Arbitration as a dispute resolution method is suitable in disputes between independent and equal positioned litigants such as independent merchants. *Lex Sportiva* is probably the first law which is trying to withdraw one typical relationship of subordination from the jurisdiction of the national state and regulate it differently.

The comparison of the historical development of *lex mercatoria* with the now arising *lex sportiva* might provide some clues as regards the future development of sports law and the harmonization of its principles world wide similarly to the uniformity achieved as regards the sporting rules of the "world" games as for example is football.

Many of the doctrines and principles of mercantile law are universally recognized and today constitute a part of the domestic law of every nation-state. Berman indicates as examples the rule that a negotiable bill of lading is a document of title through whose transfer the risk of loss or damage to goods in transit can be shifted to subpurchasers; or that a banker's letter of credit gives an exporter an absolute right of payment by the confirming bank upon his presentation of the appropriate shipping and other commercial documents[24]. Further, Berman speaks of a world law of mercantile

---

[21] Id., at p. 354.

[22] Gerard Malynes, Consuetudo vel Lex Mercatoria, or the Ancient Law Merchant (London, 1622), from the Preface, "To the Courteous Reader." as cited by Harold Berman, Law and Revolution.

[23] The expression "legal jungle" is used by Roberto Branco Martins in the Report on the Social Dialogue in European Football.

[24] Harold J. Berman, Epilogue: An Ecumenical Christian Jurisprudence, Internet Publication, available at the time of writing at http://www.argobooks.org/berman/ecumenical-christian-jurisprudence.html.

transactions "derived from the historically developing customs of the transnational community of merchants, bankers, carriers, underwriters, and their lawyers, who for centuries have constituted a world community of "friendly strangers," as Lon L. Fuller called them, held together by common traditions and common trust"[25]. Indeed, today's world community of merchants possesses its own law – *Lex Mercatoria* and their own arbitral courts to decide the disputes arisen within that community. In practice, disputes do not reach the national courts any longer.

Belonging to the international business community today's merchants consciously and voluntarily accept and observe the rules created by that community.

Many authors including Berman have supported the opinion that the rules of *Lex Mercatoria* may be applied only through the rules of national law, although *Lex Mercatoria* is "more than merely factual identity or uniformity between national systems"[26]. In France, for instance, Code of Civil Procedure provided that in arbitrations involving the interests of international commerce, the arbitrators apply the rules of law chosen by the parties and in case of absence of such a choice they may apply the rules they consider appropriate.[27] During the draft of the Swiss Law on Conflict of Laws the majority of the drafters agreed that *Lex Mercatoria* may be applied as a law with which the dispute has the closest connection[28].

In principal, arbitral tribunals could apply *Lex Mercatoria* in two ways, 1. either through application of a national law (whether explicitly chosen by the parties or on the basis of the conflict of laws rule), which has incorporated *Lex M*ercatoria or 2. through application of *Lex Mercatoria* itself as happened in the case Norsolor S.A. v. Pabalk for instance where "the arbitrators have applied the law designated by the conflict of laws rule, which they deemed appropriate, namely, the general principles of obligations generally applicable to international commerce[29]. Such general principles as good faith and commercial reasonableness are considered part of *Lex Mercatoria*. However, if *Lex Mercatoria* is not recognized as an autonomous body of law under the national law, arbitrators could be deemed of acting *ex aequo et bono* without authorization by the parties and the awards are threaten to be set aside.

National law and national courts still plays very important role in the process of the enforcement of awards which applied the rules of *Lex Mercatoria*[30]. It has to be possible for the national court to apply *Lex Mercatoria* as an independent body of law by virtue of choice of law clause in the contract concluded by the parties. It is indispensable in this respect that the national law and legal theory must recognize *Lex Mercatoria* as an autonomous body of law, which is not always the case.

Sports law is highly potential to become a world law similarly to mercantile law. The universally accepted rules of more than 200 games and universally accepted principles governing competitions at world level, significance of sport for demonstration of individual and national values, globalization of sport, are part of the conditions precedent for this to happen. However, the comparison with *Lex Mercatoria* reveals some important differences which might be relevant for the future development of sports law as a world law.

A statement saying that the community of merchants is held together by common traditions and common trust does not seem to be applicable to contemporary sport, which, especially in recent years, departs from the Corinthian values of playing a game because of the love to that game. Nowadays, the result of the competition does not have only sport implications but further determines who is going to get better sponsor. Commercialization of sport invoked the need for protection of different and very often conflicting interests of the stakeholders in sport. Sport federations are often criticised for pursuing their own commercial interests without taking into account and sometimes even in detriment of the interests of sportsmen. FIFPRO, the international trade union of professional football players, for instance, suspects that football rulers misuse their personal contacts with politicians to

---

[25] Id..

[26] F. De Ly, International Business Law and Lex Mercatoria, Elsevier Science Publishers B.V. 1992, p. 246 reffering to H. Berman, C. Kaufman, The law of international commercial transactions (lex mercatoria), p. 273.

[27] Id., at p. 249.

[28] Id., at p. 251.

[29] Norsolor S.A. (France) v. Pabalk Ticaret Sirketi S.A. (Turkey), Tribunal de grande instance of Paris, March 4 1981, Cour dapple of Paris, December 15, 1981 and November 19, 1982, Cour de cassation, October 9, 1984.

[30] See Filip De Ly, International Business Law and Lex Mercatoria, Elsevier Science Publishers B.V. 1992, p. 214.

maintain the sometimes illegal rules drafted by the football governing bodies in detriment of players[31]. The current relations in sport are everything else but relations of trust.

However, exactly in the view of the conflicting interests in sport the role of CAS is very important and the consistent resolving of the disputes might significantly contribute to the idea for the creation of an independent body of law capable to restore and maintain justice in sport. Evidence of the increasing role of CAS are the more frequent use of arbitration clauses in the contracts between sponsors, federations and clubs[32] the trend for increasing the volume of cases reaching CAS and the number of sport federations admitting the authority of CAS to resolve the disputes in their particular sports.

On the other hand, CAS cannot make up for the missing democracy and transparency in the activity of sport federations. The big problem in sport is exactly the absence of a good and democratic governance which to give credibility and fairness to sport regulations and to defend the idea for full autonomy of sport. CAS is an institution for settlement of civil law disputes, however, it is not an administrative or constitutional court, before which provisions of sport regulations could be challenged on the ground of contradiction with acts staying higher in the hierarchy of the legal instruments. Furthermore, CAS is not entitled to review the substance of the decision-making process but only the procedure and the power of the particular bodies to pass the decision in issue. Although CAS has a lot of common characteristics with international court it is not a court. An opinion has been expressed that "CAS could develop into an instrument of "constitutional" review and standard-setting in the realm of international sports law"[33]; however, this is still not the case and the regulations of sport associations may be scrutinized on the basis of national laws. The incentive for clubs and sportsmen to refer their cases to the courts as well as their mistrust and suspicion to the federations will remain present until their interests are adequately safeguarded through their participation in the decision-making process especially as regards matters of primary concern for them. The lack of democratic rule-making process and credibility in respect of the actions of sport governing bodies further handicaps the possibilities for recognition of *Lex Sportiva* by the national laws of the states.

Another difference with *Lex Mercatoria* is the fact that CAS cannot apply *Lex Sportiva* through the application of the national law of a particular state as could be the case with *Lex Mercatoria* due to the fact that national laws usually have not incorporated *Lex Sportiva*. Very often, certain cases would have diametrically opposite outcome under national laws in comparison with their potential outcome under the law of international sport federations based on the principle of freedom of association due to conflicting provisions of national sports or employment laws. *Lex Sportiva* may apply to relations in sport also as an autonomous body of law, which is to be recognized as such by national laws, however, this is still not the case either. A review of modern court practices would show a third option for enforcement of *Lex Sportiva* – if the rules of *Lex Sportiva* constitute mandatory rules reflecting a public policy so commanding that they must be applied even if the general body of law to which they belong is not competent by application of the relevant rule of conflict of laws.[34]

However, being a private arbitration system and not a universally recognized court including by the EU Member States by virtue of an international treaty the CAS awards will be subject to enforcement proceedings in the countries where the enforcement is sought and, therefore, their conformity with the public policy and mandatory rules in operation in such countries will be reviewed by the national courts. In countries like Bulgaria and Hungary, for example, employment related disputes are not subject to arbitration at all and national courts have exclusive jurisdiction over employment disputes. It is true that FIFA ensures the compliance of the parties with the award not through the assistance of national courts but rather through threatening the parties with disciplinary sanctions. The latter, however, together with the already mentioned deficits of *Lex Sportiva* as a concept, as well as the mandatory reference to arbitration of players and clubs imposed through the by-laws of their federations, could threaten the recognition of CAS as a valid arbitration system and do not in

---

[31] Such an opinion was expressed by Theo van Seggelen from FIFPro at the 6th Asser-Clingendael International Sports Lecture held at the Cliningendael Institute in the Hague on 6 June 2006

[32] Ian S. Blackshaw, Robert C.R. Siekmann, Janwillem Soek (eds), *The Court of Arbitration for Sport 1984 – 2004*, T.M.C. Asser Press 2006, page 30; Bruno Simma, article The Court of Arbitration for Sport.

[33] Ibid., p. 26.

[34] Mayer, Pierre, Mandatory Rules of Law in International Arbitration, 2 Arb. Int'l. 274 (1986) at p. 275.

any manner contribute to the idea of an objective, just, transparent, self-integrated and universally accepted international sports law or *Lex Sportiva*.

Future changes in the global governance of sport making it more democratic and transparent, future changes in the attitude of sport rulers admitting that they are subject to the law to the very same extent as any other individuals and legal entities, the inevitable, in case of absence of the first two, interaction between sports law and the legal systems of the national laws and the supranational EU law, as well as the future development of the CAS jurisprudence are the conditions needed for crystallization, promotion and recognition of the international sports law as a world law with its own universally harmonized and world valid provisions.

APPENDIX XXIV

ICANN UNIFORM DISPUTE RESOLUTION POLICY AND RULES

ICANN

Uniform Domain Name
Dispute Resolution Policy
Policy Adopted: August 26, 1999
Implementation Documents Approved: October 24, 1999

(A) ICANN UNIFORM DOMAIN NAME DISPUTE RESOLUTION POLICY

Notes:
1. This policy is now in effect. See www.icann.org/udrp/udrp-schedule.htm for the implementation schedule.
2. This policy has been adopted by all accredited domain-name registrars for domain names ending in .com, .net, and .org. It has also been adopted by certain managers of country-code top-level domains (e.g., .nu, .tv, .ws).
3. The policy is between the registrar (or other registration authority in the case of a country-code top-level domain) and its customer (the domain-name holder or registrant). Thus, the policy uses "we" and "our" to refer to the registrar and it uses "you" and "your" to refer to the domain-name holder.

Uniform Domain Name Dispute Resolution Policy
(As Approved by ICANN on October 24, 1999)
1. Purpose. This Uniform Domain Name Dispute Resolution Policy (the "Policy") has been adopted by the Internet Corporation for Assigned Names and Numbers ("ICANN"), is incorporated by reference into your Registration Agreement, and sets forth the terms and conditions in connection with a dispute between you and any party other than us (the registrar) over the registration and use of an Internet domain name registered by you. Proceedings under Paragraph 4 of this Policy will be conducted according to the Rules for Uniform Domain Name Dispute Resolution Policy (the "Rules of Procedure"), which are available at www.icann.org/udrp/udrp-rules-24oct99.htm, and the selected administrative-dispute-resolution service provider's supplemental rules.
2. Your Representations. By applying to register a domain name, or by asking us to maintain or renew a domain name registration, you hereby represent and warrant to us that (a) the statements that you made in your Registration Agreement are complete and accurate; (b) to your knowledge, the registration of the domain name will not infringe upon or otherwise violate the rights of any third party; (c) you are not registering the domain name for an unlawful purpose; and (d) you will not knowingly use the domain name in violation of any applicable laws or regulations. It is your responsibility to determine whether your domain name registration infringes or violates someone else's rights.
3. Cancellations, Transfers, and Changes. We will cancel, transfer or otherwise make changes to domain name registrations under the following circumstances:
   a. subject to the provisions of Paragraph 8, our receipt of written or appropriate electronic instructions from you or your authorized agent to take such action;

b. our receipt of an order from a court or arbitral tribunal, in each case of competent jurisdiction, requiring such action; and/or
c. our receipt of a decision of an Administrative Panel requiring such action in any administrative proceeding to which you were a party and which was conducted under this Policy or a later version of this Policy adopted by ICANN. (See Paragraph 4(i) and (k) below.)

We may also cancel, transfer or otherwise make changes to a domain name registration in accordance with the terms of your Registration Agreement or other legal requirements.

4. Mandatory Administrative Proceeding.
This Paragraph sets forth the type of disputes for which you are required to submit to a mandatory administrative proceeding. These proceedings will be conducted before one of the administrative-dispute-resolution service providers listed at www.icann.org/udrp/approved-providers.htm (each, a "Provider").
 a. Applicable Disputes. You are required to submit to a mandatory administrative proceeding in the event that a third party (a "complainant") asserts to the applicable Provider, in compliance with the Rules of Procedure, that
 (i) your domain name is identical or confusingly similar to a trademark or service mark in which the complainant has rights; and
 (ii) you have no rights or legitimate interests in respect of the domain name; and
 (iii) your domain name has been registered and is being used in bad faith.
 In the administrative proceeding, the complainant must prove that each of these three elements are present.
 b. Evidence of Registration and Use in Bad Faith. For the purposes of Paragraph 4(a)(iii), the following circumstances, in particular but without limitation, if found by the Panel to be present, shall be evidence of the registration and use of a domain name in bad faith:
 (i) circumstances indicating that you have registered or you have acquired the domain name primarily for the purpose of selling, renting, or otherwise transferring the domain name registration to the complainant who is the owner of the trademark or service mark or to a competitor of that complainant, for valuable consideration in excess of your documented out-of-pocket costs directly related to the domain name; or
 (ii) you have registered the domain name in order to prevent the owner of the trademark or service mark from reflecting the mark in a corresponding domain name, provided that you have engaged in a pattern of such conduct; or
 (iii) you have registered the domain name primarily for the purpose of disrupting the business of a competitor; or
 (iv) by using the domain name, you have intentionally attempted to attract, for commercial gain, Internet users to your web site or other on-line location, by creating a likelihood of confusion with the complainant's mark as to the source, sponsorship, affiliation, or endorsement of your web site or location or of a product or service on your web site or location.
 c. How to Demonstrate Your Rights to and Legitimate Interests in the Domain Name in Responding to a Complaint. When you receive a complaint, you should refer to Paragraph 5 of the Rules of Procedure in determining how your response should be prepared. Any of the following circumstances, in particular but without limitation, if found by the Panel to be proved based on its evaluation of all evidence presented, shall demonstrate your rights or legitimate interests to the domain name for purposes of Paragraph 4(a)(ii):
 (i) before any notice to you of the dispute, your use of, or demonstrable preparations to use, the domain name or a name corresponding to the domain name in connection with a bona fide offering of goods or services; or
 (ii) you (as an individual, business, or other organization) have been commonly known by the domain name, even if you have acquired no trademark or service mark rights; or
 (iii) you are making a legitimate noncommercial or fair use of the domain name, without intent for commercial gain to misleadingly divert consumers or to tarnish the trademark or service mark at issue.

d. Selection of Provider. The complainant shall select the Provider from among those approved by ICANN by submitting the complaint to that Provider. The selected Provider will administer the proceeding, except in cases of consolidation as described in Paragraph 4(f).
e. Initiation of Proceeding and Process and Appointment of Administrative Panel. The Rules of Procedure state the process for initiating and conducting a proceeding and for appointing the panel that will decide the dispute (the "Administrative Panel").
f. Consolidation. In the event of multiple disputes between you and a complainant, either you or the complainant may petition to consolidate the disputes before a single Administrative Panel. This petition shall be made to the first Administrative Panel appointed to hear a pending dispute between the parties. This Administrative Panel may consolidate before it any or all such disputes in its sole discretion, provided that the disputes being consolidated are governed by this Policy or a later version of this Policy adopted by ICANN.
g. Fees. All fees charged by a Provider in connection with any dispute before an Administrative Panel pursuant to this Policy shall be paid by the complainant, except in cases where you elect to expand the Administrative Panel from one to three panelists as provided in Paragraph 5(b)(iv) of the Rules of Procedure, in which case all fees will be split evenly by you and the complainant.
h. Our Involvement in Administrative Proceedings. We do not, and will not, participate in the administration or conduct of any proceeding before an Administrative Panel. In addition, we will not be liable as a result of any decisions rendered by the Administrative Panel.
i. Remedies. The remedies available to a complainant pursuant to any proceeding before an Administrative Panel shall be limited to requiring the cancellation of your domain name or the transfer of your domain name registration to the complainant.
j. Notification and Publication. The Provider shall notify us of any decision made by an Administrative Panel with respect to a domain name you have registered with us. All decisions under this Policy will be published in full over the Internet, except when an Administrative Panel determines in an exceptional case to redact portions of its decision.
k. Availability of Court Proceedings. The mandatory administrative proceeding requirements set forth in Paragraph 4 shall not prevent either you or the complainant from submitting the dispute to a court of competent jurisdiction for independent resolution before such mandatory administrative proceeding is commenced or after such proceeding is concluded. If an Administrative Panel decides that your domain name registration should be canceled or transferred, we will wait ten (10) business days (as observed in the location of our principal office) after we are informed by the applicable Provider of the Administrative Panel's decision before implementing that decision. We will then implement the decision unless we have received from you during that ten (10) business day period official documentation (such as a copy of a complaint, file-stamped by the clerk of the court) that you have commenced a lawsuit against the complainant in a jurisdiction to which the complainant has submitted under Paragraph 3(b)(xiii) of the Rules of Procedure. (In general, that jurisdiction is either the location of our principal office or of your address as shown in our Whois database. See Paragraphs 1 and 3(b)(xiii) of the Rules of Procedure for details.) If we receive such documentation within the ten (10) business day period, we will not implement the Administrative Panel's decision, and we will take no further action, until we receive (i) evidence satisfactory to us of a resolution between the parties; (ii) evidence satisfactory to us that your lawsuit has been dismissed or withdrawn; or (iii) a copy of an order from such court dismissing your lawsuit or ordering that you do not have the right to continue to use your domain name.

5. All Other Disputes and Litigation. All other disputes between you and any party other than us regarding your domain name registration that are not brought pursuant to the mandatory administrative proceeding provisions of Paragraph 4 shall be resolved between you and such other party through any court, arbitration or other proceeding that may be available.
6. Our Involvement in Disputes. We will not participate in any way in any dispute between you and any party other than us regarding the registration and use of your domain name. You shall not name us as a party or otherwise include us in any such proceeding. In the event that we are named as a party in any such proceeding, we reserve the right to raise any and all defenses deemed appropriate, and to take any other action necessary to defend ourselves.

7. Maintaining the Status Quo. We will not cancel, transfer, activate, deactivate, or otherwise change the status of any domain name registration under this Policy except as provided in Paragraph 3 above.
8. Transfers During a Dispute.
   a. Transfers of a Domain Name to a New Holder. You may not transfer your domain name registration to another holder (i) during a pending administrative proceeding brought pursuant to Paragraph 4 or for a period of fifteen (15) business days (as observed in the location of our principal place of business) after such proceeding is concluded; or (ii) during a pending court proceeding or arbitration commenced regarding your domain name unless the party to whom the domain name registration is being transferred agrees, in writing, to be bound by the decision of the court or arbitrator. We reserve the right to cancel any transfer of a domain name registration to another holder that is made in violation of this subparagraph.
   b. Changing Registrars. You may not transfer your domain name registration to another registrar during a pending administrative proceeding brought pursuant to Paragraph 4 or for a period of fifteen (15) business days (as observed in the location of our principal place of business) after such proceeding is concluded. You may transfer administration of your domain name registration to another registrar during a pending court action or arbitration, provided that the domain name you have registered with us shall continue to be subject to the proceedings commenced against you in accordance with the terms of this Policy. In the event that you transfer a domain name registration to us during the pendency of a court action or arbitration, such dispute shall remain subject to the domain name dispute policy of the registrar from which the domain name registration was transferred.
9. Policy Modifications. We reserve the right to modify this Policy at any time with the permission of ICANN. We will post our revised Policy at least thirty (30) calendar days before it becomes effective. Unless this Policy has already been invoked by the submission of a complaint to a Provider, in which event the version of the Policy in effect at the time it was invoked will apply to you until the dispute is over, all such changes will be binding upon you with respect to any domain name registration dispute, whether the dispute arose before, on or after the effective date of our change. In the event that you object to a change in this Policy, your sole remedy is to cancel your domain name registration with us, provided that you will not be entitled to a refund of any fees you paid to us. The revised Policy will apply to you until you cancel your domain name registration.

(B) ICANN UNIFORM DOMAIN NAME DISPUTE RESOLUTION POLICY RULES

Note: These rules are now in effect. See www.icann.org/udrp/udrp-schedule.htm for the implementation schedule.

Rules for Uniform Domain Name Dispute Resolution Policy
(the "Rules")
(As Approved by ICANN on October 24, 1999)
Administrative proceedings for the resolution of disputes under the Uniform Dispute Resolution Policy adopted by ICANN shall be governed by these Rules and also the Supplemental Rules of the Provider administering the proceedings, as posted on its web site.

1. Definitions
   In these Rules:
   Complainant means the party initiating a complaint concerning a domain-name registration.
   ICANN refers to the Internet Corporation for Assigned Names and Numbers.
   Mutual Jurisdiction means a court jurisdiction at the location of either (a) the principal office of the Registrar (provided the domain-name holder has submitted in its Registration Agreement to that jurisdiction for court adjudication of disputes concerning or arising from the use of the domain name) or (b) the domain-name holder's address as shown for the registration of the domain name in Registrar's Whois database at the time the complaint is submitted to the Provider.
   Panel means an administrative panel appointed by a Provider to decide a complaint concerning a domain-name registration.

Panelist means an individual appointed by a Provider to be a member of a Panel.
Party means a Complainant or a Respondent.
Policy means the Uniform Domain Name Dispute Resolution Policy that is incorporated by reference and made a part of the Registration Agreement.
Provider means a dispute-resolution service provider approved by ICANN. A list of such Providers appears at www.icann.org/udrp/approved-providers.htm.
Registrar means the entity with which the Respondent has registered a domain name that is the subject of a complaint.
Registration Agreement means the agreement between a Registrar and a domain-name holder.
Respondent means the holder of a domain-name registration against which a complaint is initiated.
Reverse Domain Name Hijacking means using the Policy in bad faith to attempt to deprive a registered domain-name holder of a domain name.
Supplemental Rules means the rules adopted by the Provider administering a proceeding to supplement these Rules.
Supplemental Rules shall not be inconsistent with the Policy or these Rules and shall cover such topics as fees, word and page limits and guidelines, the means for communicating with the Provider and the Panel, and the form of cover sheets.

2. Communications
   (a) When forwarding a complaint to the Respondent, it shall be the Provider's responsibility to employ reasonably available means calculated to achieve actual notice to Respondent. Achieving actual notice, or employing the following measures to do so, shall discharge this responsibility:
      (i) sending the complaint to all postal-mail and facsimile addresses (A) shown in the domain name's registration data in Registrar's Whois database for the registered domain-name holder, the technical contact, and the administrative contact and (B) supplied by Registrar to the Provider for the registration's billing contact; and
      (ii) sending the complaint in electronic form (including annexes to the extent available in that form) by e-mail to:
         (A) the e-mail addresses for those technical, administrative, and billing contacts;
         (B) postmaster@<the contested domain name>; and
         (C) if the domain name (or "www." followed by the domain name) resolves to an active web page (other than a generic page the Provider concludes is maintained by a registrar or ISP for parking domain-names registered by multiple domain-name holders), any e-mail address shown or e-mail links on that web page; and
      (iii) sending the complaint to any address the Respondent has notified the Provider it prefers and, to the extent practicable, to all other addresses provided to the Provider by Complainant under Paragraph 3(b)(v).
   (b) Except as provided in Paragraph 2(a), any written communication to Complainant or Respondent provided for under these Rules shall be made by the preferred means stated by the Complainant or Respondent, respectively (see Paragraphs 3(b)(iii) and 5(b)(iii)), or in the absence of such specification
      (i) by telecopy or facsimile transmission, with a confirmation of transmission; or
      (ii) by postal or courier service, postage pre-paid and return receipt requested; or
      (iii) electronically via the Internet, provided a record of its transmission is available.
   (c) Any communication to the Provider or the Panel shall be made by the means and in the manner (including number of copies) stated in the Provider's Supplemental Rules.
   (d) Communications shall be made in the language prescribed in Paragraph 11. E-mail communications should, if practicable, be sent in plaintext.
   (e) Either Party may update its contact details by notifying the Provider and the Registrar.
   (f) Except as otherwise provided in these Rules, or decided by a Panel, all communications provided for under these Rules shall be deemed to have been made:
      (i) if delivered by telecopy or facsimile transmission, on the date shown on the confirmation of transmission; or
      (ii) if by postal or courier service, on the date marked on the receipt; or

(iii) if via the Internet, on the date that the communication was transmitted, provided that the date of transmission is verifiable.

(g) Except as otherwise provided in these Rules, all time periods calculated under these Rules to begin when a communication is made shall begin to run on the earliest date that the communication is deemed to have been made in accordance with Paragraph 2(f).

(h) Any communication by
   (i) a Panel to any Party shall be copied to the Provider and to the other Party;
   (ii) the Provider to any Party shall be copied to the other Party; and
   (iii) a Party shall be copied to the other Party, the Panel and the Provider, as the case may be.

(i) It shall be the responsibility of the sender to retain records of the fact and circumstances of sending, which shall be available for inspection by affected parties and for reporting purposes.

(j) In the event a Party sending a communication receives notification of non-delivery of the communication, the Party shall promptly notify the Panel (or, if no Panel is yet appointed, the Provider) of the circumstances of the notification. Further proceedings concerning the communication and any response shall be as directed by the Panel (or the Provider).

3. The Complaint

(a) Any person or entity may initiate an administrative proceeding by submitting a complaint in accordance with the Policy and these Rules to any Provider approved by ICANN. (Due to capacity constraints or for other reasons, a Provider's ability to accept complaints may be suspended at times. In that event, the Provider shall refuse the submission. The person or entity may submit the complaint to another Provider.)

(b) The complaint shall be submitted in hard copy and (except to the extent not available for annexes) in electronic form and shall:
   (i) Request that the complaint be submitted for decision in accordance with the Policy and these Rules;
   (ii) Provide the name, postal and e-mail addresses, and the telephone and telefax numbers of the Complainant and of any representative authorized to act for the Complainant in the administrative proceeding;
   (iii) Specify a preferred method for communications directed to the Complainant in the administrative proceeding (including person to be contacted, medium, and address information) for each of (A) electronic-only material and (B) material including hard copy;
   (iv) Designate whether Complainant elects to have the dispute decided by a single-member or a three-member Panel and, in the event Complainant elects a three-member Panel, provide the names and contact details of three candidates to serve as one of the Panelists (these candidates may be drawn from any ICANN-approved Provider's list of panelists);
   (v) Provide the name of the Respondent (domain-name holder) and all information (including any postal and e-mail addresses and telephone and telefax numbers) known to Complainant regarding how to contact Respondent or any representative of Respondent, including contact information based on pre-complaint dealings, in sufficient detail to allow the Provider to send the complaint as described in Paragraph 2(a);
   (vi) Specify the domain name(s) that is/are the subject of the complaint;
   (vii) Identify the Registrar(s) with whom the domain name(s) is/are registered at the time the complaint is filed;
   (viii) Specify the trademark(s) or service mark(s) on which the complaint is based and, for each mark, describe the goods or services, if any, with which the mark is used (Complainant may also separately describe other goods and services with which it intends, at the time the complaint is submitted, to use the mark in the future.);
   (ix) Describe, in accordance with the Policy, the grounds on which the complaint is made including, in particular,
      (1) the manner in which the domain name(s) is/are identical or confusingly similar to a trademark or service mark in which the Complainant has rights; and

(2) why the Respondent (domain-name holder) should be considered as having no rights or legitimate interests in respect of the domain name(s) that is/are the subject of the complaint; and

(3) why the domain name(s) should be considered as having been registered and being used in bad faith

(The description should, for elements (2) and (3), discuss any aspects of Paragraphs 4(b) and 4(c) of the Policy that are applicable. The description shall comply with any word or page limit set forth in the Provider's Supplement Rules.);

(x) Specify, in accordance with the Policy, the remedies sought;

(xi) Identify any other legal proceedings that have been commenced or terminated in connection with or relating to any of the domain name(s) that are the subject of the complaint;

(xii) State that a copy of the complaint, together with the cover sheet as prescribed by the Provider's Supplemental Rules, has been sent or transmitted to the Respondent (domain-name holder), in accordance with Paragraph 2(b);

(xiii) State that Complainant will submit, with respect to any challenges to a decision in the administrative proceeding canceling or transferring the domain name, to the jurisdiction of the courts in at least one specified Mutual Jurisdiction;

(xiv) Conclude with the following statement followed by the signature of the Complainant or its authorized representative:

"Complainant agrees that its claims and remedies concerning the registration of the domain name, the dispute, or the dispute's resolution shall be solely against the domain-name holder and waives all such claims and remedies against (a) the dispute-resolution provider and panelists, except in the case of deliberate wrongdoing, (b) the registrar, (c) the registry administrator, and (d) the Internet Corporation for Assigned Names and Numbers, as well as their directors, officers, employees, and agents."

"Complainant certifies that the information contained in this Complaint is to the best of Complainant's knowledge complete and accurate, that this Complaint is not being presented for any improper purpose, such as to harass, and that the assertions in this Complaint are warranted under these Rules and under applicable law, as it now exists or as it may be extended by a good-faith and reasonable argument."; and

(xv) Annex any documentary or other evidence, including a copy of the Policy applicable to the domain name(s) in dispute and any trademark or service mark registration upon which the complaint relies, together with a schedule indexing such evidence.

(c) The complaint may relate to more than one domain name, provided that the domain names are registered by the same domain-name holder.

4. Notification of Complaint

(a) The Provider shall review the complaint for administrative compliance with the Policy and these Rules and, if in compliance, shall forward the complaint (together with the explanatory cover sheet prescribed by the Provider's Supplemental Rules) to the Respondent, in the manner prescribed by Paragraph 2(a), within three (3) calendar days following receipt of the fees to be paid by the Complainant in accordance with Paragraph 19.

(b) If the Provider finds the complaint to be administratively deficient, it shall promptly notify the Complainant and the Respondent of the nature of the deficiencies identified. The Complainant shall have five (5) calendar days within which to correct any such deficiencies, after which the administrative proceeding will be deemed withdrawn without prejudice to submission of a different complaint by Complainant.

(c) The date of commencement of the administrative proceeding shall be the date on which the Provider completes its responsibilities under Paragraph 2(a) in connection with forwarding the Complaint to the Respondent.

(d) The Provider shall immediately notify the Complainant, the Respondent, the concerned Registrar(s), and ICANN of the date of commencement of the administrative proceeding.

5. The Response

(a) Within twenty (20) days of the date of commencement of the administrative proceeding the Respondent shall submit a response to the Provider.

(b) The response shall be submitted in hard copy and (except to the extent not available for annexes) in electronic form and shall:
  (i) Respond specifically to the statements and allegations contained in the complaint and include any and all bases for the Respondent (domain-name holder) to retain registration and use of the disputed domain name (This portion of the response shall comply with any word or page limit set forth in the Provider's Supplemental Rules.);
  (ii) Provide the name, postal and e-mail addresses, and the telephone and telefax numbers of the Respondent (domain-name holder) and of any representative authorized to act for the Respondent in the administrative proceeding;
  (iii) Specify a preferred method for communications directed to the Respondent in the administrative proceeding (including person to be contacted, medium, and address information) for each of (A) electronic-only material and (B) material including hard copy;
  (iv) If Complainant has elected a single-member panel in the Complaint (see Paragraph 3(b)(iv)), state whether Respondent elects instead to have the dispute decided by a three-member panel;
  (v) If either Complainant or Respondent elects a three-member Panel, provide the names and contact details of three candidates to serve as one of the Panelists (these candidates may be drawn from any ICANN-approved Provider's list of panelists);
  (vi) Identify any other legal proceedings that have been commenced or terminated in connection with or relating to any of the domain name(s) that are the subject of the complaint;
  (vii) State that a copy of the response has been sent or transmitted to the Complainant, in accordance with Paragraph 2(b); and
  (viii) Conclude with the following statement followed by the signature of the Respondent or its authorized representative:
  "Respondent certifies that the information contained in this Response is to the best of Respondent's knowledge complete and accurate, that this Response is not being presented for any improper purpose, such as to harass, and that the assertions in this Response are warranted under these Rules and under applicable law, as it now exists or as it may be extended by a good-faith and reasonable argument."; and
  (ix) Annex any documentary or other evidence upon which the Respondent relies, together with a schedule indexing such documents.

(c) If Complainant has elected to have the dispute decided by a single-member Panel and Respondent elects a three-member Panel, Respondent shall be required to pay one-half of the applicable fee for a three-member Panel as set forth in the Provider's Supplemental Rules. This payment shall be made together with the submission of the response to the Provider. In the event that the required payment is not made, the dispute shall be decided by a single-member Panel.

(d) At the request of the Respondent, the Provider may, in exceptional cases, extend the period of time for the filing of the response. The period may also be extended by written stipulation between the Parties, provided the stipulation is approved by the Provider.

(e) If a Respondent does not submit a response, in the absence of exceptional circumstances, the Panel shall decide the dispute based upon the complaint.

6. Appointment of the Panel and Timing of Decision

(a) Each Provider shall maintain and publish a publicly available list of panelists and their qualifications.

(b) If neither the Complainant nor the Respondent has elected a three-member Panel (Paragraphs 3(b)(iv) and 5(b)(iv)), the Provider shall appoint, within five (5) calendar days following receipt of the response by the Provider, or the lapse of the time period for the submission thereof, a single Panelist from its list of panelists. The fees for a single-member Panel shall be paid entirely by the Complainant.

(c) If either the Complainant or the Respondent elects to have the dispute decided by a three-member Panel, the Provider shall appoint three Panelists in accordance with the procedures identified in Paragraph 6(e). The fees for a three-member Panel shall be paid in their entirety by the Complainant, except where the election for a three-member Panel was made by the Respondent, in which case the applicable fees shall be shared equally between the Parties.

(d) Unless it has already elected a three-member Panel, the Complainant shall submit to the Provider, within five (5) calendar days of communication of a response in which the Respondent elects a three-member Panel, the names and contact details of three candidates to serve as one of the Panelists. These candidates may be drawn from any ICANN-approved Provider's list of panelists.

(e) In the event that either the Complainant or the Respondent elects a three-member Panel, the Provider shall endeavor to appoint one Panelist from the list of candidates provided by each of the Complainant and the Respondent. In the event the Provider is unable within five (5) calendar days to secure the appointment of a Panelist on its customary terms from either Party's list of candidates, the Provider shall make that appointment from its list of panelists. The third Panelist shall be appointed by the Provider from a list of five candidates submitted by the Provider to the Parties, the Provider's selection from among the five being made in a manner that reasonably balances the preferences of both Parties, as they may specify to the Provider within five (5) calendar days of the Provider's submission of the five-candidate list to the Parties.

(f) Once the entire Panel is appointed, the Provider shall notify the Parties of the Panelists appointed and the date by which, absent exceptional circumstances, the Panel shall forward its decision on the complaint to the Provider.

7. Impartiality and Independence

A Panelist shall be impartial and independent and shall have, before accepting appointment, disclosed to the Provider any circumstances giving rise to justifiable doubt as to the Panelist's impartiality or independence. If, at any stage during the administrative proceeding, new circumstances arise that could give rise to justifiable doubt as to the impartiality or independence of the Panelist, that Panelist shall promptly disclose such circumstances to the Provider. In such event, the Provider shall have the discretion to appoint a substitute Panelist.

8. Communication Between Parties and the Panel

No Party or anyone acting on its behalf may have any unilateral communication with the Panel. All communications between a Party and the Panel or the Provider shall be made to a case administrator appointed by the Provider in the manner prescribed in the Provider's Supplemental Rules.

9. Transmission of the File to the Panel

The Provider shall forward the file to the Panel as soon as the Panelist is appointed in the case of a Panel consisting of a single member, or as soon as the last Panelist is appointed in the case of a three-member Panel.

10. General Powers of the Panel

(a) The Panel shall conduct the administrative proceeding in such manner as it considers appropriate in accordance with the Policy and these Rules.

(b) In all cases, the Panel shall ensure that the Parties are treated with equality and that each Party is given a fair opportunity to present its case.

(c) The Panel shall ensure that the administrative proceeding takes place with due expedition. It may, at the request of a Party or on its own motion, extend, in exceptional cases, a period of time fixed by these Rules or by the Panel.

(d) The Panel shall determine the admissibility, relevance, materiality and weight of the evidence.

(e) A Panel shall decide a request by a Party to consolidate multiple domain name disputes in accordance with the Policy and these Rules.

11. Language of Proceedings

(a) Unless otherwise agreed by the Parties, or specified otherwise in the Registration Agreement, the language of the administrative proceeding shall be the language of the Registration Agreement, subject to the authority of the Panel to determine otherwise, having regard to the circumstances of the administrative proceeding.

(b) The Panel may order that any documents submitted in languages other than the language of the administrative proceeding be accompanied by a translation in whole or in part into the language of the administrative proceeding.

12. Further Statements

In addition to the complaint and the response, the Panel may request, in its sole discretion, further statements or documents from either of the Parties.

13. In-Person Hearings

There shall be no in-person hearings (including hearings by teleconference, videoconference, and web conference), unless the Panel determines, in its sole discretion and as an exceptional matter, that such a hearing is necessary for deciding the complaint.

14. Default

(a) In the event that a Party, in the absence of exceptional circumstances, does not comply with any of the time periods established by these Rules or the Panel, the Panel shall proceed to a decision on the complaint.

(b) If a Party, in the absence of exceptional circumstances, does not comply with any provision of, or requirement under, these Rules or any request from the Panel, the Panel shall draw such inferences therefrom as it considers appropriate.

15. Panel Decisions

(a) A Panel shall decide a complaint on the basis of the statements and documents submitted and in accordance with the Policy, these Rules and any rules and principles of law that it deems applicable.

(b) In the absence of exceptional circumstances, the Panel shall forward its decision on the complaint to the Provider within fourteen (14) days of its appointment pursuant to Paragraph 6.

(c) In the case of a three-member Panel, the Panel's decision shall be made by a majority.

(d) The Panel's decision shall be in writing, provide the reasons on which it is based, indicate the date on which it was rendered and identify the name(s) of the Panelist(s).

(e) Panel decisions and dissenting opinions shall normally comply with the guidelines as to length set forth in the Provider's Supplemental Rules. Any dissenting opinion shall accompany the majority decision. If the Panel concludes that the dispute is not within the scope of Paragraph 4(a) of the Policy, it shall so state. If after considering the submissions the Panel finds that the complaint was brought in bad faith, for example in an attempt at Reverse Domain Name Hijacking or was brought primarily to harass the domain-name holder, the Panel shall declare in its decision that the complaint was brought in bad faith and constitutes an abuse of the administrative proceeding.

16. Communication of Decision to Parties

(a) Within three (3) calendar days after receiving the decision from the Panel, the Provider shall communicate the full text of the decision to each Party, the concerned Registrar(s), and ICANN. The concerned Registrar(s) shall immediately communicate to each Party, the Provider, and ICANN the date for the implementation of the decision in accordance with the Policy.

(b) Except if the Panel determines otherwise (see Paragraph 4(j) of the Policy), the Provider shall publish the full decision and the date of its implementation on a publicly accessible web site. In any event, the portion of any decision determining a complaint to have been brought in bad faith (see Paragraph 15(e) of these Rules) shall be published.

17. Settlement or Other Grounds for Termination

(a) If, before the Panel's decision, the Parties agree on a settlement, the Panel shall terminate the administrative proceeding.

(b) If, before the Panel's decision is made, it becomes unnecessary or impossible to continue the administrative proceeding for any reason, the Panel shall terminate the administrative proceeding, unless a Party raises justifiable grounds for objection within a period of time to be determined by the Panel.

18. Effect of Court Proceedings

(a) In the event of any legal proceedings initiated prior to or during an administrative proceeding in respect of a domain-name dispute that is the subject of the complaint, the Panel shall have the discretion to decide whether to suspend or terminate the administrative proceeding, or to proceed to a decision.

(b) In the event that a Party initiates any legal proceedings during the pendency of an administrative proceeding in respect of a domain-name dispute that is the subject of the complaint, it shall promptly notify the Panel and the Provider. See Paragraph 8 above.

19. Fees

(a) The Complainant shall pay to the Provider an initial fixed fee, in accordance with the Provider's Supplemental Rules, within the time and in the amount required. A Respondent electing under Paragraph 5(b)(iv) to have the dispute decided by a three-member Panel, rather than the single-member Panel elected by the Complainant, shall pay the Provider one-half the fixed fee for a three-member Panel. See Paragraph 5(c). In all other cases, the Complainant shall bear all of the Provider's fees, except as prescribed under Paragraph 19(d). Upon appointment of the Panel, the Provider shall refund the appropriate portion, if any, of the initial fee to the Complainant, as specified in the Provider's Supplemental Rules.

(b) No action shall be taken by the Provider on a complaint until it has received from Complainant the initial fee in accordance with Paragraph 19(a).

(c) If the Provider has not received the fee within ten (10) calendar days of receiving the complaint, the complaint shall be deemed withdrawn and the administrative proceeding terminated.

(d) In exceptional circumstances, for example in the event an in-person hearing is held, the Provider shall request the Parties for the payment of additional fees, which shall be established in agreement with the Parties and the Panel.

20. Exclusion of Liability

Except in the case of deliberate wrongdoing, neither the Provider nor a Panelist shall be liable to a Party for any act or omission in connection with any administrative proceeding under these Rules.

21. Amendments

The version of these Rules in effect at the time of the submission of the complaint to the Provider shall apply to the administrative proceeding commenced thereby. These Rules may not be amended without the express written approval of ICANN.

APPENDIX XXV

FREDDY ADU DOMAIN NAME WIPO DECISION

WIPO Arbitration and Mediation Center

ADMINISTRATIVE PANEL DECISION
Freddy Adu v. Frank Fushille
Case No. D2004-0682

1. The Parties
The Complainant is Freddy Adu, an individual residing in Los Angeles, California, United States of America, represented by Jared Saurer of the law firm Wyatt, Tarrant & Combs, Memphis, Tennessee, United States of America.

The Respondent is Frank Fushille, an individual residing in San Diego, California, United States of America, represented by Joel C. Golden, San Diego, California, United States of America.

2. The Domain Name and Registrar
The domain name at issue is <freddyadu.com> ("Disputed Domain Name"), and is registered with Register.com.

3. Procedural History
The Complaint was filed with the WIPO Arbitration and Mediation Center (the "Center") on August 27, 2004. On August 27, 2004, the Center transmitted by email to Register.com a request for registrar verification in connection with the Disputed Domain Name. On August 27, 2004, Register.com transmitted by email to the Center its verification response confirming that the Respondent is listed as the registrant and providing the contact details for the administrative, billing, and technical contact. The Center verified that the Complaint satisfied the formal requirements of the Uniform Domain Name Dispute Resolution Policy (the "Policy"), the Rules for Uniform Domain Name Dispute Resolution Policy (the "Rules"), and the WIPO Supplemental Rules for Uniform Domain Name Dispute Resolution Policy (the "Supplemental Rules").

In accordance with the Rules, paragraphs 2(a) and 4(a), the Center formally notified the Respondent of the Complaint, and the proceedings commenced on August 31, 2004. In accordance with the Rules, paragraph 5(a), the due date for Response was September 20, 2004. The Response was filed with the Center on September 16, 2004.

The Center appointed Richard G. Lyon as the sole panelist in this matter on September 22, 2004. The Panelist submitted the Statement of Acceptance and Declaration of Impartiality and Independence, as required by the Center to ensure compliance with the Rules, paragraph 7. The Panel finds that it was On September 22, 2004, Complainant, through his counsel, sent an email to the WIPO Arbitration and Mediation Center's Case Manager, requesting permission to add certain information to the record in this proceeding. Complainant wished to add a statement of counsel that questioned the validity of Respondent's assertion in the Response that Respondent had a registered copyright in the Disputed Domain Name. On September 25, 2004, the Respondent, through counsel, replied by a telefax to the Case Manager with evidence purporting to support the contention in the Response. In Procedural Order No. 1, issued September 27, 2004, the Panel denied these requests to supplement the record.

The Panel issued Procedural Order No. 2 on October 5, 2004, requesting that Complainant correct a discrepancy in its evidence, and requesting both parties to provide certain correspondence between them. Complainant submitted the material requested on October 8, 2004. Respondent submitted nothing further.

4. Factual Background

The pleadings indicate that the parties do not dispute the facts set out in this section of the opinion. Additional factual assertions made by each party, and factual inferences that each party wishes the Panel to draw, are set out in the section 5, "Parties' Contentions."[35]

The Complainant, Freddie Adu, is a world famous soccer prodigy. In November 2003, at age 13, he signed a major contract with United States Major Soccer League (MSL).

Respondent, an individual residing in San Diego, California, United States of America, has described himself as proficient in multimedia communications, including web design, web maintenance, webcasting, and creating educational software. He is a lifelong soccer fan. He registered the Disputed Domain Name on October 14, 2002.

The Disputed Domain Name resolves to a single page with a soccer ball and goal netting, with praise and encouragement for Complainant and his MSL team, and the phrase "coming soon." There is no evidence of any other use of the Disputed Domain Name.

Respondent has never been known, individually or in business, by the name Freddie Adu. Complainant has never authorized Respondent to use Complainant's name in any manner.

In June 2003, Respondent initiated contact with the Complainant, by sending an email to Richard Motzkin of SportsNet, LLC, an agency that represents Complainant in marketing matters. Respondent said that "the original idea for my site was going to include articles, links, photos, and a bulletin board for fans to talk about their soccer interests ... basically a fans' site," but inquiring if he could make that site an "official site." Respondent also stated, "I'd like to manage this website."

Mr. Motzkin replied promptly, asking for Respondent's contact information and "whether you would be willing to sell the domain name to [Complainant] and, if so, for how much?" Email correspondence between Respondent and representatives of SportsNet continued through March 2004. Respondent several times proposed making the Disputed Domain Name the web address for Complainant's official site.

Respondent sent his most detailed proposal on January 27, 2004. Elements of this proposal were his majority ownership of the site, participation in all corporate advertising negotiations, "open access to [Complainant] and his sponsors," "first access to all web tracking information," "special admission to all matches, charity events and all other opportunities that promote good will in which [Complainant] takes part," all "for the sole purpose of generating positive public relations opportunities for [Complainant]." Respondent requested a "primary role" in photograph and video content promoting Complainant, in which Respondent "would retain all rights to all photographs, audio and video."

Complainant's counsel sent Respondent a cease and desist letter on May 24, 2004, demanding a cessation of Respondents use of Complainant's name and transfer of ownership of the Disputed Domain Name to Complainant.

Respondent, through counsel, replied on July 16, 2004. He declined to transfer the Disputed Domain Name, and asserted his right to continued ownership and use of the Disputed Domain Name as a fan site, based upon many of the assertions that he now makes in the Response.

5. Parties' Contentions

Complainant. The Complainant contends as follows:

Rights in a mark. Complainant uses his given name commercially in a variety of ways, such as product endorsements. His skill, renown, and the commercial value likely to follow from his skills were the subject of considerable publicity in the United States for several years before his contract signing. Complainant submits several newspaper and other media articles from 2001 – 2002, as evidence that his name and its commercial potential were well known since at least those dates. Under well-settled rules of decision under the Policy, a sports star, like any other person whose name is used as a commercial identifier, may claim his name as a mark, even if not formally registered, sufficient to permit institution of a dispute under the Policy.

---

[35] The Panel commends both parties for well organized and well supported presentations of their respective cases. Each party has purported its factual allegations with an affidavit made on personal knowledge, and each has in its pleading carefully separated factual assertions from legal arguments and conclusions.

Rights or Legitimate Interests. Complainant has never authorized Respondent to use his name in any manner. He has never made any "demonstrable preparations" to use the Disputed Domain Name as a fan site or indeed for any other purpose. Respondent was put on notice of "the dispute" before he made any use of the Disputed Domain Name in connection with the bona fide offering of goods and services; in fact, he has never made any use of the Disputed Domain Name. Respondent has never been commonly known by the Disputed Domain Name, nor operated any business under the Complainant's name or anything similar. Respondent has used the Disputed Domain Name misleadingly to divert consumers seeking information about Complainant.

Bad faith. Respondent's bad faith is illustrated by the following:

- His registration of the Disputed Domain Name when he knew of Complainant's exclusive rights.
- His intention to attract fans and consumers who were seeking information about Complainant. Evidence of this is an email from Respondent, in which Respondent estimated the use of Complainant's name would generate 10-20,000 hits per month (if not more)."
- Respondent's non-use of the domain name for over two years demonstrates bad faith under the warehousing doctrine first set out in *Telstra Corporation, Limited. v. Nuclear Marshmallows*, WIPO Case No. D2000-0003.
- Respondent's unauthorized designation of his web site as the official site of Complainant. On February 9, 2004, Complainant conducted a Yahoo!® search for "Freddie Adu". The first result was the Disputed Domain Name, advertised as "official site of the young soccer phenom."
- Quoting from the Complaint, "it is difficult to conceive of any actual or contemplated or active use of the [Disputed Domain Name] that would not be illegitimate."
- Respondent's business proposal of financial participation in the official website for Complainant presents Hobson's choice: "either intimate involvement with someone who Complainant has no desire to associate with" or giving up any right to use the prime domain name incorporating his valuable mark. This "undesirable choice is the antithesis of good faith."

Respondent. Respondent contends as follows

Rights in a mark. Complainant was not well known at the time Respondent registered the Disputed Domain Name. Since Complainant did not sign a commercial contract until more than a year after Respondent registered the Disputed Domain Name, Complainant did not have enforceable rights under the Policy at that time. Respondent cites *Brooke Bollea, a.k.a Brooke Hogan v. Robert McGowan*, WIPO Case No. D2004-0383, as authority for this argument.

Rights or Legitimate Interests. Respondent's intention has always been to create a noncommercial fan site, an activity normally regarded as a bona fide non-commercial offering of services. Respondent, a lifelong soccer enthusiast, learned in October 2002, that an Italian soccer team was interested in signing Respondent to a professional contract. Respondent saw in Complainant not only a future star player but also an individual "who could make soccer more popular amongst American's youths," and an athlete who, by his character and dedication, "could be an excellent role model for American kids."

Respondent registered the Disputed Domain Name "not for profit" but as a "fan based informational news domain." After spending some time searching for associates of Complainant to contact, in June 2003, he read that Complainant had signed with a sports agent, Richard Motzkin of SportsNet, whom Respondent immediately contacted by email. His initial email mentioned establishment of "a fan-based website to honor the future star." He also raised the possibility of making his website Complainant's official website.

Respondent has copyright ownership in <freddyadu.com>.

Respondent asserts that he has made use of the Disputed Domain Name, by posting his soccer-oriented wallpaper and including his email address on the website. Respondent met and had his picture taken with Complainant. Moreover, Respondent did not further develop the website for a number of reasons. There was little information available about Complainant, and at least until May 2004, he believed that negotiations with the Complainant's agent would result in Respondent's desired collaborative commercial website. Respondent has several times responded to emails from the public requesting information about Complainant. He has been "eager to develop the site for the last two years."

Respondent never proceeded with a fan site because he believed Complainant would be interested in helping provide information. Complainant's May 2004 cease and desist letter "came as a surprise" as Respondent "believed Complainant supported Respondent's website intentions."

The term *services* in Paragraph 4(a)(i) of the Policy is not limited to commercial services and may include non commercial services. Respondent states succinctly that "it has never been [my] intention to use the domain name for commercial gain." His purpose has been educational and informational, to promote soccer in America and develop an informational site about Complainant.

Respondent never intended to divert consumers; at the time he registered the Disputed Domain Name, "there was nothing to divert them from." As one of Complainant's biggest fans, he obviously has no intention of tarnishing Complainant's image.

Bad Faith. Respondent's purpose in establishing a fan site for Complainant is "benevolent" and "wholly lacking in bad faith."

Respondent had no intent to "coerce" a business venture; he was merely excited about the possibility of working with Complainant and led by Complainant's communications to believe that he might have that opportunity. He "never asked for or took money" in return for transfer. Respondent presents his own Catch-22 for a sports fan: if he accepts money for the domain name it's bad faith because he's in it for profit, if he refuses, "that also demonstrates bad faith because it shows that [he is] holding on to the domain name against Complainant's desires."

Respondent did not register the Disputed Domain Name to prevent Complainant's development of a commercial website; Complainant has done so at <freddyadu.net> and <freddyadu9.com>.[36]

Respondent has never registered any other domain name. He never indicated that the Disputed Domain Name was Complainant's official website, and referred at least one commercial inquiry to Complainant's agent. In sum, this is not the abusive registration the Policy was enacted to prevent.

6. Discussion and Findings

Policy Standards. The Complainant must prove the elements set out in paragraph 4(a) of the Policy. These elements are as follows:

(i) Respondent's Domain Name is identical or confusingly similar to a trademark or service mark in which the Complainant has rights; and
(ii) Respondent has no rights or legitimate interests in respect to the Domain Name; and
(iii) Respondent's Domain Name has been registered and is being used in bad faith.

Complainant bears the burden of proof on each of these elements.

Rights in a Mark. Since the Disputed Domain Name is identical to the mark in which the Complainant asserts rights, the Panel's inquiry under Paragraph 4(a)(i) of the Policy is whether Complainant's rights (if any) in the mark permit him to bring an action under the Policy.

As Respondent acknowledges, athletes and other celebrities who use their given names for commercial purposes have rights in that name sufficient to invoke the Policy. In the *Brooke Hogan* case cited by Respondent, this Panel held that determination of whether the requirements of Paragraph 4 (a)(i) of the Policy are established is based upon the complainant's rights in the applicable mark when the complaint was filed. Clearly Complainant in this proceeding had such rights when the Complaint was filed. Complainant has established this element of the Policy. As in *Brooke Hogan*, the Panel addresses Respondent's timing argument below under Paragraph 4(a)(iii) of the Policy. See also *Swissvoice ag v. Chan chin sung*, WIPO Case No. D2004-0672, in which the panel similarly considered the issue of trademark status at the date of registration as an issue of bad faith.

Rights or Legitimate Interest. Paragraph 4(a)(ii) of the Policy requires a complainant to prove a negative, that the Respondent lacks rights or legitimate interests in the domain name at issue. A complainant sets forth the facts within his knowledge to make a *prima face* case, which then shifts the burden of proof to the respondent to establish that he held rights or made a permitted use.[37]

Panelists in disputes under the Policy have consistently found that noncommercial fan sites qualified as legitimate use.[38] In this proceeding, though, there is no fan site. There is no evidence of

---

[36] Complainant wears the number 9 on his jersey.

[37] *Credit Suisse Group v. Milanes-Espinach, Fernando and Milanes-Espinach, SA*, WIPO Case No. D2000-1376; *Anti Flirt S.A. and Mr. Jaques Amsellem . v. WCVC*, WIPO Case No. D2000-1553; *Intocast AG v. Lee Daeyoon*, WIPO Case No. D2000-1467

[38] *E.g., RAI Radiotelevisione Italiana S.p.A. v. Alessandro Pescetelli*, WIPO Case No. D2002-0716; *Joe Cole v. Dave Skipper*, WIPO Case No. D2003-0843

Respondent's use of the Disputed Domain Name for this or indeed any other purpose, or of "demonstrable preparations" to do so. Respondent's factual assertions, if true, demonstrate only that he *intended* to use the Disputed Domain Name for a fan site. Intentions are not "demonstrable preparations" to use a domain name. Under Paragraph 4(a)(ii), once Complainant has established his *prima face* case, "concrete evidence," not intentions, is necessary to overcome that presentation. *Kevin Garnett v. Trap Block Technologies*, FA 128073 (NAF 2002). Respondent has presented no evidence at all of preparation to use the site for any purpose. Respondent's placeholder format is inadequate evidence of preparation to use the site; like any other placeholder it merely reserves the web address for future use.

Respondent does assert that he took no action to develop a website in reliance upon the pendency of, or statements made to him during, his email negotiations with Complainant's agent. In Procedural Order No. 2, the Panel requested from both parties all written correspondence between Respondent and SportsNet in February 2004, primarily to evaluate Respondent's assertion that he was lulled into inaction by Complainant's agent. Nothing in the written communications between Complainant's agent and Respondent justifies any such reliance. In his reply to Respondent's first inquiry, Complainant's agent immediately inquired about transfer of the Disputed Domain Name. Later correspondence contains no statement by Complainant's agent acceding to Respondent's continued use of the Disputed Domain Name, much less active encouragement.

While Complainant did not send his cease and desist letter until three months after discovering Respondent's alleged use of the Disputed Domain Name as an official site, his message to Respondent was consistent throughout: he wanted the right to the Disputed Domain Name, and was willing to consider paying for it. Respondent had eight months before his initial contact with Complainant and two months before receiving the cease and desist letter to make preparations for his fan site. During this time he did nothing. There is no basis for a finding of laches or estoppel.[39]

Registered and Used in Bad Faith.Paraphrasing Respondent's timing argument in the context of bad faith, Respondent asserts that since Complainant did not sign his first professional contract until November 2003, more than one year after Respondent registered the Disputed Domain Name, his registration was could not have been in bad faith because Complainant's name had not yet achieved the fame and commercial connection necessary to make it a trademark.

The complainant in *Brooke Hogan* alleged that her name had "become famous" at the time respondent registered it as a domain name, but "offer[ed] no evidence to support her allegation." Here Complainant has submitted evidence that Complainant's name had received trademark status (or equivalent stature under the Policy) on the date Respondent registered the Disputed Domain Name.[40] Respondent not only does not contest this evidence,[41] his own theory of the case depends upon Complainant's fame and success. There is and could be little basis for a fan site for an unknown soccer player or unknown actress. Complainant's evidentiary showing distinguishes this proceeding from the *Brooke Hogan* matter.

The undisputed evidence also establishes Respondent's bad faith use of the Disputed Domain Name. The most offensive act of a cybersquatter is to hold another's mark for ransom. Such conduct has earned its own subsection in Paragraph 4(b) of the Policy. The Policy was adopted specifically to provide an owner in these circumstances with a swift and inexpensive alternative to litigation to redeem his mark. Rather than a single payment for transfer of the Disputed Domain Name, Respondent's asked for continuing participation in Complainant's affairs and promotional activities, a majority interest in Complainant's official website, and ownership of media images featuring Complainant. The financial consequences to Respondent of such an arrangement would surely have exceeded his out of pocket costs for registering the Disputed Domain Name. Although Complainant initiated the possibility of transfer for money, it was Respondent who consistently pressed the Complainant for

---

[39] Respondent's contention that his registering the disputed Domain Name as a copyright deserves at best a footnote. Copyright interests confer no trademark rights on their owner. Copyrights need not be registered; they accrue from creating a word, phrase, or other work. If copyright ownership established rights under Paragraph 4(a)(ii) of the Policy, every domain name owner could automatically defeat a UDRP proceeding.

[40] Among the information submitted are articles from *Sports Illustrated* magazine, the Cleveland *Plain Dealer*, the Washington *Post*, *USA Today*, and a transcript of an interview carried on ABC. Some of these are dated in 2001

[41] In fact Respondent claims to have heard about Complainant in an article about the possibility of a professional team's signing Complainant as a twelve year old.

official status and participation in Complainant's marketing and financial activities. Paragraph 4(b)(i) specifically encompasses "other consideration." And it would defy common sense as well as the language and intent of the Policy to limit the scope of that paragraph to one-off cash transactions.

That leaves the question of whether Respondent registered the Disputed Domain Name in bad faith. Paragraph 4(a)(iii) is conjunctive, requiring both registration and use in bad faith. A panel may infer bad faith registration from bad faith use, and the evidence in this proceeding amply justifies doing so. Respondent states that he sought out Complainant at his earliest opportunity. He approached not Complainant himself, but Complainant's commercial agent. His only proposal, and the only details for any use of the website presented by Respondent, were commercial in nature and (whether intended or not) were obviously likely to yield Respondent substantial financial rewards and commercial recognition. Respondent has presented no evidence supporting his stated alternative of a fan site or any other non-commercial use. For over two years he has made no use of his website. This record establishes bad faith in registration as well as in use of the Disputed Domain Name.

Despite the connotations of the phrase *bad faith*, motive and intent should play at best a peripheral role in a panel's decision. It would be all too easy for a cybersquatter to concoct a plausible excuse and swear to its veracity if subjectively honorable intentions alone overcame the bad faith requirement of Paragraph 4(a)(iii). As this Panelist stated in *Reliant Energy, Inc. v. Brent Graeter*, WIPO Case No. D2001-0246, another case in which the defense was based upon an intention to use the complainant's mark for a fan site,

"Bad faith, as used in the Policy and the Rules, is intended to be judged by an objective standard, based upon the proof submitted by the parties, rather than a Panel's subjective evaluation of a respondent's intentions or state of mind. The Policy's and the Rules' general prohibition on live testimony and cross-examination make it virtually impossible for a Panel to evaluate the latter. Respondent's unqualified offer to sell the Domain Names is an uncontested fact, and cannot be elided by a later self-serving statement in an adversary proceeding. To the extent possible a panel should base its decision upon objective evidence."

This case illustrates a second reason for preferring objective standards for ascertaining bad faith. The Policy condemns conduct, not motives. A pure heart will not excuse tortious behavior. The Panel here has no reason to doubt Respondents' devotion to the game of soccer or his admiration for Complainant. Since his conduct plainly constitutes bad faith under the Policy, those facts are irrelevant.

7. Decision

For the foregoing reasons, in accordance with Paragraphs 4(i) of the Policy and 15 of the Rules, the Panel orders that the domain name< freddyadu.com> be transferred to the Complainant.

Richard G. Lyon
Sole Panelist
Dated: October 17, 2004

APPENDIX XXVI

SOME SELECTED SPORTS DOMAIN NAME DISPUTES CASES

WIPO Arbitration and Mediation Center

ADMINISTRATIVE PANEL DECISION
World Wrestling Federation Entertainment, Inc. v. Michael Bosman
Case No. D99-0001

1. The Parties
The complainant is World Wrestling Federation Entertainment, Inc., f/k/a Titan Sports, Inc., a corporation organized under the laws of the State of Delaware, United States of America, having its principal place of business at Stamford, Connecticut, United States of America. The respondent is Michael Bosman, an individual resident in Redlands, California, United States of America.

2. The Domain Name(s) and Registrar(s)
The domain name at issue is <worldwrestlingfederation.com>, which domain name is registered with Melbourne IT, based in Australia.

3. Procedural History
A Complaint was submitted electronically to the World Intellectual Property Organization Arbitration and Mediation Center (the "WIPO Center") on December 2, 1999, and the signed original together with four copies forwarded by express courier under cover of a letter of the same date. An Acknowledgment of Receipt was sent by the WIPO Center to the complainant, dated December 3, 1999.

On December 3, 1999 a Request for Registrar Verification was transmitted to the registrar, Melbourne IT requesting it to: (1) confirm that the domain name at issue is registered with MelbourneIT; (2) confirm that the person identified as the respondent is the current registrant of the domain name; (3) provide the full contact details (i.e., postal address(es), telephone number(s), facsimile number(s), e-mail address(es)) available in the registrar's Whois database for the registrant of the disputed domain name, the technical contact, the administrative contact and the billing contact; (4) provide a copy of the registration agreement that was in effect at the time of the original registration of the domain name, as well as any subsequent amendments to the agreement; (5) provide a copy of the domain name dispute policy (if different from ICANN's Uniform Domain Name Dispute Resolution Policy) that was in effect at the time of the original registration of the domain name, as well as any subsequent amendments to the policy.

On December 8, 1999, MelbourneIT confirmed by reply e-mail that the domain name <worldwrestlingfederation.com> is registered with MelbourneIT and that the respondent, Michael Bosman, was the current registrant of the name. The registrar also forwarded the requested Who is details, as well as copies of the registration agreement and applicable dispute resolution policy.

The policy in effect at the time of the original registration of the domain name at issue provided that "Registrant agrees to be bound by the terms and conditions of this Registration Agreement." MelbourneIT Domain Name Registration Agreement, effective as of October 7, 1999, para. 1. Paragraph 7 of the Registration Agreement, entitled, "Dispute Policy," provides in pertinent part:

Registrant agrees, as a condition to submitting this Registration Agreement, and if the Registration Agreement is accepted by MelbourneIT, that the Registrant is bound by MelbourneIT's current Dispute Policy ("Dispute Policy"). Registrant agrees that MelbourneIT, in its sole discretion, may change or modify the Dispute Policy, incorporated by reference herein, at any time. Registrant agrees that Registrant's maintaining the registration of a domain name after changes or modifications to the Dispute Policy become effective constitutes Registrant's continued acceptance of these changes or modifications. Registrant agrees that if Registrant considers any such changes or modifications to be unacceptable, Registrant may request that the domain name be deleted from the domain name database. Registrant agrees that any dispute relating to the registration or use of its domain name will be subject to the provisions specified in the Dispute Policy.

Effective December 1, 1999, MelbourneIT adopted the Uniform Domain Name Dispute Resolution Policy, adopted by the Internet Corporation for Assigned Names and Numbers ("ICANN") on August 26, 1999 (the "Policy"). There is no evidence that respondent ever requested that the domain name at issue be deleted from the domain name database. Accordingly, respondent is bound by the provisions of the Policy.

On December 6, 1999, having received written permission from the WIPO Center, the complainant submitted (electronically and in hardcopy) a Supplemental Complaint under cover of a letter of the same date. The Complaint and Supplemental Complaint will hereafter be referred to as the "Complaint."

A Formal Requirements Compliance Checklist was completed by the assigned WIPO Center Case Administrator on December 8, 1999. The Panel has independently determined and agrees with the assessment of the WIPO Center that the Complaint is in formal compliance with the requirements of the Policy, the Rules for Uniform Domain Name Dispute Resolution Policy, as approved by ICANN on October 24, 1999 (the "Uniform Rules"), and the WIPO Supplemental Rules for Uniform Domain Dispute Resolution Policy, in effect as of December 1, 1999 (the "WIPO Supplemental Rules"). The required fees for a single-member Panel were paid on time and in the required amount by the complainant.

No formal deficiencies having been recorded, on December 9, 1999, a Notification of Complaint and Commencement of Administrative Proceeding (the "Commencement Notification") was transmitted to the respondent (with copies to the complainant, MelbourneIT and ICANN), setting a deadline of December 28, 1999, by which the respondent could file a Response to the Complaint. The Commencement Notification was transmitted to the respondent by e-mail to the e-mail addresses indicated in the Complaint and specified in MelbourneIT's Whois confirmation, as well as to <postmster@worldwrestlingfederation.com>; no e-mail addresses were found at any web page relating to the disputed domain name. In addition, the complaint was sent by express courier to all available postal addresses. Having reviewed the communications records in the case file, the Administrative Panel finds that the WIPO Center has discharged its responsibility under Paragraph 2(a) of the Uniform Rules "to employ reasonably available means calculated to achieve actual notice to Respondent." In any event, evidence of proper notice is provided by the evidence in the record of the respondent's participation in the settlement negotiations with the complainant.

On December 14, 1999, in view of the complainant's designation of a single panelist (but without prejudice to any election to be made by the respondent) the WIPO Center invited M. Scott Donahey to serve as a panelist in Case No. D99-0001, and transmitted to him a Statement of Acceptance and Request for Declaration of Impartiality and Independence.

On December 29, 1999, having received no Response from the designated respondent, using the same contact details and methods as were used for the Commencement Notification, the WIPO Center transmitted to the parties a Notification of Respondent Default.

Having received on December 14, 1999, M. Scott Donahey's Statement of Acceptance and Declaration of Impartiality and Independence, also on December 29, 1999, the WIPO Center transmitted to the parties a Notification of Appointment of Administrative Panel and Projected Decision Date, in which M. Scott Donahey was formally appointed as the Sole Panelist. The Projected Decision Date was January 11, 2000. The Sole Panelist finds that the Administrative Panel was properly constituted and appointed in accordance with the Uniform Rules and WIPO Supplemental Rules.

Following these transmittals, the WIPO Center received a series of emails from the respondent and the complainant's representative, indicating that the parties intended to settle and had reached a settlement in principle. On January 6, 2000, the WIPO Center received a copy of an unsigned settlement agreement, with assurances that a signed copy would be transmitted by facsimile. On January 6, 2000, in view of the settlement negotiations between the parties, the Case Administrator notified the parties that the time in which the Panel was to issue a decision on the merits had been extended to January 15, 2000.

Following repeated requests from the WIPO Center for a copy of the fully executed final settlement agreement, on January 12, 2000, a copy of an agreement, signed only by respondent, was received. While the Panel is aware that the parties are close to completing their settlement, the Panel is also mindful of its responsibility to issue a timely decision, and one in compliance with the deadlines established by the Uniform Rules, the WIPO Supplemental Rules, and those established by the WIPO Center in accordance with those rules. *See, e.g.*, Uniform Rules, paras. 10(c) and 15(b). Accordingly, this decision is issued prior to having received completely executed settlement documents, and, as such, does not rely on any purported settlement agreement.

The Administrative Panel shall issue its Decision based on the Complaint, the e-mails exchanged, the Policy, the Uniform Rules, the WIPO Supplemental Rules, and without the benefit of any Response from respondent.

4. Factual Background

The complainant has provided evidence of the registration of the following marks:

1. Service Mark – WORLD WRESTLING FEDERATION, registered for a term of 20 years from January 29, 1985, with the United States Patent and Trademark Office;
2. Trademark – WORLD WRESTLING FEDERATION, registered for a term of 20 years from November 7, 1989, with the United States Patent and Trademark Office.
   Complaint, Annexes B and C.

The respondent registered the domain name <worldwrestlingfederation.com> for a term of two years from October 7, 1999. E-mail dated December 7, 1999, from Jan Webster to the WIPO Center Case Administrator, providing Whois details. The respondent is not a licensee of complainant, nor is he otherwise authorized to use complainant's marks. Complaint, para. 14.

Complainant is authorized to use and has used its service mark in connection with entertainment services, namely the provision of sporting events such as wrestling exhibitions for television. Complaint, para. 17 and Annex B. Complainant is authorized to use and has used its trademark in connection with metal key chains, phonograph records, prerecorded audio and video cassettes, switch plates, computer programs concerning the sport of wrestling, watches, stickers, book markers, book plates, collection books, pictorial biographies, blowouts, paper napkins, paper table covers, memo boards, posters, stationery-type portfolios, memo pads, book covers calendars, trading cards, pens, pencils, magazines, decals, umbrellas, backpacks, roll bags, seat cushions, towels, shoes, bibs, children's pajamas, T-shirts, sweatshirts, ties, caps, sweaters, sports shirts, headbands, sweatbands, belts, fleece sets comprising warm-up pants and warm-up jacket, puzzles, board games, workout sets comprising exercise equipment in the nature of barbells, dumbbells, handgrips, wristbands. Charts, and/or audio cassette tapes. Complaint, para. 18 and Annex C. Complainant has also used its mark in connection with the promotion of wrestling entertainment services on its internet web site which may be found at <wwf.com>. Complaint, para. 19.

On October 10, 1999, three days after registering the domain name at issue, respondent contacted complainant by e-mail and notified complainant of the registration and stated that his primary purpose in registering the domain name was to sell, rent or otherwise transfer it to complainant for a valuable consideration in excess of respondent's out-of-pocket expenses. Complaint, paras. 25 and 26. By e-mail dated December 3, 1999, respondent contacted complainant's representative and offered to sell the complainant the domain name at issue for the sum of US$1,000.00. Supplemental Complaint, para. 4 and Annex A. In his e-mail, respondent stated that cybersquatting cases "typically accomplish very little and end up costing the companies thousands of dollars in legal fees, wasted time and energy." Supplemental Complaint, Annex A. The payment of US$1,000 would represent more than payment for respondent's time and money, but also and "most important" [sic] would serve as consideration for "the right of current ownership of the domain name `worldwrestlingfederation.com.'" Supplemental Complaint, para. 7.

Respondent has not developed a Web site using the domain name at issue or made any other good faith use of the domain name. Complaint, para. 28. The domain name at issue is not, nor could it be contended to be, a nickname of respondent or other member of his family, the name of a household pet, or in any other way identified with or related to a legitimate interest of respondent.

5. Parties' Contentions

A. Complainant

Complainant contends that respondent has registered as a domain name a mark which is identical to the service mark and trademark registered and used by complainant, that respondent has no rights or legitimate interests in respect to the domain name at issue, and that respondent has registered and is using the domain name at issue in bad faith.

B. Respondent
Respondent has not contested the allegations of the Complaint.

6. Discussion and Findings
Paragraph 15(a) of the Rules instructs the Panel as to the principles the Panel is to use in determining the dispute: "A Panel shall decide a complaint on the basis of the statements and documents submitted in accordance with the Policy, these Rules and any rules and principles of law that it deems applicable." Since both the complainant and respondent are domiciled in the United States, and since United States' courts have recent experience with similar disputes, to the extent that it would assist the Panel in determining whether the complainant has met its burden as established by Paragraph 4(a) of the Policy, the Panel shall look to rules and principles of law set out in decisions of the courts of the United States.

Paragraph 4(a) of the Policy directs that the complainant must prove each of the following:

1) that the domain name registered by the respondent is identical or confusingly similar to a trademark or service mark in which the complainant has rights; and,
2) that the respondent has no legitimate interests in respect of the domain name; and,
3) the domain name has been registered and used in bad faith.

It is clear beyond cavil that the domain name <worldwrestlingfederation.com> is identical or confusingly similar to the trademark and service mark registered and used by complainant, WORLD WRESTLING FEDERATION. It is also apparent that the respondent has no rights or legitimate interests in respect of the domain name. Since the domain name was registered on October 7, 1999, and since respondent offered to sell it to complainant three days later, the Panel believes that the name was registered in bad faith.

However, the name must not only be registered in bad faith, but it must also be used in bad faith. The issue to be determined is whether the respondent used the domain name in bad faith. It is not disputed that the respondent did not establish a Web site corresponding to the registered domain name. Accordingly, can it be said that the respondent "used" the domain name?

It is clear from the legislative history that ICANN intended that the complainant must establish not only bad faith registration, but also bad faith use. "These comments point out that cybersquatters often register names in bulk, but do not use them, yet without use the streamlined dispute-resolution procedure is not available. While that argument appears to have merit on initial impression, it would involve a change in the policy adopted by the Board. The WIPO report, the DNSO recommendation, and the registrars-group recommendation all required both registration <u>and</u> use in bad faith before the streamlined procedure would be invoked. Staff recommends that this requirement not be changed without study and recommendation by the DNSO." Second Staff Report on Implementation Documents for the Uniform Dispute Resolution Policy, submitted for Board meeting of October 24, 1999, para. 4.5,a.

Paragraph 4,b,i of the Policy, provides that "the following circumstances ... shall be evidence of the registration and use of a domain name in bad faith: ... circumstances indicating that you have registered or you have acquired the domain name primarily for the purpose of selling, renting or otherwise transferring the domain name registration to the complainant who is the owner of the trademark or service mark ... for valuable consideration in excess of the documented out-of-pocket costs directly related to the domain name." (Emphasis added.)

Because respondent offered to sell the domain name to complainant "for valuable consideration in excess of" any out-of-pocket costs directly related to the domain name, respondent has "used" the domain name in bad faith as defined in the Policy.

Although it is therefore unnecessary to consult decisions of United States' courts, the panel notes that decisions of those courts in cases which determine what constitutes "use" where the right to a domain name is contested by a mark owner support the panel's conclusion. For example, in the case of *Panavision International, L.P. v. Dennis Toeppen, et al.*, 141 F. 3d 1316 (9th Cir. 1998), the Court of Appeals held that the defendant's intention to sell the domain name to the plaintiff constituted "use" of the plaintiff's mark:

"Toeppen's argument misstates his use of the Panavision mark. His use is not as benign as he suggests. Toeppen's `business' is to register trademarks as domain names and then sell them to the rightful trademark owners. He `acts as a `spoiler,' preventing Panavision and others from doing business on the Internet under their trademarked names unless they pay his fee.' ... As the district court found, Toeppen traded on the value of Panavision's marks. So long as he held the Internet registrations, he curtailed Panavision's exploitation of the value of its trademarks on the Internet, a value which Toeppen then used when he attempted to sell the panavision.com domain name to Panavision." *Id.*, at 1325.

To the same effect is the decision in *Intermatic Inc. v. Toeppen*, 947 F. Supp. 1227 (N.D. Ill. 1996). In that case the Federal District Court determined that "Toeppen's intention to arbitrage the `intermatic. com' domain name constitutes a commercial use... . Toeppen's desire to resell the domain name is sufficient to meet the `commercial use' requirement of the Lanham Act. *Id.*, 1239.

The Panel notes with approval that the Policy and Rules set out by ICANN encourage thesettle-ment and that the parties in this case have engaged in extensive settlement negotiations. It was noted by the complainant in an email to the respondent regarding possible settlement that, while it was not the complainant's policy to pay individuals to stop infringing its intellectual property, it was also complainant's policy not to litigate against its fans. Email from Complainant's Representative to Respondent, dated December 09, 1999. Complainant acknowledged that it could have proceeded to litigation under the United States "Anticybersquatting Consumer Protection Act," but that it elected not to. By engaging in this proceeding, complainant has sought to protect complainant's intellectual property interests while preserving the relationship between complainant and its fans at a minimal cost to all concerned.

7. Decision

For all of the foregoing reasons, the Panel decides that the domain name registered by respondent is identical or confusingly similar to the trademark and service mark in which the complainant has rights, and that the respondent has no rights or legitimate interests in respect of the domain name, and that the respondent's domain name has been registered and is being used in bad faith. Accordingly, pursuant to Paragraph 4,i of the Policy, the Panel requires that the registration of the domain name <worldwrestlingfederation.com> be transferred to the complainant.

M. Scott Donahey
Presiding Panelist
Dated: January 14, 2000

WIPO Arbitration and Mediation Center

ADMINISTRATIVE PANEL DECISION
ISL Marketing AG, and The Federation Internationale de Football Association v. J.Y. Chung, Worldcup2002.com, W Co., and Worldcup 2002
Case No. D2000-0034

1. The Parties

The First Complainant is ISL Marketing AG ("ISL"). The Second Complainant is The Federation Internationale de Football Association ("FIFA"), a non-profit association organized in accordance with Article 60(ff) of the Swiss Civil Code. ISL and FIFA collectively are referred to herein as "the Complainants".

The First Respondent is Mr. Ji Young Chung ("Chung"), and individual of In Chon, Korea. The Second Respondent is Worldcup2002.com, the legal status of which is not clear. The Third Respond-ent is W Co., the legal status of which is not clear. The Fourth Respondent is Worldcup 2002, the legal status of which is not clear. The First Respondent, the Second Respondent, the Third Respond-ent and the Fourth Respondent collectively are referred to herein as "the Respondents".

2. The Domain Names and Registrar

The domain names the subject of this Complaint are:

(1) worldcup2002.com

(2) worldcup2002.net
(3) worldcup2002.org
(4) worldcup02.org
(5) worldcup10.com
(6) 2002worldcup.org
(7) worldcup02.net
(8) 2002worldcup.net
(9) worldcup2006.org
(10) worldcup2010.com
(11) worldcup2010.org
(12) worldcup2010.net
(13) 2006worldcup.org
(14) wc2002.com
(15) wc02.com

For ease of reference, at various points throughout this Decision identification of each of these domain names is made by way of the number associated with it in the above list.

The Registrar of each of these domain names is Network Solutions, Inc of Herndon, Virginia, USA.

3. Procedural History
Issuance of Complaint
On February 3, 2000, the Complainants submitted to the World Intellectual Property Organization Arbitration and Mediation Center ("WIPO Center") a Complaint made pursuant to the Uniform Domain Name Dispute Resolution Policy implemented by the Internet Corporation for Assigned Names and Numbers (ICANN) on October 24, 1999 ("Uniform Policy"), and under the Rules for Uniform Domain Name Dispute Resolution Policy implemented by ICANN on the same date ("Uniform Rules"). The Complainant concerned the domain names (1)-(3) inclusive.

A Supplement to the Complainant was submitted by the Complainants to the WIPO Center on February 14, 2000. This Supplement concerned domain names (4)-(15) inclusive.

Confirmation of Registration Details
A Request for Registrar Verification in relation to all the domain names the subject of this Complaint was dispatched by the WIPO Center to the Registrar by email on February 15, 2000. By emails to the WIPO Center on February 16 and February17, 2000, the Registrar in relation to each of the domain names confirmed that it had received a copy of the Complaint from the Complainant; confirmed that it was the Registrar of the domain names; identified and provided contact details for the current registrant, the Administrative Contact, the Technical Contact and the Billing Contact of those domain names; and informed that the status of each of the domain names is "active". The registrant, Administrative Contact and Record Created date for each of these domain names is as follows:

Domain Name	Registrant	Administrative Contact	Record Created
(1)	Worldcup2002.com	Chung, JY	31-Dec-1997
(2)	W Co.	Chung, JY	07-Sep-1997
(3)	Worldcup 2002	Chung, JY	26-Aug-1997
(4)	Worldcup 02	Chung, JY	15-Sep-1997
(5)	Worldcup 10 Promotions	Chung, JY	16-Sep-1997
(6)	Worldcup 2002	Chung, JY	09-Sep-1997
(7)	Worldcup 2002 News	Chung, JY	13-Sep-1997
(8)	Worldcup 2002 Update	Chung, JY	09-Sep-1997
(9)	Worldcup 2006	Chung, JY	09-Sep-1997

(10)	Worldcup 2010	Chung, JY	10-Sep-1997
(11)	Worldcup 2010 Online	Chung, JY	10-Sep-1997
(12)	Worldcup 2010 Promotions	Chung, JY	10-Sep-1997
(13)	Ji Young Chung	Chung, JY	17-Oct-1999
(14)	Worldcup	Chung, JY	13-Sep-1997
(15)	Worldcup	Chung, JY	13-Sep-1997

By an email to the WIPO Center on March 24, 2000, the Registrar confirmed that the "record created" date is the date on which the domain name was first registered.

By emails to the WIPO Center on February 16, and February 17, 2000, the Registrar also confirmed in relation to each of the domain names that either 4.0 Service Agreement or 5.0 Service Agreement is in effect. Amongst other things, both 4.0 Service Agreement and 5.0 Service Agreement provide that the registrant agrees to be bound by the domain name dispute policy incorporated therein. The policy incorporated into those Agreements is the Uniform Policy. The language of these registration Agreements is English. The case before this Administrative Panel was conducted in the English language.

Notification to Respondents

Having verified that the Complaint satisfied the formal requirements of the Uniform Policy and the Uniform Rules, and that payment of the filing fee had been properly made, the WIPO Center issued to the Respondents on February 18, 2000, a Notification of Complaint and Commencement of Administrative Proceeding, to the postal, facsimile and email contact details of the Respondents, as provided by the Registrar. Copies of this Notification of Complaint were sent to the Complainant, the Registrar and ICANN on the same date.

Records show that the facsimile transmissions to Chung and to the Technical and Zone Contacts for the domain names were received by them. Records show that the email transmissions to many of the email addresses given by the Registrar as being the contact email addresses of the registrant or of the Administrative, Technical or Zone Contact of the domain names, were not received, the addresses having "permanent fatal errors". By virtue of the fact that the facsimile transmissions to Chung and to the Technical and Zone Contacts for the domain names were received by them, and the fact that Administrative Contact of all of the domain names, Chung, filed a response to the Complaint, this Administrative Panel finds that, for each of the domain names the subject of this dispute, the WIPO Center has discharged its responsibility under rule 2(a) of the Uniform Rules "to employ reasonably available means calculated to achieve actual notice to Respondent".

Filing of Response

On March 9, 2000, the WIPO Center received from the First Respondent, Chung, a Response dated March 6, 2000. This Response was not expressed to be made on behalf of Chung alone. The tenor of the Response (which is discussed further in section 5, below) is to the effect that the Response is made on behalf of the First, Second, Third and Fourth Respondents.

Constitution of Administrative Panel

On March 8, 2000, the WIPO Center issued to the prospective sole Panelist, Dr. Andrew Christie, a request for Declaration of Impartiality and Independence. On March 13, 2000, Dr. Christie submitted to the WIPO Center a Statement of Acceptance and Declaration of Impartiality and Independence. On the same date the WIPO Center issued to both parties a Notification of Appointment of Administrative Panel and Projected Decision Date, informing of Dr. Christie's appointment and that, absent exceptional circumstances, a decision would be provided by this Administrative Panel by March 26, 2000. This Administrative Panel found that exceptional circumstances existed which required the projected date of decision to be extended. These circumstances included the fact that there are a large number of domain names the subject of the Complaint, the fact that there are multiple Complainants and Respondents, the fact that there was filed a Supplement to the Complaint, and the fact that there was some question whether the Complaint complied with the formalities of the Uniform Policy and Uniform Rules (as discussed below).

Compliance with the formalities of the Uniform Policy and the Uniform Rules
This Administrative Panel notes that pursuant to rule 1 of the Uniform Rules, the "Respondent" means "the holder of a domain-name registration against which a complaint is initiated", and that pursuant to rule 3(c) of the Uniform Rules, "the complaint may relate to more than one domain name, provided that the domain names are registered by the same domain-name holder". This Administrative Panel acknowledges three points in relation to the Complainant's naming of the Respondents to this Complaint: (i) the First Respondent, Chung, is not the registrant of any of the domain names; (ii) the domain names are not all registered by the same domain name holder; and (iii) the registrants of domain names (4), (5), (7)-(12) inclusive, (14) and (15) are not named as Respondents.

Nevertheless, it is the case that the First Respondent, Chung, is the Administrative Contact for each of the domain names. In addition, the precise legal status (including whether they in fact exist) of many of the registrants – in particular, the registrants of domain names (4), (5), (7)-(12) inclusive, (14) and (15) – is not clear. Further, in his Response Chung states that he "has been maintaining a relationship with" and has "influence over" the registrants of those names, and "may be said to be the virtual owner of" some of them. Finally, in his Response Chung did not challenge the validity of any aspect of the formalities of the Complaint. In light of these facts, it appears to this Administrative Panel that Chung is the person responsible for and beneficially entitled to the registration of each of the domain names in issue. Taking into account the general principles underlying the Uniform Policy and the Uniform Rules, this Administrative Panel finds that in substance the appropriate Respondents have been named in relation to all of the domain names the subject of the Complaint.

Accordingly, this Administrative Panel concurs with the assessment by the WIPO Center that the Complaint as supplemented by the Supplement to the Complaint complies with the formal requirements of the Uniform Policy and Uniform Rules.

4. Factual Background
The Complainants asserted, and generally provided evidence in support of, the following facts. Except where stated in section 5 below, the Respondents did not challenge these facts. Except where stated otherwise, this Administrative Panel finds these facts established.

Complainants' Activities
FIFA, founded in Paris in 1904, is the world governing body of the sport of "association football" (commonly known throughout the world as soccer or football). FIFA is comprised of the National Football Association of 203 countries around the world, and is the originator and organizer of a number of world soccer championships, including, in particular, the widely known quadrennial world football championship known as the World Cup. In 2002, FIFA will sponsor, and Korea and Japan will co-host, the first World Cup championship to be held outside of Europe and/or the Americas. The 2002 World Cup championship has attracted substantial attention and generated significant independent press coverage throughout Asia and the remainder of the world. FIFA maintains a significant presence on the Internet through its website located at www.fifa.com.

ISL is the exclusive marketing agent for FIFA, charged with the commercial exploitation and protection of FIFA's intellectual property rights including, in particular, the <WORLD CUP> mark and properties.

Complainants' Trademarks
FIFA, or an entity whose name includes the letters ISL, is the owner of numerous trademark registrations for the <WORLD CUP> mark and variations thereof in countries throughout the world, including the following:

a. Swiss Trademark Registration No. 431340 for the WORLD CUP mark covering goods in the following International Classes: 3 (cosmetics and cleaning preparations); 4 (lubricants and fuels); 6 (metal goods); 8 (hand tools); 9 (electrical and scientific apparatus); 11 (environmental control apparatus); 12 (vehicles); 14 (jewelry, precious metals); 16 (paper goods and printed matter); 18 (leather goods); 20 (furniture and articles not otherwise classified); 21 (housewares and glass); 24 (fabrics);

25 (clothing); 28 (toys and sporting goods); 29 (meats and processed foods); 30 (staple foods); 32 (light beverages); 33 (wine and spirits); 36 (insurance and financial services); 38 (communications services); 39 (transportation and storage services); 42 (miscellaneous services). A copy of the FIFA's registration certificate is attached as Exhibit 4 to the Complaint.

b. Swiss Trademark Registration No. 403353 for the mark WORLD CUP JAPAN 2002 covering goods in the following International Classes: 3, 4, 6, 7, 8, 9, 11, 12, 14, 16, 18, 20, 21, 24, 25, 28, 29, 30, 32, 33 (See descriptions provided in paragraph above); and International Classes 1 (chemicals); 5 (pharmaceuticals); 26 (fancy goods); 27 (floor coverings); 31 (natural agricultural products); and 34 (smoker's articles). A copy of ISL Football AG's registration certificate is attached as Exhibit 5 to the Complaint.

c. International Trademark Registration No. 678511 for the mark WORLD CUP for goods falling in International Classes: 3, 4, 6, 8, 9, 11, 12, 14, 16, 18, 20, 21, 24, 25, 26, 28, 29, 30, 32, 33, 36, 38, 39, 40, 41, 42. A copy of FIFA's registration certificate is attached as Exhibit 6 of the Complaint.

d. Japanese Trademark Registration No. 4012048 for the mark WORLD CUP for the following goods and services: unworked or semi-worked glass (except building glass); pans; non-electric coffee-pots (not of precious metal); Tetsubin (cast iron kettles); kettles; tableware (not of precious metal); ice pails; household whisks (non-electric); portable cold boxes; strainers; pepper pots; sugar bowls; salt shakers (not of precious metal); trays (not of precious metal); toothpick holders (not of precious metal); rice chests; bamboo bowls; shakers; rice scoops; hand-operated coffee grinders and hand-operated pepper mills; funnels; glass preserving jars; drinking flasks; wooden pestles; earthenware mortars; dining trays/stands; bottle openers; graters; tart scoops; pan-mats/trivets; chopsticks; chopstick cases; ladles/dippers; sieves/sifters; chopping boards; insulating flasks/vacuum bottles; rolling pins; grills; toothpicks; lemon squeezers; non-electric waffle irons; cleaning or laundry equipment; tub brushes; metal brushes; brushes for pipes; industrial brushes; ship scrubbing brushes; pig bristles for brushes; clothes brushes; packaging containers of glass or ceramic; troughs for livestock; poultry rings; feeding vessels for pets; brushes for pets; chewing pacifiers for dogs; flower pots; hydroponic instruments for home gardening; cinder sifters for household use; boxes of metal for dispensing paper towels; boot jacks; bird cages; bird baths; watering cans; chamber pots; coal scuttles; soap dispensers; piggy banks (not of metal); toilet paper holders; mouse traps; fly swatters; bath water stirrers; bathroom stools; bathroom pails; candle extinguishers and candlesticks (not of precious metal); vases (not of precious metal); upright signboards of ceramic or glass; koro (incense burners); flower bowls (not of precious metal); wind chimes. A copy of ISL Properties Aktiengesellschaft's registration certificate is attached as Exhibit 7 of the Complaint.

e. Korean Trademark Registration No. 348097 for the mark WORLD CUP for goods in International Class 6 (beers and ales). A copy of FIFA's registration certificate is attached as Exhibit 8 of the Complaint.

f. Japanese Trademark Registration No. 320598 for the mark WORLD CUP JAPAN 2002 for the following goods and services in Class 9: batteries; glasses; electrical communication machines and apparatus; records; metronomes; applied electronic machines and instruments; electric irons; electric hair-curlers; electric wax polishers; electric cleaners; electric buzzers; cinematographic films; transparencies; slide film mounts pre-recorded video discs and video tapes; toys for television games for home use. A copy of FIFA's registration certificate is attached as Exhibit 9 of the Complaint.

g. Japanese Trademark Registration No. 320598 for the mark WORLD CUP JAPAN 2002 and Device for the same goods identified in the paragraph above. A copy of FIFA's registration certificate is attached as Exhibit 10 of the Complaint.

h. Korean Trademark Registration No. 339323 for the mark 2002 WORLD CUP KOREA and Device for the following goods in Class 52: non-music recorded tapes; phone cards; pictorial postcards; calendars; pamphlets; credit cards; card keys; motion picture films; slide films and photographs. A copy of FIFA's registration certificate is attached as Exhibit 11 of the Complaint.

i. International Trademark Registration No. 482138 for the mark FIFA WORLD CUP Trophy and Device for the goods and services in International Classes 6, 14, 25, 28. A copy of FIFA's registration certificate is attached as Exhibit 12 of the Complaint.

According to the documentation provided by the Complainants, the trademarks identified in (b) and (d) above are registered in the name of ISL Football AG, and ISL Properties Aktiengesellschaft, respectively. The Complainants have not provided any evidence of the connection, if any, between these two entities and the Complainants. Accordingly, this Administrative Panel makes no finding, for the purpose of this Complaint, that the Complainants own the trademark registrations alleged in paragraphs (b) and (d) above.

With the apparent exception of trademark registration (c) above, each of the trademark registrations which this Administrative Panel finds is owned by the FIFA was issued on a date before the earliest date of registration of any of the domain names in issue (namely August 26, 1997, for domain name (3)).

FIFA has used the <WORLD CUP> mark in connection with the promotion of its World Cup event via its Internet website located at www.fifa.com. In addition, FIFA has used the <WORLD CUP> brand to promote its international football championship for nearly a century. The <WORLD CUP> brand name symbolizes the substantial goodwill associated with FIFA. Furthermore, due to its wide and substantial international use, the FIFA <WORLD CUP> mark and associated marks enjoy significant fame.

Respondents' Activities

Prior to the issuance of this Complaint, at a time not specified by the Complaints, Chung established web sites at http://www.worldcup2002.net and http://www.worldcup2002.org, each of which resolve to the homepage located at http://www.worldcup2002.com ("Chung's web site"). As at January 20, 2000, this web site framed content from FIFA's official web sites (including, in particular, FIFA's official web site, the official web site of FIFA's Japan Organizing Committee, and the official web site of FIFA's Korean Organizing Committee) without the Complainants' authorization or authority beneath a horizontal banner listing the disputed domain names (1)-(3) inclusive (Exhibits 15 and 16 of the Complaint). Chung's web site also included news releases taken in their entirety, and without permission, from FIFA's official website. These articles were included in a link on Chung's web site titled <Media News> (Exhibits 23, 24 and 25 of the Complaint).

The Complainants assert that Chung's web site included advertisements from competitor companies to FIFA's official WORLD CUP 2002 corporate sponsors, and that Chung likely collects advertising revenues and profits from these activities. Attached as Exhibit 26 of the Complaint is an alleged screen shot of Chung's web site displaying a VISA advertisement beneath the disputed domain names (1)-(3) inclusive. Attached as Exhibit 27 of the Complaint is an alleged screen shot of the full VISA advertisement obtained by clicking on the VISA button advertisement on Chung's web site. The Complainant states that contrary to the implication left by Chung's web sites, MASTERCARD, not VISA, is the official corporate sponsor (for financial services) of WORLD CUP 2002.

This Administrative Panel notes that the VISA advertisement in Exhibit 26 appears to be superimposed over, rather embedded within, the page of Chung's web site. Further, this Administrative Panel notes that Exhibit 27 of the Complaint is in fact a screen shot of Chung's web site displaying a list of songs which may be listened to using <Real Player>. Also, in his Response Chung asserts that "the affiliated web site Japan.CC, not this website, used to have a VISA card ad". In light of the fact that this issue is contested by the Respondents, and that the evidence of the Complainants on this issue is at best ambiguous, for the purpose of this Complaint this Administrative Panel does not find that Chung's web site included advertisements.

On December 24, 1999, Chung sent an email to Christoph P. Malms, Chairman of ISMM, the parent company of ISL (a copy of which is Exhibit 13 of the Complaint). The subject line of this email is "WORLDCUP2002.COM NET ORG". The substantive contents of this email are:

I am the owner of the above three domain names.
I understand your company is going to make a website for wo.
May I ask whether the above names cud be used as your website?
If you are interested in any of the names, I am willing to sell it to your company.
Worldcup2002.com is now in operation on the web although its contents are not so rich at the moment.
Please visit if you have any time.

5. Parties' Contentions

The Complaint

The Complainants contend that each of the three elements specified in paragraph 4(a) of the Uniform Policy are applicable to each of the domain names the subject of this dispute.

In relation to element (i) of paragraph 4(a) of the Uniform Policy, the Complainants contend that each of the domain names are confusingly similar to FIFA's <WORLD CUP> mark. In particular, the Complainants contend that the domain names "incorporate, both fully and in abbreviated form, FIFA's ... trademark WORLD CUP ... and significantly incorporate each of FIFA's marks WORLD CUP, WORLD CUP JAPAN 2002, WORLD CUP KOREA JAPAN 2002, and WORLD CUP KOREA 2002".

In relation to element (ii) of paragraph 4(a) of the Uniform Policy, the Complainants contend that Chung does not have rights or legitimate interests in the domain names "by virtue of the fact that FIFA's WORLD CUP mark(s) are distinct and famous, and Chung's use of FIFA's marks is unauthorized". Further, the Complainants contend that none of the three circumstances identified in paragraph 4(c) of the Uniform Policy apply to Chung's activities.

In relation to element (iii) of paragraph 4(a) of the Uniform Policy, the Complainants contend that evidence of bad faith registration and use is established by circumstances of the sort identified in paragraphs 4(b)(i), (ii) and (iv) of the Uniform Policy. In relation to paragraph 4(b)(i) circumstances, the Complainants point to Chung's December 24, email to Christoph P. Malms. In relation to paragraph 4(b)(ii) circumstances, the Complainants point to Chung's registration of 15 domain names containing or abbreviating the mark <WORLD CUP>. In relation to paragraph 4(b)(iv) circumstances, the Complainants point to the fact that Chung's web site framed the content of FIFA's web site, slavish copied the content of FIFA's press releases, and used FIFA's trademarks in a manner unlawfully suggesting a sponsorship or association which does not exist. In addition, the Complainants contend that bad faith on the part of the Respondents is evidenced by the fact that Chung "deliberately registers domain names under fictitious organizations, in breach of his contract with NSI, to disguise his individual connection to and evade his legal responsibility for the registration of his domain names".

Complainants' Request under Rule 12

In their Supplement to the Complaint, the Complainants requested the Panel under rule 12 of the Uniform Rules:

to compel Chung to produce a full list of his domain names associated with his NIC handles JYC6 and JC11182, and any other NIC handles registered to Chung.

The reason for this request was stated as follows:

NSI will provide, via email, reports listing all domains registered to a particular NIC contact handle. Because NSI does not respond to informal discovery requests and NSI will only send these reports to the email address listed for the NIC contact handle, Plaintiff cannot obtain a list of all trademark-related domain names currently registered by Chung.

The Response

The Respondents in general terms contend that none of the three elements specified in paragraph 4(a) of the Uniform Policy are applicable to any of the domain names the subject of this dispute.

In relation to element (i) of paragraph 4(a) of the Uniform Policy, the Respondents contend that the compound phrase <worldcup2002> "is neither identical nor similar to FIFA's 'world cup' as registered" by it. In addition, the Respondents contend their use of the domain names does not create any confusion with the Complainants, because Chung's web site "clearly states in large letters on its front page that it is not FIFA's official website".

In relation to element (ii) of paragraph 4(a) of the Uniform Policy, the Respondents contend that they have rights or legitimate interests in respect of the domain names, by virtue of the circumstances identified in paragraph 4(c). In particular, the Respondents contend that Chung's web site "had already been in use for bona fide offering of online service before the notice of dispute. It has increasingly been known as such."

Further, the Respondents contend that Chung "has been making a legitimate non-commercial or fair use of <worldcup2002.com>". The substance of this contention is best elaborated by quoting (necessarily at some length) from the Response, as follows:

At the moment, worldcup2002.com is providing several links with world cup-related websites and some information about Korea and Japan without any purpose of getting commercial gain. The intent is to provide an integrated and more convenient world cup 2002-related website for the world cup soccer fans around the world. This is motivated by [Chung's] dissatisfaction with the conventional world cup related websites. [Chung] strongly believes that there should be a fresher (in idea) and more convenient world cup website regardless of money matters. And [Chung] does not believe that FIFA or some other big corporations should be the only media of communication exchange among soccer lovers of the world. …

[Chung's web site] is based on the belief that anyone, whether individual or corporate, who has worthwhile information and ideas, opinions should be given the opportunity to freely share them with his contemporary citizens of the world. We do not believe that FIFA should be the only entity to talk about or provide information about 2002 FIFA World Cup Korea/Japan. …

It is also generally believed that one of the positive functions of the internet, which is one of the greatest human heritages, is that it provides room for anyone to freely exchange their ideas, knowledge, information, opinions beyond their national boundaries, thus contributing to the accumulation of global wealth of knowledge.

In relation to element (iii) of paragraph 4(a) of the Uniform Policy, the Respondents generally contend that "the issue of bad faith cannot exist fundamentally". The general thrust of the Response on this issue is to the effect that there cannot be bad faith registration and use where the domain name is used as the address of a web site which provides a non-commercial source of information about an event of great public interest. Further, the Respondents contend that the compound phrase <worldcup2002> is not the Complainants' exclusive property. In particular:

the word "world cup" is widely used by many organizations all around the world. Many official international sports games, other than soccer, are held under the name of "world cup".

The Respondents took issue with the Complainants' contention that bad faith was evidenced by Chung's offer to sell domain names (1)-(3) inclusive. In particular, the Respondents state:

This website [the one to which domain names (1)-(3) resolve] is not offered for sale for a significant amount of money. It is needless to say that it is absolutely possible in any free market society to ask a question of anybody whether they are interested in buying any privately-owned thing. It was once considered a good idea to sell this website to an entity, who has better financial and technical resources to improve it, for the low price of recovering its cost. But, at the present moment, this website is not being put up for sale at any price.

The Respondents also took issue with the Complainants' contention that bad faith was evidenced by Chung's deliberate registration of domain names under fictitious organizations. The Respondents claim that:

Those registered names are not fictitious names, but actual groups engaged in world cup fan club activities. It is the common practice and reality in Korea that fan clubs, art-related entities or small-scale neighborhood stores do perform their respective functions without registering their presence. [Chung] happens to be their admin contact due to his influence over them. As [the Response] mentioned earlier, if there had been any intention to use fictitious names, [Chung] would have used different contact names and addresses. There is no bad faith here.

Respondents' reply to Complainants' Request under Rule 12

The Respondents resisted the Complainants' request under rule 12 of the Uniform Rules for this Administrative Panel to compel Chung to produce a full list of his domain names associated with his NIC handles JYC6 and JC11182, and any other NIC handles registered to Chung. The Respondents contended that such a request "may constitute an undue infringement upon [Chung's] privacy".

6. Discussion and Findings

Complainants' Request under Rule 12

Rule 12 of the Uniform Rules provides as follows:

In addition to the complaint and the response, the Panel may request, in its sole discretion, further statements or documents from either of the Parties.

The sensible reading of this rule is that it permits a Panel to request further information that is relevant to the Complaint as filed by the Complainant. It is not directed towards obtaining further information that might be relevant to some other Complaint that the Complainant, or some other party, might at some time in the future wish to file.

There may be some Complaints for which it is relevant to know all the domain names registered by the Respondent. In relation to this Complaint, however, the Complainants have not shown how knowing the identity of all of Chung's domain name registrations is relevant to the Complaint filed by them. In the absence of demonstrable relevance, this Administrative Panel will not request the Respondents to provide this information under rule 12. Accordingly, the Complainants' request under rule 12 is refused. Should it subsequently become known that Chung has registered other domain names that allegedly are identical or confusingly similar to the trademarks or service marks of Complainants or some other party, and that these registrations allegedly occurred in circumstances where the other requirements of paragraph 4(a) of the Uniform Policy are satisfied, then the correct course is for the Complainants, or that other party, at that time to file a Complaint under the Uniform Policy.

Complainants' Contentions under Paragraph 4(a)

It is a close question whether the Complainants' have made out their case under paragraph 4(a) of the Uniform Policy. The Respondents joined issue on each of the three elements which need to be established for a remedy to be available. The contentions of both the Complainants and the Respondents on a number of issues are finely balanced.

Identical or Confusingly Similar Domain Names

This Administrative Panel finds that domain names (1)-(13) inclusive are confusingly similar to FIFA's registered trademark <WORLD CUP>. FIFA's registered trademark <WORLD CUP> is widely known, at least in relation to the provision of services and goods related to and associated with the conduct of the quadrennial association football world championship organized by it. Also widely known are the fact that this football championship is organized quadrennially, and the fact that the years in which the championship will be conducted include 2002, 2006 and 2010. Accordingly, the addition in domain names (1)-(13) inclusive of the number 02, 10, 2002, 2006 or 2010 does not distinguish the use of the phrase <worldcup> from the association with FIFA that these letters have in the mind of consumers. In fact, the use of these numbers serves to confirm such an association in the mind of consumers.

Because the Complainant has succeeded, in relation to domain names (1)-(13) inclusive, in its contention that paragraph 4(a)(i) of the Uniform Policy is satisfied by virtue of those domain names being confusingly similar to FIFA's registered trademark <WORLD CUP>, it is not necessary for this Administrative Panel to consider whether that paragraph of the Uniform Policy is also satisfied by virtue of those domain names being confusingly similar to FIFA's other registered trademarks. Accordingly, this Administrative Panel makes no finding on those matters.

This Administrative Panel finds that domain names (14) and (15) are not confusingly similar to any of FIFA's registered trademarks, and are not confusingly similar to the registered trademarks identified in (b) and (d) of paragraph 4.4 above. Domain name (14) contains the numbers <2002>, which most probably would be understood by most people as being a reference to the year 2002. Domain name (15) contains the numbers <02>, which arguably might be considered by a number of people to be an abbreviation of the year 2002. However, neither domain name contains the key words <WORLD CUP>.

The fact that domain names (14) and (15) both contain the letters <WC> is insufficient to satisfy the requirement of paragraph 4(a)(i) of the Uniform Policy. Whilst it can be argued that <WC> is an abbreviation of <WORLD CUP>, this Administrative Panel does not consider that this is the likely meaning which most people would give to these letters. These letters are open to being interpreted as meaning any number of things, as well as meaning nothing at all. There is nothing in the context of the use of these letters in the domain names that suggests they are an abbreviation of anything. Even if the context of their use did make clear that the letters <WC> were an abbreviation, it is quite likely many native speakers of the English language would consider they were an abbreviation either for "water closet" (and hence an allusion to "toilet") or "West Central" (see *Concise Oxford English Dictionary*, entry for "WC"), or for "without charge" (see *Merriam-Webster's Collegiate Dictionary*, entry for "WC"). As for how native speakers of other languages using the Romanised alphabet would most likely interpret these letters as an abbreviation, this Administrative Panel is unable to decide. In short, the letters <WC>, even in conjunction with the year <2002> or the year abbreviation <02>, do not likely suggest <WORLD CUP>, and hence domain names (14) and (15) are not confusingly similar to any of the trademarks referred to in paragraph 4.4 above.

Respondents' Rights or Legitimate Interests in the Domain Names
The Complainants' case in relation to the second aspect of paragraph 4(a) of the Uniform Policy is less clear. The Complainants contend that Chung does not have rights or legitimate interests in the domain names "by virtue of the fact that FIFA's WORLD CUP mark(s) are distinct and famous, and Chung's use of FIFA's marks is unauthorized". Whilst this Administrative Panel accepts that FIFA has not authorized Chung to use the <WORLD CUP> mark, it does not consider this mark to be particularly distinctive. Even (or perhaps particularly) when the context of use is limited to sporting events, the words <WORLD CUP> are not inevitably associated only with FIFA. According to *Encyclopedia Britannica CD 98 Standard Edition*, there are at least 16 sports in addition to association football which have a World Cup competition. These sports include Alpine Skiing (awarded since 1967), three-cushion Billiards, Cricket (both Women's, since 1973 and Men's, since 1975), Fencing, Field Hockey, Golf (since 1967), Rugby League, Rugby Union, Rugby Sevens, Snooker, Swimming, Wrestling, and various gymnastic, track and field sports. It may be, therefore, that any number of sporting organizations who conduct a competition under the name <World Cup> could argue that they have a right or legitimate interest in respect of domain names containing those words. However, the Respondents are not such an organization.

Nevertheless, the Respondents contend that they have a right or legitimate interest in the domain names the subject of this Complaint by virtue of the circumstances identified in paragraph 4(c) of the Uniform Policy. This claim is founded on the assertion that, prior to notice of the dispute, Chung used domain names (1)-(3) inclusive as the address of a web site which provided a bona fide offering of an on-line service (an alternative source of information about the FIFA World Cup 2002), that Chung's service has become "increasingly known" by such domain names, and that this use constituted a legitimate non-commercial use of the domain names. This Administrative Panel notes that this claim does not relate to domain names (4)-(13) inclusive, and so cannot found a right or legitimate interest in those domain names. Because no other evidence of a right or legitimate interest in those domain names was provided by the Respondents, and because the Complainants asserted that the Respondents were not authorized to use FIFA's registered trademark <WORLD CUP> in these confusingly similar domain names, this Administrative Panel finds that the Respondents have no right or legitimate interest in domain names (4)-(13) inclusive.

In relation to domain names (1)-(3) inclusive, this Administrative Panel does not find that Chung's web site offered a bona fide on-line service. As stated in paragraph 4.9 above, the Complainants have established that Chung's web site framed content from FIFA's official web sites (including, in particular, FIFA's official web site, the official web site of FIFA's Japan Organizing Committee, and the official web site of FIFA's Korean Organizing Committee) without the Complainants' authorization or authority, and included news releases taken in their entirety, and without permission, from FIFA's official website. This is not a bona fide offering of on-line services.

This does not, however, resolve the issue. It will be sufficient for the Respondents to succeed in this Complaint in relation to domain names (1)-(3) inclusive if they can establish, as they claim, that they are making a legitimate non-commercial or fair use of these domain names, without intent for commercial gain to misleadingly divert consumers or to tarnish the trademarks or service marks of FIFA. Is Chung's use of these domain names as an address for his web site such a use as contemplated by paragraph 4(c)(iii) of the Uniform Policy? The parties dispute whether Chung's web site is commercial. For the reasons stated in paragraph 4.10 above, this Administrative Panel did not find that Chung's web site contained the advertisement alleged by the Complainants. Since the Complainants did not allege any other commercial activity at the web site, it follows that this Administrative Panel finds that Chung's use of the domain names as the address of his web site is a non-commercial use. However, the question remains whether this non-commercial use is legitimate or in any event is a fair use.

The Respondents' contention is that their non-commercial use of domain names (1)-(3) inclusive as addresses for Chung's web site is legitimate and a fair use, because it provides alternative news and information about the forthcoming FIFA World Cup in 2002. As a matter of principle, this Administrative Panel agrees with the general sentiments expressed by the Respondents, extracted in paragraph in 5.9 above. However, it finds that the actual use made of the domain names is rather different from the high ideals espoused therein. The evidence of the Complainants establishes that Chung's web site framed and slavishly copied content from FIFA's official World Cup web site. This is hardly an example of a "a fresher (in idea)" offering. It is one thing to provide alternative news and information about, or even commentary and criticism on, a matter of public interest; it is another thing altogether to appropriate someone else's news and information and provide it in circumstances suggesting the provider is the creator of it, or at least is authorized to supply it. The former may well be a legitimate or fair use, but the latter is generally not. In this case, the Respondents' use of domain names (1)-(3) inclusive as the address of Chung's web site, even though non-commercial, was not a legitimate or fair use.

In light of the above facts, this Administrative Panel finds that the Respondents do not have a right or legitimate interest in domain names (1)-(13) inclusive.

Domain Names Registered and Used in Bad Faith

This Administrative Panel does not accept the Complainants' contention that bad faith is established, under paragraph 4(b)(i) of the Uniform Policy, by virtue of Chung's offer to sell domain names (1)-(3). Chung's offer to sell the domain names was rather understated. Further, it occurred more than two years after the domain names were registered, and after Chung had established the web site which used them as its address. In addition, no sale price was mentioned in the communication in which the domain names were offered for sale. These facts do not establish that the intended consideration of the sale was in excess of Chung's documented out-of-pocket costs directly related to the domain names. Indeed, these facts do not even establish that Chung acquired the domain names primarily for the purpose of selling them to the Complainant.

This Administrative Panel does accept, however, the Complainants' contention that the fact of Chung's registration of 13 similar domain names, and the circumstances of his use of three of them, are both evidence that, prior to the filing of this Complaint, the domain names have been registered and were being used in bad faith. If Chung's true motive in this case was to provide a bona fide alternative forum for fresh news and information about the FIFA World Cup 2002, why register 13 similar names? Would not one domain name be sufficient to achieve the purpose of providing a location for alternative news and information about the FIFA World Cup competition? The Respondents assert that each of the registrants of domain names (1)-(13) inclusive is "an actual fan club for world cup 2002 [that does] not have to be publicly registered under Korean law", with which Chung has "been maintaining relationship" and which has "asked [Chung] to obtain domains for them and manage their websites under his full responsibility". However, the Respondents did not state the name or even the address of the individuals, in charge of these fan clubs, whom had asked him to obtain the domain names and set up web sites under them. Also, it is noteworthy that many of the domain names were registered on the same day, and almost all were registered within two weeks of each other. It is unlikely in the extreme that 11 different fan clubs gave Chung instructions to register a domain name for them in the space of such a short time.

The only plausible conclusion to draw from these facts is that Chung intended to warehouse for his own use a large number of domain names using the words <world cup>. The effect of this warehousing is to prevent the Complainants from reflecting their trademark <WORLD CUP> in a corresponding domain name. The "pattern of such conduct" required by paragraph 4(b)(iii) is provided by the sheer volume of names registered. Accordingly this Administrative Panel finds that the Respondents have registered and used domain names (1)-(13) inclusive in bad faith. In relation to domain names (1)-(3) inclusive, this finding is supported by the established facts that the actual use to which these domain names were put was as an address to Chung's web site which framed and slavishly copied, without authorization, content and material of FIFA and its affiliates.

Appropriate Remedy

The Complainants requested this Administrative Panel to require the Registrar to transfer the domain names to FIFA. In light of the fact that FIFA has proved it is the owner of many trade mark registrations for <WORLD CUP>, it is clear that FIFA is the appropriate party to whom the domain names (1)-(13) inclusive should be transferred, if it is considered that transfer is the appropriate remedy in this case. The fundamental issue is whether a transfer of domain names is in fact the appropriate remedy in the circumstances of this case.

Cancellation of a domain name under the Uniform Policy does not amount to an exclusion of the domain name. Once the registration is cancelled, it is possible for any person to re-register that domain name. This Administrative Panel notes that, to date, in none of the previous decisions of Administrative Panels appointed by the WIPO Center has cancellation been ordered as the appropriate remedy. In a number of the decisions of Administrative Panels appointed by the National Arbitration Foundation, cancellation has been ordered. In none of those decisions, however, was a rationale given for this remedy over the remedy of transfer to the Complainant.

As discussed in paragraph 6.8 above, there are a number of other sports which have a World Cup competition, and hence there may be a party other than the Complainants who would wish to register and, having registered, could claim a right or legitimate interest in, some or all of the domain names the subject of this Complaint. It might be thought that, in such a situation, the appropriate remedy is cancellation rather than transfer, because cancellation leaves open the possibility for such other party to obtain registration. Against this view, however, is the fact that the remedy of cancellation leaves open the possibility for anyone – including the Respondent or a party related to the Respondent – to subsequently obtain registration of the domain name following the cancellation. An outcome in which a Respondent to a successful Complaint subsequently reapplied for and obtained registration of the just cancelled domain name would frustrate the intent of the Uniform Policy. Even if the unsuccessful Respondent did not do this, there is no guarantee that another party without a right or legitimate interest in the domain name would not subsequently register and use the domain name in bad faith, in which case the Complainant would need to bring another Complaint, this time against that other party. Of course, a Complainant might seek to avoid these outcomes by registering in its own name the domain name the subject of the cancellation. If that were to occur, the outcome is the same as if the domain name had been transferred to the Complainant.

As was stated in WIPO Case No. D2000-0044:

By requesting transfer of the domain name to itself, Complainant has effectively requested registration of the "toefl.com" domain name. Although there might be other legitimate users of the domain name that would seek registration subsequent to a cancellation of Respondent's registration, Complainant's request for registration should reasonably take precedence under a general first-in-time principle applicable to legitimate requests for registration.

This Administrative Panel agrees with that statement of principle. Further, a decision of an Administrative Panel under the Uniform Policy to transfer a disputed domain name to a Complainant does not mean that the Complainant obtains an invulnerable domain name registration. It remains open to any party to bring an action against a former Complainant's holding of a domain name. Thus, an order of transfer should not prejudice the position of a third party who wishes to impugn the holding of a domain name registration obtained by way of an Administrative Panel's order of transfer.

For all of the above reasons, this Administrative Panels considers that the appropriate remedy in this case is that domain names (1)-(13) inclusive be transferred to FIFA.

7. Decision

This Administrative Panel decides that the Complainant has proven each of the three elements in paragraph 4(a) of the Uniform Policy in relation to each of the domain names (1)-(13) inclusive the subject of this Complaint. This Administrative Panel also decides that the Complainant has not proven all of the three elements in paragraph 4(a) of the Uniform Policy in relation to both of the domain names (14) and (15) the subject of this Complaint.

Pursuant to paragraph 4(i) of the Uniform Policy and rule 15 of the Uniform Rules, this Administrative Panel requires that the Registrar, Network Solutions, Inc, transfer to the Second Complainant, The Federation Internationale de Football Association, the following domain names:

worldcup2002.com	2002worldcup.org	worldcup2010.org
worldcup2002.net	worldcup02.net	worldcup2010.net
worldcup2002.org	2002worldcup.net	2006worldcup.org
worldcup02.org	worldcup2006.org	
worldcup10.com	worldcup2010.com	

Andrew F. Christie
Sole Panelist
Dated: April 3, 2000

WIPO Arbitration and Mediation Center

ADMINISTRATIVE PANEL DECISION
Formula One Licensing B.V. v. Formula One Internet
Case No. D2000-0193

WIPO Arbitration and Mediation Center

ADMINISTRATIVE PANEL DECISION
Nike, Inc. v. William Coleman
Case No. D2000-1120

1. The Parties
The Complainant in this administrative proceeding is Nike, Inc., an Oregon corporation with its principal place of business in Beaverton, Oregon, U.S.A. The Respondent is William Coleman, whose address is 7440-B Canterbury Avenue, Maplewood, Missouri, 63143 U.S.A.

2. The Domain Name and Registrar
The domain name in dispute is as follows: "nike.net". The domain name was registered by Respondent with Network Solutions, Inc. (NSI) on May 31, 1998.

3. Procedural Background
On August 24, 2000, the WIPO Arbitration and Mediation Center received from Complainant via e-mail a complaint for decision in accordance with the Uniform Policy for Domain Name Dispute Resolution, adopted by the Internet Corporation of Assigned Names and Numbers (ICANN) on August 26, 1999, ("Policy"), the Rules for Uniform Domain Name Dispute Resolution Policy, approved by ICANN on October 24, 1999 ("Rules"), and the WIPO Supplemental Rules for Uniform Domain Name Dispute Resolution Policy (Supplemental Rules).

The complaint was filed in compliance with the requirements of the Rules and the Supplemental Rules, payment was properly made, the administrative panel was properly constituted, and the panelist submitted the required Statement of Acceptance and Declaration of Impartiality and Independence.

The instant Administrative Proceeding was commenced on September 26, 2000.

Respondent did not file a Response, and a "Notification of Respondent Default," dated October 18, 2000, was forwarded by WIPO to Respondent.

The decision of the Panel was due to WIPO on or before November 7, 2000.

4. Factual Background
As set forth in the Complaint, Complainant Nike is the world's leading sports and fitness company. It designs, manufactures, and markets a broad range of footwear, apparel, and equipment. Complainant also maintains an active presence on the Internet, primarily through its "nike.com" website, where Complainant promotes and sells its goods and services, and provides information about its business activities.

Since 1971, Complainant has used and promoted its NIKE trademark worldwide in connection with footwear, apparel, equipment, and retail store services. Last year alone, Complainant sold several billion dollars worth of NIKE brand merchandise.

Complainant owns numerous trademark registrations worldwide for its NIKE mark. These include U.S. Registration Nos. 1,243,248 and 1,277,066. See Complaint, Annex D.

As noted above, Respondent registered the domain name in dispute with NSI on May 31, 1998. Respondent's site is active, but contains merely a single page that makes no reference to Respondent or Complainant. Instead, it appears to be a page generated by a different company's web-authoring software program that informs the software owner of the software's successful installation. See Complaint, Annex E.

On May 23, 2000, Complainant sent a letter to Respondent seeking transfer of the domain name and offering to reimburse Respondent for his out-of-pocket costs in registering the name. See Complaint, Annex F. Respondent never responded to this letter or to other communications from Complainant. See Complaint, Annexes G and H.

Finally, Complainant contacted Respondent's Administrative Contact, Jeff Solomon. Mr. Solomon told Complainant that he had no knowledge of Respondent or of the domain name registration. Mr. Solomon also indicated that the NIC handle and e-mail address accompanying his name in the Respondent's registration record did not belong to him, but, rather, to an individual in Kuwait who, Mr. Solomon alleged, had earlier taken control of one of Mr. Solomon's domain names without proper authorization. See Complaint, Annex J.

5. Parties' Contentions

Complainant contends that the domain name in issue is identical to its NIKE mark; that there is no evidence that Respondent has any rights or legitimate interests in the domain name; and that Respondent registered and used the domain name in "bad faith."

6. Discussion and Findings

The Panel has carefully weighed the evidence presented and determines that Complainant has met the requirements set forth in § 4.a. of the Policy.

There is no question that the domain name in dispute is identical to a mark in which Complainant has rights. The domain name incorporates, in full, the NIKE mark, which has been used by Complainant since 1971. The mark also is the subject of several U.S. trademark registrations owned by Complainant.

The Panel further determines that Respondent has no rights or legitimate interests with respect to the domain name. The evidence reveals that Respondent does not appear to have used "nike" as part of its name or mark and has not used the domain name in connection with a bona fide offering of goods or services.

There is also evidence to support a determination of "bad faith" registration and use. Given the renown and widespread use of the NIKE mark, the Panel finds that Respondent could readily foresee that people would assume the "nike.net" domain name to be connected with Complainant, that the public would seek out the site in the hope of finding Complainant's site, and that Complainant would, therefore, wish to own and use the name and site. The Panel further determines that Respondent's failure to use the domain name also supports a finding of "bad faith" registration and use under the Policy. See Telstra Corp., Ltd. v. Nuclear Marshmallows, Case No. D2000-0003 (February 18, 2000). Finally, Respondent's listing of Mr. Solomon as the Administrative Contact for the domain name, when Mr. Solomon had no knowledge of Respondent or of the domain name, also constitutes evidence of "bad faith" registration and use.

7. Decision

In view of the above, the Panel GRANTS Complainant's request for transfer to it of the domain name "nike.net".

Jeffrey M. Samuels
Sole Panelist
Dated: November 6, 2000

WIPO Arbitration and Mediation Center

ADMINISTRATIVE PANEL DECISION
Jordan Grand Prix Limited v. Gerry Sweeney
Case No. D2000-0233

1. The Parties

The Complainant is Jordan Grand Prix Limited, a company incorporated in England, with its principal place of business at Silverstone, Northamptonshire, NN12 8TJ, United Kingdom.

The Respondent is Mr. Gerry Sweeney of Main Street, Loughrea, Republic of Ireland.

2. The Domain Name and Registrar

The domain name at issue is <jordanf1.com>. The domain name is registered with Network Solutions Inc., 505 Huntmar Park Drive, Herndon, Virginia 20170, United States of America ("NSI").

3. Procedural History

The Complaint submitted by Jordan Grand Prix Limited was received on March 30, 2000 (electronic version), and April 3, 2000 (hard copy), by the World Intellectual Property Organization Arbitration and Mediation Center ("WIPO Center").

On or about April 14, 2000, a request for Registrar verification was transmitted by WIPO Center to NSI, requesting it to:

(a) Confirm that a copy of the Complaint had been sent to it by the Complainant as required by WIPO Supplemental Rules for Uniform Dispute Resolution Policy, paragraph 4(a).
(b) Confirm that the domain name at issue is registered with NSI.
(c) Confirm that the person identified as the Respondent is the current registrant of the domain name.
(d) Provide full contact details, i.e., postal address(es), telephone number(s), facsimile number(s), email address(es), available in NSI's WHOIS database for the registrant of the disputed domain name, the technical contact, the administrative contact and the billing contact for the domain name.
(e) Confirm that the Uniform Domain Name Dispute Resolution Policy was in effect.
(f) Indicate the current status of the domain name.

The Complainant had nominated in its Complaint another provider as the Registrar. The Complainant did not advise WIPO Center that NSI was the Registrar until April 14, 2000.

By email dated April 14, 2000, the Registrar advised WIPO Center as follows:

(a) NSI had received a copy of the Complaint from the Complainant.
(b) NSI is the Registrar of the domain name registration <jordanf1.com>.
(c) Gerry Sweeney is the current registrant of the said domain name. His relevant information is as follows:
Mr. Gerry Sweeney as Registrant, Administrative and Billing Contact
Main Street
Loughrea
Co. Galway
Ireland
Telephone: +353 91 841 407
Fax: +353 91 842 015
Email: sween@iol.ie
Technical and Zone Contact:
Registrar, Internic
internic-free@REGISTER.COM USA
Ph: 212 627 4988
Fax: 212 627 6477
(d) NSI's 4.0 Service Agreement is in effect.
(e) The domain name registration <jordanf1.com> is in "Active" status.

NSI has adopted the policy for Uniform Domain Name Dispute Resolution adopted by the Internet Corporation for Assigned Names and Numbers ("ICANN").

The Respondent has never requested that the domain name at issue be deleted from the domain name database. The Respondent has not sought to terminate his agreement with NSI. The Respondent is accordingly bound by the provisions of the Domain Name Dispute Resolution Policy, i.e., the ICANN policy.

Having verified that the Complaint satisfied the formal requirements of the Uniform Policy and the Uniform Rules, WIPO Center, on April 6, 2000, transmitted by post/courier, facsimile and email a notification of Complaint and Commencement of Administrative Proceedings to the Respondent. A copy of the Complaint was also emailed to NSI and ICANN.

The Complainant elected to have its Complaint resolved by a single panel member: it has duly paid the amount required of it to WIPO Center.

The Respondent was advised that a Response to the Complaint was required within 20 calendar days (i.e., by April 26, 2000). He was also advised that any Response should be communicated, in accordance with the Rules, by four sets of hard copy and by email.

On April 26, 2000, the Respondent filed a Response.

On May 1, 2000, WIPO Center invited the Honourable Sir Ian Barker QC of Auckland, New Zealand, to serve as sole Panelist in the case. It transmitted to him a statement of acceptance and requested a declaration of impartiality and independence.

On May 4, 2000, the Honourable Sir Ian Barker QC advised his acceptance and forwarded to WIPO Center his statement of impartiality and independence. The Panelist finds that the Administrative Panel was properly constituted in accordance with the Rules and the Supplementary Rules.

On May 4, 2000, WIPO Center forwarded to the Honourable Sir Ian Barker QC by courier the relevant submissions and the record. These were received by him on May 10, 2000. In terms of Rule 5(b), in the absence of exceptional circumstances, the Panel is required to forward its decision by May 18, 2000.

On May 4, 2000, the Panelist advised WIPO Center pursuant to Rule 12 that he required a Reply to the Response from the Complainant by May 8, 2000. This date was later extended to May 10, 2000. This reply was received by the Panel on May 10, 2000.

The Panel has independently determined and agrees with the assessment of WIPO Center that the Complaint meets the formal requirements of the Rules for Uniform Domain Name Dispute Resolution Policy as approved by ICANN on October 24, 1999, ("the Rules") and the Supplemental Rules for Uniform Domain Name Dispute Resolution Policy ("the Supplemental Rules").

The language of the administrative proceeding is English, being the language of the registration agreement.

4. Factual Background

The Claimant is the owner of Community Trademarks numbered CTM 00442848 and CTM 00672907 for the mark "Jordan Grand Prix" in several classes. The Respondent admits these registrations which were made in 1998 and 1999.

The Complainant owns a Formula One motor racing team which has competed in FIA Formula One World Championships competitions since 1991. Because of the extensive media coverage of motor racing, Formula One-type racing and the associated expression "F1" are well-known worldwide. The Complainant operated since March 1996 a commercial website <jordangp.com>.

On March 8, 2000, the Respondent sent an email to the Complainant's agent offering to sell the domain name in question before putting it up for auction. He said: "I purchased the website domain 'www.jordanf1.com' last year. Given 'F1' is synonymous with Formula 1 racing, thought it might be an appropriate web domain for you to have going forward. Would you be interested in purchasing this domain. Would like to give you first option on the purchase of the domain before I put it up for auction".

The Complainant's solicitors replied on March 9, 2000, with a "cease and desist" letter indicating an intention to invoke the Dispute Resolution Policy. The Respondent did not reply "due to the unrealistic deadline and threatening nature of the same".

The Complainant's website has been operating under the domain name <F1.jordan.com> since April 2000. A variety of Jordan merchandise, mainly apparel, is sold on this website. The change of website name was said to have been made for marketing reasons. Various press clippings attached to the Complainant's Reply show that it is commonly referred to as "Jordan F1".

5. Parties' Contentions

The Complainant submits that the domain name is confusingly similar to the Complainant's trademark and its common law rights in the mark. The Respondent is said to have no legitimate interest in respect of the domain name, to have not used it in connection with a *bona fide* offering of services and not to have been known by the domain name. The Respondent's offer to sell the domain name to the Complainant constitutes use in bad faith.

The Respondent submits that the domain name <jordanf1.com> is neither identical nor confusingly similar to the trademark "Jordan Grand Prix". Reference to common law rules is not permitted under paragraph 3(b)(ix)(i) of the Rules. He admitted that the Complainant is known as "Jordan Grand Prix".

The Respondent's stated intention was to ensure that the domain name was registered for no commercial purpose, but rather for the exchange of information, ideas and opinions by primarily Irish motor-racing fans. The Respondent denies that he ever tried to sell, rent or otherwise transfer the domain name registration to the owner of the mark because the Complainant is not the owner of a mark "jordanf1". He characterizes the Complaint as "a clear example of the uncompromising and inequitable behavior adopted by this large, powerful multi-national company towards a single individual".

In reply, the Complainant relied on the Respondent's admission that the Complainant is known as "Jordan Grand Prix". It has a trademark application pending in respect of the mark "Jordan Grand Prix" for numerous further categories. It submitted that the Respondent's domain name is confusingly similar to the Complainant's mark in that the expressions "grand prix" and "F1" are synonymous to the public which would be confused thereby. It pointed out that the Respondent had not used the site for a year, nor had he provided any evidence that it had been established to exchange information amongst fans.

6. Discussion and Findings

Paragraph 15(a) of the Rules instructs the Panel to "decide a complaint on the basis of the statements and documents submitted in accordance with the policy, these rules and any rules and principles of law that it deems applicable".

The burden for the Complainant, under paragraph 4(a) of the ICANN Policy, is to show:

(a) That the domain name registered by the Respondent is identical or confusingly similar to a trademark or service mark in which the Complainant has rights.
(b) That the Respondent has no rights or legitimate interests in respect of the domain name.
(c) The domain name has been registered and used in bad faith.

In determining whether the domain name <jordanf1.com> is confusingly similar to the trademark "Jordan Grand Prix", the Panel has regard to various tests in trademark law as to when a mark may not be registered where "the use of which would be likely to deceive or cause confusion …". (The words cited or similar are to be found in trademark statutes in several jurisdictions). Out of many cases, the following principles relevant to the present situation emerge:

Where there is a worldwide association of ideas in connection with a particular name or figure, a mark in whatever category will not be allowed which incorporates that particular name or figure. See *Radio Corporation Pty Ltd v Disney* (1937), 57 CLR 448, where the High Court of Australia upheld a Registrar's refusal of the marks "Mickey Mouse" and "Minnie Mouse" for radio receiving kits and sets.

All surrounding circumstances have to be taken into account, including the circumstances where the applicant' s mark is likely to be used, the relevant market and the character of those involved in the market. See *Polaroid Corporation v Hannaford and Burton Ltd* [1975] 1 NZLR 566 and *Hi-Bred Corn Company v Hy-Line Chicks Pty Ltd* [1978] 2 NZLR 50.

The word "deceive" implies the creation of an incorrect belief and causing "confusion" may go no further than mixing up or perplexing the minds of the purchasing public: *New Zealand Breweries Ltd v Heineken* [1964] NZLR 115. Where deception or confusion is alleged as to the source of the goods, "deceived" is equivalent to being misled into thinking that the goods bearing the applicant's mark come from some other source and "confused" indicates being caused to wonder whether that may not be the case (*Hi-Bred Corn* case).

Although the marks must be compared as a whole in determining confusion, when each mark has a common feature, greater attention needs to be focused on the remaining parts of the marks: *re Broadhead's Application* (1950), 67 RPC 209, 215.

Allowances must be made for imperfect recollections on the part of members of the public and the effect of careless speech (*re Rysta's Application* (1943), 60 RPC 87, 188-9; *Polaroid* (supra) at 571.

The overall test is one of impression of confusion in the mind of the person making the decision: *General Electric Co. v General Electric Co. Ltd* [1972] 1 WLR 729, 738: [1973] RPC 297.

Where an application is to be rejected on the ground of confusion, the Court (or Panel) must be satisfied that there is a real danger of confusion (*Berlei (UK) Ltd v Bali Brassiere Co Inc.* [1969] 1 WLR 1306: [1969] RPC 472).

In the light of the above principles, the Panel concludes:

The name "Jordan" is well-known internationally as being associated with Formula 1 motor-racing.

The name "Jordan" and its association with Formula 1 racing will be especially familiar to motor-racing enthusiasts worldwide.

The words "Grand Prix" are similarly well-known – also in conjunction with the word "Jordan" – to the same section of people.

Persons with an interest in motor-racing or even with a vague knowledge of it would be confused or perplexed by a website <jordanf1.com>. They would think, at least, that the website had some connection with the Complainant.

Such people could easily be confused into thinking that "Jordan Grand Prix" was the same as "jordanf1", given the allowances to be made for faulty recollection and/or careless speech.

Focusing on the expressions "Grand Prix" and "F1" – both of which are used in conjunction with Jordan – confusion must be expected, given the association of both expressions with motor-racing.

The Panel's overall impression – as a "jury question" – is of a real danger of confusion between the two expressions.

Consequently, the Panel considers that the Respondent's domain name <jordanf1.com> is confusingly similar to the Complainant's mark "Jordan Grand Prix".

Paragraph 4(c) of the Policy shows how a Respondent can demonstrate rights or interest in the domain name at issue. Whilst the overall onus of proof rests on a Complainant, nevertheless failure by a Respondent to demonstrate that he comes within paragraph 4(c) can assist the Panel in deciding whether on consideration of all the evidence a Complainant has discharged the onus of proof. The following circumstances in particular, but without limitation, if found by the Panel to be proved, demonstrate rights or legitimate interests in the domain name at issue.

> "(i) before any notice to you of the dispute, your use of, or demonstrable preparations to use, the domain name or a name corresponding to the domain name in connection with a bona fide offering of goods or services; or
> (ii) you (as an individual, business or other organization) have been commonly known by the domain name, even if you have acquired no trademark or service mark rights; or
> (iii) you are making a legitimate noncommercial or fair use of the domain name, without intent for commercial gain to misleadingly divert consumers or to tarnish the trademark or service mark at issue."

The Panel finds that there is no evidence that the Respondent, before receiving notice of the dispute, used or demonstrably prepared to use the domain name in connection with a *bona fide* offering of services without intent for commercial gain. There is no evidence other than his generalized statements about providing a forum for Irish motor-racing enthusiasts by means of the website. If that were so, one wonders why the Respondent chose "Jordan", knowing, as he must have done as a motor-racing enthusiast, of the Complainant's reputation. There is no evidence that he has been commonly known by the domain name.

The Respondent has no licence or other legal right in respect of the domain name. The Panel therefore decides that the Respondent has no rights or legitimate interests in respect of the domain name.

Paragraph 4(b)(iii) and (iv) of the ICANN policy document, on which the Complainant relies, states:

> "the following circumstances ... shall be evidence of the registration and use of the domain name in bad faith:
> (iii) You have registered the domain name primarily for disrupting the business of a competitor.
> (iv) By using the domain name, you have intentionally attempted to attract, for commercial gain, Internet users to your website or other on-line locations, by creating a likelihood of confusion with the complainant's mark as to the source, sponsorship, affiliation or endorsement of your website or location or of a product or service on your website or location."

The Respondent has offered to sell the domain name to the Complainant. Numerous previous WIPO Panel decisions have shown that such conduct constitutes use in bad faith. Accordingly, the Panel finds that the Respondent has registered and used the domain name in bad faith.

7. Principles of Law Applicable

The law on confusing similarity of trademarks is well-established. It is discussed in the previous section. A useful summary is found in *Levi Strauss & Co. v. Kimbyr Investments Ltd* [1994] 1 NZLR 332. The summary is based on a consideration of authorities from a number of common law jurisdictions:

> "The tests to be applied in deciding whether there was "confusing similarity" were well established. The plaintiffs' mark as registered must be compared with the defendant's mark as it appeared in actual use – additions or variations which might be relevant in a claim for passing off would not avoid a trade mark infringement claim. The imperfect recollection of the ordinary customer must be borne in mind. The "idea of the mark" must be carefully considered. Consideration must be given to the circumstances of the trade in which the marks in question were employed. Evidence of actual confusion was not essential, but there must be a likelihood of a number of purchasers or potential purchasers or interested members of the public being confused. It was for the Court to decide the question as a matter of personal impression having due regard to the evidence." (Quoting from headnote).

The legal position in England on domain names of confusingly similar wording to registered trademarks was discussed by the Court of Appeal in *British Telecommunications Plc and Others v One in a Million Ltd and Others* [1999] 1 WLR 903. The Court there was dealing with domain names identical or confusingly similar to registered trademarks where the domain name holders had tried to sell the names to the trademark owners. Injunctions were issued. This is the situation envisaged by paragraph 4(a)(i) of the Rules.

The English position is similar to that taken in other common law jurisdictions. In the United States there are cases noted by Panelists in other WIPO Center decisions, such as *Panavision International LP v Toeppen* 141 F.3d. 1315 (9th Cir. 1998).

The Panel accordingly determines that, under the Policy, the Complainant has proved its case. Accordingly, the Complainant is entitled to the limited relief which this Panel is empowered to give. The Panel's decision is based primarily on the terms of the Policy cited earlier.

8. Decision

For the foregoing reasons, the Panel decides:

that the domain name registered by the Respondent is identical or confusingly similar to the trademark to which the Complainant has rights;
that the Respondent has no rights or legitimate interests in respect of the domain name; and
the Respondent's domain name has been registered and is being used in bad faith.

Accordingly, pursuant to paragraph 4(i) of the Policy, the Panel requires that the registration of the domain name <jordanfl.com> be transferred to the Complainant.

Hon. Sir Ian Barker, QC
Presiding Panelist
May 11, 2000

WIPO Arbitration and Mediation Center

ADMINISTRATIVE PANEL DECISION
Nike, Inc. v. Crystal International
Case No. D2001-0102

1. The Parties

The parties are Nike, Inc. of One Bowerman Drive, Beaverton, Oregon 97005, USA (Complainant) and Crystal International of Lotte APT 7-1105, Jung-Gae-2-Dong Nowon-Gu, Seoul 139-222

Korea and/or of RM609 HyoChunB/D, SeoChoDong, 1425-10 SeoChoKu, Seoul, 137-070 Korea (Respondent).

2. The Domain Names and Registrars

The domain names in dispute are <nikewomen.com>, <nikeshop.net>, <nikeshop.org>, <nike-shop.com>, <nike-shop.net> and <inike.net> ("the Domain Names"). Network Solutions, Inc. ("NSI") is the registrar of <nikewomen.com>, <nikeshop.org> and <inike.net>. Tucows, Inc ("Tucows") is the registrar of <nikeshop.net>, <nike-shop.com> and <nike-shop.net>.

3. Procedural History

The complaint was filed by the Complainant's Assistant General Counsel with the WIPO Arbitration and Mediation Center ("the Center") in hard copy on January 18, 2001 and by email on January 19, 2001. The complaint incorrectly identified NSI as the registrar of all of the Domain Names and contained a submission to the jurisdiction of the courts of Virginia, USA (in which the principal office of NSI is located). By email of January 25, 2001, NSI verified that it was the registrar of <nikewomen.com>, <nikeshop.org> and <inike.net>, that its Service Agreement incorporating the Uniform Domain Name Dispute Resolution Policy ("the Policy") applies to these domain names, and that it had received a copy of the complaint. NSI pointed out that the other domain names in dispute had been transferred to Tucows.

An amendment to the complaint to identify Tucows as the registrar of these domain names was filed with the Center by email on February 1, 2001 and in hard copy on February 2, 2001. The amendment also revised the submission to jurisdiction to refer to the courts of Korea. By email of February 1, 2001, Tucows verified that it was the registrar of nikeshop.net, nike-shop.com and nike-shop.net and that the Policy applies to these domain names in accordance with its Registration Agreement. Tucows stated in this email that it had not received a copy of the complaint, but indicated that the domain names were on hold to ensure no changes of ownership or Registrar for the duration of the dispute.

The complaint authorized payment of the correct amount of fee from the Complainant's account held with WIPO and the Center's formal requirements compliance checklist records that the correct fee has been duly paid. On a review of the file, the Panel concludes that the complaint complied with the applicable formal requirements, except that it was not sent by the Complainant to Tucows in accordance with paragraph 4(b) of the WIPO Supplemental Rules for Uniform Domain Name Dispute Resolution Policy ("the WIPO Supplemental Rules"). Since this omission has not prejudiced the Respondent the Panel has decided to disregard it.

The complaint was sent to the Respondent on February 2, 2001 (a) by email to postmaster @ each of the Domain Names; (b) by email to maxion@maxion.co.kr nikeshop@chollian.net and nike-shop@nike-shop.co.kr (the addresses indicated for the administrative and billing contacts for the various Domain Names in the NSI and Tucows whois databases); by email to dns-admin@hypermart.net (the address indicated for the technical contact in the NSI whois database); (c) by fax to +82-2-977-5604 (the fax number indicated for the Respondent in the NSI whois database); (d) by courier to the two postal addresses of the Respondent set out above (the addresses indicated for the Respondent in the NSI and Tucows whois databases respectively). The Panel concludes that the complaint was properly notified in accordance with paragraph 2(a) of the Rules for Uniform Domain Name Dispute Resolution Policy ("the Rules").

The Respondent did not submit a response within the time required by the Rules and on February 26, 2001 the Center gave notification of default by email to the above email addresses for the administrative and billing contacts. The single member Panel, Jonathan Turner, submitted a Statement of Acceptance and Declaration of Impartiality and Independence and was duly appointed on March 8, 2001. In accordance with paragraph 15 of the Rules, the Panel was required to forward its decision to the Center by March 22, 2001 in the absence of exceptional circumstances. On March 11, 2001 the Respondent sent the Center an email whose content is summarised in section 5 of this Decision. The Center replied to the Respondent stating that its email would be forwarded to the Panel which would have sole discretion to decide whether to accept and/or consider this email in deciding the case.

4. Factual Background

The Complainant is very well known throughout the world as a leading supplier of sports footwear, clothing and equipment under its name "Nike". Its activities include the operation of retail outlets under the names "Nike Town" and "Nike Shop". It has registered "Nike" as a trade mark in the US and no doubt in many other countries, although the Complaint does not include details of registrations in countries other than the US.

The Respondent registered the Domain Names at various dates between November 22, 1998 and July 17, 1999. It does not currently have any websites at present at any of these addresses.

5. Parties' Contentions

The Complainant contends that the Domain Names are similar to its well-known Nike brand in which it has trade mark rights, that the Respondent has no discernible legitimate interest in using the Domain Names, and that they were registered and are being used in bad faith and to prevent the Complainant from using them.

As noted above, the Respondent did not submit a response within the time required by the rules. In a subsequent email the Respondent stated that it intended to use certain of the Domain Names for a Nike shopping mall website and that it did not understand why this should be unlawful.

6. Discussion and Findings

The Panel has to decide first whether it should take the Respondent's email of March 11, 2001 into consideration, even though it was sent after the end of the period for filing the response. Paragraph 5(d) of the Rules provides that "at the request of the Respondent, the Provider may, in exceptional cases, extend the period of time for the filing of the response". The general power of the Panel to extend time limits in paragraph 10(c) of the Rules is likewise exercisable only in "exceptional cases".

The Panel considers that this is not an exceptional case. In particular, there is no reason to believe that the Respondent did not have a fair opportunity to file its response within the time limit. Furthermore, the email does not comply with the requirement of certification of the response specified in paragraph 5(b)(viii) of the Rules.

The Panel also has power under paragraph 12 of the Rules to request further statements or documents from the parties at its sole discretion. However, the Panel considers that this provision should not be stretched in order to circumvent the restrictions on extending time limits provided in paragraphs 5(d) and 10(c) of the Rules.

The Panel is conscious of the possible arguments in favour of considering the email that it would not in fact prejudice the Complainant or affect the outcome of this case. However, to take the email into account on the basis of such arguments could set a precedent which would be contrary to the wording of the Rules and the objective of providing an efficient and expeditious procedure for the resolution of domain name disputes. The Panel has accordingly decided not to take the Respondent's email of March 11, 2001 into consideration.

In accordance with paragraph 4 of the Policy, a complainant must prove (i) that the domain name is identical or confusingly similar to a trademark or service mark in which the complainant has rights; (ii) that the Respondent has no rights or legitimate interests in respect of the domain name; and (iii) that the domain name has been registered and is being used in bad faith.

As to the first requirement, the Panel considers that each of the Domain Names is confusingly similar to "Nike" and "Nike Shop". The Panel is also satisfied that Complainant has registered trade mark rights in "Nike" and unregistered trade mark rights in "Nike" and "Nike Shop". The Complainant has given details of some of its registered trade marks for "Nike" in the US but not in other countries. However, in the absence of any indication that the Domain Names would be used in relation to activities confined to a particular country or countries, the Panel considers that it is appropriate to take into account the Complainant's rights in any country, including the US. Furthermore, the Panel is satisfied that the worldwide goodwill and reputation of the Nike brand is such that the Complainant has unregistered trade mark rights in Korea where the Respondent is based.

As to the second requirement, the Panel is satisfied that the Respondent has no legitimate interest in using the names. In particular, the Respondent does not appear to have used or made any preparations to use any of the Domain Names in connection with any bona fide offering of goods or services prior to the dispute in accordance with paragraph 4(c)(i) of the Policy.

As to the third requirement, the Panel considers that bad faith is indicated by the registration of a series of domain names which are confusingly similar to a famous brand name followed by the absence of any legitimate use of them for over two years since the first was registered. The Panel is satisfied that the Domain Names were in fact registered in order to prevent the Complainant from reflecting "Nike" and "Nike Shop" in corresponding domain names. The Panel considers that the registration of a series of six such names is sufficient to constitute a pattern of such conduct within the meaning of paragraph 4(b)(ii) of the Policy. The Panel is also satisfied that the Domain Names were registered by the Respondent primarily for the purpose of selling for valuable consideration in excess of its costs and that the case falls within paragraph 4(b)(i) of the Policy. Further, the retention of the Domain Names for these purposes constitutes use in bad faith.

Given the reputation of the "Nike" brand, the Panel considers that the use of the Domain Names by another person would be likely to cause confusion. The Panel concludes that the Domain Names should therefore be transferred to the Complainant.

7. Decision
The Panel decides that the Domain Names <nikewomen.com>, <nikeshop.net>, <nikeshop.org>, <nike-shop.com>, <nike-shop.net> and <inike.net> should be transferred to Nike, Inc. of One Bowerman Drive, Beaverton, Oregon 97005, USA.

Jonathan Turner
Sole Panelist
Dated: March 19, 2001

WIPO Arbitration and Mediation Center

ADMINISTRATIVE PANEL DECISION
National Association for Stock Car Auto Racing, Inc. v. David Crawford, Jr.
Case No. D2001-1338

1. The Parties
The Complainant is the National Association for Stock Car Auto Racing, Inc., a Florida corporation with offices at 1801 West International Speedway Blvd., Daytona Beach, Florida 32114, U.S.A. The Complainant is represented by Elizabeth Pasquine, Esq., Kilpatrick Stockton LLP, 11130 Sunrise Valley Drive, Suite 300, Reston, Virginia 20191-4329, U.S.A.

The Respondent is David Crawford Jr., an individual whose address is 22 Foster Road, Milford, New Hampshire 03055, U.S.A.

2. The Domain Names and Registrar
The six (6) domain names in dispute are: <nascargames.com>, <nascargames.net>, <nascar-games.com>, <nascar-games.net>, <nascarinteractive.com> and <nascartvchannel.com>.

The registrar for the disputed domain names is Network Solutions Incorporated (NSI), 505 Huntmar Park Drive, Herndon, Virginia 20170, U.S.A.

3. Procedural History
This dispute is to be resolved in accordance with the Uniform Policy for Domain Name Dispute Resolution (the Policy) and Rules (the Rules) approved by the Internet Corporation for Assigned Names and Numbers (ICANN) on October 24, 1999, and the World Intellectual Property Organization Arbitration and Mediation Center's Supplemental Rules for Uniform Domain Name Dispute Resolution (the Center, the Supplemental Rules).

The Complaint was filed on November 9, 2001, by e-mail and on November 13, 2001, in hard copy. On November 16, 2001, the Center requested that the registrar NSI check and report back on the registrant for the six (6) disputed domain names, <nascargames.com>, <nascargames.net>, <nascar-games.com>, <nascar-games.net>, <nascarinteractive.com> and <nascartvchannel.com>. On November 19, 2001, NSI reported to the Center that the registrant was the Respondent, David Crawford Jr.

On November 22, 2001, the Center forwarded a copy of the Complaint to Respondent by registered mail and e-mail and this proceeding officially began. Respondent's Response was received by e-mail on December 10, 2001, and in hard copy on December 14, 2001.

The Administrative Panel submitted a Declaration of Impartiality and Independence on January 7, 2002, and the Center proceeded to appoint the Panel on January 8, 2002.

The Panel finds the Center has adhered to the Policy and the Rules in administering this Case.

This Decision is due by January 22, 2002.

4. Factual Background

The Complainant describes itself as "the world's premier regulating, governing and sanctioning body for stock car automobile racing." In this capacity, the Complainant lends its name and backing to several thousand car races per year all over the United States.

The Respondent is an individual who owns an array of Internet activities. The Respondent registered or re-registered the disputed domain names during October 2001, and uses them in conjunction with Internet games related to car races.

Both parties affirm there were some telephone exchanges in mid-2001, during which Complainant asserted trademark rights. Respondent followed up with an e-mail dated July 18, 2001 (Complaint Annex I), in which he proposed collaborating with the Complainant, but no agreement was reached.

In this proceeding the Complainant now is seeking transfer of the six (6) disputed domain names.

5. The Parties' Contentions

Complainant's Summarized Contentions:

- Complainant is the world's premier regulating and sanctioning body for stock car racing. Each year it sanctions over 2,200 races in 13 divisions on 128 tracks in 40 states across the United States.
- Complainant's racing events are the number one spectator sport in the United States.
- Most if not all of Complainant's Winston Cup series racing events are nationally televised or broadcast via radio. NASCAR's television ratings are second only to the National Football League for sporting events.
- Complainant has used its NASCAR mark in connection with stock car racing since at least 1948.
- Complainant registered its<nascar.com> domain name on December 28, 1995. The website at <nascar.com> was launched on December 7, 1999, and features car game racing and a tv section.
- Complainant licenses use of its marks to more than two hundred different licensees for such diverse goods and services as automotive products, television shows, clothing, bottled water, key chains, video games and restaurant services.
- Over its long years of extensive use, Complainant's NASCAR trademarks have acquired enormous goodwill and have become substantial assets of Complainant's business.
- Complainant has never authorized Respondent or his predecessor to use the NASCAR marks.
- The games on Respondent's website are very similar to the fantasy games featured on Complainant's website (Complaint Annex J).
- There is also a link on Respondent's website to a product called the Three Peace Salute, dedicated to a racing hero. The product is sold through a Post Office Box in Milford, N.H., the same town Respondent identified in his address (Complaint Annex K).
- One of the banner ads that appear on the website is for a company called Ready2Race, also owned by the Respondent.
- The websites for the other five domain name registrations at issue here appear to be identical to the <nascargames.com> website, all featuring multiple references to Complainant, banner advertising and links to Respondent's other websites (Complaint Annex M).
- Upon information and belief, Respondent is paid by third party advertisers on its website based upon the amount of traffic to the website (Complaint Annex F).
- The disputed domain names are confusingly similar to Complainant's mark because: the domain names at issue incorporate Complainant's mark in full.

- The inclusion of the generic terms "games" and "interactive" and the highly descriptive phrase "tv channel" in the domain names do not distinguish Respondent's domain names from Complainant's marks.
- Respondent has no rights or legitimate interests with respect to the domain name because Respondent's use of the domain names is not related to any legitimate business carried on by Respondent. Complainant on the other hand has used its mark in relation to stock car racing since at least 1948, (US Reg. No. 990, 987) and began obtaining federal Principal Register registrations for its mark in 1966, (US Reg. No. 817, 553) (Complaint Annex E).
- The inclusion of a trademark in a domain name suggests to consumers that the website found at that domain name is associated with the owner of the trademark.
- Complainant submits that by electing to register and then use domain names incorporating Complainant's mark, Respondent was intentionally attempting, for commercial gain, to attract Internet users to the site by creating a likelihood of confusion with the Complainant's mark as to the source, sponsorship, affiliation or endorsement of the web site.
- Evidence of bad faith in that the domain name was registered for commercial gain can be demonstrated in many different ways. Sales of merchandise on the site and third party banner advertising are both means of profiting from a website.
- Registration of multiple domain names that incorporate Complainant's NASCAR mark provides a valid basis for suggesting that Respondent intended to profit by using Complainant's popular mark.
- On information and belief, Respondent registered and used the domain names in order to trade upon and profit from the public's recognition of Complainant's NASCAR marks and the enormous goodwill associated with them.

Respondent's Contentions:

- As of January 7, 2000, the Respondent has been legally registered and doing business under the trade name "Virtual Thunder" for the purpose of online gaming.
- The use of the word "NASCAR" in the domain names indicates the type of games and interaction and is not confusing. The Respondent does not claim or appear to be NASCAR. Any reference to racing series and sanctions, including, but not limited to, NASCAR, are descriptive and are used to distinguish the particular events. Official sanctions, series and sponsor trademarks are not included on any of the Respondent's online properties.
- Domain History: Business goals at the time of initial registration of the "nascargames" domains were to provide online entertainment to the online racing community. Attaining an "Official" status from NASCAR was explored in December of 1999. (Response Annex B-NASCAR Prospective Licensee Application Form).
- In July of 1999, the Respondent started designing a website to provide a variety of games related to motor sports.
- In November 1999, affiliate programs were very popular as the dot.com boom was quickly evolving. In an effort to explore revenue models, the Respondent joined the affiliate programs at Amazon.com and Etoys.com and decided to use the nascargames domain to list NASCAR items offered by these affiliates. The Amazon.com affiliate program generated $12.56 in referral revenue and payment has never been collected due to their minimum payment restrictions. The eToys.com affiliate program generated $0.00 and has been dissolved (Response Annex D).
- In September 2000, a letter from the Complainant was received about the confusion of the NASCAR mark in the "nascargames" domain. At that time, a disclaimer was added to the main page of the "nascargames" website to prevent confusion and a notification letter was sent to the Complainant (Response Annex C).
- Contrary to the Complainant's suspicion and belief, the Respondent is not generating revenue from the domain name in question or any online properties.
- Contrary to what Complainant alleges, there does not exist any page that solicits third party advertisers.
- The Respondent believes that the Complainant promised exclusive rights for any online NASCAR gaming to undisclosed affiliates and therefore has targeted the Respondent to set a precedent for future domain acquisitions.

– The Respondent requests that the Panel make a finding of reverse domain name hijacking based upon the grounds of the illicit tactics, false assumptions and incorrect allegations issued by the Complainant after learning the actualities of the Respondent's situation and intentions.

6. Discussion and Findings

In order for Complainant to prevail and have the six (6) disputed domain names transferred, the Complainant must prove the following (the Policy, para. 4(a)(i-iii):

– the domain name is identical or confusingly similar to a trademark or service mark in which the Complainant has rights; and
– the Respondent has no rights or legitimate interests in respect of the domain name; and
– the domain name was registered and is being used in bad faith

Identical or Confusingly Similar

The Complainant has exhibited copies of a number of mark registrations for NASCAR on the principal register of the United States Patent and Trademark Agency. The Panel notes for example service mark no. 2205056 dated November 24, 1998, in international class 41 for a database providing news on auto and truck racing. The Panel also notes NASCAR service mark registration no. 1054100 dated December 7, 1976, in international class no. 41 for regulating and promoting stock car racing (Complaint Annex E).

The only distinctive part of all the disputed domain names is the Complainant's NASCAR mark: the words "games, interactive and tv channel" are merely descriptive and in no case create a mark different from the Complainant's. The Panel therefore finds the Complainant has satisfied section 4a(i) of the Policy with regard to all six (6) of the disputed domain names, i.e., the disputed domain names are confusingly similar to Complainant's NASCAR trademark. (see e.g. WIPO/ICANN Case No. D2000-0464, *Kabushiki Kaisha Toshiba d/b/a/ Toshiba Corporation v. Distribution Purchasing & Logistics Corp.*, July 27, 2000, where adding "store" to the Toshiba mark did not negate confusing similarity)

Legitimate Rights or Interests

The Complainant has asserted it has not given the Respondent any type of license or permission to use its NASCAR mark.

For its part, the Respondent has made conflicting arguments under the Policy about why he should be allowed to continue using the word NASCAR in the six (6) disputed domain names. The Respondent argues that his websites using the Complainant's NASCAR mark are noncommercial and thus should be allowed under Section 4c(iii) of the Policy: "you are making a legitimate noncommercial or fair use of the domain name, without intent for commercial gain to misleadingly divert consumers or to tarnish the trademark or service mark at issue." In this regard, the Respondent asserts he provided all investment money for the websites from his personal funds and that he does not accept advertising or seek any other type funding for the disputed domain name websites (Response p. 3).

However, at various other junctures in his Response, the Respondent admits to having had agreements with Etoys.com and Amazon.com whereby these companies would pay the Respondent for clients arriving via the Respondent's website (Response p. 2). Respondent asserts he made very little money from these arrangements, but the Panel finds this argument disingenuous: clearly it does not matter under the Policy how much or how little money a party makes from the commercial use of a domain name. What is controlling is whether the Respondent's website was commercial, and the Panel finds this is the case. The Respondent also acknowledges that at one point he sought to become licensed to use the Complainant's NASCAR mark (Response p. 2). Thus, the Respondent can not benefit from the non-commercial fair use provision of the Policy at 4c(iii) in order to claim a legitimate right or interest in the disputed domain names.

Nor can the Respondent benefit from the Policy provisions at 4c(i): "before any notice to you of the dispute, your use of, or demonstrable preparations to use, the domain name or a name corresponding to the domain name in connection with a bona fide offering of goods or services". The Panel is certain that the Respondent's activities and interests made him intimately familiar with the Complainant's strong and famous mark. The Respondent could not have been engaging in a bona fide offering of goods and services prior to being contacted by the Complainant.

The Panel finds the Respondent has no legitimate rights or interests in the disputed domain names.

Registered and Used in Bad Faith
The Complainant has shown that the Respondent at various points in the past has had third party advertisement on his websites at, or linked to, the disputed domain names. The Respondent himself has alluded to his affiliation with Etoys.com and Amazon.com for commercial gain. The Respondent has also stated he cross-promotes with other Internet organizations without money changing hands. However, the Panel believes that a barter arrangement can result in commercial gain to the Respondent just as paying money can.

The Panel finds the Respondent's actions and contentions distill into a clear violation of the bad faith provisions of the Policy at 4b(iv), i.e., the Respondent is trying to tap into the good will of the Complainant's NASCAR mark in order to reap economic benefit through a variety of schemes, but all having to do with racing games inspired by the Claimant's real-life NASCAR events and by the Complainant's own NASCAR internet games. (Many previous ICANN decisions note that where a website is used to advertise other websites that sell goods, it is appropriate to assume the former website owner is being paid for this service. See e.g. WIPO/ICANN Case No. D2000-0102 *Nokia Corporation v. Nokiagirls.com a.k.a. IBCC*, April 18, 2000).

In view of the above bad faith findings, the Panel finds untenable the Respondent's request that the Complaint be found to constitute an attempt at Reverse Domain Hijacking.

7. Decision

The Panel finds the six disputed domain names are confusingly similar to the Complainant's NASCAR mark. The Panel also finds the Respondent is not making a fair, non-commercial use of the Complainant's famous mark, but is instead making a non bona fide commercial use, and thus has no legitimate rights or interests in the domain names. Finally, the Panel finds the Respondent registered and is using the disputed domain names in bad faith by attempting to take advantage of the Complainant's famous mark for commercial gain for the Respondent.

Therefore, in accordance with ICANN Policy para. 4(i) and Rule 15, the Panel orders that the six (6) disputed domain names, <nascargames.com>, <nascargames.net>, <nascar-games.com>, <nascar-games.net>, <nascarinteractive.com> and <nascartvchannel.com> all be transferred from the Respondent, David Crawford Jr., to the Complainant, National Association for Stock Car Auto Racing, Inc.

Dennis A. Foster
Sole Panelist
Dated: January 20, 2002

WIPO Arbitration and Mediation Center

ADMINISTRATIVE PANEL DECISION

Tottenham Hotspur plc v. Kirsch Securities Ltd
Case No. D2003-0363

1. The Parties

The Complainant is Tottenham Hotspur plc of London, United Kingdom
The Respondent is Kirsch Securities Ltd of Middlesex, United Kingdom

2. The Domain Name and Registrar

The disputed domain name <tottenhamhotspur.com> is registered with Tucows.

3. Procedural History

The Complaint was filed with the WIPO Arbitration and Mediation Center (the "Center") on May 12, 2003. On May 13, 2003, the Center transmitted by email to Tucows a request for registrar verification in connection with the domain name at issue. On May 13, 2003, Tucows transmitted by email to the Center its verification response confirming that the Respondent is listed as the registrant and providing the contact details for the administrative, billing, and technical contact. The Center verified that the Complaint satisfied the formal requirements of the Uniform Domain Name Dispute Resolution Policy (the "Policy"), the Rules for Uniform Domain Name Dispute Resolution Policy (the "Rules"), and the WIPO Supplemental Rules for Uniform Domain Name Dispute Resolution Policy (the "Supplemental Rules").

In accordance with the Rules, paragraphs 2(a) and 4(a), the Center formally notified the Respondent of the Complaint, and the proceedings commenced on May 15, 2003. In accordance with the Rules, paragraph 5(a), the due date for Response was June 4, 2003. The Respondent did not submit any Response. Accordingly, the Center notified the Respondent's default on June 5, 2003.

The Center appointed David Perkins as the sole panelist in this matter on June 17, 2003. The Panel finds that it was properly constituted. The Panel has submitted the Statement of Acceptance and Declaration of Impartiality and Independence, as required by the Center to ensure compliance with the Rules, paragraph 7.

4. Factual Background

4.1 The Complainant

4.1.1 The Complainant operates the well-known English football (soccer) club TOTTENHAM HOTSPUR. The club was founded in 1882, as the Hotspur Football Club and in 1884 was renamed Tottenham Hotspur Football Club.

4.2 The TOTTENHAM HOTSPUR registered trademarks

The Complainant is the registered proprietor of United Kingdom Trademark No. 1,199,577 for the words TOTTENHAM HOTSPUR in Classes 6: 14: 16: 18: 20: 21: 24: 25 and 28. That mark has been registered with effect from 1983. This is a merged registration for marks separately registered for each of the classes of goods, all dating from 1983. The Complaint states that trademark applications for TOTTENHAM HOTSPUR are pending in the European Community, Korea, Japan, the United States of America and Canada.

4.3 Reputation in the TOTTENHAM HOTSPUR mark

The Club plays in the United Kingdom Football Association's Premier League. It has won both English National and European competitions on numerous occasions. It is well-known in football playing countries worldwide. The Complainant's website at <www.spurs.co.uk> launched in July 1996, currently receives over 3 million page hits a month. The Complainant also sells under the TOTTENHAM HOTSPUR brand a range of goods and services including clothing, badges, credit cards, travel to away matches in TOTTENHAM HOTSPUR branded coaches, glasses, lighters, umbrellas, soft toys, stationery, confectionery, books and audio visual products about TOTTENHAM HOTSPUR. In 2002, the value of this merchandise exceeded £1.7 million.

4.4 The Respondent

4.4.1 The Respondent appears to be a property [real estate] company. The domain name in issue was registered on December 17, 1999.

4.4.2 In the absence of a Response, the only additional information relating to the Respondent is contained in the Complaint and in correspondence with Mr. Brian Kirsch exhibited to the Complaint. Mr. Kirsch would appear to be the principal of the Respondent company. He is also the Administrative Contact for the domain name in issue.

4.4.3 According to the Complaint, as at December 2001, the domain name in issue resolved to a website for Webcreation. The home page for that website exhibited to the Complaint reads:

Webcreation

Within five years, one billion people will do five billion pounds worth of business on the internet. If you are looking for a quality customer website at a sensible price then look no further We offer a comprehensive and efficient service to get your business on the Web.

The Complaint states that subsequent to that date, presumably as a result of the correspondence between the parties [paragraph 4.3 below], the domain name in issue no longer resolves to the Webcreation website and currently does not appear to be used. That website can now be accessed through the <disneyland-paris.com> domain name, which was registered by Mr. Brian Kirsch on December 10, 1998, who is also listed in the WHOIS Search as the Administrative Contact.

4.5 Correspondence between the Parties

The correspondence exhibited to the Complaint can be summarized as follows:

August 24, 2001:
DR Ltd [agents on behalf of the Complainant] contacted Mr. Kirsch personally requesting transfer of the domain name in issue and offering to meet the costs related to such transfer.

July 2002:
The Complainant's solicitors instructed a firm of Private Investigators, .com investigations [a division of Carratu International plc], to establish the identity of the individual or business underlying the Registration and the potential uses (if any) of the domain name which the Registrant might intend to conduct. This involved a series of emails over the period of July 4 – 8, 2002. Those involved were Richard Carrington [of .com investigations], Jeremy Freeman [Managing Director of Bamps Ltd] and Mr. Brian Kirsch.

Mr. Carrington addressed his opening email of July 4, 2002, to Mr. Kirsch at the email address given by Mr. Kirsch as Administrative Contact for his <disneyland-paris.com> domain name Mr. Carrington posed as a Tottenham Hotspur fan interested in buying the domain name in issue for the purpose of using it for a fan site. Mr. Freeman replied stating:

> "My client has no intention of selling this domain."

Mr. Kirsch subsequently emailed Mr. Carrington stating:

> "… you are welcome to make me an offer."

Mr. Carrington offered £500 – £700, which Mr. Kirsch described as "laughable". Mr. Carrington then increased his offer to £3,000.00 and, later, to £5,000.00. Mr. Kirsch replied:

> "I have never advertised the site for sale nor do I particularly wish to sell the name unless what I consider is too good a price to turn down."

Adding that he had already rejected another offer to purchase the domain name in issue for £8,500.00 but saying that he would accept £15,000.00. Mr. Carrington took the matter no further.

September 2002 to January 2003:
The Complainant's solicitors wrote a cease and desist letter to Mr. Kirsch on September 26, 2002, seeking transfer of the domain name in issue and various undertakings.

The Respondent's solicitors [Whitehorns] replied on November 12, 2002, denying trademark infringement, passing off or the suggestion made in the cease and desist letter that the domain name had been registered or used in bad faith. In material part, Whitehorn's letter stated:

> "It is accepted that my clients are the owners of the above domain name but it is not (as you seem to allege) true that my clients have offered the name for sale, nor invited offers. Indeed the purpose of the purchase was as a gift to one of the director's sons; himself a keen Spurs supporter, with the intention of using it as a personal internet address.
>
> Someone (your agent I presume) approached my client and made, I am told, two offers which my clients refused. I am instructed that no offer was made to sell the domain name for £15,000, and that such figure was mentioned only with the intention of dissuading your correspondent from pestering my clients further."

The Complainant's solicitors responded that this version of events was inconsistent with previous use of the domain name issue for the Webcreation website. They also pointed to Mr. Kirsch and the Respondent being registrants of two other domain names incorporating well-known trade marks, namely <disneyland-paris.com> [Mr. Kirsch] and <thefacupfinal.com> [the Respondent]

On the Respondent's headed notepaper Mr. Kirsch replied in the following terms:

> "Your Clients were free to register the above dotcom as recently as 3 years ago but instead chose to use spurs.co.uk. They obviously felt that there was no need to register the dotcom as above and did not even secure their trading name so that nobody else could take it. This mistake on the part of Tottenham Hotspur is just that, A MISTAKE.
>
> When I found that the name was available I took it and as a lifelong Spurs supporter was very proud to own the name. I have never traded the fact that I own this name and resent your suggestions that have ever sought to profit by the ownership."

This was followed by rejection of the Complainant's request for transfer of the domain name and undertakings and ended:

> "I will however ensure that the Press is made aware of these threats by Tottenham Hotspur in trying to force a fan into submission."

This, effectively, terminated the correspondence and this Complaint was filed some 4 months later in May 2003.

5. Parties' Contentions

5.1 Complainant

5.1.2 Identical or Confusingly Similar

The domain name in issue is identical to the TOTTENHAM HOTSPUR trademark, save for the .com suffix, which is irrelevant in terms of meeting the requirements of paragraph 4(a)(i) of the Policy.

5.1.3 Rights or Legitimate Interests

The Complainant's case is as follows:

- The Respondent is not licensed or otherwise authorised by the Complainant to use the TOTTENHAM HOTSPUR trademark.
- The Respondent is not commonly known by the domain name in issue.
- Before notice of this dispute, the Respondent did not use or make demonstrable preparations to use the TOTTENHAM HOTSPUR mark in connection with a *bona fide* offering of goods or services.
- The Respondent's story that the domain name was intended as a gift for one of his sons, a keen supporter of the Football Club, for use as a personal internet address is contradicted by the unauthorised commercial use made in relation to Webcreation website [paragraphs 4.2.3 and 4.3 above].
- Further, no evidence has been provided by the Respondent of any use or preparations to use the domain name in issue as an internet address.

Still further, use of a third party trademark as a domain name for an unauthorised fan football club website does not amount to a *bona fide* offering of services or a fair use [*Juventus F.C. S.p.a v Claudio Sacco Interactive*, WIPO Case No. D2001-0260].

5.1.3 Registered and used in Bad Faith

The Complainant's case is as follows:

- Because of the notoriety of the TOTTENHAM HOTSPUR trademark, including the registered mark dating from 1983, and by reason of his being "a lifelong Spurs supporter" [see, paragraph 4.3 above], the Respondent and Mr. Kirsch were obviously well aware that that mark referred to the Complainant.
- Use of the domain name in issue for the Webcreation website was to attract Internet users to that website for commercial gain and clearly amounted to trading off the very considerable reputation of the Complainant's TOTTENHAM HOTSPUR trademark.
- Registration by the Respondent / Mr. Kirsch of the domain name in issue, coupled with the <disneyland-paris.com> and <thefacupfinal.com> domain names, is evidence of *a pattern of conduct* designed to prevent the owners of those trademarks from reflecting those marks in corresponding domain names. As such it amounts to registration in bad faith.
- The fact that the Respondent has no rights or legitimate interests in respect of the domain name is also indicative of registration in bad faith.
- Further, having regard to the email exchange [see, paragraph 4.3 above], it is plain that the domain name in issue was registered primarily for the purpose of selling it to the Complainant trademark owner for a sum greatly in excess [for example, £15,000.00] of the out of pocket costs directly related to that domain name.
- Finally, the present non-use of the domain name can amount to bad faith use if circumstances of the type indicted in *Telstra Corporation v Nuclear Marshmallows*, WIPO Case No. D2000-0003 apply. Inaction in the form of a passive holding of a domain name can amount to bad faith

use depending upon the facts of the case. Examples of circumstances indicating such bad faith can include the fact that the Complainant's trademark has a strong reputation and is well known, failure by the Respondent to provide credible evidence of any actual or contemplated good faith use, and where it is not possible to conceive of any plausible actual or contemplated use of the domain name by the Respondent that would not be illegitimate. Furthermore, the fact of taking down the original Webcreations website does not expiate prior bad faith use [*Ingersoll-Rand Co. v Frank Gurry*, WIPO Case No. D2000-0021].

5.2 Respondent

In the absence of a Response, the Panel must look at the Respondent's assertions made in the Correspondence. These have been identified in paragraph 4.3 above. They are:

- The domain name in issue was acquired for one of Mr. Kirsch's sons, a fan of the football club, for use as an internet address.
- The domain name was not acquired with a view to selling it, whether to the Complainant for an over-value or at all.
- The Respondent never offered to sell the domain name for £15,000.00. Mr. Kirsch says he has not sought to profit in that way from registration of the domain name.
- The domain name cannot be of any real concern to the Complainant, otherwise they would have registered and used it. Instead, they have registered and used the <spurs.co.uk> domain name.

6. Discussion and Findings

6.1 The Policy paragraph 4(a) provides that the Complainant must prove each of the following in order to succeed in an administrative proceeding:

- that the Respondent's domain name is identical or confusingly similar to a trademark or service mark in which the Complainant has rights; and
- that the Respondent has no rights or legitimate interests in respect of the domain name; and
- that the domain name has been registered and is being used in bad faith.

6.2 The Policy paragraph 4(c) sets out circumstances which, in particular but without limitation, if found by the Panel to be proved shall demonstrate the Respondent's rights or legitimate interest in the domain name in issue.

6.3 The Policy paragraph 4(b) sets out circumstances which, again in particular but without limitation, if found the Panel to be present shall be evidence of the registration and use of a domain name in bad faith.

6.4 As stated, the circumstances set out in paragraph 4(b) and 4(c) of the Policy are not exclusionary. They are without limitation. That is, the Policy expressly recognises that other circumstances can be evidence relevant the requirements of paragraphs 4(a)(ii) and (iii) of the Policy.

Identical or Confusingly Similar

6.5 The Panel agrees with the Complainant that the .com suffix is irrelevant. Hence, the domain name in issue is identical to the Complainant's TOTTENHAM HOTSPUR trademark and the Complaint meets the requirements of paragraph 4(a)(i) of the Policy.

Rights or Legitimate Interests

6.6 In the Panel's opinion, on the facts the Respondent has not brought itself within any of the circumstances specified in paragraph 4(c) of the Policy. The Panel agrees that where a Complainant makes a *prima facie* showing that the Respondent lacks a legitimate interest, the burden then shifts to the Respondent to demonstrate rights or such interest [*World Wrestling Federation Entertainment v Ringside Collectibles*, WIPO Case No. D2000-1306] and *F.C. Bayern München v Miguel Garcia*, WIPO Case No. D2000-1773].

6.7 Here, the Panel is satisfied that such a *prima facie* showing has been made. The Panel does not regard discontinued use of the domain name in issue for the Webcreation website a *bona fide* offering of services within paragraph 4(c)(i) of the Policy. The knowledge of Mr. Kirsch of the reputation and activities of the Complainant under the TOTTENHAM HOTSPUR trademark must clearly be imputed to the Respondent. There is nothing to suggest that Mr. Kirsch is other than the alter ego of the Respondent. The fact that the Complainant used the domain name <spurs.co.uk> for its website does not legitimise the Respondent's attempt to hijack their TOTTENHAM HOTSPUR trademark for its own commercial purposes.

6.8 Furthermore, the Respondent has chosen not to respond to this Complaint from which the Panel is entitled to and does draw an adverse inference. In all the circumstances, the Panel finds that the Respondent has failed to show rights or legitimate interest in respect of the domain name in issue and, accordingly, the Complaint meets the requirements of paragraph 4(a)(ii) of the Policy.

Registered and Used in Bad Faith

6.9 On the facts, the Panel takes the view that the Complainant has demonstrated registration and use in bad faith under paragraph 4(b)(iv) of the Policy. This is by reason of the Respondent's use of the domain name for commercial gain in relation to the Webcreation website, which can only be construed as a blatant attempt to take advantage of the well-known TOTTENHAM HOTSPUR trademark and the inevitability that this would create a likelihood of association with the Complainant's Football Club.

6.10 Does the Complaint established *a pattern of conduct* as required by paragraph 4(b)(ii) of the Policy? Registration by Mr. Kirsch of <disney-paris.com> might, on its own, have been insufficient evidence of such a pattern. However, given the facts of this dispute as a whole, the Panel would tend towards a finding in favour of the Complainant under this provision of the Policy. But, given the Panel's finding in paragraphs 6.9 and 6.12 of this Decision, it is not necessary to come to a decision on this point.

6.11 As to paragraph 4(b)(i) of the Policy there is a conflict of evidence The Complainant points to the Respondent's willingness to sell the domain name for £15,000.00 [see, paragraph 4.3 above]. The Respondent says he did not register the domain name with the intention of selling and he only advanced the £15,000.00 figure with the intention of dissuading Mr. Carrington from pestering him any further [Whitehorn's letter of November 12, 2002]. Then in a later letter [letter dated December 18, 2001] Mr. Kirsch himself took a somewhat contradictory position when he stated that he considered £15,000.00 to be the appropriate value of the domain name:

> "Finally, as a Property Dealer I have spent my life dealing with values of property and by suggesting that £15,000 was my price I only sought to establish what someone else was prepared to pay."

6.12 As noted by the Panellist (Sir Ian Barker Q.C.) in *Veuve Clicquot Ponsardin, Maison Fondee en 1772 v The Polygenix Group Co.*, WIPO Case No. D2000-0163, the Respondent's offer to treat with persons with a "property interest" in the domain name there in issue was "powerful evidence of bad faith". Also, as stated in *Educational Tertiary Service v Toefl*, WIPO Case No. D2000-0004 cited by Sir Ian in the *Veuve Clicquot* case:

> "The value which Respondent seeks to secure from sale of the domain name is based on the underlying value of Complainant's trademark. This value is grounded in the right of Complainant to use its mark to identify itself as a source of goods or services. Respondent has failed to establish any legitimate domain name-related use for Complainant's trademark, in a context in which such legitimisation might be possible. The Respondent having failed to present any such justification, the Panel may reasonably infer that Respondent neither intended to make or has made any legitimate use of Complainant's trademark in connection with the domain name at issue."

6.13 Although in that case, the Respondent clearly stated in its website its intention to sell domain names for a profit, the principle of the Respondent being prepared to treat with the Complainant trademark owner, in effect, to buy back its own rights is, in the Panel's opinion, strongly indicative of bad faith. Again, the Panel would tend to find in favour of the Complainant under this provision of the Policy.

6.14 Finally, as noted, the circumstances set out in paragraph 4(b) of the Policy are not exhaustive of the acts which can give rise to a holding of bad faith registration and use [see the *Telstra* case (supra)]. Added to the circumstances advanced in the Complaint [see, paragraph 5.1.4 (final bullet point)], there is, again, the fact that the Respondent has not chosen to defend this Complaint by filing a Response.

6.15 In all the circumstances, the Panel find that the domain name in issue was registered and is being used in bad faith and, accordingly, the Complaint meets the requirements of paragraph 4(a)(iii) of the Policy.

7. Decision
For all the foregoing reasons, in accordance with Paragraphs 4(i) of the Policy and 15 of the Rules, the Panel orders that the domain name <tottenhamhotspur.com> be transferred to the Complainant.

David Perkins
Sole Panelist
Dated: June 23, 2003

WIPO Arbitration and Mediation Center

ADMINISTRATIVE PANEL DECISION
Ralph Maltby Enterprises, Inc. v. Women With Balls (W.W.B. Accessories)
Case No. D2004-0917

1. The Parties
The Complainant is Ralph Maltby Enterprises, Inc., Newark, Ohio, United States of America, represented by Dinsmore & Shohl LLP, Dayton, Ohio, United States of America.

The Respondent is Women With Balls (W.W.B. Accessories), Laguna Beach, California, United States of America.

2. The Domain Name and Registrar
The disputed domain name <womensgolfworks.com> is registered with Dotster, Inc..

3. Procedural History
The Complaint was filed with the WIPO Arbitration and Mediation Center (the "Center") on November 3, 2004. On November 3, 2004, the Center transmitted by email to Dotster, Inc. a request for registrar verification in connection with the domain name at issue. On November 4, 2004, Dotster, Inc. transmitted by email to the Center its verification response confirming that the Respondent is listed as the registrant and providing the contact details for the administrative, billing, and technical contact. The Center verified that the Complaint satisfied the formal requirements of the Uniform Domain Name Dispute Resolution Policy (the "Policy"), the Rules for Uniform Domain Name Dispute Resolution Policy (the "Rules"), and the WIPO Supplemental Rules for Uniform Domain Name Dispute Resolution Policy (the "Supplemental Rules").

In accordance with the Rules, paragraphs 2(a) and 4(a), the Center formally notified the Respondent of the Complaint, and the proceedings commenced on November 8, 2004. In accordance with the Rules, paragraph 5(a), the due date for Response was November 28, 2004. The Respondent did not submit any response. Accordingly, the Center notified the Respondent's default on November 29, 2004.

The Center appointed Lynda J. Zadra-Symes as the sole panelist in this matter on December 13, 2004. The Panel finds that it was properly constituted. The Panel has submitted the Statement of Acceptance and Declaration of Impartiality and Independence, as required by the Center to ensure compliance with the Rules, paragraph 7.

4. Factual Background
The following facts and statements are derived from the Complaint and its annexed documents. The Respondent has not contested any of these facts and statements.

For over twenty-five years, Complainant, Ralph Maltby Enterprises, Inc., has used both GOLFWORKS and THE GOLFWORKS in various formats as trademarks and service marks in connection with golf clubs and golf equipment. Complainant is the owner of several United States federal registrations covering its GOLFWORKS marks, including the following registrations that have become incontestable under the provisions of U.S. trademark law:

THE GOLFWORKS (Stylized), U.S. Reg. No. 1,211,844, issued October 5, 1982, and used since 1976, in connection with the custom manufacture and repair of golf clubs and the custom design of golf clubs;

THE GOLFWORKS (Stylized), U.S. Reg. No. 1,304,735, issued November 14, 1984, and used since 1977, in connection with hand tools and gauges used in the manufacture and repair of golf clubs;

THE GOLFWORKS, U.S. Reg. No. 1,749,856, issued February 2, 1993, and used since 1978, in connection with tools and gauges for use in the manufacture and repair of golf clubs, golf bags; golf clubs and components thereof and accessories therefor, and other golf-related items.

Under U.S. trademark law (15 U.S.C. Section 1115), these incontestable registrations provide conclusive evidence of Complainant's ownership of the marks in the U.S. and of its exclusive right to use the marks in connection with the goods and services identified in the registrations.

Complainant also owns registrations of THE GOLFWORKS mark in other countries, including Canada, Japan and the United Kingdom for use in connection with golf clubs and golf equipment. Complainant submitted with its Complaint copies of the certificates of registration for all of the trademarks referenced above.

Complainant registered the domain name <golfworks.com> on November 17, 1995, and has maintained the registration continuously since that date. Complainant uses the domain name in connection with a web site that promotes Complainant's products and services marketed under the GOLFWORKS marks, and through which consumers can purchase those goods and services. In addition to the goods and services listed in Complainant's above registrations, Complainant's web site also offers clothing and sportswear items, and educational services, books and videos in the field of golf equipment.

According to the Complaint, Complainant and its founder, Ralph Maltby, are well known in the field of golf and golf equipment, and they are particularly recognized for their expertise in the custom manufacture and design of golf clubs and the repair of golf clubs.

Respondent registered the disputed domain name <womensgolfworks.com> on July 9, 2000. As shown in Annex 7 attached to the Complaint, the domain name resolves to a web site used to promote golf accessories and golf clothing items directed primarily to women golfers. Pages printed from the web site in November 2004, show Respondent's use of the phrase "An Original Golfworks product" to describe Respondent's golf-related items promoted on the web site.

5. Parties' Contentions

A. Complainant

Complainant contends that it has prior rights in the GOLFWORKS mark which is incorporated in its entirety in Respondent's domain name, with the addition of the descriptive term "womens" and the top-level domain designation ".com." Complainant contends that the disputed domain name is confusingly similar to its registered GOLFWORKS marks and <golfworks.com> domain name, that Respondent has no legitimate rights or interests in respect of the disputed <womensgolfworks.com> domain name and that Respondent has registered and is using the disputed domain name in bad faith to sell golf-related products, mislead Internet users and disrupt the Complainant's business. Complainant therefore contends that the domain name should be transferred to the Complainant.

B. Respondent

The Respondent did not reply to the Complainant's contentions.

6. Discussion and Findings

Paragraph 15(a) of the Rules instructs the Panel to "decide a complaint on the basis of the statements and documents submitted in accordance with the Policy, these Rules and any rules and principles of law that it deems applicable."

In view of the Respondent's failure to submit a Response, the Panel shall decide this administrative proceeding on the basis of Complainant's undisputed representations pursuant to paragraphs 5(e), 14(a) and 15(a) of the Rules and draw such inferences it considers appropriate pursuant to paragraph 14(b) of the Rules.

Paragraph 4(a) of the Policy directs that the Complainant must prove each of the following to obtain an order that a domain name should be cancelled or transferred:

(i) the domain name registered by the Respondent is identical or confusingly similar to a trademark or service mark in which the complainant has rights;
(ii) the Respondent has no rights or legitimate interests in respect of the domain name; and
(iii) the domain name has been registered and is being used in bad faith;

A. Identical or Confusingly Similar

Complainant has established its prior rights in the mark GOLFWORKS as indicated in its U.S., Canadian, Japanese and UK trademark registrations. Complainant is also the owner and operator of a web site located at the domain name <golfworks.com>, which it registered in 1995, and which promotes and offers for sale golf equipment and related clothing and accessories.

Respondent's domain name <womensgolfworks.com> incorporates Complainant's registered trademark GOLFWORKS in its entirety. Complainant argues that the addition of the descriptive term "womens" adds nothing distinctive and does not substantially alter the impression conveyed by the domain name. Instead, according to Complainant, this descriptive term merely suggests that the products advertised at Respondent's site are a line of GOLFWORKS products directed toward women and that the addition of such a descriptive term is not sufficient to avoid a finding of confusing similarity. Complainant submits that Respondent's <womensgolfworks.com> domain name is sufficiently similar to Complainant's GOLFWORKS marks that a reasonable Internet user would mistakenly assume that the domain name and any associated web site are affiliated with Complainant. Complainant submits further that the potential for confusion is aggravated by the reference in the content of Respondent's web site to the phrase "An Original Golfworks product," to promote certain products offered for sale on Respondent's web site. Complainant states that the use of GOLFWORKS alone, without the word "womens," in the content of the website to promote golf-related goods reinforces the impression that the <womensgolfworks.com> web site and/or the products promoted on that site are affiliated with Complainant's GOLFWORKS trademarks or business.

Accordingly, the Panel finds that the <womensgolfworks.com> domain name is confusingly similar to Complainant's GOLFWORKS trademarks under Policy paragraph 4(a)(i).

B. Rights or Legitimate Interests

Complainant submits that the Respondent is not affiliated with the Complainant, and Complainant has never assigned, sold, licensed or transferred any rights in any of its GOLFWORKS marks to Respondent. There is no evidence indicating that Respondent was known by the name "womensgolfworks" prior to registration of the disputed domain name. Indeed, Respondent's disputed domain name registration was issued in the name of a business named "Women With Balls (W.W.B. Accessories)," and not a name incorporating the term "womens golfworks."

Finally, Respondent's offering of golf equipment and accessories at the web site located at the disputed domain name does not create a legitimate interest in the domain name because Respondent's use of the confusingly similar domain name (as well as use of Complainant's GOLFWORKS mark in the text of the web site) to promote and sell identical or closely related goods and services constitutes infringing use in the United States. Such infringing use does not give rise to a legitimate right or interest on the part of the Respondent. *Chase Manhattan Corp. v. John Whitely*, WIPO Case No. D2000-0346 (June 12, 2000); *Chanel, Inc. v. Estco Technology Group*, WIPO Case No. D2000-0413 (September 18, 2000).

Moreover, based on the Respondent's failure to respond to the Complainant's allegations, the Panel may assume that the Respondent has no rights or legitimate interests in the disputed domain name.

Accordingly, the Panel finds that the Complainant has established Policy paragraph 4(a)(ii).

C. Registered and Used in Bad Faith

All of Complainant's above-referenced U.S. trademark registrations were issued many years before Respondent's registration of the disputed domain name. Moreover, Complainant's domain name <golfworks.com> was registered in 1995, five years prior to the year in which Respondent registered the disputed domain name. The opportunities for Respondent, also a U.S. business, to become aware of Complainant's prior U.S. trademark rights were numerous. Indeed, a simple Internet search results in numerous references to Complainant's GOLFWORKS trademark supporting Complainant's claims that it is well-known in the field of golf and golf equipment and has established significant customer association in the GOLFWORKS marks in the United States over the last twenty-five years. It is therefore likely that anyone working in the field of golf equipment in the United States has some knowledge of Complainant's business and its use of the GOLFWORKS marks.

In addition, under U.S. trademark law, Respondent had at least constructive knowledge of Complainant's rights in the GOLFWORKS marks at the time it registered the contested domain name. (15 U.S.C. Section 1072). Registration of a domain name that is confusingly similar to another's registered mark that is done with knowledge, whether actual or constructive, has been found to evidence bad faith. See, e.g., *Mobil Oil Corporation v. John S. Flynn*, WIPO Case No. D2000-1562 (January 27, 2001).

These findings, together with the finding that the Respondent has no legitimate rights or interests in the domain name, lead the Panel to conclude that the domain name <womensgolfworks.com> has been registered by the Respondent in bad faith.

7. Decision

For all the foregoing reasons, in accordance with Paragraphs 4(i) of the Policy and 15 of the Rules, the Panel orders that the domain name, <womensgolfworks.com> be transferred to the Complainant.

Lynda J. Zadra-Symes
Sole Panelist
Dated: December 27, 2004

WIPO Arbitration and Mediation Center

ADMINISTRATIVE PANEL DECISION
The Orange Bowl Committee, Inc. v. Front and Center Tickets, Inc/ Front and Center Entertainment
Case No. D2004-0947

1. The Parties

The Complainant is The Orange Bowl Committee, Inc, Miami, Florida, of United States of America, represented by Hunton & Williams, United States of America.

The Respondent is Front and Center Tickets, Inc/ Front and Center Entertainment, Fort Lauderdale, Florida, of United States of America, represented by Mark Halpern.

2. The Domain Names and Registrar

The disputed domain names <orangebowl.net> and <orangebowltickets.net> ("Domain Names ") are registered with Dotster, Inc.

3. Procedural History

The Complaint was filed with the WIPO Arbitration and Mediation Center (the "Center") on November 10, 2004. On November 11, 2004, the Center transmitted by email to Dotster, Inc. a request for registrar verification in connection with the domain names at issue. On November 11, 2004, Dotster, Inc. transmitted by email to the Center its verification response confirming that the Respondent is listed as the registrant and providing the contact details for the administrative, billing, and technical contact. The Center verified that the Complaint satisfied the formal requirements of the Uniform Domain Name Dispute Resolution Policy (the "Policy"), the Rules for Uniform Domain Name Dispute Resolution Policy (the "Rules"), and the WIPO Supplemental Rules for Uniform Domain Name Dispute Resolution Policy (the "Supplemental Rules").

In accordance with the Rules, paragraphs 2(a) and 4(a), the Center formally notified the Respondent of the Complaint, and the proceedings commenced November 16, 2004. In accordance with the Rules, paragraph 5(a), the due date for Response December 6, 2004. The Response was filed with the Center December 6, 2004.

The Center appointed Mark Partridge, Frederick M. Abbott and Neil A. Smith as panelists in this matter on December 23, 2004. The Panel finds that it was properly constituted. Each member of the Panel has submitted the Statement of Acceptance and Declaration of Impartiality and Independence, as required by the Center to ensure compliance with the Rules, paragraph 7.

4. Factual Background

Complainant has used the ORANGE BOWL mark since 1935, for one of the nation's best-known college football tournaments. It has also expanded use of the mark to a variety of other goods and services, including a tennis tournament, a basketball championship, a golf tournament and various types of merchandise.

The ORANGE BOWL tournament has been the subject of extensive advertising and media attention and is watched annually by millions of spectators. The television rights alone to broadcast the ORANGE BOWL game involve fees in excess of $100,000,000.00.

Complainant sells millions of tickets and hundreds of thousands of goods under the ORANGE BOWL mark, some of which are sold via Complainant's websites at "www.orangebowl.com" and "www.orangebowl.org".

Complainant obtained a federal trademark registration for the mark ORANGE BOWL on December 12, 1995, but inadvertently allowed that registration to lapse on September 14, 2002, due an administrative error. Complainant is the co-owner federal trademark registrations for FEDEX ORANGE BOWL (Reg. No. 2,129,760; 2,037,172) and reapplied for federal registration of the mark ORANGE BOWL on December 10, 2002. Respondent admits that ORANGE BOWL is a famous name.

Respondent is engaged in the online resale of tickets for sporting and entertainment events. The domain name <orangebowltickets.net> was registered on April 14, 1999. The domain name <orangebowl.net> was registered on June 24, 1999.

Complainant sent a letter of objection on August 11, 2000, regarding Respondent's use of <orangebowl.net>. At that time, it appears that it used that domain name for a site stating "Welcome to the Orange Bowl" on the homepage. On August 29, 2000, Respondent answered that it operates about 250 website portals directing traffic to sites where it resells event tickets.

Respondent's conduct has been the subject of prior UDRP claims, including *National Collegiate Athletic Association and March Madness Athletic Association, LLC v. Mark Halpern and Front & Center Entertainment,* WIPO Case No. D2000-0700, which found that Respondent violated the Policy by registration and use of domain names incorporating the marks NCAA, FINAL FOUR and MARCH MADNESS; and *HBP, Inc. v. Front and Center Tickets, Inc.*, WIPO Case No. D2002-0802, in which the majority found that Respondent's registration and use of <daytona500tickets.net> and <daytona500tickets.org> violated the Policy (the later case involved members of this Panel: Mr. Abbott was the presiding panelist for the majority and Mr. Smith issued a dissent).

At the time the Complainant in this action was filed, Respondent used the respective Domain Names for a site that offered tickets to various events, including college bowl game tickets and National Football League tickets, as well as "all concert tickets – all sporting event tickets – all theater tickets." The site included a disclaimer stating: "The National Collegiate Athletic Association (NCAA) has neither licensed or endorsed Front and Center Entertainment Group to sell goods and services in conjunction with NCAA and regular season or championship games." There was no disclaimer relating to Complainant.

The domain name <orangebowl.net> is no longer active, and Respondent has agreed to transfer it to Complainant.

The domain name <orangebowltickets.net> now leads to a modified site that prominently bears the heading "Orange Bowl National Championship Tickets." There is also a new disclaimer stating:

"Orangebowltickets.net is a private ticket broker and the FedEx Orange Bowl has neither licensed nor endorsed Front and Center Entertainment Group to sell goods and services in conjunction with The FedEx Orange Bowl and regular season or championship games."

The page continues to offer tickets for other events, including other college bowl games, NFL games and the Superbowl, with several links from the site leading to Respondent's "frontrow.com" website where it offers tickets to other events, including tickets to Las Vegas Shows, Broadway Shows, NASCAR races, and concerts by performers such as Celine Dion, Elton John and Cher.

5. Parties' Contentions

A. Complainant

Complainant contends that the domain name <orangebowl.net> is identical in materials part to the mark ORANGE BOWL in which it has rights.

Complainant further contends that the domain name <orangebowltickets.net> is virtually identical to its ORANGE BOWL mark and that the addition of generic term "Tickets" is not a distinguishing feature.

Complainant asserts that Respondent does not have any right or legitimate interest in the Domain Names because it is not authorized to use Complainant's marks as domain names, is not known by those names, and is not making bona fide use of the trademark. More specifically, Complainant contends that Respondent's resale of ORANGE BOWL tickets is contrary to the terms and conditions printed on the ticket. Complainant also contends that Respondent is not making non-commercial or fair use of the Domain Names, but instead is making commercial use of the Domain Names to divert Internet users to a site where it sells tickets to Complainant's event and other events at inflated prices. Finally, Complainant contends that Respondent's conduct is bad faith use and registration of the Domain Names because Respondent deliberately uses Complainant's mark to misdirect Internet users to Respondent's site for commercial gain.

B. Respondent

Respondent concedes that Complainant owns the mark ORANGE BOWL and that the mark is famous. Respondent also concedes that it has been the subject of prior decisions which found similar conduct to violate the Policy.

Respondent further agrees that it "cannot make any argument" regarding the domain name <orangebowl.net> and agrees to transfer the name to Complainant.

Nevertheless, Respondent claims it has a legitimate interest and right to use the domain name <orangebowltickets.net> because he is a legitimate ticket broker using the domain name to sell genuine ORANGE BOWL tickets to persons who search for such tickets online and has done so for almost five years.

Respondent contends his use of the domain name allows him to provide a valuable service to persons seeking event tickets and that such persons will not be confused because it is apparent from the fact that he sells tickets to other events that the site is not an "official" ORANGE BOWL site and because there is a disclaimer on the site.

Respondent further contends that his conduct is justified because many people in the secondary market for event tickets use similar names and because another ticket broker was allowed to keep similar domain names in *NCAA v. Randy Pitkin,* WIPO Case No. D2000-0903 (a split decision in which Mr. Smith sided with the majority in favor of the domain name owner).

6. Discussion and Findings

The Respondent states that it has no argument regarding the domain name <orangebowl.net> and agrees to transfer the name to Complainant. Therefore, the entirety of the Panel finds in favor of Complainant on that domain name.

With respect to the domain name <orangebowltickets.net>, Paragraph 4(a) of the Policy requires the Complainant to establish each of the following elements:

(i) that the domain name registered by the Respondent is identical or confusingly similar to a trademark or service mark in which the Complainant has rights;

(ii) that the Respondent has no rights or legitimate interest in respect of the domain name; and

(iii) that the domain name has been registered and is being used in bad faith.

The majority of the Panel finds as follows on these elements.

A. Identical or Confusingly Similar

Respondent does not dispute that Complainant owns trademark rights in the mark ORANGE BOWL. Respondent further concedes that the ORANGE BOWL name is famous.

The issue is whether the addition of "tickets" is sufficient to avoid a finding of confusingly similarity. In reaching a conclusion under this element of the Policy, prior decisions primarily base the test on a comparison of the mark and the domain name on their own, without regard to the content of the site. See *AT&T Corp. v. Amjad Kausar*, WIPO Case No. D2003-0327.

It is generally well-established the addition of merely descriptive or non-distinctive matter to another's mark is not sufficient to avoid confusion. See *NCAA v. Randy Pitkin*, WIPO Case No. D2000-0903. Thus, the addition of ".com" is held to be insufficient to avoid confusion. *Id.*

Similarly, in the other Panel decisions considering the issue, including decisions involving this Respondent, the addition of "tickets" to the name of an event has uniformly been held to be insufficient to avoid confusion. See *National Collegiate Athletic Association and March Madness Athletic Association, LLC v. Mark Helpern and Front & Center Entertainment,* WIPO Case No. D2000-0700 (transferring domain names including <finalfourtickets.net> to the complainant); *HBP, Inc. v. Front and Center Tickets, Inc.*, WIPO Case No. D2002-0802 (transferring the domain name <daytona500tickets.net> to the complainant); *ISL Worldwide and The Federal Internationale de Football Association v. Western States Ticket Service,* WIPO Case No. D2001-0070 (transferring <fifatickets.com>); *The Professional Golfers' Association of America v. 24/7 Ticket Service,* WIPO Case No. D2002-0258 (transferring <pgachampiontickets.com>); *NCAA v. Randy Pitkin*, WIPO Case No. D2000-0903 (finding in favor of complainant on this issue, but ruling in favor of respondent on other grounds); *Southwest Airlines Co. v. Patrick Orly,* WIPO Case No. D2003-0761 (transferring <southwestairlinestickets.com>).

Similarly, the Panel finds that Respondent's addition of "tickets" is not sufficient to avoid confusion since it is a generic or merely descriptive term for the goods offered by Complainant under the ORANGE BOWL mark. Accordingly, we conclude that the remaining domain name at issue is confusingly similar to a mark in which Complainant has rights under Paragraph 4(a)(i) of the Policy.

B. Rights or Legitimate Interests

Complainant contends that Respondent has no rights or legitimate interest in the Domain Name. The record shows that Respondent has no relationship with or authorization from Complainant for the use of the ORANGE BOWL mark. Further, it appears that Respondent is known as Front & Center Entertainment, not the name ORANGEBOWLTICKETS.NET.

Respondent contends that it is using the domain name for a bona fide offering of ORANGE BOWL tickets. Indeed, the record shows that Respondent sells ORANGE BOWL tickets, along with tickets for a wide range of other events. However, whether or not this use is a bona fide use depends on whether or not Respondent's use of the ORANGE BOWL is legitimate, non-infringing use. Otherwise, a respondent could rely on an intentional infringement to demonstrate a legitimate interest. See *Madonna Ciccone, p/k/a Madonna v. Dan Parisi and "Madonna.com"*, WIPO Case No. D2000-0847 (holding that infringing use of <madonna.com> to sell services did not create legitimate interest).

Respondent acknowledges that it is using Complainant's trademark in a domain name to promote its commercial ticket brokering services. Thus, our inquiry focuses on whether that use is permitted or not.

Paragraph 4(c)(iii) of the Policy states that a registrant can demonstrate rights or a legitimate interest in the domain name if the registrant is:

> "making a legitimate noncommercial or fair use of the domain name without intent for commercial gain to misleadingly divert consumers or to tarnish the trademark or service mark at issue."

Respondent's use is commercial, so we must determine if it constitutes fair use.

We conclude that the Respondent's use of Complainant's mark in Respondent's domain name fails to meet the test for fair use because the ORANGE BOWL mark is used in Respondent's domain name not merely to describe, but also as an attention-getting device to attract Internet users to Respondent's site to sell other products, and because the domain name is used to sell products that it does not describe (e.g., Broadway show tickets, Las Vegas tickets, NFL tickets and tickets for competing college bowl events). By using the mark in the domain name, Respondent is using Complainant's mark more prominently than is necessary merely to describe its services. Moreover, the Complainant's mark is used in a way that triggers initial interest confusion regarding the relationship with Complainant in a way that is not adequately dispelled, for reasons more fully discussed below.

We recognize that the resolution of domain name disputes depends on the specific facts involved, and that prior decisions involving similar names may not be apposite due to factual differences. Nevertheless, it is significant to note that Respondent has been involved in at least two other ICANN UDRP decisions involving the use of another's trademark as a domain name to sell tickets online.

National Collegiate Athletic Association and March Madness Athletic Association, LLC v. Mark Helpern and Front & Center Entertainment, WIPO Case No. D2000-0700 (transferring domain names including <finalfourtickets.net> to the complainant); and *HBP, Inc. v. Front and Center Tickets, Inc.*, WIPO Case No. D2002-0802 (transferring the domain name <daytona500tickets.net>). In each case, a decision was rendered finding that similar conduct by Respondent to that at issue here was not fair use and was a violation of the Policy.

Similarly, other panels have addressed disputes involving the addition of "tickets" to the name of an event. *ISL Worldwide and The Federal Internationale de Football Association v. Western States Ticket Service,* WIPO Case No. D2001-0070 (transferring <fifatickets.com>); *The Professional Golfers' Association of America v. 24/7 Ticket Service,* WIPO Case No. D2002-0258 (transferring <pgachampiontickets.com>). These decisions also conclude that the type of use made by Respondent is not fair use.

The exception to these cases is *NCAA v. Randy Pitkin*, WIPO Case No. D2000-0903, where the majority concluded that the respondent's use of the domain name <womensfinalfourtickets.com> and similar names was fair use and did not violate the Policy. A dissenting opinion concluded that respondent's use of the domain names at issue was not fair use. The *NCAA v. Randy Pitkin,* of course, turns on the specific facts of the case, and relied at least in part on Complainant's failure of proof, stating:

The Complainant fails to address the "fair use" defense, with the exception of the unsupported assertion in Complaint paragraph 18, Sentence 5 which states: "Respondents are able to conduct their business without using NCAA trademarks."

Here, Complainant has provided points and authorities to support a conclusion in its favor on the question of fair use.

The panel majority considered the U.S. Supreme Court's recent decision in *KP Permanent Make-Up v. Lasting Impression*, No. 03-409, decided December 8, 2004 (slip opinion) in making its determination. In that case, the Supreme Court held that a party invoking a fair use defense to trademark infringement does not carry a burden of proving that its descriptive use of a trademark term carries no likelihood of confusion.[42] The Court, however, declined to provide other guidance regarding the fair use defense, and it noted that its holding "does not foreclose the relevance of the extent of any likely consumer confusion in assessing whether a defendant's use is objectively fair."

The facts in *KP Permanent Make-Up* are rather different that those here. *KP Permanent Make-Up involved* a claim of fair use of a descriptive term ("microcolor") by an alleged infringer in reference to its own product. This case involves asserted fair use of a famous and distinctive mark to attract Internet users to a website offering products in competition with the trademark holder's product. The panel majority has determined that Respondent's use of Complainant's mark goes beyond fair use and does not find *KP Permanent Make-Up* to the contrary.

Accordingly, for the reasons discussed above, we conclude that Respondent's use of Complainant's ORANGE BOWL mark in a domain name used in connection with the resale of tickets not only to the ORANGE BOWL game but also for tickets to a variety of unrelated and competing events is not fair use under the Policy. We further conclude, therefore, that Respondent lacks any right or legitimate interest in the use of ORANGE BOWL in its domain name and find in Complainant's favor on Paragraph 4(a)(ii) of the Policy.

C. Registered and Used in Bad Faith

The Policy lists several nonexclusive criteria to show bad faith registration and use of a domain name. Paragraph 4(b)(iv) indicates that bad faith use and registration may be found when the Respondent is intentionally attempting to attract, for commercial gain, Internet users to its website, by creating a likelihood of confusion with the complainant's mark.

Respondent concedes that it intentionally registered and is using Complainant's mark to attract Internet users to its website. It does this for commercial gain. We believe Respondent does so by creating a likelihood of confusion with and by trading on Complainant's mark. Persons initially

---

[42] The Court noted that a fair use defense virtually presupposes some degree of confusion between a mark and the term used in its descriptive sense. There is no reason to raise a fair use defense unless a prima facie case of infringement is made out.

encountering Respondent's domain name are likely to be confused as to the source, sponsorship, affiliation or endorsement of the domain name due to the use of the famous ORANGE BOWL mark. They may thus be drawn into the site trusting that they may obtain tickets from an authorized source.

Respondent is using Complainant's well known mark as a principal means (i.e., via the domain name) to advertise and sell products of third parties. A disclaimer may or may not be sufficient to dispel confusion as to the source of products at the "point of sale" (i.e. on Respondent's website). However, at this point Respondent has already misused Complainant's mark to bring consumers into its shop. Once in the shop, consumers are offered competitors' products. In the words of the Seventh Circuit, this is "plain misdescription, in fact false advertising" (*Ty Inc. v. Perryman*, No. 02-1771, (7th Cir.), decided October 4, 2002). The panel majority does not consider that Respondent's disclaimer is adequate to cure this exercise of bad faith use of Complainant's famous and distinctive mark.

Even assuming that a disclaimer might be effective to remedy initial interest confusion in a way that would remedy the initial problematic use, Respondent's disclaimer does not dispel the initial interest confusion caused by the domain name itself and is inadequate to avoid likelihood of confusion at the site. Prior to this action, Respondent's website featured a disclaimer of affiliation with the NCAA that did not mention Complainant or the ORANGE BOWL mark. This was obviously inadequate to dispel confusion about the relationship of Respondent and its site with Complainant. Subsequent to the filing of this action, Respondent has modified its site and disclaimer.

The new disclaimer is also problematic. It states that "the FedEx Orange Bowl has neither licensed or endorsed Front and Center Entertainment Group to sell goods and services in conjunction with the FedEx Orange Bowl." The disclaimer is confusing in that it is limited the sale of "goods and services" in conjunction with the event and fails to address Respondent's relationship to Complainant with respect to the sale of "tickets." A person reading and understanding the disclaimer is not clearly informed whether or not Respondent as "a private ticket broker" is authorized by Complainant to resell ORANGE BOWL tickets.

We acknowledge that Respondent in part uses the domain name to resell ORANGE BOWL tickets, and in that limited sense persons are accurately informed about some of Respondent's products. However, they are not adequately informed about the relationship of Complainant to Respondent's site and tickets, and may incorrectly conclude Respondent's conduct, including pricing and sale of tickets to other events, is endorsed by Complainant, when in fact that is not the case.

In sum, as a result of Respondent's use of the famous and distinctive ORANGE BOWL mark in its domain name, consumers are likely to be brought to Respondent's website mistakenly believing it is authorized, "official" or endorsed by Complainant. Respondent is thereupon offering to sell tickets to events which compete with that of Complainant. This is a bad faith use of Complainant's mark. Once at the website, consumers are likely to continue to believe mistakenly that Complainant has authorized or endorsed Respondent's use of the ORANGE BOWL mark in connection with the resale of tickets to the ORANGE BOWL game and for other events.

Therefore, we conclude that Complainant has established bad faith registration and use under Paragraph 4(b)(iv) of the Policy.

7. Decision

For all the foregoing reasons, in accordance with Paragraphs 4(i) of the Policy and 15 of the Rules, we order that the domain name <orangebowl.net> and <orangebowltickets.net> be transferred to the Complainant.

Mark V.B. Partridge
Presiding Panelist
Dated: January 20, 2005

DISSENTING OPINION

I believe that the Panel should rule for the Respondent for the reasons enunciated in the prior decision of the WIPO panel in *NCAA v. Randy Pitkin* WIPO Case No. D2000-0903.

In this case the portion of the domain name that is at issue is also the name of an event, which cannot otherwise easily be otherwise described, coupled with the word "tickets," where the website is being used for the purpose of advertising the sale of tickets to the event. It is my belief that the use of such a domain name including, as it does, the word "tickets" is not cybersquatting under the rules governing the Uniform Dispute Resolution Policy.

While the Internet domain name using only the trademark name of the event might be cybersquatting, and thus I agree with the award of the Internet domain name <orangebowl.net> to Complainant, a concession which apparently Respondent makes in its Reply Brief, without admission, I do not believe that this applies to the use of the name of the actual event coupled with the generic word "ticket."

When the trademark is also the name of an event, such as the Orange Bowl, use of the name of the event is not always a trademark use, but may be a nominative fair use, where the words "Orange Bowl" although they be a trademark, are being used for the name of the event. It is difficult to identify the event, particularly this one, since it is one of several "bowl" games, and cannot be identified by its date, which varies from year to year, and this year, for some reason, is on a Tuesday!

I submit that the Orange Bowl event is even harder to identify, without using the words which also are a trademark, then even the Super Bowl, since various words preceding the word Bowl are used to distinguish this game from others on nearby dates, which mark also apparently indicates a major product of the Florida location in which this particular bowl game is played. It cannot be distinguished by the identification of the teams, since USC, which often commands a seat at the Rose Bowl, this year is in the Orange Bowl.

To the extent that the Orange Bowl is the name of a venue, *i.e.*, the particular coliseum or stadium where the Orange Bowl game is played, then it is also the name of venue for which the ticket will provide a seat license for the holder to sit in, and likewise the identification of this venue, together with the generic word "tickets" where the sale of tickets for this event in this location is being held, is also not, in my view, an unfair use.

It is my belief therefore that it is not bad faith to register the domain name which is also the "name of the game," together with the generic word "tickets" in this circumstance. Respondent has also placed a prominent disclaimer of sponsorship or association with the Orange Bowl on the face of its website, and understands the need to avoid a likelihood of confusion or mistake, if such exists. It may well be that selling a plethora of tickets to the named event at much higher prices then are normally garnered for this game, will also help avoid any likelihood of confusion or mistake in the use of the Internet domain name <orangebowltickets.com>.

Finally, I take note of the decision of the United States Supreme Court in *KP Permanent Make Up v. Lasting Impressions*, –U.S.–, No. 03-409 decided December 8, 2004 S.C. (December 2004), where the United States Supreme Court, in the jurisdiction where both respondent and complainant reside, and the jurisdiction where the tickets and event were sold and is held, determined that where a trademark is being used by a defendant fairly to describe, in this case, the event and/or the event tickets, then the possible existence of even actual confusion does not provide a basis for the finding of trademark infringement and unfair competition under United States law. The United States Supreme Court, specifically rejected the view of the United States Court of Appeals for the Ninth Circuit which had held that the existence of confusion might trump infringement, and/or that there would be a burden on one party or another to prove the existence of, or absence of, confusion, when a mark is being used fairly and descriptively.

The panel majority attempts to distinguish this case as one where the famous mark is being used by another "to attract Internet users to a website offering products in competition with the trademark holder's product." I do not believe this to be the case, since the tickets being offered are the trademark holder's product, and are to attend the trademark holder's product, its Orange Bowl games.

Finally, I note that the new phenomenon of corporate sponsorship has made even the trademark use of the Orange Bowl trademark, less likely to cause confusion, since it is now the, presumably "FedEx" or "Federal Express" "brand" Orange Bowl game, stadium, venue, and/or ticket therefor.

Neil Smith
Dissenting Panelist

WIPO Arbitration and Mediation Center

ADMINISTRATIVE PANEL DECISION
The Football Association Premier League Limited v. Trademark
Case No. D2005-0014

1. The Parties

The Complainant is The Football Association Premier League Limited, London, United Kingdom of Great Britain and Northern Ireland, represented by McCormicks Solicitors, Leeds, United Kingdom of Great Britain and Northern Ireland.

The Respondent is Trademark, Georgetown, Grand Cayman GT, Cayman Islands of United Kingdom of Great Britain and Northern Ireland.

2. The Domain Name and Registrar

The disputed domain name <fapremierleague.com> is registered with NamesDirect.com on May 16, 2003.

3. Procedural History

The Complaint was filed with the WIPO Arbitration and Mediation Center (the "Center") on January 5, 2005. On January 6, 2005, the Center transmitted by email to NamesDirect.com a request for registrar verification in connection with the domain name at issue. On January 6, 2005, NamesDirect.com transmitted by email to the Center its verification response confirming that the Respondent is listed as the registrant and providing the contact details for the administrative, billing, and technical contact. The Center verified that the Complaint satisfied the formal requirements of the Uniform Domain Name Dispute Resolution Policy (the "Policy"), the Rules for Uniform Domain Name Dispute Resolution Policy (the "Rules"), and the WIPO Supplemental Rules for Uniform Domain Name Dispute Resolution Policy (the "Supplemental Rules").

In accordance with the Rules, paragraphs 2(a) and 4(a), the Center formally notified the Respondent of the Complaint, and the proceedings commenced on January 7, 2005. In accordance with the Rules, paragraph 5(a), the due date for Response was January 27, 2005. The Respondent did not submit any response. Accordingly, the Center notified the Respondent's default on January 31, 2005.

The Center appointed Ian Blackshaw as the sole panelist in this matter on February 4, 2005. The Panel finds that it was properly constituted. The Panel has submitted the Statement of Acceptance and Declaration of Impartiality and Independence, as required by the Center to ensure compliance with the Rules, paragraph 7.

4. Factual Background

The Complainant is a company registered in England under the name "The Football Association Premier League Limited", whose members are the football clubs that participate in the Football Association Premier League competition, currently known as the Barclays Premiership (the "Competition"), which is the elite league of football in England and Wales. The Complainant organizes and acts as the governing body of the Competition. The Football Association Premier League Limited was formed on February 20, 1992, and has organized successive seasons of the Competition in each football season since 1992/1993. One of its founding shareholders is the Football Association Limited, the governing body of football in England and Wales, which is universally known as "The F.A.".

The Complainant is commonly and inevitably referred to as "The F.A. Premier League". It is the Premier League of football in England and Wales, as opposed to the many other Premier Leagues in other sports and other areas, and to refer to it as the FA Premier League is an almost automatic adaptation. Indeed, the Complainant refers to itself as the same on its headed paper, a copy of which has been submitted to the Center, and within its corporate logo, which can also be seen on the headed paper, and which also forms the basis of the sleeve badge worn by every football player at every match within the Competition. Both the Complainant and the Competition organized by the Complainant are well known not only to football enthusiasts but also to non-football enthusiasts.

The Complainant is the proprietor of several trademark registrations, both in the UK and the European Union, for the mark "PREMIER LEAGUE". Such registrations, which date back to 1992 (when the Complainant was formed) and 1998 respectively, cover a wide range of goods in various

Classes and also services in Class 41 for, amongst other things, "services relating to sports' events and matches; all relating to the promotion of Association football". Copies of printouts from the relevant Trademark Registry databases in respect of the Complainant's trademark registrations for "PREMIER LEAGUE" (including that relating to Class 41) have also been submitted to the Center in support of the Complaint.

The Complainant's name, fame and reputation and that of the Competition promoted and organized by it has spread throughout the world in terms of worldwide media coverage; worldwide dissemination of branded goods; and – not least – as a result of worldwide broadcasts of both complete matches and excerpts in the form of highlights from the Competition in some 192 countries worldwide, reaching some 600 million people worldwide.

Use of the trademarks referred to above, together with, amongst others, the Complainant's logo and the unregistered mark "F A PREMIER LEAGUE", are licensed to the Official Partners and suppliers of the Complainant. By way of illustration of some of the licensing and sponsorship deals, which have been undertaken by the Complainant, the current sponsor of the Competition is Barclays, one of the largest financial services groups in the world. Other Official partners of the Complainant include Nike in respect of, *inter alia*, match balls for the Competition; Anheuser Busch with Budweiser being the Official Beer of the F. A. Premier League; and GlaxoSmithKline the Official Drinks Supplier of the F.A. Premier League with, *inter alia*, its Lucozade Sport drink.

The Complainant, as mentioned above, also enters into licensing deals for the production of officially licensed products. For example, the Complainant has an agreement with E A Sports (one of the most well known and respected producers of computer games) for the development of an F.A Premier League computer game. Copies of the covers of some previous computer games produced on behalf of the Complainant, which clearly identify and make reference to the Complainant as "The F.A. Premier League", have also been submitted to the Center. A further example of branded goods produced in association with the Complainant is the F.A. Premier League Sticker and Collector Album produced by Topps Europe Limited under its Merlin brand; copies of some of the covers of the sticker albums, clearly incorporating the Complainant's branding and the term "F.A. Premier League", have also been submitted to the Center in support of the Complaint.

With regard to the worldwide broadcasting of the Complainant's name and the Competition organized and promoted by the Complainant, one of the most notable and publicized deals is that with Sky Television. Back in 1992, at the time of the formation of the Complainant, the agreement with Sky Television (covering five seasons) was worth approximately £191 million. The three-Season deal with Sky Television, which commenced at the beginning of the 2004/2005 Season, was worth approximately £1.1 billion. The fame and reputation of the Complainant can be illustrated by the fact that the broadcasting rights associated with the Competition are hotly contested.

In addition to the registered trademarks and unregistered rights the Complainant has in the term "F.A. Premier League" (referred to above), the Complainant has also registered a number of domain names incorporating not only the term "Premier League" but also "F.A. Premier League". For example:

<fapremierleague.co.uk>;
<fapremierleague.net>;
<fa-premier-league.co.uk>;
<premier-league.com>.

And the Complainant's main website is located at: "www.premierleague.com".

It is not unknown for members of the general public, where they do not know the official website of an entity, to type in a URL utilizing the name of such an entity in the hope that they will reach the correct website. Consequently, the Complainant registered the above domain names, being variations of its trade marks and the accepted and commonly used abbreviation of the Complainant's corporate name, and directed all of the same to the Complainant's main website. The Complainant's main website during the first quarter of the 2004/2005 Season received a total number of 53,775,557 'hits' through approximately 1,205,599 users. The Complainant (as mentioned above) has registered the domain name <fapremierleague.co.uk> (the .co.uk version of the domain name being the subject matter of this complaint). During the period December 2003 to November 2004, it has received a total number of 294 'hits', being not an insignificant amount.

5. Parties' Contentions
A. Complainant
1. The domain name is identical or confusingly similar to a trademark or service mark in which the Complainant has rights:
(Policy, para. 4(a)(i), Rules, paras. 3(b)(viii), (b)(ix)(1))
The Complainant asserts that it can be clearly seen from the above background information that the Complainant has rights – registered and/or unregistered – in the terms "Premier League" and "F.A. Premier League". The domain name, <fapremierleague.com>, which is the subject of this Complaint, is clearly similar to the trademark registrations held by the Complainant. The only difference between the two being the addition of the term "FA". The term "FA" is well recognized within the football world as referring to the "Football Association", being the governing body of football in England and Wales and it is with the consent of that body that the Complainant is permitted to use the term "FA" within its trading name. The term "FA" is also a registered trademark of such governing body. Copies of printouts from the relevant Trademark Registry databases in respect of the trademark registrations for "FA" have been submitted to the Center in support and part of the Complaint.

The reference to "FA" within the domain name in issue is obviously intended to infer a connection to the premier league of football taking place in England as opposed to any other sporting premier league. Furthermore, the website associated with that domain name clearly contains links to websites for some of the top teams participating in the Competition organized by the Complainant.

In addition, the domain name in issue is identical to the unregistered and/or common law rights, which the Complainant holds in respect of the term "F.A. Premier League" and/or "The F.A. Premier League". This reasoning, namely the assertion that the Domain Name is identical, is based on the findings by the Administrative Panel in *The Sportsman's Guide, Inc v. Modern Limited, Cayman Islands*, WIPO Case No. D2003-0305, where the Panel held that "*the addition of generic top-level domains name 'com' or the omission of the term 'the', are without legal significance and certainly do not render the disputed domain name different....*".

2. The Respondent has no rights or legitimate interests in respect of the domain name:
(Policy, para. 4(a)(ii), Rules, para. 3(b)(ix)(2))
In accordance with Rules, paragraph 3(b)(ix)(2), the Complainant asserts that the Respondent has no rights or legitimate interests in respect of the domain name in issue.

In support of such assertion, the Complainant points to the fact that:

1. Prior to any notice to the Respondent of this Complaint, the Respondent was not using the domain name in connection with a bona fide offering of goods and/or services, nor had it made any preparations to do so. The domain name was and is instead being used by the Respondent unfairly to trade on the Complainant's name and marks, by associating the domain name, by way of hypertext links, to other sites and online stores offering information, goods and/or services, many of which are associated with merchandise websites and/or unofficial websites for football clubs forming part of the Competition organized and promoted by the Complainant.
2. The Respondent is not commonly known by the terms forming the domain name or any proportion thereof, nor has it registered and/or attempted to register the domain name as a trademark.
3. The Respondent is not making a legitimate non-commercial or fair use of the domain name, without intent for commercial gain to misleadingly divert consumers or to tarnish the trademark or service mark in issue. The Respondent has a clear intention to use the domain name for a commercial basis with the further intent of making commercial gains. This can be illustrated by the fact that there are sponsored links and pop-up advertising on the website associated with the domain name in dispute, evidence of which has been submitted to the Center in support of the Complaint. Furthermore, as the Respondent is not utilizing the domain name in issue for the bona fide offering of goods and/or services, the Respondent can have no reason to register the disputed domain name other than misleadingly to divert consumers to the website in the belief that they are being directed to the website of the Complainant. Once on the website, the Respondent clearly hopes that they will then proceed to click onto one of the hypertext links contained within the website. Finally, the Respondent, by implication, has an intent to tarnish the marks in which the Complainant has rights, due to the fact that, within that section of the

website purportedly associated with the Complainant, there is a link to an online store dealing in "Sex Toys & Sexy Lingerie". Again, evidence of this has been submitted.

4. The Complainant has never assigned, licensed, authorized or given permission to the Respondent to use or register as a domain name the marks identified above as being marks in which the Complainant has rights

3. The domain name was registered and is being used in bad faith:
(Policy, paras. 4(a)(iii), 4(b); Rules, para. 3(b)(ix)(3))

In accordance with Rules, paragraph 3(b)(ix)(3), the Complainant asserts that the disputed domain name was registered and is being used in bad faith.

In support of such assertion, the Complainant, as shown above, clearly has a significant amount of goodwill and reputation (not only in respect of the UK but also worldwide) in respect of the term "F.A. Premier League". The Respondent, given the content of the website associated with the domain name (being in the majority references to and hypertext links to websites and online stores associated with certain football clubs being participants of the Competition organized by the Complainant), clearly has prior knowledge of the Complainant and the Competition organized by the same. In light of such obvious prior knowledge of the Respondent, the Respondent's registration and use of the disputed domain name is effectively an intentional attempt to create confusion with the Complainant's marks and thereby attract, for commercial gain, internet users to the website. The commercial gain, in this instance, would be afforded by means of sponsored hypertext links on the website associated with the disputed domain and pop-up advertising, which appear when that website is accessed.

A further indicator that the disputed domain name was registered in bad faith is the fact that the website associated with the disputed domain name contains no contact details for the Respondent (these have to be obtained from the "Whois" database of information) and the fact that the name contained within the "Whois" database does not appear necessarily to be a genuine one.

Furthermore, on October 14, 2004, the Complainant wrote to the Respondent with regard to the disputed domain name and requested that the Respondent transfer the disputed domain name to the Complainant. A copy of the letter sent to the Respondent has been annexed to the Complaint. This letter was sent to the Respondent by International Signed For Post at the address specified in the "Whois" database (whilst this letter left the UK on October 16, 2004, the Complainant has not been notified if it has been signed for); by facsimile utilising the number obtained from the "Whois" database; and by email to the email addresses specified in the "Whois" database. The Complainant has not received any delivery failure notices in respect of such emails. The Complainant has not received any response from the Respondent, which indicates that the Respondent does not believe they have a legitimate right and/or interest in the domain name.

B. Respondent

The Respondent, having been duly notified and kept informed of the proceedings by the Center, did not file any Response to the Complaint.

6. Discussion and Finding

To qualify for transfer or cancellation, the Complainant must prove each of the following elements of paragraph 4(a) of the Policy, namely:

(i) The disputed domain name is identical or confusingly similar to a trademark or service mark in which Complainant has rights; and
(ii) Respondent has no rights or legitimate interests in respect of the domain name; and
(iii) The disputed domain name has been registered and is being used in bad faith.

In accordance with paragraph 15(a) of the Rules, the Panel shall decide the Complaint on the basis of the statements and documents submitted and in accordance with the Policy, the Rules, and any rules and principles of law that it deems applicable.

In accordance with paragraph 14(a) of the Rules, in the event that a Party, in the absence of exceptional circumstances, does not comply with any of the time periods established by the Rules or the Panel, the Panel shall proceed to a decision on the Complaint and (b) if a Party, in the absence of exceptional circumstances, does not comply with any provision of, or requirement under, the

Rules or any request from the Panel, the Panel shall draw such inferences there from as it considers appropriate.

In accordance with paragraph 10(d) of the Rules, the Panel shall determine the admissibility, relevance, materiality and weight of the evidence.

In previous cases in which the Respondent failed to file a Response, the Panel's decisions were based upon the Complainant's assertions and evidence, as well as inferences drawn from the Respondent's failure to reply. See *The Vanguard Group, Inc. v. Lorna Kang*, WIPO Case No. D2002-1064; and also *Köstritzer Schwarzbierbrauerei v. Macros-Telekom Corp*, WIPO Case No. D2001-0936. The failure by the Respondent to dispute the Complainant's allegations allows the inference to be drawn by the Panel that they are true.

Nevertheless, the Panel must not decide in the Complainant's favor solely based on the Respondent's default (*Cortefiel S.A. v. Miguel García Quintas*, WIPO Case No. D2000-0140). The Panel must decide whether the Complainant has introduced elements of proof, which allow the Panel to conclude that its allegations are true.

A. Identical or Confusingly Similar

It is clear that the Complainant holds several trademark registrations in the UK, dating back to its foundation in 1992, and also one in the European Union, dating back to 1998, in the name "Premier League" covering a wide range of goods and services. Additionally, the Complainant has rights, granted by the England and Wales Football Association, to use the term "F.A." – the commonly referred to and recognized abbreviation for and also a registered trademark of this organization – in the Complainant's corporate and trading names. Furthermore, the Complainant has also registered a number of domain names incorporating not only the name "Premier League" but also "F.A. Premier League" including <fapremierleague.co.uk>. The Complainant's main website is located at: "www.premierleague.com".

The Respondent incorporates in the domain name in issue, the Complainant's trademark "PREMIER LEAGUE" with the addition of the letters "FA". This is clearly confusingly similar. And the addition of the letters "FA" rather than eliminating any confusion, in fact, compounds that confusion because of the rights the Complainant has in the name "Premier League" and also in the abbreviation "F.A" as mentioned above. The elimination of the "dots" after each of the letters is irrelevant for the purposes of confusion. In any case, there is a general stylistic tendency in print not to use dots in abbreviations.

In any event, it is established case law that where a domain name incorporates a complainant's registered mark, this is sufficient to establish that the domain name is identical or confusingly similar for the purposes of the Policy. See *Magnum Piering, Inc. v. The Mudjackers and Garwood S. Wilson, Sr.*, WIPO Case No. D2000-1525.

Furthermore, for the purposes of the Policy and the Rules, the Respondent's domain name is identical to the above-mentioned Complainant's registered domain name – <fapremierleague.co.uk> – notwithstanding that the Respondent's domain name is a ".com" level one. See the decision in *The Sportsman's Guide, Inc v. Modern Limited, Cayman Islands*, WIPO Case No. D2003-0305 and, in particular the extract, cited above, where such a difference was held to be legally immaterial.

All in all, consumers and Internet users will be confused and misled into thinking that the domain name in issue belongs to the Complainant, which is not, in fact, the case.

Thus, the Panel concludes that there is no doubt that the domain name in issue if not identical is certainly confusingly similar to the trade or service marks in which the Complainant demonstrably has rights.

B. Rights or Legitimate Interests

In order to determine whether the Respondent has any rights or legitimate interests in respect of the domain name (Article 3 (b)(ix)(2) of the Rules and Article 4 (c) of the Policy), attention must be paid to any of the following circumstances, in particular, but without limitation:

- Whether before any notice to the Respondent of the dispute, there is any evidence of the Respondent's use of, or demonstrable preparations to use, the domain name or a name corresponding to the domain name in connection with a bona fide offering of goods or services;

- Whether the Respondent (as an individual, business, or other organization) has been commonly known by the domain name, even if the Respondent has acquired no trademark or service mark rights;
- Whether the Respondent is making a legitimate non-commercial or fair use of the domain name, without intent for commercial gain misleadingly to divert consumers or to tarnish the trademark or service mark at issue.

There is no evidence that the Respondent has been using or preparing to use the domain name in issue prior to these proceedings for a bona fide offering of goods and services. On the contrary, the Respondent's website contains links to other online stores offering goods and/or services.

Likewise, the Respondent is not commonly known by the domain name in issue.

It is clear that the Respondent has registered and is using the domain name unfairly to attract and divert traffic to its own website, for its own commercial and financial gain, which otherwise would have gone to the Complainant's websites. Apart from general harm to the Complainant's trademark rights and other interests, especially its substantial investment in the Premier League football Competition and related broadcasting and merchandising activities, there is evidence that the Complainant's valuable trade and service marks have been tarnished through the sponsored link on the Respondent's website to an online store selling "Sex Toys and Sexy Lingerie" with the 'strap line' "make her day". Having nothing to do with the game of football or the Complainant's Competition, this is clearly a serious and unjustified misuse of the Complainant's well-known and valuable trade and service marks.

Again, there is no evidence that the Respondent has been authorized or licensed in any way whatsoever to use the Complainant's trade and service marks for its own commercial and business purposes. As has been demonstrated, the Complainant has an extensive licensing and merchandising program and the Respondent does not figure in it at all.

Thus, for all these reasons, the Panel concludes that the Respondent has no rights or legitimate interests in respect of the domain name in issue.

C. Registered and Used in Bad Faith

Regarding the bad faith requirement, paragraph 4(b) of the Policy lists four examples of acts, which *prima facie* constitute evidence of bad faith. This list is not exhaustive but merely illustrative. See *Nova Banka v. Iris*, WIPO Case No. D2003-0366.

Paragraph 4(b)(iv) of the Policy is relevant to the present case and provides that there is evidence of bad faith in the following circumstances:

"(iv) by using the Domain Name, the Respondent has intentionally attempted to attract, for commercial gain, Internet users to its website or other on-line location, by creating a likelihood of confusion with the Complainant's mark as to the source, sponsorship, affiliation, or endorsement of the Respondent's website or location or of a product or service on its website or location."

In view of the unauthorized incorporation of the Complainant's valuable and well-known trade and service marks in the domain name in issue and the references and links in the Respondent's corresponding website to online stores associated with certain football clubs that participate in the Complainant's competition, the Respondent is using the domain name to create confusion on the part of consumers and Internet users with a view to reaping commercial and financial gains. The commercial nature of the Respondent's website is emphasized by its slogan: "What you need, when you want it". In other words, the Respondent is not operating the website associated with domain name in issue for fun. The Respondent is, therefore, acting in bad faith within the meaning of para. 4(b)(iv) of the Policy.

Furthermore, the unauthorized use of the Complainant's trade and service marks in the domain name in issue also implies that the Complainant has, in some way, sponsored or endorsed the Respondent's website and its commercial activities carried on through it, which is not, in fact, the case. This is further evidence of bad faith.

Also, by failing to respond to the Complainant's 'cease and desist' letter of October 14, 2004, and also to answer the Complaint and participate in the present proceedings, this, in the view of the Panel, is additional evidence of bad faith on the part of the Respondent. If the Respondent had any justification for registering the domain name in issue in the first place it is reasonable to assume that the Respondent would have taken these opportunities to put forward an answer in defense of its actions.

Again, the fact that the Respondent's website does not contain any contact details also suggests some element of bad faith on its part.

Based on all the above, the Panel, therefore, concludes that the domain name in dispute was registered and is being used by the Respondent in bad faith.

7. Decision

For all the foregoing reasons, in accordance with Paragraphs 4(i) of the Policy and 15 of the Rules, the Panel orders that the domain name <fapremierleague.com> be transferred to the Complainant.

Ian Blackshaw
Sole Panelist
Dated: February 9, 2005

WIPO Arbitration and Mediation Center

ADMINISTRATIVE PANEL DECISION
Triple Crown Productions, LLC v. 4URLS.COM
Case No. D2006-0083

1. The Parties

The Complainant is Triple Crown Productions, LLC, Louisville, Kentucky, United States of America, represented by Wyatt, Tarrant & Combs, United States of America.

The Respondent is 4URLS.COM, Kansas City, Missouri, United States of America.

2. The Domain Name and Registrar

The disputed domain name <thetriplecrown.com> is registered with Intercosmos Media Group d/b/a directNIC.com.

3. Procedural History

The Complaint was filed with the WIPO Arbitration and Mediation Center (the "Center") on January 18, 2006. On January 19, 2006, the Center transmitted by email to Intercosmos Media Group d/b/a directNIC.com a request for registrar verification in connection with the domain name at issue. On January 19, 2006, Intercosmos Media Group d/b/a directNIC.com transmitted by email to the Center its verification response confirming that the Respondent is listed as the registrant and providing the contact details for the administrative, billing, and technical contact . The Center verified that the Complaint satisfied the formal requirements of the Uniform Domain Name Dispute Resolution Policy (the "Policy"), the Rules for Uniform Domain Name Dispute Resolution Policy (the "Rules"), and the WIPO Supplemental Rules for Uniform Domain Name Dispute Resolution Policy (the "Supplemental Rules").

In accordance with the Rules, paragraphs 2(a) and 4(a), the Center formally notified the Respondent of the Complaint, and the proceedings commenced on February 1, 2006. In accordance with the Rules, paragraph 5(a), the due date for Response was February 21, 2006. The Respondent did not submit any response. Accordingly, the Center notified the Respondent's default on February 22, 2006.

The Center appointed Dennis A. Foster as the sole panelist in this matter on March 7, 2006. The Panel finds that it was properly constituted. The Panel has submitted the Statement of Acceptance and Declaration of Impartiality and Independence, as required by the Center to ensure compliance with the Rules, paragraph 7.

4. Factual Background

The Complainant has used United States of America-registered TRIPLE CROWN service marks uninterruptedly since 1950.

The Complainant uses its TRIPLE CROWN trademarks in conjunction with the three most famous horse races in the United States, viz., The Kentucky Derby, The Preakness, and The Belmont Stakes.

The disputed domain name, <thetriplecrown.com>, was registered by the Respondent on April 29, 1999. Recently, the Respondent has been offering the disputed domain name for sale on the Internet for $8,000.

5. Parties' Contentions

A. Complainant

Due to its long, continuous and extensive use, the Complainant's TRIPLE CROWN service mark has become one of the most famous trademarks in sports, recognized by millions of people in the United States and abroad.

The disputed domain name, <thetriplecrown.com>, is virtually identical to the Complainant's registered TRIPLE CROWN service marks.

The Respondent is a buyer, seller and registrant of domain names.

On the website linked to the disputed domain name, <thetriplecrown.com>, Respondent makes it clear that this domain name is for sale and that it would be perfect for Complainant's business. For this domain name, Respondent is seeking the hefty sum of $8,000 (Complaint Exhibits 1g and 1h).

Respondent is not using the disputed domain name for a bona fide offering of goods and services. Instead of using the domain name, the Respondent seeks to sell it for $8,000.

Respondent is not commonly known by the name "The Triple Crown", but is rather known as 4urls.com.

The Respondent is not engaged in criticism, scholarship, political advocacy or the exercise of any First Amendment right.

A strange alignment of Jupiter and Mars did not cause Respondent to register the disputed domain name. At the time Respondent took this action, it was fully aware that the famous TRIPLE CROWN mark was used in reference to the three most famous horse races in the United States: The Kentucky Derby, The Preakness and The Belmont Stakes.

The Respondent has violated the bad faith provision of paragraph 4(b)(i) of the Policy. The Respondent took the Complainant's famous mark, incorporated it into a domain name, and then advertised that the domain name would be perfect for Complainant to own. The fact that Respondent knew of Complainant's famous mark at the time of registration also is evidence of Respondent's bad faith registration.

Respondent's bad faith is also shown by its demand for a selling "price well in excess of Respondent's reasonable out-of-pocker expenses". (*Experian Information Solution, Inc. v. BPB Prumerica Travel (a/k/a SFXB a/k/a H. Bousquet a/k/a Brian Evans*, WIPO Case No. D2002-0367, July 8, 2002)

B. Respondent

The Respondent did not reply to the Complainant's contentions.

6. Discussion and Findings

In order to prevail in this proceeding and obtain transfer of the disputed domain name, the Complainant must prove per paragraphs 4(a)(i) through 4(a)(iii) of the Policy:

- the disputed domain name is identical or confusingly similar to a trademark or service mark in which the Complainant has rights; and
- the Respondent has no rights or legitimate interests in respect of the domain name; and
- the domain name was registered and is being used in bad faith.

A. Identical or Confusingly Similar

The Complainant has exhibited copies of its TRIPLE CROWN service mark registrations on the United States principal register. These include service mark no. 0984679 dated May 21, 1974, in international class 042 for promoting the competitiveness of thoroughbred horse racing. Next there is a device plus words service mark registration no. 1479895 dated March 8, 1988, in international class 035 for nominating thoroughbred horses for races. And registration no. 1902003 dated June 27, 1995, in international class 041 is for a system of awarding prizes to thoroughbred horse owners.

The disputed domain name, <thetriplecrown.com>, is confusingly similar to the Complainant's TRIPLE CROWN service mark. As the Complainant points out, it has long been established in decisions under the Policy that the article "the" does not influence an analysis under the Policy for identity or confusing similarity. (See.e.g., *Vie de France Yamazaki Inc. v. Donna Sayada*, Inc., WIPO Case No. D2000-1081, October 13, 2000; also *Belo Corp. v. George Latimer,* WIPO Case No. D2002-0329, May 16, 2002).

The Panel thus finds the Complainant has met its burden of proof in paragraph 4(a)(i) of the Policy.

B. Rights or Legitimate Interests

The Complainant contends the Respondent has no legitimate rights or interests in the disputed domain name pursuant to paragraphs 4(c)(i-iii) of the Policy. That is to say, the Complainant contends the Respondent is not in bona fide offering goods and services per (4(c)(i)), is not commonly known by the disputed domain name ((4(c)(ii)), and is not making a non-commercial fair use of the disputed domain name per (4(c)(iii)). The Respondent is in default and thus has not attempted to show any legitimate rights or interests in the disputed domain name.

The Panel observes that the only use the Respondent is making of the disputed domain name is to try to sell it for $8,000. The Panel agrees with the Complainant that this is not a legitimate right or interest in the disputed domain under the Policy, and the Panel goes further and states that the Respondent's use is best dealt with in the Bad Faith section of this decision.

C. Registered and Used in Bad Faith

The Respondent has for some time attempted to sell the disputed domain name on the Internet for $8,000 (Complaint Exhibits 1(g) and (h)). There is no evidence the Respondent ever tried to do anything else with the disputed domain name, so this appears to have been Respondent's primary purpose when Respondent registered the disputed domain name. Obviously, $8,000 is much more than the Respondent paid for the disputed domain name when he registered it on April 29, 1999. This is a square-on violation of the bad faith provision of the Policy in paragraph 4(b)(i).

The Panel finds the Complainant has carried its burden of proof under paragraph 4(a)(iii) of the Policy to show that the Respondent registered and is using the disputed domain name in bad faith.

7. Decision

For all the foregoing reasons, in accordance with paragraphs 4(i) of the Policy and 15 of the Rules, the Panel orders that the domain name, <thetriplecrown.com> be transferred to the Complainant.

Dennis A. Foster
Sole Panelist
Dated: March 21, 2006

WIPO Arbitration and Mediation Center

ADMINISTRATIVE PANEL DECISION
Stoneygate 48 Limited and Wayne Mark Rooney v. Huw Marshall
Case No. D2006-0916

1. The Parties

The Complainants are Stoneygate 48 Limited ("the First Complainant") and Wayne Mark Rooney ("the Second Complainant") both c/o Grant Thornton, Heron House, Albert Square, Manchester M60 8QT, United Kingdom of Great Britain and Northern Ireland, represented by Kilburn & Strode, United Kingdom of Great Britain and Northern Ireland.

The Respondent is Huw Marshall, of Wrexham, United Kingdom of Great Britain and Northern Ireland ("the Respondent"), represented by Trowers & Hamlins, United Kingdom of Great Britain and Northern Ireland.

2. The Domain Name and Registrar

The disputed domain name <waynerooney.com> ("the Domain Name") is registered with Register.com ("the Registrar").

3. Procedural History

The Complaint was filed with the WIPO Arbitration and Mediation Center (the "Center") on July 19, 2006. On July 20, 2006, the Center transmitted by email to the Registrar a request for registrar verification in connection with the Domain Name. On July 25, 2006, the Registrar transmitted by email to the Center its verification response confirming that the Respondent is listed as the registrant and providing the contact details for the administrative, billing, and technical contact. The Center verified that the Complaint satisfied the formal requirements of the Uniform Domain Name Dispute Resolution Policy (the "Policy"), the Rules for Uniform Domain Name Dispute Resolution Policy (the "Rules"), and the WIPO Supplemental Rules for Uniform Domain Name Dispute Resolution Policy (the "Supplemental Rules").

In accordance with the Rules, paragraphs 2(a) and 4(a), the Center formally notified the Respondent of the Complaint, and the proceedings commenced on July 26, 2006. In accordance with the Rules, paragraph 5(a), the due date for Response was August 15, 2006. The Response was filed with the Center on August 15, 2006.

The Center appointed Mr. Tony Willoughby as the sole panelist in this matter on August 30, 2006. The Panel finds that it was properly constituted. The Panel has submitted the Statement of Acceptance and Declaration of Impartiality and Independence, as required by the Center to ensure compliance with the Rules, paragraph 7.

On September 18, 2006, the Panel sought a further submission from the Complainants in respect of two matters raised in the Response. The Complainants responded on September 25, 2006, and the Respondent responded by way of a further filing on October 2, 2006.

On October 4, 2006, the Center forwarded to the Panel an email from the Registrar asking the Center whether the Registrar was compelled to answer some questions put to it by the Respondent. The Panel's reply, forwarded to the Registrar by the Center, was to the effect that it was a matter for the Registrar whether or not it responded to the Respondent's questions.

The issue is academic in that for the purposes of this decision the Panel will assume that the Registrar, if it were to reply, would provide answers consistent with the Respondent's contentions.

4. Factual Background

The First Complainant, a company incorporated in England on February 22, 2002, is the registered proprietor of CTM number 00298905 dated December 23, 2002, WAYNE ROONEY (words) covering a variety of goods and services.

The Second Complainant assigned to the First Complainant his trademark rights along with certain other image/merchandising rights in January 2003.

The Second Complainant is a very well-known professional footballer who was born in Liverpool in 1985. He made his name with Everton for whom he first started playing (in their youth team) as a 15 year old in 2000. He played his first game in the Premiership in August 2002, but by then he was well-known in footballing circles and particularly in the Liverpool area. The Liverpool Echo in the early months of 2002 featured several reports of Everton's youth team's matches in which the Second Complainant merited a headline.

One example from the February 7, 2002 issue read: "WAYNE STARS IN SHOW OF MAGIC". Others from around the same time read: "No rest for Blues hotshot, Rooney" and "Rooney to lead Blues Youth Cup charge". At the time the Second Complainant was earning about £100 per week.

The Second Complainant turned professional with Everton in January 2003. He moved to Manchester United in August 2004 and rapidly achieved international status.

The Respondent is an actor. He is an ardent Everton fan and recognised the Second Complainant's star properties at an early stage. He registered the Domain Name on April 16, 2002. On the same day he registered the domain name <waynerooney.co.uk>.

On May 20, 2003, a sports management agency representing the Second Complainant wrote to the Respondent noting that the Respondent had registered the Domain Name and <waynerooney.co.uk> and asking the Respondent what plans he had for those domain names. There is a dispute as to what did or did not ensue following that letter.

As at the date of the Complaint, the Domain Name was connected to a directory site operated by the Registrar which feature links to a variety of other sites ranging from football related sites to online dating sites.

Following receipt of the Complaint the Respondent instructed the Registrar to remove the link to the directory site and the link was duly removed.

5. Parties' Contentions

A. Complainants

The Complainants contend that the Domain Name is identical to a trademark in which the Complainants have rights. The Complainants claim unregistered rights in addition to the trademark registration referred to above.

The Complainants contend that the Respondent has no rights or legitimate interests in respect of the Domain Name, pointing out that it is not the Respondent's name and that the Complainants have granted the Respondent no licence to use the Second Complainant's name in any shape or form.

The Complainants contend that the Domain Name was registered and is being used in bad faith. The Complainants point to the Respondent's lack of any rights in respect of the Domain Name and the use of it to connect to the Registrar's directory site which, while it contains references to the Second Complainant, is also linked to sites in respect of which the Complainants have no interest of any kind. The Complainants contend that the Respondent is deriving income from the directory site.

The Complainants allege that they have approached the Respondent with a view to acquiring the Domain Name, but the Respondent has never replied.

The Complainants' primary contention under the heading of "bad faith", which effectively wraps up within it the subsidiary contentions, is that the Respondent registered the Domain Name with a view to exploiting the Second Complainant's name, thereby causing damage to the Complainants in the form of loss of business opportunity and dilution and/or tarnishment of the WAYNE ROONEY trademark.

The Complaint concludes as follows:

> "The [Domain Name] is an obvious Internet address for consumers to use when looking for the Complainants' website. Instead of locating the Complainants' website when waynerooney.com (sic) is entered in the Internet browser, consumers are directed to a directory of Internet websites which have no connection whatsoever with the Complainants.
>
> It is evident that [the Respondent] is through the use of the website at "www.waynerooney.com" attempting directly to target and attract consumers in the UK, where the bulk of the Complainants' fans (and potential customers) are based. The fact that the registrant's website contains "sponsored" Internet links indicates that [the Respondent] has obtained payment for displaying these Internet links or obtains revenue through a click/pay arrangement. [The Respondent] has therefore used the [Domain Name] for the purpose of attracting Internet users for commercial gain. This has resulted in a potential loss of opportunity for the Complainants to exploit the WAYNE ROONEY name."

B. Respondent

The Respondent denies the Complainants' allegations.

While he accepts that the Complainants have trademark rights, he says that they should be ignored. He points out that the CTM which dates back to the application date in December 2002 (a) post-dated the registration of the Domain name and (b) in any event did not in fact mature into a registration until 2004, long after the Domain Name was registered. Publication of the registration did not occur until August 2004.

The Respondent denies that the unregistered rights existed at the time he registered the Domain Name. At that time the Second Complainant was a 16 year-old boy whose reputation and goodwill (such as it was) was very local. He had not at that stage turned professional. The Respondent observes that the Second Complainant was a junior employee of Everton and that not all employees attract reputation and goodwill sufficient to acquire common law rights in passing off.

Additionally, the Respondent argues that trademark rights (registered and unregistered) are not so broad that they cover all uses of the mark in question. In particular, they do not cover uses other than in the course of trade.

The Respondent, an ardent Everton fan, claims that he registered the Domain Name in good faith having watched the Second Complainant play in a youth team football match in early 2002. He says that he immediately recognised the boy's potential and planned to set up a non-commercial fan site.

However, not then having the know-how necessary to set-up a website and being too busy as an actor to devote time to the matter, he did not immediately get around to doing anything about it. The

Second Complainant then "betrayed" Everton by moving to Manchester United in August 2004, and the Respondent lost all interest in him. Certainly, there was now no question of the Respondent using the Domain Name for a fan site. Accordingly, he did nothing with the Domain Name.

Following receipt of the Complaint he learnt that the Registrar was using the Domain Name to connect to its directory site featuring sponsored links to other sites. He immediately contacted the Registrar and instructed the Registrar to remove the link to its directory site and this was done.

The Respondent denies all responsibility for any commercial use made of the Domain Name and denies too that he derived any commercial benefit.

The Respondent denies that at the relevant time he had no rights or legitimate interests in respect of the Domain Name. He claims that his intended use of the Domain Name for a non-commercial fan site gives rise to a legitimate interest. He claims that for such a site it is legitimate to use the name of the subject of the site. By way of illustration he points to two such sites, namely "www.wayneroon-eyonline.com" and "www.davidbeckham.ws".

The Respondent denies that the Domain Name was registered and is being used in bad faith. He reiterates that he had a legitimate interest in registering the Domain Name. He denies that he has blocked the Complainants from registering an appropriate domain name. He observes that there are several available including <wayne-rooney.com>. Insofar as the bad faith allegations concern the content of the website connected to the Domain Name, that is historical and in any event it had nothing to do with him, everything to do with the Registrar and he derived no commercial benefit of any kind. He knew nothing of it until the Complaint arrived.

Finally, the Respondent denies that he ever failed to respond to the Complainants when they approached him. He received a letter, which was followed by a telephone call. He says that he told them that he had never thought of selling the Domain Name and the call ended on that note. There were then a couple of follow-up calls from the agency, but the people to whom he spoke appeared to be unaware of the original call. The conversations led nowhere.

C. The Responses to the Procedural Order

The Procedural Order, directed to the Complainants, gave the Complainants an opportunity to respond to two matters raised in the Response, namely the Respondent's denials that he (a) failed to respond, as alleged by the Complainants, to an approach made by the Complainants to acquire the Domain Name and (b) derived any income from the content of the website connected to the Domain Name.

The Complainants dealt with the first of those matters by saying that they could not verify the position because of changes to the personnel at the Second Complainant's sports management agency. They went on to say that because the Respondent had produced nothing to verify his story they declined to accept it.

As to the second matter they produced a substantial argument in support of the proposition that even if the Respondent did not benefit from the content of the website and was not responsible for selecting the content, he should nonetheless bear the responsibility for the result – he had demonstrated by getting the content removed that he could control the Registrar and when he registered the Domain Name the agreement he signed made it clear that unless he rejected the option the Domain Name would connect to a site featuring content selected by the Registrar including advertisements. He elected not to reject the option. While it may be the case that he did not derive any commercial benefit from the advertising links, the Registrar certainly did so and paragraph 4(b)(iv) of the Policy still applied.

The Complainants also disclosed that the Respondent had registered the domain name, <wayn-erooney.co.uk> on the same day that he registered the Domain Name. They contend that this is inconsistent with the Respondent's stated intention of creating a non-commercial fan site.

In relation to the first matter the Respondent produces a letter from the Second Complainant's sports management agency dated May 23, 2003, asking the Respondent what his plans were for the Domain Name and the domain name, <waynerooney.co.uk>. He has not retained notes of his telephone conversations. He stands by his story and contends that if the Complainants expect any weight to be given to their allegation, they should support it with evidence.

As to the second matter, the Respondent argues strongly that for a bad faith allegation under the Policy to succeed there has to be a bad faith intention on the part of the Respondent. The Respondent was completely unaware of what the Registrar was doing with the Domain Name until the content of the site was drawn to his attention in the Complaint.

Since the Panel does not intend to decide this case on the basis of the use made by it by the Registrar, it is unnecessary for the Panel to set out in full the weighty arguments advanced on the issue.

6. Discussion and Findings

General

According to paragraph 4(a) of the Policy, for this Complaint to succeed in relation to the Domain Name, the Complainants must prove that

(i) The Domain Name is identical or confusingly similar to a trademark or service mark in which the Complainants have rights; and
(ii) The Respondent has no rights or legitimate interests in respect of the Domain Name; and
(iii) The Domain Name has been registered in bad faith and is being used in bad faith.

A. Identical or Confusingly Similar

There is no dispute that the Complainants have trademark rights in the name WAYNE ROONEY, nor is there any dispute that the Domain Name is identical to that trademark if one discounts the generic domain suffix.

That being so, the Panel finds that the Domain Name is identical to a trademark in which the Complainants have rights.

As will be noted from section 5B above, the Respondent argues that the Complainants' rights should be ignored because they did not exist at the date of registration of the Domain Name.

The Panel refers to the passage in paragraph 1.4 of the WIPO Overview of WIPO Panel Views on Selected UDRP Questions (accessible on the WIPO website), which reads:

> "1.4 Does the complainant have UDRP-relevant trademark rights in a mark that was registered, or in which the complainant acquired unregistered rights, after the disputed domain name was registered?
>
> Consensus view: Registration of a domain name before a complainant acquires trademark rights in a name does not prevent a finding of identity or confusing similarity. The UDRP makes no specific reference to the date of which the owner of the trade or service mark acquired rights. However it can be difficult to prove that the domain name was registered in bad faith as it is difficult to show that the domain name was registered with a future trademark in mind."

The Panel adopts the consensus view and stands by his finding above that the Domain Name is identical to a trademark in respect of which the Complainant has rights.

B. Rights or Legitimate Interests

The Respondent claims that as an ardent Everton fan, having watched the Second Complainant play in a youth team match for Everton in early 2002 and recognizing the latter's potential, he resolved to set up a non-commercial fan site devoted to the Second Complainant. He says that this gives him a legitimate interest in respect of the Domain Name. He says that it makes eminent sense for him to select a domain name for the website which features the name of the subject of the site. In support he draws the Panel's attention to two other such sites, namely "www.waynerooneyonline.com" and "www.davidbeckham.ws".

The Panel confesses to finding this a difficult story to swallow.

The Respondent admits that he has no knowledge or experience of web design, yet following a football match he develops an urge to register not one domain name, but two domain names, the Domain Name and the '.co.uk' equivalent, featuring the name of a 16 year old footballer whose reputation and goodwill barely exists (see the Respondent's submission in relation to common law rights), but in whom he sees the potential for a fan site.

Thus far, while the story is unusual, it could be made good if this ardent fan, so motivated to do something wholly outside his knowledge and experience, actually took some steps to realize his ambition. But he did nothing. He registered the Domain Name in April 2002, but did absolutely nothing until the event occurred in August 2004, some two and a quarter years later, which is said to have dashed his dreams. The Second Complainant moved from Everton to Manchester United.

What might he have been expected to have done? He could have produced some plans for the fan site. He could have entered into talks with someone with the relevant expertise. He could even have booked himself on a course to acquire the relevant expertise. But he did nothing. His reason is that at that time his acting career precluded him from devoting the time to it.

Paragraph 4(c) of the Policy, which is addressed to respondents, includes a non-exhaustive list of what a respondent can produce to the Panel to demonstrate rights or legitimate interests for the purpose of paragraph 4(a)(iii) of the Policy. The only sub-paragraph relevant here is sub-paragraph (i) which reads:

> "(i) before any notice to you of the dispute, your use of, or demonstrable preparations to use, the domain name or a name corresponding to the domain name in connection with a bona fide offering of goods or services;"

As indicated, the Panel has nothing before him, other than the Respondent's assertion, to demonstrate his intention. Whether his stated intention would have been enough for this purpose is an open question. What is unquestionable is that without any supporting evidence the Panel has no alternative but to find that the Respondent has no rights or legitimate interests in respect of the Domain Name.

Before departing this section of the decision it should be explained that while it is for the Complainants to prove all three elements of paragraph 4(a) of the Policy, proving that the Respondent has no rights or legitimate interests is often impossible for a complainant to prove and particularly where, as here, the stated justification for registering the Domain Name is entirely in the hands of the Respondent. In these circumstances it is for the Complainants to make out a *prima facie* case and for the Respondent to answer that case. Here there is no question but that the Respondent deliberately adopted the Second Complainant's name, the only issue is as to the reason, hence the need for some demonstrable support as referred to in paragraph 4(c)(i) of the Policy.

C. Registered and Used in Bad Faith

Under this head it is necessary to re-visit the issue as to the date on which the Complainants acquired trademark rights in the WAYNE ROONEY mark. The Panel refers again to the WIPO Overview of WIPO Panel Views on Selected Questions. Paragraph 3.1 states:

> "3.1 Can bad faith be found if the disputed domain name was registered before the trademark was registered/common law trademark rights were acquired?
>
> Consensus view: Normally speaking, when a domain name is registered before a trademark right is established, the registration of the domain name was not in bad faith because the registrant could not have contemplated the complainant's non-existent right. However: In certain situations, when the respondent is clearly aware of the complainant, and it is clear that the aim of the registration was to take advantage of the confusion between the domain name and any potential complainant rights, bad faith can be found. This often occurs after a merger between two companies, before the new trademark rights can arise, or when the respondent is aware of the complainant's potential rights, and registers the domain name to take advantage of any rights that may arise from the complainant's enterprises."

Clearly, on that basis, it is open to the Panel to find bad faith under the Policy even if the Complainants' rights post-dated the Domain Name registration. There can be no doubt that the Respondent registered the Domain Name with full knowledge of the existence of the Second Complainant and in contemplation of the reputation and goodwill that he knew the Second Respondent would develop.

However, the Panel is satisfied on the balance of probabilities that as at April 2002, an English court would have entertained a passing off action at the suit of the Second Complainant based upon the Second Complainant's reputation and goodwill in existence at that date. Goodwill for this purpose need not be national. All the evidence points to the Second Complainant being very well-known in the Liverpool area at that time. Certainly, readers of the Liverpool Echo with an interest in football cannot have missed the headlines in which he featured.

The specific allegation of bad faith levelled at the Respondent is that he registered the Domain Name, knowing it to be the name of the Second Complainant, the name under which the Second Complainant carried on his profession, and intending to use it to connect to a commercial website. Thus, Internet users would be encouraged to visit the Respondent's website erroneously believing it to be the official website of the Complainants. The cause of the confusion is the web address, the principal element of which is the Domain Name. On the back of that so-called "confusion" visitors to the site would be faced with various commercial links and advertisements. Whether or not those visitors to the site then appreciated that it was not an official site, nonetheless they might be tempted to click on the links and make purchases. At any rate, that (according to the Complainants) would be the Respondent's hope and expectation.

If this can be proved, the Complaint succeeds under paragraph 4(b)(iv) of the Policy which reads:

> "by using the domain name, you have intentionally attempted to attract, for commercial gain, Internet users to your website ..., by creating a likelihood of confusion with the complainant's mark as to the source, sponsorship, affiliation, or endorsement of your website ...or of a product or service on your website ..."

The Complainants thought when they lodged the Complaint that they had clear evidence to support the claim. The Domain Name was connected to a directory page of the Registrar and featured sponsored advertisements.

However, it now turns out that the website in question was a creation of the Registrar, not the Respondent and the Respondent knew nothing about it. As soon as he read the Complaint and learnt of the website, he contacted the Registrar and the link to the offending site was removed. That is the evidence of the Respondent and the Panel accepts it.

The Complainants say that that is not the end of the matter because even if all that is true, the Respondent signed up to the Registrar's terms and could have rejected that option. In not having rejected it, the Respondent, while not actually operating the site or responsible for the selection of the advertisements on the site, should nonetheless bear the overall responsibility for it. The Complainants produce a WIPO UDRP decision in support of that argument, but the Panel would prefer to deal with the matter on another basis.

As indicated under the previous head, the Panel has serious doubts as to the truth of the Respondent's story. It is an extraordinary story. It asks the Panel to assume that out of ardent fervour the Respondent behaved totally out of character registering a domain name for the first time and with a view to setting up a website devoted to the Second Complainant at a time when he (the Respondent) had no relevant knowledge or expertise and apparently without access to anyone having that knowledge or expertise. The Panel is then asked to believe that that ardent fervour died a death for over 2 years as the second Complainant's career was going from strength to strength until his move to Manchester United.

If the Respondent's story is a complete fabrication, then it is but a short step to conclude that the Respondent's purpose all along was abusive.

Nonetheless, truth can sometimes be stranger than fiction so the Panel explores the Respondent's story further. The Respondent says that he was going to set up a fan site and he points to two fan sites of the kind in question, "www.waynerooneyonline.com" and "www.davidbeckham.ws". The Panel has visited those websites and they are commercial sites. The links connect to sites many of which have no connection with Wayne Rooney and David Beckham. They both offer merchandise (directly or indirectly) and feature sponsored links. It is inconceivable to the Panel that the operators of those sites do not derive any commercial benefit.

The Panel has no idea what the Respondent means by a non-commercial fan site if, as appears to be the case, those two fan sites, which he identifies, are typical of what he had in mind. The existence of the potential commercial benefit renders his story credible. In any event the Panel is unable to accept that the Respondent had no eye to the potential commercial benefit. The Panel does however accept that the idea was dependent upon the Respondent's support for the Second Complainant and the latter's move to Manchester United would have killed the idea off, if it was not already dead by then.

The Panel finds that when the Respondent registered the Domain Name he knew that the Second Complainant was likely to become a very hot property indeed and saw a benefit in registering the Domain Name with a view to creating a site and deriving a commercial benefit via that site. A high proportion of visitors to a site with the URL "www.waynerooney.com" would believe it to be the official website of the Complainants (in precisely the same way that people would expect "www.evertonfc.com" to be the official website of Everton Football Club) and would be visiting it for that reason. On reaching the site they might or might not appreciate that it is not an official site, but by then the deception will have occurred. If as is likely the site is offering (directly or indirectly) Wayne Rooney merchandise, there is a high chance that visitors will consider purchasing it. If they see other links that interest them, they will click on those links and thereby generate click revenue for the Respondent, the operator of the site.

The Panel finds that registration of the Domain Name with that intent in the circumstances of this case constitutes bad faith registration and use. The fact that, as things have turned out, the Respondent has never actually got around to using the Domain Name is neither here nor there.

This finding stems in part from the Panel's inability to accept as plausible the Respondent's claim that his fan site would be non-commercial and because the fan sites which the Respondent himself has cited as examples ("www.waynerooneyonline.com" and "www.davidbeckham.ws") are indeed commercial fan sites.

Accordingly, the Panel finds for the Complainant under the third element of the Policy.

7. Addendum

In the Complaint the Complainants asserted that they had attempted to contact the Respondent regarding ownership of the Domain Name, but that no response had ever been received. Clearly they regarded this failure on the part of the Respondent to be reprehensible.

The Respondent's response to that allegation was that he had been approached by a sports management agency and had responded to the effect that he had never thought of selling the Domain Name. There were then a couple of further telephone calls from the agency but to no purpose or effect.

In the face of that story one might have expected the Complainants either to come out with evidence to disprove the Respondent's response or to withdraw the allegation. They have done neither. They maintain the allegation, but say that they cannot verify it due to personnel changes at the agency. Effectively, they say that it is for the Respondent to disprove it.

In the view of the Panel that approach is, to say the least, most unfortunate. If factual allegations of that kind, the details of which ought to be in the possession of the party making the allegation, are made, they should be properly particularised. If they cannot be particularised because there is nobody around to verify them, the allegation should be suitably qualified to indicate to the Panel the limitations to be placed on it. This is particularly important in a procedure such as this where for any number of reasons a response to the complaint may not be forthcoming.

8. Decision

For all the foregoing reasons, in accordance with paragraphs 4(i) of the Policy and 15 of the Rules, the Panel orders that the Domain Name, <waynerooney.com>, be transferred to the Complainants.

Tony Willoughby
Sole Panelist
Dated: October 6, 2006

WIPO Arbitration and Mediation Center

ADMINISTRATIVE PANEL DECISION
National Football League v. Peter Blucher d/b/a BluTech Tickets
Case No. D2007-1064

1. The Parties

The Complainant is National Football League, New York, New York, United States of America, represented by Debevoise & Plimpton, United States of America.

The Respondent is Peter Blucher d/b/a BluTech Tickets, Miami Shores, Florida, United States of America.

2. The Disputed Domain Names and Registrar)

The disputed domain names are: <superbowlxliiipackages.com>, <superbowlxliiitours.com>, <superbowlxliipackages.com>, <superbowlxlipackages.com>, <superbowlxlitours.com>, <superbowl xlivpackages.com>, <superbowl41packages.com>, <superbowl41tours.com>, <superbowl42 packages.com>, <superbowl42tours.com> <superbowl43packages.com>, <superbowl43tours.com>, <superbowl44packages.com> and <superbowl44tours.com>, all of which are registered with Go Daddy.com, Inc. ("Registrar").

3. Procedural History

The Complaint was brought pursuant to the Uniform Domain Name Dispute Resolution Policy (the "Policy"), which was adopted by the Internet Corporation for Assigned Names and Numbers ("ICANN") on August 26, 1999, and approved on October 24, 1999, and in accordance with the Rules for Uniform Domain Name Dispute Resolution Policy (the "Rules") as approved on October 24, 1999, and the World Intellectual Property Organization Supplemental Rules for Uniform Domain Name Dispute Resolution Policy in effect as of December 1, 1999, (the "Supplemental Rules").

The Complaint was filed with the WIPO Arbitration and Mediation Center (the "Center") in email form on July 18, 2007, and in hard copy form, along with accompanying Exhibits A-S, on July 20, 2007.

Pursuant to paragraph 4(d) of the Policy, the Complainant selected the Center as the ICANN approved administrative dispute resolution service provider to administer this proceeding. Through the Complaint, the Complainant requested a single-member panel.

After receiving the original Complaint, the Center, in accordance with paragraph 5 of the Supplemental Rules, verified that the Complaint complied with the formal requirements of the Rules and the Supplemental Rules. In that regard, on July 23, 2007, the Center requested confirmation from the Registrar as to whether the Registrar received a copy of the Complaint from the Complainant and to confirm contact and registrant information set forth in the Complaint relative to the disputed domain name. The Center also requested the Registrar to specify, for the domain name: (a) whether the Policy applies to that name, (b) whether the registrant has submitted, in its registration agreement, to the jurisdiction at the location of the principal office of the registrar for court adjudication of disputes concerning or arising from the use of that name, (c) the language of the registration agreement, and (d) whether that name will remain "locked" during the proceeding.

Subsequently, on July 23, 2007, the Registrar provided its response to the Center through which the Registrar specified name and contact information pertinent to each of the disputed domain names to the extent present in its WhoIS database, and confirmed that the Respondent is listed as the registrant for all the names. The response also confirmed that for each of the names: (a) GoDaddy.com, Inc. is the registrar, (b) the Registrant has submitted to jurisdiction at the location of the principal office of the Registrar for court adjudication and (c) the registration agreement is in English; and all the names will remain locked during the pendency of this proceeding.

The Center verified that the Complaint satisfied the formal requirements of the Policy, the Rules and the Supplemental Rules.

On August 3, 2007, the Center formally notified the Respondent, by email letter, of the filing of the Complaint, including an indication that the Center was forwarding a complete copy of the Complaint to the Respondent, together with all its Exhibits, by both courier and email. The Complaint and its accompanying documents, and all subsequent communications associated therewith, were provided in the preferred manners and to the addresses as mandated by paragraphs 2(a), 2(b) and 4(a) of the Rules.

Hence, the notification to the Respondent having occurred on August 3, 2007, under paragraph 4(c) of the Rules, this administrative proceeding is deemed to have commenced on that date.

Having reviewed the Complaint and all the correspondence, including that between the Center and the Registrar, the Panel agrees with the determination of the Center that the Complaint and its handling met the requirements of the Rules and the Supplemental Rules.

The Respondent was then provided with a 20 calendar day period, expiring on August 23, 2007, to file its Response with the Center and serve a copy of the Response on the Complainant.

As of August 24, 2007, the Center had not received a formal Response to the Complaint from the Respondent; hence, the Center, in an email letter August 24, 2007, notified the Respondent of his default.

Accordingly, pursuant to the Rules and Supplemental Rules, by email letter dated September 4, 2007, the Center contacted the undersigned, Mr. Peter L. Michaelson, requesting his service as a Sole Panelist for this dispute. Subsequently, on the same day, Mr. Michaelson accepted and returned, by facsimile to the Center, a fully executed Statement of Acceptance and Declaration of Impartiality and Independence. The Panel finds that it was properly constituted. The Center, through an email letter dated September 10, 2007, notified the Parties of the appointment of Mr. Michaelson as Sole Panelist.

Based on the deadline set forth in paragraph 15 of the Rules, a decision was to be issued by the Panel to the Center on or before September 24, 2007.

This dispute concerns fourteen domain names, specifically:

<superbowlxliiipackages.com>, <superbowlxliiitours.com>,
<superbowlxliipackages.com>, <superbowlxlipackages.com>,
<superbowlxlitours.com>, <superbowlxlivpackages.com>,
<superbowl41packages.com>, <superbowl41tours.com>,
<superbowl42packages.com>, <superbowl42tours.com>,
<superbowl43packages.com>, <superbowl43tours.com>,
<superbowl44packages.com> and <superbowl44tours.com>.

The language of this proceeding is English.

4. Factual Background

A copy of the WhoIS registration records for all the disputed domain names appears in Exhibit A to the Complaint. As indicated on these records, the following names were all registered on September 27, 2006: <superbowlxliiipackages.com>, <superbowlxliiitours.com>, <superbowlxliipackages.com>, <superbowlxlivpackages.com>, <superbowl42packages.com>, <superbowl42tours.com>, <superbowl43packages.com>, <superbowl43tours.com>, <superbowl44packages.com> and <superbowl44tours.com>; on January 24, 2006: <superbowl41packages.com>; on January 18, 2006: <superbowl41tours.com>; and on September 27, 2005: <superbowlxlipackages.com> and <superbowlxlitours.com>.

A. Complainant's SUPER BOWL Marks

The Complainant owns four United States trademark registrations and over fifty counterpart foreign trademark registrations for the term SUPER BOWL in block letters and on which this dispute is based. The Complainant has provided, in Exhibit E to the Complaint, a copy of the US registration certificate for each of its marks and the accompanying entries for that mark from the public web-accessible Trademark Electronic Search System (TESS) and the Trademark Applications and Registrations Retrieval (TARR) databases provided by the US Patent and Trademark Office (PTO). Pertinent details of these registrations are as follows:

1. SUPER BOWL

United States registration 3,138,590; registered: September 5, 2006 filed: August 9, 2005.

This mark is registered for use in connection with "football helmets, cell phone covers, cell phone straps, special holsters and accessories in connection thereof for carrying cellular telephones, cell phone face plates, decorative magnets, prerecorded compact discs, audio tapes, videotapes and DVDs all featuring the sport of football, computer mouse pads", all in international class 9; "jewelry, watches, clocks, pins, earrings, necklaces, bracelets, belt buckles made primarily of precious metals, charms, money clips made primarily of precious metals, tie pins, rings, collectible coins, commemorative coins", all in international class 14; "posters, trading cards, series of books relating to football, magazines relating to football, newsletters relating to football, notepads, stickers, bumper stickers, paper pennants and greeting cards, printed tickets to sports games and events, pens and pencils, rub on decorative transfers, note paper, pictorial prints, picture postcards, art pictures, wrapping paper, paper table cloths, paper napkins, paper party invitations, paper gift cards, paper gift bags, paper decorations, collectible cards; collectible card and memorabilia holders, souvenir programs for sports events" all in international class 16; and "toys and sporting goods, namely plush toys, stuffed animals, play figures, golf balls, golf club covers, footballs, toy banks, playing cards, Christmas tree ornaments, balloons, jigsaw puzzles, miniature helmets" all in international class 28. The registration certificate states that both first use and first use in commerce of this mark, when used in conjunction with the goods in classes 16 and 28, commenced as of January 1, 1975, and in classes 9 and 14 commenced as of January 1, 1980.

2. SUPER BOWL

United States registration 2,954,420; registered: May 24, 2005
filed: January 29, 2004

This mark is registered for use in connection with "men's, women's and children's clothing, namely, fleece tops and bottoms, caps, headwear, t-shirts, sweatshirts, shorts, tank tops, jeans, sweaters, pants, jackets, turtlenecks, jumpsuits, golf shirts, woven shirts, knit shirts, jerseys, wristbands, warm up suits, wind resistant jackets, raincoats, parkas, ponchos, gloves, ties, suspenders, cloth bibs, sleepwear, namely, robes, night shirts and pajamas, mittens, knit hats and caps, scarves, aprons, headbands, ear muffs, underwear, sneakers and slippers", all in international class 25. The registration certificate states that both first use and first use in commerce of this mark, when used in conjunction with these services, commenced as of January 30, 1971.

3. SUPER BOWL
United States registration 882,283; registered: December 9, 1969
renewed: November 27, 1989
filed: March 7, 1969

This mark is registered for use in connection with "entertainment services in the nature of football exhibitions" in international class 41. The registration certificate states that both first use and first use in commerce of this mark, when used in conjunction with these services, commenced as of January 15, 1967.

4. SUPER BOWL
United States registration 846,056
registered: March 12, 1968 on the Supplemental Register
renewed: March 12, 1988 on the Supplemental Register
filed: December 19, 1966
Amended on December 20, 1967 to the Supplemental register

This mark is registered for use in connection with "equipment (or apparatus) sold as a unit for playing a football-type board game" in international class 28. The registration certificate states that both first use and first use in commerce of this mark, when used in conjunction with these goods, commenced as of December 6, 1966.

B. The Complainant
The Complainant, The National Football League (NFL), is an unincorporated association of 32 member clubs, each of which owns and operates a professional football team. For over 80 years, the NFL and its member clubs have provided entertainment to sports fans worldwide in the form of professional American football games. NFL football is, and for many years has been, one of the most popular spectator sports in the United States. The NFL has televised live broadcasts of its football games on American television since 1939.

The SUPER BOWL football game is usually among the highest-rated of all television programs in the United States of America, if not the highest rated such program. According to press reports, the SUPER BOWL game held on February 4, 2007 in South Florida (SUPER BOWL XLI (41)) was the third most-watched television program ever in the United States of America with an average US viewing audience of more than 93 million people. See the web article "Super Bowl Draws Third-Largest TV Audience Ever", a copy of which appears in Exhibit D to the Complaint). In addition, since the first SUPER BOWL game in 1967 (Super Bowl I (1)), the SUPER BOWL game and related festivities have attracted large crowds of fans and tourists, with the attendance at SUPER BOWL XLI having been 74,512. Thousands more individuals travel to the host city of any SUPER BOWL game to attend events surrounding the game without actually attending the game itself.

The Complainant's advertising, promotional and marketing efforts in connection with the SUPER BOWL game have resulted in widespread public acceptance and recognition for that game and its associated events and exhibitions.

The Complainant's website for its SUPER BOWL game is located at "www.superbowl.com". The Complainant registered that domain name on December 23, 1995. In addition to providing extensive information about that game, the website also provides information about official related activities and event sponsors. A hard-copy printout of the home page of that website appears in Exhibit F to the Complaint.

The Complainant also operates a service called "NFL ON LOCATION" which provides SUPER BOWL packages for corporate groups. These packages include tickets, accommodations and "NFL Extras" with those "extras" including admission to special events, parking and gift bags. Exhibit G to the Complaint provides hard-copy screenshots of the home pages of the NFL ON LOCATION website for Super Bowl XLI game and for the upcoming Super Bowl XLII game.

The Complainant authorized the SUPER BOWL XLI game host committee to operate an official fan reservation service for that game. As indicated by the home page of the website for this committee – a copy of that page appears in Exhibit H to the Complaint, this service provided lodging to individuals and groups that came to the South Florida area for this game. Similarly, and as indicated by a copy of a corresponding home page provided in Exhibit I to the Complaint, the host committee for the upcoming SUPER BOWL XLII game in Arizona is offering an official fan reservation service which will provide hotel accommodations to individuals and groups coming to the Arizona area for that particular game.

C. The Respondent

Without authorization from the Complainant, the Respondent, on September 27, 2005, registered the disputed domain name <superbowlxlipackages.com>. Any Internet user who enters that name will reach the Respondent's website.

Until the occurrence of the SUPER BOWL XLI game on February 4, 2007, the Respondent's website was apparently directed to selling tour packages (such as a game ticket and hotel package) to that game – as shown in Exhibit J to the Complaint by a hard-copy printout of the home page of the Respondent's website as it then existed. The name of the Respondent's business was prominently shown as "Super Bowl XLI Tours, Inc." Moreover, two football helmets with the official AFC (American Football Conference) and NFC (National Football Conference) logos and an image of the Vince Lombardi trophy were featured on the Respondent's website.

D. Interactions between the Parties, the Respondent's further activities

On September 6, 2006, the Complainant's in-house counsel sent a letter to the Respondent objecting to his use of the Complainant's marks and the disputed domain name <superbowlxlipackages.com> (a copy of this letter appears in Exhibit K to the Complaint). That letter was returned to the Complainant unopened. Subsequently, that counsel telephoned the Respondent and, during that conversation, obtained the Respondent's correct mailing address. The Complainant in a follow-up letter to the Respondent dated September 19, 2006 (a copy of which appears in Exhibit L to the Complaint) enclosed a copy of its September 6th letter.

On September 29, 2006, the Respondent, responded by letter to the Complainant – a copy of that letter appears in Exhibit M to the Complaint – stating that he deleted the image of the Lombardi Trophy from his site and that he was "in the process of transferring" the <superbowlxlipackages.com> domain name to the Complainant. No subsequent transfer of that domain name ever occurred. Other than the removing the image of the Lombardi Trophy from his site, the Respondent made no other apparent changes to that site (see a hard-copy printout in Exhibit N to the Complaint of the home page of that site at it then existed). By e-mail message dated October 12, 2006 (a copy of which appears in Exhibit O to the Complaint), the Complainant reiterated its demand that Respondent transfer the domain name and cease using the Complainant's marks. No response was then forthcoming.

On November 14, 2006, Complainant's outside counsel sent another cease and desist letter (a copy of which appears in Exhibit P to the Complaint) to the Respondent. By this point in time, the Complainant learned that Respondent also had registered, without authorization from the Complainant, the domain names <superbowlxlitours.com>, <superbowl41tours.com> and <superbowl41packages.com>, each of which directed Internet users to the Respondent's website located at <superbowlxlipackages.com>. The November 14th letter demanded transfer of all four of those names to the Complainant.

In a responding letter dated on or about December 21, 2006 – a copy of which appears in Exhibit Q to the Complaint, the Respondent merely claimed that he had removed "all NFL related items" from his website. That letter did not mention any of the four domain names then at issue.

Subsequently, the Complainant learned that, back on September 27, 2006, the Respondent had registered the ten remaining disputed domain names, namely: <superbowlxliipackages.com>,<superbowlxliiipackages.com>, <superbowlxlivpackages.com>, <superbowlxliiitours.com>,

<superbowl42packages.com>, <superbowl43packages.com>, <superbowl44packages.com>, <superbowl42tours.com>, <superbowl43tours.com> and <superbowl44tours.com>. All the disputed domain names, which the exception of <superbowl41packages.com> (in that regard, see Exhibit R to the Complaint for a web page resolution error message), currently resolve to the Respondent's website located at <superbowlxlipackages.com>.

On or about February 7, 2007 (a few days after SUPER BOWL XLI game), the Respondent's website was changed to a page promoting "Blu-Tech Tickets" and advertising upcoming concerts (for example, for John Mayer and Gwen Stefani) and shows (such as The Lion King). See Exhibit S in the Complaint for a hard-copy printout of the home page and several lower level pages of that site as it then existed.

5. Parties' Contentions

A. Complainant

(i) Identical or Confusingly Similar

The Complainant contends that each of the disputed domain names is confusingly similar to the Complainant's SUPER BOWL Marks.

Specifically, the Complainant contends that the differences between each such name and the marks is that each domain name contains, as a suffix, a specific number, whether in Arabic or Roman numeral notation, followed by a generic term "packages" or "tours", all of which are insufficient to adequately distinguish each such name from the marks and thus preclude confusion of Internet users.

Further, the Complainant contends that, given the similarity of the names to the marks, confusion is even more likely to occur in light of the ongoing activities of the Complainant's NFL ON LOCATION service and the SUPER BOWL host committee's fan reservation service – for which the Respondent appears to provide directly competitive services through his website. Consequently, any of the disputed domain names by virtue of its inclusion of the mark SUPER BOWL will convey to Internet users that the Respondent's associated website, as well as the services offered there through, is affiliated with or authorized by the Complainant or the host committee, when in fact it is not.

Hence, the Complainant believes that, for each of these names, it has satisfied the confusing similarity/identicality requirement in paragraph 4(a)(i) of the Policy.

(ii) Rights or Legitimate Interests

The Complainant contends that the Respondent has no rights or legitimate interests in any of the disputed domain names pursuant to paragraph 4(a)(ii) of the Policy.

First, the Complainant states that there is no relationship of affiliation between it and the Respondent that gave rise to any license, permission or other right through which the Respondent could own or use any domain name which incorporates the Complainant's SUPER BOWL Marks.

Second, the Complainant contends that the Respondent, in choosing to incorporate the Complainant's mark SUPER BOWL in each of the disputed domain names and then using that name to resolve to a commercial website, is trading off the Complainant's goodwill and fame. Such use does not constitute a *bona fide* offering of goods or services. Consequently, the Respondent's use of each name does not qualify under paragraph 4(c)(i) of the Policy.

Third, the Complainant alleges that the Respondent is not commonly known by any of the names – given his business name as "Blu-Tech Tickets" or "Blu-Tech Company", and is not making a legitimate noncommercial or fair use of any such name without intent for commercial gain to misleadingly divert consumers, thus, failing to qualify under either of paragraphs 4(c)(ii) or 4(c)(iii) of the Policy.

(iii) Registered and Used in Bad Faith

The Complainant contends, for several reasons, that the Respondent registered and is now using each of the disputed domain names in bad faith under paragraph 4(a)(iii) of the Policy.

First, the Complainant alleges that the Respondent registered each of these names to intentionally confuse Internet users and exploit that confusion by diverting Internet users, who, by virtue of the inclusion of the mark SUPER BOWL in the name, expect to reach a website authorized by or affiliated with the Complainant, but are diverted to the Respondent's commercial site instead where the Respondent, for its own commercial benefit, offers tickets and other packages involving the Complainant's SUPER BOWL games as well as SUPER BOWL related services that directly compete with those provided by entities authorized by Complainant. This constitutes bad faith under paragraphs 4(b)(iii) and 4(b)(iv) of the Policy.

Second, the Complainant contends that the Respondent knew of the Complainant's mark SUPER BOWL prior to registering each of the disputed names. Yet, in spite of that knowledge, the Respondent registered those names, hence establishing a pattern of abusive registrations which aim to prevent the Complainant from reflecting its SUPER BOWL Mark in a corresponding domain name, thus evidencing bad faith under paragraph 4(b)(ii) of the Policy.

Third, although the disputed domain name <superbowl41packages.com> does not resolve to the Respondent's website, nevertheless the Respondent has made no use of that name since it was registered on January 18, 2006, thus reflecting passive holding which, under the circumstances here, amounts to bad faith under paragraph 4(b) of the Policy.

B. Respondent

The Respondent failed to file any Response to the allegations raised in the Complaint.

6. Discussion and Findings

In view of the lack of a Response filed by the Respondent as required under paragraph 5 of the Rules, this proceeding has proceeded by way of default. Hence, under paragraphs 5(e), 14(a) and 15(a) of the Rules, the Panel is directed to decide this administrative proceeding on the basis of the Complainant's undisputed representations.

A. Identical or Confusingly Similar

The Panel finds that each of the disputed domain names is confusingly similar to the Complainant's SUPER BOWL Marks.

From a simple comparison of each name to the marks, no doubt exists that all the disputed domain names are, for all practical purposes, confusingly similar to the SUPER BOWL Marks. The only differences between each name and the mark SUPER BOWL is the addition of a number and a generic word "tours" or "packages", collectively as a suffix, and the appending of a gTLD (generic top level domain) ".com" to the mark – with the latter being totally irrelevant in assessing confusing similarity or identicality under paragraph 4(a) of the Policy and thus ignored.

It is now very well-established in UDRP precedent, including numerous decisions previously rendered by this Panel, that minor variations, such as adding short letter or number groups or even generic words to a mark, are each insufficient in and of itself, when used in forming a domain name that results from modifying the mark, to confer requisite and sufficient distinctiveness to that name to avoid user confusion. Adding a number, whether in Arabic or Roman numerals, and/or a generic word "tours" or "packages" to the mark SUPER BOWL are clearly such minor variations. See, e.g., *Toilets.com, Inc. v. Rons Porta Johns*, WIPO Case No. D2007-0952 (August 27, 2007); *Associated Bank Corp. v. Texas International Property Associates*, WIPO Case No. D2007-0334 (June 28, 2007); *Gerber Childrenswear Inc. v. David Webb*, WIPO Case No. D2007-0317 (April 24, 2007); *SPX Corp. v. Hevun Diversified Corp.*, NAF Case No. FA791657 (November 13, 2006); *Google Inc. v. Burns*, NAF Case No. FA 726096 (August 16, 2006); *The Cheesecake Factory Inc. and The Cheesecake Factory Assets Co., LLC v. Say Cheesecake,* WIPO Case No. D2005-0766 (September 12, 2005); *Napster, Inc. v. Vinscani*, WIPO Case No. D2005-0531 (July 19, 2005); *Caesars Entertainment Inc. v. Nova Internet Inc.*, WIPO Case No. D2005-0411 (June 22, 2005); *Lockheed Martin Corporation v. The Skunkworx Custom Cycle*, WIPO Case No. D2004-0824 (January 18, 2005); *Lockheed Martin Corp. v. Deborah Teramani*, WIPO Case No. D2004-0836 (December 1, 2004); and *National Collegiate Athletic Assoc. v. Dusty Brown*, WIPO Case No. D2004-0491 (August 30, 2004); *Lane-Labs USA, Inc. v. Powell Productions*, NAF Case No. FA 155896 (July 1, 2003); and *Cable News Network LP, LLP v. Elie Khouri d/b/a Channel News Network et al.*, NAF Case No. FA 117876 (December 16, 2002). While a sufficient number of variations or even one such significant variation itself made to a mark may suffice, under a specific factual situation, to impart requisite distinctiveness to a resulting domain name and there through dispel user confusion (see, e.g., *Citgo Petroleum Corporation v. Richard Antinore*, WIPO Case No. D2006-1576 (March 14, 2007); and *CP Films, Inc. v. Solar Lunar Performance Film*, NAF Case No. FA861127 (February 6, 2007)), such is clearly not the case here when both each of the names at issue and the marks are viewed, as they must, in their entirety with respect to each other.

Such confusion, should it occur, would undoubtedly cause Internet users intending to access Complainant's website, but who were to reach the Respondent's site instead, to think that an affiliation of some sort exists between the Complainant and its affiliates and the Respondent, when, in fact, no such relationship would exist at all. See, e.g., *Google Inc. v. Jennifer Burns,* NAF Case No. FA 726096 (August 16, 2006); *Cheesecake Factory, Napster, Caesars Entertainment, Lockheed v. Skunkworx,* and *Lockheed v. Teramani,* all cited *supra*; see also *Register.com, Inc. v. Reile*, NAF Case No. FA 208576 (January 27, 2004); *Caesars World, Inc. and Park Place Entertainment Corp. v. Japan Nippon,* WIPO Case No. D2003-0615 (September 30, 2003); *Leiner Health Services Corp. v. ESJ Nutritional Products,* NAF Case No, FA 173362 (September 16, 2003); *American Family Life Assurance Company of Columbus v. defaultdata.com aka Brian Wick*, NAF Case No. FA 123896 (October 14, 2002); *AT&T Corp. v. Abreu*, WIPO Case No. D2002-0605 (Sept. 11, 2002); *L.F.P., Inc. v. B and J Properties,* NAF Case No. FA 109697 (May 30, 2002); *Peter Frampton v. Frampton Enterprises, Inc.,* WIPO Case No. D2002-0141 (April 17, 2002); *Spence-Chapin Services to Families and Children v. Stanley Wynman*, NAF Case No. FA 100492 (December 10, 2001); *Meijer, Inc. v. Porksandwich Web Services,* NAF Case No. FA 97186 (July 6, 2001); *MPL Communications, Limited et al v. 1WebAddress.com*, NAF Case No. FA 97092 (June 4, 2001); *American Home Products Corporation v. Malgioglio,* WIPO Case No. D2000-1602 (February 19, 2001); *Surface Protection Industries, Inc. v. The Webposters a/k/a Mark's Paint Store, Inc.,* WIPO Case No. D2000-1613 (February 5, 2001); *Dollar Financial Group, Inc. v. VQM NET,* NAF Case No. FA 96101 (January 25, 2001); *eBAY Inc. v. G L Liadis Computing, Ltd. and John L. Liadis d/b/a G L Liadis Computing Ltd.,* WIPO Case No. D2000-1463 (January 10, 2001); *Treeforms, Inc. v. Cayne Industrial Sales Corp.,* NAF Case No. FA 95856 (December 18, 2000); *Pep Boys Manny, Moe and Jack of CA v. E-Commerce Today, Ltd.,* e Resolution Case No. AF-0145 (May 3, 2000).

Moreover, this Panel firmly believes that here the Respondent's use of the mark SUPER BOWL when followed by a number and either the generic word "tours" or "package" only serves to exacerbate, rather than diminish, that confusion. This is plainly evident given the substantial recognition, notoriety and fame now enjoyed by Complainant's SUPER BOWL Marks, of which this Panel takes judicial notice, and particularly so since the Complainant over many years – certainly commencing well before the earliest date of September 27, 2005 on which the Respondent registered some of the disputed domain names – has routinely used and continues to use its mark SUPER BOWL followed by a number when referring to each one of its football games.

Therefore, the Panel finds that each of the disputed domain names is confusingly similar to the Complainant's SUPER BOWL Marks as to cause confusion; hence, the Complainant has satisfied its burden under paragraph 4(a)(i) of the Policy.

B. Rights or Legitimate Interests

By virtue of its default, the Respondent has not provided any basis that, under the circumstances here, would legitimize a claim to any of the disputed domain names under paragraph 4(c) of the Policy.

No evidence exists of record that the Complainant has ever authorized the Respondent to utilize its SUPER BOWL Marks or any mark confusingly similar thereto in conjunction with the goods and services which the Complainant and its affiliates, such as the SUPER BOWL host committee, uses those marks, nor does the Complainant or its affiliate apparently have any relationship or association whatsoever with the Respondent. As such, any use to which the Respondent were to put the SUPER BOWL Marks or one confusingly similar thereto in connection with the identical or similar goods and services to those currently provided by the Complainant and its affiliates under the SUPER BOWL Marks would violate the exclusive trademark rights now residing in the Complainant. See, e.g., *Toilets.com, Inc.,* cited *supra; Associated Bank*, cited *supra*; *GoDaddy.com, Inc., v. GoDaddysDomain.com, Clark Signs, Graham Clark,* WIPO Case No. D2007-0303 (May 7, 2007); *Citgo Petroleum Corporation v. Richard Antinore*, WIPO Case No. D2006-1576 (March 14, 2007); *New Destiny Internet Group, LLC and Xplor Media, Inc. v. SouthNetworks,* WIPO Case No. D2005-0884 (October 14, 2005); *The Cheesecake Factory Inc., Napster* and *Caesars Entertainment, Inc.,* all cited *supra*; *Pelmorex Communications Inc. v. weathernetwork*, WIPO Case No. D2004-0898 (December 28, 2004); *Sybase, Inc. v. Analytical Systems*, WIPO Case No. D2004-0360 (June 24, 2004); *Caesars World, Inc. and Park Place Entertainment Corporation v. Japan Nippon,* WIPO Case No. D2003-0615 (September 30, 2003); *Leiner Health Services Corp. v. ESJ Nutritional Products,* NAF Case

No. FA 173362 (September 16, 2003); *AT&T Corp. v. Roman Abreu d/b/a Smartalk Wireless, cited supra*; *MPL Communications, Limited et al v. 1WebAddress.com*, NAF Case No. FA 97092 (June 4, 2001); *America Online, Inc. v. Xianfeng Fu,* WIPO Case No. D2000-1374 (December 11, 2000); and *Treeforms,* cited *supra.* Consequently, the United States of America – located Respondent could not legally acquire any public association between it and any of the SUPER BOWL Marks or one similar thereto, at least for the goods and services rendered by the Complainant, including its affiliates, or those similar thereto. Hence, based on the evidence before the Panel, the Respondent does not fall within paragraph 4(c)(ii) of the Policy.

Further, there is absolutely no evidence of record that the Respondent has ever been commonly known by any of the domain names. Nor could the Respondent in this case ever become so known, in light the Complainant's continuous use of its mark SUPER BOWL for nearly 40 years prior to the earliest date (September 27, 2005) on which the Respondent registered some of the names, without infringing on the exclusive trademark rights of the Complainant. See, *Treeforms, Inc.,* cited *supra.*

Moreover, since Respondent's use of the names, which intentionally infringes the Complainant's trademark rights, does not constitute a *bona fide* use and is unquestionably commercial in nature, Respondent's conduct does not fall within paragraphs 4(c)(i) or 4(c)(iii) of the Policy either.

Accordingly, the Panel concludes that the Respondent has no rights or legitimate interests in any of the disputed domain names within paragraph 4(a)(ii) and 4(c) of the Policy.

C. Registered and Used in Bad Faith

The Panel believes that the Respondent's actions constitute bad faith registration and use of all of the disputed domain names.

In light of no evidence to the contrary, the Panel infers, based on the record and the default of the Respondent, that the Respondent was well aware of the Complainant and its mark SUPER BOWL when the Respondent registered each of the disputed domain names. Yet, in spite of that knowledge, the Respondent intentionally chose and registered each of those names to opportunistically exploit its potential to generate user confusion, for the Respondent's eventual pecuniary benefit and to the Complainant's ultimate detriment.

Moreover, nothing exists on the Respondent's website which would lead any Internet user to reasonably infer other than that a connection, affiliation or relationship of some sort likely exists between the Respondent's website and the Complainant – when, in actuality, none exists. Thus, the Respondent's use of the names is highly likely to confuse, if not actually deceive, Internet users who visit that site but do so with the intention of visiting the Complainant's site instead. See *Toilets.com, Inc.* and *Associated Bank,* both cited supra; *Christian Dior Couture v. Alex Roché,* WIPO Case No. DTV2007-0004 (June 15, 2007) and *Gerber Childrenswear*, cited *supra.*

The evidence of record indicates that, while 13 of the 14 disputed domain names each resolves to the Respondent's website at "www.superbowlxlipackages.com", one name <superbowl41packages. com> does not and is apparently not yet in use. Nevertheless, the Panel infers from the lack of any Response and the nearly identical nature of this remaining name to some of those that are already in use, with the sole difference being the number 41 rather than 42, 43 or 44 (ignoring whether that number is in Arabic or Roman numeral notation – a difference without any significance here), that the Respondent, given the pattern of his actions, had every intention of so using this remaining name in the same exact fashion as he did with each of the 13 names now in use but for reasons unknown has not yet done so. The fact that the Respondent has been passively holding that one name for nearly two years since its registration on September 27, 2005 rather than actually using it is of no consequence, as the Panel views this passive holding as evidencing bad faith use and registration to the same extent as if the Respondent actually used that name in the same fashion as he had used the others.

Hence, the Panel concludes that the Respondent violated paragraph 4(a)(iii) of the Policy and specifically paragraph 4(b)(iv) thereof.

Thus, the Panel concludes that the Complainant has provided sufficient proof of its allegations, with respect to all the disputed domain names, to establish a case under paragraph 4(a) of the Policy upon which the relief it now seeks can be granted.

7. Decision

Accordingly, under paragraphs 4(i) of the Policy and 15 of the Rules, the Panel grants the relief sought by the Complainant.

All the disputed domain names, <superbowlxliiipackages.com>, <superbowlxliiitours.com>, <superbowlxliipackages.com>, <superbowlxlipackages.com>, <superbowlxlitours.com>, <superbowlxlivpackages.com>, <superbowl41packages.com>, <superbowl41tours.com>, <superbowl42packages.com>, <superbowl42tours.com> <superbowl43packages.com>, <superbowl43tours.com>, <superbowl44packages.com> and <superbowl44tours.com>, are ordered transferred to the Complainant.

Peter L. Michaelson
Sole Panelist
Dated: September 24, 2007

WIPO Arbitration and Mediation Center

ADMINISTRATIVE PANEL DECISION
The Arsenal Football Club Public Limited Company v. Official Tickets Ltd
Case No. D2008-0842

1. The Parties

The Complainant is The Arsenal Football Club Public Limited Company, of London, United Kingdom of Great Britain and Northern Ireland, represented by SafeNames Ltd., United Kingdom of Great Britain and Northern Ireland.

The Respondent is Official Tickets Ltd, of South Carolina, United States of America.

2. The Domain Name and Registrar

The disputed domain name <official-arsenal-tickets.com> (the "Domain Name") is registered with GoDaddy.com, Inc.

3. Procedural History

The Complaint was filed with the WIPO Arbitration and Mediation Center (the "Center") on June 1, 2008. The named Respondent was Domains by Proxy, Inc. On June 2, 2008, the Center transmitted by email to GoDaddy.com, Inc. a request for registrar verification in connection with the Domain Name. On June 2, 2008, GoDaddy.com, Inc. transmitted by email to the Center its verification response, advising that the Respondent Official Tickets Limited is listed as the registrant, and providing the contact details. The Center sent an email communication to the Complainant on June 3, 2008, providing the registrant and contact information disclosed by the Registrar, and inviting the Complainant to submit an amendment to the Complaint. The Complainant filed an amendment to the Complaint on June 5, 2008, naming Official Tickets Limited as Respondent. The Center verified that the Complaint together with the amendment to the Complaint satisfied the formal requirements of the Uniform Domain Name Dispute Resolution Policy (the "Policy"), the Rules for Uniform Domain Name Dispute Resolution Policy (the "Rules"), and the WIPO Supplemental Rules for Uniform Domain Name Dispute Resolution Policy (the "Supplemental Rules").

In accordance with the Rules, paragraphs 2(a) and 4(a), the Center formally notified the Respondent of the Complaint, and the proceedings commenced on June 9, 2008. In accordance with the Rules, paragraph 5(a), the due date for Response was June 29, 2008. The Respondent did not submit any response. Accordingly, the Center notified the Respondent's default on June 30, 2008.

The Center appointed Warwick Smith as the sole panelist in this matter on July 9, 2008. The Panel finds that it was properly constituted. The Panel has submitted the Statement of Acceptance and Declaration of Impartiality and Independence, as required by the Center to ensure compliance with the Rules, paragraph 7.

As no response was filed, the Panel has checked the record to ensure that the amendment to the Complaint was properly notified to the Respondent. The Panel is satisfied that the Center has discharged its responsibility in that regard.

4. Factual Background
The Complainant
The Complainant is the owner of the well known London-based football club, Arsenal. It holds numerous registrations for the mark ARSENAL in the United Kingdom of Great Britain and Northern Ireland, the European Union, and the United States of America. The Complainant also holds international registrations of the ARSENAL mark.

It is not necessary to refer to all of these trade mark registrations. It is enough for present purposes to refer to the two United States of America registrations relied upon by the Complainant. First, the Complainant registered the word mark ARSENAL, in various classes and covering a variety of goods and services, with effect from September 1997. Secondly, the Complainant holds an ARSENAL device mark, consisting of the word "Arsenal" on a shield device. Again, this registration covers numerous goods and services in various classes, including "arranging and conducting... football competitions... providing facilities for soccer and football matches... provision of sports information services... organisation of sporting events" in International Class 41. This registration has effect from February 2003.

In addition to its ARSENAL trade mark, the Complainant owns a number of domain names which incorporate the word "Arsenal".

The Complainant's principal website is at "www.arsenal.com" ("the Complainant's Website"). The Complainant's Website contains an area where Internet users can purchase authentic tickets and information on ticket retailers for football matches featuring the Arsenal Football Club.

The Respondent and the Domain Name
The Domain Name was registered on October 24, 2007. The original registrant appears to have been Domains by Proxy, Inc., and the WhoIs particulars produced by the Complainant show that that company was the registered holder of the Domain Name as recently as March 19, 2008. At some time between that date and the date of filing the Complaint, the registration of the Domain Name appears to have been transferred to the Respondent, Official Tickets Limited.

The Complainant has produced a screen shot taken from the website to which the Domain Name resolves ("The Respondent's Website"), taken on March 19, 2008. On that date, the Respondent's Website prominently featured the Complainant's ARSENAL word and shield device marks, and contained the introductory words:

> "*Welcome to Official Arsenal Tickets. Book your official tickets online through our secure system. All tickets booked are confirmed and guaranteed.*"

To the left of the screen, there appeared prominently the words:

> "*Official Tickets*"
> "*Get it, Enjoy it!*"

The Respondent's Website then featured click-on icons, where the site browser could view tickets available for various Arsenal fixtures in the English premier football league. The Respondent's website also provided click-on links to web pages offering "Top Official Tickets" for various other clubs in the English premier league, as well as for a number of named clubs in the Spanish and Italian football leagues. In addition, there were click-on links for websites or web pages offering tickets to various other sporting events and concerts. Contact phone numbers were listed in France, Italy, Germany, Spain, and the United Kingdom of Great Britain and Northern Ireland.

In addition to ticket sales for various events, the Respondent appears to have been running a hotel reservations service through the Respondent's Website. There was also advertising for major courier and credit card companies.

The Complainant has also produced screen shots from the Respondent's Website taken on May 20, 2008. These also featured the Complainant's marks and the introductory text referred to above, but the "view tickets" links were to events which seemingly had nothing to do with the Complainant or its football operations (e.g. concerts and formula 1 motor racing events).

The Complainant says that the Respondent is not an authorized distributor and retailer of Arsenal tickets, and had no authority to use the Complainant's ARSENAL mark in the registration of the

Domain Name. Moreover, there has been no reference on the Respondent's Website to the Complainant's Website, nor any disclaimer stating that the Respondent's Website is not affiliated with or endorsed by the Complainant.

The Complainant produced screen shots, taken on May 29, 2008, from the websites at the domain names:

<official-chelsea-tickets.com>
<official-fulham-tickets.com>
<official-liverpool-tickets.com>
<official-intermilan-tickets.com>
<official-manchester-tickets.com>
<official-milan-tickets.com>
<official-tottenham-tickets.com>
<official-westham-tickets.com>

As at June 3, 2008, the registered owner of all of these domain names was Domains by Proxy, Inc.

The websites to which these domain names resolved, appeared to be identical in style to the Respondent's Website, except that each featured the particular football club whose name formed part of the particular domain name. Arsenal only featured as a click-through link on a side-bar on the websites at these domain names.

The Complainant says that the websites at each of these domain names contained similar colours, fonts, images, and logos to those employed by the owners of the trade marks under which the corresponding football clubs carry on business. None contained any disclaimer or reference to the legitimate website operated by the corresponding football club. All contained the word "official" throughout.

The Complainant says that it has run a trade mark search on "Official Tickets Limited" at the United States Patents & Trade Marks Office, and that the Respondent possesses no trade marks, under its business name, registered with that office. The Complainant also says that it has searched for registered United States companies in the South Carolina region which contain the word "Tickets" in their title. The search yielded no results. A search run by the Complainant on the Dun & Bradstreet Inc. website at "www.smallbusiness.bnb.com" did not yield any hits either.

Pre-Commencement Correspondence

The Complainant's representative sent emails to the Respondent at the email address official-arsenal-tickets.com@domainsbyproxy.com, on March 31 and April 24, 2008. The emails both referred to the Complainant's rights in the mark ARSENAL, and the Respondent's lack of authority to register and use the Domain Name. The emails requested the immediate transfer of the Domain Name to the Complainant.

The Respondent did not reply to those emails.

5. Parties' Contentions

A. Complainant

The Complainant contends:

1. The Complainant has rights in the ARSENAL word and device marks, and the Domain Name is confusingly similar to those marks. The addition of the generic words "official" and "tickets" is insufficient to avoid the confusing similarity, as the Domain Name incorporates the Complainant's mark in its entirety.
2. The Respondent has no rights or legitimate interest in respect of the Domain Name:
   (a) the Respondent is not known as "Arsenal".
   (b) the Respondent possesses no trade marks under that name registered in the United States Patents & Trade mark Office;
   (c) the Complainant has not authorised the Respondent to use its ARSENAL mark, whether by incorporating that mark into a domain name or otherwise;
   (d) the Respondent is using the Complainant's mark as an attention-getting device to attract more traffic to the Respondent's website and generate additional revenue;

(e) a use which intentionally trades on the fame of another cannot constitute a *bona fide* offering of goods or services (citing *Madonna Ciccone v. Dan Parisi,* WIPO Case No. D2000-0847). In this case, the Respondent is using the Complainant's ARSENAL mark to sell not only tickets to Arsenal football fixtures, but also tickets to other sporting events and concerts.

(f) the Respondent has used the Complainant's logo and shield device mark throughout the Respondent's Website. Also, there are frequent references to the term "official" on the Respondent's Website. Those usages demonstrate that the Respondent is purposefully misleading Internet users, and tarnishing the Complainant's reputation. Therefore, the Respondent is not making a fair use of the Domain Name.

(g) The Respondent has no conceivable legitimate reason to use the Complainant's trade marks in the way that it has.

3. The Domain Name was registered and is being used in bad faith:

(a) the Respondent is selling football tickets for the Complainant's matches in competition with the Complainant, in circumstances where the Respondent was fully aware of the Complainant and registered the Domain Name with the intention of disrupting the Complainant's business, and promoting its own business. Those activities constitute bad faith registration and use under paragraph 4(b)(iii) of the Policy.

(b) The Respondent's use of the Complainant's registered mark (not only in the Domain Name but also throughout the Respondent's Website), its deliberate use of colors, fonts, images and logos which are similar to those used by the Complainant, and its consistent use of the term "official", show that the Respondent has been intentionally attempting to attract Internet users to the Respondent's Website by creating a likelihood of confusion with the Complainant's mark as to the source, sponsorship, affiliation or endorsement of the Respondent's Website or location or of a product or service on the Respondent's Website (Policy paragraph 4(b)(iv)).

(c) The Respondent has failed to post any disclaimer on the Respondent's Website, which would serve to distinguish it from the Complainant and its activities. The Respondent is effectively misleading Internet users into believing that the Respondent's Website is an "official site" sponsored, endorsed, or supported by the Complainant.

(d) The Respondent failed to respond to the Complainant's cease and desist emails.

(e) The Respondent has used a WhoIs privacy service to evade detection and ensure that it could continue to generate revenue without being identified.

(f) The Respondent is not a registered company in either the United States of America or the United Kingdom of Great Britain and Northern Ireland. The Respondent has used false and inaccurate registration particulars, contrary to paragraph 2(a) of the Policy.

(g) The Respondent registered the Domain Name to prevent the Complainant from reflecting its ARSENAL trade mark in a corresponding domain name. The Respondent has engaged in a pattern of such conduct, registering a series of domain names that wholly incorporate registered trade marks of which the Respondent is not the proprietor or licensee, and using the corresponding websites to sell tickets to sporting events and concerts which cannot be verified as authentic or genuine. The domain names featuring the names of the other football clubs are all linked to each other, and are part of a scheme to promote the Respondent's online ticket store. All of them have active websites that contain similar colours, fonts, images, and logos to those used by the trade mark owners whose marks have been used by the Respondent in these domain names. None of these websites contain disclaimers or references to the legitimate websites operated by the relevant football clubs or other trade mark owners. All contain the use of the word "official" throughout. Together, these registrations are sufficient to demonstrate that the Respondent has been involved in a pattern of bad faith conduct.

B. Respondent

The Respondent did not reply to the Complainant's contentions.

6. Discussion and Findings

A. What the Complainant Must Prove

Under paragraph 4(a) of the Policy, a complainant has the burden of proving the following:

(i) That the disputed domain name is identical or confusingly similar to a trade mark or service mark in which the complainant has rights; and

(ii) That the respondent has no rights or legitimate interests in respect of the disputed domain name; and

(iii) That the disputed domain name has been registered and is being used in bad faith.

Paragraph 15(a) of the Rules requires the panel to:

> "... decide a complaint on the basis of the statements and documents submitted in accordance with the Policy, these Rules and any Rules and principles of law that it deems applicable".

If a respondent does not submit a response, paragraph 5(e) of the Rules requires the panel to "decide the dispute based on the complaint". Under paragraph 14(b) of the Rules, the panel may draw such inferences from a respondent's failure to comply with the Rules (e.g. by failing to file a response), as the panel considers appropriate.

B. Identical or Confusingly Similar

The Complainant has established that it has rights in the mark ARSENAL. The question is whether the Domain Name is confusingly similar to that mark.

The Panel is satisfied that it is. First, the Domain Name incorporates the Complainant's ARSENAL mark in its entirety. Numerous WIPO UDRP panels have regarded the fact that a disputed domain name wholly incorporates the complainant's mark, as sufficient to establish confusing similarity for the purposes of the Policy – see, for example, *Nokia Group v. Mr. Giannattasio Mario*, WIPO Case No. D2002-0782, and the decisions referred to at pages 4 to 5 of the decision in that case.

While there may be some cases where a disputed domain name which incorporates in full a complainant's trade mark will not be confusingly similar to that trade mark (because sufficient additional letters or numbers have been added to the mark to remove any confusion), that is not the position here. The distinctive part of the Domain Name is the word "Arsenal". The words "official", and "tickets" are generic, and do not reduce the confusing similarity between the Domain Name and the Complainant's mark. If anything, the use of those words increases the likelihood of confusion, because both words are suggestive of one of the Complainant's main business activities (selling "official tickets" to Arsenal matches). The word "official" in particular, strongly suggests that the Domain Name is owned by or connected with a genuine entity known as "Arsenal". On the evidence which has been produced, it is clear that a very large number of Internet users would connect the word "Arsenal" where it occurs in the Domain Name, with the Complainant.

C. Rights or Legitimate Interests

Paragraph 4(c) of the Policy sets out a number of circumstances which, without limitation, may be effective for a respondent to demonstrate that it has rights to, or legitimate interests in, a disputed domain name, for the purposes of paragraph 4(a)(ii) of the Policy. Those circumstances are:

(i) Before any notice to [the respondent] of the dispute, use by [the respondent] of, or demonstrable preparations to use, the disputed domain name or a name corresponding to the disputed domain name in connection with a bona fide offering of goods or services; or

(ii) Where [the respondent] (as an individual, business, or other organization) [has] been commonly known by the disputed domain name, even if [the respondent has] acquired no trade mark or service mark rights; or

(iii) Where [the respondent is] making a legitimate noncommercial or fair use of the disputed domain name, without intent for commercial gain to misleadingly divert consumers or to tarnish the trade mark or service mark at issue.

If the circumstances are sufficient to constitute a *prima facie* showing by the Complainant of absence of rights or legitimate interests on the part of the Respondent, the evidentiary burden shifts to the

Respondent to show, by plausible, concrete evidence, that it *does* have a right or a legitimate interest in the Domain Name.

That approach is summarized at paragraph 2.1 of the Center's online document "WIPO Overview of WIPO Panel Views on Selected UDRP Questions", as follows:

> "A Complainant is required to make out an initial prima facie case that the respondent lacks rights or legitimate interests. Once such prima facie case is made, respondent carries the burden of demonstrating rights or legitimate interests in the domain name. If the respondent fails to do so, a complainant is deemed to have satisfied paragraph 4 (a)(ii) of the UDRP".

In this case, the Complainant has clearly made out a *prima facie* case of "no rights or legitimate interests". The Domain Name is confusingly similar to the Complainant's mark, and the Complainant has not authorized the Respondent to use its mark, whether in a domain name or otherwise. There is nothing to suggest that the Respondent might be commonly known by the Domain Name (a circumstance which might have formed the basis for a right or legitimate interest defense under paragraph 4(c)(ii) of the Policy), and nor is there any evidence that the Respondent has been making a non-commercial or fair use of the Domain Name, without intent for commercial gain – the Domain Name has quite clearly been used for commercial purposes. Paragraph 4(c)(iii) of the Policy therefore could not apply.

Nor is there anything to suggest that the Respondent might have been able to claim a right or legitimate interest under paragraph 4(c)(i) of the Policy. For the reasons which are set out in the next section of this decision, the Panel finds that the Respondent has registered and used the Domain Name in bad faith. Bad faith registration and use of a disputed domain name can never form the basis for a right or legitimate interest claim. The same factors which point to the conclusion of bad faith registration and use, necessarily preclude a finding that the Respondent's use of the Domain Name has been in connection with a *bona fide* offering of goods or services.

As the Complainant has made out a *prima facie* case which has not been answered by the Respondent, the Complainant must succeed on this part of its Complaint.

D. Registered and Used in Bad Faith

Paragraph 4(b) of the Policy lists a number of circumstances which, without limitation, are deemed to be evidence of the registration and use of a disputed domain name in bad faith. Those circumstances are:

(i) circumstances indicating that [the respondent has] registered or acquired the disputed domain name primarily for the purpose of selling, renting, or otherwise transferring the disputed domain name registration to the complainant who is the owner of the trade mark or service mark or to a competitor of that complainant, for valuable consideration in excess of [the respondent's] documented out-of-pocket costs directly related to the disputed domain name; or

(ii) [the respondent has] registered the disputed domain name in order to prevent the owner of the trade mark or service mark from reflecting the mark in a corresponding domain name, provided that [the respondent has] engaged in a pattern of such conduct; or

(iii) [the respondent has] registered the disputed domain name primarily for the purpose of disrupting the business of a competitor; or

(iv) by using the disputed domain name, [the respondent has] intentionally attempted to attract, for commercial gain, Internet users to [the respondent's] website or other on-line location, by creating a likelihood of confusion with the complainant's mark as to the source, sponsorship, affiliation, or endorsement of [the respondent's] website or location or of a product or service on [the respondent's] website or location.

The Complainant has also sufficiently proved this part of the Complaint. The Panel has come to that view for the following reasons.

1. The Domain Name is confusingly similar to the Complainant's ARSENAL mark, and the Complainant has not authorized the Respondent to use that mark, whether in a domain name or otherwise. The Respondent has no rights or legitimate interests in respect of the Domain Name.

2. The Complainant and its ARSENAL mark are well known around the world. The incorporation of the word "Arsenal" in the Domain Name, and the content of the Respondent's Website, together leave no room for doubt that the Respondent was well aware of the Complainant and its marks when the Domain Name was registered in October 2007.
3. The Respondent is clearly not some innocent reseller of tickets to Arsenal Football Club fixtures. Through the Respondent's website it offers tickets to matches organized by other clubs, tickets to various concerts or other events, and a hotel reservation service, none of which has anything to do with the Arsenal Football Club. The consensus view of WIPO UDRP panels deciding cases under the Policy, is that the use of a third party trade mark owner's mark in a domain name by an authorized reseller of that third party's products, will only be regarded as a use in connection with a *bona fide* offering of the third party's products, if certain conditions are satisfied. One of those conditions is that the respondent reseller must use the relevant website to sell *only* the trade marked products; otherwise, the reseller could be using the trade mark to bait Internet users and then switch them to other goods (see *Oki Data Americas, Inc. v. ASD Inc.*, WIPO Case No. D2001-0903). Another "*bona fide* use" requirement for such a reseller, is that the website must accurately disclose the reseller's relationship with the trade mark owner. In this case, the Respondent's Website offers (directly or indirectly) tickets to events run by numerous parties who have no connection with the Complainant – even if it is offering genuine tickets to Arsenal fixtures, it does not meet the "only the trade mark owners products" aspect of the "authorized reseller" test articulated by the panel in *Oki Data Americas Inc. v ASD Inc.* Nor does the Respondent meet the other "limb" of the *Oki Data Americas Inc.* "*bona fide* reseller" test referred to above: the Respondent's Website does not contain anything to advise visitors to the Respondent's Website that the site is not owned by or connected with the Complainant.
4. Not only does the Respondent duplicate the Complainant's ARSENAL word mark on the Respondent's Website, it also reproduces the Complainant's Arsenal shield device mark. The unauthorized use of the Complainant's marks, and the frequent use of the word "official", all point clearly to an intention to mislead Internet users into believing that the Respondent's Website is somehow associated with or authorized by the Complainant.
5. The Panel is also satisfied on the evidence produced, that the Respondent is responsible for the registration of the domain names containing the names of other well known football clubs which were referred to by the Complainant. While each of these domain names appears to have been registered by Domains by Proxy Inc. (also the registered holder of the Domain Name until shortly before the Complaint was filed), all of them appear to be similar in style, and each lists the same contact telephone numbers in France, Italy, Germany, Spain, and the United Kingdom of Great Britain and Northern Ireland, as are listed on the Respondent's Website. Each of these other domain names incorporates the word "official", and each appears to be designed to mislead Internet browsers into believing that the linked websites are operated or authorized by the owners of the relevant football clubs. The Panel accepts the Complainant's submission that these other domain names have been registered and used by the Respondent as part of a scheme designed to promote the Respondent's online ticket store, by attracting browsers looking for ticket sites operated or authorized by the relevant football clubs.
6. In the foregoing circumstances, the Panel is satisfied that the Respondent registered and has been using the Domain Name, for the bad faith purpose described in paragraph 4(b)(iv) of the Policy: by using the Domain Name, the Respondent has intentionally attempted to attract, for commercial gain, Internet users to the Respondent's website, by creating a likelihood of confusion with the Complainant's ARSENAL mark as to the source, sponsorship affiliation or endorsement of the Respondent's Website (and of the tickets being offered for sale on the Respondent's Website).
7. The use of the WhoIs privacy shield in this case, the apparently late change of the Domain Name registration into the name of the Respondent, and the Complainant's difficulty in locating any registration information for a company called "Official Tickets Limited", are all, in the absence of any Response, factors adding to the Panel's overall impression that the Domain Name was registered and has been used in bad faith.

7. Decision

For all the foregoing reasons, in accordance with paragraphs 4(i) of the Policy and 15 of the Rules, the Panel orders that the Domain Name, <official-arsenal-tickets.com> be transferred to the Complainant.

Warwick Smith
Sole Panelist
Dated: July 22, 2008

APPENDIX XXVII

TABLE OF WIPO SPORTS DOMAIN NAME CASES

The following is a list of Sports Domain Name Cases decided by the WIPO Arbitration and Mediation Center with Case References; the Domain Names at issue; and the outcomes of the Decisions:

CASE DETAILS	DOMAIN NAME(S)	DECISION
D1999-0001	worldwrestlingfederation.com	Transfer
D2000-0034	wc02.com wc2002.com worldcup02.net worldcup02.org worldcup10.com worldcup2002.com worldcup2002.net worldcup2002.org worldcup2006.org worldcup2010.com worldcup2010.net worldcup2010.org 2002worldcup.net 2002worldcup.org 2006worldcup.org	Transfer, cancellation in part
D2000-0108	niketown.com	Transfer
D2000-0128	arizona-cardinals.com arizonacardinals.com arizona-cardinals.net greenbay-packers.com greenbaypackers.com greenbay-packers.net jacksonvillejaguars.com kansascity-chiefs.com kansascitychiefs.com kansascitychiefs.org philadelphia-eagles.com philadelphiaeagles.com philadelphiaeagles.net	Transfer
D2000-0147	carolinapanthers.com	Transfer
D2000-0149	girondinsdebordeaux.com	Transfer
D2000-0153	uefachampionsleague.com	Transfer
D2000-0167	e-nike.com enike.com	Transfer
D2000-0189	usolympicstore.com	Transfer
D2000-0193	f1.com	Complaint denied
D2000-0202	Sgma.com	Transfer
D2000-0206	columbia-sports-wear-company.com columbiasportswearcompany.com	Transfer
D2000-0230	euro2000.com	Complaint denied
D2000-0233	jordanf1.com	Transfer
D2000-0256	wwwstonecold.com wwwwwf.com	Transfer
D2000-0290	Iwwf.com wwfshop.com	Transfer
D2000-0339	pgadeals.com	Transfer
D2000-0427	rollerblading.com	Complaint denied

D2000-0429	rollerblade.net	Transfer
D2000-0431	bandondunes.com	Transfer
D2000-0435	olympiconlinestore.com usaolympiconlinestore.com	Transfer
D2000-0461	corinthians.com	Transfer
D2000-0481	holmes-place.com holmesplace.com holmesplace.org	Transfer
D2000-0532	sampdoria.com	Complaint denied
D2000-0700	final-four.org finalfour-tickets.com finalfourticketsforsale.com finalfour-tickets.net finalfourtickets.net final-4.net final-4.org final4.org march-madness.org ncaatickets.org	Transfer
D2000-0710	championsleague.com	Transfer
D2000-0715	cruzeiro.com	Transfer
D2000-0829	fluminense.com	Transfer
D2000-0903	bigdancetickets.com final-four-seats.com finalfourseats.com final-four-tickets.net final-4-tickets.com final4-tickets.com ncaatickets.com sweet-sixteen-tickets.com sweetsixteentickets.com thebigdancetickets.com womensfinalfour.com womensfinalfourtickets.com	Complaint denied with dissenting opinion
D2000-0908	americangolf.net	Transfer
D2000-1120	nike.net	Transfer
D2000-1172	Bmw-williamsf1.com bmw-williamsf1.net bmw-williamsf1.org	Transfer
D2000-1211	knicks.com	Complaint denied
D2000-1218	wembleystadiumonline.com	Transfer
D2000-1233	wembleystadium.net	Transfer
D2000-1306	wwfauction.com wwfauction.net	Transfer
D2000-1359	Facup.com	Transfer
D2000-1378	bettingncaabasketball.com bettingncaafootball.com finalfour2001.org gamblingncaabasketball.com gamblingncaa.com gamblingncaafootball.com marchmadness2001.net ncaafinals.net ncaagames.net ncaaplayoffs.net ncaapostseason.com ncaapreseason.net ncaateamstore.com	Transfer

	wagerncaabasketball.com wagerncaa.com wagerncaafootball.com	
D2000-1397	nike-shoes.com	Transfer
D2000-1466	juvestore.com	Transfer
D2000-1471	euronike.com nike-europe.com nikeeurope.com nikeurope.com	Transfer
D2000-1499	wwfwcw.com	Transfer
D2000-1598	nikesportstravel.com niketravel.com	Transfer
D2000-1620	washingtonwizards.com	Transfer
D2000-1626	mynba.com	Transfer
D2000-1707	nike-soccer.com nike-soccer.net nike-soccer.org	Transfer
D2000-1773	fcbayern.com	Transfer
D2000-1779	Ryder-cup.org	Transfer
D2000-1805	realmadrid.org	Transfer
D2001-0097	worldcup.org worldcup-tv.com	Transfer
D2001-0102	inike.net nike-shop.com nike-shop.net nikeshop.net nikeshop.org nikewomen.com	Transfer
D2001-0157	thelondonmarathon.com	Transfer
D2001-0218	pgamagazine.com	Transfer
D2001-0234	nhlcoolshots.com	Transfer
D2001-0260	juventus.net	Complaint denied
D2001-0335	fulhamfc.com	Transfer
D2001-0372	adidasadidasadidas.com adidas3stripe.com	Transfer
D2001-0396	juvefans.net juve.net juventusfans.com juventusfans.net	Complaint denied, transfer in part
D2001-0424	fifaworldcup.net	Transfer
D2001-0546	ballysfitness.com	Transfer
D2001-0583	juvetv.com	Transfer
D2001-0688	uefaeuro2004.com	Transfer
D2001-0717	uefa2004.com	Complaint denied
D2001-0852	bitegolf.com	Transfer
D2001-0896	juvebiz.com juvecard.com juvemobile.com juvepark.com juvetravel.com	Transfer
D2001-0963	veagasinsider.com vegasinsder.com vegasinsidr.com vegasnsider.com vegsinsider.com	Transfer

	vgasinsider.com	
D2001-0979	bongoboard.com	Complaint denied
D2001-1115	wwwnike.com	Transfer
D2001-1156	adidascasino.com	Transfer
D2001-1185	nhlpenguins.com	Transfer
D2001-1232	juventusnews.com	Transfer
D2001-1338	nascar-games.com nascargames.com nascar-games.net nascargames.net nascarinteractive.com nascartvchannel.com	Transfer
D2001-1347	goretexbags.com goretexfilterbags.com goretexfilter.com goretexfilters.com	Transfer
D2001-1350	nascaracing.com	Transfer
D2001-1387	nascarnowmag.com	Transfer
D2002-0046	liverpoolfc.com	Transfer
D2002-0258	pgachampionshiptickets.com	Transfer
D2002-0390	just-do-it.org	Transfer
D2002-0543	nikeshoes.com	Transfer
D2002-0544	justdoit.net	Complaint denied with dissenting opinion
D2002-0624	victorbaccarat.com victorbingo.com victorblackjack.com victorpoker.com victorroulette.com victorslots.com	Transfer
D2002-0680	adidassalomon.com	Transfer
D2002-0726	galatasaray.com	Transfer
D2002-0802	daytona500tickets.net daytona500tickets.org	Transfer
D2002-0814	oakleykorea.com	Transfer
D2002-0917	galatasaray.net	Transfer
D2002-1011	minorleaugebaseball.com	Transfer
D2002-1143	bowflexexercise.com	Transfer
D2003-0006	gsstore.com	Complaint denied
D2003-0018	galatasaraystore.com	Transfer
D2003-0042	porschetennis.com	Transfer
D2003-0121	realmadridshop.com	Transfer
D2003-0137	ternana.com	Transfer
D2003-0145	sportsmanguides.com sportsmenguides.com	Transfer
D2003-0325	Rallyedespharaons.com rallyedespharaons.net	Transfer
D2003-0363	tottenhamhotspur.com	Transfer
D2003-0411	torino2006.net	Transfer
D2003-0464	bayernmuenchen.net bayernmunchen.net	Transfer
D2003-0466	littlegym.com	Transfer

D2003-0468	realracingclub.com	Transfer
D2003-0489	www-adidas.com	Transfer
D2003-0490	wwwadidas.com	Transfer
D2003-0598	madrid2012.com 2m12.com 2m12.info 2m12.org	Transfer
D2003-0617	madrid2012.org	Transfer
D2004-0009	valenciacf.com	Transfer
D2004-0097	prodive.com	Transfer
D2004-0210	formula-1.net	Transfer
D2004-0255	mizunosports.com	Transfer
D2004-0433	nordicwalker.net nordicwalker.org	Transfer
D2004-0500	atletica.com	Transfer
D2004-0543	antiguasport.com	Transfer
D2004-0576	Ryder2004.com	Transfer
D2004-0628	godzillagolf.com godzillagolf.net godzillagolf.org golfgodzilla.com	Transfer
D2004-0708	worldblackbelts.com	Transfer
D2004-0719	lifetimeproducts.com	Transfer
D2004-0795	bridgestonegolf.com	Transfer
D2004-0882	rallydesign.com	Transfer
D2004-0917	Womensgolfworks.com	Transfer
D2004-0947	orangebowl.net orangebowltickets.net	Transfer with dissenting opinion
D2004-0983	houstonrockets.com newjerseynets.com	Transfer
D2004-1004	golfalenda.com	Transfer
D2004-1028	arai.com	Transfer
D2004-1079	adidasone.com adidas1.com	Transfer
D2004-1087	nyjets.com	Transfer
D2005-0014	fapremierleague.com	Transfer
D2005-0234	Nflpa.com	Transfer
D2005-0386	addidas.com	Transfer
D2005-0541	extremesports.com	Complaint denied
D2005-0822	williamspinball.com	Transfer
D2005-0825	kalenji.com	Complaint denied
D2005-1083	primalquest.com	Complaint denied
D2005-1107	bfgoodrichsuperchallenge.com	Transfer
D2005-1260	lasvegasmotorspeedway.com	Transfer
D2005-1262	maxfligolf.com	Transfer
D2006-0083	thetriplecrown.com	Transfer
D2006-0126	delongsportswear.com	Transfer
D2006-0199	flyersalumni.com	Transfer
D2006-0475	adidastunit.com	Transfer
D2006-1250	huntersspecialties.com	Transfer

D2006-1262	hibbettsporting.com	Transfer
D2006-1360	hibbettsportinggoods.com	Transfer
D2007-0024	zoomies.com	Transfer
D2007-0032	adidas.mobi	Transfer
D2007-0283	hibbett.net	Complaint denied
D2007-0430	hibbats.com hibbertssoporting.com hibbertssports.com hibbetsportsstore.com hibbetsshoestore.com hibbettsorts.com hibbiett.com hibbitesports.com hibbitsshoes.com hibbitsshoestore.com hibbitssporting.com hibbitz.com hibitsport.com hibitssport.com sportaddition.com sportshibbet.com wwwhibbets.com wwwhibbettsports.com	Transfer
D2007-0861	divex.com	Complaint denied
D2007-0896	mlbtv.com	Transfer
D2007-0947	pedalo.com	Complaint denied
D2007-1000	superbowlxliv.com	Transfer
D2007-1064	superbowlxliiipackages.com superbowlxliiitours.com superbowlxliipackages.com superbowlxlipackages.com superbowlxlitours.com superbowlxlivpackages.com superbowl41packages.com superbowl41tours.com superbowl42packages.com superbowl42tours.com superbowl43packages.com superbowl43tours.com superbowl44packages.com superbowl44tours.com	Transfer
D2007-1162	buggieunlimtted.com	Transfer
D2007-1218	donsbest.com	Transfer
D2007-1256	kalenji.com	Transfer
D2007-1274	onceaweekworkout.com	Transfer
D2007-1320	ihategunbroker.com	Transfer
D2007-1321	pga2012.com	Transfer
D2007-1346	richharvestlinks.com richharvestlinks.net richharvestlinks.org	Transfer
D2007-1400	nascarcollectibles.com	Transfer
D2007-1415	proforcekarate.com proforcemartialarts.com	Transfer
D2007-1500	specilized.com	Transfer
D2007-1524	nascartours.com	Complaint denied
D2007-1631	seracing.com	Transfer
D2007-1839	nationalfootballleague.com	Transfer

D2007-1871	panathinaikos.com	Transfer
DAU2005-0004	bigbanger.com.au luxilon.com.au	Complaint denied
DAU2005-0005	espn.com.au	Transfer
DES2006-0012	uefa.es	Transfer
DIE2006-0004	adidas.ie	Transfer
DNU2001-0001	volvooceanrace.nu	Transfer
D1999-0001	worldwrestlingfederation.com	Transfer
D2000-0034	wc02.com wc2002.com worldcup02.net worldcup02.org worldcup10.com worldcup2002.com worldcup2002.net worldcup2002.org worldcup2006.org worldcup2010.com worldcup2010.net worldcup2010.org 2002worldcup.net 2002worldcup.org 2006worldcup.org	Transfer, cancellation in part
D2000-0108	niketown.com	Transfer
D2000-0128	arizona-cardinals.com arizonacardinals.com arizona-cardinals.net greenbay-packers.com greenbaypackers.com greenbay-packers.net jacksonvillejaguars.com kansascity-chiefs.com kansascitychiefs.com kansascitychiefs.org philadelphia-eagles.com philadelphiaeagles.com philadelphiaeagles.net	Transfer
D2000-0147	carolinapanthers.com	Transfer
D2000-0149	girondinsdebordeaux.com	Transfer
D2000-0153	uefachampionsleague.com	Transfer
D2000-0167	e-nike.com enike.com	Transfer
D2000-0189	usolympicstore.com	Transfer
D2000-0193	f1.com	Complaint denied
D2000-0202	Sgma.com	Transfer
D2000-0206	columbia-sports-wear-company.com columbiasportswearcompany.com	Transfer
D2000-0230	euro2000.com	Complaint denied
D2000-0233	jordanf1.com	Transfer
D2000-0256	wwwstonecold.com wwwwwf.com	Transfer
D2000-0290	Iwwf.com wwfshop.com	Transfer
D2000-0339	pgadeals.com	Transfer
D2000-0427	rollerblading.com	Complaint denied
D2000-0429	rollerblade.net	Transfer

D2000-0431	bandondunes.com	Transfer
D2000-0435	olympiconlinestore.com usaolympiconlinestore.com	Transfer
D2000-0461	corinthians.com	Transfer
D2000-0481	holmes-place.com holmesplace.com holmesplace.org	Transfer
D2000-0532	sampdoria.com	Complaint denied
D2000-0700	final-four.org finalfour-tickets.com finalfourticketsforsale.com finalfour-tickets.net finalfourtickets.net final-4.net final-4.org final4.org march-madness.org ncaatickets.org	Transfer
D2000-0710	championsleague.com	Transfer
D2000-0715	cruzeiro.com	Transfer
D2000-0829	fluminense.com	Transfer
D2000-0903	bigdancetickets.com final-four-seats.com finalfourseats.com final-four-tickets.net final-4-tickets.com final4-tickets.com ncaatickets.com sweet-sixteen-tickets.com sweetsixteentickets.com thebigdancetickets.com womensfinalfour.com womensfinalfourtickets.com	Complaint denied with dissenting opinion
D2000-0908	americangolf.net	Transfer
D2000-1120	nike.net	Transfer
D2000-1172	Bmw-williamsf1.com bmw-williamsf1.net bmw-williamsf1.org	Transfer
D2000-1211	knicks.com	Complaint denied
D2000-1218	wembleystadiumonline.com	Transfer
D2000-1233	wembleystadium.net	Transfer
D2000-1306	wwfauction.com wwfauction.net	Transfer
D2000-1359	Facup.com	Transfer
D2000-1378	bettingncaabasketball.com bettingncaafootball.com finalfour2001.org gamblingncaabasketball.com gamblingncaa.com gamblingncaafootball.com marchmadness2001.net ncaafinals.net ncaagames.net ncaaplayoffs.net ncaapostseason.com ncaapreseason.net ncaateamstore.com wagerncaabasketball.com wagerncaa.com	Transfer

	wagerncaafootball.com	
D2000-1397	nike-shoes.com	Transfer
D2000-1466	juvestore.com	Transfer
D2000-1471	euronike.com nike-europe.com nikeeurope.com nikeurope.com	Transfer
D2000-1499	wwfwcw.com	Transfer
D2000-1598	nikesportstravel.com niketravel.com	Transfer
D2000-1620	washingtonwizards.com	Transfer
D2000-1626	mynba.com	Transfer
D2000-1707	nike-soccer.com nike-soccer.net nike-soccer.org	Transfer
D2000-1773	fcbayern.com	Transfer
D2000-1779	Ryder-cup.org	Transfer
D2000-1805	realmadrid.org	Transfer
D2001-0097	worldcup.org worldcup-tv.com	Transfer
D2001-0102	inike.net nike-shop.com nike-shop.net nikeshop.net nikeshop.org nikewomen.com	Transfer
D2001-0157	thelondonmarathon.com	Transfer
D2001-0218	pgamagazine.com	Transfer
D2001-0234	nhlcoolshots.com	Transfer
D2001-0260	juventus.net	Complaint denied
D2001-0335	fulhamfc.com	Transfer
D2001-0372	adidasadidasadidas.com adidas3stripe.com	Transfer
D2001-0396	juvefans.net juve.net juventusfans.com juventusfans.net	Complaint denied, transfer in part
D2001-0424	fifaworldcup.net	Transfer
D2001-0546	ballysfitness.com	Transfer
D2001-0583	juvetv.com	Transfer
D2001-0688	uefaeuro2004.com	Transfer
D2001-0717	uefa2004.com	Complaint denied
D2001-0852	bitegolf.com	Transfer
D2001-0896	juvebiz.com juvecard.com juvemobile.com juvepark.com juvetravel.com	Transfer
D2001-0963	veagasinsider.com vegasinsder.com vegasinsidr.com vegasnsider.com vegsinsider.com vgasinsider.com	Transfer

D2001-0979	bongoboard.com	Complaint denied
D2001-1115	wwwnike.com	Transfer
D2001-1156	adidascasino.com	Transfer
D2001-1185	nhlpenguins.com	Transfer
D2001-1232	juventusnews.com	Transfer
D2001-1338	nascar-games.com nascargames.com nascar-games.net nascargames.net nascarinteractive.com nascartvchannel.com	Transfer
D2001-1347	goretexbags.com goretexfilterbags.com goretexfilter.com goretexfilters.com	Transfer
D2001-1350	nascaracing.com	Transfer
D2001-1387	nascarnowmag.com	Transfer
D2002-0046	liverpoolfc.com	Transfer
D2002-0258	pgachampionshiptickets.com	Transfer
D2002-0390	just-do-it.org	Transfer
D2002-0543	nikeshoes.com	Transfer
D2002-0544	justdoit.net	Complaint denied with dissenting opinion
D2002-0624	victorbaccarat.com victorbingo.com victorblackjack.com victorpoker.com victorroulette.com victorslots.com	Transfer
D2002-0680	adidassalomon.com	Transfer
D2002-0726	galatasaray.com	Transfer
D2002-0802	daytona500tickets.net daytona500tickets.org	Transfer
D2002-0814	oakleykorea.com	Transfer
D2002-0917	galatasaray.net	Transfer
D2002-1011	minorleaugebaseball.com	Transfer
D2002-1143	bowflexexercise.com	Transfer
D2003-0006	gsstore.com	Complaint denied
D2003-0018	galatasaraystore.com	Transfer
D2003-0042	porschetennis.com	Transfer
D2003-0121	realmadridshop.com	Transfer
D2003-0137	ternana.com	Transfer
D2003-0145	sportsmanguides.com sportsmenguides.com	Transfer
D2003-0325	Rallyedespharaons.com rallyedespharaons.net	Transfer
D2003-0363	tottenhamhotspur.com	Transfer
D2003-0411	torino2006.net	Transfer
D2003-0464	bayernmuenchen.net bayernmunchen.net	Transfer
D2003-0466	littlegym.com	Transfer
D2003-0468	realracingclub.com	Transfer

D2003-0489	www-adidas.com	Transfer
D2003-0490	wwwadidas.com	Transfer
D2003-0598	madrid2012.com 2m12.com 2m12.info 2m12.org	Transfer
D2003-0617	madrid2012.org	Transfer
D2004-0009	valenciacf.com	Transfer
D2004-0097	prodive.com	Transfer
D2004-0210	formula-1.net	Transfer
D2004-0255	mizunosports.com	Transfer
D2004-0433	nordicwalker.net nordicwalker.org	Transfer
D2004-0500	atletica.com	Transfer
D2004-0543	antiguasport.com	Transfer
D2004-0576	Ryder2004.com	Transfer
D2004-0628	godzillagolf.com godzillagolf.net godzillagolf.org golfgodzilla.com	Transfer
D2004-0708	worldblackbelts.com	Transfer
D2004-0719	lifetimeproducts.com	Transfer
D2004-0795	bridgestonegolf.com	Transfer
D2004-0882	rallydesign.com	Transfer
D2004-0917	Womensgolfworks.com	Transfer
D2004-0947	orangebowl.net orangebowltickets.net	Transfer with dissenting opinion
D2004-0983	houstonrockets.com newjerseynets.com	Transfer
D2004-1004	golfalenda.com	Transfer
D2004-1028	arai.com	Transfer
D2004-1079	adidasone.com adidas1.com	Transfer
D2004-1087	nyjets.com	Transfer
D2005-0014	fapremierleague.com	Transfer
D2005-0234	Nflpa.com	Transfer
D2005-0386	addidas.com	Transfer
D2005-0541	extremesports.com	Complaint denied
D2005-0822	williamspinball.com	Transfer
D2005-0825	kalenji.com	Complaint denied
D2005-1083	primalquest.com	Complaint denied
D2005-1107	bfgoodrichsuperchallenge.com	Transfer
D2005-1260	lasvegasmotorspeedway.com	Transfer
D2005-1262	maxfligolf.com	Transfer
D2006-0083	thetriplecrown.com	Transfer
D2006-0126	delongsportswear.com	Transfer
D2006-0199	flyersalumni.com	Transfer
D2006-0475	adidastunit.com	Transfer
D2006-1250	huntersspecialties.com	Transfer
D2006-1262	hibbettsporting.com	Transfer

D2006-1360	hibbettsportinggoods.com	Transfer
D2007-0024	zoomies.com	Transfer
D2007-0032	adidas.mobi	Transfer
D2007-0283	hibbett.net	Complaint denied
D2007-0430	hibbats.com hibbertssoporting.com hibbertssports.com hibbetsportsstore.com hibbetsshoestore.com hibbettsorts.com hibbiett.com hibbitesports.com hibbitsshoes.com hibbitsshoestore.com hibbitssporting.com hibbitz.com hibitsport.com hibitssport.com sportaddition.com sportshibbet.com wwwhibbets.com wwwhibbettsports.com	Transfer
D2007-0861	divex.com	Complaint denied
D2007-0896	mlbtv.com	Transfer
D2007-0947	pedalo.com	Complaint denied
D2007-1000	superbowlxliv.com	Transfer
D2007-1064	superbowlxliiipackages.com superbowlxliiitours.com superbowlxliipackages.com superbowlxlipackages.com superbowlxlitours.com superbowlxlivpackages.com superbowl41packages.com superbowl41tours.com superbowl42packages.com superbowl42tours.com superbowl43packages.com superbowl43tours.com superbowl44packages.com superbowl44tours.com	Transfer
D2007-1162	buggieunlimtted.com	Transfer
D2007-1218	donsbest.com	Transfer
D2007-1256	kalenji.com	Transfer
D2007-1274	onceaweekworkout.com	Transfer
D2007-1320	ihategunbroker.com	Transfer
D2007-1321	pga2012.com	Transfer
D2007-1346	richharvestlinks.com richharvestlinks.net richharvestlinks.org	Transfer
D2007-1400	nascarcollectibles.com	Transfer
D2007-1415	proforcekarate.com proforcemartialarts.com	Transfer
D2007-1500	specilized.com	Transfer
D2007-1524	nascartours.com	Complaint denied
D2007-1631	seracing.com	Transfer
D2007-1839	nationalfootballleague.com	Transfer
D2007-1871	panathinaikos.com	Transfer

DAU2005-0004	bigbanger.com.au luxilon.com.au	Complaint denied
DAU2005-0005	espn.com.au	Transfer
DES2006-0012	uefa.es	Transfer
DIE2006-0004	adidas.ie	Transfer
DNU2001-0001	volvooceanrace.nu	Transfer

Indices

NATIONAL AND INTERNATIONAL LEGISLATION AND REGULATIONS

INTERNATIONAL LEGISLATION

WORLD INTELLECTUAL PROPERTY ORGANIZATION (WIPO)

NATIONAL LEGISLATION

CHINA

ENGLAND

FRANCE

SWITZERLAND

COURT OF ARBITRATION FOR SPORT (CAS)

INTERNATIONAL ASSOCIATION OF AMATEUR ATHLETIC FEDERATIONS (IAAF)

INTERNATIONAL BADMINTON FEDERATION (IBF)

INTERNATIONAL CHAMBER OF COMMERCE (ICC)

INTERNATIONAL CYCLING UNION (UCI)

INTERNATIONAL EQUESTRIAN FEDERATION (FEI)

INTERNATIONAL FEDERATION OF ASSOCIATED WRESTLING STYLES (FILA)

INTERNATIONAL ICE HOCKEY FEDERATION (IIHF)

INTERNATIONAL MOTORCYCLING FEDERATION (FIM)

INTERNATIONAL OLYMPIC COMMITTEE (IOC)

INTERNATIONAL SWIMMING FEDERATION (FINA)

UNION OF EUROPEAN FOOTBALL ASSOCIATIONS (UEFA)

WORLD ANTI-DOPING AGENCY

NATIONAL REGULATIONS

TABLE OF CASES

INTERNATIONAL PUBLIC ORGANISATIONS

EUROPEAN COURT OF HUMAN RIGHTS

EUROPEAN COURT OF JUSTICE

WORLD INTELLECTUAL PROPERTY ORGANISATION (WIPO)

NATIONAL COURTS

AUSTRALIA

CANADA

NATIONAL AND INTERNATIONAL ARBITRAL TRIBUNALS

NATIONAL ARBITRATION FORUM (NAF)

COURT OF ARBITRATION FOR SPORT (CAS)

INDEX OF PERSONS AND ORGANISATIONS

PERSONS

ORGANISATIONS

SUBJECT INDEX

Asser International Sports Law Series

Editors
Robert C.R. Siekmann and Janwillem Soek

ISSN 1874–6926

Basic Documents of International Sports Organisations, R.C.R. Siekmann and J.W. Soek, eds. (The Hague/Boston/London, Kluwer Law International 1998)

Doping Rules of International Sports Organisations, R.C.R. Siekmann, J.W. Soek and A. Bellani, eds. (The Hague, T.M.C.Asser press 1999)

Professional Sport in the European Union: Regulation and Re-regulation, A. Caiger and S. Gardiner, eds. (The Hague, T.M.C.Asser press 2000)

Arbitral and Disciplinary Rules of International Sports Organisations, R.C.R. Siekmann and J.W. Soek, eds. (The Hague, T.M.C.Asser press 2001)

Mediating Sports Disputes: National and International Perspectives, I.S. Blackshaw (The Hague, T.M.C.Asser press 2002)

The European Union and Sport: Legal and Policy Documents, R.C.R. Siekmann and J.W. Soek, eds. (The Hague, T.M.C.Asser press 2005)

Sports Image Rights in Europe, I.S. Blackshaw and R.C.R. Siekmann, eds. (The Hague, T.M.C.Asser press 2005)

The Court of Arbitration for Sport 1984–2004, I.S. Blackshaw, R.C.R. Siekmann and J.W. Soek, eds. (The Hague, T.M.C.Asser press 2006)

The Strict Liability Principle and the Human Rights of Athletes in Doping Cases, J.W. Soek (The Hague, T.M.C.Asser press 2006)

The Council of Europe and Sport: Basic Documents, R.C.R. Siekmann and J.W. Soek, eds. (The Hague, T.M.C.Asser press 2007)

European Sports Law: Collected Papers, S. Weatherill (The Hague, T.M.C.Asser press 2007)

Players' Agents Worldwide: Legal Aspects, R.C.R. Siekmann, R. Parrish, R. Branco Martins and J.W. Soek, eds. (The Hague, T.M.C.Asser press 2008)

The Sporting Exception in European Union Law, R. Parrish and S. Miettinen (The Hague, T.M.C.Asser press 2008)

The Jurisprudence of the FIFA Dispute Resolution Chamber, F. de Weger (The Hague, T.M.C.Asser press 2009)

EU, Sport, Law and Policy: Regulation, Re-regulation and Representation, S. Gardiner, R. Parrish and R.C.R. Siekmann (The Hague, T.M.C.Asser press 2009)

TV Rights and Sport: Legal Aspects, I.S. Blackshaw, S. Cornelius and R.C.R. Siekmann, eds. (The Hague, T.M.C.Asser press 2009)

The Law of the Olympic Games, A.M. Mestre (The Hague, T.M.C.Asser press 2009)

The International Sports Law Journal (ISLJ)

Dr Robert Siekmann
Director
ASSER International Sports Law Centre
P.O. Box 30461
2500 GL THE HAGUE
The Netherlands

Telephone: + 31-(0)70-3420342/345/300
Fax: + 31-(0)70-3420346
E-mail: R.C.R.Siekmann@asser.nl
URL: www.sportslaw.nl

SPRINGER NATURE

GPSR Compliance

The European Union's (EU) General Product Safety Regulation (GPSR) is a set of rules that requires consumer products to be safe and our obligations to ensure this.

If you have any concerns about our products, you can contact us on ProductSafety@springernature.com

In case Publisher is established outside the EU, the EU authorized representative is:

Springer Nature Customer Service Center GmbH
Europaplatz 3
69115 Heidelberg, Germany

FSC
www.fsc.org
MIX
Papier | Fördert gute Waldnutzung
FSC® C083411

Kolibri 360 GmbH
Ferdinand-Jühlke-Straße 7
99095 Erfurt, Deutschland
produktsicherheit@kolibri360.de